MW01514917

A Buyer's and Enthusiast's Guide to

Flying Eagle
and Indian Cents

A Guide, Commentary, Catalogue Raisonné,
Source Book, and Armchair Companion
for Both Series

1856 to 1909

by

Q. David Bowers

Bowers and Merena Galleries, Inc.

ABOUT THE AUTHOR:

Q. David Bowers, with Raymond N. Merena, is an owner of Bowers and Merena Galleries, Inc. He has been in the rare coin business since 1953 when he was a teenager. The author is recipient of the Pennsylvania State University College of Business Administration's Alumni Achievement Award (1976), has served as president of the American Numismatic Association (1983-1985) and president of the Professional Numismatists Guild (1977-1979), is a recipient of the highest honor bestowed by the ANA (the Farran Zerbe Award), was the first ANA member to be named Numismatist of the Year (1995), is a recipient of the highest honor given by the Professional Numismatists Guild (The Founders' Award), and has received more "Book of the Year Award" and "Best Columnist" honors given by the Numismatic Literary Guild than has any other writer. He is the author of over 40 books, hundreds of auction and other catalogues, and several thousand articles including columns in *Coin World* and *The Numismatist.*

Dave enjoys buying, selling, studying, and writing about coins. His other interests include American history, books, music, natural history, and art.

CAVEAT: Prices, rarity ratings, and other information were gathered from various sources. Over a period of time there are many variables in the rare coin market including but not limited to changes in grading interpretations, market prices, market strength, popularity, and numbers of pieces known or reported. In all instances readers are urged to buy or sell carefully and to consult current outside market prices. No recommendation of any kind is made with regard to Flying Eagle and Indian cents as an investment, what grades or appearances are suitable for investment, or whether prices in the future will be higher, lower, or the same as they are now.

The author and publisher are not responsible for typographical errors (although any called to our attention will be corrected in any future edition), price changes, or changing market conditions.

ISBN # — 0-943161-68-1

© **1996 by Bowers and Merena Galleries, Inc.**

All rights reserved including duplication of any kind, or storage in electronic or visual retrieval systems. Permission is granted for writers to use a reasonable number of brief excerpts and quotations in reviews, magazine articles, and coin catalogues. Written permission is required for other uses including in reference books or any use of illustrations.

Published by
Bowers and Merena Galleries, Inc.
Box 1224
Wolfeboro, NH 03894-1224.

Retail and wholesale inquiries invited, Attention: Publications Department.

TABLE OF CONTENTS

ACKNOWLEDGMENTS

Vic Bozarth provided a newly discovered 1882 misplaced date variety for examination.

Larry Briggs provided information about the rarity of the 1857 quarter dollar showing a clash mark from a Flying Eagle cent die.

Frank Campbell, librarian, American Numismatic Society, furnished a citation from a Thomas L. Elder catalogue.

Lynn Chen, librarian of the American Numismatic Association, provided copies of *Mint Reports* not in the Bowers and Merena Reference Library, furnished early PCGS and NGC publications, and provided copies of several articles.

John Dannreuther discussed various aspects of grading and die varieties, especially the characteristics and history of 1856 Flying Eagle cents.

Edmund Deane of the Harry W. Bass, Jr. Research Foundation, translated certain information to the Macintosh format for the author and furnished many possibilities for citations.

Thomas K. DeLorey reviewed the manuscript and made valuable suggestions including concerning the curious overstrikes of 1857 and various technical matters. He also contributed a commentary concerning the 1870 sale of James B. Longacre's numismatic effects.

Dr. Richard Doty, Smithsonian Institution, provided a copy of die records kept at the Philadelphia Mint in the 1880s by A.W. Downing, general foreman of the Coining Department (and also bearing a few notes by A.W. Straub, a machinist in the Engraving Department, who by 1884 identified himself as "foreman of the Die Makers Room").

George Elling loaned several coins for photographcy.

Michael C. Ellis provided a clashed die 1857 cent for examination.

Dr. Alan Epstein formed a high-grade collection of Indian cents, and photographs of certain of his coins were furnished for study and possible reproduction by Richard Snow and Brian Wagner.

Michael Fahey, ANACS, reviewed selected parts of the manuscript, made several suggestions and comments, discussed the 1856 Flying Eagle cent, and provided a copy of the ANACS *Population Report* for use in this work.

Bill Fivaz reviewed the manuscript, commented on several unusual varieties, furnished several illustrations, and helped in other ways.

Kevin J. Flynn shared his ideas concerning die making and misplaced dates.

David Hall, Professional Coin Grading Service (PCGS), granted permission to use information concerning quantities of coins graded and helped in other ways.

Ken Hill photographed an 1870 Shield nickel clashed with an Indian cent obverse and provided an image of it.

Michael J. Hodder reviewed the manuscript and made many valuable suggestions and contributions.

R.W. Julian provided copies of his numerous excellent research articles (citations in the Bibliography reflect his working titles) and files on Flying Eagle and Indian cents; included were valuable data pertaining to die production, coinage dates, and Mint correspondence.

David W. Lange, Numismatic Guaranty Corporation of America, reviewed selected parts of the manuscript, shared observations concerning grading, discussed the 1856 Flying Eagle cent, and made suggestions and comments.

Julian Leidman provided a group of 1858 pattern copper-nickel cents for examination.

Sam Lukes related his personal experiences with certain rare varieties, commented on the manuscript, and helped in other ways.

Bill Metropolis reviewed the manuscript, made valuable comments, and offered certain coins for photography.

Dr. Joel Orosz read the manuscript and made several suggestions and additions, particularly concerning historical notes.

Jay Parrino provided several Proof Flying Eagle cents for examination.

Chris Pilliod reviewed the manuscript, made many valuable suggestions (particularly on technical and die matters), provided photographs, and helped in many other ways.

Emily Ramey provided several sets of high-grade Flying Eagle and Indian cents for study.

James Reardon discussed the current market availability of certain Indian cents in worn grades.

P. Scott Rubin provided historical auction listings for 1856 Flying Eagle cent appearances.

Harry Salyards, M.D., reviewed the manuscript and made many valuable suggestions and contributions.

Mark Salzberg, Numismatic Guaranty Corporation of America (NGC), granted permission to use information concerning quantities of coins graded.

Craig B. Sholley provided information and early Mint data about die making processes, sent two coins for examination, and made several comments on the manuscript.

Richard Snow reviewed the manuscript, furnished a number of illustrations, commented on various issues, furnished copies of catalogues and price lists, gave a list of proposed grading guidelines, wrote the preface to the book, and helped in many other ways.

Edgar E. Souders contributed information concerning die making procedures and created illustrations of the die-making process for Indian cents.

Stanley Spurgeon, M.D., made certain specimens from his collection available for study and discussed the intricacies of several die varieties.

Stack's provided a photograph of the 1860 Washington Cabinet medal.

J.T. Stanton provided several illustrations of die varieties for study and possible use.

Larry R. Steve reviewed the manuscript and made many valuable suggestions and comments, reviewed certain technical comments and theories of the author, and was generous in other ways as well; he also provided permission to use information from *Longacre's Ledger,* journal of the Fly-In Club, and provided specimens of certain rare varieties for examination and photography. His insights concerning die preparation and striking procedures were of special importance.

David Sundman discussed the relative rarity of certain issues.

Brian Wagner helped with photographs and other information and provided 1996 retail price suggestions for numerous issues (which I considered in conjunction with other data on hand).

Bob Wilhite of *Numismatic News* furnished 1965 coin market price information from the files of that publication.

Jerry Wysong contributed valuable information, particularly concerning die making and, separately, Flying Eagle cents.

Keith Zaner, editor of *Coin World* "Trends," reviewed the manuscript and many several valuable comments concerning current pricing levels and related philosophy.

Bowers and Merena Galleries staff credits:

Mark Borckardt helped answer several inquiries and discussed technical matters including die making and die varieties. **Roberta French** transcribed information from PCGS and NGC reports, helped with other aspects of gathering data, and assisted with formatting of the pages. **Jennifer Meers** proofread, designed, and laid out the book. **Rosalie Minnerly** helped with correspondence and contact with historians and specialists. **Beth Piper** engaged in price research. **Douglas Plasencia** took and developed the photographs (except for historical coin pictures and other images from the Bowers and Merena archives and those separately credited). **Andrew W. Pollock III** reviewed certain information concerning pattern issues and made suggestions.

Note: Contributions cited as "letter" in footnotes are a combination of narrative letters, marginal notes in manuscript copies, and other notes sent to the author; if such a submission was not day-dated by the sender, the date of receipt is cited.

PREFACE AND APPRECIATION

by Richard Snow

Flying Eagle and Indian cents are one of the most fascinating series of United States coinage. Spanning an era from before the Civil War to well into the twentieth century, these small pieces were the most familiar of all American coins to the general public.

Considered ordinary and little appreciated in their own time, these cents have become prime objects of collecting importance and numismatic scholarship. In recent years many hitherto unknown varieties have come to light.

Mysteries remain to be solved, such as the background of the famous 1856 Flying Eagle cent and which are originals and which are restrikes; at present, some seem to have the characteristics of both!

The intriguing puzzle of clashed dies among 1857 Flying Eagle cents comes close to solution in Dave Bowers' book, and perhaps it is indeed solved, not only through the author's efforts and insights, but with a generous measure of help from some of the leading students of the series.

Just as noted sculptor Augustus Saint-Gaudens believed the Flying Eagle cent to be the high point in American coinage artistry, you will enjoy collecting this short-lived (1856-1858) series and contemplating its beautiful design.

Similarly, Indian cents hold their own beauty and fascination, and among the varieties there are secrets to be learned and puzzles to be solved. New information regarding such rarities as the 1864 with L Proof issues are among the contributions that Dave has incorporated into this work. Dozens and dozens of other new discoveries, findings, and facts await as you peruse the pages.

As Dave Bowers' book shows, the series is filled with interesting coins with great stories. In fact, he seems to have collected stories, anecdotes, and facts with the same excitement that you might feel when chasing a rare 1877 cent! Not only is there enough numismatic information to fill TWO books on these cents, but you'll find lots of worthwhile hints, suggestions, and advice on buying coins, grading them, and evaluating market prices. Perhaps, as Dave suggests, when you finish reading it you'll be in the expert class, or close to it!

Flying Eagle and Indian cents are common enough that almost everyone in the United States can own a representative collection of many varieties, and rare enough that there are some key issues that represent true high points in any numismatic search or endeavor. Along the way there is something for everyone. This book is your passport to learning about them.

And, who knows, you might solve the riddle of the "1875 Mystery Cent." Someone will!

Dave's book is a worthy update to my 1992 book *Flying Eagle and Indian Cents*. My congratulations go to him for a fine, well-researched book. I am sure that as a reader you will share my enthusiasm.

FOREWORD

by the author

Let me tell you how I began my interest in coins. Indian cents played an important part:

My maternal grandfather, Chester L. Garratt, an attorney by profession, was a hobbyist and researcher in many areas. The Book of Daniel in the Bible fascinated him, as did Revelation, and he had bookshelves devoted to these subjects. He also explored trisecting the angle and squaring the circle, and when I was in the second grade, suggested I give the trisecting and squaring puzzles a try. Of course, I thought I could solve both, but I soon learned otherwise. He copyrighted a perpetual calendar of which he was quite proud—whereby you could insert any date in recent centuries or in the future, and find out what day of the week it fell upon.

In my grandfather's two-story red-brick, slate-roofed Victorian home, said to have been built in 1857, in Honesdale, Pennsylvania, I lived for several years as a youngster. I recall with fondness the countless hours spent in his library which was at the top of a long flight of wooden stairs, with books lining all four walls. It was Grandpa Garratt who gave me my first "rare" coin, a well worn 1893 Columbian half dollar. He also had a cigar from the Columbian Exposition, sealed in an aluminum tube, to be opened and smoked 100 years after the fair. I wonder what happened to it.

In the same town a friend of our family had a home in which a dozen or more Indian pennies were embedded face-up in a concrete walk near the front door. I remember looking at these strange coins and their long-ago dates and marveling how wonderful it would be to own even one of them. This must have been about 1945 or 1946. Sometime about then the Episcopal Church in Honesdale had a fund-raising auction featuring donated items, and I was the successful bidder for a few dollars on a cast iron bank filled with worn Indian and Lincoln cents.

At an early age, I began accumulating miscellaneous information, not necessarily intentionally, but as a matter of interest. I bought used copies of anthologies of Robert Ripley's *Believe It or Not* column and found it fascinating to learn that the Lord's Prayer could be written on a grain of rice, and that Chinese people—if marching four abreast day and night—kept increasing their number sufficiently quickly that a parade passing a given point would never end. My aunt, artist Elsa L. Garratt, shared my interest in obscure things, and was very proud of an autographed book Ripley had sent her when she contributed information about a huge iron anchor that was cast in Sweden, but never used on a ship. I don't have the citation on hand today, but I recall seeing Ripley's sketch of it sitting on dry land looking like a forlorn monument. In the same vein, I enjoyed the books of globetrotter Richard Halliburton, especially his almost-like-being-there descriptions of the Seven Wonders of the Ancient World (the Temple of Diana, the Colossus of Rhodes, the lighthouse of Pharos, etc.). Years later while on a trip to Turkey I was shown a cornfield near Ephesus and was told that was where the great Temple of Diana once stood (not quite as romantic as Halliburton's sketch of what it looked like millennia ago).

In 1948 my parents, sister Eve, and brother Bill moved to Forty Fort, about an hour away from Honesdale and in the same state.

By 1952 I was 13-year-old high school student fascinated with the world around me. My interests continued to be diverse and included reptiles, scouting (my friend Bob King and I secured a scoutmaster and re-activated Troop 123), short-wave radio, building balsa wood Strombecker kit models of World War II airplanes (the P-38, B-17, and B-29 were favorite types), picture postcards, rocks and minerals, and astronomy. Having a modest budget—my wages at the time were 25 cents per hour for cutting grass, pulling weeds, and shoveling snow—I had to spend wisely. I chose books over just about anything else.

Raymond L. Ditmars' *Reptiles of North America* was given to me by my mother as a Christmas gift in 1952 and was added to a small library of a half dozen books I had on the subject of herpetology. From Ditmars I learned, for example, that turtles might have a common name such as "box turtle," but in addition had nesting and mating habits, territorial ranges, physical characteristics, and other attributes which made them interesting. Ditmars, who was curator of reptiles at the New York Zoological Garden (Bronx Zoo), had a way of making just about *anything* sound fascinating. Reading about a box turtle was tantamount to developing an aching desire to own one as a pet! Today, years later, I still like turtles, and one of my favorite coin types is the common 1837 Hard Times token showing a diamondback terrapin.

From such experiences I learned the power of the written word and how it can spur one to a great enthusiasm for acquisition.

About that time I was deeply immersed in the study of rocks and minerals, subscribed to a couple of publications on the subject, and had a few reference books. I contemplated it would be nice to visit Franklin, New Jersey someday (where all sorts of fluorescent minerals could be found). I had heard about E.S. Dana's multiple-volume *System of Mineralogy,* the standard reference in the field. I took the bus (not being old enough to drive) to the Osterhout Memorial Library in nearby Wilkes-Barre to see if it had a set, which, fortunately, the institution did. However, unfortunately, one had to be 16 years of age even to examine it—apparently, it was in a stack or section reserved for adults. Therefore, whatever Dana had to report on his chosen subject was lost to me.

Someone told me that Robert L. Rusbar, tax collector for our town, had a very nice collection of rocks and minerals, so I made it a point to give him a call. I was greeted cordially, taken into the basement office of his home, and shown box after box of colorful garnets, Herkimer "diamonds," sulfur clusters, quartz crystals, and the like. Bob Rusbar, as I later called him, gave me a mineral catalog from Ward's Natural Science Establishment in Rochester, New York, but like a nickel-less kid looking through the window of a candy store, I didn't have money to buy the beautiful crystals and other things arrayed on its pages.

After a session with rocks and minerals, Bob asked me if I collected coins, to which I replied in the negative. He brought out from a safe a small green-covered album of Lincoln cents, pointed to one of the first openings, and told me he had paid $10 for that particular coin. He carefully explained that it was a Lincoln cent made in the first year of issue, 1909, with the initials of the designer, Victor David Brenner, V.D.B., on the reverse—but that alone did not make it valuable. With only these features, it would be worth just a few cents. However, beneath the date was a tiny "S" signifying it had been made in San Francisco. This letter or mintmark, hardly visible, jumped the value from a few cents up to the $10 he had paid.

I felt certain that as soon as I left his office and looked through some pocket change I would find *several* 1909-S V.D.B. cents—after all, a copy of the *Guide Book* that he showed me revealed that 484,000 had been minted. Certainly, in the town of Forty Fort alone there must be hundreds just waiting for me to find!

Bob Rusbar gave me a couple of blue Whitman coin folders and a few mintmarked Lincoln cents to get me started. Inspired with the idea of making money more quickly than by cutting grass and other such mundane chores, I went to the Forty Fort State Bank, traded a $10 bill for 1,000 mixed Lincoln cents, and began looking for 1909-S V.D.B., 1914-D, and 1931-S pieces—the varieties I was told were the most valuable.

The first 1,000 pennies were looked through, then another 1,000, then another 1,000. Soon, my two Lincoln cent folders were nearly full—with no 1909-S V.D.B., 1914-D, or 1931-S—but with most everything else. Unfortunately, during the next several months I found just one Indian cent—hardly enough to even attempt building a collection of these from circulation. On the other hand Barber dimes were seen occasionally and Barber quarters even more often. Barber halves—nearly always worn to the point of virtual smoothness—were available with some frequency, perhaps one Barber half out of every 200 or 300 half dollars examined.

From finding Lincoln cents in circulation I went to other series, including Mercury dimes and Standing Liberty quarters. Meanwhile, I sought to gain more knowledge. Not one to do things half way, I decided to take the bull by the horns and write to the Philadelphia, Denver, and San Francisco mints to see how many older coins they could supply, and order Proofs from each.

Back came mimeographed form letters from each institution informing me that Proofs were made only at Philadelphia, that no back-dated coins were available, and giving me other basic information.

Soon, I discovered the *Numismatic Scrapbook Magazine,* a monthly journal put out by the Hewitt brothers (Lee and Cliff) in Illinois. This was like discovering Ali Baba's cave! Each month brought dozens of pages filled not only with stories and tales about coins and coin collecting but, better yet, dozens of advertisements offering things for sale. Today it is very difficult as an adult who has seen quite a few things over the years to describe how exciting it was one day each month when the *Scrapbook* arrived. Everything else would be forgotten for an hour or two as I digested almost every word.

My horizons continued to expand, and George P. Williams, an insurance agent from nearby Kingston and a long-time numismatist, took me under his wing, gave me a tour through his beautiful personal collection housed in Wayte Raymond's "National" albums and took me each month to the meeting of the Wilkes-Barre Coin Club held in the YMCA. Although George had some Indian cents, he liked early half dollars better and had album pages full of them.

The first coin I ever ordered through the mail was an Indian cent—an 1859 Proof from the Copley Coin Company run by Maurice Gould and Frank Washburn in Boston. The price paid was $11, the full market price at the time. It was a glittering little gem. What a treasure!

It is impossible to convey how exciting it was for me to look at the description of a coin in the *Guide Book,* check its mintage and market value, and dream of owning it—and then send a check to an advertiser in the *Scrapbook* to order it, and in person actually own this dream coin a few days later.

I liked my beautiful Proof 1859 cent and decided to buy some other Proofs to go along with it. I recall contemplating an 1877 offered for $90, but passed it by in favor of buying most of the later, more common dates from 1879 to 1909 at $2.50 to $3.50 each.

By that time, I had decided to become a *dealer*—possibly a stretch of the use of that word—by running advertisements in the classified section of the local paper seeking coins. At one point, I got the brilliant idea of running some classified advertisements in Denver, believing that there must be lots of rare 1914-D Lincoln cents in circulation there, and that Colorado readers would be happy to sell them to me. However, no coins ever materialized, just bills for the advertisements. Learning was indeed a step-by-step process!

As time went on and my small but growing dealership prospered, my capital increased, finally to the point at which I had several thousand dollars' worth of inventory. I would buy coins locally from the public and from other collectors and then sell them at the coin club and to collectors I met there.

The more I became involved in coins, the more I wanted to learn about them. I soon found that while spending $10 or $20 for a rare coin was enjoyable, the same amount spent on books brought a lot more pleasure. Soon, I had back copies of the *Numismatic Scrapbook Magazine* dating to 1935, and a file of several decades of *The Numismatist.* I wasn't old enough to join the American Numismatic Association—you had to be 17 at the time—but in 1955, my father, Quentin H. Bowers, joined, and I read the magazines as they came in.

Becoming a dealer wasn't easy in the 1950s. There were no guides to go by, no written rules, and experience was the great teacher. Moreover, buying and selling coins, as in many other walks of life, didn't come with guarantees. With relatively few exceptions, if I bought a coin and it turned out to be an alteration, forgery, or something else, that was my tough luck. (Today, most rare coin dealers guarantee the authenticity of the things they sell.)

Grading? There were no published standards, and what one person called Gem Uncirculated another might call About Uncirculated, or even less.

I learned by doing, and I am happy to say that my favorable experiences outnumbered the problems by probably one hundred to one. Important to the present book, I gained as much knowledge as possible, and did not rely upon anyone else when it came to making decisions. By now, over 40 years later, I have handled many important collections and major rarities and have dealt with many thousands of numismatists. I have seen it vividly demonstrated time and again that those who have the most fun, those who make the most profit from their collections, and those who stay with the hobby longest, are those who take the time to learn about coins. This is true whether one is collecting worn Indian cents or Proof $20 gold coins—or, for that matter, anything else.

Today, my quest for knowledge still continues. There are many things to learn, and while I am quite conversant with most basic things in American numismatics, there are still areas that invite research. Indeed, in the entire history of collecting, no person has known everything, nor will anyone ever. In recent years I have become quite interested in American monetary history of the nineteenth century. From a numismatic viewpoint, just one book has been written on the subject, the deceptively titled *Fractional Money* by Neil Carothers, "fractional money" not referring to familiar Fractional Currency paper notes, but to coins of various denominations. Much of what Carothers wrote pertains to the small cent series.

The longer I am involved with coins, the more I appreciate the history behind them. Writing the present book may seem to be backward, inasmuch as I have written books on many other topics, some esoteric, others mundane, but probably on no other series as basic as small cents. However, as a perusal of the comments and footnotes will reveal, there are still many mysteries within the Flying Eagle and Indian cent series.

I like Flying Eagle and Indian cents and probably always will, perhaps a reflection of my long-ago first purchase of an 1859 Indian cent. Although I have handled my share—or perhaps more than my share—of great American rarities, there will always be a place in my heart for an 1856 Flying Eagle cent, 1864 Indian cent with a tiny "L" initial hidden below the headdress, or the first branch mint minor coin, the scarce 1908-S cent. Some small cents are rare, others common, but each has its own story.

One of the "missed deals" I think about every so often is a cigar box filled with worn Indian cents that a family near my town owned when I was a teenager. In response to one of my advertisements to buy old coins I was invited to visit their home. After looking through several hundred coins and finding one 1872, but no 1877 or 1909-S, something came up, the owners had to leave, and I was told to come back another day. That other day never came, as they decided against parting with the old "pennies." Apparently, my enthusiasm for them rekindled their own interest. I've often wondered what happened to the coins.

At another time—this was from about 1954 to the early 1960s—I tried to buy every 1858 pattern Indian cent I could find—specifically, the type with laurel wreath reverse as regularly adopted in 1859. These were known as the AW-264 variety from the Adams and Woodin text on pattern coins. In the late 1950s when Abe Kosoff sponsored and encouraged Dr. J. Hewitt Judd to write a new book on patterns, I furnished Dr. Judd with the information that AW-264 cents existed in multiple die varieties—something not known before. This was the era of re-examination of many American series, and numerous hitherto overlooked die varieties were identified in such series as pattern coins, state copper coins of the 1785-1788 era, federal silver and gold coins from the 1790s to the 1830s, and tokens. Concerning federal coins, while cents and half cents had been studied intensely, many other series had been overlooked.

From nearly day one in my collecting endeavors, the 1856 Flying Eagle cent was a landmark. At the current price of about $200 to $300 in the early 1950s I could not afford to order one through the mail. It was a great day when I saw my first specimen—a nice Proof owned by Dr. Albert Thomas, who brought it and his other small cents to a meeting of the Wilkes-Barre Coin Club. As usual for fine private collections, his coins were displayed in "National" light brown cardboard album pages, a favorite way to house coins and enjoy them at the same time. I came to like and appreciate the Raymond pages, and I feel the hobby lost something when they were no longer being made. They were a "warm" and "friendly" place to house your collection and watch it grow coin by coin as the empty holes were filled.

Anyway, I have derived a good measure of enjoyment from Flying Eagle and Indian cents over the years. Quite possibly, Indian cents are the "playground" of numismatics. Made in large quantities, they are inexpensive today, and at the same time they offer enough interesting varieties to keep the most astute numismatist reaching for his or her magnifying glass.

The current state of research and enthusiasm in the Flying Eagle and Indian cent series is of a high order of excellence and is far in advance of the methodology applied to most other series of the second half of the nineteenth century (possibly with Morgan dollars excepted). There are differences of opinion, but most in the field work together, share their findings, and are willing to accept new ideas. From such a foundation, progress continues to be made.

Writing this book has brought back many nice memories and has brought me a renewed appreciation of our hobby and what fine people there are in it. The research has been a lot of fun, and I thank each and every person mentioned in the Acknowledgments as well as those noted in the text.

————Q. David Bowers

CHAPTER 1
USING THIS BOOK

The Purpose of the Book

This book is about the two major early types of small-diameter cents, more specifically known as Flying Eagle cents (1856-1858) and Indian cents (1859-1909). In the pages to follow I share with you some of my observations, opinions, and ideas combined with a generous measure of historical information, grading guidelines, and price data.

My opinions, especially those concerning grading, are apt to differ from "conventional wisdom." They are simply my opinions, and I certainly respect anyone who has other views.

Interestingly, when I began work on this book a few years ago I thought that just about all varieties worth discovering in the Flying Eagle and Indian cent had already been found, and so far as Mint procedures were concerned, Don Taxay (in *U.S. Mint and Coinage*), Walter Breen (various texts), and others had exhausted the subject.

I was very wrong.

Probably more discoveries have been made in these series in the past 10 years than in any other 25-year or 50-year period. And, discoveries are still being made.

During the course of writing the present text I and certain contributors may have unraveled the long-standing 1857 clashed dies mystery, or perhaps we have not. Then there is the complex situation surrounding the famous 1856 Flying Eagle cent: how many die varieties are there, and can business strikes and Proofs be neatly divided into these two categories? As this book goes to press, the answers are not complete. There is much "left on the table" for readers to contemplate and discover. Doubtless, 10 years hence many of the suppositions and comments I and others give will be supplanted by new discoveries. This is the way it should be in any dynamic area of numismatics, and if the field of Flying Eagle and Indian cents is anything it is indeed dynamic.

If you are beginning your interest in numismatics or in the small cent series, I hope this book will repay its cost in terms of useful knowledge.

If you are an old-timer I hope you'll find some new information and insights that will lend value and appreciation to your collecting endeavors. If your forte is Mint history or other technical matters, perhaps you'll find some useful ideas to contemplate and some theories to revise.

Even more important, the main reason to read about, study, and collect Flying Eagle and Indian cents is to *enjoy* the experience. If the following pages help increase your enjoyment, I will be sufficiently rewarded.

Organization of the Book

The book is divided into the chapters and appendices listed below. The purpose of the appendices is to permit the inclusion of technical, historical, analytical, and grading material to supplement the text, but in a position that it does not interfere with the flow of the main book.

For each of the two major types—Flying Eagle cents and Indian cents—I give introductory information about their history, striking characteristics, and other aspects of their creation and minting. In effect, each date has a "sub-chapter" of its own. Thus, 1856 has its own sub-chapter as does 1909-S.

In instances in which mintages are known, figures are given for business strike and Proof production. The availability today of each issue in Mint State, circulated grades, and Proof is discussed. Average market prices are given and trace the advance (usually) in value of each variety on the numismatic market in the past several decades.

For various issues I give additional comments including collecting information and historical notes. Hopefully, reading about each issue will enhance its value and enjoyment to you.

Here is what the book contains:

Chapter 1: Using the Book. You are there now. Basic information, rarity scale ratings, etc.

Chapter 2: How Dies are Made. How dies are made; general processes. It was a judgment call where to insert chapters 2, 3, and 4 in this book, as they are somewhat of a technical nature and could have been placed after such subjects as grading and the coin market. However, understanding how coins are struck is a useful background to just about every other aspect of Flying Eagle and Indian cents.

Chapter 3: Dies and Coin Making: Flying Eagle Cents. From master hubs to working dies, plus the coining process.

Chapter 4: Dies and Coin Making: Indian Cents. From master hubs to working dies, plus the coining process

Chapter 5: The Grading Challenge. Commentary, somewhat icono-clastic, but I hope realistic, on various aspects of numerical grading including Mint State and Proof levels, "brown," "red and brown," "red," etc. Lots of opinion will be found here.

Chapter 6: Aspects of Collecting. Forming a collection. Elements of con-noisseurship. How to buy "smart" and effectively. Much opinion will be found here, too.

Chapter 7: Numismatic and Market Trends. The development of nu-mismatic interest in Flying Eagle and Indian cents over the years, chang-ing price levels, popularity considerations, etc.

Chapter 8: Flying Eagle Cents 1856-1858: History and Background: Origin of the design, distribution, introduction to the public, and other aspects.

Chapter 9: Flying Eagle Cents 1856-1858: Date-by-date Study and Analysis: Detailed view of each of the three years (each as a separate sub-chapter with its own year date heading), the 1858/7 overdate, plus selected unusual die varieties, the latter being especially abundant and fascinating among 1857 Flying Eagle cents. Historical market prices are given for a long span of years and for many different grade categories.

Chapter 10: Indian Cents 1859-1909: History and Background. The new design and how it came to be. The Sarah Longacre question. Alloys used. Dies and their characteristics. Changes over the years.

Chapter 11: Indian Cents 1859-1909: Date-by-date Study and Analy-sis: Detailed study of each year (each as a separate sub-chapter with its own year date heading) plus selected unusual die varieties. Historical market prices are given for a long span of years and for many different grade categories.

Appendix I: Die Quantities for each Year, Commentary and Analy-sis. Often such statistics contribute to a better understanding of the availability and rarity of the coins themselves.

Appendix II: Pattern Small Cents. Overview and commentary con-cerning patterns related to the Flying Eagle and Indian cent series. Also discussed are the origins of designs, restriking, and other topics.

Appendix III: Scott catalogue listings. Selected late nineteenth- and early twentieth-century price guides to Indian cents.

Appendix IV: Third-Party Grading. A discussion and thought-pro-voking commentary concerning populations of certified coins in cer-tain levels—particularly Mint State and Proof—and to what extent such information is useful to the intending buyer.

How to Use This Book

There are two basic ways to use this book:

First, there is the quick way. If you want to find a lot of information about the 1858/7 overdate Flying Eagle cent, 1872 Indian cent, 1909-S Indian cent, or any other particular date, mintmark, or major variety, simply turn to that listing and read what I have presented.

Second, after doing a bit of skimming, start at the beginning of the book and read at least all of the narrative and introductory material to the various sections. If you are motivated, read the individual coin listings as well. If you do this, I believe you'll be as conversant with Flying Eagle and Indian cents as 95% or more of all *general dealers* in these and will be able to hold your own in conversations with *specialist dealers.* In the meantime, you'll become a smarter buyer and will enjoy your collection more than ever before.

Terminology

While I have always preferred to call them *cents,* the term *pennies* is part of the American idiom and even seems to be somewhat official. Any reading of the annual reports of the director of the Mint will reveal numerous mentions of "pennies," the standard numismatic reference book on old American copper cents of the 1793-1814 years is titled *Penny Whimsy,* and visitors to the Denver Mint can secure a little booklet, *How to Make a Penny.*[1]

Small cents are the most ubiquitous of all American coins. Hundreds of billions have been coined—primarily of the 1909 to date Lincoln cents—and untold quantities are unaccounted for today.

What should we call the cent design used from 1859 to 1909? *Indian Head cent* is perhaps more descriptive than simply *Indian cent,* but in practice the *Head* is often dropped. *Longacre's Ledger* notes on its cover that it is the official publication of the Flying Eagle and Indian Cent Collectors Society, with no "Head" mentioned. *The Guide Book of United States* coins—the most popular of all annual price guides—directs the reader to Indian Head cents, while *Walter Breen's Complete Encyclopedia of U.S. and Colonial Coins* serves up a lot of information on "Indians." Richard Snow's book is titled *Flying Eagle & Indian Cents,* while the tome by Larry R. Steve and Kevin J. Flynn bears *A Comprehensive Guide to Selected Rare Flying Eagle and Indian Cent Varieties* on its cover. This commentary could be extended, but in summary it seems that "Head" is usually omitted in the titles of books, articles, and catalogue descrip-

---

[1] This publication was reprinted in *The Numismatist,* April 1971.

tions. Thus, in the present work the term "Indian cent" is used in reflection of popular preference.

Now, a few other comments before the main text begins:

Rarity of Flying Eagle and Indian Cents

The relative "rarity" of Flying Eagle and Indian cents is demonstrated by these cumulative mintage figures for business strikes (coins intended for circulation):

1857-1858 Flying Eagle cent: 42,050,000

1859-1909 Indian cent: 1,849,560,942

—

1909-1958 Lincoln cents, "wheat" reverse: 25,817,554,493

1959-1982 Lincoln cents, bronze, Memorial reverse: 158,150,469,076

1982 to date Lincoln cents, plated zinc: Over 140,000,000,000

In 1970 at the Philadelphia Mint, some 1,898,315,000 Lincoln cents were struck. Today in its own context, the 1970 is considered a bit "scarcer" than certain other modern Lincoln cents and lists for 25¢ in Mint State in the 1996 *Guide Book,* whereas truly "common" modern Lincoln cents list for 10¢ apiece. The entire mintage of Indian cents 1859-1909 was less than for this single Lincoln cent variety!

Sheldon's Rarity Scale

Although many shorthand annotations for rarity ratings have been devised over the years, including my Universal Rarity Scale (URS), the most popular is that created by Dr. William H. Sheldon for use in *Early American Cents,* 1949, as part of a *market formula* explained under the "ANA Grading System" in Chapter 5.

A knowledge of these numbers is useful when reading reference books, auction catalogues, and price lists.

Under the Sheldon Rarity Scale, an "R" or "Rarity" number is given, such as "R-5" or "Rarity-5." This can be translated per the following scale:

SHELDON RARITY SCALE
Rarity-1: Over 1,250 estimated known today.
Rarity-2: 501 to 1,250.
Rarity-3: 201 to 500.
Rarity-4: 76 to 200.
Rarity-5: 31 to 75.
Rarity-6: 13 to 30.
Rarity-7: 4 to 12.
Rarity-8: 2 or 3.
Unique: 1

Sometimes intermediate descriptions are used. Thus, "High Rarity-7" in a catalogue description indicates that there are more likely 4, 5, or 6 known than 10, 11, or 12.

Rarity ratings are apt to change. For example, if I discovered an 1887/6 overdate Indian cent—to create a mythical example—at the outset it would be unique; just one known. After it was publicized in *Longacre's Ledger, Coin World, COINage, Coins* magazine, *Numismatic News, The Numismatist,* and other places, perhaps a half dozen more would be reported to me. Now, the 1887/6 overdate is Rarity-7. However, experience and logic indicates that if a half dozen more turn up within a short time of being publicized nationally, there are probably many more among 1887 cents that have not been inspected for the overdate feature. Dr. Sheldon related that if Jones was seen in a crowd, then he certainly was there. However, if he was not seen he might also have been there. In the present example, as an experienced numismatist I would estimate the 1887/6 as Rarity-6 or even Rarity-5, but I could not cite coin-by-coin all the pieces in existence to back up my estimate.

Because of the nature of such estimates, rarity ratings tend toward the common end of the scale over a period of time, but, occasionally, a coin is discovered and remains rare. True examples of the latter situation include the Mint State 1888/7 Indian cent, two examples of which were discovered by James F. Ruddy in 1970, who at the time thought that examples might be plentiful, and hundreds of Mint State coins would come to light once collectors knew what to look for. Additional discoveries were very few.

Further, rarity ratings are interesting, but sometimes they have little to do with market values, because popularity is a greater factor. As an example, the famous 1856 Flying Eagle cent is Rarity-1 (over 1,250 known) and yet is one of the most desired and most expensive issues in the series. A 1895 Indian cent with minor evidence of repunching at the 1 of the date may be scarce or rare, perhaps many times harder to find than an 1856 Flying Eagle cent, but few people care, and such an 1895 Indian cent would bring only a small premium.

Where are They Now?

Doubtless, today there are Indian cents on the ocean floor in the hull of the *Titanic,* others under the sand on the beach at Coney Island, some moldering in the sod of the Gettysburg battlefield, and still more in attics and dresser drawers. Hundreds of millions of worn Indian cents were withdrawn by the Treasury Department and melted. More than likely, of the 1,849,560,942 originally coined from 1859 to 1909, probably no more than about 2% to 3% are in collectors' hands today, or, say, about 37 million to 55 million, most of which are of the later dates in the series (1879-1909). Of course this is just an estimate.

Tens of millions of copper-nickel Flying Eagle cents (1856-1858) and Indian cents (1859-1861) have never been redeemed by the Treasury Department, and hundreds of millions of bronze Indian cents (1864-1909) are presently unaccounted for. Most will probably forever remain that way and, quite likely, were destroyed long ago.

Evoking the Past

Each Flying Eagle and Indian cent in existence today has its own story hidden between its obverse and reverse surfaces. If only it could speak!

A glittering Proof 1859 Indian cent might relate that Joseph J. Mickley gazed down upon it in 1860, and that T. Harrison Garrett admired it in his upstairs study in Evergreen House in Baltimore in 1880. Or, another sparkling little 1859 Proof cent might relate that J.M. Clapp took time from his activities in the oil fields of north central Pennsylvania in early October 1896, to read a slim catalogue received in the mail from dealer Charles Steigerwalt, and to post a bid for this piece offered in the Henry Blair Collection auction held on October 14th.

A well-worn 1879 Indian cent worth just a few dollars probably was in most states of the Union in its time, was spent hundreds of times for penny candy, saw the inside of a piggy bank or two or three, was dropped in many gum and amusement machines, and was prized many times as a part of a kid's allowance—perhaps even more than a numismatist prizes it today. One can just imagine a freckle-faced, pigtailed little girl running down the street to the store to get rid of this little but quite valuable coin as fast as possible! What treasures it could buy!

Flying Eagle and Indian cents were the most egalitarian of all American coins in their day. Anyone could own one—and did. In 1863, when all silver and gold coins were being hoarded and the two-cent, nickel three-cent, and nickel five-cent denominations had not yet been made, the cent was the *only United States coin in circulation.* Remarkable!

I have always enjoyed American history, and when coins are related to history the appreciation of both is enhanced. A good almanac will be of great help with history, especially one or another of the popular volumes telling of events year-by-year in America's past.

And just to think: these little copper-nickel and bronze "messengers from the past" can be in your own collection today—yours to enjoy. No wonder they are so popular with numismatists.

Effective Observation

As baseball player and some-time philosopher Yogi Berra said, "You can see a lot by just looking." I use an inexpensive "Swift" brand doublet hand magnifier with two lenses, each about an inch in diameter, and each of 4X magnification. Used singly, one lens gives 4X, which permits the entire obverse or reverse of a Flying Eagle or Indian cent to be seen at one time. Used doubly, the magnification is 8X, or enough to readily detect date repunching, die lines, or other features of the coin, including those discussed below. For grading a coin I like the 4X level best as it permits a good overall view of an entire side of a coin.

Such a magnifying glass will permit you to appreciate the curved, straight, wide, narrow, repunched, and other date styles and to check other features, leading to the enjoyment I just mentioned.

If need be, I have a Bausch & Lomb stereo-zoom microscope, but it is used only occasionally except when checking specific characteristics such as date repunchings or other small details, but never for grading.

This said, before you become too serious in your acquisition of Flying Eagle and Indian cents, buy a good magnifier.

To observe effectively takes time. The story is told that famed naturalist Alexander Agassiz asked his Harvard students to observe the eye of a fish. An eye is an eye is an eye, the typical student thought, and in a few moments the observation was done. Then Agassiz insisted that the students try again, and this time take many minutes. Upon careful study, they learned that each fish had different scale patterns and different characteristics. With the Agassiz experiment in mind, when I used to teach the "All About Coins" course for the American Numismatic Association I suggested that my students take five to 10 minutes to examine three different 1794 cents and compare them. Everyone in the class soon found that these "identical" coins were in fact quite different, and, more important, each came to like 1794 cents and to gain an appreciation of early die making.

Enjoyment

It's a curious fact that many if not most coin collectors receive pleasure from seeking and buying coins, but do not enjoy their coins once they own them.

In my own business, Bowers and Merena Galleries, I certainly derive a good measure of satisfaction in the buying and selling of coins, but by far the greatest measure of enjoyment for me comes with the studying, classifying, and examining of the pieces. As unbelievable as it may seem to someone who does not know me, I can have just as much fun with a common or slightly scarce coin as I can have with a landmark rarity.

How can you *enjoy* a coin once you own it? For starters, use the magnifying glass I just mentioned.

Examining a Flying Eagle or Indian cent carefully under magnification can often yield much information and perhaps create a puzzle or two. A good way to appreciate die differences is to take a coin early in a given series and compare it to one later in the series. For example, under magnification compare an 1860 Indian cent (the first year with the oak wreath and shield reverse design) with the last year in the series, 1909. You will see differences in die relief and details and much else. Or, pick a dozen different Indian cents at random and look at their date numerals under a glass. Some have the date in a straight line, others curved. On some the date is small and tightly spaced, on others large and wide.

Don't be in a hurry. Like Agassiz's budding zoölogy students or my beginning "All About Coins" class attendees, take your time. Look and then look again. Lest you think this is something so basic that only beginners should do it, you might be heartened to know that while writing this book I often spent 10 to 20 minutes *per coin* taking notes on certain pieces. And, these are coins I was already quite familiar with, or at least thought I was.

Repunched dates, planchet defects, die breaks, die finish lines, and much more await the patient observer and are all discussed in the pages of this book. Among Indian cents there were so many different dies used that without doubt many presently unknown interesting varieties await discovery, perhaps by you!

Further, each Flying Eagle and Indian cent has its own Mint history (how it was struck, what alloy was used, etc.) and numismatic history (market trends, hoards, prices, etc.).

If you can bring all of these aspects together—the studying under magnification of a coin's surface, a knowledge of its tie with American history, and its Mint and numismatic history—each coin in your collection will come *alive*. It will no longer be simply a date in a specific grade with a market price, but it will be an object of history, art, and admiration.

Further, there is the joy of assembling a collection—perhaps starting with a few common dates, adding some scarcer ones, and finally achieving completion with the long-desired 1871, 1872, 1877, and 1909-S issues, but possibly discovering along the way that some "ordinary" date was also very hard to find in the grade you desired.

CHAPTER 2
HOW DIES ARE MADE

Introduction

As a key to understanding the various characteristics of Flying Eagle cents and Indian cents it is important to know how they were made.

I have found the following commentaries useful for the general knowledge they impart, and I am sure you will find them to be of help as well.

However, as will be seen later in chapters 3 and 4, die-making procedures were not necessarily standard, historical records are sometimes contradictory and are often incomplete, and today there are differing opinions as to how certain dies were produced. Taken as a trilogy, chapters 2, 3, and 4 give much information concerning Mint technology, perhaps more than has appeared in any other single printed source thus far.

How Dies Were Made In 1861

The following description of die making is excerpted and adapted from "Making Money: The Mint at Philadelphia," by Waldo Abbott, in *Harper's New Monthly Magazine,* March 1861:

> We visit the Die Room to learn how the dies are made.
>
> A coin has an impression on both sides, requiring, of course, a die for each. These are to be made with extreme care, to be of the finest workmanship, and all exactly alike. Their manufacture is one of the most important operations in the Mint.
>
> Look at the bas-relief of Liberty on one side of a coin. It would be exceedingly difficult to design this in hard steel and of so small a size; so they first make the design in wax, probably six times as large as the coin, by which means the beautiful proportions can be obtained. From this a brass cast is taken, and reduced on steel to the size of the coin by a transfer or reducing lathe. This ingenious instrument was introduced from France by Mr. Peale, who also operated it for some time.
>
> The brass cast is fastened to the large wheel at the right-hand side of the lathe. On the small wheel to the left of the cast is fastened a piece of soft steel, on which the design is to be engraved. Both of these wheels revolve in the same way and at the same speed. There is a long iron bar or lever fastened by a joint to an iron

support at the extreme left, which runs in front of the two wheels. A spring at the upper end draws it in toward the wheels. Fastened to the lever is a pointed steel stub, which touches the cast. A very sharp "graver" is fastened to the lever below, which touches the steel. The wheels revolve, and the stub, when it is pushed back by the heavy relief of the cast, forces back the lever, which draws back the graver, and prevents it cutting the steel. So where there is a raised place in the cast the graver is prevented from cutting into the steel, but where there is a depression in the cast the graver cuts the same in the steel.

As the lever is jointed at the left, the nearer the graver is placed to that end the less motion it will have. The distance of the steel from the joint regulates the proportion of the reduction from the cast.

After the graver has cut one small shaving around the steel, a screw is turned, which lowers the right end of the lever slightly, just enough to allow the graver to cut another shaving, and the stub to touch the cast very little farther from the centre. Thus the graver cuts very little at a time; but the work is cut over several times, until the design is sufficiently blocked out. This machine will not finish off the die perfect enough to use; but it reduces the design in perfect proportion, and performs most of the rough work. The original dies for coins being now all made, the lathe is used mostly for medals, of which a great many are struck, by order of Congress, for various purposes. A very fine one was presented to the Japanese while they were in this country [QDB note: Japanese Embassy medal by Anthony C. Paquet]. There is now in the machine a cast of Washington's bust, merely to show how the cast is placed.

After the die comes from the lathe it is carefully finished off by hand, and when all polished is a beautiful piece of work. It is still very soft, requiring to be hardened before it can be used, which is done by heating it very hot, and holding it under a stream of water until cold. The relief is exactly like the coin—that is, the device is raised as in the coin. It will not do to use this in stamping, as it would reverse the appearance on the coin. Therefore this "hub," or "male die," as it is named, is used only to make other dies.

Round pieces of very soft steel, a little larger than the die, are smoothed off on the top, the centre being brought to a point a little higher than the sides. It is placed on a solid bed, under a very powerful screw-press, and the hub placed on top of it—the centre of the hub on the point of the steel, like a seal on the sealing-wax. The screw is turned with great force by several men, and presses the hub a little into the steel. It is necessary to have the steel higher in the centre, as if the centre impression is not taken first, it can not be brought out sharp and distinct. The steel is softened again by being heated and allowed to cool slowly, and the operation is repeated. This is done several times, until the whole impression is full and distinct. If there is any little defect it is rectified with the engraver's tool. The surplus steel around the edge is cut off, and the date put in by hand, when it is hardened and ready for use.

The date is not cut on the hub or on the first die—which is called a "female"—as perhaps the hub will last for two years, and the date can not be altered. This die is never used to stamp with, but preserved, so that if the hub breaks it can be used to make another. The dies for use are prepared in the same way. About 1,300 a year are made for the various branch mints, and those for the New Orleans Mint were sent on just before the state seceded, which the authorities have not yet had time to return. Sometimes a die will wear for a couple of days, and again they will break while stamping the first coin. Steel is treacherous, and no dependence can be placed in its strength. As nearly as can be ascertained their cost is $16 a pair.

How Dies Were Made In 1896

The following description of die making is excerpted and adapted from "Manufacture of Dies," by Chief Engraver Charles E. Barber, 1896:

After the design for the coin or medal is decided upon, the engraver prepares a model in wax, or any material he may prefer to use, of the design selected, or as much of it as he may think most desirable for the medal or coin. The model is generally made three, four, or five times as large as the finished work is intended to be. When the model is finished an electrotype [a.k.a. galvano] is made. This electrotype when sufficiently strong is prepared for the reducing lathe, and a reduced copy is made the size required for the coin or medal, as the case may be.

The reducing lathe is a machine, working somewhat upon the principle of the pantograph, only in this case the one point traces or follows the form of the model, while another and much smaller point made in the form of a drill cuts away the material and thus produces a reduction of the model. This process of reducing the design from the model is necessarily a very slow operation, as accuracy of the reduction depends upon the slow motion of the machine and delicate handling of the operator. While it is not in the power of the operator or machine to improve the model, it is quite an easy matter, if not properly managed, for the machine to distort or the operator to lose the delicacy of the model.

The reducing machine can work either from a model in relief or intaglio, though the relief is more often used and is considered the better way.

In describing the process, I have said the engraver makes a model of the design he wishes to produce, or as much as he thinks desirable. To explain more fully, I would say some designs or parts of a design are not calculated for reducing by machine, and therefore the engraver only reduces so much of the design as he knows from experience will give the desired effect; the rest he cuts in...namely with gravers and chisels. [Dates, letters, ornaments, wreath elements such as berries, etc., were often added by the use of punches or gravers.]

When the reduction is made by the machine from the model it is then taken by the engraver and worked over and finished in all the detail and delicate parts, as the machine does not produce an entirely finished work. When finished by the engraver it is hardened and tempered. If the reduction has been made intaglio [cut into the die, rather than in relief], when hardened it is completed and is called a [master] die, and coins or medals can be struck from it;[1] but if in relief, it is called a hub, and the process of making a die from it commences, which is done as follows:

The hub or relief being made hard, a piece of steel is prepared in the following manner to receive the impression of the hard hub: Take a block of steel sufficiently large to make your die, and carefully anneal it until it is quite soft. This is done by heating the steel to a bright red and allowing it to cool very gradually, being careful to exclude the air by packing the steel in carbon. The steel being soft, turn off the surface of the block of steel [by using a lathe] and smooth it before you com-

---

[1] QDB note: As the inserted [master] indicates, this was the process to make the master die. Coins were not struck from master dies but, rather, were struck from working dies made later in the process.

DIE ROOM, 1901: Showing some of the lathes used to trim and finish dies and, along the far wall, a swing-arm press used for hubbing. (*The United States Mint at Philadelphia,* James Rankin Young, 1903, p. 64)

mence the process called hubbing, which is as follows:

Place the block of soft steel under the plunger of a strong screw press; then put the hard relief or hub on top of the soft steel, and bring down your plunger with a good sharp blow. This will give you an impression upon the soft steel. In order to make a proper impression, the process of annealing the steel and the one just described, called hubbing, must be repeated many times, until you have a perfect impression of the hub. This being obtained, you have a die which only requires being hardened and tempered to be ready for use....

To harden the steel dies, they are packed in cast-iron boxes filled with carbon to exclude the air, and when heated to a bright red are cooled suddenly with water. As this would leave them too hard, and liable to crack and break on the edges, the temper is technically what is called drawn, which is done by gently heating until you notice a color appearing upon the surface of the steel. A light straw color is a good color for cutting tools [such as letter punches fabricated at the Mint], but dies are generally brought to a deeper color, and in some cases to a blue.

How Dies Are Made Today

The following description of die making is adapted from a letter written in 1988 by Eleanor McKelvey, public services manager of the Philadelphia Mint, to numismatist Bill Fivaz. The process in use in 1988 differs from Charles E. Barber's method of 1896, but there are many similarities. The terms *master hub, master die, working hub,* and *working die,* used in numismatics today, are explained below (but were not specified under these terms in the preceding 1896 narrative):

Once a coin design has been approved, it is then modeled in plastilene or wax in relief (positive image), just as it will appear on the coin itself only larger. The next step is to cast the design in plaster. This produces an incuse (negative, recessed) image as it will eventually appear on the die itself. This negative plaster model is refined and the date is engraved into it. Several positive and negative plasters are produced to further refine the design. Finally a positive master plaster is cast. Then a silicon rubber mold is made (negative image). The mold is filled with epoxy resin which dries and hardens producing an extremely durable model. This epoxy model can be anywhere from three to ten times the size of the actual coin to be produced.

The next step is to reduce the size of the image on the epoxy model to the actual size of the coin to be produced. To do this, the Mint uses a Janvier Transfer-Engraving Machine. This machine has two "arms," one of which is applied to the epoxy model and the other to the end of a cylindrical-shaped steel blank. Using the principle of the fulcrum, the Janvier Transfer-Engraving Machine can trace the design of the epoxy model and engrave the same design onto the face of the blank in the size of the coin to be produced. This becomes the *master hub* (positive image) for that coin design.

The Master Hub is then used to make a *master die* by placing the master hub into a press opposite another steel blank. With several hundred tons of force, the master hub is pressed into the end of the blank, creating what is called the master die. However, it will always take more than one impression of the master hub into the steel blank to produce a satisfactory image upon the die. With at least two

Creating the Raised Hub
from the Reducing Machine

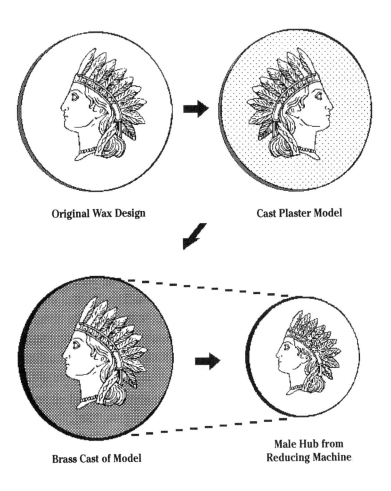

Original Wax Design   Cast Plaster Model

Brass Cast of Model   Male Hub from
Reducing Machine

(Drawings by Edgar E. Souders)

Obverse Working Die Creation

Master Hub Receives
impression of Liberty
Head from punch.

Dentils are added
around the border.

The lettering UNITED STATES OF
AMERICA is added. This com-
pletes the hub. From this master
hub a working die is made. The
working die is shown above

The date is added to the working
die. If other working dies are
made, dates are added separately
to them, resulting in slight
differences in date placement.

(Drawings by Edgar E. Souders)

hubbings (impressions, the process just described) needed, we now have the first point at which doubled dies could occur, if the hub and the die are not properly aligned between hubbings. However, because of the stringent quality control measures for inspecting the master tool, the possibility of a double master tool is extremely remote. These measures include inspection by the die shop foreman, quality control inspector, the chief sculptor engraver and the die division head. Location lugs are ground into the sides of the master die to assist in repositioning the die.

There is generally only one master hub produced, and two master dies, one of which is unfinished and held in reserve until and unless absolutely needed. The master die is then used to produce a *working hub,* then the working hub is used to produce *working dies,* of which there are very many produced. If a die is doubled, it is most likely to occur at this stage of manufacture as a result of alignment problems. The working dies are then used to actually strike the coins.

Of course, in the nineteenth century when Flying Eagle and Indian cent dies were being made, plaster, copper alloys, and iron (possibly) were used instead of modern materials, and dates from a four-digit logotype were punched individually into each working die (until 1909, when dates were incorporated into the master die).

Ms. McKelvey's detailed description also reveals how doubled die coins (such as the 1873 Doubled LIBERTY Indian cent) could have been made (most probably from the doubling of a working hub into a working die).

Models and Galvanos

During the general period under discussion— from the latter part of the decade of the 1830s to about 1880—artists at the Mint created large models of designs in wax or plaster, transfer molds were made in plaster, these molds were filled with molten metal, and from this process a metal copy of the model was created. This metal copy was then placed on a transfer lathe and reduced in size for use in the die-making process explained in detail in chapters 3 and 4.

Beginning sometime after 1880, the Philadelphia Mint used the electrodeposition of copper to create galvanos, these being metal copies or electrotypes of an artist's design, thus replacing the casting method.

In many other mints around the globe, electrotypes of models were used long before the 1880s. The Philadelphia Mint was certainly a laggard in this technology. However, electricity from galvanic batteries had been employed at the same institution decades earlier to make electrotypes, but for other purposes, as evidenced by this commentary in Jacob R. Eckfeldt and William E. DuBois' 1842 book, *A Manual of Gold and Silver Coins of All Nations,* p. 189.[1] Eckfeldt and DuBois were discussing

---

[1] Citation suggested by Craig B. Sholley.

use of Joseph Saxton's medal-ruling machine to prepare illustrations of coins for the book. This device employed a tracer pressed against the metal surface of a coin, and by a linking mechanism created a two-dimensional engraving of the coin's design. However, the use of the tracer against the surface of valuable coins would have damaged the specimens. Hence:

> We must then have been at a loss, except for the seasonable invention of the *electrotype,* of M. Jacobi. By this apparatus, a coin suspended in an electro-galvanic battery, with certain adjustments not to be described here, gradually becomes coated with copper, which, when removed in a solid cake, presents as complete a counterpart to the coin, as if produced from the die, under a coining press.
>
> Copies of all the coins were first taken in this way, and from these the rulings were made. It may be added, that the finest specimens of coin, belonging to the cabinet of the Mint, were at our command for this purpose.

Electrotyping was used widely elsewhere during the middle of the nineteenth century, including to make copies of rare coins and to prepare ornamental plaques.[1]

The Transfer Process

Hubs and dies are created as follows:

Each hub or die is made of soft steel. In its soft state it receives an impression from a transfer lathe, punches, or another hub or die.

With an impression on its surface, a given hub or die is locally hardened. Thus made hard, this hub or die can in turn be used to transfer its design into another hub or die made of soft steel. This new hub or die is then hardened and can be used, in turn, to impress into another piece of soft steel.

These transfers are done on a screw (later, beginning in 1893, on a hydraulic) press operated slowly by four or five men on the lever arms. This multiplying process can go through several generations of transfers without losing significant detail. The following two chapters explore Flying Eagle cent and Indian cent die making and striking procedures.

Mint Procedures

However, even though the Mint may have had procedures or equipment in place at a given time, other methods of hub and die preparation may have been used. As an example, the 1900 Lafayette commemora-

---

[1] Sample citations: *American Journal of Numismatics,* 1867, Vol. 1, No. 11, p. 87, in which coin dealer Edward Cogan tells of buying an electrotype 1792 Washington cent in 1856; *AJN* Vol. 2, No. 1, p. 9, in which Augustus B. Sage relates that S.H. Black, located on Broadway, New York City, "has been for years a professional electrotypist." It is related (Pollock, *United States Patterns and Related Pieces,* p. 66, and other references) that of the 1854 pattern cent (Judd-159, Pollock-186), "electrotypes [are] said to have been made at the Mint."

tive silver dollar exists today in multiple obverse die varieties, differing in the position and alignment of the letters. This indicates that letter punches were used directly on the several working dies, certainly an anachronistic procedure by 1899 (the year the dies were made), but one used, perhaps, because of time constraints and/or an anticipated limited production run.

Chapters 3 and 4 address various aspects of die making. During the preparation of this book it became evident that standard information in the excellent works of Walter Breen and Don Taxay (see Bibliography) was in many cases incomplete. A new generation of students (acknowledged in the fore part of the book and also the footnotes) has taken the Breen and Taxay work forward and has made possible a greater understanding of the processes, although many questions remain.

What started as a seemingly simple recitation of die making evolved into a rather complex, but very interesting study, of Mint procedures.

CHAPTER 3
DIES AND COIN MAKING:

Flying Eagle Cents

Flying Eagle Cent Obverse Dies

A typical Flying Eagle cent obverse die may have been made in the manner described below.

A reverse die was probably created in a somewhat similar manner, but without a date. The reverse "agricultural wreath" motif, created by Longacre in wax in 1854 for use on the $3 gold coin, was employed on the 1856 cent and was reduced from a copy of Longacre's model by use of the portrait lathe.[1]

Creating the Master Hub:
Revisiting the Gobrecht Era

The Flying Eagle motif on the 1856 cent was copied from that on the 1836 Gobrecht silver dollar. Examples of these silver dollars were struck at the Mint in December 1836 and placed into circulation at face value shortly thereafter. As will be seen, 1836 was a time of transition at the Mint.

To create a punch or master hub of the flying eagle motif years later in 1856 when creating the new small-size one-cent piece, Chief Engraver James B. Longacre may have secured an actual specimen of an 1836 Gobrecht silver dollar. Gobrecht is believed by some to have cut the eagle design for the dollar directly into soft steel, this being before the Contamin portrait lathe was used for regular die making (which first happened in spring 1837). Thus, if the Contamin lathe was the only reducing device in use, there were no large plaster, wax, or other models of the eagle used in die making. Consequently, if this were true, 20 years later in 1856 Longacre had no large original models to use. However, the scenario may have been different.

---

[1] Portrait lathe, a.k.a. transfer lathe and reducing lathe. From 1837 to 1867 a Contamin lathe, made in France, was used; in September 1867 a lathe invented by C.J. Hill of London was purchased and was used from about 1868 until the early 20th century, by which time it had been found unsatisfactory and was replaced by a Janvier lathe made in France (Taxay, *U.S. Mint and Coinage*, p. 314 and elsewhere).

PHILADELPHIA MINT IN APRIL 1865: From an old photograph showing the Mint draped in mourning cloth after President Lincoln's death. The man wearing a high hat and standing at the base of the third column from the left is Mint Director James Pollock. James Booth, the melter and refiner, is standing two steps below. (*The United States Mint at Philadelphia,* James Rankin Young, 1903, p. 8)

A glimpse of the coinage procedures in 1836 may be of interest. Unfortunately, information is somewhat contradictory, and the precise situation may never be known:

On June 18, 1836, Director Robert Maskell Patterson wrote to Secretary of the Treasury Levi Woodbury, noting in part: "Mr. Gobrecht will commence the die for the reverse immediately." This silver dollar reverse die was completed by the last week in August.

Meanwhile, the Mint had placed its order in Paris through a friend of Director Robert M. Patterson, Samuel Fisher, for a Contamin portrait lathe on November 6, 1835. Franklin Peale of the Philadelphia Mint had visited the Paris Mint, had seen one in operation, and desired to install one at the Philadelphia facility.[1]

The Contamin lathe order had been renewed on June 6, 1836. The device was scheduled to be shipped to America on the *Erie* on December 24, 1836, but delays ensued and transport did not take place until early in 1837. Thus, the Contamin lathe was of no relevance to the production of Gobrecht silver dollars which were struck in December 1836.[2]

On March 20, 1837, Director Patterson reported that the Contamin lathe had arrived "after a long and alarming delay." It was found to be poorly packed, and injuries had been sustained.[3]

Although the Contamin device may not have been used, there was technology in place for portrait-ruling and various types of pantograph copying devices were in widespread use. Circa 1817 Gobrecht had devised a medal ruling machine by which a three-dimensional medal or bas-relief object could be converted to a two-dimensional illustration for use in a publication using a linear (not slow spiral or circular as in later transfer lathes) process. An improved version of his 1817 invention was brought by Gobrecht to the Mint when he joined the staff. Numismatic historian Craig B. Sholley commented:[4]

> [At the Mint, Christian Gobrecht used his reducing pantograph] to etch the

---

[1] Peale made a report to the director of the Mint, June 17, 1835, detailing his European trip and the mints visited. Peale returned to America with several models of coin presses used in Europe, which were then studied and used in the construction of similar equipment later used at the Philadelphia Mint. "One of the coining presses constructed from a model brought from England is still used in the Mint," James Ross Snowden commented in a letter dated July 29, 1856. (Citation provided by Craig B. Sholley)

[2] Also see Walter Breen, *The Secret History of the Gobrecht Coinages*, p. 12. The Contamin portrait lathe is said to have come to America "on the next boat" after the June 6, 1836, order renewal arrived in Paris; this statement differs from the *Erie* scenario. The first regular use of the Contamin lathe is said by Breen to have been to reduce the Gobrecht dollar obverse (from a model? from a dollar coin? not stated) to create the 1837 Liberty Seated half dime and dime obverse hubs.

[3] Citation courtesy of Craig B. Sholley from a document located and copied by R.W. Julian.

[4] Letter, June 3, 1996. Craig B. Sholley furnished copies of several early Mint documents and citations to the author. More information about and an effusive tribute to Gobrecht's pantograph is found in Eckfeldt and DuBois, *A Manual of Gold and Silver Coins of All Nations,* 1842, pp. 186-188.

design on a steel blank from a model of a medal or coin. Having done this, Gobrecht then followed the etched pattern in hand cutting the master die for the medal or coin. The model for the medal or coin being oversized, the term "reduction" is used when referring to the use of this device.

With the combined ingenuity of Christian Gobrecht and Franklin Peale and the presence of Gobrecht's invention suggests that a reduction process may have been employed. Such copying lathes had been in use for decades in Europe by 1836.

That there was some kind of a reducing device in use at the Mint by mid-December 1836 is further evidenced by instructions given to Gobrecht by Franklin Peale sometime before December 14, "to proceed immediately with the *reduction* of the new device for the 1/2$ dies," to which Gobrecht agreed.[1] Whether a reducing lathe was on hand at the Mint earlier in the year—in June 1836, when Gobrecht began his work on the flying eagle reverse die for the silver dollar—is not known, but it is not out of the question in view of the mechanical prowess of Gobrecht and Peale. If a large model for Gobrecht's flying eagle was made in 1836, it is not known to exist today.

The scenario of the first use of the French (Contamin) transfer device to copy models or designs is confused by the reminiscences of George Escol Sellers. A visitor to various world mints and an engineer familiar with the machinery in use at the Philadelphia Mint, Sellers mentioned specifically the flying eagle design. However, he wrote his recollections decades later, as an old man, and his dates and facts were sometimes inaccurate:[2]

> There was imported, I think from France, a die sinking lathe. To use this lathe to do its portion of the die sinking a template die [was made] for the dollar about 6 inches in diameter. For this Uncle Titian [Peale] modeled the flying eagle and Mr. Thomas Sully, the female figure of Liberty. From these, plaster casts were made and from them plaster [molds] from which to cast bronze templates. I think the

---

[1] Citation furnished by Michael J. Hodder, letter, May 14, 1996.

[2] *Early Engineering Reminiscences of (1815-40) of George Escol Sellers,* edited by Eugene S. Ferguson, p. 74-76. Sellers, born in 1808, was 75 years old when he began writing his memoirs and observations; thus, the Gobrecht era could not have been a bright, fresh memory, even if he referred to older notes. QDB note: Alternatively, Sellers, although he mentions the dollar denomination, may have recalled some other Liberty Seated obverse and Flying Eagle reverse design combination other than that for the 1836 silver dollar; for example, the 1838 Liberty Seated figure and Flying Eagle reverse used on pattern half dollars, which would have been made during the normal period use of the Contamin lathe. In other inaccurate recollections, Sellers claimed that the first Thonnelier-type press was forged at his family's works and then assembled at the Mint by his uncle, Franklin Peale. However, Mint records and correspondence dated 1836 must take precedence over Sellers' later writing, and Mint information identifies Merrick, Agnew & Tyler as the press makers. As Craig B. Sholley (letter, June 10, 1996) suggested, "While we can use Sellers to corroborate or augment the Mint records, I do not think it is appropriate to use Sellers in counterpoint to them." Sellers' hagiographic view of his uncle Franklin Peale differs sharply from the view of Peale as a self-serving opportunist in Don Taxay's *U.S. Mint and Coinage.*

bronzes were cast at Merrick's[1] but were not satisfactory; then a lamp maker's foundry was tried with no better results.

I told Dr. Patterson and Uncle Franklin [Peale] of what I had seen Henri Mogeme do to mould the fine Berlin iron and his crucible castings and what he had told me of the importance of moulding by pressure and not tamping, [which] he called kneading or dry facing. Uncle Franklin suggested that we should try to make an iron casting from the medallion patterns, and for that purpose he went out to Cardington[2] with me. [The medallion pattern was covered with tiny sand particles taken from on top of a beam where they had fallen over a period of time. This dust is layered gently and carefully with successive layers of moist sand. This material was pressed into the face of the medallion pattern, then turned over carefully, the pattern removed, and a recessed mold remained. The process was repeated for the second side of the medallion. The casting process, in two halves, was a success.]

Further from Sellers:[3]

A total change was made on the face of the [silver dollar] coins. The female figure, with liberty shield, staff and cap. was designed by Thomas Sully. I do not recollect who made the model in relief from his design, but that of the flying eagle on the reverse, surrounded by United States of America, One Dollar, with twenty-six stars on the plain surface, was designed and modeled by Titian R. Peale. From these relief models, which were about 6 inches in diameter, castings were made to be used as templates or tool guiders in the die-sinking lathe. To get these castings satisfactory many experiments were tried in our foundry, finally settling on a kind of speculum alloy not too hard for finishing.

Although the die-sinking lathe was a labor-saving tool in the rougher portions of die sinking, it did not dispense with the final delicate hand finish, yet Mr. Charles [sic] Gobrecht, who was then the die sinker, was much opposed to its use....

On August 25, 1836, Director Patterson sent Treasury Secretary Woodbury a trial impression struck from Gobrecht's flying eagle reverse die. Designs were approved and dies were ready for striking silver dollars by September 22. Striking of coins took place sometime between that time and December.

Walter Breen has stated that production of the Gobrecht dollars did not occur for several months as it was desired to make the coins on a new steam press, and it was not ready for full-scale coinage production until about November 8, when 1836 reeded-edge half dollars were made (the silver dollars had plain edges).[4]

---

[1] QDB note adapted from Eugene S. Ferguson's note as editor of *Reminiscences,* p. 74: Probably Merrick & Towne of the Southwark Foundry; Merrick was also a partner at one time in Merrick, Agnew & Tyler.
[2] QDB note: Cardington was the name of a group of machine shops operated by Coleman Sellers (George's father) and John Brandt in Upper Darby Township, not far from Philadelphia. The shops were under Sellers family management from their founding circa 1829 until they were sold at auction shortly after the Panic of 1837.
[3] Sellers, p. 77.
[4] Walter Breen, *The Secret History of the Gobrecht Coinages,* pp. 12, 13, 23, 24; and other sources. *Gleason's Pictorial Drawing Room Companion,* July 17, 1852, illustrates the primary steam engine at the Philadelphia Mint with a pulley driving a wide belt.

CONTAMIN PORTRAIT LATHE: Illustration of the Contamin portrait lathe tracing a model (white object mounted on largest vertical disc on table) and, to its left, cutting a hub in reduced size. This general type of device, first installed at the Mint in 1837, is still used today. (*Illustrated History of the United States Mint*. George G. Evans, 1892, p. 15)

However, the Breen commentary is directly contradicted by at least two documents.[1] The first is a letter (memorandum) from R.M. Patterson, director of the Mint, to Chief Coiner Adam Eckfeldt, September 22, 1836:

> The dies for the new dollar having been sunk by Mr. Gobrecht, and the impressions approved by the Treasury Department, I am exceedingly desirous that you shall take, without delay, the necessary measures for an early issue of dollar coins. For this object I pray you to have the hubs and working dies prepared, and the proper arrangements adopted for cutting and milling the planchets, and coining them in the large screw press, the pieces being struck in a close reeded or grooved collar.[2]
>
> The employment of the screw-press is only to be temporary, and you are aware that it is of great importance that the lever-press for dollars should be completed at as early a day as possible.
>
> For this purpose, the machine shop being now ready, I beg you to use any execution to find suitable workmen, in addition to those already in the Mint, who may be employed upon the new press till it is finished—these men to be enrolled among the [unclear] hands, but to be engaged only for this special object; and paid from the appropriation for new machinery, &c.

Additional information is provided by the 1836 *Mint Report,* which noted in part:

> On the 23d of March last, the first steam coinage in America was executed at this Mint; and the performance of the press, in which the power of the lever is substituted for that of the screw, has answered all our expectations. Since that time, all the copper coins have been struck by this press, and it has been lately used with success for coining half dollars.
>
> The workmen are now engaged in making other steam presses; and, as these are completed, the coining by human labor will be abandoned, and the work that can be executed in this department of the Mint will be greatly increased.

The preceding indicates that by the close of the year 1836, all copper coins (large cents, as there was no business strike production of half cents) and some half dollars had been produced by steam. Could the 1836 Gobrecht dollars have been produced by a screw press, as per Patterson's letter of September 22?

The same 1836 *Mint Report* told of improvements in die making:

> Before the last year, the dies were formed only in part from the hub—much work still remaining to be executed by the engraver before they were ready for coining. By a modification of the process lately introduced, the entire impression on the die is transferred by the aid of the press alone; thus, not only saving much unnecessary labor to the engraver, but securing the desirable object of making the dies, for the same denominations of coins, exact facsimiles of one another.

Notwithstanding the preceding, certain Liberty Seated silver denomination dies produced for the next several years employed hand-punch-

---

[1] Citations furnished by Craig B. Sholley.
[2] QDB note: The finished 1836 Gobrecht silver dollars were made with a plain edge using a plain collar.

ing of stars.[1] As is readily apparent in the review of numerous dies and manufacturing methods employed over a period of time at the Mint, it was often the case that certain refined technologies and improvements were used at the same time older techniques were employed.

A letter from Director Patterson to Secretary of the Treasury Levi Woodbury, June 30, 1837, reveals that the Contamin device was performing satisfactorily:[2]

> I have the honor to send you enclosed some specimens of a new coinage of dimes, which I pray you to submit to the inspection of our President.
>
> To have prepared the hub for the original die for the head [obverse] of this coin, by the ordinary process, would have occupied our Engraver two months, and would have been a task requiring great skill and close labor. But by means of an instrument which I caused to be made at Paris, and which the French call a tour à portrait, the hubs both for the dime and half dime were cut in one afternoon, and required afterwards only retouching and some finishing by hand. They have, besides, the advantage of being exact facsimiles, reduced, of the larger dies.
>
> [The director went on to say that after many problems had been resolved, the steam presses were now functioning satisfactorily, and one had turned out] 400,000 cents within the last few weeks, without interruption or accident, and our largest press has been coining half dollars with perfect success.

Creating the Master Hub:
Longacre In 1856

Years later in 1856, Longacre used the pantograph method on a Contamin reducing lathe, similar to the process described in the preceding chapter, to reduce the flying eagle on the dollar coin (alternatively, from an early brass or bronze casting of the eagle motif, if such existed) to an appropriate size for the new Flying Eagle cent.[3]

If a large flying eagle matrix or model was not used on the copying lathe during the creation of the Flying Eagle cent in 1856, it may have been the case that an actual 1836 silver dollar *coin* was employed as the model. Under this scenario, this coin was affixed to a very slowly rotat-

---

[1] See the writer's further comments in the Louis E. Eliasberg, Sr., Collection catalogue, May 1996; *e.g.*, note under Lot 947: "It is apparent that stars on the obverse of half dimes of the Liberty Seated, No Drapery varieties were hand-punched individually and thus show *rotational* double punching in some instances."

[2] Letter copy furnished by Craig B. Sholley. No coinage of silver dollars was contemplated in June 1837, and the reference is to other denominations.

[3] Several different varieties of portrait and copying lathes were developed, primarily in France, the source in 1836 of the Contamin device, which arrived at the Philadelphia Mint in spring 1837. A collection of such machines is currently in the Arts et Métiers Museum in Paris. Several European die-making innovations were introduced into the Philadelphia Mint by Franklin Peale who toured European minting facilities in the 1830s; Taxay's *U.S. Mint and Coinage* gives details. For additional information on die making and striking, *The Art and Craft of Coinmaking*, by Denis R. Cooper is highly recommended. Portrait lathes were in use at the Paris Mint circa 1780 and at Matthew Boulton's Soho Mint in the 1790s; by the early nineteenth century "reducing machines were in use in many European mints" (Cooper, pp. 164-165).

EAGLE MOTIF ON 1836 GOBRECHT DOLLAR: 1836 Gobrecht
silver dollar. Dies by Christian Gobrecht. Mint mascot "Peter"
is said to have been the model. It seems likely that the eagle
motif on the reverse of an actual specimen of this dollar was
mechanically copied by a reducing lathe in 1856 to create the
flying eagle on the new cent.

ing vertically-mounted disc, while at the same time a soft steel blank, somewhat smaller in size, was affixed to another part of the lathe, with its face in a vertical position, and was synchronized by means of connecting gears to rotate at the same speed as the larger model.[1]

A tiny needle at one end of the pantograph traced the relief features of the eagle on the dollar coin (alternatively, a large model), while at the other end, a tiny cutter was adjusted to cut away the soft steel blank and create a reduced-size version of the eagle for use on the cent.[2] For a large coin or medal, the process took many hours, even a day or so, to complete. A smaller coin such as a half dime or dime could be done in a few hours.

The slower the tracing of the model and the smaller the tracing needle and cutting point, the sharper the details would be in the master hub. Even with a relatively fine tracing needle and cutting point, many of the delicate features on the silver dollar eagle (if such was used) were not transferred, such lost features including minute feather details. This is because the $1 coin eagle was less than twice the size (lateral dimensions) of the eagle on the cent. Normally, to achieve excellent details, the model or master had to be much larger, often four to six times the dimensions of the hub and sometimes even much larger.

The soft steel blank with the tiny flying eagle in relief was trimmed on a lathe, heated to a cherry-red color, then quenched to make the steel hard (and somewhat brittle). After this was done, the master hub (a.k.a. device or design punch), as it was called, was cleaned to remove any roughness or scale. From this point, probably another transfer was made to impress the flying eagle design *incuse* in soft steel.[3]

At that point, Longacre did extensive retouching to the small incuse image in soft steel. The eagle's eye, which on the dollar had a prominent eyelid covering the top part of the eyeball, was created on the cent by punching a circle from a ring punch. The eagle's claws were modified as were certain feather details and outlines. However, the general configuration, arrangement of the feathers, etc., remained the same as on the dollar.

---

[1] Don Taxay, *U.S. Mint and Coinage,* p. 150, describes the process in detail.

[2] Craig B. Sholley, letter, June 3, 1996, commented that the Contamin lathe had a fixed cutter (which produced metal shavings), but years later other devices such as the Janvier lathe had rotating drill points or cutters (the latter being milling machines; these produced spiral shavings and metal particles; this residue was carried away by a recirculating bath of mineral oil).

[3] Alternatively, the portrait lathe could have cut the design incuse to begin with in the soft steel blank. The portrait lathe could make either an incuse or a relief copy of the model or master, and it could also be adjusted to vary the relief of the design. Chris Pilliod, letter, June 2, 1996, commented concerning *modern* procedures: "I talked with two current Mint engravers. As you relate in your text, the transfer lathe can operate either way. Traditionally an artist prefers to make his model in relief so that the master hub is incuse. However, Tom Rodgers prefers the opposite."

By another transfer, a master hub was made of the flying eagle hub and was kept on hand for further use.

Master Hub Variations

There were two master hubs used to make 1856-1858 Flying Eagle cent obverses:

Obverse Master Hub 1: The first flying eagle motif was used to make at least two master dies (see below), one with Style of 1856 letters used for all 1856 cents and some early 1857 cents; and the Style of 1857 letters used to make most 1857 and about half of the 1858 cents. This first flying eagle motif had smoothed feathers at the top of the neck, a complete circle or ring around the eye, and a few other features differing from the following.

Obverse Master Hub 2: The flying eagle motif was slightly revised (different neck feathers, now somewhat ruffed at the top; eagle eye treatment with circle incomplete at top, etc.). Used to make the master die for 1858 Small Letters cents.

Reverses: Reverse differences exist among 1856-1858 cents, often identified by the topological relationship of the letters in ONE CENT with the wreath elements. On some later issues the veins in the first and second cotton leaves (which some have called "maple" leaves from their appearance) in the wreath are incised (the third or top cotton leaf is not incised on any variety).

Other Tools

Every engraver had at his fingertips several sets or fonts of letters and numbers arranged on the faces of individual punches. These were typically kept in a wooden rack with each punch upright in a hole drilled to receive it. Each punch was in relief and appeared identical to a finished letter or number on a coin. The face of each punch was slightly tapered. Punch sets were kept separate and arranged by size. Sometimes there would be extra punches for commonly used letters such as vowels.

These punches were often ordered from machine shop suppliers or engravers outside of the Mint, although they were sometimes made at the Mint as well. Sometimes a flat strip or matrix containing many letters, numerals, and ornaments was employed, and soft steel rods were simply tapped into the orifices to create the characters in relief.[1]

---

[1] An illustration of such a matrix is in *The Art and Craft of Coinmaking,* p. 80. The Philadelphia Mint had extensive machining and tool-making facilities, and in later decades sometimes made its own coin presses (cf. John Sinnock, "Making Dies At the Philadelphia Mint." *The Numismatist,* October 1941).

As punches were used they tended to wear or become damaged, the latter often taking the form of delicate serif tips breaking off. Sometimes punches would be lightly ground down to recondition their faces, causing some slight differences in later impressions made by these punches, such as making the elements seem thicker and the interior spaces (such as at the inside top of the letter A) seem smaller.

In instances in which a series of numbers or letters was to be used in the same sequence repeatedly, multiple-letter or multiple-number ("logotype") punches were made, usually at the die shop in the Mint. Examples of multiple-subject punches include four-digit date punches and so-called "ring punches," more properly arc punches, with groups of letters. These logotype punches were made by the transfer process (hard steel into soft steel, hardened, then into soft steel, etc.) used to make working hubs from master hubs.

Creating the Master Die

The steel hub punch with the flying eagle in raised relief was used to create a master die. The eagle motif was punched into a soft steel blank. Next, the engraver punched in the letters UNITED STATES OF AMERICA, probably individually (as alignments are irregular), although some have suggested that ring punches were used. Some type of an arc-like jig was probably employed to ensure that the letters were all about the same distance from the outside border of the die and that they were spaced regularly (more or less).[1] These features were all intaglio (recessed) in the master die.

At this point the master die for the obverse of a Flying Eagle cent consisted of the eagle and the inscription UNITED STATES OF AMERICA. The master die was then turned on a lathe, trimmed, and the dentils (a.k.a. denticles; toothlike projections along the rim) impressed, probably by a punching machine to ensure that they were consistent in spacing and regular in size.[2]

The entire master die was then hardened by quenching. By another heating and quenching process the face of the master die was made

---

[1] Craig B. Sholley commented, letter, June 3, 1996: "It is my conclusion that a punching machine was employed for this purpose. There is a record of the purchase of such a machine many years earlier (cf. Frank Stewart, *History of the First United States Mint*, p. 174, showing the payment on July 20, 1793, of $24.67 to Jacob Craft for "a punching machine for the die sinker"). The punching machine likely had an adjustable arm which held the punch over the die and perhaps "click stops" ever degree or so to allow exact positioning of the punch around the circumference."

[2] The addition of dentils to early master and other dies is not addressed in detail in current numismatic literature. Craig B. Sholley, letter, June 3, 1996, suggested that a punching machine, such as that purchased by the Mint in 1793, would have provided the necessary uniformity. Moreover, although no description of dentil making has been located for Flying Eagle cents, it is known that a punching machine was in use to make dentils in the 1870s for the Morgan silver dollar.

very hard, while the shank or back part of the master die was softer so as to absorb blows without shattering. The entire master die could then be tempered (softened) to give it needed ductility to prevent shattering.[1]

Master Die Variations

In 1856 one master die was made for the Flying Eagle cent (today the letters are called the Style of 1856 letters and, among other characteristics, have a somewhat squared center in the O in OF; A and M in AMERICA touch, but the M is slightly higher than the A). This identical master die was used to make all 1856-dated dies and, very early in 1857, to make 1857-dated dies with Style of 1856 letters. In all probability, the letter punches used to make this and other master dies were ordered from a private source outside the Mint.

In early 1857, probably by March but certainly by April, a new master die was made with "Style of 1857" letters. These letters are slightly heavier than the Style of 1856 and in some instances have thicker upright or vertical members. The interior of the O in OF is irregular, but not squared (the new style is called by some a D-shaped interior); A and M touch and are each of the same height where they join. This master die was used for the balance of 1857 and in 1858 for the Large Letters coinage.[2]

In 1858 another master die was made, this with small, heavy, and widely separated letters (including A and M). This also employed a new master hub (Hub 2 as described above, only the second to be used in the series) which differed in slight respects from the earlier one. This is the 1858 Small Letters variety.

Working Hubs and Dies

From a hardened master die, working hubs (in raised relief, appearing similar to a coin itself, but without date) were made in soft steel by the transfer method. In turn, working hubs were hardened and used to make working dies, the latter in soft steel, later hardened.

Along these transfer processes, working hubs and working dies sometimes exhibited slightly different characteristics, even if made from the same master die. For example, a hub or die impressed deeply into another during the transfer process would give the letters the appearance of being slightly thicker, larger and closer together. However, as the let-

---

[1] Certain information in this paragraph is adapted from Chris Pilliod, letter, June 2, 1996.
[2] However, certain 1857 Flying Eagle cents are believed to exist with mixed fonts (see 1857 sub-chapter). This may indicate one or more additional master dies or, alternatively, strengthening of letters by hand punching.

ters did not move in their positions, all relational and topological aspects remained the same.

On deeply impressed working dies for the reverse of the Flying Eagle cent the leaves on the agricultural wreath appeared larger at their tips, the "buds" (corn ear tips) at the top of the wreath appeared closer together, and the E in ONE appeared closed or nearly so, among other minute differences. On lightly impressed working dies the elements appeared lighter and farther apart, and the E seemed to be less closed.

In 1858 two different master dies (each from a different hub, with the eagle styled slightly differently) were employed to make working hubs and, down the line by transfer, working dies.

Relief vs. Incised Cotton Leaf Veins

On the original reverse master hubs of 1856 and 1858, the three cotton leaves near the top of the wreath (here numbered from the bottom, first leaf, second leaf, and third leaf) were in the form of relief or raised veins.[1]

As time went on, these raised veins became less prominent, and in many strikings of 1857 and 1858 cents they are poorly defined. Although the circumstances were not recorded, it seems that in the working hub—which showed the wreath and other reverse features in relief—a graving tool was used to cut or incise outlines at the veins in the first and second cotton leaves on each side. This incise veins were cut on top of or next to what remained of the raised veins. This did not represent a new design, but was an effort to strengthen the prominence of a pre-existing feature. The procedure was somewhat clumsily done, as examination of a coin under magnification will reveal.

All coins seen with incised veins at leaves 2 and 3 have been on the die style first used in 1858 with very short leaves ("Low Leaves") below C and T of CENT. Virtually nothing on the subject of incised veins has appeared in the literature, and the distribution of this feature among various 1858 Low Leaf reverse dies remains to be learned.[2]

The 3rd (highest) cotton leaf was not altered, and the raised veins, quite visible in 1856, fade to veritable obscurity by 1858, including on the issues with the first and second leaves incised.

Relief of Working Die Features

Some working dies for Flying Eagle cents were relapped (reground),

---

[1] The original wax model of the "agricultural wreath" made by Longacre in 1854 for use on the 1854 $3 has prominent raised veins in the cotton leaves (cf. Thomas K. DeLorey, present owner of the model, letter, May 17, 1996).

[2] During research for the present work, several specialists commented that they had never paid attention to this feature.

lightly polished, or otherwise resurfaced during their production life. When a die was resurfaced, features in lower relief were ground away, making dentils, letters and date numerals, and leaf elements (on the reverse) look thinner and more open at their low areas (where design or element meets the plane surface of the field).

On some dies, certain features such as letters in ONE CENT may have been strengthened by hand.

Different-appearing coins struck at different times from the same die are referred to as *die states,* not die varieties.

Dates on Flying Eagle Cent Dies

Dates were added separately to working dies of Flying Eagle cents, all from the same 1856, 1857, and 1858 logotypes. Thus, for a given year, date varieties occurred with regard to positioning on the die, but not in respect to the alignment of the numerals with each other. While only the most dedicated specialist is interested in collecting minute date position differences, such are interesting to observe.

Among Flying Eagle cents a quick way to determine date positions is to note the distance from the left side of the bottom serif of the 1 and the dentils (rounded nubs in the border, a.k.a. denticles) below. Further, if an imaginary line is drawn downward from that tip, and perpendicular to the base of the 1, where does it intersect the dentils? If you want to be very technical, the best way to really determine if there is even a slight difference is to compare two coins side by side with a stereoscopic device or a photographic overlay. Even so, considering that over 100 different obverse dies were made for the 1857 Flying Eagle cent alone, some minor differences may not be detectable.

At least two 1857 cent dies were overpunched with 1858 date logotypes, thus creating 1858/7 overdates.

Dates can vary in their appearance even if they are made from the same four-digit logotype punch. A date punched lightly into a die will appear to have thinner numerals and be more "open" (the ball on the 5 separated from the vertical element above it; on 1856 cents, the top knob of the 6 separated from the curved part below, etc.). The entire date may appear smaller than one punched deeply into the die. Similarly, if a die with a deeply punched date was reground or repolished during its life, parts of the lower areas of the date would be removed, making the date seem smaller, thinner, and more open.

If the same four-digit logotype was punched twice or more, a repunched date occurred, which showed repunching at one, two, three, or all four date numerals; these are collected as separate varieties if the repunching is distinctive or unusual.

Flying Eagle Cent Die Finishing

After working dies were made to strike Flying Eagle cents, the dies were dressed or finished to remove burrs and surface irregularities. This was probably done on some type of a reciprocating or rotary lapping device (if the latter, the flat edge of the device would have been used edge-on, as the finish lines in dies are absolutely parallel, not arc-like.[1]

Proof dies were given special mirror finishes. Often tiny parallel *raised* lines can be seen on business strikes and Proofs, these being die finishing marks. While these can occur anywhere on a coin, typically they are in the field or flat area and are most readily seen in the field close to the border dentils. Magnification is required to discern them. Hold a coin carefully and turn it so that light from a bulb reflects from the coin's field into your eye.

Among Proof dies, those dated 1856 were polished less fully than those dated 1857 and 1858.[2] Among nearly all Proof Flying Eagle cents, the Proof surface is not as mirrorlike as that found, for example, on 1857 and 1858 Proof silver or gold coins.

Die Injuries

Clash marks were caused by one die impressing into the other. This was probably most often done during the set-up process for the coining press or when a die was adjusted. Conventional wisdom[3] has it that these clash marks were *always* created during *coinage,* but upon reconsideration of the matter, this seems unlikely except in a few circumstances. The type of press used to coin business strike Flying Eagle and Indian cents was driven by a rotating flywheel actuating a knuckle-type device (a.k.a. lever press). In such a press, the top or hammer die comes downward a specific distance, then retreats upward to begin the cycle anew. Whether or not there is a planchet between the dies, the top die comes down to a specified distance from the bottom die. If there is a planchet, a coin is struck. If there is no planchet, the top die simply goes down to its normal position, strikes nothing, and then retreats. There is no mechanism on a flywheel-type press by which the top die, if secured in its holder, will go farther down and impact the bottom die if a planchet is not there.

---

[1] Adapted from a commentary by Craig B. Sholley, letter, June 3, 1996.
[2] A detailed discussion of the finish on 1856 Flying Eagle cent dies is given in the 1856 sub-chapter.
[3] Including past comments by the present writer; future comments will be revised!

Among 1857 Flying Eagle cents there are three die varieties known with clash marks from dies of *different denominations,* probably caused during the press set-up process (see detailed commentary in the 1857 Flying Eagle cent sub-chapter). More often in various other series from half cents through gold during this time period, clash marks were caused by the obverse and reverse dies for the same coin hitting each other during the press set-up process.[1]

However, there is an exception to the foregoing: In addition, clash marks could occur during the normal coining process "if the mechanism that raises the lower die to eject the struck coin malfunctions and does not lower the die before the upper die comes down, and there is no planchet between the dies."[2] Similarly, if one die or the other became loose in its chuck or matrix, die clashing could occur during a coinage run.

Flying Eagle Cent Die Wear

As dies were used they became worn. Fields sometimes became pebbly and grainy, especially toward the borders where the metal flow was the greatest. Coins struck from worn dies often appear somewhat satiny or "greasy" and lack frosty lustre.

Dies sometimes broke, causing tiny raised hairline die breaks. Sometimes a small piece would chip or spall from the edge, causing coins to have a small blob or "cud" near the border.

Striking (Business Strikes)

If the dies were spaced slightly more apart than they should have been in the coining press, the coins would not strike up properly. Among Flying Eagle cents this usually manifested itself with weak areas on the eagle's tail (in particular), the eagle's head, and on the reverse, certain areas of the wreath; these reverse details being deep in the die and opposite the aforementioned obverse areas. The requirement that metal flow in opposite directions to fill die recesses could not be easily met under normal high-speed coinage conditions.

These indistinct features are seen on Mint State coins and are not

---

[1] In earlier times before steam coinage, when hand-operated presses were used, clash marks were indeed caused by dies coming together without intervening planchets. Sometimes an early die pair would clash multiple times (*e.g.,* on the 1828 Small Date dime, JR-1, known with three or four distinct clashes on the reverse; on the 1799 BB-161 silver dollar which has more multiple clashes on the obverse below the bust than can be readily counted).

[2] Thomas K. DeLorey, note, April 12, 1996; also in same note: "I have seen clash marks appear on late-state Morgan silver dollar dies, long after set-up is finished." QDB note: Of course, there is the possibility that one or both dies had been used, removed from the press for one reason or another, then put back in the press later—involving another set-up process. (Coinage procedures are rarely simple!)

wear. Sometimes the surface of the *original planchet* can be seen in areas that are not struck up. These areas did not have metal flow and thus show any marks, nicks, etc., that were present on the original planchet before coinage. Noted variety specialist Bill Fivaz refers to these as "planchet abrasions."

In contrast, if the dies were spaced slightly too close together, the coin would be very sharply struck, and any excess metal would be forced up between the restraining collar and the dies to create a wire rim. While such coins are pleasing to numismatists, at the Mint spacing the dies too close together caused rapid die wear and breakage.

Occasionally a business strike Flying Eagle cent will be seen with *bifurcated* letters in which the bottoms of the letters in UNITED STATES OF AMERICA will be split, thus, for example, giving a fork-like appearance to the bottom of the I. Among numerals, there will also be irregularities, such as indentations or scallops on what otherwise would be rounded areas of the 8's. The letters and numerals appear to be "fancy" or "frilly." These occur on many denominations within the American series, but perhaps most often on copper, nickel, and silver denominations, and less frequently on gold coins. Some writers (*e.g.,* M.H. Bolender in his 1950 book on silver dollars) have considered these to be different die states or even varieties, but they are nothing but artifacts of the striking process and are due to metal flow outward (with lessened upward and into-the-die-orifice emphasis at the borders) as the planchet spreads, especially if the retaining collar is not in place (such pieces can be of larger than usual diameter and are referred to as "broadstruck"). Bifurcations are sometimes seen on off-center strikes as well, these also being struck outside the collar.

Business strikes were made on Thonnelier-type knuckle-action presses, advanced versions of the models first installed at the Mint in March 1836 and later improved by Rufus Tyler of the firm that built the presses (Merrick & Agnew).[1] Chief Coiner Franklin Peale is traditionally credited, wrongly, for these innovations, due in part to his self-serving articles in the *Journal of the Franklin Institute* and by George Escol Sellers' glowing praise in his *Engineering Reminiscences* for his uncle.

Peale was a devious man at the Mint and was fired in 1854. During his tenure he used its facilities to make kites, magician's apparatus, a "noisy

---

[1] The Merrick & Agnew firm was best known as a builder of hand-pumped fire engines. Rufus Tyler later became chief coiner at the New Orleans Mint. A letter from Mint Director James Ross Snowden to Secretary of the Treasury James Guthrie, July 29, 1856, gave certain historical accounts and noted that Tyler had a contract with the government to supply the Philadelphia Mint and its branches (Charlotte, Dahlonega, and New Orleans) "with coining presses, milling machines, and cutting presses. Mr. Tyler was, I am informed, a scientific and practical mechanic and eminent machinist." (Letter copy provided by Craig B. Sholley)

sofa" (which wheezed, honked, and squawked when someone sat upon it), and other things for his personal amusement and who sent Mint workmen to his home to perform cleaning and repairs. He also conducted a private medal-making business there.[1]

This basic knuckle-action coining press mechanism, also called the lever press mechanism, was pioneered in 1817 in Köln, Germany, by D. Uhlhorn. The striking was much more uniform than that accomplished by the old screw-type press driven by weighted arms. In general, coins of all kinds struck by a screw press were apt to be sharper in definition (coins were "squeezed") than those produced by quick-action steam-powered presses (quickly "stamped"), but there are numerous exceptions.

The first steam press employed in Philadelphia was a copy of the Uhlhorn-Thonnelier style mechanism and was made in Philadelphia by Merrick, Agnew & Tyler, following experimentation at the Mint in 1835 from sketches and models made in France and England by Peale.

In 1858 David Gilbert improved the Mint presses. In 1874 a larger and more powerful type of knuckle-action press made in Philadelphia by Morgan & Orr was installed.

It was Mint practice over the years to keep old presses on hand as new presses were added, so that at any given time the age of the equipment was mixed.[2] In virtually all instances, the addition of a new piece of die-making or coining equipment at a given time did not mean that all earlier methods were immediately abandoned.

Power was from a vertical "steeple" type steam engine located at a distance in the building and transmitted to the press via shafts and pulleys.[3]

---

[1] For expanded information about Peale's misuse of Mint facilities see Don Taxay, *U.S. Mint and Coinage*, pp. 183-184 (and other pages). A letter from James Ross Snowden to Secretary of the Treasury James Guthrie, July 29, 1856, cited earlier in another context, examined Peale's claims to have invented certain things, and in the majority of instances specifically attributed the innovations to other people; this was in response to Peale's own testimony and memorial, and statements made to an investigative committee (Senate document dated May 23, 1856), crediting Peale for vastly improving the operations and efficiency of the Mint. Peale left behind a trail of admirers, however, and scattered references in later articles portray him in a favorable light (*e.g.,* Abbott's 1861 story of the Mint in *Harper's New Monthly Magazine,* and in several privately published tourists' guides to the Mint).

[2] Morgan & Orr made powerful presses used to strike the new trade dollar denomination in 1873; one of these, used for years at the San Francisco Mint, is on display today at the ANA Headquarters building in Colorado Springs, CO. Relative to the use of old presses, during the coin shortage of the 1960s long-stored presses from the New Orleans Mint and an old press from the Carson City Mint were again pressed into service to make new coins. In the 1970s and 1980s old-style knuckle-action business strike presses were run at slow speed at the San Francisco Mint and used to make modern Proof coins for collectors; this despite widespread conventional wisdom that hydraulic presses were always used to make Proofs.

[3] Probably the one built 1829-1830 by Rush & Muhlenberg, 30 h.p. (cf. George Escol Sellers, *Early Engineering Reminiscences,* pp. 72, 75). Adam Eckfeldt disliked the horizontal type of steam engine, which was thought by many technicians to be superior. The Charlotte, Dahlonega, and New Orleans mints used horizontal engines.

EARLY STEAM-POWERED PRESS: Presses of this type—built in Philadelphia by Merrick, Agnew & Tyler using systems developed by Uhlhorn and Thonnelier—were driven by a belt attached to the calf wheel at the left of the device and powered by a steam plant located at a distance. Steam-powered presses were first used at the Philadelphia Mint in March 1836. Gobrecht's famous 1836-dated Flying Eagle silver dollars were struck on a press of this type as were Flying Eagle cents in 1857 and 1858. In the latter year the press shown here was remodeled and rebuilt by David Gilbert. (*Coins and Coinage: The United States Mint, Philadelphia,* A.M. Smith, undated edition from the 1880s, p. 12)

Planchets for Flying Eagle cents were made within the Mint from ingots of copper-nickel. These ingots were flattened into long strips by a rolling mill, whose steel rollers were moved closer together until the required thickness was obtained. From each strip, planchets were cut by a punch press, much in the manner of a cookie cutter.

Planchets were tumbled to remove rough edges, then annealed by heating and slow cooling to soften them, cleaned in a light acid bath, rinsed, then run through a milling (a.k.a. upsetting) machine which gave each planchet a raised rim. This made it easier for metal to flow into finished high rims during the coining process.[1]

Planchets with raised rims were hand-fed into a brass tube on the front of the press, from which point mechanical pincers grabbed each planchet and put it in striking position within the retaining collar and atop the bottom or anvil die. The top or hammer die descended, compressed the planchet against the bottom die and outward to the collar, and then retreated, while the anvil die rose slightly and pushed the finished cent out of the collar, at which point it was mechanically retrieved and placed into a chute, emptying into a small metal container.

Striking (Proofs)

Proof coins are said to have been struck during this era by using a screw press which operated more slowly than a steam-powered press. However, it is possible that knuckle-type presses of the regular steam-driven variety were employed, but at a slower speed than in the Coining Department. Production took place in the Medal Department, which was separate from the mass-production coinage facility and which was loosely supervised. No records survive of the specific quantities struck of Proof Flying Eagle cents, if indeed any records were ever kept.

To create a Proof Flying Eagle cent, polished obverse and reverse dies compressed a cleaned and lightly polished planchet that was placed into the die and removed by hand, so as to prevent marks. It was recommended to strike each coin twice to fully bring up the sharpness of the design, but in practice many if not most seem to have been struck just once. Further, it seems likely that certain specimens made for collectors were struck on ordinary (not cleaned or lightly polished) planchets. Thus, Proofs among certain copper-nickel cents of this era cannot be as easily differentiated as can be contemporary silver and gold Proof coins.

---

[1] The copper-nickel metal caused problems with the tumbling machines as traces of this metal adhered to gold planchets when gold was later tumbled in the same devices. The annealing of planchets varied over the years; sometimes this was done before adding the upset rim and other times after. The rolling of the metal strip, cutting of planchet discs, and upsetting the rim "work hardened" the planchets and made them more difficult to strike; annealing softened them.

Challenge

The exact methods from beginning to end by which dies were made and coins struck during the days of the Flying Eagle cent are not known today. While the above processes represent those known to have been in use at the Mint during the time indicated, there is a good possibility that some procedures varied from those I have delineated. The entire subject of die preparation and coin striking is undergoing a renaissance of research, and without doubt new findings and theories will be published in the future.

CHAPTER 4
DIES AND COIN MAKING:

Indian Cents

Indian Cent Obverse Dies

A typical Indian cent obverse die was made in the same general manner as just described for Flying Eagle cents, but with different devices.

As is the case with the making of Flying Eagle cent dies, the exact steps for making Indian cent dies were not recorded at the Mint, and some aspects of the process can only be theorized today. Fortunately, there are some excellent minds at work on this subject, and knowledge today is much greater than it was even a decade ago.

A wax model of the Indian by Longacre survives today in the National Coin Collection at the Smithsonian Institution. However, it differs in some important details from the first Indian cents struck.

From a related basic model, perhaps with different treatment of the headband (see discussion by Larry R. Steve below), an incuse plaster impression (the galvano process did not go into general use until after the early 1880s and quite probably not until the early 1890s),[1] would have been taken of the relief model and used as a mold for molten brass (the usual metal used at the time; quite possibly, other copper alloys were also employed). This large brass duplicate, in relief, would have been placed on the transfer lathe and reduced mechanically.[2]

After the portrait was reduced to smaller size by the lathe, engravers used a system of actual-size hard-steel to soft-steel transfer processes, adding raised letters (as appearing on finished coins) by punching letters into intaglio hubs and masters and adding incuse letters by punching letters into relief hubs and masters. I theorize that this general multiplying process was used for Indian cents, and that the models

---

[1] Walter Breen, *Dies & Coinage*, p. 18; more specifically, John R. Sinnock, "Making Dies at the Philadelphia Mint," in which he stated that the galvano process was one of the die-making innovations instituted within the past half century (*e.g.*, since 1891).

[2] Denis R. Cooper, *The Art and Craft of Coinmaking*, p. 161. Cooper specifies iron or bronze in use in Britain and, presumably, certain other mints, but the present writer can locate no reference to iron having been used at Philadelphia in the general period from the 1850s through the 1880s; typical references are to brass (*e.g.*, see 1861 die-making process described in Chapter 2).

over the years consisted of the portrait as described above, but not the inscription UNITED STATES OF AMERICA. The lettering is so finely detailed that I doubt if it could have been transferred while retaining sharpness.

Alternatively, some scholars believe that Longacre modeled the obverse—Indian portrait, letters in UNITED STATES OF AMERICA, letters in LIBERTY, and everything else except the date—on an oversize raised (relief) wax or plaster model comparable to the way entire coin designs and inscriptions were translated later in the nineteenth century.

Processes apparently varied from denomination to denomination and over a period of time. Craig B. Sholley furnished for examination an 1840 Liberty Seated half dollar, Philadelphia Mint, which clearly shows arc-like portrait lathe lines in the incuse letters of LIBERTY on the shield, proving conclusively that LIBERTY was in the original large model for this half dollar issue (this motif, with drapery, was introduced in 1839).

The steel master hub punch, in raised relief, with the Indian portrait was used to create a master die by impressing the portrait into its center.

LIBERTY in the Headband:
Larry Steve's Comments

How and at what point was the word LIBERTY added to the headband of the Indian cent? Larry R. Steve offers these ideas:[1]

This question can be answered in many different ways, all with the same conclusion.

Although I have not taken any specific measurements, a casual observation of LIBERTY on the headband reveals that it is consistently positioned throughout the entire series, both among the different dates and among the different dies of the same date. If the letters of LIBERTY were individually punched into the master die *after* the motif of the Indian had been impressed through the hubbing process, then there should be evidence of irregular spacing between the letters, or of the alignment along the bases. None has been detected.

Even if some sort of jig were used to insure proper base alignment, or spacers between the letters, or even if a matrix of letters was used to create a single punch, there would still be some evidence of irregular positioning between the upper and lower edge of the headband. Again, none has been detected. Other evidence of letter punching for LIBERTY would manifest itself either through broken serifs, or as "outline images" from the base of the punch itself. Once again, none has been detected.

Based upon all these observations, I can only conclude that LIBERTY was part of the brass or other model and transferred to the master hub, and that it was subsequently "impressed' into the master die through the hubbing process rather than being "punched" into the die by hand.

---

[1] Letter, May 9, 1996.

LONGACRE SKETCHES: Three different sketches of Liberty by James Longacre. The top and lower left sketches were used on gold dollars, the sketch at lower right shows the feather headdress modified for use on the Indian cent. (Library Company of Pennsylvania; reproduced in Taxay, *U.S. Mint and Coinage*, p. 213)

Arguments may be presented that both the [brass casting] and master hub were sans LIBERTY, based upon the wax model now at the Smithsonian Institution. It could be argued further that LIBERTY was then subsequently punched into the master die (this would imply that there was just one master die). I believe that as the wax model has a broad bust point [unlike the narrow bust point first used to make Indian cents in pattern form in 1858] and has a beaded top and bottom edge to the headband, it is impossible that this was used to create a brass casting.... As there were multiple master dies made in the Indian cent series (with different bust points, with different spacing of letters as in the dividing line at the 1886 Type I and II, with L on ribbon, etc.) and as the position and arrangement of the word LIBERTY remained constant, LIBERTY must have been part of the brass casting.

As an alternative theory (and I raise the point simply for discussion), a LIBERTY-less incuse portrait of the Indian could have been made in soft steel, the letters L-I-B-E-R-T-Y added by individual punching,[1] and this image could have been multiplied (by the soft steel hardened, impressed into soft steel, hardened, etc., repetitive process) to create later Indian image punches that could have been modified by reshaping the bust point. I agree with Larry R. Steve that LIBERTY was added to the design very early (in 1858 when the first pattern Indian cents were made), and it did not vary after the beginning.

Craig Sholley's Comments

Craig B. Sholley has furnished a specimen of an 1864 bronze (without L) Indian cent with many raised circular lines on the portrait, artifacts from the transfer lathe process. While to my eye these lines are between and near the letters in the word LIBERTY, none seem to be on the letters themselves. Perhaps other specimens exist which would show such a feature on the letters, and the answer would be resolved.

His commentary on this and other matters is germane to the present discussion:[2]

On the question of which elements were in the model and which were entered at the master hub or master die stage, I think that the enclosed coins [1840 Liberty Seated half dollar and 1864 bronze Indian cent] and photos will assist in a rather straightforward analysis.

On the 1840 Liberty Seated half dollar, note that the lathe lines can be seen within the letters of LIBERTY. Therefore LIBERTY was in the model, since any punching of the letters after the reduction would have destroyed the machining lines. Likewise, note that some lines can be seen going up the sides of the crossbars and stripes in the shield. This demonstrates that these lines were also in the mode. However, note that the reverse shield lines on all Liberty Seated halves prior to 1858 are hand cut. This effectively demonstrates the limitation of the lathe high

---

[1] If so, perhaps the letters from this same punch font can be found elsewhere among contemporary (circa late 1850s) Mint productions such as medals; I have not explored this possibility.

[2] Letter, June 3, 1996.

1864 BRONZE INDIAN CENT, without L on ribbon. Close-up of portrait details showing raised arcs from the portrait lathe used to create the master hub. These arcs are most prominent in the area of Miss Liberty's eye. (Craig B. Sholley Collection)

aspect ratio (height to width) elements cannot be reproduced. In 1858 a new re-duction was made to produce the Type II half dollar hub. The shield lines were cut into the new master die and reproduced by hubbing from that point on.

On the 1864 bronze Indian cent, note that the lathe lines can be seen within the upper loop of B and between the middle and upper crossbar of E in LIBERTY. I also believe that the lines can be seen crossing the right lower serif of I and the left upper serif of E. However, note that I've only looked at this on my home 'scope (20X); this should be checked at higher magnification. Regardless, this still shows that LIBERTY was in the model for the same reason as with the 1840 Liberty Seated half dollar.

Regarding the peripheral lettering UNITED STATES OF AMERICA, I believe the lettering was entered in the master dies. I have never seen lathe lines on this period coinage passing through the peripheral lettering. Also, Charles Hoskins and R.W. Julian have informed me that the lathe was not capable of reproducing the lettering unless the sides of the letters were raked 15° to allow the tool point to pass over. The first series to show lettering in the reduction is the Peace silver dollar series begin-ning years later in 1921 (note the beveled lettering on such silver dollars).

As to the reverse of the Indian cent, I can only draw parallels from the Liberty Seated half dollar series. I have several pieces which show the lathe lines on the reverse passing over details in the feathers, arrows, claws, etc. From this and the obverse of both the 1840 Liberty Seated half dollar and the 1864 bronze Indian cent, I would conclude that the wreath and entire shield, including lines, were in the model. The inscription ONE CENT was punched into the master die.

Border Lettering

The letters UNITED STATES OF AMERICA around the border of the obverse of the Indian cent were punched into master dies and remain constant in their alignment through part of 1886, at which time the Type II master die was created with the lettering more closely spaced. Prob-ably arc-type punches with the complete UNITED STATES OF AMERICA inscription were used in each instance.

Within these time frames (1858-1886 and 1886-1909) several other changes took place including bust point shape alteration and the addi-tion of an L to the ribbon. Exactly how various changes were made and during which steps of the transfer process is not known today.

The depth of impression probably accounts for the "shoulders" or "outlines" seen in the inscription UNITED STATES OF AMERICA on bronze Indian cents of the hub style from 1864 L through early 1886. This leg-end in its entirety may be impressed from its own arc-style punch, as noted.[1]

Larry R. Steve has suggested that the Type II (1886-1909) design had UNITED STATES OF AMERICA as part of the galvano and thus was re-duced mechanically on the portrait lathe.

---

[1] Adapted from Chris Pilliod, letter, June 2, 1996.

No matter what the scenario, it is evident that there were multiple master dies over the years.

From a master die, working hubs (in raised relief, appearing similar to a coin itself, but without date) were made, which in turn made working dies.

Each working die (intaglio) was impressed with a four-digit date logotype, such as 1876. Thus, as in fact 39 different obverse dies were created for 1876 cents, each of these 39 differed from the others by minute positioning of the date numerals.

Master Hub and Die Changes

Throughout the course of the Indian cent series there were several notable changes made to the master hubs and dies, as noted. In addition, there were some minor modifications. Thus, working dies made from the various master hubs and master dies show these *major* differences:

Obverse Hubs: Indian Cents

Obverse Hub 1: 1858-1860. Narrow Bust (pointed end to neck point).

Used on a small number of pattern Indian cents dated 1858, all 1859 regular issue cents, and on a small percentage of business strike 1860 cents. Designer: James B. Longacre.

Obverse Hub 2: 1860-1864. Broad Bust (large, thick end to neck point).

Field dished or basined more than the preceding. Used on most business strike cents dated 1860; all Proofs dated 1860; all coins dated 1861, 1862, and 1863; 1864 copper-nickel cents; and 1864 bronze cents without L. Also used circa 1860-1861 to create 1858-dated pattern dies from which many restrikes were made (see Appendix II for details).

Obverse Hub 3: 1864-1886. Narrow Bust (pointed end to neck point similar to 1858-1860).

Last feather of Indian's headdress points between the I and C of AMERICA. L on ribbon. Somewhat similar to Hub 1, but with obverse die more dished or basined and with slight other differences including faint extra outlines—usually flat and close to the field—on the legend and portrait (not visible on dies that were lightly hubbed or resurfaced). A different arc-style punch was used with the letters in UNITED STATES OF AMERICA slightly more widely spaced than on Type I.[1] There is also a slightly different treatment of Miss Liberty's eyebrow. Used on 1864 bronze cents with L on ribbon and all other later cents 1865 through

---

[1] This difference is not readily noticeable upon quick observation, but the use of an optical comparator reveals that the Type II letters are more closely spaced in the legend.

part of the year 1886. Among 1886 cents, coins from this hub are popularly called the 1886 Type I design.

Obverse Hub 4: 1886-1908. Narrow Bust. Last feather of Indian's headdress points between the C and A of AMERICA.

Among 1886 cents, coins from this hub are popularly called the 1886 Type II design. No extra outlines to legend or portrait.

Obverse Hub 5: 1909. Narrow Bust. Larger L on ribbon.

In 1909 the obverse hub was changed to include a larger letter L (for Longacre) on the ribbon, with the L moved slightly downward from its previous position. The right side of the bottom right serif on the L is vertical on the earlier issues and on the 1909 is sloped to the right. The change is not dramatic, but can be observed by comparing a 1909 Indian cent with an earlier date. The entire date 1909 was included on the hub for the first time; this date was punched into the hub and then transferred to the master die and working dies (thus, all 1909 cents have the date position the same with reference to the bust point, denticles, etc.).

Chris Pilliod commented: "One might ask why a new hub was made for just one year's issuance, 1909. In fact, *all* denominations including the Barber coinage, gold coins, and Liberty Head nickel had new master hubs made with the date added."[1]

Reverse Hubs: Indian Cents[2]

Reverse Hub A: 1858-1859. Laurel wreath (called "olive" leaf in some citations).

Each cluster in the wreath has six leaves. Used on some (but not all; some have five leaves) pattern laurel wreath reverse cents of 1858 and all regular issue cents of 1859. Designer: Anthony C. Paquet or James B. Longacre.[3]

Reverse Hub B: 1859-1864. Oak wreath with narrow shield at apex. Strong bottom to N in ONE and tops of EN in CENT.

Used on pattern transitional cents of 1859 and all regular copper-nickel Indian cents 1860-1864. The wreath is not completely oak, for at the lower part of the left side of the wreath are a few laurel ("olive" in some citations) leaves; on the oak leaves the veins are in relief, on the laurel they are incised.[4] ONE CENT lettering details are somewhat dif-

---

[1] Letter, June 2, 1996.
[2] Thanks to Thomas K. DeLorey for certain information (notes, April 12, 1996).
[3] The National Portrait Gallery has a sketch of the Indian cent, attributed to Longacre, with a laurel-type wreath as the reverse, but differently executed than the final version.
[4] This wreath is essentially an adaptation of the oak (mostly) wreath used on various pattern cents dated 1858, but now with a narrow shield at the top.

ferent from that used on 1859 regular issues. Designer: Anthony C. Paquet or James B. Longacre.

Reverse Hub C: 1864-1877. Oak wreath with narrow shield at apex. Shallow or weak bottom to N in ONE and, to a lesser extent, the tops of EN in CENT.

E's with T-shaped serifs (appearing similar to a push-pin, with a tapered underside to the head and with a distinct stem) at centers. This reverse was used on bronze 1864 cents, all 1865-1869 cents, and some cents dated 1872 and 1877, the last two overlapping with issues from Reverse Hub D.

Reverse Hub D: 1870-1909. Oak wreath with narrow shield at apex. Normal strength letters in ONE CENT.

E's with flared or trumpet-shaped serifs (with the tapering gradually blending into the stem) at centers. Used on some cents 1870-1877, overlapping with the preceding, and on all cents 1878-1909. Hub D exists in several minor variations:

Certain Proofs (but not business strikes nor all Proofs) of the 1872-1878 years are struck from a reverse die with a high-relief "blob" taking the place of the right top serif of the T in CENT. This is a die flaw or accident and does not represent an intended change.

Reverse Hub D/C: 1870. Hub D struck over Hub C, showing doubling, especially at top left of E in CENT. E in ONE has T-shaped serif at center, E in CENT has flared serif. Seen on some cents dated 1870.

The preceding hub variations are most readily discernible on high-grade specimens and under magnification. Little commercial attention has been paid to them.

In all instances, if a working hub was lightly impressed into a working die, certain features would also be lightly impressed. On deeply impressed working dies the outside leaves on the reverse wreath sometimes are closer to the dentils.

Dates on Indian Cent Dies

On Indian cent obverse dies, dates were added separately, all from the same four-digit logotype for a given year. However, exceptions are the dates 1865, 1871, and 1873, known from two different logotypes for each year, each of the four-digit type, but differing from each other in some details. These are:

1865 "Plain 5" and 1865 "Fancy 5" dates.

1871 Wide Date (usual style) and Close Date.

1873 "Closed 3" and 1873 "Open 3" dates.

Thus, while different years may have dates larger or smaller than other years, within a given year such as 1859, 1872, 1876, 1904, or whatever, the same date logotype was used.[1]

Within a specific year, date varieties can occur with regard to positioning. For example, all Proof 1872 cents seen by me have the date centered between the neck point of Miss Liberty and the border dentils, while most (but not all) business strikes have the date very low and close to the dentils.

Among Indian cents a quick way to determine date position is to note the distance from the left side of the bottom serif of the 1 and the dentils below. If an imaginary line is drawn downward from that tip, and perpendicular to the base of the 1, where does it intersect the dentils? The distance of the top of the 1 and the neck truncation and the distance of the bottom left tip of the 1 and the dentils can be observed to determine, approximately, a "high date," "centered date," or "low date" for certain issues. Further, some issues have the date close or far, as measured left to right, from the tip of the neck point (see discussion in the sub-chapter on 1864 L Proof cents as an example). Sometimes these left-to-right differences can be quite dramatic within a given date. As many differences in date positions are microscopic, it is unlikely that a great interest will ever arise in collecting any but the most obviously different examples.

As is the case described earlier for Flying Eagle cents, on Indian cent dies dates can be punched shallowly or deeply into working dies, creating slight differences in the spacing and thickness of the numerals or even in their apparent size. The numerals are slightly tapered (this facilitates the removal of the coins from the die) and have smaller tops or faces as their highest parts and larger bases where the numerals meet the field of the coin.

If a date logotype is slightly tilted at the top or bottom of the date when punched into the die, the date will appear slightly shorter, as either the top or the bottom will be more deeply impressed than the other. These are not collected as separate varieties, however.

If the same four-digit logotype is punched twice or more, a repunched date occurs, which shows repunching at one, two, three, or all four date numerals; these are collected as separate varieties if the repunching is distinctive or unusual. The discussion of the 1867 repunched date cent in the 1867 sub-chapter may be of interest in this regard.

In 1894 there were 55 different obverse dies prepared to strike cents. Thus, in theory there is the possibility of eventually locating 55 differ-

---

[1] Larry R. Steve, letter, April 29, 1996, noted that the matter of the same punch being used for all dies of a given year is under his study, and that dates meriting further examination include 1880, 1882, 1883, and 1889. Chris Pilliod, letter, May 19, 1996, prompted the present writer to investigate date varieties of 1871; these are also listed in Richard Snow's 1992 text, p. 100.

ent die varieties, although it is possible that a few dies were destroyed without being used. Some of these theoretical 55 varieties differ from each other only by microscopic differences in date placement and alignment and are of no particular added numismatic interest. In fact, unless one uses an optical comparator of high magnification, they could not be identified. However, in one instance the date numerals were punched in the die, then punched again with a dramatically different alignment so that two sets of overlapping figures can be seen even under a low-power glass. Known as the 1894 Doubled Date variety, it is several dozen times rarer than a "normal" 1894. In theory, assuming average use of all 55 obverse dies, one in 55 cents of this date in existence today is of the Double Punched Date variety. In practice the ratio may be a bit more or less depending upon how long this particular 1894 obverse die was used and the average use of the 54 other dies. However, knowledge of the method of creating the coin (double-punching of the same four-digit 1894 date logotype) combined with the number of dies prepared for that year can at least indicate that the 1894 Double Punched Date is very scarce.

In addition, when overdates were created—as with the previously mentioned 1858/7 Flying Eagle cent and with the 1888/7 Indian cent—logotype punches from two different dates were used. For the 1888/7 cent die, the first punch, 1887, was placed on the die in the year 1887. It is believed that this die was not used in 1887,[1] and rather than destroy it as obsolete early in 1888, the first date was mostly effaced and then was overpunched with an 1888 logotype, creating the overdate.

Numerous dates—with the 1864 with-L bronze issues being particularly notable—are known with several or even many varieties caused by repunching of the date numerals. From one to all four digits can show doubling ranging from slight to dramatic (the Snow and Steve-Flynn books cited in the Bibliography are rich in information concerning date doubling).

So-called "misplaced dates" were caused by the four-digit date logotype being impressed against the working die in an area not intended. The 1888/7 Snow-2 overdate thus in addition to having its overdate feature has the lower left serif of an extraneous 1 in the date protruding from the neck of Miss Liberty above her necklace, caused by an inadvertent impression of part of the logotype into the working die. More often seen are the several misplaced dates in which one or more date numerals are seen hidden among the dentils in the border below the date.

---

[1] In general in American numismatics, overdates were made from unused earlier-dated dies that had not been hardened. However, there are exceptions (such as the 1806/5 quarter dollar made from an obverse die previously used in 1805; thanks to Thomas K. DeLorey for this citation).

MISPLACED DATES occur on quite a few Indian cent obverses. This 1870 shows the top of a stray 0 emerging from the dentils below the 7 in the date. (Chris Pilliod Collection)

For example, among 1870 cents at least two varieties are known which show parts of the date logotype in the dentils below the correct 1870 date, apparently the result of the four-digit punch coming into hard contact with the working die while not being even near the correct position. One of these 1870 dies shows the upper part of a 0 protruding from the dentils below the 7 of the date. Another under strong magnification shows a garbled mess of digit segments (at least eight according to Larry R. Steve and Kevin J. Flynn) within the dentils.

These and related misplaced dates may have been done by the engraver to test the hardness of the die by using an unobtrusive location to determine its suitability for impressing the entire date punch. However, if this is the case, then it seems reasonable that numerous related misplaced dates will be found on other dies of the era, for example nickels and dimes. As of 1996, other series have not been studied as intensely as have Indian cents, and in any event, fewer dies were made for other denominations. The prevalence of misplaced dates in other series and their frequency as expressed as a percentage of dies made, awaits further study.

Alternatively, Kevin J. Flynn presented this theory:[1]

> With more dies needed for lower denominations, I believe that less attention was paid to details for these, and resulted in punching the dates in the dentils. Cents were not as important as gold dollars. Because there are many misplaced dates known for certain Indian cent years and none for others, I believe that the person or persons who performed this task for those years was sloppy. The best theory is that the date punch was placed on the face of the working die. The person punching the date used the bust of the Indian as a reference point for placement, then struck the date punch with a hammer.
>
> It is very easy to misjudge relative position and punch south 1/8 of an inch. I have tried experimenting with this theory using a 3/4" clay model and a 1/4"-wide punch. It is very easy to misjudge unless you are experienced. If the person struck it, lifted up the punch, and saw no sign of the date, he would just try it again.

---

[1] Kevin J. Flynn, letter, May 9, 1996, here slightly edited. He also reported that he had identified 140 different misplaced dates in various series including 81 on Indian cents from 1865 to 1908.

A decade or so ago the term "misplaced date" was largely unknown. Since then, alert students of various series in the mid-nineteenth century have identified misplaced dates on various series from Indian cents to gold denominations. The search continues, although relatively few specialists are interested in date positions of Liberty Head nickels, for example (in contrast, there are many date-position aficionados for Indian cents). Kevin J. Flynn recently reported that *10 different* misplaced-date dies have been found so far for the 1908 cent alone.[1]

Date positions and variations thereof are a playground for the Indian cent specialist, and doubtless many more interesting varieties await discovery. The reason for misplaced dates during die making process is just beginning to be explored, and perhaps the true reason differs from the ideas just presented.

In some instances in American coinage, the same date logotype punch was used on more than one denomination in American coinage. A familiar example is the 1885 gold $20 and 1885 silver trade dollars which share date logotypes. The interchangeability of Indian cent punches with other denominations awaits further study, with the two-cent piece, nickel three-cents, nickel five-cent piece, and dime dies being the most likely hunting grounds. It is known that the same four-digit logotypes were employed to make two different styles of dates on the 1871 Indian cent (see sub-chapter for details) and also two different styles on 1871 two-cent pieces. Ditto for the 1865 "Plain 5" and "Fancy 5" cents and two-cent pieces.

Beginning in 1909, the date was incorporated into the master die. Thus, from this point onward there are no variations of date placement among Indian and Lincoln cents. Of course, this has little relevance with the solo Indian cent date (1909) involved, but it does influence greatly the methodology of collecting the Lincoln cents of a later era.

On May 24 and 25, 1910, Director of the Mint A. Piatt Andrew supervised the destruction of many old dies and hubs on hand at the Philadelphia Mint, some dating back to the 1830s.[2] On May 24, two master dies and two hubs were destroyed of the "one-cent (old design)."

Mintmarks in Dies

For 1908-S and 1909-S cents, mintmarks were punched separately into the reverse working dies, thus causing minute differences in position-

---

[1] Letter, April 24, 1996. Further on the subject, *The Gobrecht Journal,* organ of the Liberty Seated Collectors Club, has printed many notices of misplaced dates on Liberty seated silver coins.

[2] A complete listing was printed in *The Numismatist,* October 1913, pp. 541-542.

ing. All dies including those used in San Francisco were made at the Philadelphia Mint.[1]

Die Preparation

Dies for Indian cents were prepared in the same basic manner as described above for Flying Eagle cents. In a few instances, the creation of working dies from working hubs involved multiple impressing of the working die, with the final impression slightly off register from the earlier impression(s). The most dramatic instance of this is the 1873 Indian cent with LIBERTY in the headband fully doubled.

Die Injuries

As in the case of Flying Eagle cents, Indian cents sometimes show clash marks caused when the obverse and reverse dies came together during the press set-up process or, probably more rarely, without a planchet between them. Thus far, all known clash marks are from cent dies; there are no bi-denominational clashes as in the Flying Eagle series (but see related bi-denominational clashes described in notes in the 1864 Bronze, 1868, 1870, and 1899 sub-chapters).

Die Wear

Worn dies are common in the Indian cent series. They seem to be most prevalent for Civil War years and from the 1880s through the 1900s; in other words, the high-production years. Die breaks and cuds were formed in the same manner as with Flying Eagle cents described above.

Metal Alloy Subtleties

There seem to have been slight differences in the bronze alloy over the years. While these differences were probably minute and virtually undetectable when the coins were first struck, over a period of decades Indian cents from different alloy mixes have toned somewhat differently. Thus, an uncleaned, undipped Mint State red and brown bronze Indian cent of the 1864 to early 1870s years (and also 1908-S and 1909-S, but not the Philadelphia coins of those later years) is apt to have a "woodgrain" effect to the toning, with streaks or "pellets" of brown toning, elongated, over yellowish-red mint red background, these streaks being oriented in a specific direction (caused by the distending of the minute alloy differences during the planchet strip rolling process). The same woodgrain effect is seen among certain dates of Mint State red

---

[1] Philadelphia continued to be the source for dies for United States coinage until May 1996 when a supplementary die shop was opened at the Denver Mint.

COINING ROOM: View at the Philadelphia Mint in the 1880s. Visitors were allowed to watch coining in progress, and upon departing from the Mint they could buy freshly-struck coins for face value as souvenirs, or could pay a premium and buy Proofs. Indian cents were the most popular purchases. (*Visitor's Guide and History of the United States Mint, Philadelphia, Pa.* A.M. Smith, 1885, p. 19)

and brown two-cent pieces. To my eye, this type of red and brown woodgrain toning is very beautiful. Chris Pilliod seconded this sentiment, noting: "I agree and find these pieces *very* attractive, but the grading services apparently do not."[1]

Striking (Business Strikes)

Striking of Indian cents for circulation was accomplished in essentially the same manner as outlined in Chapter 3 for Flying Eagle cents, except that over a period of time the presses were made more efficient, and certain processes were simplified.

If the dies were spaced slightly more apart than they should be in the coining press, the coins would not strike up properly. Among Indian cents this usually manifested with weakness on the high points of the Indian portrait, especially on the ribbon and the tips of the feathers, and on the reverse, the top part of the shield. Border dentils appear incomplete or "mashed" on many such cents. In general, copper-nickel Indian cents of the 1859-1864 years presented more problems in obtaining sharp strikes than did the later (1864-1909) bronze cents in softer metal.

If the dies were spaced slightly too close together, the coin will be very sharply struck, and any excess metal will be forced up between the restraining collar and the dies to create a wire rim (a.k.a. "knife rim" or, in Mint nomenclature, a "fin"). Spacing the dies too close together caused rapid die wear and breakage. However, the problem was not as great with bronze Indian cents as it was with copper-nickel issues.

If either the obverse or the reverse die was not fixed in its position, it might rotate, causing the reverse of a struck coin to have other than the normal 180° alignment with the obverse.

Business strikes were made on steam presses throughout most of the Indian cent series. At the new Mint beginning in 1901 the old presses plus some new presses (the latter made locally by T.C. Dill) were electrically driven.

Planchets for copper-nickel Indian cents were made within the Mint from ingots of copper-nickel. The policy during the bronze cent era 1864-1909 varied, and some planchets were made internally, while others were obtained under contract from various outside suppliers. All planchets purchased from the private sector were finished with raised rims.

Striking (Proofs)

Proof coins are said to have been struck using a screw press which operated more slowly than the steam-type press. Beginning in 1893 a

---

[1] Letter, June 2, 1996.

WHERE PROOFS WERE MADE, 1903: Medal Department of the Philadelphia Mint, a separate division which used hydraulic presses and other
types of presses to strike medals, badges, and Proof coins. (*The United
States Mint at Philadelphia,* James Rankin Young, 1903, p. 66)

hydraulic press was employed.[1] However, it is also possible that regular
knuckle-action presses were used, but at a slower speed than utilized to
coin business strikes. The slower the press speed, the more the effect is
of "squeezing" rather than "stamping," and more details are obtained
from the deepest recesses of the dies.

Production of Proofs was accomplished in the Medal Department,
which was separate from the mass-production coinage facility.

It was recommended to strike each coin twice, so as to fully bring up
the sharpness of the design, but in practice many seem to have been
struck just once. During the period from the 1880s through the early
1900s—the 1886-1889 years seem to have been especially egregious—

---

[1] "Early Proofs Struck on Screw Press." *Numismatic Scrapbook Magazine,* January 1964, p. 33.

production was often careless, even sloppy, and the finished Proofs were often less than satisfactory. Some Proofs from this era have beveled edges in the manner of business strikes. Making matters complicated for numismatists is the fact that some Proof dies were put on high-speed production presses and used to make business strikes, these having prooflike surfaces (see below).

On a few 1868 Proofs, both dies are oriented in the same direction, a die set-up error (this die alignment variety is recognized by ANACS, but not by NGC or PCGS).

Proof vs. Prooflike Cents

Among Indian cents there seem to be some issues that are neither fish nor fowl, so to speak. These coins have certain attributes of Proof issues and certain of Mint State coins. While certain coins may never be precisely attributed to everyone's satisfaction, the following commentary from Chris Pilliod gives a view of the topic:[1]

> As far as distinguishing Proof Indian cents from Mint State examples, these ideas may be useful:
>
> Proof Indian cents were struck from specially prepared dies and planchets. It is definitely true that Proof dies were not retired from use after having struck 500 to 1,000 Proof issues. For the sake of economy they were then employed to make business strike coins. This is verifiable for several Indian cent varieties for which the same repunched date found on a Proof can also be found on a very "mushy" late die state business strike (for example, 1879). So, what do you call a coin struck from freshly retired Proof dies on a business planchet? This gets down to semantics and subjectivity.
>
> Probably the best statement I ever heard was from Jack Beymer[2] who said this concerning a puzzling coin in another series:
>
> "All 1864 Liberty Seated dimes are Proofs, but some are more Proof than others."
>
> I tend to believe that once a Proof die was taken out of the Proof press and installed into a production press, any subsequent coin must be a business strike as this piece was intended to be placed into general circulation. The problem is figuring them out.

---

[1] Letter, May 19, 1996, here adapted.
[2] Prominent West Coast professional numismatist and discoverer of numerous die varieties in various series over the years.

CHAPTER 5
THE GRADING CHALLENGE

Grading

Much has been written about coin grading in recent decades. Too much. This chapter does not help reduce the information overload, and if you are already familiar with grading you might want to skim it lightly or skip it completely. However, if you are interested in the subtleties of the subject, reading the commentary may be worthwhile. Unfortunately, it takes a lot of words to *try* to explain grading. Even so, I probably have left certain questions unanswered.

I am coming from this angle: I am trying place myself in the position of an intelligent, enthusiastic, and well-meaning collector who has discovered Flying Eagle and Indian cents, and who wants to spend his or her money wisely. My assumption is that you, as this theoretical collector, would rather have a high quality collection than a low quality one, and you realize that one cannot have at the same time the highest quality and the lowest price. Now to the subject:

Often, the advice is given that the higher the numerical grade, the better the coin. This is repeated so often that the owner of a Mint State-65 coin, a gem, comes to believe that this is the ultimate or close to it, while a grade such as Extremely Fine-40 is not worthwhile. This is unfortunate, for within the bronze Indian cent series a glossy brown EF-40 coin can be more beautiful than a blotchy MS-65. *More than in any other area of numismatics, the astute collecting of copper and bronze coins requires a degree of connoisseurship.*

And yet, scarcely a mention of connoisseurship is to be found in popular grading guides or population reports!

If you read this chapter carefully and also Appendix IV, and absorb what you read, I believe you will be as knowledgeable as 95% of the people who have ever written out a check for a Flying Eagle or Indian cent.

Grading Aspects: Various Sources

Grading is a matter of opinion. Is now. Always has been. Always will be. At least that is how I feel.

Given this, the sharing of opinions stated by authorities over a span of time can be valuable to you as a buyer today.

Over the years many different grading guidelines and systems have appeared in print, including one using Roman numerals I, II, III, etc., published in *The Numismatist* in the 1890s. There were no commonly accepted standards until recent decades, and one person's "Extremely Fine" might be another's "Uncirculated."

The following is from the *Coin Collectors' Illustrated Guide of the United States,* by Philadelphia dealer A. M. Smith, and was published January 1886. It was boldly titled A.M. SMITH'S AUTHORITATIVE STANDARD CLASSIFICATION OF COINS. So far as can be determined, no one but Mr. Smith paid much attention to it, although in retrospect it seems to have been one of the better schemes of its time:

Poor coins are those on which the design, lettering and date are almost intelligible, or the least degree visible.

Fair are those well worn, but which still retain every portion of the design, all letters and the entire date, almost distinguishable.

Very Fair is the rating given to coins in which lettering, design and date are clearly readable.

Good applies to those where every mark, letter and figure is well defined, with only the high, fine hair lines, such as the hair, feathers in wings, and like delicate lines, worn off.

Very Good coins are somewhat worn, but nearly "Fine."

Fine coins are those which are barely worn, but which, under critical examination, show traces of wear in the rubbed surfaces of the finer lines. No scratches or nicks are permissible in "Fine" coins unless so stated.

Very Fine means that the coin has the well defined lines and surface of a piece that has been little in circulation, and shows the slightest traces of wear, and is not scratched or nicked in the least.

Uncirculated, implies that the coin is free from the least wear or scratches, and has the appearance of a piece just dropped from the coining press.

Brilliant Proof coins have a burnished mirror-like reflective surface; the dies and planchets being both polished before striking these coins, which are exclusively for collectors. As soon as soiled or tarnished even by much handling, they are no longer to be considered as equal to "Brilliant Proofs," but are still called "Proofs."

Modern Grading

Below are given overviews of several existing grading standards and guidelines followed by a delineation of grade levels from well-worn to perfect (Poor-1 to MS-70). Then follows a grade-by-grade combined listing.

It will be seen that among Mint State Flying Eagle and Indian cents in the two separate listings, published grading standards are quite similar.

ANA-Sheldon Grading System

Here is my explanation of the origin, rationale, and characteristics of the American Numismatic Association Grading Scale, which is based on and expanded from the Sheldon Scale given by Dr. William H. Sheldon in his 1949 book, *Early American Cents.*

This is the scale that started the "numbers craze." Actually, it was devised by Dr. Sheldon in 1949 as a *market formula to determine the value of 1793-1814 copper cents.* His theory was that if a coin were in a certain grade such as VF-20, were Rarity-5 (the Sheldon Rarity Scale is also widely used today), and had a Basal Value (a value assigned to a variety depending upon its rarity and popularity) of $2, the market price would be 20 x 5 x $2 = $200. The reason we have MS-60 and MS-70, rather than a scale going up to MS-100 or MS-1000, is that in 1949, a typical MS-60 early large cent had a market value of about twice that of a VF-30 coin. Sheldon devised his numbers to fit the market conditions of that time.

Today in the 1990s, for most coins an MS-60 coin is worth much more than just twice the value of a VF-30, and if Dr. Sheldon were alive and were devising this system today, MS-60 might be MS-300 or MS-500 instead! Back in 1949 a small difference in grade did not necessarily make a big difference in price. Today in the 1990s a small difference in grade can make an astronomical difference in price! Thus, the Sheldon or, as it is sometimes called today in its vastly expanded form, the American Numismatic Association (ANA) Grading Scale, has *no scientific or mathematical basis at all.*

However, it remains alive and well and is considered by many—including me—to be better than the old adjectives-only method. The latter method deteriorated into "gem Uncirculated," "super gem Uncirculated," "wonderful choice Uncirculated," etc., with no one being quite sure which description indicated a better grade. Today, even if we can't all agree whether a coin is MS-63 or MS-65, at least we know that a coin described by the same person at the same time as MS-65 is better than one listed as MS-63 or MS-64.

The ANA Grading Scale ranges from grade 1, or Poor-1, upward. A Poor-1 coin is at the bottom of the scale of wear. It is nearly smooth with most lettering worn away. In contrast, at the top of the scale is Mint State (a.k.a. Uncirculated), topped by Mint State-70, or perfection—a blemish-free coin as nice as the moment it left the dies.

In practice, few if any coins are absolutely perfect. Mint State-65 (abbreviated MS-65), or gem quality, represents about the best Flying Eagle or Indian cent to be found under normal circumstances.

The ANA Grading Scale is given in general terms. Each grade is better than the one before it:[1]

There are two major problems with the ANA-Sheldon Scale:

1. Grading was, is, and will probably always be a matter of opinion.

2. Many people—and not just neophytes either—consider that if a coin has a number such as MS-64 attached to it, it is *precisely* and *scientifically* graded. Thus a newcomer to numismatics might say, "At long last, here is a collecting field in which grading is precise, uniform, and easy to understand." In actuality, one might just as well call MS-64 grade "Mmm" (as in delicious) and Abt. Good-3 "Ugh" (as in not so desirable)— these two terms being adapted from Dr. Harry Salyards' poignant commentary given at the end of this chapter.

Photograde Grading Guidelines

The *Photograde* guide to grading United States coins, featuring pictures for various grade levels, was written by James F. Ruddy and first published in 1970. Since that time it has gone through many editions. At present it is printed and distributed by Western Publishing Company, which also publishes the *Guide Book of U.S. Coins* and the *Official ANA Grading Standards for U.S. Coins,* among other titles.

Photograde is most useful for its illustrations and descriptions of worn coins through AU, as points of wear can be delineated in photographs. In addition, a narrative accompanies each illustration. Higher levels of Mint State and Proof coins cannot be photographed in a consistently definitive manner and are treated only in passing by this book.

Richard Snow's Guidelines

After the grading listings for Flying Eagle cents I give the grading standards for *Indian* cents proposed and published by Richard Snow, with some modifications made by Snow for use in the present text. These are somewhat more detailed than the ANA standards. (There are no equivalent Snow standards for Flying Eagle cents.)

The Richard Snow standards are reflective of this well-known author's thinking specifically with regard to Indian cents, and in combination with your own experience, viewing of different specimens, etc., they may be of value as a source of knowledge.

---

[1] For more details refer to the book, *Official A.N.A. Grading Standards for United States Coins* and to *Photograde,* by James F. Ruddy.

Combined Grading Guidelines
Flying Eagle Cents 1856-1858
ABOUT GOOD
(AG; AG-3)
Flying Eagle Cents

ANA-Sheldon grading definition: Outlined design. Parts of date and legend worn smooth. Obverse: Eagle is outlined with all details worn away. Legend and date readable but very weak and merging into rim. Reverse: Entire design partially worn away. Bow is merged with the wreath.

Photograde definition: Obverse: The date will be weak but readable. Reverse: The rim will be worn down into the wreath.

QDB (commentary): Copper-nickel Flying Eagle cents tended to wear quite attractively, and the typical coin even at the AG-3 level is apt to have rather "clean" surfaces without dents or corrosion.

GOOD
(G; G-4)
Flying Eagle Cents

ANA: Heavily worn. Design and legend visible but faint in spots. Obverse: Entire design well worn with very little detail remaining. Legend and date are weak but visible. Reverse: Wreath is worn flat but completely outlined. Bow merges with wreath.

Photograde: Obverse: The lettering and the date will be readable although the rim may be worn down to the tops of the letters. Reverse: The wreath will be completely outlined but worn flat.

QDB (commentary): Considering that higher grade pieces are available quite inexpensively, the demand for 1857 and 1858 Flying Eagle cents in G-4 grade is mostly with beginners, not with specialists.

Only a few 1856 Flying Eagle cents are known in this low grade, but when they are offered the response is enthusiastic. Such pieces are very worthwhile for the budget-minded buyer.

VERY GOOD
(VG-8)
Flying Eagle Cents

ANA: Well worn. Design clear but flat and lacking details. Obverse: Outline of feathers in right wing ends show but some are smooth. Legend and date are visible. The eye shows clearly. Reverse: Slight detail in wreath shows, but the top is worn smooth. Very little outline showing in the bow.

Photograde: Obverse: About one-third of the feathers on the eagle will show but will be weak. Reverse: The wreath will show some detail but be worn smooth on top.

QDB (commentary): In the 1930s and 1940s Flying Eagle cents in the G to VG level were available in quantity, and such dealers as Tatham Stamp & Coin Co. (Springfield, MA) and B. Max Mehl (Fort Worth, TX) had thousands. Such hoards are long gone. Today in the 1990s they are usually found one, two, or several at a time, although they are not rare.

FINE
(F-12)
Flying Eagle Cents

ANA: Moderate to heavy even wear. Entire design clear and bold. Obverse: Some details show at breast, head, and tail. Outlines of feathers in right wing and tail show with no ends missing. Reverse: Some details visible in the wreath. Bow is very smooth.

Photograde: Obverse: About half of the feathers on the eagle will show. The detail of the eagle's head will be very clear. Reverse: More detail will appear on the wreath.

QDB (commentary): A pleasing grade for the buyer filling in a date set, but who does not want to spend the money for higher condition pieces.

VERY FINE
(VF-20; also VF-30)
Flying Eagle Cents

ANA: VF-20. Light to moderate even wear. All major features are sharp. Obverse: Breast shows considerable flatness. Over half of the details are visible in feathers of the wings. Head worn but bold. Thigh smooth, but feathers in tail are complete. Reverse: Ends of leaves and bow worn smooth. • **VF-30.** Obverse: Small flat spots of wear show on breast and thigh. Feathers in wings still show nearly full details. Head worn but sharp. Reverse: Ends of leaves and bow worn almost smooth.

Photograde: Obverse: About three-quarters of the feathers will show sharply. The eagle's tail feathers will be complete. There will be considerable flatness on the eagle's breast. Reverse: The ends of the leaves will be worn smooth. Note: The words "ONE CENT" are sometimes weak due to striking.

QDB (commentary): Same comment as for F-12. At the VF level occasional 1856 Flying Eagle cents come on the market, reflective of patterns that were spent, quite possibly by congressmen and others who received them in 1856 and early 1857.

EXTREMELY FINE
(EF-40; also EF-45)
Flying Eagle Cents

ANA: EF-40. Very light wear on only the highest points. Obverse: Feathers in wings and tail are plain. Wear shows on breast, wing tips, head, and thigh. Reverse: High points of the leaves and bow are worn. • **EF-45.** Obverse: Wear shows on breast, wing tips and head. All feathers are very plain. Reverse: High points of the leaves and bow are lightly worn. Traces of mint lustre still show.

Photograde: Obverse: There will be wear on the eagle's breast and left wing tip. All other details will be sharp. Reverse: There will be wear on the high points of the leaves and ribbon bow.

QDB (commentary): Specimens at the EF level can be very attractive. While the ANA standards suggest that "traces of mint lustre still show," it has been my experience that any coin with significant lustre is apt to be graded higher than EF and will fall into the AU range.

ABOUT UNCIRCULATED
(AU-50; also 53, 55, 58)
Flying Eagle Cents

ANA: AU-50. Small trace of wear visible on highest points. Obverse: Traces of wear show on the breast, left wing tip, and head. Reverse: Traces of wear show on the leaves and bow. Half of the mint lustre is still present. • **AU-55.** Obverse: Only a trace of wear shows on the breast and left wing tip. Reverse: A trace of wear shows on the bow. Three-quarters of the mint lustre is still present. • **AU-58.** Has some signs of abrasion: feathers on eagle's breast, wing tips.

Photograde: Obverse: There will be only a trace of wear on the eagle's breast and left wing tip. Note: Weakness of lettering and date may appear on some 1857 cents due to striking. Reverse: Only a trace of wear will show on the highest points of the leaves and bow. (Highest grade defined in detail in *Photograde*.)

QDB (commentary): AU coins can vary considerably in their aesthetic appeal. It is important to find one that is lightly and attractively worn and without stains or splotches.

MINT STATE-60
(MS-60)
Flying Eagle Cents

ANA: A strictly Uncirculated coin with no trace of wear, but with blemishes more obvious than for MS-63. May lack full mint lustre, and surface may be dull or spotted.

Photograde: This grade, at the low end of the Uncirculated scale, represents a coin which has never been in the channels of circulation, but which has numerous bagmarks and other evidences of coin-to-coin contact. However, traces of sliding wear, friction in the fields, and heavy rubbing are not seen. (Definition used for all denominations.)

QDB (commentary): Cherrypicking is needed for quality here. Most MS-60 coins are somewhat heavily marked and nicked (if they were not, they would be graded higher). From MS-60 onward, published grading standards are somewhat hard for anyone to follow in the absence of having coins on hand to view and seeing in advance what is called MS-60 (or some other Mint State grade) in the market. This is not a criticism, for I do not know of anyone in numismatics who using the medium of words and/or illustrations can clearly define MS-60 as opposed to MS-61, and the latter as opposed to MS-62, etc.

At all Mint State levels, the aesthetic appearance of the coin is often a more important indicator of market desirability and value than is the numerical grade.

MINT STATE-61
(MS-61)
Flying Eagle Cents

ANA: Lustre may be diminished or noticeably impaired, and the surface has clusters of large and small contact marks throughout. Hairlines could be very noticeable. Scuff marks may show as unattractive patches in large areas or on major features. Small rim nicks, striking or planchet defects may show, and the quality may be noticeably poor. Eye appeal is somewhat unattractive.

QDB (commentary): See comments under MS-60.

MINT STATE-62
(MS-62)
Flying Eagle Cents

ANA: An impaired or dull lustre may be evident. Clusters of small marks may be present throughout with a few large marks or nicks in prime focal areas. Hairlines may be very noticeable. Large unattractive scuff marks might be seen on major features. The strike, rim, and planchet quality may be noticeably below average. Overall eye appeal is generally acceptable.

QDB (commentary): Once again, quality is important. If I were forming a collection I would ignore a coin with "large unattractive scuff marks" and move on to a higher grade, or at the very least I would do a lot of checking around at this MS-62 level before buying a coin.

MINT STATE-63
(MS-63)
Flying Eagle Cents

ANA: A Mint State coin with attractive mint lustre, but noticeable detracting contact marks or minor blemishes. Mint lustre may be slightly impaired. Numerous small contact marks, and a few scattered heavy marks may be seen. Small hairlines are visible without magnification. Several detracting scuff marks or defects may be present throughout the design or in the fields. The general quality is about average, but overall the coin is rather attractive.

QDB (commentary): The MS-63 level is a happy compromise between low price and high quality, and with some looking around you should be able to acquire nice pieces.

MINT STATE-64
(MS-64)
Flying Eagle Cents

ANA: Has at least average lustre and strike for the type. Several small contact marks in groups, as well as one or two moderately heavy marks may be present. One or two small patches of hairlines may show under low magnification. Noticeable light scuff marks or defects might be seen within the design or in the field. Attractive overall quality with a pleasing eye appeal.

QDB (commentary): We are now in the gem level. The typical MS-64 coin to my eyes is one that is lustrous and frosty, quite attractive overall, but has a few too many contact marks to merit MS-65. Often these marks are more prominent on the obverse fields than anywhere else on the coin. At any grade level—MS-64 or otherwise—I would avoid pieces with gashes, rim cuts, or any heavy marks.

MINT STATE-65
(MS-65)
Flying Eagle Cents

ANA: No trace of wear; nearly as perfect as MS-67 except for some small blemish. Has full mint lustre but may be unevenly toned or lightly fingermarked. A few barely noticeable nicks or marks may be present. Shows an attractive high quality of lustre and strike for the date and mint. A few small scattered contact marks, or two larger marks may be present, and one or two small patches of hairlines may show under magnification. Noticeable light scuff marks may show on the high points of the design. Overall quality is above average and overall eye appeal is very pleasing.

QDB (commentary): Look for a brilliant or lightly toned coin with lots of lustre. Search for a sharp strike as well. Do this, and you will have a very beautiful coin.

MINT STATE-66
(MS-66)
Flying Eagle Cents

ANA: Must have above average quality of strike and full original mint lustre, with no more than two or three minor but noticeable contact marks. A few very light hairlines may show under magnification, or there may be one or two light scuff marks showing on frosted surfaces or in the field. The eye appeal must be above average and very pleasing for the date and mint.

QDB (commentary): This grade is rather "new" in the Flying Eagle series and was scarcely heard of a decade or so ago. Such a coin should be a very lustrous, very beautiful specimen with very few marks. This and other very high grades elude definition in print.

MINT STATE-67
(MS-67)
Flying Eagle Cents

ANA: Virtually flawless but with very minor imperfections. Has full original lustre and sharp strike for date and mint. May have three or four small contact marks and one more noticeable but not detracting mark. On comparable coins, one or two small single hairlines may show under magnification, or there may be one or two light scuff marks showing on frosted surfaces or in the field. The eye appeal must be above average and very pleasing for the date and mint.

QDB (commentary): Same comment as for MS-66.

MINT STATE-68
(MS-68)
Flying Eagle Cents

ANA: Attractive sharp strike and full original lustre for the date and mint, with no more than four light scattered contact marks or flaws. No hairlines or scuff marks can be seen. Has exceptional eye appeal.

QDB (commentary): Same comment as for MS-67. It is important to keep an eye out for value at any high grade level such as this. If an offered coin is an 1856 Flying Eagle cent—a classic and highly desired rarity at any level—you can be more comfortable, in my opinion, than if a coin is an 1857 which is quite common in MS-65, but which may sell for thousands of dollars more in MS-67 or MS-68, although the grade is only *slightly* higher. I admit that I am somewhat conservative in my thinking, and I am always more comfortable if a coin offers a generous measure of *basic rarity* as a date in addition to *condition rarity.*

MINT STATE-69
(MS-69)
Flying Eagle Cents

ANA: Must have very attractive sharp strike and full original lustre for the date and mint, with no more than two small non-detracting contact marks or flaws. No hairlines or scuff marks can be seen. Has exceptional eye appeal.

QDB (commentary): No particular comment.

MINT STATE-70
(MS-70)
Flying Eagle Cents

ANA: The perfect coin. Has very attractive sharp strike and original lustre of the highest quality for date and mint. No contact marks are visible under magnification. There are absolutely no hairlines, scuff marks, or defects. A flawless coin exactly as it was minted, with no trace of wear or injury. Must have full mint lustre and brilliance or light toning. Any unusual die or planchet traits must be described. Attractive and outstanding eye appeal.

Photograde: An absolutely perfect coin. Under magnification with a hand glass, no contact or other marks are to be seen. In general, such perfection is only found among modern coins specifically issued at a premium price for collectors. (Definition for all denominations.)

QDB (commentary): At present the MS-70 grade has not extended to Flying Eagle cents.

Combined Grading Guidelines
Indian Cents 1859-1909

POOR
Indian Cents

ANA grading guidelines: Poor-1 (not abbreviated): Worn nearly smooth; minimum grade. Barely identifiable as to type. Date may be worn away.

Photograde guidelines: This grade not discussed.

Snow grading guidelines: This grade not discussed.

QDB (commentary): This grade is not collectible in the Indian series if the date cannot be read, for except for the 1859 (the only year with the laurel wreath reverse) and the 1864 without-L bronze cent (with Broad Bust) it would not be possible for the typical collector to determine in what year the coin was struck. As these two exceptions are not rare dates, dateless Indian cents in Poor grade are not desired by numismatists.

FAIR
Indian Cents

ANA: Fair-2 (not abbreviated): Very worn, most inscriptions missing.

Photograde: This grade not discussed.

Snow: This grade not discussed.

QDB (commentary): A Fair-grade coin with the date readable, but barely, is mainly useful as a filler for a rare date, perhaps 1871, 1872, or 1877.

ABOUT GOOD
(AG; AG-3)
Indian Cents

ANA: Obverse: Head is outlined with nearly all details worn away. Legend and date readable but very weak and merging into rim. Reverse: Entire design partially worn away. Bow is merged with the wreath.

Photograde: Obverse: The rim will be worn down well into the letters. The date will be weak but readable. Reverse: The rim will be worn down into the wreath.

Snow: Heavy wear. Only partial rims. All letters in UNITED STATES OF AMERICA visible. Minimum: All letters of the legend are visible, though they may not be legible. Maximum: Rim just merges with the field on one side.

QDB (commentary): The date should be unequivocally readable. About Good is a nice "filler" grade for some of the rarities such as 1871, 1872, and 1877. However, on the key 1864 L cent the L will not be visible (such L-less coins can be identified by having the date 1864 and the Narrow Bust hub, not found on the without-L coins, but nearly all numismatists want to see the L they have paid for!).

When a coin is in About Good grade it has seen a lot of life experience, and some surface marks, etc., are normal, but notable damage such as cuts and gouges should be mentioned.

GOOD
(G; G-4)
Indian Cents

ANA: Obverse: Entire design well worn with very little detail remaining. Legend and date are weak but visible. Reverse: Wreath is worn flat but completely outlined. Bow merges with wreath.

Photograde: Obverse: the outline of the Indian will be distinct. LIBERTY will not show on the headband. The rim may be worn down to the tops of the letters. Reverse: The wreath will be completely outlined but worn flat.

Snow: Heavy wear. Full rims on both sides. All letters in UNITED STATES OF AMERICA are readable. Minimum: All rims are clear. Maximum: Two letters of the word LIBERTY are visible.

QDB (commentary): The Richard Snow guidelines imply that on some specimens NO letters in the word LIBERTY are visible. Years ago, a Good-grade coin with a couple letters visible would have been called G-VG or "strong Good." It is nice if you can buy G-4 coins with two letters in view, but don't expect it.

The G-4 grade is a standard condition level for a set containing pieces picked out of circulation several or more decades after they were minted. In this grade coins can be cherrypicked for quality, and if you do this you will find that a G-4 1877 or other rare cent can be an attractive part of your set. A great misconception in numismatics, in my opinion, is that a well-circulated coin is not desirable. The correct philosophy is that a worn coin, if attractive and rare, can be very desirable, and while it is usually always better to have a Mint State example, no one should refrain from completing a set simply because Mint State coins are too expensive. Remember, in some series a G-4 coin would be about the finest condition available—certain rare varieties of 1785-1788 Vermont and Connecticut copper coins being examples.

In the field of large cents sometimes G-6 is used to describe a particularly nice Good coin. In the Indian cent market this and certain other intermediate numbers are not as widely used, but if they are this is an excellent practice, as if correctly applied they designate an especially desirable example.

VERY GOOD
(VG-8)
Indian Cents

ANA: Obverse: Outline of feather ends show but some are smooth. Legend and date are visible. At least three letters in LIBERTY show clearly, but any combination of two full letters and parts of two others is sufficient. Reverse: Slight detail in wreath shows, but the top is worn smooth. Very little outline showing in the bow.

Photograde: Obverse: A total of any three letters of LIBERTY will show. This can be a combination of two full letters plus two half letters as not all dates of Indian cents wore uniformly. Reverse: The wreath will begin to show some detail. On some issues the bottom of the N in ONE may be weak due to striking.

Snow: At least 3 letters of LIBERTY will show. Minimum: Three letters of LIBERTY will show, usually L and RT, but any combination of parts of letters is acceptable. Maximum: All but one letter of LIBERTY is visible.

QDB (commentary): The "three letters of LIBERTY" rule dates back a long time, and doubtless B. Max Mehl used it. While a coin with six of the seven letters visible is technically below F-12 and is thus VG, if you are offered such a coin, expect to pay a premium for it.

The word LIBERTY wears at different rates on different dates within the series. On some varieties the word wears away more rapidly than do other features of the coin. Thus, two different coins can have, for example, L, R, and T visible, and one will have another part of the coin, say the reverse, somewhat weak, and on the other the reverse can be very sharp. As an example of an exception, among 1866 Indian cents some specimens are struck with bulged obverses due to die characteristics, and on these pieces the word LIBERTY can wear away quickly, yielding a lower grade such as VG-8, but overall the coin can have the sharpness of Fine or better.

Sometimes VG-10 is used for a particularly nice VG coin.

FINE
(F-12)
Indian Cents

ANA: Obverse: One-quarter of details show in the hair. Ribbon is worn smooth. LIBERTY shows clearly with no letters missing. Reverse: Some details visible in the wreath and bow. Tops of leaves are worn smooth.

Photograde: Obverse: A full LIBERTY will be visible, but it will not be sharp. Reverse: The top part of the leaves will be worn smooth. The ribbon bow will show considerable wear.

Snow: All letters of LIBERTY will be at least partly visible. The lower edge of the headband is indistinct. Minimum: All letters of LIBERTY must be partly visible, though they need not be entirely legible. Maximum: All letters of LIBERTY clearly readable. The base of the headband is not complete.

QDB (commentary): This is a twilight-type grade, and often if the word LIBERTY is fairly strong, but the headband borders are not complete, a coin will be called VF-20 by some collectors and dealers. In practice, there are relatively few Indian cents within the strict F-12 category; there seem to be many more VG-8 and VF-20 pieces.

Sometimes F-15 is used for a particularly nice Fine coin.

VERY FINE
(VF-20; also VF-30)
Indian Cents

ANA: VF-20. Obverse: Headdress shows considerable flatness. Nearly half of the details show in hair and on ribbon. Head slightly worn but bold. Reverse: Leaves and bow are almost fully detailed. • **VF-30.** Obverse: Small flat spots of wear on tips of feathers, ribbon, and hair ends. Hair still shows half of details. LIBERTY slightly worn, but all letters are sharp. Reverse: Leaves and bow worn but fully detailed.

Photograde: Obverse: A full sharp LIBERTY will be visible even though there is some wear. The feathers will be worn on the tips. Note: Indian cents cannot be graded by the diamond designs on the ribbon as this feature was not always sharply struck. Reverse: There will be more detail in the leaves and on the ribbon bow.

Snow: VF-20. The borders on the headband will be visible. The lower ribbon and hair curl will be connected. Minimum: The lower edge of the headband at LIBERTY just shows. Some major contact marks may show. Maximum: The lower edge of the headband is very plain. Many small marks may show. • **VF-30.** Minimum: The lower edge of the headband and LIBERTY are clear and distinct. Only a few marks show. Maximum: The lower ribbon and the hair curl just touch.

QDB (commentary): We are getting into a twilight zone: trying to define the somewhat undefinable. In practice, there seem to be different ideas in the marketplace as to where Fine ends and VF begins.

EXTREMELY FINE
(EF-40; also EF-45)
Indian Cents

ANA: EF-40. Obverse: Feathers well defined and LIBERTY is bold. Wear shows on hair above ear, curl to right of ribbon and on the ribbon end. Most of the diamond design shows plainly. Reverse: High points of the leaves and bow are worn. • **EF-45.** Obverse: Wear shows on hair above ear, curl to right of ribbon and on the ribbon end. All of the diamond design and letters in LIBERTY are very plain. Reverse: High points of the leaves and bow are lightly worn. Traces of mint lustre still show.

Photograde: Obverse: There must be a full sharp LIBERTY. The ends of the feathers (except on certain weakly struck issues, such as 1859-1864 copper-nickel pieces) will be sharply detailed. Reverse: There will be wear on the high points of the leaves and ribbon bow.

Snow: EF-40. Some light wear on the highest points. Ribbon and lower hair curl are separated. A trace of lustre may show. Minimum: The ribbon and lower hair curl are just separated. A few lines of the diamond design show. A few large marks or many small marks may be present. Maximum: Most, but not all of the diamond design shows plainly. Many small marks may be present. • **EF-45.** Minimum: All diamonds on the ribbon are visible. The coin may have a few marks. Maximum: Less than 25% mint lustre shows. The highest points will show some wear.

QDB (commentary): Experience is the great teacher in this and higher grades. Ten different coins are apt to show 10 different gradations. Again, one rule does not fit all. The best way to understand EF-40 is to view a selection of coins already classified in this grade. Even so, you might call a few VF-35 and others EF-45. No problem here. It's the nature of the grading game. Further, the sharpness of the diamond design on certain issues is more of a factor of striking than of wear.

In the marketplace you will often find that coins offered as EF-45 have little lustre at all (if they did, they would be offered as AU-50 or better).

EF-45 can be a very beautiful grade for an Indian cent, and a set of matched pieces, with glossy fields, can be a joy to behold.

David W. Lange of the Numismatic Guaranty Corporation of America noted that "Indian cents do not always have complete feather details, as made."[1] This is an important point to remember; in instances in which the feather details were not sharply struck to begin with, examples seen today cannot be sharp.

ABOUT UNCIRCULATED
(AU-50; also 53, 55, 58)
Indian Cents

ANA: AU-50. Obverse: Traces of wear show on the hair above ear and curl to right of ribbon. Reverse: Traces of wear show on the leaves and bow knot. Half of the mint lustre is still present. • **AU-55.** Obverse: Only a trace of wear shows on the hair above the ear. Reverse: A trace of wear shows on the bow knot. Three-quarters of the mint lustre is still present. • **AU-58.** Has some signs of abrasion: hair above ear, curl to right of ribbon; bow knot.

Photograde: Obverse: Only a trace of wear will show on the highest points such as above the ear and the lowest curl of hair. Reverse: Only a trace of wear will show on the highest points of the leaves and ribbon bow.

Snow: AU-50. Some mint lustre will show. There will be a small trace of wear visible on the highest points of the coin. Minimum: No less than 25% original mint lustre. May have a few heavy contact marks or many small marks. Maximum: Slight wear. Less than 50% mint lustre. A moderate amount of contact marks. • **AU-55.** Minimum: Slight wear on the high points. A moderate amount of light contact marks. 50% mint lustre. Maximum: Less than 75% mint lustre. Very few contact marks. • **AU-58.** Minimum: Slight wear on the high points of the coin. Only a few light marks may be present. 75% mint lustre. Maximum: A virtual gem with full lustre. Very few or no contact marks. The coin cannot be called Mint State because of a very minor abrasion.

QDB (commentary): The AU grade is highly subjective. It is worth noting that some grading services insert AU-53 between the AU-50 and AU-55 levels. For years AU-55 or Choice AU was the standard designation for a nice AU Indian cent that was just short of the Uncirculated category. Some AU pieces have tinges of red or orange mint color in protected areas.

AU-58 is a loosely defined category. What are "some signs of abrasion" (ANA) or "a few light marks" (Snow)? Again, viewing a number of pre-graded coins is a good way to gain knowledge of the AU category. In practice in the marketplace there isn't much difference in some instances in appearance between AU-58 and MS-60 grades. As an added comment, David W. Lange of NGC noted that "a nice AU-58 is typically worth more in the market than an MS-60."[2]

The entire area of grading from AU-58 to MS-62 is fraught with contradictions, and among coins seen in the marketplace there is little consistency.

---

[1] Letter, May 16, 1996.
[2] Letter, May 16, 1996.

The following grades apply to Mint State (also Proof coins in the Snow listings).

MINT STATE-60
(MS-60)
Indian Cents

ANA: A strictly Uncirculated coin with no trace of wear, but with blemishes more obvious than for MS-63. May lack full mint lustre, and surface may be dull or spotted. Further: Unattractive, dull, or washed out mint lustre may mark this coin. There may be many large detracting contact marks, or damage spots, but absolutely no trace of wear. There could be a heavy concentration of hairlines, or unattractive large areas of scuff marks. Rim nicks may be present, and eye appeal is very poor. Copper coins may be dark, dull, or spotted.

Photograde: This grade, at the low end of the Uncirculated scale, represents a coin which has never been in the channels of circulation, but which has numerous bagmarks and other evidences of coin-to-coin contact. However, traces of sliding wear, friction in the fields, and heavy rubbing are not seen.

Snow: No wear. May have many spots and marks. Unattractive eye appeal. A below average coin. The typically encountered coin in a typical group.

QDB (commentary): I disagree with the ANA and Snow contentions that a MS-60 coin is unattractive. *Proof*-60 coins, usually, but in my opinion, a MS-60 coin, if not spotted and simply with some contact marks, can be very beautiful. However, in the market the grades of MS-60 and MS-61—sometimes even MS-62—are ignored if the coins are attractive, and the grade jumps to MS-63. In other words, an attractive MS-61 becomes a MS-63 coin, while an ugly MS-61 stays at MS-61.

Among Proofs, the Proof-60 category nearly always refers to a coin that is stained or spotted. Such coins got that way from having been cleaned and retoned (either artificially or over a long period of time) or, less often, from being stored in damp or other unfavorable conditions. In general, quality Proofs begin about at the Proof-63 level. At *all* Proof levels coins have to be cherrypicked if choice specimens are desired.

MINT STATE-61
(MS-61)
Indian Cents

ANA: lustre may be diminished or noticeably impaired, and the surface has clusters of large and small contact marks throughout. Hairlines could be very noticeable. Scuff marks may show as unattractive patches in large areas or major features. Small rim nicks, striking or planchet defects may show, and the quality may be noticeably poor. Eye appeal is somewhat unattractive. Copper pieces may will be generally dull, dark, and possibly spotted.

Photograde: Intermediate grade; not defined.

Snow: Many have many spots and marks. Somewhat attractive eye appeal.

QDB (commentary): MS-61 coins can be quite attractive, but not many coins with high aesthetic appeal are graded in this category (see description under MS-60 above). Proofs are apt to be unattractive. Definitions of Mint State coins are becoming increasingly wordy with less useful definition. This is no fault of the grading standard compilers; grading is a matter of opinion, and coins are apt to differ widely. How the heck anyone can figure out how many or how few scuffs, rim nicks, planchet defects, etc., are permissible for MS-61 (see ANA above) is beyond me.

David W. Lange noted this:[1] "In practice, low grades such as MS-61 are applied fairly consistently by the grading services by simply judging where a coin falls relative to more distinguishable grades."

MINT STATE-62
(MS-62)
Indian Cents

ANA: An impaired or dull lustre may be evident. Clusters of small marks may be present throughout with a few large marks or nicks in prime focal areas. Hairlines may be very noticeable. Large unattractive scuff marks might be seen on major features. The strike, rim, and planchet quality may be noticeably below average. Overall eye appeal is generally acceptable. Copper coins will show a diminished color and tone.

Photograde: Intermediate grade; not defined.

Snow: May have some spots and marks. Attractive eye appeal.

QDB (commentary): MS-62 coins can be beautiful if you can find them. Nearly all Proof-62 coins are unattractive (if they were attractive, they would be graded higher). A close study of the wording in the definitions of Mint State and Proof listings and this and nearby levels will reveal that a lot is left to individual interpretation: what is "attractive"? What are "some" spots? What are "some" marks? Are three large marks equal to 14 tiny marks? I am not trying to be difficult, just to point out that once you are offered a coin in a certain grade, it is up to YOU to do some further thinking.

MINT STATE-63
(MS-63)
Indian Cents

ANA: Specific grading for Indian cents: A Mint State coin with attractive mint lustre, but noticeable detracting contact marks or minor blemishes. Further: Mint lustre may be slightly impaired. Numerous small contact marks, and a few scattered heavy marks may be seen. Small hairlines are visible without magnification. Several detracting scuff marks or defects may be present throughout the design or in the fields. The general quality is about average, but overall the coin is rather attractive. Copper pieces may be darkened or dull. Color should be designated.

Photograde: Intermediate grade; not defined.

Snow: Only a few light spots or marks. An average coin. Typical for an average group of Mint State coins. Attractive eye appeal.

QDB (commentary): Same philosophy as foregoing, except that in practice *Proof* coins at this level have a chance at being attractive. I have found that some coins called Proof-63 BN (brown) are especially worthwhile and, for my money, can be nicer than a Proof-65 RB (red and brown). Lots of opportunities at this level for the alert buyer.

---

[1] Letter, May 16, 1996.

MINT STATE-64
(MS-64)
Indian Cents

ANA: Has at least average lustre and strike for the type. Several small contact marks in groups, as well as one or two moderately heavy marks may be present. One or two small patches of hairlines may show under low magnification. Noticeable light scuff marks or defects might be seen within the design or in the field. Attractive overall quality with a pleasing eye appeal. Copper coins may be slightly dull. Color should be designated.

Photograde: Intermediate grade; not defined.

Snow: Very few minor spots or marks. Very attractive eye appeal. Choice. One of the best from a typical group of Mint State cents.

QDB (commentary): I really cannot see much difference in the verbal definitions given for the 64 grade vs. the 63 grade. Again, the situation is highly subjective. I, for one, would rather have two "marks" than one "spot," as I can tolerate marks (the result of coin-to-coin or other contact) but don't care for spots (caused by corrosion or undue oxidation). Of course, if you don't mind spots, you'll find *many* coins— numismatic leopards, so to speak—to add to your collection at this level.

The MS-64 and Proof-64 levels are generally called "gem" quality. Such terms as RD, RB, and BN are used to describe the surface coloration, and beginning about this level often cause widely different values to be assigned within the same numerical grade.

If I were assembling a gem (MS-64 or MS-65, or Proof-64 or Proof-65) set of Indian cents and did not have a clear rapport or understanding with a dealer, and were simply "surfing" various advertisements, etc., I would use these two grade levels as starting points, and look only at certified coins. While certified coins can be erratic and often are, uncertified gems are usually worse, especially if offered by dealers who emphasize their low prices. With a certified coin in hand as a *starting point,* I would examine it closely. If it were ugly I would not buy it, nor would I if it had other problems. However, with some looking, a great deal of patience, and with your bargain-hunting instinct (which we all have) kept in check, over a period of time you can assemble a *truly* gem set this way. The Proofs will be harder to find spot-free than will be the Mint State coins.

MINT STATE-65
(MS-65)
Indian Cents

ANA: Specific grading for Indian cents: No trace of wear; nearly as perfect as MS-67 except for some small blemish. Has full mint lustre but may be unevenly toned or lightly fingermarked. A few barely noticeable nicks or marks may be present. Further: Shows an attractive high quality of lustre and strike for the date and mint. A few small scattered contact marks, or two larger marks may be present, and one or two small patches of hairlines may show under magnification. Noticeable light scuff marks may show on the high points of the design. Overall quality is above average and overall eye appeal is very pleasing. Copper coins have full lustre with original or darkened color as designated.

Photograde: An Uncirculated (or Proof) coin which possesses only a few scattered bagmarks or hairlines, none of which is disfiguring. By current definition such a coin is one of excellent quality with an overall pleasing aspect.

Snow: Virtually spot or mark free. Very attractive eye appeal. A gem. Typically the finest quality found in an above average group of Mint State coins.

QDB (commentary): Same as preceding. The assigning of the MS-65 or Proof-65 number to a coin is no assurance of eye appeal or quality. However, if hand picked, coins can be very beautiful at this level. If you compare the differences in wording among the grades in this range you will realize (again) that in-person inspection of pre-graded coins is the best way to gain knowledge.

MINT STATE-66
(MS-66)
Indian Cents

ANA: Must have above average quality of strike and full original mint lustre, with no more than two or three minor but noticeable contact marks. A few very light hairlines may show under magnification, or there may be one or two light scuff marks showing on frosted surfaces or in the field. The eye appeal must be above average and very pleasing for the date and mint. Copper coins display full original or lightly toned color as designated.

Photograde: Intermediate grade; not defined.

Snow: Virtually spot and mark free, a nearly flawless beauty. Very attractive eye appeal. Rarely encountered.

QDB (commentary): A few years ago this grade wasn't often used. Now it is seen all the time. What a few years ago was a very nice MS-65, cherrypicked for its outstanding quality, is now sometimes graded MS-66 or MS-67. Ditto for Proofs.

MINT STATE-67
(MS-67)
Indian Cents

ANA: Specific grading for Indian cents: Virtually flawless, but with very minor imperfections. Further: Has full original lustre and sharp strike for date and mint. May have three or four small contact marks and one more noticeable but not detracting mark. On comparable coins, one or two small single hairlines may show under magnification, or there may be one or two light scuff marks showing on frosted surfaces or in the field. The eye appeal must be above average and very pleasing for the date and mint. Copper coins display full original or lightly toned color as designated.

Photograde: Intermediate grade; not defined.

Snow: Spot and mark free. A nearly perfect coin. Extremely attractive eye appeal.

QDB (commentary): On Mint State coins there should be no spots. However, among certified Proof coins some have spots at this level (not that they should). Again, make your own decisions about quality.

In practice, if I were writing out a check for a MS-67 Indian cent I would not want scuff marks, "two small single hairlines," or anything else like this on the coin. Reality among coins graded at this level may be somewhat different. To date, this grade is rarely used, but who knows what the future will bring?

MINT STATE-68
(MS-68)
Indian Cents

ANA: Attractive sharp strike and full original lustre for the date and mint, with no more than four light scattered contact marks or flaws. No hairlines or scuff marks can be seen. Has exceptional eye appeal. Copper coins must be bright with full original color and lustre.

Photograde: Intermediate grade; not defined.

Snow: Almost perfect in all respects.

QDB (commentary): Currently this grade is used only rarely. Perhaps tomorrow it will be common, if grade interpretations escalate. When I mention escalation I am not referring to the present ANA or Richard Snow standards, but to what one finds among commercially graded and certified coins.

MINT STATE-69
(MS-69)
Indian Cents

ANA: Must have very attractive sharp strike and full original lustre for the date and mint, with no more than two small non-detracting contact marks or flaws. No hairlines or scuff marks can be seen. Has exceptional eye appeal. Copper coins must be bright with full original color and lustre.

Photograde: Intermediate grade; not defined.

Snow: Essentially perfect in all respects.

QDB (commentary): What is a non-detracting mark or flaw? How does "essentially perfect" (MS-69) differ from "perfect" (MS-70)? David W. Lange, representing NGC, noted:[1] "We agree and have not used this grade for Indian cents."

MINT STATE-70
(MS-70)
Indian Cents

ANA: Specific grading for Indian cents: A flawless coin exactly as it was minted, with no trace of wear or injury. Any unusual die or planchet traits must be described. Further: The perfect coin. Has very attractive sharp strike and original lustre of the highest quality for date and mint. No contact marks are visible under magnification. There are absolutely no hairlines, scuff marks, or defects. Attractive and outstanding eye appeal. Copper coins must be bright with full original color and lustre.

Photograde: An absolutely perfect coin. Under magnification with a hand glass, no contact or other marks are to be seen. In general, such perfection is only found among modern coins specifically issued at a premium price for collectors.

Snow: MS-70 or Proof-70: Perfect in all respects.

QDB (commentary): In theory, a carefully made Proof coin kept carefully since the time of manufacture should qualify, but as of 1996 this grade is not used. If one grading service has a "breakthrough" and offers 70-graded coins, perhaps we'll see a lot of them. Re the ANA listings: What are the "unusual planchet traits" that are important to mention at the MS-70 level, but, apparently, not if a coin is MS-63 through MS-69? Planchet defects were last heard from in the ANA grading scale at the MS-62 level.

---

[1] Letter, May 16, 1996.

Alternative Grading Suggestions

Grading is a matter of opinion. Although over the years many guidelines and standards have reached print, no system has ever been good enough that it can be scientifically replicated from print alone; that is, no system has ever enabled someone without experience and knowledge to read the guidelines and at that point grade a group of coins expertly.

However, among circulated grades from Poor-1 to AU-58, where *actual wear* rather than *attractive appearance* is most important, grading guidelines are easier to follow. Among Mint State categories the definitions are much more subjective. Most advanced specialists in the Indian cent field can agree if a coin is VG-8, but few can agree on such levels as MS-65, MS-66, and MS-67.

Still further, grade is only a part of the consideration determining a coin's *value,* and a glossy brown VG-8 coin can be more desirable to own than an ugly or corroded VF-20.

Ideally, when describing a coin of significant value the grade should be given together with notation of any major problems such as cleaning, scratches, digs, corrosion, etc. In practice, if a coin is of very low value (a well-worn 1907 cent for example), it is not practical to do this. However, when it is possible to describe a coin beyond simple grades, a better understanding is imparted.

In addition to the above or any other published ideas or standards, your own standards, experience, or whatever system you use, the value of a given coin will in addition be determined by its striking quality, surface quality, problems or lack thereof, and, especially, aesthetic appeal. These considerations may not be important for a VF-20 1907 Indian cent, but they certainly are for some of the more expensive issues. And, there is no reason why you shouldn't be "fussy" with a VF 1907 cent, too.

Larry R. Steve on Grading and Quality

Larry R. Steve—well-known student of Indian cents and the Mint processes that made them, long-time collector of the series, and current editor of *Longacre's Ledger*— contributed his ideas as to grading.[1]

While he does not give grade-by-grade differentiation or guidelines, I believe that his thoughts are exceedingly valuable as they reflect technical or numerical grade as only one element of a coin's desirability:

I am a student of the "old school" of grading and am concerned with strike,

---

[1] Letter, April 29, 1996.

surface, lustre, and eye appeal, all of these in combination with an emphasis on originality.

With respect to Mint State coins, some aspects that I consider most important are fullness or weakness of strike (fullness being better of course), satiny surfaces vs. flowlined (from die wear) surfaces, unimpaired lustre vs. impaired or subdued lustre, and distribution or blend of color.

Spots, marks, scrapes, rim nicks, etc., are netted out as cumulative fractional grades depending upon number, severity, and location (a small spot embedded within the feathers of the headdress is less obtrusive than an equally sized, or even smaller, spot in the middle of the field).

Circulated coins descend from Mint State coins, and their grading should begin with the same aforementioned considerations, upon which varying degrees of wear are then described. Should any official guidelines for the grading of Indian cents ever be formulated, they should at the very least include separate grades for the obverse and reverse and be explicitly detailed enough to create a visual image.

Surfaces: Color and Spotting

When first struck, copper-nickel Flying Eagle cents 1856-1858 and Indian cents 1859-1864 were a light golden, brilliant color. Over a period of time they tend to tone to a medium golden brown.

Bronze Indian cents made from 1864 onward tone differently. When first coined they were a bright, light orange color. Copper is a chemically active metal, and almost immediately cents began to combine with atmospheric elements and tone, first a reddish-orange, then a deeper reddish orange, then with traces of light brown, then a mix of red and brown, and, finally, light brown.

If a bronze Indian cent is exposed to moisture drops (from the atmosphere, from tiny saliva drops when someone holds a coin and speaks, etc.), contact with skin (causes brown fingerprints to develop over a period of time), contact with sulfur-content paper (in a paper roll for wrapping cents, in an album with cardboard pages, etc.), toning will occur.

In all cases, gradual, blended toning is more desirable than spotty or irregular toning. The brown toning of a prominent fingerprint on the reverse of an Indian cent is less desirable than the same amount of brown toning evenly distributed around the rim. In fact, the former would lessen the value of the coin considerably while the latter would have little effect at all. And yet, both coins can have the same numerical grade.

Tiny moisture droplets often develop into black or green oxidation patches. In no instances are these desirable, but if microscopic they can be accepted with grace. It is the current practice of leading certification services to simply downgrade a coin a number or two to reflect such tiny spots or flecks. Thus, a MS-65 coin, but with spots, may be graded as a MS-63 or MS-64. If a Proof Indian cent has enough spots to make a Dalmatian jealous, it might be graded simply as Proof-61 or Proof-62, without any further indication of quality.

In the absence of any accompanying narrative, the only way to tell if there are spots is to see the coin itself. Presumably, a more detailed description such as "MS-65, but with microscopic flecks, net grade MS-63" would, somehow, be perceived as negative.

Among graded coins on the market there are plenty of Proof-65 and MS-65 coins, marked as Proof-65 or MS-65, with spots! Concerning this, David W. Lange, a representative of NGC, commented:[1]

> Such coins presumably would have graded higher without the spots. This is the compromise which reflects "market grading" versus "technical grading." Certified grades seem to present a coin's market value as currently recognized.

Color: Red to Brown

While copper-nickel Flying Eagle and Indian cents can be graded by the amount of wear, marks, etc., as generally described in the ANA Grading Scale, Richard Snow's grading guidelines, *Photograde,* and other published standards, *bronze* Indian cents from 1864 to 1909 are often classified by color as well, especially in Mint State and Proof levels.

It is widely believed that "brilliant is best." Thus, the more *original* orange color a coin has, the better.

Indian cents with most or all of the surface colored orange or reddish orange are typically called "red," abbreviated "RD" on certified coin holders. You will note among the price charts given in this book that values are heavily skewed toward coins with "red," particularly at the MS-65 or Proof-65 levels.

Indian cents with a mixture of red and brown—a generous measure of each, but with no particular percentages defined—are usually called "red and brown," abbreviated "RB." Coins that are nearly completely or fully brown are called "brown," abbreviated "BN." Indeed, it would be very difficult for anyone to measure a percentage of color, as shadings often blend into each other. NGC uses these benchmarks:[2]

> BN designates a coin that shows no mint red at all or no more than about 15% of its original color. To be designated RD, a coin must show at least 85% to 90% of its original color. Those that fall between these extremes are labeled RB.

---

[1] Letter, May 16, 1996.
[2] David W. Lange, letter, May 16, 1996, enclosing his article, "From One to Seventy," *The Numismatist,* May 1996, p. 610.

Thus, in grading nomenclature for bronze cents we have not only the numerical grade such as MS-63, but a suffix indicating color, such as MS-63 RD (considered best to own, per conventional wisdom), MS-63 RB (next best), and MS-63 BN (least).

Color on Bronze Cents: A Closer Look

If you want a really *nice* set of bronze Indian cents 1864-1909, you must cherrypick for quality. If you are a connoisseur you will want to buy these one at a time. Expect to pay a premium for quality pieces. This advice cannot be overemphasized, in my opinion. Bottom-feeders and bargain-seekers wind up with the dregs, of which there are many in coin market channels in virtually every series, but especially among bronze Indian cents.

Certification services can be a good *beginning* for your search. However, as aesthetic value is not considered by the grading services, except in a general way, it is not unusual to find a bronze Indian cent certified as MS-64 or Proof-64 but with unsightly spots. The quality of certified and other coins is apt to vary widely, with such terms as "RB" (red and brown) having no standard definition at all. Sometimes Indian cents certified as "RD" (for "red") have less red than do pieces certified as "RB" (red and brown). Among copper-nickel Flying Eagle cents 1856-1858 and Indian cents 1859-1864 there are fewer problems as the surface toning color is not part of the grading and market system. Still, even these should be selected with care.

Many Indian cents have been dipped or cleaned and recolored. This is less of a problem with certified coins than with "raw" ones, but there are many cleaned and recolored coins in certified holders as well.

While no test I can give in print can assure you of determining these, in general if a coin is brilliant or partly brilliant, and if when examining it under a 4X or 8X glass in bright light, turning the coin slowly as you inspect it, if you see tiny parallel hairlines in the obverse field or brush marks on the Indian's cheek, these are warning signals.

What is acceptable as to cleaning and what is not has never been defined. In 1995 and 1996 there was some flurry in the letters to the editors columns of *Coin World* and *Numismatic News* expressing surprise to the news that the Professional Coin Grading Service (PCGS) and the Numismatic Guaranty Corporation of America (NGC), the two leading grading services, occasionally clean silver and gold coins if requested to do so, but do not mark the coins as having been "cleaned" or "dipped." On the other hand, the very same grading services are known to have returned coins to submitters with notations such as "altered surface," implying cleaning. While there can be "good" cleaning and "bad" cleaning, most is in the latter category. However, it seems that such dipping has been of coins other than copper or bronze.[1]

Moreover, for a Proof Indian cent to be in a lower grade such as Proof-60, Proof-61, or Proof-62, it probably has hairlines and thus was cleaned at one time. This is true of certified coins as well as non-certified ones. Quite possibly, the true description—but not used at all by the hobby—for a Proof coin of any denomination, copper, nickel, silver, or gold, in a lower Proof grade should be something like "Proof-60 due to cleaning." There has to be *some reason* that a Proof is not in a higher grade. The existence of a high level Proof-64 or Proof-65, which is short of perfection but still often of excellent quality, can be explained by a few handling marks, but most lower grade Proofs have been cleaned. Others that may have not been cleaned have some other problem such as staining or corrosion. This point is moot, for as long as collectors, grading services, dealers, and others simply accept "Proof-60," "Proof-61," etc., without elaboration, all should be satisfied.

Bronze Indian cents marked "BN" (brown) should be an attractive medium or light brown, perhaps with some tinges of nicely blended red, in order to be suitable for a connoisseur's collection, although in the marketplace quality varies widely. Mint lustre may or may not be present.

Bronze Indian cents marked "RB" (red and brown) should have a nice blend of red and brown, not bright red with brown spots or patches, but red with a gradual transition to brown. It is not unusual for one side to have more red or more brown than the other.

Bronze cents marked "RD" (red) should be fully or nearly fully brilliant. Any tinges of natural light brown toning should be delicately blended. Copper is a very active metal chemically, and even the reddest of "RD" coins have some natural light toning (unless they have been cleaned). On red coins the outer edge (as viewed edge-on) is virtually always toned brown. If the edge of a coin is bright red, this probably means the coin has been dipped. Of course, if a coin is in a slab, you will have no clue as to what the edge looks like, but you can hope that the graders took this aspect into consideration.

You should be your own judge as to quality. I find that buying quality Indian cents for inventory takes a lot of plain old-fashioned work and is a great deal more difficult than buying, for example, Morgan silver dollars.

Just as Rome was not built in a day, no outstanding collection of

---

[1] John Dannreuther (principal of PCGS) comment, letter, May 11, 1996: "We no longer dip coins for customers and have *never* dipped copper and *never* will." David Lange (of NGC) comment, letter, May 16, 1996: "NGC does not clean copper coins; we won't go beyond a neutral solvent, and then only if requested by the submitter."

Indian cents was ever built quickly. Take your time, buy the inexpensive varieties first, and be "fussy."

Striking vs. Value

Some Flying Eagle and Indian cents are well struck, others have a few areas of weakness, and still others have major weaknesses. However, certification services don't mention the sharpness of striking at all, although the element of sharp strike is mentioned in some ANA grading classifications in the higher levels, but not in others. For MS-60, MS-61, MS-63 in the ANA standards, strike is not mentioned at all. For MS-62 strike can be "noticeably below average," for MS-64 "average," for MS-65 "high quality," for MS-66 "above average," for MS-67 "sharp," and for MS-68, 69, and 70 "attractive sharp strike." While such definitions are interesting, it would be rather difficult for a new collector on a desert island to determine the difference between "high quality" and "above average."

Further, it has been my observation that most coins on the market today are graded by lustre and surface appearance, and sharpness of strike is generally ignored by grading experts, unless there is a flat spot or other *blatant* area of weakness.

If you see a description for a MS-65 1857 Flying Eagle or 1896 Indian cent you haven't any idea, unless you see it, if it is sharp as a needle or if it has flat spots. Poorly struck pieces tend to be offered at "bargain" prices. In the sub-chapter descriptions of individual dates and mintmarks in this book I give indications as to what type of striking to expect if a given date of Flying Eagle or Indian cent is known with differences.

Suppose you are offered two Flying Eagle cents, each in the same degree of Mint State. One is priced at $1,000 and the other at $650. Which is the better buy?

If the $650 one is flatly struck, it may be a poor buy in comparison to a sharply struck specimen for $1,000. However, unless you know the series and inspect the coin, you have absolutely no way to compare values. Unfortunately for those who have it that the computer age has brought with it all of the answers, to date there is no substitute for visually inspecting a coin to determine its worth. Once again, simple grading numbers just won't work. Sorry!

Changing Interpretations

If you have a scientific turn of mind, please stay with me, even though I have indicated that grading "numbers" alone will have only limited usefulness to you. If you demand precise numbers and enjoy calculations, then when you are *finished* enjoying your Indian cent collection, simply turn to the stock market, the calculation of pi to umpteen decimal places, or to the study of planetary orbits.

In addition to the variables introduced by grading numbers, surface color, and lack of consideration for aesthetic descriptions, in recent years the grading interpretations used by certain leading grading services have slipped (at least this is my opinion). This is due in large part (again, my opinion) to the services competing with each other for the business of dealers, who represent the largest segment of coin submitters. If a service is "easy" and liberal, it will get more business. If it is "tight," dealers may well go elsewhere. The result is that in the mid-1990s, certified coins are often highly erratic in their consistency, quality, and interpretations.

I dare say that an Indian cent graded "MS-64 RB" if bought in 1988 would be of better quality than one certified in the same grade in the mid-1990s.

Don't take my word for the existence of wide actual differences within coins graded alike, for I am a dealer and also a very minor stockholder in PCGS (but have nothing to do with grading coins there). Take your own test. Assemble in one spot a group of 10 certified or uncertified or a combination—whatever you prefer—Indian cents called Proof-64 RB or MS-64 RB. The dates can be mixed. You will see a *few* beauties, some with spots, and some that are very unattractive. As published prices on electronic exchanges are often based upon certified coins, and as dealers with "dogs" offer them at bargain prices in order to get rid of them, it has been my experience that many published price guides are highly unreliable.

Where does this leave you?

It offers an excellent opportunity to gain an advantage over your fellow collectors simply by becoming educated on the subject and knowing what to avoid and what to buy.

If you demand to be able to buy Flying Eagle and Indian cents by simply looking at grading numbers and picking the cheapest pieces offered at a given level, good luck! (You'll need it.) However, if you take the time to become a connoisseur, I believe you will build a beautiful collection and also have an enjoyable challenge while doing it.

Don't take grading numbers too seriously. Think for yourself. In addition to considering whether a coin is MS-63 or MS-65 or whatever, keep in mind some of Larry R. Steve's ideas given earlier; thoughts about strike, lustre, spotting, etc. Grading is an art, not a science.

Remember, in numismatics the hobby has painted itself into a corner. A large, complex grading system is in place, and because of its inconsistency, there have been many misunderstandings and many hard feelings over the years. If you were to collect old books or music boxes instead (two of my hobby interests), you would find virtually no problems expressed in collectors' publications about grading. On the other hand, if it was necessary in the marketplace to assign a specific number such as MS-61, MS-62, or MS-63 to a first-edition copy of Jack London's *Sea Wolf,* or to a Link Style 2E coin-operated piano, then attention would turn, at least in part, from enjoying the hobby at hand to hair-splitting about grading.

I do not mean to make light of grading in numismatics. I simply encourage you to understand what it is all about and form your own conclusions. Above all, trust your own judgment once you have gained a modicum of experience, and buy a coin *only if you think it is attractive.*

Before leaving the grading subject in this chapter, I think you'll find the next few paragraphs to be interesting:

Dr. Salyards on Grading "Precision"

Penny-Wise, March 15, 1996, contained an editorial commentary by Harry E. Salyards, M.D., and also a detailed article by William C. Noyes, relating to coin grading as applied to large cents. Without attempting to discuss that particular article, let me say that it addressed the long-popular idea in large cent circles of not only assigning a numerical grade to a coin such as VF-30, but also grading both sides of the coin (as a coin does have two sides and often the two are different), and after that is done, giving the opinion as to whether a particular piece is "choice," "average," or "scudzy," the latter being a name for an unattractive piece. It was large-cent expert and author Jack Robinson, I believe, who introduced "scudzy" into the nomenclature (so far it hasn't spread to Indian cents).

In his editorial Dr. Salyards, quoting John D. Wright—lots of quotes here—noted that "coin grading is only a science as music is a science," but further went on to say, "Like music, grading is first and foremost an aesthetic response: beauty or the lack of it. Like music, it is susceptible to endless verbal and numerical dissection; but no inherent satisfaction derives from labeling a given coin VF-35/30, net 20/25, or MS-63 PQ—any more than deriving a mathematical theorem of a chord progression can 'explain' the effect of a particular Mozart sonata. At bottom, music is nothing but vibrating air, and a coin nothing but a bit of metal. Once we've 'graded' it to the ultimate degree of 'precision,' we find we're no closer to the *truth* about it than when our conception of music consisted of 'mmm' versus 'ugh,' or our coin grading scale equaled 'new' or 'used.'"

QDB note: Now there's an idea for some new coin grading terms. I would rather have an "Mmm" 1856 Flying Eagle cent than an "Ugh" one!

For additional reading on grades vs. rarity vs. market prices please see Appendix IV, which is devoted to a detailed discussion of certified coins, especially those in Mint State and Proof categories.

CHAPTER 6
ASPECTS OF COLLECTING

Introductory Remarks

Now that grading is behind us—or at least has had its own chapter—I go on to some other aspects of collecting. These and other considerations are, of course, all interrelated so far as market value and desirability are concerned.

I would like you to be a connoisseur, and along the way it is as important to know what to avoid as what to buy. Thomas A. Edison is said to have made 500 non-working light bulbs before *the* light bulb was invented in 1879. If you consider 20 coins before buying *the* coin, you have accomplished much.

Cleaning

Immersing a brown-toned Indian cent in silver dip or another cleaner will make it "brilliant," perhaps a bright orange somewhat similar to what it looked like when first minted, but to the expert's eye, ever so slightly paler and not quite the "right" hue. Cleaning a bronze coin strips the surface of its toning and makes chemically active copper metal even more susceptible to atmospheric effects. Soon, most dipped pieces become blotchy or unevenly colored. Most mottled and stained bronze cents in certified holders marked "BN" or "RB" have probably been cleaned. Some blotchy "RD" coins may represent recently dipped pieces that have been certified, but which changed color within the holders.

I don't like blotchy coins, and if I were putting together a collection of cents, I would rather own a run of nicely matched, brown-toned AU-55 cents than a series of blotchy MS-63 RB pieces. I've mentioned this earlier and will come back to it again. *Quality* is the key word that you as a connoisseur should always keep in mind. *Quality* first, *price* second.

The "secret" to success in buying is simply to avoid coins that are stained and ugly, even if the price is a bargain. Let someone else buy them. The popular coin publications are filled with all sorts of claims and offers, and all too often that bargain "gem brilliant Uncirculated" or "selected brilliant Uncirculated" proves to be a scrubbed-up About Uncirculated coin. Or, that certified Proof-61 cent may indeed be Proof-61, but so spotted that it is ugly as a toad, and will be something you'll always regret buying, no matter how much of a "bargain" it is.

Bill Fivaz commented: "Don't buy a problem. It will always be a problem. It doesn't get any better, and it could get worse!"[1]

Similarly, Richard Snow remarked, "There is no price *too low* for a problem coin."[2]

"Good" Cleaning

And yet, some cleaning and techniques can improve a coin's surface. A bright unnatural orange coin that has been dipped will retone a nice brown if it is exposed to the atmosphere, such as on a windowsill under a little wire basket to prevent it from slipping away. Or, a mixture of sulfur powder and mineral oil applied with a cotton swab may do the trick. This is not a suggestion for you, but merely an indication of what can be done to bring back the latent beauty of a cent that has been made ugly. Dr. Sheldon in *Early American Cents* gives some good advice, and James F. Ruddy's *Photograde* book also has a worthwhile discussion.

A *copper-nickel* cent that is stained or blotched, if it is in a higher grade may sometimes be dipped with good effect. However, as mentioned in *Photograde,* repeated dipping will yield only a dull, unattractive surface, a coin with no "life."

Dipping a *bronze* Indian cent usually lessens its value from the outset.

Brushing a circulated bronze coin with a camel's hair brush may remove dust and impart a glossy surface. Again, consult Dr. Sheldon on this one.

Acetone (a volatile solvent available at drug and hardware stores, and which must be carefully used) or plain old soap and water can be used effectively to remove dirt and verdigris from the surface of an Indian cent.

In all in instances, do your experimenting with a common, cheap bronze Lincoln cent, not a numismatically valuable Indian cent.

A Bit of Philosophy

I am a dealer, and I make my living by buying and selling coins. Because of this, you might think that I've wasted a lot of print telling you of some of the pitfalls to avoid. Certainly, you might loosen up your purse

---

[1] Letter, March 29, 1996.
[2] Letter, April 10, 1996.

strings if I were to state unequivocally:

Indian cents advertised as MS-65 RD are incredible bargains on today's market. Buy as many as you can find, even if you have to borrow money to do it.

And, indeed, a lot of advice you see is like this.

However, my philosophy is that if you are knowledgeable about the problems and pitfalls, you will buy coins more effectively, and the pleasures of making a good buy will be more exciting, more real. If you buy that MS-65 Red Indian cent and know full well what the grading game is about, then you are home free. If you have looked at 16 coins and have passed them by, and finally have found Coin No. 17, the sparkling gem you've been hoping for, you will be happy and satisfied. You'll really appreciate what you have, just as Edison realized the importance of Light Bulb No. 501.

On the other hand, if you buy a coin described as MS-65 Red, but are not sure whether the price is right or what the coin should look like or whether quality is important, but are relying simply upon someone else's sales message or the inducement of a low price, the day of reckoning awaits you.

There are pleasures in collecting Flying Eagle and Indian cents, and these pleasures are *delicious* once you have some knowledge. There is an Unclouded Sky in numismatics if you are a connoisseur. Take my word for it: become a connoisseur, a smart buyer, and you'll have a really great time.

Mint State and Proof Prices

Market prices of bronze Indian cents in Mint State and Proof categories are apt to vary. In the price listings in the sub-chapters for each date I give estimated figures based upon historical listings, but no one price is really applicable to all coins of a given grade and color. As noted, coins within a specific category—MS-63 RB for example—can vary as to specific value.

In the listings a MS-65 RD cent is valued higher than a MS-64 RD, and the last is valued higher than a MS-63 RD.

A MS-65 RB cent is valued higher than a MS-64 RB, and the last is valued higher than a MS-63 RB.

A MS-65 BN cent is valued higher than a MS-64 BN, and the last is valued higher than a MS-63 BN.

However, in the real world among coins you are offered, a MS-64 RD coin in some instances can be more aesthetically pleasing than a MS-65 RD, and so on.

There are so many variables among the numbers, colors, and the coins themselves that it is often impossible to state, for example, whether a MS-63 RD cent is worth more or less than a MS-65 RB. Certainly, the MS-63 RD should be "brighter," but perhaps the MS-65 red and brown is nicer overall.

Market Prices of Years Past

Over the years, price trends have varied. In the sub-chapters for each date of Flying Eagle and Indian cent I give historical values under the heading "Market Prices" for the market in 1938, 1944, 1965, and 1996. In general, each later year lists prices higher than earlier years, but there are exceptions. In recent times there has been a wide differential among categories in the Mint State and Proof ranges. Years ago, such differences were small.

Among Indian cents in historical price listings including 1938, 1944, and 1965—the three benchmark years used in this text—there were no such refinements. Thus, such retroactive listings are highly subjective and are simply estimates, reflecting in most instances that a "brilliant" or "bright" coin would sell for more than a deeply toned one and that a coin with a surface with few marks would sell for more than one with numerous marks.

For further reading Appendix III gives historical prices of Indian cents listed in selected Scott *Standard Catalogue* editions 1878 to 1913. These are more curious than informative, but they show what kind of erratic information our numismatic forebears had to work with.

Today's Market Prices

Within "Market Prices" I give estimated values for Flying Eagle and Indian cents in various grades, not only the estimated prices of years ago, but suggested values for 1996. These prices are for *quality* examples of each grade. Stained, spotted, and unattractive coins will usually sell for less, often far less if the numerical grade is high but the aesthetic value is low. However, as per the grading commentary in Chapter 5, a Proof-60, Proof-61, or Proof-62 coin is apt to be unattractive.

Today in the 1990s, Indian cents in higher grade levels are typically graded by the American Numismatic Association's numerical grading system, with 1-point divisions between 60 and 70, as described earlier in the present text. Thus, Mint State coins are classified into MS-60, MS-61, MS-62, etc., through MS-70, the higher numbers representing the higher grades. Similarly, Proof-60, Proof-61, etc., grades are used. In the bronze series, color indications are added such as BN (brown), RB (red

Rolling mill at the Philadelphia Mint, 1880s. Metal strips were subjected to high pressure which squeezed them to ever increasing thinness. Once the desired thinness was achieved, planchets were cut from the strip in the manner of a cookie cutter

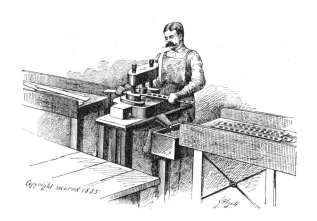

Cutting planchets from a strip. (Both pictures on this page from *Visitor's Guide and History of the United States Mint, Philadelphia, Pa.* A.M. Smith, 1885, pp. 12 and 16.)

and brown), and RD (red). A few dealers use old-time adjectival grading such as Uncirculated, Choice Uncirculated, and Gem Uncirculated.

Related to this, it is worth noting that among listings for high-grade coins in *The Coin Dealer Newsletter* are many prices which seem to be far above certain other listings published elsewhere. In large part these high prices are values for selected quality coins carefully inspected by discriminating buyers; these are *not* for run-of-the-mill certified coins, some of which, if unattractive, can be worth *far* less.

If someone publishes a bid price of $3,000 for Cent X in MS-65 RD grade, you can bet your last dollar that he or she wants to *personally inspect* that coin before laying out $3,000 for it. Often, a coin has to be cherrypicked for quality, indeed quite special, to merit the bid price. The vast majority of the examples of Coin X in MS-65 RD grade may be worth, say, $1,500 to $2,000 or even less.

In the same vein Keith Zaner, editor of the weekly market column in *Coin World,* is "fussy" about quality and uses these guidelines:[1]

> *Coin World* Trends values for Mint State-65 and Proof-65 bronze Indian cents and Lincoln cents are for ones which retain 100% of their original mint red or orange color.
>
> This was the color they possessed when they first entered circulation. It is important to keep in mind that as the original color changes toward brown the value often drops. Initially, the value can drop rather dramatically. Many key and semi-key date Indian cents from the mid-1860s through the 1870s have tremendous differences in value depending upon the extent or percentage of the original mint color which remains. An 1872 Indian cent grading MS-65 and exhibiting its full red original mint color can command a very large premium above an example which has 90% of its original color. *Coin World* Trends takes color into consideration before a value is listed.

If you buy a "bargain" specimen for $1,500 and think you are buying a $3,000 coin, think again. The entire concept of *quality* is largely overlooked by many purchasers. However, in my opinion it should be important to *you.*

Prices are a composite of information found in standard sources such as *Coin World* "Trends" (by Keith Zaner), *Numismatic News* "Coin Market" listings (by Bob Wilhite), *Coin Dealer Newsletter, Certified Coin Dealer Newsletter, Guide Book of United States Coins,* suggestions by Brian Wagner, auction prices, personal experience, mathematical interpolation and extrapolation, and that catch-all: guesswork (hopefully, somewhat educated). In addition, in some instances the *Standard Catalogue of U.S. Coins* and other historical sources are cited. Another valuable source is the 1993 article in *Longacre's Ledger,* Vol. 3, No. 1, "Pricing MS-65 RED Bronze Indian Cents," by Brian Wagner and Richard Snow.

---

[1] Letter, April 15, 1996.

Notwithstanding the preceding, there is no such thing as a *precise* market price for a given grade of Flying Eagle or Indian cent at a specific point in time. If you doubt this statement, simply secure a copy of the annual compilation of auction prices assembled by Krause Publications and see how divergent prices are for the same dates of coins in the same described grades sold in the same time period. As an illustration, 1857 Flying Eagle cents listed in MS-63 grade (I picked this as there are no "red," "red and brown," or "brown" differences to contend with in copper-nickel listings) sold in 1995 for prices ranging from a low of $242 to a high of $1,100.[1]

No analysis of auction results or price list entries can be a valid measurement unless two coins in the same advertised grade are compared side-by-side by the same person at the same point in time using the same lighting conditions. It could be that the above mentioned $242 coin was ugly and the $1,100 coin was a "high end" MS-63 or even MS-64 or finer, or perhaps two competitors at the sale each realized it was a rare die variety and bid accordingly. Such distinctions and refinements are extremely difficult for the lay person to understand. After all, the same share of common stock in John Doe Enterprises on the New York Stock Exchange sells for just about the same price no matter from which stock broker you buy it. Moreover, the "quality" of two shares is identical.

Not so with coins. Two pieces with identical numerical grades and descriptions can have a significant differential in market price.

Buying "Smart" (Summary)

No one rule or set of rules fits all situations, especially among Flying Eagle and Indian cents. However, I believe that these guidelines will be helpful in nearly all instances:

1. Look at the coin, not at the numerical grade or color designation, except as a starting point. If it is stained, spotted, ugly, or unappealing, don't buy it. Wait for another. You'll have a later chance. As noted above, a gem $1,100 coin in a particular grade can be a better buy than an ugly $242 piece in the same grade.

2. There are a lot of "traps" among certified coins and even more among those that are not certified. Some pieces are very ugly. And, as grading interpretations loosen, the average quality is getting worse. To put it simply, the typical certified MS-65 RD cent on the market in 1989 was better in quality than the same grade today. A lot of yesterday's MS-64 coins are today's MS-65s! Outside of certified coins, grading of Mint State and Proof

---

[1] *Auction Prices Realized, U.S. Coins, Auction Results for 1995,* p. 42.

bronze Indian cents is often a minefield for the unwary or uneducated buyer. Unless you have some grading savvy, at least start by examining certified coins. You may not bat 1000, but you stand a better chance of batting 300 than if you buy non-certified pieces. Certification by ANACS, NGC, and PCGS has become so popular, that most dealers have sent in their coins for grading to these services. High-value coins that are *not* certified may represent coins that have been cleaned, retoned, or have other problems and have been rejected by these services. This is not always true as some dealers don't like certified coins, and many collectors stay away from them as well, but for the beginner certification is a good first step when considering coins. It is notable that ANACS also attributes Flying Eagle and Indian cents to certain die varieties (such as the clashed dies of 1857), while NGC and PCGS do not.

3. Think independently. Don't let someone fool you into believing that all MS-65 RD coins are better than, for example, MS-63 BN specimens. This is not the case. There are nice coins and there are ugly coins within each grade category.

4. Don't be a bargain hunter. If the quality is there and the coin is *rare,* don't be afraid to pay the going rate or even more. No one ever bought the best quality for the cheapest price. This is true throughout the Flying Eagle and Indian cent series and is especially so among the bronze Indian cents 1864-1909. On the other hand, among later Lincoln cents, if a coin is common in gem condition (as are, for example, Proof Lincoln cents of the past two or three decades), then finding a gem will be a snap, just about every vendor has high quality, and the effort of cherrypicking for quality will not be important. Stated another way, the discipline needed to buy a modern Proof-65 RD 1990-S Lincoln cent is one thing, and that needed to buy a Proof-65 RD Indian cent of 1890 is another.

5. Study the specific variety of the coin you intend to buy in order to determine its characteristics, its availability in various grades, and its other aspects. This book will be a help in this regard. As the aforementioned Yogi Berra once said, "If you don't know where you are going, you might end up someplace else." Fortunately for you, there is much information available on Flying Eagle and Indian cents—in this book and elsewhere (see Bibliography)—so you can indeed know where you are going. It takes more savvy to buy a MS-65 or Proof-65 RD Indian cent of any date than it does to buy an MS-65 1881-S Morgan dollar or a gem Proof 1964 Kennedy half dollar.

6. Take your time. No matter how well endowed your checking account may be, allow yourself a year or two or three to put together a nice set. This will prolong the thrill of the hunt as well. No one has ever

put together a quality collection of Flying Eagle and Indian cents by buying in a hurry.

Solidity of the Pricing Structure

In my opinion, the solidity or strength of a market price for a given cent at a given grade level depends on a number of factors. Even if you become a connoisseur to a high degree and have a bottomless checking account, I believe that you should still seek *good value* for the money you spend. At least I would if I were assembling a set of Flying Eagle and Indian cents.

Here are some points to ponder:

1. Basic rarity: If a coin is recognized as a key issue—a rare date— and if it has been highly prized by several generations of numismatists, is has a more solid price structure than if it has only recently become valuable. Thus, an 1856 Flying Eagle cent, 1859 Indian cent (only year of the laurel wreath reverse design), 1877 cent (low-mintage rarity), or other key issue will probably always be in demand.

2. Condition rarity: This applies to a coin that might be very common in a grade such as Proof-63 BN, but which in Proof-65 RD may be very rare. While I do not question that such rarity is a good reason for a higher price, watch out if the differential is too great. *Just be careful.* You read it here! Also, if you are a fan of the population and census reports issued by grading services, remember this rule: *As time goes on, coins in a given grade become more plentiful in the reports, never less plentiful.* Few people stop to think about this, but you should.

In 1996 there has been quite a "play" on MS-65 RD and Proof-65 RD Indian cents, with some aggressive buyers willing to pay record prices for these, while expressing no interest at all in buying, for example, MS-65 RB and Proof-65 RB coins. As a result, some truly wide gaps have developed in the pricing structure. Moreover, as reiterated earlier, *quality* does play a part, often major, and perhaps someone willing to pay $5,000 for a certain Proof-65 RD might not want to buy *your* coin for even $2,000, if yours is spotted or if the buyer simply doesn't want it. Again, *please be careful.*

Here are two hypothetical small cents, one a *basic rarity* and the other a *condition rarity:*

Basic Rarity, Coin A, selected market prices: VF-20 $250; MS-65 BN $800; MS-65 RB $1,200; MS-65 RD $2,200.

Commentary: This coin seems to be quite valuable all along the line. While an MS-65 RD coin is more expensive than one with RB surfaces, the differential seems to be reasonable.

Condition Rarity, Coin B, selected market prices: VF-20 $7; MS-65 BN $200; MS-65 RB $350; MS-65 RD $2,200.

Commentary: The value of this coin in MS-65 RD grade seems to be based virtually entirely upon the surface color, as in lower grades the coin is not expensive. While it may be a dandy value at $2,200, for my money I would be more careful about buying this coin than I would Coin A. There is not much of a fallback position, and it is a long way from $2,200 back to the next highest level at $350.

Dealing With Dealers

As you build a collection of Flying Eagle and Indian cents I suggest that you develop a good relationship with several dealers who are interested in your business and deliver good quality. A dealer with your "want list" on hand can often help you find pieces that might not be openly advertised.

Also, do not begrudge a dealer a fair profit. After all, he or she is a human being, too, and has expenses, a business to run, a family to support, likes to go on an occasional vacation, etc. Consider the value of the coin only. What the dealer paid for it is not important. At the risk of oversimplification, I present two instances. Which coin is the better buy for you?:

Coin A, a certified Proof-65 RB Indian cent, cost the dealer $1,200, is not particularly attractive, and can be yours for $1,350.

Coin B, a certified Proof-65 RB cent of the same date and variety, is a gorgeous gem any connoisseur would be proud to own. The dealer paid $900 for it and is asking $1,600.

For my money I would buy Coin B in a heartbeat and might not buy Coin A even if the dealer offered it to me at the price he paid. Further, if the dealer had paid $2,000 for Coin A and was willing to sell it to me at a loss and take just $1,350, I would still take Coin B.

Another suggestion: If a dealer offers you a coin for $1,600, and you think it is worth $1,600, don't automatically make a counter-offer on it. After all, he or she probably set the price with some reason for doing so. Otherwise, you'll be viewed as being a somewhat "cheap" customer, and the dealer's cherrypicks and new purchases will be offered to someone else first.

There is no steadfast rule on the above, and if a coin with a $1,600 asking price is really worth only $1,500, then perhaps $1,500 is a fine offer. However, if you already think it is a good buy at $1,600, pay that and thank the dealer for saving it for you. Dealers like to hear compliments, too! And, the next time the dealer has a coin on your "want list," chances are he or she will give you a chance to buy it.

When time comes to sell—and virtually everyone sells someday—you will probably place them in the hands of a dealer, either for a cash offer or for sale at auction. Again, realize that the dealer is running a business for profit and will want to buy at a significant discount from retail listings. Also, problem-free coins in any grade will find a more ready market and at a better price than will weakly struck, spotted, stained, or other coins which in one way or another are not attractive.

Storage and Display

It is not known what the long-term effects of storing copper coins in certified holders is. Be careful, and in any event keep your coins away from dampness, harmful fumes (such as sulfur), heat, and intense light. Do not store coins in soft plastic holders with PVC (polyvinyl chloride) content. If you buy coins in these holders in auction sales—where they are commonly used to permit easy viewing of coins without handling them—remove them immediately. No exceptions here.

In the course of buying collections I have noticed that most types of albums with protective slides (Raymond-National, Meghrig, Whitman Bookshelf, Library of Coins, and similar brands) or custom plastic holders (Capital, Leffler, etc.) have served well to display coins from both sides and to protect them, provided the coins are kept dry and away from the influences just mentioned. If an album has clear slides, it is important to push the coin down into its hole (using a piece of cellophane or polyethylene to avoid skin contact with the copper surface) so that the slide will not come into contact with the coin when it is slid back and forth. Otherwise, tiny parallel "slide marks" are apt to be put on the cheek of Miss Liberty. Bright Mint State or Proof coins tend to tone slightly over a long period of years, often to a warm yellow-golden hue.

KoinTains, commercially available two-part plastic capsules, seem to be quite effective as well and are easy to handle—almost like handling a "bare" coin.

If a coin has a greasy surface or has PVC (polyvinyl chloride) contamination, it can be de-greased using certain solvents available in coin shops. I am not necessarily recommending this; just mentioning that some collectors do it. However, de-greasing exposes the surface of a coin to faster changes from the atmosphere, so such a coin must be protected.

When I first collected Lincoln cents and had worn examples of earlier dates and Uncirculated (today's "Mint State") specimens of most from the 1930s onward, and graduated from the Whitman folder stage, I painted each coin with a thin layer of clear fingernail polish, let it dry thoroughly, and then put it in a Raymond album page. Later, when I sold the pieces I used fingernail polish remover. The coins seemed to be perfectly preserved in the meantime. Doubtless, this technique would work equally well with Flying Eagle and Indian cents, although if either the polish or the remover contained trace amounts of acid or contaminants, there might be problems. Again, I am not recommending this; just mentioning it.

In any event, handle and store your coins with care. In all instances, check your coins periodically, regardless of what type of holders they are in, to ensure that they are not developing "problems."

Flying Eagle and Indian cents have been around for a long time, and with some basic care they will remain unchanged during your custodianship.

Further Thoughts on Collecting

Collecting Flying Eagle and Indian cents is a pleasant, affordable pursuit. The series of dates and, beginning in 1908, just two mintmark issues, contains several scarce and rare coins, but none are "impossible."

Among the over 50 dates and two mintmark issues (1908-S and 1909-S) made from 1856 to 1909, the only dates costing over $100 for a well-circulated, but still attractive specimen are the 1856 Flying Eagle, 1877 Indian, and 1909-S Indian.

The only circulated one costing more than $2,000 is the 1856 Flying Eagle. You can excuse yourself from collecting one of these if you wish, as it is technically a pattern, not a regular issue.

Flying Eagle and Indian cents can be collected in several different ways. A set of basic design types is affordable, even in high grades, and is easily assembled. A collection with a run of Philadelphia Mint dates plus the two mintmark varieties is the most popular way to acquire these cents and is studded with a handful scarce varieties, a few rare ones, and dozens that are readily obtainable.

Beyond that there are many interesting die varieties in the series including the curious clashed die issues of 1857, the seldom-seen 1888/7 overdates (two dies), several doubled dies, and enough repunched and misplaced date varieties to keep you busy for a month of Sundays.

CHAPTER 7
NUMISMATIC AND MARKET TRENDS

Introduction

Over the years the collecting of small cents has experienced many trends and cycles. The following outline is by decades and discusses the state of the collecting art at these intervals:

Numismatics in the 1850s

At the beginning of the decade there were about 100 serious coin collectors in the nation.[1] These aficionados were not organized, had no periodicals or value guides to serve them, and mainly thrived on their own enthusiasm. "Large" copper cents were in circulation, and few envisioned that they would be discontinued.

In 1856—when the 1856 Flying Eagle cent made its debut—the numismatic hobby was beginning a rapid growth stage. In 1857-1858 this accelerated when it became known throughout America that the familiar old "large" copper cents would be called in, to be replaced by small-diameter Flying Eagle cents.

A scramble to build sets of large cents ensued, and much attention was paid to such rare dates as 1793, 1799 (in particular), and 1804.

In 1858 Edward D. Cogan became America's first full-time rare coin dealer, a line of trade he followed until 1879, in the meantime establishing himself as a person of knowledge and fairness.[2] Thus it can be said that American small cents and the widespread popularity of numismatics in this country began about the same time. Even though Cogan may have become a numismatist by profession, he and virtually every other dealer of the era also bought, sold, and traded other items such as Indian relics, birds' eggs, autographs, and, eventually, stamps as philately grew popular. There was hardly enough profit to be made in coin deal-

---

[1] Edward D. Cogan estimate given in a retrospective comment in the *American Journal of Numismatics,* 1867. Cogan began his numismatic interest in 1856 when he purchased an electrotype (copy) of a 1792 Washington cent.
[2] See note about Cogan in the sub-chapter about 1856 Flying Eagle cents

ing to support a home and family. Cogan's offering of a set of large cents via a modest listing on November 1, 1858, became a guidepost for later generations of numismatic bibliophiles and, as historian John W. Adams has commented, it was "a landmark in popularizing the hobby."[1]

As collectors concentrated their quests on older and more classic coins, the new Flying Eagle cents were generally ignored at first, except for the well-known 1856. There does not seem to have been much interest in 1857 in acquiring current Proof cents of that date, and today they are great rarities.

This soon changed, and in 1858, pattern small cents became a fad, but business strikes and regular Proofs were more or less overlooked.

There were perhaps several thousand coin collectors in America by the end of the decade of the 1850s, but all but a few hundred were very casual in their interest. The American Numismatic and Archaeological Society, founded in 1858, catered to the more erudite collectors, and beginning in 1866 its *American Journal of Numismatics* would become the first regularly-published coin periodical in the United States.

Numismatics in the 1860s

Small cents were still the new kids on the block. One of the most desired varieties continued to be the 1856 Flying Eagle cent, which commanded a market price of $1 to $2. Pattern small cents of 1858 were also quite popular, as they had been since 1858, and at the Mint they were restruck as fast as they could be sold or traded to dealers and collectors.

Flying Eagle and Indian cents—except for the famous 1856—being relatively new, were seldom mentioned in print. Instead, emphasis was on earlier types such as 1793-1857 large copper cents.

In 1864 virtually no numismatic attention—and, most probably *none at all*—was paid to the addition of a tiny L (for Longacre) to the obverse of the Indian cent. A few collectors who bought Proof bronze Indian cents late in the year happened to get specimens with the L, but they did not realize their good fortune at the time.

Numismatics in the 1870s

Collecting small cents by date sequence became popular in this decade. The typical cabinet included one of each date, plus the copper-nickel and bronze types of 1864 (but the 1864 L was not widely noticed). Likely as not, the coins in a typical collection were Proofs. It was also

---

[1] John W. Adams, *United States Numismatic Literature*, Vol. I, pp. 17, 20.

STRIKING COINS: An elegantly dressed lady operates a coining press at the Philadelphia Mint in the 1860s while visitors gaze from behind an iron railing. Planchets were stored in a wooden drawer at the front of the press. The attendant fed them into a vertical brass tube. Finished cents or other coins were ejected at the rear into a metal container. Power was provided by steam via a system of shafts and pulleys. The drive belt is at the left side of the press. (*Coins and Coinage: The United States Mint, Philadelphia,* A.M. Smith, undated edition from the 1880s, p. 25; this illustration was widely reproduced elsewhere)

popular to mix various patterns among regular issue Flying Eagle and Indian cents, particularly those patterns dated 1858. Limited restriking of certain varieties of such pieces probably continued in the early 1870s. Pattern cents that reached the market were exceedingly popular stock in trade items with dealers.

By 1871 at least a few collectors realized that the 1864 cents with the tiny L were in existence and that in Proof format they were rare. Accordingly, someone at the Mint made up a new obverse 1864 L die and ran a few "restrikes" off the press, including for good measure some in aluminum. The restriking remained undiscovered for over a century, until in the mid-1990s Richard Snow unraveled the history of this issue.[1]

Flying Eagle and Indian cents in circulation were generally ignored in the 1870s, although the Treasury was busy redeeming millions of the copper-nickel issues. The hobby of coin collecting was growing, but there were no published grading standards and no special albums or holders for the display of coins.

In Philadelphia the young Chapman brothers—S. Hudson and Henry— hung out their shingle as "numismatists and antiquaries." On the coin collecting scene, auctions were the focal point of attention, and most significant cabinets were formed through competitive bidding in sale rooms. However, Indian cents were apt to be offered in bulk lots, if they were listed at all. They simply were not valuable enough for serious commercial attention or market discussions in the pages of the *American Journal of Numismatics*.

Numismatics in the 1880s

The coin hobby continued to grow. The low-mintage 1877 cents were largely ignored, and, so far as is known, only a handful of people picked them out of circulation for resale or possible price appreciation. The "investment" word, although not unknown, was not central to numismatic activities. No doubt, anyone examining a handful of Indian cents from pocket change would have found several of the scarce and relatively recent dates such as 1871, 1872, and possibly even an 1877 or two. As the years slipped by, numismatists came to realize that there was something special about 1877 Indian cents, and they became recognized as rarities.

Proof coins were popular, and "minor Proof sets" consisting of the Indian cent, nickel three-cent piece, and Shield nickel were made in record numbers—several thousand in most years. During the decade of the 1880s the Mint was very "sloppy" in its manufacture of Proof coins

---

[1] See 1864 L cent sub-chapter to follow.

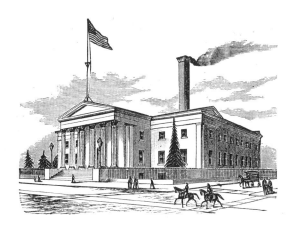

Two 1885 engravings taken from *Visitor's Guide and History of the United States Mint.* At top is shown an engraving of the Philadelphia Mint located at the northwest corner of Chestnut and Juniper streets. This facility served until 1901. All Flying Eagle and most Indian cents were minted here. The lower engraving shows the Mint Cabinet gallery with rare coins on display.

and, particularly, the handling of them after they were struck. It was common practice at the Mint to mix Proof coins together in drawers or containers and for clerks to handle them carelessly, often putting fingerprints on the coins' surfaces. Harlan P. Smith, one of America's best known collectors and dealers, filed a formal complaint alleging that in June 1886 he went to the Philadelphia Mint to buy a Proof gold dollar, and:

> The clerk opened a small writing desk and took out a round paper box which contained numerous gold Proofs. He scraped them over with his fingers and rubbed them together, upon which proceeding deponent looked with utter astonishment as it defaced the coins with pin marks and scratches....[1]

If Proof gold coins—considered the *creme de la creme* of the Mint's output for collectors—were treated this way, one can imagine how this same clerk handled "lowly" Proof Indian cents! Because of this type of treatment, certain high-mintage Proof cents of this decade, if brilliant and with high-quality surfaces, would become recognized as rarities a century later.

As the decade of the 1880s progressed, the nation experienced a boom in collecting activity, and many different disciplines gained numerous devotees. These were good times for armchair pursuits and hobbies, and an atmosphere of interest and excitement prevailed. There was a renewed appreciation of the American past, and throughout the country many town and county histories were published and large and finely detailed map portfolios were issued. Today, I view the 1880s as the Golden Era of Historical Publishing.

Meanwhile, on the coinage scene the design error 1883 Liberty Head nickel five-cent piece without CENTS on the reverse created a sensation and gave impetus to an increased focus on coin collecting.

In numismatics the early 1880s saw the rise of publications on minute die varieties of federal coins, particularly *A Description of 268 Varieties of U.S. Cents, 1816-1857, in the Collection of Frank D. Andrews;* John W. Haseltine's[2] *Type Table of United States Dollars, Half Dollars, and Quarter Dollars;* and Dr. Edward Maris' *Historical Sketch of the Coins of New Jersey.*

The last-named book was Maris' second *chef d'oeuvre* and was a worthy companion to his 1869 study, *Varieties of the Copper Issues of the United States in the Year 1794.*

In 1883 Harold P. Newlin's *Classification of the Early Half Dimes of the*

---

[1] Quoted in full by Walter Breen in his *Proof Coins Encyclopedia,* p. 182; here excerpted.

[2] Actually, dealer J. Colvin Randall is believed to have been the author; as demonstrated by numismatic bibliophile Charles Davis in the Fall 1993 issue of *The Asylum* (journal of the Numismatic Bibliomania Society).

United States filled an obvious gap in the 1881 Haseltine study. Unusual among numismatic references, the Newlin work imparted the author's great enthusiasm for the subject discussed. Newlin *loved* half dimes, and even today it is hard to read what he said about the rare 1802 half dime without wanting to rush right out and buy one, even though virtually all examples are well worn.

Meanwhile, just about every numismatic bookshelf of consequence included a copy of Sylvester S. Crosby's 1875 seminal work, *The Early Coins of America.*

While a few dedicated specialists used magnifying glasses to pick out varieties of colonial coins, 1793 and 1794 large cents, and some other early issues, the idea of collecting die varieties of coins produced in the mid-nineteenth century was viewed by many as being absurd. Andrews' 1881 work on 1816-1857 cents met with unfavorable reviews, and if you had visited a dealer or auction room in the 1880s, large copper cents of the 1816-1857 era would not have been attributed in detail.

Even more remote would have been the attribution of Flying Eagle and Indian cents by minute varieties. If someone had taken an interest in the repunched date varieties of 1864 bronze cents, for example, they would have been viewed as having a strange numismatic orientation. The relevancy of this situation to the present book is that no one studied curiosities in the Flying Eagle and Indian cent series during the era they were produced, and technical questions that could have been asked of employees in the Engraving Department or Coining Room at the Philadelphia Mint were never raised. Thus, in the second half of the twentieth century when die varieties became of paramount interest—mainly after about 1960 when the "Collectors' Clearinghouse" column in *Coin World* drew many inquiries and the new 1960 Small Date and Large Date Lincoln cents aroused nationwide interest—the field of Flying Eagle and Indian cent varieties was largely *terra incognita.* There were a few exceptions such as the 1858 Large Letters and Small Letters cents, the 1864 with L on the ribbon, and the "types" of 1886, but nothing in comparison to the number of interesting variations that would later reach the medium of print.

Numismatics in the 1890s

Collectors of small cents were more plentiful in the 1890s as were dealers in them, although in most if not all instances, such cents were a sideline to other interests.

The 1856 Flying Eagle cent maintained its fame, and the various pattern cents—especially the die combinations dated 1858—were eagerly sought, but circulation strikes of Indian cents were simply too "com-

No.	Good.	Fine.	Unc.
145 1857 Small date....	25	50	1 50
146 1857 Large "	25	50	1 50

COPPER-NICKEL AND BRONZE CENTS.

Type. Flying eagle *l.* *Rev.* Value in cotton, tobacco and grain wreath.

	Fine.	Unc.	Proof.
147 1856 Copper-Nickel	4 00	6 00	—
148 1856 Pure Copper..	5 00	7 50	—
149 1856 Pure Nickel ..	—	7 50	—
150 1857 Copper-Nickel	05	25	1 00
151 1858 Copper-Nickel, large letters	10	30	1 00
152 1858 Copper-Nickel, small letters	20	50	—
153 1858 Pure Copper, small letters	5 00	7 50	—

Type. Indian head in profile *l.* *Rev.* Value in olive wreath.

| 154 1858 Copper-Nickel | — | 1 00 | 1 50 |
| 155 1858 Copper....... | — | 3 50 | 4 50 |

| 156 1859 Copper-Nickel | 05 | 25 | 50 |
| 157 1859 Copper... ... | — | 2 50 | 4 00 |

Obv. as last. *Rev.* Value beneath shield in oak wreath.

158 1859 Copper-Nickel	—	1 50	2 00
159 1860 "	05	25	50
160 1861 "	05	30	65
161 1862 "	05	15	30
162 1863 "	05	15	40

No.	Fine.	Unc.	Proof.
163 1863 Bronze........	—	1 00	1 50.
164 1864 "	—	10	1 25
165 1864 Copper-Nickel	05	10	1 00

L.(ongacre) on ribbon, on all following.

166 1864 Bronze	05	15	85
167 1865 Copper-Nickel	2 50	3 50	4 00
168 1865 Bronze	05	15	40
169 1866	05	15	40
170 1867	05	15	40
171 1868	05	15	40
172 1869	05	15	35
173 1870	05	15	35
174 1871	05	20	35
175 1872	05	25	35
176 1873	05	15	30
177 1874	05	10	30
178 1875	05	10	25
179 1876	05	10	25
180 1877	10	75	75
181 1878	05	10	20
182 1879	05	10	20
183 1880		10	25
184 1881		10	30
185 1882		10	15
186 1883		10	15
187 1884		10	15
188 1885		05	15
189 1886		05	15
190 1887		05	15
191 1888		05	15
192 1889		05	15
193 1890		05	15
194 1891		05	15
195 1892		05	10

BRONZE TWO CENTS.

Type. Shield on crossed arrows, surmounted by scroll and wreath. *Rev.* Value in wheat wreath.

| 1 1864 .... | 10 | 15 | 1 50 |
| 2 1865 .... | 10 | 15 | 80 |

MARKET PRICES IN 1893: A page from The Scott Stamp & Coin Co. *Standard Catalogue*, 1893 edition.

SCOTT'S STORE IN 1893: Headquarters of the Scott Stamp & Coin Co., 18 East 23rd Street, New York City. The firm published a series of *Standard Catalogue* coin price guides over the years.

mon" and "ordinary" to attract attention. This situation was not unusual then or in any other early era—until decades later when collecting current coinage via albums and folders became popular. Coins are rarely the focus of attention in their own time, and as strange as it may seem today, in the late 1890s virtually no one cared whether the San Francisco Mint had struck dimes in 1894 (they had made just 24 of them, and later they would be recognized as great rarities), and in 1922 no one at all paid attention to Lincoln cents so weakly struck that the D mintmark was not present (today these are the famous and expensive 1922 "Plain" cents).

Most serious numismatists continued to buy Proof Indian cents each year as part of minor Proof sets, although in the coming decade the numbers of Proofs minted would trend downward from the figures of the 1880s. In part this was due to widespread collector disillusionment and dissatisfaction with the practices of the Philadelphia Mint, which was getting a lot of "bad press" for its restriking activities and at the same time was becoming increasingly careless with the quality of its Proof coins. Harlan P. Smith's 1886 complaint about the careless clerk must have been ignored.

It was common practice for numismatists to clean their coins, often using silver polish or acid. Potassium cyanide—a deadly poison[1]—was in special favor and had the advantage of taking minute scuffs, scratches, and friction on a coin's surface and converting the whole to a matte-like finish. Today, such coins would be viewed as ugly or "lifeless." If today in the 1990s you peruse the pages of Walter Breen's 1977 *Proof Coins Encyclopedia* you'll find many notations reflective of such practices, such as these:

> **1891 Proof cents:** Usually brilliant to gray when not cleaned to death.
> **1895 Proof cents:** Normal date. This the one usually found. Brilliant golden to brown when not cleaned to death.

Thank heaven for David U. Proskey, the New York dealer who bought up unsold remainders of Proof minor coins and who did nothing but ignore them for decades (later they passed to Wayte Raymond and others and, uncleaned, into the market).

Something happened to the hobby in the late 1890s. Perhaps it was the tough economic times that began in 1893, perhaps the populace was tired of all of the silver dollar discussions attendant to the 1896

---

[1] In 1916 noted collector J. Sanford Saltus died when he inadvertently sipped a glass of potassium cyanide, mistaking it for a nearby glass of ginger ale. Today, the American Numismatic Society gives an award in his name each year, as it has for decades—not an award for cleaning coins—but for medallic sculpture designs. Most recipients probably don't know "the rest of the story" about the endowment behind the award!

presidential campaign of McKinley vs. Bryan, perhaps it was the Spanish-American War in 1898 or the distraction of gold in the Klondike. Whatever it was, the coin hobby paused for breath, stumbled, and had several difficult years. For a time it was likely that the American Numismatic Association, born in 1891, would die before becoming a teenager. However, good times were ahead, and the ANA wakened from its moribund state, and its publication, *The Numismatist,* founded in 1888, went on to become the longest-lived monthly coin-collecting periodical (and is still popular today in the 1990s).

In the 1890s, coin-operated machines were just beginning to become popular, and by inserting an Indian cent into a beckoning slot, one could hear a two-minute tune on an Edison phonograph or receive a stick of gum while a Regina music box played *Old Folks at Home.*

Numismatics in the 1900s

The American Numismatic Association entered an expansion period by the turn of the century. Two contributors to *The Numismatist*—founder Dr. George F. Heath and Augustus G. Heaton—were two of the most brilliant and enthusiastic figures in the hobby and each did much to spur growth.

The 1877 Indian cent was recognized as a scarce date, but one that could be found in pocket change with a little luck. In his touring exhibit, "Money of the World," set up at the Lewis and Clark Exposition, Portland, Oregon, in 1905, Farran Zerbe posted a large sign at the entrance illustrating an 1877 Indian cent.

In 1903 the *Wall Street Journal* printed this:[1] "HISTORY IN SIX WORDS: War, poverty, peace, prosperity, pride, war." These same precepts relate in a strong way to coinage. In times of war, coinage of small cents has always increased tremendously. In times of peace, mintages have been small, and when poverty is widespread, the figures have been smaller yet.

Way down in Fort Worth, Texas, B. Max Mehl, a shoe clerk, took a fancy to numismatics and began to buy and sell coins, leading to a highly publicized career that would extend over a half century and make "that coin man in Texas" known to millions.

Teddy Roosevelt was in the White House, and what a "bully" time he had. Along the way he influenced the designs of American coinage via a commission given to artist-sculptor Augustus Saint-Gaudens, who planned to replace the Indian cent with a new flying eagle design, but

---

[1] As quoted in the *Granite State News,* July 18, 1903.

fate intervened. To this date, Roosevelt remains the only president who took a deep and abiding interest in current American coin designs.[1]

A continuing surge in the diversity and popularity of coin-operated amusement machines and penny arcades prompted record coinages of cents and nickels, an expansion that would continue in the next decade. The high water mark in Indian cent production for circulation was achieved in 1907, but, ironically, the same year saw fewer Proof Indian cents made than in any other year since the 1870s.

In many cities the local transportation company would build a "trolley park" at the end of its line, a few miles out of town, and create a new destination for weekend riders on otherwise slow days for business. Typically, an Indian penny was prince in such a park, and the Liberty nickel was king. All sorts of attractions were to be had in exchange for a pocketful of loose change. In Chicago the Mills Novelty Company turned out dozens of different peep-shows, fortune-telling machines, perfume sample dispensers, and other gadgets that offered a minute or two of diversion upon receipt of an Indian cent. The penny postcard became a nationwide sensation, and countless millions were turned out. The visitor to Coney Island, Pikes Peak, or the Washington Monument was apt to buy a handful of cards for a cent apiece, and a stamp to go on them for another cent, and mail them to friends.

Pennies for thoughts, pennies from heaven, pennies for candy, pennies saved and pennies earned—all were apt to be Indian pennies.

On August 2, 1909, the old order changed, and the Indian cent that American citizens had known since their childhood was replaced with a new design featuring the portrait of Abraham Lincoln.

Numismatics in the 1910s

The great hullabaloo about the 1909 V.D.B. Lincoln cent in August 1909 and its controversial initials, and the recognition of the 1909-S V.D.B. cent as a scarce, low-mintage variety, gave numismatics a great boost. Thousands of new devotees entered the field. The 1909-S V.D.B. and 1909-S (without V.D.B.) Lincoln cents were offered for sale by several West Coast dealers, who usually had some 1909-S Indian cents on hand, too. Interestingly, the higher-mintage 1908-S Indian cent was largely ignored,

---

[1] Runner-up may be George Washington, who is said to have visited the Philadelphia Mint frequently in the 1790s, but who, sadly, left little or no written records of what he did there. On April 2, 1992, when speaking at a ceremony in Philadelphia to observe the 200th anniversary of the 1792 Mint Act, I conversed with Mint and Treasury Department officials, who could not cite any instance in which a sitting president had ever visited any United States Mint, and certainly none had been to the new (built in the late 1960s) Mint on Independence Square in Philadelphia, although several presidents had been close by (such as to visit Independence Hall).

A PENNY KINGDOM: A turn of the century scene at Automatic Vaudeville, 48 East 14 Street, New York City, captioned "The Greatest Place of Amusement on Earth for One Cent." Machines taking Indian cents offered flip-card peep shows, metal name plates, rifle practice, a two-minute phonograph tune, breath testing (who can blow the hardest through a rubber tube, never mind sanitation), weight lifting, a chance at the Corbett (after Gentleman Jim Corbett) punching machine, fortune telling, and other delights.

and I believe that most slipped into circulation before the August 1909 interest in small cents began. I have often thought that even today the 1908-S Indian cent just might be slightly rarer in Mint State than the 1909-S Indian, and I know for sure it is dozens of times rarer than a 1909-S V.D.B. Lincoln cent.

A complete date set of bronze Indian cents from 1864 onward could be picked from circulation, and a survey of pocket change would reveal a few scattered Flying Eagle and copper-nickel Indian cents of the early years 1857-1864. The copper-nickel pieces were typically called "white cents," nomenclature that would remain common in numismatic circles for several decades thereafter. The gradual replacement of the Indian design by the Lincoln motif during the 1910-1920 era spurred many to begin looking more closely at Indian cents.

Late in the decade, on January 1, 1919, E.S. Thresher of Kansas City, Missouri, began an intense search for coins in circulation. Six years later he reported his finds which included one of each bronze Indian cent from 1864 to 1909. His supply of cents came from the cash drawers of about 200 coin-operated machines that accepted this denomination.[1]

In numismatic circles there was a small cadre of collectors interested in die varieties of Flying Eagle cents, and for J.W. Scott & Co., Ltd.'s 1913 *Standard Catalogue,* David U. Proskey contributed listings of various "re-engraved" (today we use the term *repunched*) dates and reverse leaf positions. Proskey, quite unheralded by historians today, was ahead of his time, and doubtless had he been born a century later, he would take his place today alongside Walter Breen as a pivotal contributor to numismatic knowledge. What a shame it is that Proskey never wrote an autobiography or at least a recitation of his extensive transactions and experiences.

In 1916 and again in 1920 and 1921, Commodore W.C. Eaton published exhaustive studies of Flying Eagle cent die varieties in *The Numismatist.* Notwithstanding this, the average collector simply wanted one coin for each date.

Most Indian cents—including Mint State and Proof coins—sold for fairly low prices on the numismatic market, and as a result they tended to be catalogued together in groups and sets in auction offerings. Thus,

---

[1] "Coins That Can Be Found In Circulation." *The Numismatist,* July 1925, pp. 356-357. Coins of larger denominations were acquired from "pocket money." In other series Thresher found such prizes as a 1916 Standing Liberty quarter and an 1895 Philadelphia Mint silver dollar plus 67 Shield nickels (of which only eight had the date readable), 21 Liberty Seated dimes, 12 Liberty Seated quarters, 16 Liberty Seated half dollars, two Missouri No Star commemorative half dollars, an 1839-O Capped Bust half dollar, and other items. He also had the good fortune of buying for face value a pair of 1915-S Panama-Pacific round and octagonal $50 gold coins from a bank teller who received them in a deposit.

a perusal of nineteenth- and early twentieth-century auction descriptions provides little in the way of useful or interesting information for Indian cent specialists today.

In New York City, dealer Proskey continued to parcel out coins from large quantities of Proof Indian cents that he had bought years earlier—unsold Mint remainders mainly from the 1880s. He had lots of nickel three-cent pieces, too, but fewer Shield and Liberty Head nickels—perhaps these latter "high denomination" coins were more enticing to spend (just a guess) at a time when they were worth very little on the collectors' market.

When storm clouds rose in August 1914 and foretold World War I, the American economy started to boom, as factories in the United States worked overtime to supply munitions and other goods to the beleaguered nations of Europe. Mintage quantities of Lincoln cents went to unprecedented highs in the last several years of the decade, and the numbers of Indian cents in circulation became diluted.

On November 11, 1918, a truce was declared in Europe. Headlines in the November 23 *Granite State News,* published in Wolfeboro, New Hampshire, read as follows, whimsically perhaps, but perhaps not: "Nation is wholly unprepared for peace's arrival. Industry is thrown almost in panic at sudden armistice."

Numismatics in the 1920s

The end of the wartime boom economy and the onset of hard times in the agricultural areas of America brought a slump to American business in the early 1920s. The market for coins seemed largely immune to such influences, but there certainly were many numismatists who had to cut back on their purchases. Stimuli to numismatics early in the decade included a spate of new commemorative coins and "rare" varieties (1921 Alabama, 1921 Missouri, 1920-1921 Pilgrim, 1922 Grant, and other half dollar issues) and expanded retail offerings of Proof Indian cents and other date listings by such dealers as David U. Proskey, John Boss, John Zug, William Pukall, Henry Chapman, F.C.C. Boyd (who was better known as a collector), and Wayte Raymond.

The American Numismatic Association was alive and well, with its popular president, Moritz Wormser, being re-elected several times to the post. However, its publication, *The Numismatist,* fell into the groove of printing long and tedious (unless you were interested in the topic) listings of counterstamped coins, broken bank notes, Lincoln medals, and other numismatic esoterica. There was little editorial "spark" in evidence. In the meantime, the formerly glorious *American Journal of Numismatics,* earlier published quarterly by the American Numismatic

Society, had changed over to the occasional issuance of monographs on technical subjects.

In the 1920s the collecting of Flying Eagle and Indian cents continued its limited popularity. Prices were very low, and a nearly complete set of dates in Uncirculated grade from 1857 to 1909 could be purchased for just a few cents per coin. In Pittsburgh, John A. Beck hoarded 1856 Flying Eagle cents—the most famous and most desired of all small cent varieties—and had several hundred of them. By 1924, the year of Beck's death, his inventory of these little rarities touched the 531 mark.[1]

In Fort Worth, Texas, B. Max Mehl electrified America with his dazzling offers to pay premiums for coins in pocket change via his *Star Rare Coin Encyclopedia,* which he sold by the hundreds of thousands for $1 each. Famous numismatic personalities of the decade could be divided into two classes: 1. B. Max Mehl. 2. Everyone else.

Mehl had a two-faceted business, and besides selling his *Encyclopedia,* he conducted mail bid sales of numerous large collections formed by leading numismatists.

Along the way on May 17, 1921, Mehl sold for a widow in Albany, New York, the 1804 silver dollar in the collection of her late husband, Judge James H. Manning. It went for $2,500, plus a handling fee, to Elmer S. Sears, a well-known dealer. Somehow, this numismatic transaction was transmogrified through the wonderful medium of advertising to a sketch of a cashier in a movie theatre taking coins for tickets, and a caption that went something like this, and I paraphrase, "I paid Mrs. Manning over $2,000 for her old silver dollar. What treasures do *you* have in your pocket change?" Well, the U.S. Post Office took issue with what it viewed as deception,[2] and the ever accommodating Mr. Mehl switched advertising campaigns, including one used a few years later which informed readers that if they could find an 1894 dime with a little S mintmark on it, they could send it to Mehl in Texas and get a check to send Junior to college or forestall foreclosure on the deed to the ranch.

It is certain that Mehl's nationwide advertising resulted in a greatly increased awareness of coins and numismatics, and as a result many scarce Indian cents and other coins were rescued from circulation.

By decade's end, America had experienced flappers, the Charleston, bathtub gin, bootlegging, player pianos, Harold Lloyd on the silver screen, Duesenberg automobiles, the Florida land boom, Lucky Lindy and his *Spirit of St. Louis,* the "Monkey Trial" with Darrow vs. Bryan, and everyone being an expert on the rising stock market.

---

[1] These pieces were inventoried by Pittsburgh collector George H. Clapp (of large cent specialty fame) in 1931; this information was later disseminated to collectors.

[2] Recollection of the author, conversation with Mehl, circa 1956.

On the coinage scene, pocket change was apt to contain some really beautiful silver coins including the "Mercury" dime, Standing Liberty quarter, and Liberty Walking half dollar. Peace silver dollars, also beautiful, tended to remain in Treasury storage or bank vaults, except in the mountainous areas of the American West, where they were familiar sights.

Numismatics in the 1930s

The Depression was just beginning in the early part of the decade, but coin collecting continued to be a popular avocation. Mehl was flying high, touching only the mountaintops, and even had his own radio program to sell his *Star Rare Coin Encyclopedia*. The American Numismatic Association gave him a special award in recognition of all the publicity he generated. Meanwhile, in homes all across America anyone with a copy of Mehl's dandy little book knew that the 1856 Flying Eagle cent was a highly-valued rarity worth all of $3 to $5 if in "new condition," not quite in the class of the famous 1913 Liberty Head nickel for which Mehl would pay $50, but still worthy of notice.[1]

Prices of Flying Eagle and Indian cents remained firm in the early 1930s, primarily because they had not risen sharply during the boom years of the 1920s and thus had no great height from which to fall. This was not true, however, for common stocks, rare books, art, real estate, Currier & Ives prints, and other items that had been the darlings of the big spenders in recent years.

Indian cents were becoming scarce in circulation. It became a popular pastime to sort through pocket change and cull them out to save (in the same manner, in the 1950s many citizens would save 1943 steel Lincoln cents, and in the 1960s saving pre-1959 Lincoln "wheaties"—with the wheat sheaf motif—became popular).

In autumn 1934, William D. Hogan of Parrottsville, Tennessee, reported that during the preceding 18 months he had tried to put together from circulation a date set of Indian cents from 1880 onward and had acquired all but the 1880, 1882, 1885, 1889, and 1894.[2] Of a given 1,000 cents in circulation in 1935, about 10 to 20 were apt to be of the Indian design. As time went on and Lincoln cents were made in ever-increasing quantities, Indian cents became proportionately harder to find.

In July 1937, H.B. Combest of Chicago reported that he had looked through 5,000 cents and had found just three Indians (dates not speci-

---

[1] Prices from *The Star Rare Coin Encyclopedia and Premium Catalog,* 38th edition, 1933. Mehl's buying prices in this guide were typically far below retail numismatic values. His main purpose was to sell books, not to buy coins.

[2] *The Numismatist,* November 1934.

fied). More ambitious was the search of B.S. Moore of Greenville, South Carolina, who in September of the same year revealed that in sorting 100,000 cents he had found 116 of the Indian type (again, dates not given).[1]

In Shippensburg, Pennsylvania, M.L. Beistle—whose main collecting interest was half dollars—was in the cardboard specialty products business. In 1928 he produced an album page with openings for coins, faced on each side with celluloid slides to permit viewing. Sales were slow to begin with, but soon an alliance was made with Wayte Raymond, who ran the coin department of J.W. Scott & Co. in New York City, and in the 1930s such pages were aggressively marketed to collectors.

While collecting coins in small paper envelopes (the most popular way to store them) or in open trays or drawers may have been convenient, the advent of holders and folders—including by Whitman Publishing Company—made it possible for John Q. Numismatist to tell at a *glance* that he still needed an 1877 Indian cent—a gaping hole stared back at him each time he looked at his album.

Hole filling became the order of the day, the demand for date and mintmark sequences of affordable, low-denomination coins skyrocketed, and by the end of the decade the pricing structure of Indian cents and other minor coins was vastly different from what it had been in 1930.

Helping spur the hobby horse forward was the production in 1931 at the San Francisco Mint of a Lincoln cent variety with a mintage of fewer than one million pieces. Granted, it was Depression time in the economy, but while the request, "Brother, can you spare a dime?" may not have yielded a ten-cent piece, saving a few rare 1931-S pennies was hardly a financial strain. The coin market boomed.

In the spring of 1933 Uncle Sam via newly-inaugurated President Franklin D. Roosevelt stopped paying out gold coins, further increasing interest in numismatics. In Baltimore, banker Louis E. Eliasberg shifted gears from being an casual collector, his style since about 1925 when he started his interest, to assembling the foundation of what would become the only complete collection of United States coins by date and mintmark sequence (an accomplishment finally achieved on November 7, 1950, with his purchase of the only known 1873-CC without-arrows Liberty Seated dime).

The 1930s also saw many other watershed activities that would profoundly influence the hobby including the launching of the *Standard Catalogue of United States Coins* (Wayte Raymond) and the inauguration

---

[1] *Numismatic Scrapbook Magazine,* July 1937, pp. 154-155 (Combest); September 1937, p. 212 (Moore); Moore also found one 1909-S V.D.B. Lincoln cent, five 1914-D cents, but none of 1931-S.

of the *Numismatic Scrapbook Magazine* (Lee F. Hewitt). Not to be over-looked is the unforgettable commemorative half dollar boom of 1936 precipitated by the curious actions of C. Frank Dunn in his office on the second floor of the Phoenix Hotel in Lexington, Kentucky, in autumn 1935.

Out on Long Island, young John Jay Ford, Jr., became interested in rare coins and, among other things, bought scarce Indian cents, includ-ing some rare unattributed patterns, in dealers' stocks in New York City, as well as some regular Proofs called "copper patterns," but priced *less than* regular Proofs. I can appreciate the latter as I did the same thing with dealers' stocks in the 1950s.

Numismatics in the 1940s

"Penny boards" issued by Whitman Publishing Company and others and new versions of the Beistle-made "National" albums issued by Wayte Raymond continued to be very popular.

Indian cents were by now very diluted in circulation by the hundreds of millions of Lincoln cents minted since 1909, but it was still possible with patience to pick most of the turn-of-the-century dates out of pocket change. In the summer of 1943 Mint Director Nellie Tayloe Ross urged citizens to raid their piggy banks and return worn Indian cents to circu-lation, stating that most dates were worth only face value anyway.

One person not wanting to do any such thing may have been Marvin Winsett, who penned an article, "Collect Indian Head Cents For Plea-sure and Profit," for *The Numismatist,* October 1943, noting in part:

> Collecting small cents, and particularly the Flying Eagle and Indian Head cents, is a fascinating hobby, and considered from an investment angle (and every collec-tor likes to contemplate that point of view) it can be very profitable too. Most Indian Head cents can be purchased in Fine condition for a nominal sum, while the Uncircu-lated and Proof coins in nearly all dates bring a high premium. And so it is with Indian Head cents as with other coins; it pays to collect condition, preferably Uncir-culated and Proof; certainly nothing less than Fine, if you want your collection to increase in value....
>
> Sometimes we wonder where prices on small cents will stop. Of course, they will not actually ever stop. Rarities will continue to be rarities and become even rarer as time goes on, and as the demand increases the prices will continue to rise. There are occasional slumps in the coin market as in other markets, but values on the whole remain fairly consistent. It may well be that the seemingly high prices asked for some of these coins today will prove to be a bargain tomorrow.

Depression aftermath notwithstanding, coin collecting was in a boom period. Leading periodicals included *The Numismatist* and the *Numis-matic Scrapbook Magazine.* Beginning in 1943—quite possibly with Abe Kosoff's remarkable auction of the Michael F. Higgy Collection—numis-matic prices increased dramatically—almost overnight. At the Higgy sale,

SMALL CENTS

Flying Eagle
Copper-Nickel

	Fine	Unc.	Proof
1862	.15	.75	3.00
1863	.15	.50	3.50
1864	.35	1.00	5.00

Indian Head
Bronze

	Fine	Unc.	Proof
1864	.35	2.50	7.50
1864 L on ribbon	3.50	15.00	
1865	.25	1.00	5.00
1866	.75	4.50	7.50
1867	.75	4.50	7.50
1868	.75	3.50	6.00
1869	1.00	3.50	6.00
1870	1.50	5.00	6.00
1871	2.50	6.00	12.50
1872	3.00	7.50	12.50
1873	.35	2.00	3.00
1874	.35	3.00	4.00
1875	.50	3.00	4.00
1876	.50	3.00	4.00
1877	5.00	12.50	20.00
1878	.75	3.50	5.00
1879	.35	1.25	1.50
1880	.25	1.00	1.25
1881	.25	1.00	1.25
1882	.25	1.00	1.25
1883	.25	1.00	1.25
1884	.35	1.00	1.25
1885	.50	2.00	3.00
1886	.25	1.00	1.50
1887	.25	.75	1.50
1888	.35	1.00	1.25
1889	.25	.75	1.25
1890	.25	.75	1.25
1891	.25	.75	1.25
1892	.25	1.00	1.50
1893	.25	.75	1.50
1894	.25	1.00	1.50
1895	.25	.75	1.50
1896	.25	1.00	1.50
1897	.35	1.00	1.50
1898	.35	1.00	1.50
1899	.25	1.00	1.50
1900	.15	1.00	1.50
1901	.15	1.00	1.50
1902	.15	.35	1.00
1903	.15	.50	1.00
1904	.15	.50	1.00
1905	.15	.35	1.25
1906	.15	.35	1.25
1907	.15	.50	1.25
1908	.15	.35	1.25
1908 S	1.00	3.00	
1909	.15	.35	2.50
1909 S		6.00	

	Fine	Unc.	Proof
1856	25.00	50.00	60.00
1857	.35	1.50	15.00
1858 Large letters	.50	3.50	25.00
1858 Small letters	.50	5.00	20.00

Indian Head
Copper-Nickel

	Fine	Unc.	Proof
1859	.25	2.50	5.00
1860	.25	2.50	4.00
1861	.75	4.50	15.00

MARKET PRICES IN 1941: A page from Wayte Raymond's *Standard Catalogue of United States Coins and Tokens*, 1941.

138

Uncirculated coins previously considered common, ordinary, and easy to find in dealers' stocks startled onlookers by bring five to 10 times current *Standard Catalogue* and other listings. In a period of wartime inflation when cash was common and consumer goods were scarce, hard assets such as rare coins were attractive to many investors.

In 1946 Richard S. Yeoman of Whitman Publishing Company, a producer of books for children and hobbyists, launched *A Guide Book of United States Coins* as a competitor to Raymond's *Standard Catalogue.* Unlike the Raymond book which appeared occasionally, the Yeoman guide to prices came out like clockwork each year. Even more important, it was sold in grocery stores, gift shops, and a lot of other places were it acted as a missionary for the coin hobby, right along with Whitman folders for Indian cents, Lincoln cents, and other coins.

Proof coins, which had been issued since 1936—following suspension since 1916—were minted continuously until 1942, after which year the exigencies of World War II forced curtailment of production.

In 1947 a West Coast numismatist was standing in line in front of a bank teller's cage when another customer with a bag of 850 one-cent pieces commented, "I've got a lot of pennies here that I heard years ago there was a premium on, but as I don't know where to get it I thought I might as well cash them in." The teller told the would-be depositor that a coin collector was in line right behind him, and a deal was made on the spot. The lucky collector became the owner of 28 1908-S and 17 1909-S Indian cents, 150 1909-S V.D.B. Lincoln cents, and other key items.[1]

In March 1948, Herman L. Boraker advised Lee F. Hewitt, editor of *The Numismatic Scrapbook Magazine,* that he had just sorted through an accumulation of 1,040 Indian cents that had been picked out of circulation years earlier, but had never been inspected by a numismatist. Grading from Fair to Fine were these dates:[2]

1860: 1	1882: 8
1864 (metal not specified): 1	1883: 8
1871: 1	1884: 6
1873: 2	1886: 5
1874: 1	1887: 19
1875: 1	1888: 13
1876: 1	1889: 27
1879: 1	1890: 18
1880: 7	1891: 16
1881: 10	1892: 16

[1] "Finds Are Still To Be Made," *Numismatic Scrapbook Magazine,* January 1948, p. 91.
[2] *Numismatic Scrapbook,* p. 300. Not delineated were about 40 assorted damaged coins.

1893: 32	1902: 69
1894: 9	1903: 69
1895: 22	1904: 53
1896: 25	1905: 67
1897: 34	1906: 112
1898: 22	1907: 127
1899: 50	1908: 23
1900: 44	1908-S: 2
1901: 63	1909: 2

It is not known when the preceding coins were saved from circulation, but a guess would be the late 1920s or very early 1930s. Note that among later issues there were no 1885 and no 1909-S cents found. To my way of thinking, such listings are extremely interesting as they reflect the circulation patterns of these coins. Much information is available about how coins were designed and struck and in what quantities, but precious little can be found about the everyday use of Indian cents and their availability in circulation over a period of time.

By the late 1940s Flying Eagle and Indian cents were foundation stones in the structure of American numismatics, and just about anyone interested in United States coins had a folder or album of them, often complete with the Philadelphia Mint issues from 1879 through 1909, but lacking the 1908 and 1909 mintmarks and missing a few earlier varieties, most often the dates 1871, 1872, and, especially, 1877. The 1856 Flying Eagle cent maintained its fame and was the Holy Grail for just about anyone beyond the amateur level. Common date Indian cents from the 1880s through the end of the series typically cost about $1 if Uncirculated and $2 or $3 if Proof.

The publication of Dr. William H. Sheldon's *Early American Cents* in an uncertain coin market in 1949 soon engendered a new interest in 1793-1814 large cents and years later would have a profound effect upon the grading of *all* coins.

Numismatics in the 1950s

Collecting Flying Eagle and Indian cents by date and mintmark continued to be a popular pastime. Like as not, the typical collector checked values each year in the *Guide Book of U.S. Coins* and continued to order coins from dealers who advertised in *The Numismatist* and, in particular, the *Numismatic Scrapbook Magazine*. Many brands of folders and albums were on the market.

In 1951 the *Cleveland Plain Dealer* newspaper solicited donations from the public to its charitable "Milk Fund," and 11,653 Indian cents were received as piggy banks and other caches were emptied. Members of the Cleveland Coin Club sorted the coins and found eight 1864 bronze cents with L on ribbon, just one dated 1871, seven of the 1872 year, four of the rare 1877, and a like number of 1908-S.[1]

Only a few scattered Indian cents were still to be seen in everyday pocket change, these mainly worn nearly smooth. By 1953, perhaps one cent in 10,000 to 20,000 cents in circulation was of the Indian design.

In early 1954, William E. Janvrin of Dover, Minnesota, announced that he had just completed spending about 500 hours looking through one million cents taken from circulation. Included among his finds were 95 Indian cents, dates not stated.[2]

In 1957-1958 Daniel D. Wiseman of Austin, Minnesota, looked through a million cents and found "35 or 40 Indian cents among which was one Fine 1864 and one Good 1868." Further from Wiseman, "Now for some facts about 1,000,000 cents. Did you know that they would make a pile one foot square and 22 feet high, weigh 35 tons, and if laid end to end would stretch 12.75 miles?"[3]

After a market slump in the late 1940s, the advent of new Proof coin issues in 1950 and the sensation caused by the low-mintage 1950-D Jefferson nickel pumped new energy into the hobby. A long boom started, which would peak in 1956, at which time the rare 1936 Proof set, which had been bid up to $600 or more, plummeted to about $300. Rolls and Proof sets were the investment darlings of the period, but Flying Eagle and Indian cents received their share of publicity as well.

A new generation of numismatic students came into being, and for the first time in several decades there was a rapidly growing interest in colonial and state coins by die varieties, in large cents by technical differences (with many new disciples who had Dr. Sheldon's 1949 book in hand), and other specialties.

The decade of the 1950s saw the rise in prominence of Walter Breen, John Jay Ford, Jr., Ned Barnsley, Eric P. Newman, Ken Bressett, and others who studied coinage history and published their findings. These were heady days on the research scene, and I remember first hand the thrill of discovering new die varieties and sharing knowledge with others. New Netherlands Coin Company catalogues were the fountainhead of published commercial information on coin history and technicali-

---

[1] "Indian Cent Charity Auction," *Numismatic Scrapbook Magazine,* September 1951, p. 814. Many of these cents were auctioned, with the top price being garnered by an Uncirculated 1859, catalogue value $5.50, which was bid up to $38.50. Michael Kolman, Jr., was auctioneer, and music for the festive fund-raising event was provided by the Willard Band of radio station WHK.

[2] "Examines One Million Cents," *Numismatic Scrapbook Magazine,* March 1954, p. 280. Among Lincoln cents he found one 1909-S V.D.B and 19 1914-D cents.

[3] *Numismatic Scrapbook Magazine,* July 1958, p. 1552.

ties, and even an ordinary coin, if presented in a New Netherlands sale, was apt to attract a lot of attention. Clearly, people liked a measure of interesting information along with a sales presentation. However, New Netherlands had little competition for, as John Ford was fond of saying, it took a lot of work to write his catalogues, and it was far easier for others to use "one-line descriptions."

Several of us banded together in the 1950s and had frequent discussions about die varieties and in 1960 formed the Rittenhouse Society as a small circle of research-oriented friends who had an informal breakfast meeting each summer at the ANA convention.

Scattered undistributed groups of Proof and Mint State Indian cents were still here and there on the market, leftovers from the days of David U. Proskey, Wayte Raymond, William Pukall, and others. As exciting as these coins may be now in the 1990s, back then they were hardly fast sellers. Undaunted, I bought quite a few such coins wrapped in thin tissue paper as packaged by the Mint back in the 1880s. Proofs were apt to be rich chocolate brown with virtually perfect surfaces, tinged with a flash of iridescent blue or purple seen when a coin was held at a certain angle to the light. Nickel three-cent pieces of the 1880s were also around in original Mint-wrapped groups as were occasional other delicacies. In the latter category, Wayte Raymond had a bunch of 1903-1908 Philippine Islands Proof sets wrapped in the same type of tissue paper as the Indian cents. Occasionally a hoard of undistributed silver commemorative half dollars minted in the 1930s would come on the market.

In Johnson City, New York, James F. Ruddy, a partner with me in the Empire Coin Company, spearheaded a mini-campaign to accumulate a quarter million common worn Indian cents, and by the late 1950s had done so, after which we sold them to a young man in Connecticut. At the time the wholesale buying price was about 5¢ to 7¢ or so per coin, with the typical grade being Good to Very Good and the dates ranging from 1879 to 1909.

Numismatics in the 1960s

Numismatic News, founded by Chet Krause in 1952, was a popular periodical, joined in spring 1960 by *Coin World.* The 1960 Small Date Lincoln cent became a nationwide sensation, and all of a sudden there were millions of new faces on the coin collecting scene, many of whom found Indian cents to be interesting to acquire. The 1956 break in the investment market had been forgotten by old-timers, and newcomers did not know about it.

In New York City, Robert Friedberg popularized his "Library of Coins" albums with cardboard pages. Particularly popular were those for type sets of United States coinage designs. I recall that virtually overnight many hundreds of new customers wanted just one date of an 1857-1858 Flying Eagle cent, the stand-alone 1859 Indian cent (the only year of the laurel wreath reverse), any copper-nickel Indian cent of the 1860-1864 years, and any bronze cent 1864-1909. I recall that a lot of coin buyers who were clueless as to why an 1859 Indian cent was important or desirable, all of a sudden had to have a gem Uncirculated or Proof specimen, and it had to be *brilliant*. Toned coins, even if attractive, were not in favor with most buyers back then, although sophisticated collectors enjoyed them and you could find them in New Netherlands auction catalogues and a few dealers' stocks.

The old or traditional numismatic hobby became a thing of the past. Now, *investment* was the key word, with *collecting* being an also-ran. The market boomed. Especially popular were bank-wrapped rolls of Lincoln cents (the 1955-S was especially in demand) and Proof sets purchased in quantity for investment. Rolls of Indian cents, never plentiful to begin with, were not a part of this boom. The most popular investment coin issue—the one that everyone kept an eye on—was the low-mintage 1950-D nickel that had provided a rocket boost to the market a decade earlier.

Several Teletype systems—with rolls of yellow paper and noisy typewriter keys—linked dealers together. Even the prestigious Professional Numismatists Guild, founded by Abe Kosoff in 1955, had its own system. Now a dealer in New York could type out a message that would be read instantly by others in the trade in Colorado, Florida, and dozens of other states. The *Coin Dealer Newsletter* was launched and was devoted to market commentary, particularly as viewed through Teletype transactions.

Unfortunately for upward investment trends, the speculative section of the coin hobby became weak-kneed in 1964 and collapsed in 1965. The 1950-D nickel, after having sold for $1,200 or more per bank-wrapped roll of 40 coins (equal to $30 apiece), fell from grace (and has hardly been heard from since).

During the 1950s Flying Eagle and Indian cents were graded adjectivally including "brilliant Uncirculated" (popularly abbreviated as BU) or "brilliant Proof," with a particularly nice piece called "choice" or "gem." Numbers were not used in the field of small cents, nor was the term "Mint State." Grading continued to be largely undefined in popular use, although a handy guide to the subject was published by Messrs. Brown & Dunn in 1958.

Indian cents became very popular in the 1960s, and the market was deluged with pieces that had been cleaned or polished (to play to the "brilliant is best" demand) masquerading as "gem Uncirculated" or other such wording. The emphasis was on low price and bargains, and those with the lowest prices on "gem Uncirculated" coins did the most business. The market became highly confused, the bad drove out the good, and the entire market for small cents eventually suffered. It was simply too much work for even the knowledgeable numismatist to order 10 "gem Uncirculated" Indian cents, only to find that only one or two were *really* even in Uncirculated grade, and even those one or two might not be gems at all. Worse yet, investors who didn't know any better poured money into such "gems" and years later found out they had nothing but scrubbed-up EF and AU coins. The market for bronze Indian cents suffered a body blow from which it would not recover for over two decades.

Meanwhile, I continued to really like Flying Eagle and Indian cents and commented from time to time about the good values that could be had by anyone caring to investigate the dormant market. One of America's leading dealers, and a strong competitor, telephoned one day in 1969 to say that he had just bought a complete set of gem Proof Indian cents (except for 1864 L), but had no customers for such coins. Would I buy it? I would and did.

On another occasion Jerry Cohen and Abner Kreisberg, leading dealers in California, mentioned to me that they had a large stock of hundreds of Proof Indian cents left over from the days of the Numismatic Gallery, in which Abner had been a partner in New York City in the 1940s. These were mostly dated in the 1880s (as were most old-time groups I encountered) with a few in the 1890s and 1900s. Would I buy them? I would and did.

Don Taxay appeared on the numismatic scene, became interested in numismatic research, and with encouragement from several others (Harry J. Forman, Walter Breen, John J. Ford, Jr., and I were the main ones; Forman and Taxay were business associates briefly) spent a lot of time in the National Archives and other sources of Mint records and turned out a really great book, *U.S. Mint and Coinage,* which became to minting technology and history what S.S. Crosby's 1875 *Early Coins of America* book was to colonial coins—a timeless classic.

Walter Breen decamped from New Netherlands Coin Co. and became the research "staff" for dealer Lester Merkin, who soon began producing first-rate auction catalogues in the New Netherlands style. Later, Breen moved to Berkeley, California, but was in the employ of Stanley Apfelbaum's publicly-traded company, First Coinvestors, Inc., based on Long Island, New York.

Both Breen and Taxay tended to divide nineteenth-century Mint patterns and Proofs into "good" and "bad" categories, the latter if a coin had been minted sometime other than the date stamped on it and/or not openly sold to collectors. Breen in particular did a lot of groundwork identifying die characteristics of such pieces. I took a somewhat different view and found most restrikes and "fancy pieces" to have added interest because of their history. "You are a *dealer,* and you *would* think that way," Walter Breen was fond of telling me.

Numismatics in the 1970s

In the early 1970s the entire coin market was licking its wounds from the investment market crash of 1965, and prices were beginning to recover (1950-D nickels not included), but Flying Eagle and Indian cents remained in the doldrums. They had not been celebrants in the investment party to begin with, and there remained that thorny problem of cleaned coins being offered as gems.

The Teletype trading networks were still going strong, and the *Coin Dealer Newsletter* remained the weekly guide to the values of rolls, Proof sets, and other investment-oriented coins, including in a small way Flying Eagle and Indian cents that went along for the ride. However, such small cents were not popular with the average investor, and in many quarters there was actually an anti-copper sentiment. The reasons for this were never clear, but may have been because while a newcomer to the hobby could instantly recognize a silver or especially a gold coin as being valuable, it took some education to realize that an old copper cent could have a substantial worth. Thus, to sell an investor on a copper coin seemed to be a "stretch" compared to an easy sell for gold.

Broader market coverage was to be found in the pages of *Numismatic News* and *Coin World.* Unfortunately for tradition, the venerable monthly *Numismatic Scrapbook Magazine* was on the ropes, and within the decade it would cease publication, despite having added R.W. Julian, researcher *par excellence,* to its stable of authors which included Raymond Williamson, Walter Thompson, Walter Breen, and other notables. *Photograde,* written by James F. Ruddy and first published in 1970—the same year that Jim Ruddy publicized his two discovery specimens of the hitherto unknown 1888/7 Indian cent—went through many editions and became a popular guide to grading coins including Flying Eagle and Indian cents. One branch of the Detroit Public Library told Jim that for a time *Photograde* was the most requested volume on their shelves!

The "Collectors' Clearinghouse" column in *Coin World* remained a forum for the publication and discussion of interesting die varieties—as it had since the early 1960s—and in 1977 Thomas K. DeLorey, editor and talented numismatist (who later went to Colorado Springs to work with the American Numismatic Association Certification Service and, later, to the dealership of Harlan Berk), introduced the numismatic world to the first clashed-die variety of the 1857 Flying Eagle cent.

Numismatics rapidly became a world of enjoyment through the looking glass. It is probably correct to say that in the 35+ years from 1960 to now in the 1990s, more die varieties have been discovered, more people have become interested in minute die differences, and more good numismatic books have been published than in any other 35-year span in history. And, it is worth noting that a new breed of specialist began to become prominent on the scene: the dealer in out-of-print numismatic books and other publications. Many printed items became highly desired collectibles in their own right.

Jerry Cohen and Abner Kreisberg sold the John Beck hoard of over 500 1856 Flying Eagles in the mid-1970s, doing so carefully and deliberately in a fashion that the market price remained fairly stable. Most of us who were interested in such things envisioned the long-hidden hoard of Beck coins to be an array of glittering gem Uncirculated and Proof coins. Reality was different. Most were dull, and only a few would be graded MS-64 or Proof-64 or finer (if they were classified today), and none of the latter were brilliant. Still, each piece was very desirable, and the market eagerly absorbed all of the coins.

However, except for key dates such as the 1856 Flying Eagle cent and a demand for some Indian cents for inclusion in type sets (the 1859 for example), the market for Indian and Lincoln cents remained sluggish.

Hope for buyers of dramatically overgraded coins began to emerge in the formation of the American Numismatic Association Certification Service with fund raising and enthusiasm led by Virgil Hancock, John J. Pittman, and others, and with dealer members of the Professional Numismatists Guild chipping in a lot of money to help. Cleaned and artificially colored coins were becoming a big problem in many numismatic areas, and Virgil Hancock found out that in one large Midwest city an enterprising man had a entire "factory" devoted to turning out such things.

Eventually, most "processed," "whizzed," and other artificially prepared or recolored coins disappeared from the market. While most whizzed coins were of silver issues, there were quite a few half cents, large cents, and Indian cents as well. While I am certainly no expert on how these were made, it was generally felt by the ANA Certification Service that a whizzed Indian cent labeled as "Uncirculated" was made by taking a high-grade coin such as an AU or basic Uncirculated example and rotating the surface of the piece under a fine wire brush. This process provided microscopic lines arranged in a circular manner, giving the coin a "lustrous" appearance. Then such a coin would be toned by heat or chemicals. The result was a fairly passable "gem Uncirculated" Indian cent that would not fool a knowledgeable collector or dealer, but was very enticing and deceptive to the beginner.

Most collectors of Flying Eagle and Indian cents stored and displayed them in Whitman "Bookshelf," Library of Coins, Meghrig (successor in style to Raymond's line), or other albums, or in plastic holders such as those made by Capital. The philosophy and prime motivational force in the collectors' marketplace continued to be to fill in as many album holes as possible.

The sale of the Garrett Collection at auction in 1979-1981 electrified the numismatic community, gold and silver prices rose to unprecedented levels, and there was a great boom in coin investment—all adding up to a peak in the market. However, Indian and Lincoln cents played only a minor role in the run-up. Then followed a slump.

Numismatics in the 1980s

Numbers became very popular in coin classification, and the Sheldon Grading System, devised in 1949 as a market formula for large cents of the 1793 to 1814 era, was expanded to include everything from half cents to double eagles and commemoratives. Numbers became the focus of attention and gave "scientific precision" to grading. Now there was such a thing as an MS-61 Indian cent, a grading "accuracy" not found in print in earlier eras. I recall that many sellers expanded grading "accuracy" to a fare-thee-well, and it was not unusual to see such numbers as "MS-65+," "MS-65+++," or even decimals such as MS-63.5 in print.

The American Numismatic Association Certification Service (ANACS) in Colorado Springs did a land-office business grading coins for a fee, at first using limited numerical categories, but eventually following the lead of the market and using the MS-60, MS-61, MS-62, etc., divisions that we all know today. Each coin was accompanied by a loose photographic certificate. Some dealers made the rounds of coin shows with boxes of coins in one briefcase and a shoebox full of ANA certificates in another. Unprecedented revenue poured into the ANA, enabling it to vastly expand its staff, facilities, and services under the executive directorship of Ed Rochette working with the ANA Board of Governors. Years later, ANACS was sold lock, stock, and barrel to Amos Press, publishers of *Coin World,* and moved to Ohio.

The Professional Coin Grading Service (PCGS) and the Numismatic Guaranty Corporation of America (NGC), founded in 1986 and 1987 respectively by David Hall and John Albanese, brought the element of *encapsulated,* certified coins to the market as did several other firms including ANACS (which had graded coins in the early 1980s, but did not encapsulate them; later ANACS began issuing "slabs" as well). In the early years, many if not most certified coins packaged by PCGS and NGC were hand-picked quality examples within their grade categories, which served to increase the demand for them. However, there was a problem: a certified or "slabbed" coin could not be put into an album. Typically, such "slabs" were stored in plastic boxes. The thrill of filling in the last space in an album, holder, or folder was gone and with it a good deal of collecting spirit.

In the second half of the 1980s there was another sharp rise in the coin market, culminating in 1989, during which year rumors were rife that "Wall Street money" would be pouring into numismatics by the untold hundreds of millions of dollars (but only a small amount of money actually dribbled in). Investors were often told that to be of "investment quality" (whatever that means) a coin should be silver or gold (but definitely not copper or bronze) and in MS-65 or Proof-65 or finer grade. No investor in his "right mind" in 1989 would have bought an MS-63 Red and Brown Indian cent. (Too bad, for if he or she had, their investment would have far outperformed most of the "recommended" silver and gold issues!)

Meanwhile, the long-ignored Flying Eagle and Indian cent series were gaining advocates on two fronts:

First and most attention-getting: Some investors became interested in these coins by "types"—not caring if an MS-65 Red cent was dated 1888 or whether it was dated 1909. Ditto for Proofs. "Bid" and "ask" prices were posted weekly in the *Coin Dealer Newsletter,* and investment buyers who didn't know the difference between a Proof-65 Indian cent and a collar button were eager to add a few gem Indian cents to their holdings, unless they had heard some "stay away from copper" warnings from investment advisors.

Second and more subtly, there was a rapidly increasing awareness of die varieties. I ascribe this to several causes including the continued popularity of the "Collectors' Clearinghouse" column in *Coin World,* the technical monographs and other writings of Walter Breen, several editions of Frank Spadone's book on major varieties and oddities, and the popular *Cherrypickers' Guide* by Bill Fivaz and J.T. Stanton, to give just a short list.

In 1988 a giant appeared on the numismatic scene. *Walter Breen's Complete Encyclopedia of United States and Colonial Coins,* published by

Doubleday, served up a virtual university course on the technical and historical side of numismatics, and anyone who spent a dozen or two hours with it stood a good chance of being shifted from the "amateur collector" to the "serious numismatist" category. Included was much valuable information about Flying Eagle and Indian cents. At Bowers and Merena Galleries, Ray Merena and I marveled that within the first year of this large and expensive book's availability we sold over 8,500 copies to our clients! Even today it remains a best seller, and deservedly so.

Numismatics in the 1990s

Copper cents were largely absent from the boom of the late 1980s, except for the aforementioned "type" coin interest as reflected in the *Coin Dealer Newsletter.* As the prices of silver dollars, commemoratives, and other "investment quality" series slid, interest in Flying Eagle and Indian cents, dormant since the mid-1960s, began to reawaken on the part of collectors. Demand increased. Prices began to rise for scarce, rare, and interesting issues. Prices for common "type" Indian cents in high grades fell, as knowledgeable specialists were not about to bid sky-high prices for common dates, and investors were all hiding behind bushes.

In January 1991 the first issue of the journal of the Flying Eagle and Indian Cent Collectors Society, *Longacre's Ledger,* appeared and contained articles by Richard Snow, Larry R. Steve, Q. David Bowers, Joe Haney, and Chris F. Pilliod. Founders of the Society were Snow and Steve, who went on to make many contributions of immeasurable value to the specialty and to help greatly with the present book.

Numismatics in 1996

Today in 1996 as these words are being written, Flying Eagle and Indian cents are enjoying an all-time high popularity, primarily with collectors, as investors (what few there are) still tend to shun copper coins.[1] Prices of many copper issues are higher than ever. Much of this interest has been fueled by a vastly expanded collector base. New devotees have been drawn to the series by the publication of several excellent reference books (centered upon Richard Snow's *Flying Eagle and Indian Cents* and to a lesser extent—as it was published later and was not as widely distributed—*A Comprehensive Guide to Selected Rare Flying Eagle and Indian Cent Varieties,* by Larry R. Steve and Kevin J. Flynn) and a new

---

[1] As a student of price and investment cycles in numismatics, I have always found it interesting that investors love to buy at the top of the market, but when prices are low, few investors are to be seen. Of course, this is in part a cause and effect relationship.

appreciation for interesting die varieties (repunched dates, the curious 1857 clashed dies, the 1873 Doubled LIBERTY, etc.).

Meanwhile, more than ever it is important to search for quality. Reflective of this search, the prices for Mint State-65 RD and Proof-65 RD coins have jumped sharply from the levels of just a few years ago, too sharply some might say. However, these prices are not just for *any* coin marked with these grades; the values are for coins hand-selected for their beauty. Other coins may be worth much less.

The market has become very stratified—more so than at any other time in the history of collecting Flying Eagle and Indian cents. In some instances a Proof-65 red coin is valued at many multiples of a Proof-65 with brown or red and brown surfaces. This worries me somewhat. For my money, I would rather have 10 different dates of Proof-65 *red and brown* Indian cents than just one Proof-65 *red.*

These are good times for cherrypickers, and some discrimination when buying can yield a "lot of coin for the money." If you had been on the numismatic scene 20 years ago, you might have shared the common feeling, even among dedicated researchers, that most important discoveries had already been made. However, back then no one knew about bi-denominational clashed dies, and no one knew about misplaced dates—these being two areas of exceptional study and collecting interest in the Flying Eagle and Indian cent series today. One cannot help but wonder what discoveries the next several decades will hold for all of us.

While much emphasis in print is on higher-grade and more valuable coins, the basic foundation of American numismatics is and perhaps always will be the "modest" collector who does not buy MS-65 Indian cents or any other old coins in this grade, but who enjoys well-worn, but quite interesting, pieces from the past—much as I enjoyed Indian cents when I saw my first ones embedded in a concrete sidewalk when I was a kid in grammar school.

Often worn coins are overlooked. Today in 1996 it is easier to learn about the availability of gem Proof 1877 Indian cents than it is for well-worn cents of 1907. With this mind I sought some advice on the *other* end of the grading scale in the series. Jim Reardon, chief buyer for the Littleton Coin Company, a leading purveyor of old American coins to hobbyists and the general public and a major buyer of obsolete coins in large quantities, had this to say:[1]

> Bags of worn Indian Head cents are not as available today in 1996 as they were in past years. Quantities are apt to be found a few dozen or a few hundred at a time.

---

[1] Letter, May 3, 1996.

The dates are mostly from 1900 to 1908. No longer are there any pre-1900 dates, these being pulled out and sold at higher prices. The most common date is 1907.

1909 is becoming difficult to buy in quantity due to promotions. 1864, 1885, and 1886 are all much scarcer than mintage or price would indicate in Good to Fine grades.

1883 is the most common of the 1880 to 1886 dates in Good through Fine grades. 1871 is the scarcest of the dates in the 1870 to 1876 range in the same grades. In similar grades 1876 and 1878 are the most common of the 1873 to 1878 years excluding the rare 1877.

1863 is the most common copper-nickel cent. Promotions have made it difficult to buy them in quantity, however. These and other copper-nickel cents are in special demand by our customers.

The information explosion has brought with it a lot of data in print as well as in electronic media. The collector of Flying Eagle and Indian cents who regularly reads such periodicals as *Coin World, COINage, Coins* magazine, *The Numismatist,* and *Numismatic News* will over a period of time learn much. In my opinion, more useful, information-filled articles are being written in the 1990s than in any other time in numismatic history. However, the specialist in a particular series such as Indian cents has to do a lot of sorting to find items of special interest in publications that cover a broad spectrum. In the meantime, there's no harm—in fact, it is very enjoyable—to learn about what is new or significant in other series. Quite possibly an article on the research methodology for Liberty Seated quarter dollars will yield ideas applicable to Indian cents.

Leading grading services such as PCGS, NGC, and ANACS are becoming increasingly responsive to the needs of *collectors,* especially since investors—once a main segment of the market—are on the sidelines now. ANACS attributes Flying Eagle and Indian cents to certain varieties such as those in the Snow and Fivaz-Stanton books—and deserves a nod of appreciation for this. I expect that it is just a matter of time until other grading services respond to what seems to be a growing demand for knowledge.

Although the storied collections of the past always attract attention when they come on the market—and in our generation we have had a nice share of them—in my opinion there are more high-quality collections being formed in the 1990s than in any other time. Unlike collectors of years past, today's serious numismatists tend to be specialized. No longer is it practical or even possible to have a high-quality collection complete from half cents to $20 gold pieces. However, by concentrating on a specialty—whether it be Flying Eagle and Indian cents, commemorative coins, middle-date large cents 1816-1839, Capped Bust halves 1807-1836, or something else—a high degree of satisfaction is obtained, an enjoyment not experienced by the generalist or broad interest collector.

Looking to the Future

The future is unknown, and even the government—which spends billions of dollars trying to forecast employment rates, manufacturing trends, inflation, interest rates, etc.—cannot determine what will happen a year from now, let alone a decade hence.

Thus, any attempt I give at forecasting the future must of necessity be guesswork.

Coin collecting has been called the world's greatest hobby. It is a pursuit in which a laborer can find as much enjoyment as a millionaire can. It is a hobby which is stimulating, exciting, and which can represent a solid store of financial value. If a collection is carefully built, and if market trends are favorable, a fine collection of small cents has the potential for being an excellent investment. At least this has been true in years past.

No special equipment is needed other than a magnifying glass and a few reference books. A worthwhile collection can be assembled in a cozy apartment in Manhattan or in a great mansion overlooking the Mississippi River. A client who lived in a mobile home park near Utica, New York, put together one of the finest sets of Indian cents I have ever purchased. In contrast, in his Evergreen House mansion on North Charles Street in Baltimore, in the 1880s Baltimore & Ohio Railroad heir T. Harrison Garrett had as much fun as anyone by acquiring Indian cents and other coins each year as the Mint issued them. A teenager can enjoy being a numismatist as can an octogenarian.

There are no rules. There is no "right way" to form a collection of Indian cents or anything else. Each collection is different.

In today's world of computers, automation, numbers, and de-personalization, coin collecting offers an outlet for individual expression, enjoyment, and creativity. At the same time, such automation makes it possible to gather more information, and more quickly, than ever before.

The chances are excellent that if someone "discovers" coin *collecting* and takes the time to read about and study coins, and to build a collection slowly and carefully, he or she will remain with the hobby for a long time.

As I see it, the future bodes well for numismatics. More leisure time, more disposable income, more sources of information (books, *Longacre's Journal,* Internet, coin periodicals, or whatever), and more appreciation for personal enjoyment all add up to a good outlook for the hobby.

CHAPTER 8
FLYING EAGLE CENTS 1856-1858

History and Background

New Design and Format

Concern was expressed in 1849 that Treasury Department profits from copper coinage had fallen sharply. In an effort to find a replacement for the 168-grain "large" copper cent, which was considered cumbersome to handle and too expensive to produce,[1] the Mint experimented with reduced-diameter and lower-weight cents as early as 1850 with several "annular" (ring-shaped) designs in various metals.

The idea of a smaller format cent was hardly new, and in 1837 Dr. Lewis Feuchtwanger spent much time and effort in trying to interest Congress in adapting "Feuchtwanger's composition"—a type of "German silver" made of nickel, copper, and zinc, with a silvery appearance—to make coins. The alloy was said to have been "clean, white and durable material, of specific value, from which coins and all articles can be advantageously manufactured as are now wrought out of silver."[2]

His proposal rejected by Congress, Feuchtwanger took matters into his own hands and caused many thousands of small-diameter tokens to be privately struck. These bore on the obverse the depiction of an eagle killing a snake, while the reverse featured a wreath and the inscriptions: FEUCHTWANGER'S COMPOSITION and ONE CENT.[3]

---

[1] That an all-copper "large" cent might be cumbersome was realized in the planning stages of the one-cent series in 1792 when reduced-diameter patterns were made of copper mixed with silver ("fusible alloy") and from copper planchets with an inserted silver center plug.

[2] 25th Congress, Document No. 7, House of Representatives, 1st Session, titled *Substitute for Copper. Memorial Lewis Feuchtwanger,* September 13, 1837. Further concerning a later effort, *Numismatic Scrapbook Magazine,* February 1963, p. 318, quotes correspondence years later, March 28, 1865, from Feuchtwanger to Mint Director James Pollock in which Feuchtwanger offers to furnish finished nickel-alloy planchets for three-cent pieces for $2 per pound, noting that he had available 50,000 pounds of alloy. Pollock replied on March 30 that "Other parties having bid much lower than yourself your proposal cannot be accepted." Apparently, multiple suppliers had nickel stocks at that time.

[3] These are catalogued today as Low-120, per the numbering system devised by Lyman H. Low at the turn of the 20th century and described in his book, *Hard Times Tokens.* Over a dozen different dies (obverse and reverse combined) were made for these tokens, indicating a large coinage at the time. Feuchtwanger was a man of many talents and interests, and today in the 1990s he is recognized by numismatists for his coinage, but in mineralogy and gemology he is likewise famous for being a pioneering author and student. Meanwhile, among other business interests, he compounded patent medicines (such as Kreosote) and had a small museum of natural history oddities.

CENT COINAGE.

LETTER

FROM

THE SECRETARY OF THE TREASURY,

TRANSMITTING

*A copy of a letter from the melter and refiner at the mint in reference to
the proposed change in the cent coinage.*

JULY 23, 1856.—Referred to the Committee of Ways and Means.

TREASURY DEPARTMENT,
July 21, 1856.

SIR: I have the honor to enclose, for the consideration of the Committee of Ways and Means, a copy of a letter received from the melter and refiner at the mint at Philadelphia, on the subject of the proposed change in the cent coinage.

I remain, very respectfully,
JAMES GUTHRIE,
Secretary of the Treasury.

Hon. N. P. BANKS,
Speaker of the House of Representatives.

MINT OF THE UNITED STATES,
Philadelphia, July 18, 1856.

DEAR SIR: The interest you expressed to me in a cent coin, nearly two years since, emboldens me to address you on the subject of the alloy, which I have lately made for the purpose, and a few samples of which were lately sent to you, I suppose, by the Director.

At your suggestion, I made, during leisure hours at the mint, a large number of alloys, and obtained one with which I was satisfied, although it failed to please generally by its resemblance to silver. I subsequently made a large number of other alloys, on the same basis as the former, keeping one principle in view, viz: to make an alloy which shall retain the red tone of copper, lightened by the alloying metals, so that it would be distinct from brass, bronze, copper, gold or silver, and yet would retain all other qualities of wear, boldness of impression, and beauty of color. Prior to the commencement of the

1856 commentary on new copper-nickel alloy.

mint repairs, I had approached my aim so nearly that I felt confident of success as soon as I could recommence my experiments. I have therefore regretted that the law now before the House should have been urged so far before I had a good opportunity of obtaining my point. The alloy which I have now made meets the approbation of all the officers of the mint without exception, and they all regret that I had not succeeded before the present bill had passed the Senate. If it be not too late, I would respectfully urge your attention to this alloy as one so very superior to the one proposed in the bill.

The latter will be scarcely superior to pure copper in wear, although beautiful when freshly issuing from the press, and I have urged this argument against its substitution from the first. The samples which I made more than a year ago, nearly of the same composition as the one I now propose, have scarcely tarnished in that time. The new alloy I propose will be even less liable to tarnish, and the extent of darkening change which it will undergo can be ascertained by wearing the samples of coin for a week in the present weather, which is most severely trying to the surface of all metals. The advantages that occur to me in the use of my new alloy may be summed up thus—

1. It is made of metals which have as definite a value as the usual articles of commerce, and the supply of which is unlimited. They are copper and nickel.

2. It is sufficiently soft metal to receive a bold impression in coinage.

3. It was a distinctive color, and cannot be confounded with the metals or alloys used or proposed for coinage.

4. It will abrade by wear less than copper, gold, or silver, or even than the proposed bronze alloy.

5. It will change color, by darkening to a slight extent, but less than the bronzed cent, and much less than copper. It will alter less than the ordinary silver coin used on the continent of Europe.

6. It is made up of copper and nickel in such proportions that a cent-piece may be made of about seventy grains weight, and yet the seignorage on their manufacture and issue will not be exorbitant, much less, in fact, than on the bronze cent proposed.

The seignorage will be ample to recall the old Spanish coin from circulation.

7. The peculiar tone of color will render it difficult of close imitation; and even if it could be counterfeited by a cheaper alloy, the difference in value would not yield a remuneration sufficient to cover the cost of manufacture and danger of detection, because a vast amount would have to be forced on the community before the aggregate profit would compensate cost. In view of these points of character, I think that the alloy in question will prove a happy result from the suggestions on the subject in your official report, and I doubt not that you could directly or mediately procure in the House (or its committee) a modification of the existing or proposed law. The admixture of the valuable metal, nickel, will tend to give character to the new cent, and render it popular.

I have the honor to be, dear sir, your obedient servant,

JAMES C. BOOTH.

In 1851 and early 1852 the price of copper subsided somewhat, and within the Treasury Department urgency for a new cent was diminished. Later in 1852 and in 1853 the price rose again—at one point to 42¢ per pound. The Mint estimated that when the price was over 40¢ per pound (which was enough metal to make 42-2/3 one-cent pieces), a loss was sustained if the costs of manufacturing were added to the calculation. In 1853 some patterns were struck in a nickel-copper composition utilizing an 1853 quarter eagle obverse die with a pattern reverse; these pieces appeared silvery in the manner of 1837 Feuchtwanger cents.

Momentum for a new-style cent increased sharply in 1854 and 1855 when really serious investigation began. Some of the pattern cents of these two years used an adaptation of Christian Gobrecht's flying eagle design created in 1838 for use on half dollars.[1] Other 1854-1855 pattern cents utilized Liberty Heads. One notable variant was made by mechanically copying the obverse of an 1854 Liberty Seated dollar (the crossbar and diagonal element did not copy, and the date appeared as 1851).

In spring 1856, James Booth, the Mint's melter and refiner, concluded that a mixture of 88 parts copper and 12 parts nickel would be ideal for a new cent.[2] This alloy became known as copper-nickel. Booth suggested that a weight of 72 grains would be convenient, as this was equivalent to 80 pieces to the Troy pound (although the avoirdupois, rather than Troy measure, was usually employed for base metals). The resultant coins were to be of small diameter and fairly thick, to eliminate any confusion with silver coins at quick glance.

On July 11, 1856, Mint Director James Ross Snowden recommended the new format. Chief Engraver James B. Longacre was instructed to prepare patterns. Nickel came from a private mine at Lancaster Gap, Pennsylvania, the owners of which obligingly furnished free samples of the copper-nickel alloy to the Mint, from which patterns were struck.[3]

---

[1] The eagle on the 1854 and 1855 pattern cents was stylistically different from that used on Gobrecht dollars of 1836, 1838 and 1839, and was similar to that used on pattern half dollars of 1838 and 1839.

[2] Booth was born in Philadelphia in 1810, was educated in the same city, and graduated from the University of Pennsylvania in 1829. He achieved renown in metallurgy and chemistry and at one time published the *Encyclopedia of Chemistry* which contained many of his writings. In 1849 he was appointed melter and refiner of the Mint. He served the institution during many important periods including the great influx of gold from the California fields 1849 onward and the adoption of nickel-content alloys for the cent in 1857 and other denominations in 1865-1866. He stayed at the Mint through 1887 and died on March 21, 1888.

[3] In a letter to a correspondent, Director Snowden on December 10, 1858, advised that present nickel supplies were mostly from Pennsylvania while copper was from Lake Superior, the latter copper being the best quality in the world; moreover, neither metal "contains arsenic and there is no danger in swallowing a new cent." (Citation provided by R.W. Julian, letter, April 24, 1996.) Carothers, *Fractional Money*, p.197, notes that the Pennsylvania nickel mine was purchased by Joseph Wharton in 1863. Steve-Flynn, *Flying Eagle and Indian Cent Varieties*, p. 207, quotes a letter from Director Snowden, February 2, 1857, to Senator S.D. Campbell, noting that "There is no charge for the [200] specimens [of pattern 1856 Flying Eagle cents] inasmuch as the alloy was presented to the Mint, and they have been struck at times when the workmen were not engaged in our normal operations."

Motifs Not Original

Longacre's new obverse design for the cent depicted an eagle flying to the left, with UNITED STATES OF AMERICA around, and the date below. Longacre adopted the eagle motif created by Christian Gobrecht 20 years earlier and used on the 1836 silver dollar and said to have been modeled from a real eagle, Peter, once a mascot at the Mint. The reverse was not original either, but was a copy of the "agricultural" wreath containing, as usually stated, "wheat, corn, cotton, and tobacco," devised by Longacre earlier for use on the 1854 gold $1 and $3.[1] In modern literature the cotton leaves are often referred to as *maple* leaves, as they more closely resemble the latter in a botanical sense; besides, few numismatists are aware of what a cotton leaf looks like.[2] However, cotton leaf is correct. The wreath composition, beginning at the ribbon, seems to be: tobacco, wheat, corn, cotton, and a corn ear, the last hardly true to nature.[3]

While the reincarnation of Peter on the Flying Eagle cent and the reuse of an old wreath created a design admired by numismatists and others, it remains a puzzle why original motifs were not used on such a momentous change in the most utilitarian of all American coin denominations.

However, at the time the cent received very little attention in either the Engraving Department or the director's office at the Mint. This denomination was more or less taken for granted. When experiments in new and artistic motifs were undertaken, likely as not they were in precious metal denominations.[4] Similarly, annual issues of the *Mint Report* typically devoted a great deal of space to silver and gold coins, but said very little about one-cent pieces. There were exceptions, of course.

Moreover, Chief Engraver Longacre was known for the slow pace at which he performed his work. Perhaps Snowden thought it would simplify matters if new motifs did not have to be created. Similarly and at a later time, Longacre copied his own designs and those of others to cre-

---

[1] Director Snowden in *A Description of Ancient and Modern Coins...*, 1860, p. 120, specifically called this a cereal wreath. In the nineteenth century it was occasionally called a tobacco wreath.

[2] *E.g.,* Breen, Proof coins *Encyclopedia,* p. 246; Snow p. 28.

[3] Although the top ends of the wreath do not particularly resemble corn ears, this is what they were intended to be. Thomas K. DeLorey, letter, June 3, 1996, commented: "The original wax model for the agricultural wreath, now in my possession, shows the detail of the two corn ears at the tops of the wreath as long, feathery fronds, signifying the tassel normally found on a corn ear. However, none of this detail survived the transfer to the various incarnations of this wreath, and in each case Longacre was forced to replace it with a series of dots resembling kernels of corn themselves." In his Proof coins *Encyclopedia,* p. 246, reference to state of reverse die B, Walter Breen calls this an "open wheat stalk."

[4] Perhaps the most elegant and varied array of new art created in a short period of time at the Mint is found among silver pattern half dollars of the year 1877.

ate several other issues including imitating the face of Miss Liberty on the 1854 $3 for use on the Indian cent, copying the shield on the 1864 two-cent piece for the obverse of the 1866 Shield nickel, and borrowing the 1859 laurel wreath cent reverse for use on the 1865 nickel three-cent piece.

Apparently, much of the new artistic work on various coins, patterns, and medals was eventually (after October 1857) given to *Assistant* Engraver Anthony C. Paquet, whose contribution to the small cent field is just now beginning to be recognized for its true importance. Appendix II discusses certain other aspects of Paquet's artistry.

Saint-Gaudens and the Flying Eagle Cent

On January 13, 1905, Mint Director George E. Roberts wrote to Augustus Saint-Gaudens, America's greatest living sculptor, asking if he would be interested in redesigning the American coinage. On January 20, 1905, the artist said he would like to explore the matter further in March during a visit to Washington, D.C.[1]

Eventually, President Theodore Roosevelt commissioned Saint-Gaudens to create new motifs for all denominations from the cent to the $20. Working in his home-studio (now a National Historic Site) in Cornish, New Hampshire, he created motifs for the $10 and $20 gold coins before succumbing to cancer in the summer of 1907.

During the course of his work, on June 28, 1906, Saint-Gaudens wrote to President Roosevelt stating he was working on designs for a replacement of the Indian Head cent, in the process paying tribute to what he considered to be the high point in historical American coinage:

> Now I am attacking the cent. It may interest you to know that on the "Liberty" side of the cent I am using a flying eagle, a modification of the device which was used on the cent of 1857. I had not seen that coin for many years, and was so impressed by it that I thought if carried out with some modifications, nothing better could be done. It is by all odds the best design on any American coin.

Saint-Gaudens died in August 1907 before he completed his coinage motifs for various denominations. As it turned out, Saint-Gaudens' flying eagle was indeed used for coinage, but not on the cent. Today it is familiar as the reverse of the $20 gold coins minted from 1907 to 1933.

In another context Saint-Gaudens stated that the best representation of "Liberty" he could think of was a young boy leaping.

Vermeule and the Flying Eagle Design

In his book, *Numismatic Art in America,* 1971, Cornelius Vermeule, of the Boston Museum of Fine Arts, commented on Gobrecht's design as

---

[1] Original Saint-Gaudens letter owned by Les Perline.

seen on early silver dollars and later adapted for the copper-nickel cent:

> The famous flying eagle...is one of the greatest symphonies of die design and cutting to be performed on any flan at any period in the history of western civilization. This is cold observation, not mere national pride.
>
> Only the most sensitive, most penetrating photograph can bring out the bold yet subtle relief and foreshortening of the bird as he flies across our vision from right front to left rear. Feathers, wing tips, beak, and curled talon are presented with a naturalistic power and precision as advanced in American numismatic art as was Benedetto Pistrucci's 1818 portrait of aged George III [on British coinage]....
>
> This vision of the national bird on the wing was as magnificent a presentation in depth, detail, and silhouette as the human mind could conceive and the human hand translate into the mechanics of coining processes....

In view of the admiration of Saint-Gaudens, Vermeule, and others for Longacre's "recycled" design borrowed from Gobrecht, and the enthusiasm collectors have for Flying Eagle cents today, perhaps it is all for the best that some other motif was not created in the 1850s at the Mint when experiments to eliminate the cumbersome large copper cent were conducted.

A few comments concerning Peter, the putative model for the Flying Eagle cent, and the engraver, Christian Gobrecht, who first translated the motif to coin form may be of interest, followed by notes about James B. Longacre, who adapted Gobrecht's design for the 1856 Flying Eagle cent:

"Peter" the Eagle

The *American Journal of Numismatics,* Vol. 27, 1893, p. 85, reprinted this from *Harper's Young People* (similar accounts also appeared elsewhere):

> On the dollars of 1836, 1838 and 1839, and the nickel cent coins in 1856 is the portrait of an American eagle which was for many years a familiar sight in the streets of Philadelphia. "Peter," one of the finest eagles ever captured alive, was the pet of the Philadelphia Mint, and was generally known as the "Mint bird." Not only did he have free access to every part of the Mint, going without hindrance into the treasure vaults where even the treasurer of the United States would not go alone, but he used his own pleasure in going about the city, flying over the houses, sometimes perching upon lamp posts in the streets. Everybody knew him, and even the street boys treated him with respect.
>
> The government provided his daily fare, and he was as much a part of the Mint establishment as the superintendent or the chief coiner. He was kindly treated and had no fear of anybody or anything, and he might be in the Mint yet if he had not sat down to rest upon one of the great flywheels. The wheel started without warning, and Peter was caught in the machinery. One of his wings was broken, and he died a few days later. The superintendent had his body beautifully mounted, with his wings spread to their fullest extent; and to this day Peter stands in a glass case in the Mint cabinet. A portrait of him as he stands in the case was put upon the coins named.

In stuffed form Peter was exhibited widely including at the Treasury exhibit at the World's Columbian Exposition in Chicago in 1893. Today the bird is on view in the lobby of the Philadelphia Mint on Independence Square.

Artist Titian Peale, son of artist and museum proprietor Charles Willson Peale,[1] was asked by Mint Director Robert Maskell Patterson to create drawings of a "lifelike" flying eagle motif for use on coinage, a departure from the perched and heraldic eagles in use for many years.

Whether Peter was actually the model for Peale and Gobrecht may never be known with certainty, but it may have been this unfortunate bird that was mentioned in a letter dated April 9, 1836, from Mint Director Robert Maskell Patterson to Secretary of the Treasury Levi Woodbury, here quoted in part. At the time, sketches were being prepared for new coinage motifs:

> The die[2] for the reverse is not yet commenced, but I send you the drawings which we propose to follow—the pen sketch being that which we prefer. The drawing is true to nature, for it is taken from the eagle itself—a bird, recently killed, having been prepared and placed in the attitude which we had selected. The eagle is flying, and like the country of which it is the emblem, its course onward and upward....
>
> It was my intention to begin the new coinage with the dollar, but it has occurred to me that it might be more proper, and more agreeable to the government, that it should be begun with the indemnity gold.[3] Besides, it would really be a pity that six millions worth of gold coins should be spread over the country with that thing on the reverse which courtesy may call an eagle, but which nature and art refuse to recognize....

The preceding indicates that Gobrecht's flying eagle was recommended for use on gold coins rather than the silver dollar, Patterson strongly disliking the perched eagle design on current gold coins (which were of the denominations $2.50 and $5). Considering that Director of the Mint Robert Maskell Patterson liked the flying eagle, and that he served as director until July 1851, it is curious that the motif was used only ephemerally on American coinage under his watch. It is further curious that "that thing on the reverse" which Patterson detested was used on the reverse of the new Liberty Seated quarter (1838), half dollar (1839), and silver dollar (1840).

---

[1] Who named his sons after famous creative people; *e.g.*, Titian Peale, Rubens Peale, Rembrandt Peale, Franklin Peale.

[2] QDB note: This and other references from most of the year 1836 refer to *dies* rather than models, perhaps verifying that the pantograph method of model-to-hub reduction was not yet in use.

[3] QDB note: Gold shipments received as indemnification from France. In addition, many gold coins of heavy weight ("old tenor" coins) minted prior to the Act of June 28, 1834, came into the Mint and were converted to coins of the new standard, which was instituted on August 2, 1834.

TITIAN PEALE SKETCH: One of over 30 sketches made in 1835 depicting an eagle in flight. This version shows the bird carrying heraldic emblems—arrows and olive branch—quite unlike the finished version used on the 1836 Gobrecht silver dollar and, years later, on the 1856 Flying Eagle cent. (Sketch filed with the Longacre papers; as reproduced in *The Secret History of the Gobrecht Coinages*)

Christian Gobrecht

Christian Gobrecht (December 23, 1785-July 23, 1844) was an accomplished clockmaker, reed organ builder, medal-ruling machine inventor (1817), engraver of rolls for printing designs on calico, speaking doll or automaton maker, and most important to his career, bank-note engraver and medalist.

Born in Hanover, York County, Pennsylvania, Gobrecht showed an aptitude for mechanical things by an early age. After serving an apprenticeship in clockmaking in Manheim (Lancaster County, Pennsylvania) he moved to Baltimore (where in 1810 he engraved an excellent portrait of George Washington for J. Kingston's *New American Biographical Dictionary*), then in 1811 relocated to Philadelphia, where he engaged in bank note plate engraving. By 1816 he was on the staff of Murray, Draper, Fairman & Company, of Philadelphia, where he prepared vignettes for currency plates ordered by various private banks. Gobrecht's signature on vignettes of this era is not known, but this is not necessarily unusual as most such works of art by various engravers were very small and not signed.

Gobrecht came to the Mint in September 1835 to work as "second engraver" (not "assistant") on the staff while William Kneass held the chief engravership. Kneass had suffered a stroke on August 28,[1] 1835, and never fully recovered. By that time Gobrecht had done contract work for the Mint for over a decade, including the production of letter and number punches. He assumed his work at the Mint with a running start, and set about creating dies from sketches prepared by Thomas Sully and Titian Peale for what we know today as the Liberty Seated coinage. After Kneass' death (August 27, 1840), Gobrecht was appointed chief engraver on December 21, 1840, although in fact Kneass had done very little work after his stroke.[2]

Relevant to the Flying Eagle cents of the 1850s, a sketch by artist Titian Peale of an eagle in flight, traditionally ascribed as a representation of Mint mascot "Peter," was used to create a motif for a silver dollar pattern dated 1836. In final form, the dollar depicted Miss Liberty, seated, on the obverse and on the reverse an eagle in flight amid a galaxy of 26 stars.[3]

---

[1] Some accounts say August 27.

[2] There seems to be no valid reason to attribute the new Liberty Head device used on certain 1838 pattern half dollars to Kneass, for he was incapable of doing engraving work at that time. The only possibility, other than the catch-all "tradition," is that they may have been made by Gobrecht using sketches prepared by Kneass before his 1835 stroke. Also see Breen, *The Secret History of the Gobrecht Coinages*, p. 24.

[3] In anticipation of Michigan joining the Union as the 26th state, which occurred on January 26, 1837 (cf. note from Thomas K. DeLorey; also Walter Breen, *The Secret History of the Gobrecht Coinages*, p. 8).

Following the production of pattern silver dollars, Gobrecht's flying eagle design was used only briefly on circulating coinage for a limited number of silver dollars dated 1836 and 1839, comprising fewer than 2,000 coins totally. It was also used in modified form (with ruffed neck feathers and somewhat "lumpier" body) on pattern half dollars dated 1838 and 1839. However, when Liberty Seated half dollars in 1839 and silver dollars in 1840 were made in large numbers for circulation, Gobrecht's flying eagle motif was abandoned in favor of a traditional perched-eagle design for the reverse.

Years later in 1854, a decade after Gobrecht's death, the flying eagle from his pattern half dollars of 1838 and 1839 reappeared on copper pattern cents of this date and, shortly thereafter, on pattern 1855 cents as well. However, Peter's most famous and enduring reincarnation was on copper-nickel, small diameter Flying Eagle cents dated 1856, 1857, and 1858.

James Barton Longacre

Born on August 11, 1794, in Delaware County, Pennsylvania, to Peter and Sarah Barton Longacre, James Barton Longacre was chief engraver at the Philadelphia Mint from 1844 to 1869.

Young Longacre served as an apprentice to James F. Watson of Philadelphia for a short time, then continued his apprenticeship with George Murray, prolific bank-note engraver of the same city who at one time also employed Christian Gobrecht.

Longacre set out on his own in 1819 and engraved metal plates for bank notes and book illustrations, including for a work on signers of the Declaration of Independence and another on stage personalities, but particularly for the *National Portrait Gallery of Distinguished Americans,* of which the first of four volumes was published in 1834.[1] This last work was published in multiple large print runs, was widely circulated, and brought great fame to Longacre and others whose work was included.

Longacre was appointed as chief engraver at the Mint on September 16, 1844, to succeed the late Christian Gobrecht. While Gobrecht had been a medalist and coin engraver of high repute, Longacre's experience in the medium of struck pieces was limited or non-existent. Certain numismatic historians (*e.g.,* Walter Breen) have ascribed many repunching blunders to him and have called him incompetent as a coin

---

[1] Sets of this work in various formats are readily available today from antiquarian booksellers. Longacre's engravings are signed in the plates. In the 1830s most newspapers and other periodicals had very few illustrations, and although illustrious figures from American history were often mentioned in print in popular literature, many readers did not know what these people looked like.

designer and engraver.[1] Nevertheless, the coins he designed serviced a very long span of American history. Longacre remained chief engraver until his death on January 1, 1869.[2]

While numismatists—especially readers of the present text—may consider Longacre's memory dear for the 1856 Flying Eagle and 1859 Indian cents, he is also remembered for the 1864 two-cent piece, 1851 and later silver three-cent designs, the 1865 nickel three-cent piece, the 1866 Shield nickel, 1849 and later gold dollars, 1854 $3, and 1850 double eagle, as well as many patterns, not the least of which are the beautiful Indian Princess pattern silver coins of 1869, the latter issued after his death.

Anthony C. Paquet

Anthony C. Paquet was born in Hamburg, Germany, in 1814, probably the son of Touissaint François Paquet, a bronze worker in that city. He came to America in 1848, and in the mid-1850s had an engraving shop in New York City. Unfortunately, there seems to be virtually nothing in present numismatic literature to identify tokens, medals, or any other metallic items he may have created prior to coming to the Mint.

Paquet did contract work for the Mint in early 1857, and on October 20 of that year joined the Mint staff as an assistant engraver. He remained in that post through early 1864, after which he returned to the private sector, but continued to do important commissions for the government, including two designs for Indian Peace medals.

Paquet furnished the letter punches for certain patterns and possibly regular coins as well, one recorded shipment arriving in late May, 1857, although he could have done earlier work as well. Apparently, the same engraver made up punches for various denominations including the dime, quarter, and half dollar.[3] However, these fonts were not used at the time for circulating coinage.

His coinage work at the Mint included numerous patterns as well as several regular-issue dies, among the latter being the short-lived modified obverse for the 1859 Liberty Seated half dime (Philadelphia Mint only) and the equally short-lived "Paquet reverse" for the 1861 $20 gold coins, the latter made at the Philadelphia and San Francisco mints.

---

[1] Sample citation, Breen, *Dies & Coinage*, p. 16: "Many of the dates which he punched into working dies show imperfections very revealing of the processes then in use...." Further information: "Prior to 1854 some of the dies were made in the chief coiner's department and were not under Longacre's control; it is not clear at present which dies Longacre controlled." (R.W. Julian, letter, April 24, 1996)

[2] An obituary and eulogy on Longacre by Dr. Henry Linderman appeared in the *American Journal of Numismatics*, 1869, Vol. 3, No. 9, p. 72.

[3] A curious one-sided trial impression illustrating several of these fonts was sold in the Abe Kosoff Estate Sale, 1985, Lot 1159, and is listed as Pollock-3131.

ANTHONY C. PAQUET LETTER PUNCHES: Test impressions of three punch fonts, believed to be the work of Anthony C. Paquet. The inscriptions, within concentric rings outlining the approximate diameters of the dime, quarter, and half dollar, are all part of a one-sided white metal striking. The innermost UNITED STATES OF AMERICA font is from a punch set virtually identical to that used on the 1858 Small Letters Flying Eagle cent (an example of which is also shown here), but more widely spaced on the cent than on the dime format. (Trial piece from the estate of Abe Kosoff, Bowers and Merena sale, November 1985, Lot 1159; illustrated in Andrew W. Pollock III's *United States Patterns and Related Issues,* p. 403, and in several other references)

1858 Small Letters cent employing similarly styled letters.

Paquet died in 1882. Certain of his later medallic work for the Mint is discussed in Appendix II.

The 1856 Flying Eagle Cent

By the mid-1850s American children and adults had grown up with the old copper "large" cents that had been in circulation ever since their introduction in 1793. The change to the lightweight, small-diameter, lightly-hued copper-nickel cent would require some education Mint officials figured.

Accordingly, beginning in late November 1856, approximately 1,000 or more 1856-dated pattern Flying Eagle cents were struck for distribution to newspaper editors, congressmen, and others of influence, with some coins held in reserve for distribution to numismatists. Included in the dispersal were one to each senator and representative, four to President Franklin Pierce, about 200 to the Committee on Coinage, Weights and Measures, and other pieces to Treasury Department officials.[1] However, it seem apparent that any congressman who wanted a few extra pieces had no trouble getting them.[2] Exactly how many promotional pieces of the 1856 Flying Eagle cent were struck in 1856 and early 1857 is not known, and it could have been far in excess of 1,000 coins.

These initial specimens of the 1856 Flying Eagle cent were of the "Uncirculated" or business-strike format, not Proof, and were intended to be similar in finish to what the average citizen would see when mass production of the new format began. The "advertising campaign" was a success, and the Act of February 21, 1857, was signed into law, making the copper-nickel Flying Eagle cent a reality.

Collectors Take Notice

Word of the curious, interesting, new, little 1856 Flying Eagle cents spread, and these coins began to have a premium value among the small but rapidly growing community of coin collectors. Specimens soon traded for 50¢ to $1 each when they could be found, which was not often. By 1859, Edward D. Cogan sold a copper-nickel specimen for $2. As $2 was more than a day's pay for many people in the late 1850s, this was indeed a significant premium.

Around the same time the Mint was busily engaged in restriking rarities for collectors. In 1859, Director James Ross Snowden announced that he could supply scarce coins to numismatists who had Washington

---

[1] Walter Breen, *The United States Minor Coinages 1793-1916*, p. 14; modified by his *Encyclopedia of Proof Coins*, p. 245. Also R.W. Julian, "The Flying Eagle Cent," *COINage*, October 1987. See additional information under the 1856 Flying Eagle sub-chapter in the present text.

[2] *E.g.*, Congressman Whitney who received multiple specimens sent to him by Director Snowden on December 24, 1856 (*cf.* Steve-Flynn, p. 206).

tokens and medals to trade for them. Snowden had been director since June 4, 1853 (and would continue until he was replaced by the new president, Abraham Lincoln, in spring 1861).[1] Under his administration facilities for what became known as the Mint Medal Department were set up on March 7, 1855, to provide a dedicated area for the production of Proof coins, medals, and, as it came to pass, restrikes. Beginning in 1859, Snowden, William E. DuBois, and other Mint officials kept busy augmenting the Washington Cabinet section of the Mint Collection (this display would be dedicated on February 22, 1860).

Snowden offered such numismatic delicacies as recognized rarities, Proofs, patterns, and low-mintage coins in exchange for Washington medals and other desired items. Such trades were pleasing to Mint officials and collectors alike. By this process and by selected purchases, the Washington display was increased from a nucleus of "four or five specimens" to 138 pieces by February 1860.[2]

In addition to whatever rarities Snowden and his close associates may have made, it is likely that others also had access to dies and coining equipment at the Mint and sought to feather their own nests (quite literally when it came to Flying Eagle cents) by producing rarities for their own accounts. (See Appendix II for additional information about patterns and restrikes.)

Whatever the unrecorded circumstances may have been, during the late 1850s and early 1860s—probably from about 1858 and continuing through the early years of the Civil War—additional 1856-dated Flying Eagle cents were struck, but apparently from original obverse dies (there is no evidence that new dies were made after early 1857). The year a particular reverse die was made—1856, 1857, or 1858—made no difference as reverses bore no dates and superficially looked alike. While three of the reverse dies used to coin 1856-dated cents seem to be contemporary with 1856, a fourth is of a style first used in 1858.

At the time, it was felt by collectors that Proof was a *better* finish than Uncirculated (Mint State). Thus, all of the restruck 1856 cents were made with prooflike or even full Proof surfaces by resurfacing existing dies. However, the surface of these Proofs was not quite as deeply mirrored as would be the Proofs of the later dates 1857 and 1858.

Exactly how many Proof 1856 Flying Eagle cents were restruck is not known. I believe that the truth may be around 1,500 to 2,500 coins. To-

---

[1] June 4, 1853, is the date personally stated by Snowden in his *Medallic Memorials of Washington*, p. 194: "entered upon the duties of the office on the 4th day of June, 1853." Numerous later accounts state June 3, 1853. Although he began serving in 1853, he was not officially confirmed until February 4, 1854.
[2] James Ross Snowden, *The Medallic Memorials of Washington*, page v (part of an account of how the Washington Cabinet was formed).

day, Proof 1856 Flying Eagle cents are much more plentiful than are frosty-surface Mint State coins, the latter being originals from the distribution in 1856 and early 1857 to congressmen and others. Clouding the situation are the facts that many Proof coins have been certified as Mint State and that in any event for many specimens there is no sharp delineation as to what constitutes a Mint State coin and what defines a Proof. Thus, population reports are of little help to the specialist seeking information.

As time went on, the 1856 Flying Eagle cent became one of the most popular of all United States coins. Although it is a pattern—as the design was not adopted until February 21, 1857—the 1856 has been "adopted" into the regular series, as have a number of other patterns (1838 Gobrecht silver dollars, 1859-1860 transitional half dimes and dimes, 1879-1880 $4 gold stellas, and a few more).

Coinage in Transition

In the meantime the coinage of the soon-to-be-old-style large copper cents continued with a vigor in 1856, and in January 1857, some 333,456 additional large cents were struck.

The Act of February 21, 1857, abolished the old, large cents and provided for the production of the new-format cents made of 88% copper and 12% nickel, weighing 72 grains (with the tolerance in weight to be no greater than 4 grains per coin). Although not specified by law, the diameter was ultimately set at 3/4 of an inch (thus laying four coins end to end is a handy way to measure 3 inches, a convenience if a ruler is not at hand).[1]

The design of the new cent was not specified, but was whatever the director of the Mint wanted, so long as approval was secured from the secretary of the Treasury. While in its draft stages there was a provision that the new cents be legal tender up to a total of 10¢ per transaction, this proviso did not appear in the final version. This was hardly novel, as the old-style cents were not legal tender either (the Mint Act of April 2, 1792, regulating the coinage, gave legal tender status to silver and gold coins only). As cents were not legal tender, anyone including government officials could refuse to accept them!

Apparently, many of the already-struck 1857 large copper cents went to the melting pot early in the same year. In consequence, this date became scarce on the collectors' market.

---

[1] Today it is more popular to state the diameter as 19.1mm, obscuring the "useful" diameter originally intended.

Snowden Makes Plans

Director of the Mint James Ross Snowden wrote to Secretary of the Treasury James Guthrie on February 20, 1857, seeking approval of the new cent and explaining its features:[1]

In anticipation of the approval by the President of the bill entitled "An Act relating to foreign coins and to the coinage of cents at the Mint," and for the purpose of submitting to you at as early a period as possible after it may be signed the question of fixing the "shape and device" for the new cent, I make this communication.

Heretofore, from time to time, I have had the honor to communicate with you in reference to the adoption of the most suitable alloy and the proper weight of the coin. These have been established in the bill in accordance with our views. I have to submit for your approval the selection of dies to be used in the coinage, and I recommend an adoption of the dies from which the enclosed specimens have been struck.

The obverse is a flying eagle with the legend "United States of America" and the date of the piece. The reverse is simply a wreath compiled of the principal staple production of our country, enclosing the denomination. The propriety, simplicity and symmetry of this arrangement I think is apparent on inspection of the coin.

The wreath is similar in design to the three-dollar gold coin, but the greater thickness of the cent enabled it to be brought out in higher and more perfect relief, and it fills more completely the face of the coin. The devices and general appearance of the cent, its thickness and smooth edge, render it so dissimilar as to prevent its being mistaken for any other denominations. The last named characteristic will enable persons...where there is an absence of light, to ascertain the denomination.

The weight of the piece is 72 grains or 3 pennyweights, equal to three twentieths of an ounce troy. The diameter is fifteen twentieths or 3/4 of an inch, and the thickness of the planchet is sixty-five thousandths of an inch. It will be seen that the relative proportions are most obviously variant from the other coins. Retaining nearly the thickness of the old copper cent, its diameter is but one twentieth of an inch greater than the dime. This familiarity of the portion is also relied upon as an important safeguard against mistaking it for other coins issued from the Mint.

I may add that I have caused some dies to be prepared, and if the "shape and devices" meet with your approval we will be able to commence the issue of a new cent at an early day, that is to say as soon as we can procure and prepare the materials necessary for the coinage.

I also take this opportunity to ask for instructions as to the "purchase of the materials necessary for the coinage of the cent," in accordance with the 5th section of the bill. The copper and nickel for these coins must be the best quality and free from other metals. I suggest that they be purchased in an open market on the most advantageous [terms] that they can be obtained in like manner as we have before purchased material for the copper cent. A superior quality of nickel mined and manufactured in the United States is obtainable in any desired quantity at the lowest market rate which will enable us to proceed with the coinage without delay.

I have the honor to be with great respect your faithful servant

James Snowden
Director of the Mint

---

[1] Quoted by Kevin Flynn in "Two Obverse Types Used on 1857 Flying Eagle Cents." *Numismatic News*, April 2, 1996, here slightly edited. Certain other letters were quoted by Larry R. Steve and Kevin Flynn in *Flying Eagle and Indian Cent Die Varieties*.

While this letter was being considered, the Coinage Act of February 21, 1857, became a reality and provided for the redemption of certain old coins and the issuance of the new copper-nickel cents.

On February 24, Secretary Guthrie wrote to Director Snowden to approve the new cent, but also to suggest a change:

> I have now to ask your attention to the edge of the piece, and to suggest the propriety of such attention in the die, as will render it less sharp.

To Guthrie's letter the director replied in part:

> I have noticed the remarks contained in your letter of yesterday approving the dies for the cent coinage, and will...have the coin changed in the manner as suggested.

Presumably, the unwanted sharp feature was simply a wire rim—or "fin" as it was called at the Mint—and no true alteration of the rim, dentils, or other design features took place.

Flying Eagle cents were struck in quantity beginning in April 1857, and were stockpiled for several weeks awaiting their initial release.

New Cents for Old Coins

A fascinating account of what happened when the new Flying Eagle cent made its debut was printed in *The Bankers' Magazine and Statistical Register,* August 1857, and was extracted from an article in *The Philadelphia Bulletin.* The time was May 25, 1857, and the place was Philadelphia:

> Every man and boy in the crowd had his package of coin with them. Some had their rouleaux of Spanish coin done up in bits of newspaper wrapped in handkerchiefs, while others had carpet bags, baskets and other carrying contrivances, filled with coppers—"very cheap and filling," like boarding-house fare.
>
> The officiating priest in the temple of mammon had anticipated this grand rush and crush, and every possible preparation was made in anticipation of it. Conspicuous among these arrangements was the erection of a neat wooden building in the yard [interior courtyard] of the Mint, a special accommodation of the great crowd of money-changers. This temporary structure was furnished with two open windows which faced the south. Over one of these windows were inscribed the words CENTS FOR CENTS, and over the other CENTS FOR SILVER. Inside the little office were scales and other apparatus for weighing and testing coin, a goodly pile of bags containing the newly-struck compound of nickel and copper, and a detachment of weighers, clerks, etc.
>
> The bags containing the "nicks" were neat little canvas arrangements, each of which held 500 of the diminutive little strangers, and each of which bore upon the outside the pleasant inscription "$5." Just as the State House bell had finished striking 9 o'clock the doors of the Mint were thrown open, and in rushed the eager crowd—paper parcels, well-filled handkerchiefs, carpet bags, baskets and all. But those who thought there was to be a grand scramble, and that the boldest pusher would be first served, reckoned without their host. The invading throng was arranged into lines which lead to the respective windows; those who bore silver had the post of

honor signed them and went to the right, while those who bore nothing but vulgar copper [old half cents and large cents] were constrained to take the left.

These lines soon grew to be of unconscionable length, and to economize space they were wound around and around like the convulsions of a snake of a whimsical turn of mind. The clerks and the weighers exerted themselves to the utmost to meet the demands of all comers, and to deal out the little canvas bags to all who were entitled to receive them; the crowd grew apace, and we estimated that at one time there could not have been less than 1,000 persons in the zigzag lines, weighed down with small change, and waiting patiently for their turn.

Those who were served rushed into the street with their moneybags, and many of them were immediately surrounded by an outside crowd, who were willing to buy out in small lots and in advance on first cost. We saw quite a number of persons on the steps of the Mint dealing out the new favorites in advance of from 30% to 100%, and some of the outside purchasers even huckstered out the coin again in smaller lots at a still heavier advance. The great majority of those who came out "made tracks" with their bags of money, and not an omnibus [horse-drawn enclosed carriage] went eastward past the Mint for several hours that did not, like the California steamers, carry "specie[1] in the hands of the passengers."

Those who made their way homeward a-foot attracted the attention of passersby by their display of specie bags, and we doubt much whether, in the history of the Mint, there was ever so great a rush inside the building, or so animated a scene outside of it. It was, in effect, at once a funeral of the old coppers and of the ancient Spanish coins, and the giving of a practical working existence to the new cents.

In a few weeks the coin will be plentiful enough at par, the Spanish coins will go out at the hands of the brokers just as they already have disappeared from ordinary circulation, and as regard for the old cents there will be "nary red" to be seen, except such as will be found in the cabinets of coin collectors.

On May 25, 1857, the day that the 1857 Flying Eagle cent made its debut, Mint Director Snowden wrote to Secretary of the Treasury Guthrie:

> The demand for them is enormous.... We had on hand this morning $30,000 worth, that is 3,000,000 pieces. Nearly all of this amount will be paid out today. The coinage will go forward, however, at the rate of 100,000 or more pieces per day and the demand will be met as well as we can.

A "Review" of the New Cent

Not everyone loved the new Flying Eagle cent. This scathing commentary appeared in *Life Illustrated,* New York, June 27, 1857, reprinted from a recent issue of the *Albany Journal:*

> The new cent coin wins opinions anything but golden. Its color—like copper counterfeiting pinchbeck and blushing at being caught in the cheat—is the ground of objection with some. Others revile the ambiguous figure which the Mint officers

---

[1] QDB note: Specie here refers to gold coins. Passengers from California typically brought their profits (if they had them) in the form of privately-minted as well as San Francisco Mint gold coins and arrived in the East aboard steamers. Copper-nickel cents were never considered to be specie; this term was reserved for coins struck in silver or gold, although the newspaper reporter used the word in the cent connection.

interpret to mean a flying eagle, but which, to the uninstructed, resembles a table napkin, or pen wiper got up for sale at a fancy fair.

The latest objection we have noticed is that children swallow it, with great consequent irritation of the stomach and bowels, from the corrosive nature of the metals of which it is composed.

There is just one good thing in the new cent. It weighs precisely the hundredth part of a pound. People inclined to decimals may turn it to some good purpose as a convenient mode of determining fractional weights; sixpence worth is an ounce; three of them can be sent by mail for three cents more.

Those of our readers who desire to see what the new cent ought to have been in color and material, can step into the State Library and admire the beautiful collection of bronze medals of the French kings, presented by Napoleon the Little. They are nearly black. A cent of this hue could not be mistaken for a half-eagle, or a dime, while the present abortion is of a compromise tint between the two. Our Mint is the more inexcusable, because the French have, within the last three years, replaced their old and cumbrous copper coinage by one of bronze, in which the defect of weight was compensated not so much by superior value in the material as by artistic taste and elegance in the devices and execution. Their example was before us for instruction and imitation.

Who cares whether a penny is worth the hundredth part of a dollar, or only the one hundred and fiftieth? Not a soul. It is mere counter change, not designed for keeping. But our Mint is scrupulous on this. Honesty, which has deserted pretty nearly every other civil department of the federal government, still keeps a lingering foothold there. And thus it comes that an administration which sticks at no outrage upon Liberty—whose effigy is banished from the cent—insists upon mixing preposterous German silver with its copper, to the end that the purchaser of a penny may get his dirty penny's worth. So did the Pharisees pay tithes of mint, anise, and cumin, while neglecting the weightier matters of the law.

Redemption of Silver

In exchange for the new copper-nickel cents the Mint and two other Treasury branches redeemed outstanding large cents from circulation and also took in worn Spanish-American silver coins, as noted above. The silver denominations consisted nearly entirely of 1/2-real, 1-real, and 2-real pieces (the larger 4 and 8 reals were rarely encountered; reals were also called "bits"), primarily made at the Mexico City Mint. Director Snowden had estimated that about $3 million worth of these foreign silver coins were in circulation by early 1857. Most were severely worn, often to the point of virtual smoothness.

Up to this point, these Spanish-American silver coins had been received at Treasury offices, Post Offices, and government land agencies at these discounted rates:

1/16th dollar or half bit: $0.05
1/8th dollar or one bit: $0.10
1/4th dollar or two bits: $0.20

Redemptions were permitted for two years from the passage of the

Act of February 21, 1857, but an extension was later granted, and coins were exchanged until the Act of June 25, 1860, ended the practice.

To facilitate their exchange for new one-cent pieces, the government raised the rate to par with United States coins, subject to several rules to prevent severely worn coins from being turned in.[1] Redemptions took place at the Philadelphia Mint, New Orleans Mint, and the New York Assay Office.

1/16th dollar or half bit: $0.0625

1/8th dollar or one bit: $0.125

1/4th dollar or two bits: $0.25

Although the accounting was sloppy, and figures varied among reports, the *Mint Report* for the fiscal year ended June 30, 1862, gave these totals redeemed as of two years earlier, by June 30, 1860: 1/16 dollars: $114,182; 1/8th dollars: $249,330; and 1/4 dollars: $440,858. The total of $804,380 was equivalent to 80,438,000 one-cent pieces.

Coinage for Circulation

By most accounts, the new small-diameter Flying Eagle cents were a great success. Over 17 million were made for circulation in 1857, followed by over 24 million in 1858. The old-style large copper cents became an anachronism within the following decade.[2]

However, the Mint was not satisfied with the design. Parts of the relatively large Flying Eagle motif on the obverse were opposite in the coining press from the heavy agricultural wreath on the reverse, and the demand was made at the moment of striking for metal to flow into deep orifices which could not be completely filled under normal die spacing and production conditions. The result was that some coins showed weakness, particularly at the eagle's head and tail.

In 1857 Mint Director James Ross Snowden suggested that the head of Columbus replace the eagle on the cent. Chief Engraver Longacre replied on July 17 that while the idea was certainly entitled to consideration, as earlier objections had been raised to the use of the portrait of George Washington on coinage the portrait of Columbus would probably meet with the same problem.[3]

---

[1] $5 worth of 1/16th dollars had to weigh more than $4.30 face value worth of current silver coins (half dimes to half dollars); $5 worth of 1/8th dollars had to weigh more than $4.50 worth of silver coins; $5 worth of 1/4th dollars had to weigh more than $4.80 in silver coins.

[2] However, millions were taken north to Canada, and in the early and mid-1860s large cents circulated actively there at a time when they were no longer plentiful in everyday transactions in the United States, having been mostly replaced by copper-nickel cents.

[3] Don Taxay, *U.S. Mint and Coinage*, p. 239. In 1892 a fanciful head of Columbus was created for use on the World's Columbian Exposition commemorative half dollar. Opinion is divided as to whether a true likeness of Columbus exists. Re: presidential portraits on coins, Washington was offered the honor in

THOSE IN CHARGE: Mint directors and superintendents during much
of the Flying Eagle and Indian cent era. Clockwise from top: James
Pollock, Henry R. Linderman (of restriking fame), James Ross
Snowden (father of the Flying Eagle and Indian cent first made under his administration), Daniel M. Fox, Adam Eckfeldt, and Col. A.
Loudon Snowden. Center: Col. O.C. Bosbyshell. (*Illustrated History
of the United States Mint.* George G. Evans, 1892, opposite p. 103)

Pattern copper-nickel cents were made in 1858 with a very small or "skinny" eagle on the obverse, thus obviating the metal flow problem, but this motif (which Richard Snow fancifully described as "a quail in the throes of death"[1] and Mint Director Snowden called an "eagle volant"[2]) was not deemed satisfactory. The lettering around the obverse border was fairly heavy in its vertical elements, somewhat similar to that associated with the work of Anthony C. Paquet on other denominations of the era, and was entirely unlike the "Small Letters" or "Large Letters" fonts used on regular issue 1858 Flying Eagle cents.

In the same year pattern Indian cents were produced by James B. Longacre. These had an Indian Head motif in the center of the obverse. The face of the new Miss Liberty was copied from Longacre's 1854 $3 (and is related somewhat to his 1849 gold $1 and $20), now outfitted with a ceremonial headdress.

On the reverse—designed by James B. Longacre or, alternatively, Anthony C. Paquet—a low-relief laurel wreath was used instead of the heavy agricultural wreath. The words ONE CENT were in shallow relief as well. This solved the metal-flow and striking problem.

Months after patterns had been made, Director Snowden wrote to the Treasury Department, November 4, 1858, stating that the present Flying Eagle cent coinage was not very acceptable to the general population, partly as the public was now used to seeing birds drawn from nature and not the "heraldic eagle which bears but little resemblance to the bald eagle." Snowden went on to say that the new experimental dies were in lower relief and have "an ideal head of America—the sweeping plumes of the North American Indian giving it the character of America," and that there was "a plain laurel wreath" on the reverse enclosing the denomination ONE CENT. Snowden requested that coinage commence as of January 1, 1859, as changes should not be made mid-year.[3]

Exit the Flying Eagle cent.

A Set of Flying Eagle Cents

A "collection" of Flying Eagle cents is one of the shortest in American numismatics. If you include the 1856 pattern, the set has three dates

---

the 1790s, but rejected the idea as "too monarchial." If suggestions for patterns with the portrait of Washington were made at the Mint in the 1840s or 1850s—recently enough for Longacre to have knowledge of them—the author is not aware of any sketches or impressions surviving today. Years later in 1863 pattern two-cent pieces were made with the likeness of Washington, and in 1866 pattern nickel five-cent coins were made with the portrait of Lincoln.

[1] *Flying Eagle & Indian Cents*, p. 49.

[2] Snowden, *A Description of Ancient and Modern Coins...*, 1860, p. 120. "Eagle volant" simply means "flying eagle."

[3] Citation supplied by R.W. Julian, letter, April 24, 1996; also "The Adoption of [the] Indian Head Cent," Walter Thompson, *Numismatic Scrapbook Magazine*, July 1961.

and no mintmark varieties. Excluding the 1856 there are just two dates.

In its basic form a set of regular issue Flying Eagle cents consists of these:

1857
1858

In an elegant, expanded form a date and *major* variety set of Flying Eagle cents consists of these:[1]

1856
1857 Obverse lettering Type of 1856.
1857 Regular obverse lettering (the type usually seen).
1857 Clashed reverse die with Liberty Seated 25¢.
1857 Clashed obverse die with Liberty Seated 50¢.
1857 Clashed obverse die with Liberty Head $20.
1858/7 Overdate.
1858 Large Letters.
1858 Small Letters.

Plus, perhaps, a counterstamp or Civil War token overstrike or two for interest and a handful of Flying Eagle patterns.

Notes on the Issues

In general, 1856-dated cents are fairly well struck. Those dated 1857 and 1858 can be found well struck with some searching, but there are many lightly struck pieces on the market. Weakness is sometimes present at the head, top of the wing, wing tip of the eagle, and upper tail feathers on the obverse and parts of the wreath on the reverse.

The 1856 is one of America's most famous rarities. Over the years several people have attempted to corner the market in these, the most successful effort being that of George W. Rice who advertised for these for many years and by early in the twentieth century amassed 756 pieces. These were sold in 1911. Many of Rice's coins went to Col. John A. Beck of Pittsburgh, whose holding of 531 pieces was kept intact until the mid-1970s, when the trustees of his estate consigned the coins to California dealers Abner Kreisberg and Jerry Cohen.[2] Most of these were sold privately including in groups to dealers. I had the opportunity to examine most of these and found that nearly all were somewhat dull, mostly ranging from about Proof-58 to Proof-62 or so (per today's grading; no

---

[1] Beyond these there are many minor date repunching varieties among 1857 and 1858 cents, die varieties of 1856 cents, etc.

[2] Kreisberg and Cohen traded as Coin Gallery; their auction division was called Quality Sales. The partners maintained a street-level store on North Beverly Drive, Beverly Hills. Earlier (circa 1944 to 1954), Kreisberg had been a partner with Abe Kosoff in the Numismatic Gallery, New York City, which opened a branch in California and, still later, moved all of its operations to the Golden State. Before joining forces with Kreisberg in the late 1950s, Cohen operated the Old Pueblo Coin Shop in Tucson, Arizona.

such refinement of numbers existed in the 1970s). There was not even one sparkling, brilliant piece in the lot. Since that time the Beck hoard coins have been distributed into the coin market.

Among other groups of note, the R.B. Leeds Collection, sold at auction by Henry Chapman on November 27-28, 1906, had 106 1856 Flying Eagle cents.[1] Probably, some of these later became a part of the Beck holdings. Today I am not aware of any hoard of these scarce cents. The aforementioned hoards are described in further detail under the 1856 Flying Eagle cent sub-chapter below.

The late Abe Kosoff, founder (in 1955) of the Professional Numismatists Guild, considered it good luck to start an auction sale with an 1856 Flying Eagle cent. Thus, Lot No. 1 in certain of his auctions was apt to be one of these, even though small cents were not particularly an emphasis elsewhere in the catalogue.

As noted above and also below under the analysis of the 1856 Flying Eagle cent, many Proofs of this particular date are sold as business strikes. As a class, high-grade Proofs are much more plentiful than high-grade business strikes, but existing population data do not reflect this. Proof prices and Mint State prices have achieved more or less parity over a long period of years, due in large part because of the traditional belief—fading in the modern market in face of more scholarly analysis of minting processes—that Proofs are "better" than business strikes. In reality, Proofs are *different from* business strikes. In more recent times, prices for Mint State coins in higher grade levels have edged ahead of prices for Proofs.

As both Mint State and Proof coins were struck from the same dies, resurfaced in some instances and at different times, and as some coins have hybrid characteristics, the entire situation of Mint State vs. Proof is somewhat of a conundrum among 1856 Flying Eagle cents. Anyone who has determined how many angels can dance upon the head of a pin is advised to take up and resolve this 1856 cent question.

The 1857 Flying Eagle cent is plentiful in worn grades and in Mint State is also the most often seen, by a slight margin, of the two regular dates in the series (excluding the 1856).

The best known 1858/7 overdate variety is recognized by a tiny tip of the under-digit 7 visible at the upper right of the terminal 8. This variety is usually lightly defined at the eagle's wing tip at the right side of the obverse; sometimes the tip appears as a disconnected line. A second 1858/7 die has come to light recently and differs slightly; see listing be-

---

[1] This was Henry Chapman's first solo auction sale following the dissolution in the same year of his long-standing partnership with his brother, S. Hudson Chapman.

low under the 1858/7 sub-chapter. Although this variety has been listed in references for years, many 1858 Flying Eagle cents have not been closely examined for the overdate feature. A few years ago I found a gem in the Bowers and Merena inventory, a certified coin I had bought simply as a regular 1858 cent. Thus, cherrypicking is a distinct possibility.

The 1858 Flying Eagle cents are usually collected by two letter sizes, the Large Letters (with larger letters and identifiable at a glance by having the letters AM in AMERICA connected at their bottoms) and the Small Letters variety with a space between the A and the M. The Large Letters style seems to be the norm for the series and more closely approximates the style used on all 1857 Flying Eagle cents. The Small Letters variety has no counterpart among letters on either of the earlier 1856 or 1857 issues and may be from a font originally considered for use on the dime. Quite possibly, it was felt at the Mint that the smaller letters would ease the metal flow problem and make possible the striking of sharper coins.

Curiosa

Three of the most curious coins in American numismatics are found in the Flying Eagle cent series and were not generally known to numismatists until relatively recent times. These are from clashed dies, are each quite scarce, and are described separately below under 1857 business strikes. The origin of the unusual "damaged" dies is not known with certainty, but is now believed to have occurred during the die set-up process.[1] The writer discounts that they were deliberately made for collectors, for if they were they would have been known to numismatists generations ago and, further, if they had been "special pieces" struck for collectors, likely as not they would have been given a Proof finish. These curious clashed-die 1857 Flying Eagle cents seem to have been struck during the ordinary course of Mint operations and were put into circulation.

These coins are heaven on earth at the fingertips of the cherrypicker. Unlike ANACS, the PCGS and NGC services do not recognize these varieties as of this time, and the opportunity exists to make a windfall purchase as a regular issue among certified coins of the latter two firms.

Catalogue Prices From 1878 to 1913

A window on prices of Flying Eagle cents is provided by various catalogues issued by the stamp (primarily) and coin firm of Scott. This work

---

[1] An opinion advanced by R.W. Julian and by Chris Pilliod and finessed by the author; see discussion in the 1857 cent section of this book.

appeared under several different titles including *The Standard Coin Catalogue (Copper)*, published in 1878; *J. W. Scott's Standard Catalogue No. 5, Copper Coins*, in the 1880s and 1890s; and *J. W. Scott's Standard Coin Catalogue No. 2, The Copper Coins of the World*, 1907.

While Scott had evidently employed amateurs to compile the 1878, 1887, 1893, and 1907 listings, pre-eminent dealer David U. Proskey was tapped to do the 1913 values. Thus, the last are probably more reflective of the actual market than were earlier listings. Proskey expanded the 1913 listings to include several varieties and patterns (the latter not cited here). Possibly reflective of a growing interest in die varieties was Proskey's notation, not reprinted below, that "about 35 different varieties of 1858 eagle cents" were known. (For Scott prices on Indian cents see Appendix III.)

1856 Flying Eagle cent (1878 edition): Uncirculated $3.50.

1856 (1887 edition): Good $4.00, Brilliant Unc. $4.50, Proof $5.00.

1856 (1893 edition): Fine $4.00, Unc. $6.00, Proof (not priced).

1856 (1907 edition): Fine $10.00, Unc. $12.00, Proof (not priced).

1856 (1913 edition): Fair $7.50, Good $9.00, Fine $12.00, Unc. (not priced), Proof (not priced). Note: These prices seem to have been listed under the wrong column headings and probably should have been: Good $7.50, Fine $9.00, and Unc. $12.00.

1856 High Leaf at C of CENT. (1913 edition): Good $7.50, Fine $10.00, and Unc. $12.00.

1856 Low Leaf at C of CENT. (1913 edition): Good $8.00, Fine $11.00, and Unc. $14.00.

1856 Re-engraved date. (1913 edition): (listed but not priced).

1857 (1878 edition): Fine $0.05, Unc. $0.25, Proof $0.50

1857 (1887 edition): Good $0.05, Brilliant Unc., $0.10, Proof $0.20.

1857 (1893 edition): Fine $0.05, Unc. $0.25, Proof $1.00.

1857 (1907 edition): Good $0.05, Fine, $0.25, Unc. $1.00, Proof (not priced).

1857 (1913 edition): Good $0.05, Fine $0.20, Unc. $0.50 Proof (not priced).

1857 Re-engraved date. (1913 edition): (listed but not priced).

1858 (1878 edition); no letter size specified: Fine $0.05, Unc. $0.25, Proof $0.50.

1858 Small Letters (1887 edition): Good $0.05, Brilliant Unc., $0.10, Proof $0.30.

1858 Small Letters (1893 edition): Fine $0.20, Unc. $0.50, Proof (not priced).

1858 Small Letters (1907 edition): Good $0.20, Fine, $0.50, Unc. (not priced), Proof (not priced).

1858 Small Letters, Low Leaf at C of CENT. (1913 edition): Good $0.05, Fine $0.25, Unc. $0.50, Proof (not priced).

1858 Small Letters, thin High Leaf at C. (1913 edition): Good $0.50, Fine $1.25, Unc. $2.00, Proof (not priced).

1858 Small Letters, thick High Leaf at C. (1913 edition): Good $0.40, Fine $0.75, Unc. $1.50, Proof (not priced).

1858 Large Letters (1887 edition): Good $0.20, Brilliant Unc., $0.30, Proof $0.50.

1858 Large Letters (1893 edition): Fine $0.10, Unc. $0.30, Proof $1.00.

1858 Large Letters (1907 edition): Good $0.10, Fine $0.30, Unc., $1.00, Proof (not priced).

1858 Large Letters, High Leaf at C of CENT. (1913 edition): Good $0.05, Fine $0.20, Unc. $0.50, Proof (not priced).

1858 Large Letters, re-engraved date (1913 edition): (listed but not priced).

1858 Large Letters, Low Leaf at C of CENT. (1913 edition): Good $0.05, Fine $0.20, Unc. $0.50, Proof (not priced).

1858 Large Letters, Low Leaf at C, re-engraved date and letters. (1913 edition): Good $0.50, Fine $1.25, Unc. $2.00, Proof (not priced).

1858 Large Letters, Low Leaf at C, re-engraved date. (1913 edition): Good $0.40, Fine $0.70, Unc. $1.00, Proof (not priced).

The Market in 1996

A Guide Book of United States Coins, Kenneth E. Bressett, editor, issued by Whitman Publishing Company, gives these values in its 1996 edition:

1856: Good-4 $2,800, VG-8 $3,200, F-12 $3,500, VF-20 $4,000, EF-40 $4,400, MS-60 $5,000, Proof-63 $6,000.

1857: Good-4 $14, VG-8 $15, F-12 $22, VF-20 $34, EF-40 $75, MS-60 $250, Proof-63 $3,000.

1858/7: VG-8 $65, F-12 $135, VF-20 $250, EF-40 $350, MS-60 $1,200.

1858 Large Letters: Good-4 $14, VG-8 $15, F-12 $22, VF-20 $34, EF-40 $75, MS-60 $250, Proof-63 $3,000.

1858 Small Letters: Good-4 $14, VG-8 $15, F-12 $22, VF-20 $34, EF-40 $75, MS-60 $250, Proof-63 $3,000.

It is seen that the *Guide Book* considers the market values of the 1857, 1858 Large Letters, and 1858 Small Letters to be precisely identical in all grades. Most probably this will change, if for no better reason than the knowledge you are gaining while reading my book will become known to *Guide Book* contributors in due course. Watch future editions and see!

Caveat: In all markets and eras, prices listed in popular guides have been approximate. Higher or lower prices often prevailed in actual transactions.

Collecting Circulated Flying Eagle Cents

Assembling a set of the basic varieties of the Flying Eagle cent—the 1857 and both letter sizes of 1858—is easy to do today in the 1990s.

Beyond these basics, the following can be added:

The 1856 is quite rare in worn grades, and a Fine or Very Fine coin is more elusive than a Proof. Because of the basic demand for the 1856 even well-worn pieces are expensive.

The interesting 1857 varieties from clashed dies are of necessity usually collected in various circulated grades, simply because of the extreme rarity of Mint State coins.

The 1858/7 is typically found in worn grades. However, for the overdate to be satisfactorily defined, a specimen should be Very Good grade or better, with Very Fine or Extremely Fine being better yet. Late die state coins with a very weak overdate feature command very little premium.

Counterstamped and Overstruck Coins

Occasionally a worn Flying Eagle cent dated 1857 or 1858 will be found counterstamped with the name of a tradesman or other person.[1] These were done as a novelty or as an advertisement to promote a person or product. As a class, counterstamped Flying Eagle cents are fairly rare. There is, however, a notable exception. At least several hundred exist bearing the imprint of DR. G.G. WILKINS, a dentist who practiced in Pittsfield, NH, during the 1860s and 1870s.

The counterstamp of N.J. TRACY, location and occupation unknown, occasionally is seen on Flying Eagle cents.

Several privately-produced Civil War store cards (tokens) of the 1863 era exist overstruck on Flying Eagle cents and are very rare. Parts of the original Flying Eagle cent designs and inscriptions are still visible on the store cards if one looks closely, an example being the Dr. Larkin M. Wilson specimen of Fuld 60-346, dated 1863, clearly and dramatically struck over an 1858 Flying Eagle cent, which crossed the auction block in 1995.[2]

Collecting Mint State Flying Eagle Cents

Choice Mint State 1856 Flying Eagle cents are quite rare. Most Mint State pieces are in lower grades, hovering around MS-60 or just a bit better. True MS-64 and MS-65 coins, brilliant and lustrous and with no prooflike surface, are exceedingly difficult to find. Nearly all such pieces advertised or certified seem to be misattributed Proofs.

The most often encountered Flying Eagle cent in Mint State is the 1857. This is quite satisfactory numismatically as it provides a good opportunity for the collector to acquire the first year of issue for a type set. Moreover, the 1857 is very historical, playing as it did a vital part in

---

[1] One overstruck on an 1856 Flying Eagle cent is reported, but not verified (George and Melvin Fuld, *U.S. Civil War Store Cards*, first edition, p. iii).

[2] Auctions by Bowers and Merena Inc., November 13, 1995, Lot 1202. Attribution to Dr. George Fuld's work on Civil War tokens. Civil War token overstrikes were in some instances deliberately produced to create numismatic delicacies for collectors such as J.N.T. Levick.

CIVIL WAR TOKEN OVERSTRIKE: 1863 Civil War token struck over an 1858 Large Letters Flying Eagle cent. The top photographs, enlarged, are oriented to show the Flying Eagle undertype. Note the "ghost" 1858 date at the lower rim and on the reverse, ONE CENT in ghost form under the shield. Among Civil War tokens this is Fuld catalogue no. F 60-346. Only a few different Civil War tokens are known overstruck on Flying Eagle cents, as contrasted to well over 50 varieties of Indian cents. Quite probably, such pieces were made in the 1860s as delicacies for collectors, not so much because of the overstrike (which makes it of commanding interest and importance today), but to create a copper-nickel version of a token otherwise seen in bronze. (Dr. Larkin M. Wilson Collection, Part I, Lot 1202, Bowers and Merena, 1995)

the redemption of Spanish-American silver coins and old "large" cents.[1]

The Flying Eagle cents of 1858 are slightly scarcer than those dated 1857, but market prices do not reflect this difference as many buyers need but a single date for "type" and select an 1857. As the 1858 cents are usually divided into the Large Letters and Small Letters categories, each of these varieties is at least twice as scarce as the date 1857.

When buying a Mint State Flying Eagle cent for your collection, care must be taken to select for sharpness of strike, especially as the certification services as well as most dealers do not mention sharpness at all on their holders or in their advertisements. To commercial graders an MS-64 is an MS-64 is an MS-64, and that's it. To *you* there should be a difference. Be fussy, and pick and choose wisely. This same advice is applicable to all other small cents from the Flying Eagle series down to the Lincoln cents of our own era.

What is a Proof Flying Eagle Cent?

Many if not most Proof Flying Eagle cents lack the deep mirror finish characteristic of, for example, later *Indian* cents, and were struck from dies that were incompletely polished. This is particularly true of 1856 Flying Eagle cents, for which even the experts disagree. The situation is not made easier by the prolonged use of certain dies which, apparently, were repolished from time to time.

In recent times there has been a growing interest in sorting 1856 Flying Eagle cents by die varieties—mainly based upon guidelines given by Walter Breen in his encyclopedia on Proof coins (published in 1977, reprinted in 1987) and Richard Snow's *Flying Eagle & Indian Cents* (1992). Several specialists are currently engaged in research on the same subject.

I anticipate that over the next few years a number of refined theories will be published concerning die combinations, die states, and estimated issue times. A question that has already arisen is this: Should an 1856 Flying Eagle cent with an incomplete Proof surface and having some characteristics of a business strike and some of a Proof, but generally acknowledged as being a restrike made for collectors, be classified as Mint State or as Proof?

While among 1857 and 1858 Proof cents the situation is not as confused as with the 1856, still it seems that the *majority* of specimens classified as Proofs years ago might equally well be called Mint State.

The question of Proof vs. Mint State or business strike finish on various copper-nickel cents of this era is examined further in Appendix II

---

[1] What we call "large" cents today were not called large until the "small" Flying Eagle cents appeared. They were simply "cents" or "copper cents," familiarly called pennies.

and specifically for 1856 is addressed in the 1856 sub-chapter below. That the confusion, even among experts, is hardly new is evidenced by the use of "Uncirculated" and "Proof" within the description of the *same specimens* by B. Max Mehl in his 1941 catalogue of the William Forrester Dunham catalogue (italics ours):

> **Lot 1412. 1856 Flying Eagle cent.** Bright *Uncirculated* with full mint lustre, raised borders, with considerable *Proof* surface. Very likely purchased as a *Proof*....
>
> **Lot 1709. 1859 Indian head pattern.** Reverse, olive wreath. *Proof,* but not in full brilliancy. Can be classed as *Uncirculated* with *Proof* surface....

Collecting Proof Flying Eagle Cents

Most 1856 Flying Eagle cents encountered in higher grades are Proofs and are restrikes made 1858 or later, but from original dies made in 1856 or very early 1857. Little notice has been paid in the marketplace concerning restrikes vs. originals. So far as is known, *all* Mint State coins (frosty and lustrous, with no prooflike or Proof surface) are originals. The distinction is often unclear, as stated above.

The 1857 Flying Eagle cent is a notable rarity in Proof finish. However, once again the situation is complicated by some prooflike business strikes being certified incorrectly as Proofs. Be careful, and use certification as a *starting point.* Conventional wisdom in the field of Flying Eagle and Indian cents is changing—this book will help—and certification services are learning, too.

In my opinion there are fewer than 20 to 30 authentic Proof 1857 Flying Eagle cents known, and I have seen estimates that there are only 10 to 20 true Proofs. This rarity is explained by the fact that most contemporary numismatists interested in 1857 Proof coins ordered them in early 1857 and received half cents and large copper cents of the old style.[1]

The Proof 1857 Flying Eagle cents were not ready until May, by which time most minor (half cent and cent) and silver Proof sets had been distributed with the older-style copper coins. Probably, most 1857 Proof Flying Eagle cents were sold singly later, not with silver sets.

1858 Proof Flying Eagle cents are likewise rare, but as a date they are more often seen than are those dated 1857. Both the Large Letters and Small Letters varieties were made with mirror Proof finish, with the Small Letters being the style usually seen. The 1858 Large Letters Proof is a *major rarity,* although most price guides and popular references have

---

[1] For comparative numbers, Breen (*Encyclopedia of Proof Coins*, pp. 103-104) cites an odd delivery of $1.33 on January 24, 1857, which "may mean 266 half cents"; and a similar odd delivery of $2.38 on February 7, 1857, which "may mean 238 Proof [large] cents," presumably Newcomb-3. (Note suggested to the author by Harry Salyards, M.D.)

not recognized this. Some 1858 Proof Flying Eagle cents, especially of the Small Letters style, are believed to have been sold as part of 12-coin sets containing 11 patterns and one regular issue; more is told about these in Appendix II.

As a class, Proof Flying Eagle cents of 1857 and 1858 are sharply struck with "square" vertical edges (when viewed from the side).

In summary, Proof Flying Eagle cents have the following availability, listed from most plentiful to most rare:

1857: The rarest; estimated 20 to 30 known.

1858 Large Letters: Second rarest, in a league with the 1857.

1858 Small Letters: Third rarest, probably 50 to 100 known.

1856: Most plentiful. Many hundreds known.

Historical prices for 1857 and 1858 Flying Eagle Proofs are lower for the 1938, 1944, and 1965 citations below because of business strikes being offered as Proofs; these diluted the market.

A sharp price differential between various levels within the Proof category such as Proof-60, Proof-63, etc., did not begin in a widespread way until the late 1980s. In earlier times a particularly choice Proof would sell for more, but not a great amount more, than a heavily toned or spotted example. Usually a Proof was simply offered as a Proof, and what few truly "fussy" collectors that were in the market could, with some searching, buy a beautiful coin for no higher price than an average one.

As unusual as it may seem to the present-day reader, connoisseurship was not emphasized decades ago. While such numismatists as Mrs. R. Henry Norweb, Floyd Starr, Louis E. Eliasberg, James A. Stack, and F.C.C. Boyd—to give just a short list—were indeed particular as to their purchases, most collectors were not. Even these discriminating collectors did not own complete sets of Proof-65 or finer Flying Eagle and Indian cents.

Historical Prices

Today in the 1990s, small cents in higher grade levels are typically graded by the American Numismatic Association's numerical grading system—as described in Chapter 5—with one-point divisions between 60 and 70. Thus, Mint State coins are classified into MS-60, MS-61, MS-62, etc., through MS-70, the higher numbers representing the higher grades. Similarly, Proof-60, Proof-61, etc., grades are used.

Among Flying Eagle cents in historical price listings including 1938, 1944, and 1965—the three benchmark years used in this text—there were no such refinements. Thus, such retroactive listings are highly subjective and are simply estimates, reflecting in most instances that a "brilliant" or "bright" coin would sell for more than a deeply toned one and that a coin with a surface with few marks would sell for more than one with numerous marks.

Trends in Collecting

Today in the 1990s, collecting specialized varieties of Flying Eagle cents is a popular pursuit for at least several hundred people, and a vastly wider circle of numismatists seek a single specimen for a type set or basic varieties for a date set. Flying Eagle cents are nearly always collected in conjunction with a cabinet of Indian cents.

During the 1980s and 1990s there arose a vastly expanded interest in die varieties, due no doubt to the writing of Walter Breen in his remarkable *Encyclopedia* (1988) and Bill Fivaz' and J.T. Stanton's enthusiastically received *Cherrypickers' Guide* (latest edition, 1994).[1] Both of these called attention to the rarity and desirability of unusual varieties and, by implication, the potential profit to be made by "cherrypicking" such pieces from among unattributed coins.

Interest increased further when *Flying Eagle & Indian Cents,* by Richard Snow (with photographs by Chris Pilliod), was published in 1992. The Fly-In Club (Fly-In = Flying Eagle and Indian cents, not a club for pilots on weekend trips!) attracted many members, and its journal, *Longacre's Ledger,* furnished a forum for many contributors—Larry R. Steve especially prominent among them—to publish new discoveries. More recently, a book by Larry R. Steve and Kevin J. Flynn, *A Comprehensive Guide to Selected Rare Flying Eagle and Indian Cent Varieties,* has been well received by enthusiasts.

---

[1] Through the popularity of its various editions this book has made "cherrypicking" an often-used word in the connoisseur's numismatic vocabulary.

CHAPTER 9

FLYING EAGLE CENTS 1856-1858

•

Date-by-Date Study and Analysis
Arranged in Sub-Chapters

1856 Flying Eagle Cent

Business Strikes:

Business strike mintage: 1,000 or more (estimate).

Number of business strike obverse dies made: Possibly as many as five, but certainly at least three, including two made in 1856 and one, two, or three 1856-dated dies made early in 1857, before the Act of February 21, 1857. These dies each have the "Style of 1856" lettering. R.W. Julian has located Mint records showing that two pairs of dies were actually made in 1856, presumably two obverses and two reverses. Thus, I conclude that the additional obverses were made early in 1857.[1]

There is absolutely no evidence to indicate that any 1856-dated Flying Eagle obverse dies were made after spring 1857.

Die commentary: Presumably, "originals" were struck with lustrous, frosty fields, not prooflike or Proof fields. Complicating the matter is the seeming situation that original dies were later resurfaced and given prooflike or Proof finish.

Original strikings: On all 1856 Flying Eagle cents struck in 1856 or very early 1857 and considered "originals," on the reverse the left leaf extends upward slightly above the baseline of the C in CENT; the leaf on the right is about even with the right bottom of the T in CENT; one variety (Reverse A below) has a slightly different alignment.

Restrikes: Struck from original dies, now repolished, as described above. In addition, on a few restrikes made in 1858 or later a new reverse was employed with the leaves at C and T shorter and with ends below the baseline.

The differentiation of originals vs. restrikes has been a focal point for many writers in the field, beginning with Walter Breen who devoted a chapter to the 1856 cent in his 1977 Proof coins *Encyclopedia*. However, in my opinion some of the conventional wisdom on the subject is due for a re-evaluation, a comment prompted by the excellent suggestions of several people who have contributed to the present book

---

[1] Mint records are often incomplete, and this finding of two die pairs does not preclude the possibility that other dies were made as well.

including John Dannreuther, Michael Fahey, Richard Snow, Larry R. Steve, and a few others. See additional commentary below.

Average number of coins struck from typical obverse die: About 1,000 originals in 1856 and early 1857, these being with frosty and lustrous surfaces. Other coins were restruck from 1858 to possibly the 1870s, possibly to the extent of 1,500 to 2,500 pieces, mostly from two obverse dies, plus a few from a third die. The average number of strikes is not known, but may have been 1,500 or more from the two most-used obverses.

Availability in Mint State: Very rare, especially if choice, frosty, and without any prooflike surface. Virtually non-existent in true MS-65 grade, uncleaned, brilliant, lustrous and frosty. Most graded as Mint State by commercial services are prooflike (and thus arguably Mint State) or Proofs and were probably restrikes made after spring 1857. In any event, the distinction between business strikes and Proofs is rarely clear—except for two extremes: lustrous and frosty coins (very rare) and deep mirror Proofs (somewhat elusive). Most specimens in high grades are prooflike and have some characteristics of business strikes and some earmarks of Proofs. In his *Encyclopedia* Walter Breen made a comment in this regard, noting that "many unworn 1856 coins are undecidable if made as Proofs or business strikes"—this from the man who wrote the book on Proofs.

The "Q word"—*quality*—is as important here as with any other popular American rarity. Probably not one in 10 or 20 Mint State or Proof coins is truly choice and attractive. Thus, while market prices can serve as a guide, in my opinion it would very worthwhile to "reach" should an especially pleasing coin be offered.

Availability in circulated grades: Rare. Probably about 400 to 800 exist including originals and quite a few Proofs that were later "spent," the latter being restrikes. Circulated coins typically are evenly worn and have a yellowish-brown color. Most are in grades from Fine to EF. Very few remained undetected in circulation long enough to wear down to such levels as Good or Very Good.

Characteristics of striking: Usually well struck. On a very few pieces there is weak striking on the eagle's breast.

Caveat: This present discussion of 1856 business strike cents must be read and considered in combination with the discussion of Proofs below, for both finishes are intertwined.

Market Prices (1856 business strikes)

YEAR	G-4	VG-8	F-12	VF-20	EF-40	AU-50
1938	$10.00	$12.50	$15.00	$17.00	$19.00	$21.00
1944	30.00	35.00	40.00	45.00	55.00	65.00
1965	600.00	725.00	875.00	1,100.00	1,900.00	2,050.00
1996	3,950.00	4,350.00	4,600.00	5,250.00	6,000.00	6,500.00

YEAR	MS-60	MS-63	MS-64	MS-65		
1938	$25.00	$25.00	$25.00	$25.00		
1944	65.00	65.00	65.00	65.00		
1965	2,350.00	2,450.00	2,550.00	2,750.00		
1996	8,000.00	10,000.00	11,000.00	22,000.00		

Note about market prices: The 1938 and 1944 values in the above and other charts in the present work are adapted from the *Standard Catalogue of U.S. Coins,* by Wayte Raymond, with the present author's extrapolations and interpolations to obtain listings for more grades than in those two editions. The 1965 prices are similarly adapted from the *Guide Book of U.S. Coins.* The 1996 prices are a composite of auction records, the author's own experience and knowledge, and listings in the *Guide Book, Coin Dealer Newsletter,* "Coin Market" column in *Numismatic News,* Keith Zaner's "Trends" in *Coin World,* suggestions by Brian Wagner, and other sources.

As noted above, most coins graded as "Mint State" and offered on the market over the years were in fact struck as specimens for collectors. Although probably intended as Proofs, the coins do not have the deep mirror surface characteristic of later Proofs and are sometimes classified as "Mint State." True Mint State coins, somewhat elusive of definition, are many orders rarer than specimen or intended Proof restrikes.

In the past, prices for business strike and Proof cents have tended to blend together. At present in 1996 there is a call for Mint State coins by Flying Eagle cent specialists, but definitions are neither consistent nor necessarily accurate.

Proofs:

Proof mintage: Mintage not known, but estimated at about 1,500 to 2,500 Proof restrikes from "original" dies with the Style of 1856 obverse letters. At least three obverse dies were used in combination with several reverse dies. See "Die Varieties" below. The term "Proof" as used here refers to coins with surfaces ranging from partially prooflike to deeply and fully Proof, the latter somewhat scarce and probably among the restrikes made long after 1858, say in the 1860s or even the 1870s.[1]

Number of Proof obverse dies made: At least three including two believed to have been made in 1856 and one very early in 1857. The two earlier dies were used to make "originals" with lustrous frosty surfaces, then resurfaced to make prooflike coins and Proofs.

Proof commentary: Most Proofs are toned yellow-brown, often with surfaces that fall far short of mirrorlike (the typical 1856 Proof compares in no way with the gem mirror quality of selected 1857 and 1858 Proof Flying Eagle cents). This is due in large part to the way they were made; apparently, the dies on Proof 1856 Flying Eagle cents were not as polished as their later Proof cousins in the series.[2] Moreover, some may have been struck on regular planchets while others may have been struck on specially prepared planchets, further increasing the number of surface differences on finished coins.

Many hundreds of Proof 1856 cents exist today and are more plentiful than all other years of Proof Flying Eagle cents combined.

Most if not all mirror-surface 1856 Proofs are restrikes, but they are only occasionally designated as restrikes in the general marketplace (Walter Breen, New Netherlands Coin Co., and a few others have noted them in years past, but such mentions

---

[1] It seems virtually certain that in 1871 various parties at the Mint were restriking 1864 L cents (see listing) and Proof 1864 Small Motto two-cent pieces, and it does not strain credulity that they may have been making other numismatic delicacies as well; it is believed that during the mid-1870s the so-called Proof restrike silver dollars dated 1801, 1802, and 1803 were coined.

[2] The same is true of 1858 pattern cents, all of which were made for pattern or numismatic purposes, but most of which have incompletely polished surfaces; some call these "business strikes," which is a misnomer, and others routinely call them Proofs; see Appendix II.

have been infrequent). Quite possibly, the point is moot if all prooflike and Proof coins are restrikes anyway. (Similarly, the vast majority of 1879-dated $4 gold Flowing Hair stellas were made in 1880, a year after the date on them; few numismatists seem to care.)

In recent times there has been an increased interest in minute die varieties of Flying Eagle cents, and as time goes on there will probably be new ideas and theories presented as to the order of striking.

Market Prices (1856 Proofs)

YEAR	PR-60	PR-63	PR-64	PR-65		
1938	$35.00	$35.00	$35.00	$35.00		
1944	85.00	85.00	85.00	85.00		
1965	2,500.00	2,600.00	2,740.00	3,000.00		
1996	5,500.00	7,000.00	9,000.00	19,000.00		

Notes

Die Varieties of the 1856 Cent

Several different obverse and reverse dies were used in various combinations to strike 1856 Flying Eagle cents. The information I give here concerning obverse dies is in some aspects different from that found in Walter Breen's 1977 Proof coins *Encyclopedia* and in Richard Snow's 1992 *Flying Eagle & Indian Cents* book although the basic Breen numbering system (1 to 5) for obverse dies and lettering system (A to D) for reverse dies has been employed.

I recommend that these and other references be consulted for conventional wisdom as to originals and restrikes. The die discussions (mainly by QDB and, as identified, Walter Breen from his earlier listings and 1992 as well as additional 1996 comments by Richard Snow) may help students of the series decipher what has been a puzzle for a long time. However, answers and theories are better defined now than ever before.

Richard Snow and Walter Breen each list five different obverse dies dated 1856 (1 through 5), but I have only examined three (1, 2, and 5) during the course of research for this book. Richard Snow in his "additional comments" notes that he has not observed the other two (nos. 3 and 4) recently; thus, parallel die descriptions for the missing two are incomplete.

Not helping research matters as to rarity of die combinations and identity of dies is the duplicated use of certain obverse and reverse photographs in reference books and auction catalogues; illustrations not necessarily representing a specific coin being described.[1] Further, most photographs reproduced in print are not sufficiently sharp to permit date orientation with dentils or other minute die information. I expect that more research will be done, and that future editions of various works will bring the 1856 situation up to date. In particular, can the two "missing" Breen obverse dies be

---

[1] For example, the Adams-Woodin, Judd, and Pollock texts all use "standard" obverse and reverse photographs and combine these pictures to illustrate certain mulings in the pattern coin series; often, photographs are not of the particular varieties indicated.

studied, and, if so, is there the possibility that one or both may be different die states of obverses 1, 2, or 5?

Meanwhile, the following paragraphs constitute a "forum"—a sharing of opinions—on the 1856 Flying Eagle cent and give a diversity of thoughts and theories.

About the Dies (general comments)

No "restrike" obverse dies?: As of spring 1996, conventional wisdom based upon Walter Breen's 1977 Proof coins *Encyclopedia* suggested that there were five different obverse dies made for the 1856 Flying Eagle cent, and these were combined with four reverses. John Dannreuther has suggested that the number of different obverse dies may be fewer, and that the same dies were resurfaced multiple times in some instances.[1] This resurfacing would account for various thickness and thinness differences in letters, numbers, and other features. His ideas were pondered by me and largely led to the 1856 "situation" as expanded and presented here, with valuable help and modification from Richard Snow.[2]

My opinion that no 1856-dated obverse dies were made after spring 1857 is based upon the lettering styles used on 1857 cents (see 1857 cents sub-chapter, discussion of Style of 1856 lettering, for complete details). In brief, in 1857 when Flying Eagle cents were first struck in quantity for circulation, the obverse lettering was of the so-called Style of 1856 with "squared" center to the O in OF and with other specific characteristics. By mid-May 1857 new punches were employed, and after this point in time the letters in certain instances are slightly differently formed, the so-called Style of 1857 lettering.

If *new dies* had been made for 1856 Flying Eagle cents after spring 1857, it is a virtual certainty that they would have had later, or Style of 1857, letters. As no 1856 Flying Eagle cents are known with Style of 1857 letters, it seems certain that *all* obverse dies were made before mid-spring 1857. As Mint records show that in 1856 there were two obverse and two reverse dies made for experimental cents, and as I have seen one other obverse (and Breen and Snow have seen this additional obverse die plus two more that I haven't seen), at present this gives a grand total of at least three and possibly four or five different obverse dies.

There seems to be no evidence at all that any 1856-dated obverse dies were made at a later date, although at a later date pre-existing 1856-dated dies seem to have been resurfaced, thus causing certain features to appear lighter or more "open." This is particularly evident at such features as the 5 and 6 in the date and certain letters (the E being prime in this regard) in the inscription. So far as I am able to determine, there was just one four-digit 1856 date logotype used. However, the lightness or openness of the figures and their spacing can vary not only from resurfacing, but also from the depth to which the logotype was punched into the working die.

The obverse dies listed below are by Walter Breen's numbers (also used by Richard Snow). The reverses are Breen letters (likewise used by Richard Snow).

As the resurfacing and repolishing of dies caused certain features to become thinner and more "open," I have endeavored to select more permanent topological features as descriptive guidelines. There may be other dies than those given below, but this is a start on what may be a new classification. Hopefully, the "missing" Breen-3 and Breen-4 obverse dies can be located so that positional differences can be studied and they can be described in parallel with the criteria given below.

---

[1] Letter, May 2, 1996.
[2] Letter, May 3, 1996, and later comments.

OBVERSE DIES USED ON 1856 FLYING EAGLE CENTS:

Breen-Snow OBVERSE Die 1: Date:[1] All four numerals thick, ball of 6 much closer to curve of 6 and ball of 5 closer to vertical element of 5 than on Obverse 2. 5 shows very light repunching on early impressions.

Left edge of base of 1: Over space between dentils; on very early impressions the edge is ever so slightly to the left of the space. Note: This characteristic is not easy to observe on photographs or even on actual coins, as lighting, shadows, and various die states all play a part and can give the appearance of subtle differences among different examples of the same die.

Ball of 6: Close to curve of 6.

U in UNITED: No notable extra features.

Dentils: Open "field" space between many dentils, especially at upper right.

Commentary: This die was used to strike originals in 1856. Whether it was used later to make restrikes is not known. This is a very rare die. Obverse 1 and obverse 2 appear somewhat similar with regard to date alignment with the dentils below. (Breen-1, Snow-1)

Breen-Snow description: "Closed E's. Thin date, open 6. *Part of an extra 5* (slanting stroke) *shows immediately to left of 5,* slightly below normal position. Left base of 1 over space or extreme left edge [of dentil]." • Richard Snow: "Repunched 5. Closed E's (the center joins the upper and lower serifs). Open 6. Left base of 1 between dentils."

Additional Richard Snow description:[2] (Repunched 5) Used in its earliest die state on the rare Snow-1, with a mirrored surface. Next used on S-3 for an extended press run where the mirror fields fade to a frosty surface.

Breen-Snow OBVERSE Die 2: Date: All numerals appear thinner and slightly more widely spaced than on Obverse 1; the 1 in the date 1856 appears to be slightly bolder than the 856 digits.

Left edge of base of 1: Over space between dentils; on very early impressions the edge is ever so slightly to the left of the space.

Ball of 6: Distant from curve of 6.

U in UNITED: Prominent spike extends from base of U.

Dentils: Usually seen tightly spaced; little field space between them. However, on very late impressions (with Reverse C) the dentils do have some open space, for example opposite the eagle's tail.

Commentary: Perhaps about 25% to 30% of known 1856 Flying Eagle cents are from this obverse die.

John Dannreuther suggests that this may be a later state of my Obverse 1, now with thinner letters and a die mark at the base of U in UNITED.[3]) In 1858 or later this die, resurfaced, was combined with the oak wreath and ornamented shield reverse to create a few special pieces for collectors (Judd-184, Pollock-220).

Breen-Snow description: Breen: "Open E's, *very thin shallow date,* open 6, left base of 1 over right part of dentil." However, the Breen photograph, p. 246, shows

---

[1] Description based upon Norweb Collection, Part I, Lot 142 coin, there called Proof-63.
[2] All "Additional Richard Snow description" entries for dies are from his letter, June 10, 1996, lightly edited.
[3] Letter, May 2, 1996.

the left base of 1 over left side of dentil. • Snow: "A small spike extends from the base of U in UNITED. Shallow date, with the 1 strongest. Open 6. Left base of 1 between dentils." Middle die state: "With all sharpness worn out of the rim, and letters."

Additional Richard Snow description: (Point at the base of U) This die shows diagonal die polish lines when used first for S-2 and later for S-5.

Breen-Snow OBVERSE Die 3: Not seen by QDB. • Breen: "Closed E's, heavier date, closed 6, plain recutting within loop of 6 and on top left serif of 1, and on bases of CA (not double striking). Left base of 1 right of left edge [of dentil]." Not illustrated. • Snow: "Slight repunching at the left top of 1 and in the upper loop of the 6. Closed 6. Closed E's. Heavy date."

Additional Richard Snow description: (Repunched 1) Not seen recently enough to comment on its surface. Used only on S-6.

Breen-Snow OBVERSE Die 4: Not seen by QDB. • Breen: "Closed E's, heavier date, 6 almost closed (later states have it open—repolished die), left base of 1 over space; none of the stigmata [apparently a euphemism for recutting] of obverses 3 or 5." Not illustrated. • Snow: "Very similar to Obverse 3, but no repunching. Left base of 1 between dentils. Closed E's. The 6 varies from being almost open to fully open, due to die polishing." Illustrated is the date area of the coin.

Additional Richard Snow description: (No repunching) Not seen recently enough to comment on its surface. Used only on S-7.

Breen-Snow OBVERSE Die 5: Date: A break develops connecting the center of the bottom right serif of the 1 to the outer curve of the 8. Later this break extends to the left of the date, over three full dentils, and contacts the border at or past the left of the third full dentil; the same break extends right through the bases of 185, later connecting to the 6.

Left edge of base of 1: Over and ever so slightly to the left of center of a dentil; sometimes referred to as being *centered* over a dentil.

Ball of 6: Close to curve of 6 and on some impressions connected to it; this date was punched into the die more deeply than Obverse 1. "Heavy date." Faint repunching at top of curved part of 6, tip and top of 6, below top of the loop in 6. These repunchings are clear on early states, blurry on intermediate states, and not visible on the final uses of the die; on most (all) there is a tiny raised line barely connecting the bottom of the ball of the 6 with the curved part of the 6 below.

U in UNITED: Die line or file mark slants downward from the lower right of dentil, going left through the upper right of the U in UNITED, continues in a straight line through the lower left of the U, exits, and terminates at the top of the eagle's beak; this is most prominent on later die states, indicating it may be an artifact of die resurfacing.

Dentils: Typically with open field spaces between dentils at the upper right, especially near S OF AMER. Tiny die line or file mark extends from the left side of a dentil to the upper right of the I in UNITED; this is weaker in later die states, indicating it was on the die earlier than the aforementioned line through U. Small mark nearly joins dentils above N in same word.

Commentary: About 75% or so of known 1856 Flying Eagle cents are from this "workhorse" obverse die. Among these are most of the originals for distribution to congressmen, newspaper editors, and others, as well as later restrikes.

On some specimens there is a prominent lump at the upper left of the letter I (on all 1856 obverses the upper left serif is defective).

Breen-Snow description: Breen: "Closed E's, heavy date, closed 6, left base of 1 left of center [of dentil]; faint recutting atop 8, at very tip of 6, atop 6, and below top of hollow loop. Die file mark up to border from right upright of I in UNITED; small mark about joins two dentils above N. On earliest states (rare) the recuttings are fairly clear (they are never pronounced, usually blurry, and on later states not visible); no cracks, no repolishing, no marks through U." Die State I: "With die file mark at I as above; recutting on date shows." Die State II: "Die repolished, recutting blurry, mark above N weaker, that above I only microscopically visible or not at all." Die State III: "As above but obverse again repolished, no trace of recutting on date." Die State IV: "Obverse again repolished; new die file mark through U to border above N; the earlier die file marks almost or completely invisible. Varying strengths of a crack from beak nearly vertically down to border; this becomes plain." Die states V, VI, and VII: Obverse crack now extends through beak and UNI (base of U, middle of N, nearer to top of I)." The obverse die remains about the same, but these states have different progressions of cracks on the reverse. Obverse 5, Die State II illustrated. • Snow: "Die line from I in UNITED to rim. Closed E's. Closed 6. Heavy date. Earliest die states show repunching of the 8 and 6, later die states do not. (Snow also describes several die states.)

Additional Richard Snow description: (Left of edge 1 centered on a denticle) Always with a small die line from the I in UNITED to the rim. The commonly encountered die. Its first use is on S-8 where the surface is somewhat frosty, though without flowlines. The second use is on S-9 for an extended press run of coins which I believe were all *intended* as Proofs, although their appearance varies as I will describe. The earliest die states are frosty, like the S-8. Later the dies were polished for the first time to a semi-mirrored or prooflike finish; in this state there are now die lines diagonally through the U in UNITED to the rim. Even later die states show flowlines. A die crack forms from the eagle's beak and extends downward progressively until the die is terminated. These later die state pieces are still Proofs although they go against some of the popularly-used attribution rules such as "no die cracks" and "no flow lines" are found on Proofs.

REVERSE DIES USED ON 1856-DATED FLYING EAGLE CENTS, AGRICULTURAL WREATH STYLE OF 1856-1858:

Breen-Snow REVERSE Die A ("Reverse of 1856"):

Left leaf: Even with the baseline of the C and precisely in line with the baseline of the CENT letters.

Right leaf: Very slightly higher than normal, about even with the middle of the right serif of the T.

Left vertical edge of strawberry-shaped leaf (intended as a cotton boll) above E in ONE, if extended downward: Intersects well to the left of the angle between the top right serif of the E and the top arm of the E.

Veins in first and second cotton leaves (maple-leaf shaped leaves) on each side: Raised.

Veins in third (top) cotton leaf on each side: Raised and very sharply delineated.

Lower right fork in ribbon end terminates: Over center of dentil.

Dentils: Short and thick.

Center dot: None.

Commentary: This is Breen's Reverse A with so-called "tilted ONE CENT." Breen reports two copper strikings; Snow reported three specimens including one listed in his 1992 book and two handled by Bowers and Merena (one of these being Norweb I: 142).[1] E in ONE open and with absolutely no traces of extra material between the two serif tips. Outlines around some wreath edge areas including below left ribbon, resulting in an incomplete area of die polish between the ribbon and dentils at this point.

Called a "prototype" by Breen. He felt this was the first of the 1856 reverse dies, but did not say why. As this is a very rare die, there seems to be no reason to believe it was one of the two actually made in 1856, as two *other* reverse dies each are known to have made multiple business strikes. This same general style of wreath was also used on all 1857 cents and some of 1858. It is a "High Leaves" style intended to be similar to Breen reverse B and D, but when the master die was made, the inscription ONE CENT was rotated ever so slightly in a clockwise direction, "lifting" the lower left of the denomination inscription and making the leaf appear low at C and "lowering" the lower right side of the inscription and making the leaf at T appear very slightly higher than normal. To the uninitiated observer, this slight difference in alignment would probably not be noticeable. I do not consider it to be a reason for rejection or limited use of the die at the Mint.

Richard Snow writes: "Reverse A and Reverse B were both used to make copper die trials similar to normal Mint procedure, and these and the copper-nickel pieces from these dies represent the earliest die state of their use...."

Research possibility and some guesswork: What happened to this reverse die? Did it break early in its life, or was it placed on the shelf and used later, say in 1857, for regular coinage? The latter seems to me to be a good possibility. A search of 1857 cent reverses might be productive. As there were 130 reverse dies made in 1857, most of which were probably used, a search of several hundred business strikes would likely yield one or more specimens, if this die was used in 1857.

Additional Richard Snow description: (Tilted ONE CENT) All have mirrored finish. Used only on S-1.

Breen-Snow REVERSE Die B ("Reverse of 1856"):

Left leaf: Slightly above the baseline of the C.

Right leaf: At (on business strikes) or just below (on later strikes from refinished die) lower right of T. Leaves are thicker on earlier (before refinishing) version.

Left vertical edge of strawberry-shaped leaf (cotton boll) above E in ONE, if extended downward: Intersects the angle between the top right serif of the E and the top arm of the E.

Veins in first and second cotton leaves on each side: Raised, but not as sharp as on Reverse A.

Veins in third (top) cotton leaf on each side: Raised, but not as sharp as on Reverse A.

Lower right fork in ribbon end terminates: Slightly to the right of the space between two dentils.

Dentils: Longer than on Breen-C or D. Thick and closely spaced.

Center dot: Above N in CENT; fades away on later strikes from resurfaced die.

---

[1] 1992 book; conversation with the author, May 10, 1996.

Commentary: Probably first used in 1856 to make business strikes. In later (re-finished) versions the right side of the E in ONE is more open (than on earlier states, in which the serifs are very close) and certain kernels on the lower part of the top right bud at the wreath apex become "islands" in the field. New patches of Proof field are created on the inside of the left opposite the E in ONE, this patch being between the left and the top of the corn ear to its right; another patch of Proof field is created in the tiny center opening in the wreath bow between the two larger openings.

Breen states, "The 1857 Proof die believed to be a repolished state of [1856] Reverse B, with second kernel on open wheat stalk at top right disconnected; unconfirmed."

Additional Richard Snow description: (No center dot) Early die states are mirrored. First used on S-2 with mirrored fields. Next used on S-3 for an extended press run, with early die states being prooflike and later die states frosty. Last found on S-8 coins which show flowlines from die wear.

Breen-Snow REVERSE Die C ("Reverse of 1858"):

Left leaf: Below the baseline of the C.

Right leaf: Significantly below lower right of T; smaller and thicker than the preceding.

Left vertical edge of strawberry-shaped leaf (cotton boll) above E in ONE, if extended downward: Intersects very slightly to the right the angle between the top right serif of the E and the top arm of the E.

Veins in first and second cotton leaves on each side: *Incised* over earlier raised veins, the latter now faded. The only 1856 Flying Eagle cent reverse with incised veins.

Veins in third (top) cotton leaf on each side: Raised, very indistinct.

Lower right fork in ribbon end terminates: Slightly to the right of the space between two dentils. Lower left fork in ribbon is only a small extension—a fraction of the length and size of the top left fork.

Dentils: Short, thin and widely separated, probably from resurfacing, on the single specimen seen; the space between each dentil is open and is nearly as wide as the dentil itself.

Commentary: Style of 1858 with short leaves at C and T and probably first used to strike coins in 1858 or later; pieces from this die would seem to be *de facto* restrikes regardless of grade or surface finish. Typically seen with Proof finish, but not in high polish. Hub deeply impressed into die giving a particularly bold aspect to wreath features such as the corn kernels at the top of the wreath apex. However, the words ONE CENT are in low relief in the die. Small diagonal die line in dentils below the right ribbon. This reverse was used on certain 1858 copper-nickel patterns and also 1856 Flying Eagle cents struck in "nickel" (described as such in the pattern references, but probably not pure nickel; however, these pieces are of lighter color than normal).

Minor technical differences were not noted by restrikers at the Mint or collectors in the private sector in the 1850s and 1860s. Sometime in 1858 or later when this new-style (1858 hub) reverse was combined with an 1856 obverse, it remained undiscovered for over a century. Probably, had an 1856 obverse been made with the later-style (Style of 1857) letters, it also would have passed unnoticed for a century or more.

This reverse was clearly made later than reverses A, B, and D, and should have been listed last by Breen.

Additional Richard Snow description: (Low Leaves) Since this die is found on 1858 Proofs and patterns in an earlier die state than seen on the 1856-dated Flying Eagle cent, it is obvious that 1856 Flying Eagle cents from this reverse die could not have been made before 1858. Diagonal die polish lines are visible on the die state used to coin S-4.

Breen-Snow REVERSE Die D ("Reverse of 1856"):

Left leaf: Slightly above the baseline of the C. On early states this leaf is tapered, becoming thinner at its end; to the left of where this leaf joins the wreath there is a large unpolished area of the field. On very late die states this leaf becomes a bit thinner near where it joins the wreath, giving the leaf a fairly uniform appearance throughout its length, and with polished field to the left of where it joins the wreath; later, additional polishing makes the top part of the leaf thicker than its bottom (on this late state the center dot remains sharp).

Right leaf: At (on business strikes) or just below (on later strikes from refinished die) lower right of T. Leaves are quite thin on early business strikes (as evidenced on worn pieces) as well as later strikings. Evidently, the hub was not impressed as deeply into the die.

Left vertical edge of strawberry-shaped leaf (cotton boll) above E in ONE, if extended downward: Intersects slightly to the left of the angle between the top right serif of the E and the top arm of the E.

Veins in first and second cotton leaves on each side: Raised, but not as sharp as on Reverse A.

Veins in third (top) cotton leaf on each side: Raised, but not strongly defined on specimens seen.

Lower right fork in ribbon end terminates: Slightly to the right of the center of a dentil.

Dentils: Shorter than on Breen-B. Thick and closely spaced on all die states seen. As the dentils are shorter, there is more open space between the bottom of the ribbons and the dentils.

Center dot: Incomplete (small part of top of dot missing) and tucked under upper left serif of N in CENT.

Commentary: Probably first used in 1856 to make business strikes. Surface finish varies from somewhat mirrored Proof to somewhat lustrous and prooflike and not mirrored, some of the latter being made among later die states.

Breen noted that this reverse develops a break from the cotton leaf (what he called a maple leaf elsewhere) at left side of wreath in the 11 o'clock position to rim; later another break is on the right from another cotton leaf to rim in the 1 o'clock position.

Richard Snow noted:[1] "So far as when Reverse D was made and first used we cannot tell. It was not used on any regular issue 1857 or 1858 example. It is possible, though impossible to prove, that it was manufactured after the Flying Eagle series ended, say in 1860. This reverse die also was paired with the dateless dies (which have Style of 1857 letters, the Large Letters style also used in 1858) and the no date / no legend pattern pieces. No real conclusions can be drawn from this, but it does fit if these Reverse D pieces are restrikes."

---

[1] Letter, June 6, 1996.

Additional Richard Snow description: (Center Dot) Earliest die states are frosty, but without flowlines. Used on S-5, S-6, S-7, and S-8 in an order not yet known with certainty. What is known is that they all precede the S-9 usage, which is the usually-found 1856. In this die pair early die states are again frosty, with semi-mirrored fields being applied after a short while. Die cracks appear at the 11 o'clock and 1 o'clock positions in the latest die states; heavy rim deterioration is evident on these late coins as well.

Die Combinations:

1-A: Probably struck in 1856 or early 1857. Reverse very boldly delineated. Very rare combination, possibly Rarity-7.[1] (Snow-1)

Additional Richard Snow description: Original issue. Proof. Rarity-8. Very rare. Norweb:142 was an unequivocal Proof.

1-B: (Business strikes) and restrikes (prooflike or Proof) coined from this pair beginning in early 1857. Early impressions are prooflike and show the doubling at the 5. Later impressions are less prooflike and lack the doubling. Probably all were made as business strikes as part of the distribution to congressmen, editors, etc., in 1856 and very early 1857. Richard Snow commentary: "I have never seen an example of this die pair that was convincing as a Proof, including the four or five prooflike examples I have seen. Weak breast feathers."[2] Second most available die combination. (Snow-3)

2-B: Very rare. (Snow-2)

Additional Richard Snow description: Original issue. Proof. Rarity-7. Unquestioned Proofs. I believe these were normal Proof production possibly for presentation purposes.

2-C: Restrikes (prooflike or Proof) coined from this pair no earlier than 1858. Very rare. Richard Snow assigns a Rarity-7 rating (4 to 12 known). (Snow-4)

Additional Richard Snow description: Restrike issue. It can be easily shown that this was struck no earlier than 1858, because the reverse is linked to the 1858 patterns. An abnormally large (Rarity-6) production of copper pieces in Proof was made probably for collector demand, as opposed to the normal population of die trials made for official testing purposes. Copper-nickel pieces produced in somewhat limited quantities in Proof format. I call this the "1858 restrike" of the 1856 Flying Eagle cent.

2-D: Not seen by QDB. • Listed as Snow 5.

Additional Richard Snow description: Restrike issue. A limited striking. Called variously Mint State and Proof by the commercial grading companies; Mint State seems to be the favored term if the *surface* characteristics are used, and Proof if the *striking* characteristics are used. They are well struck with wide rims, probably intended as collector pieces, thus Proofs. This die combination was not known to Breen and came to light in 1990. Since then a small quantity of unusually high-grade

---

[1] All rarity ratings for die combinations are of necessity tentative; relatively few extant specimens of 1856 Flying Eagle cents have been checked for their die varieties. Further, nearly all collectors are satisfied with owning just a single specimen of the 1856. Thus, a rare die variety, while interesting to specialists, is not necessarily significantly more valuable.

[2] Letter, June 6, 1996. By this commentary it would seem that Richard Snow would attribute *all* high-grade (60 or better) examples of this combination as Mint State rather than Proof.

examples have been identified including one graded MS-66 by PCGS and another called Proof-65 by NGC.

3-D: Not seen by QDB. • Listed as Snow 6.

Additional Richard Snow description: Restrike issue. The only use of this obverse die. Limited striking. Labeled "Mint State" by Breen.

4-D: Not seen by QDB. • Listed as Snow 7.

Additional Richard Snow description: Restrike issue. The only use of this obverse die also. Very limited striking. Labeled "Mint State" by Breen.

5-B: Not seen by QDB. • Listed as Snow 8.

Additional Richard Snow description: Restrike issue. Scarce. Labeled "Mint State" by Breen.

5-D: Originals (business strikes) and restrikes (prooflike or Proof, more mirrorlike than the typical 1856 Flying Eagle cent) coined from this pair beginning in 1856. Most specimens seen today in all grades are from this die combination. Many different die states exist. (Snow-9)

Additional Richard Snow description: Restrike issue. The usually-seen issue. Most if not all are Proofs if the intention of striking is used as a determinant. As the dies were frosty on early die states, mirrored on middle die state pieces, and developed die cracks on later dies the Mint State designation has been liberally given to many of these. I believe that all of these were intended for collectors and struck as Proofs. Such a large production of Proofs (1,000 to 2,000) with one die pair is unprecedented in the early 1860s. Problems with strike, planchets, die cracks, strike-throughs and strike doubling are commonly seen, notwithstanding these being intended as Proof strikings. This is why there is so much confusion regarding 1856s. With this die combination, die cracks do not automatically point to Mint State strikings, nor do die striations and planchet flaws.

Research Forum:
Proof vs. Business Strike 1856 Flying Eagle Cents

What constitutes a business strike and what determines a Proof among certain 1856 Flying Eagle cents has long been a matter of discussion and debate. There is probably no one answer that will please everyone, and perhaps there is no absolute definition.

The following comments are by Richard Snow, followed by three well-known numismatists associated with leading grading services: Michael G. Fahey, senior numismatist for ANACS; and John Dannreuther, co-founder of and consultant to PCGS; and David W. Lange, senior numismatist for NGC:

Richard Snow commentary:[1]

On reviewing the updated 1856 information in the draft of the Bowers manuscript I decided to step back and re-examine all the information as objectively as possible so that the multiple situations of Proof vs. Mint State and original vs. restrike can be clarified and presented in a clear, concise manner with all the known facts justifying my conclusions. Part of the confusion may be because of these multiple issues. The following are my ideas.

---

[1] Letter, June 10, 1996, here slightly edited and paraphrased.

First let me separate the two questions:

1) Original vs. restrike: This concerns the date of manufacture of the coins with the date of die manufacture being of some importance also. It is important to keep *die* manufacture and *coin* manufacture separate to avoid conclusions such as "As all 1856 obverse dies are of the pre-1857 style, thus all 1856s must be struck prior to 1857," which just about everyone among specialists agrees is obviously false, but which might not be obvious to a beginning collector.

2) Mint State vs. Proof. We can only look at the coins surviving and try to reconstruct a proper conclusion. However just looking at coins is not enough, we must show how they relate to each other and to the historical record to draw conclusions about the intention of the Mint at the time. Circulated coins are not of use in this regard.

Die characteristics: First the facts, as I perceive them, about obverse dies: All 1856 Flying Eagle cents are from the same hub—the so-called obverse style of 1856 (some 1857-dated coins also have this lettering style). All 1856 Flying Eagle cents are from the same date punch. A strong case can be made that all obverse dies for the 1856 cents were made prior to the middle of 1857. Following the conclusions drawn years ago by Walter Breen and published in his 1977 book on Proof coins, and expanded in my own 1992 book on Flying Eagle and Indian cents, I believe that these are all separate dies, not reworked or repolished examples of the same die. I have had the opportunity to examine many coins from these different dies together for side by side comparison. I have linked the die pairs by die state which helps in dating the production of the coin by stating which die pair came before another. This also helps in determining Proof or Mint State status. Breen-Snow numbers and letters are used.

It seems to me that copper die trials would be made prior to any test run of a quantity of copper-nickel patterns for *official* use. (Coins made specifically as numismatic rarities were produced for different reasons.) Based upon the rarity of surviving specimens, it seems to me that, typically, only two or three copper pieces were made for each official copper die trial variety. These Rarity-8 copper die trials were quite probably struck with the four original dies that R.W. Julian found mentioned in the archives. There also exist copper die trials of the S-4 (Obv. 2/Rev. C, the Low Leaves 1858 reverse) in quantities greater than all the others combined! This R-6 (13-30 pieces) striking in copper sure looks like a "delicacy" striking for numismatists. Edward D. Cogan's auction in 1859 shows higher prices paid for the copper pieces over the copper-nickel pieces. Perhaps this shows new demand for copper 1856s and is why so many S-4s were produced in copper. I believe that the four dies that exist on the three die pairs struck in copper in *limited* quantities are the *original* dies.

Copper:

Original (die trials):

Snow-1: (Obv. 1/Rev. A) Rarity-8. Proof.

S-2: (Obv. 2/Rev. B) Rarity-8. Proof.

S-3: (Obv. 1/Rev. B) Rarity-8. Proof.

Restrikes (numismatic issues):

S-4: (Obv. 2/Rev. C) Rarity-6. Proof.

Originals are of the same pairs as the Rarity-8 copper die trials listed above. While copper die trials are all Proofs, the format of the following copper-nickel issues will vary depending on the intended use of the coins.

My conclusion: Only by examining the die states, die marriages, striking qualities and matching them with historical records can we get the truth about the 1856 Flying Eagle cents. Looking at the surface and strike of examples in a random order without developing connections in a scientific manner will not yield real conclusions and can only complicate matters. The original pieces were struck for government use and were made in Proof and Mint State format. These early (1856 and early 1857) Proofs were made for die testing and presentation purposes, while the Mint State pieces were made for a test run for Congressional approval of the new small cent. Restrikes were made later to sell to collectors, who preferred Proofs.

It seems obvious that simply labeling Mint State pieces as "originals" and Proof pieces as "restrikes" is not only simplistic, but inaccurate. I do believe that the die pairings give specialists the clearest indication as to whether a coin was intended as a Proof or Mint State or as an original or restrike. Because there are so many different die pairings and striking periods, the situation may not be so clear to the casual observer.

However, if we narrow our focus to just the two die pairs that produced the most coins seen on the market today, varieties S-3 and S-9, then, and only then, can we say Mint States are originals and Proofs are restrikes.

Michael G. Fahey (ANACS) commentary:[1]

ANACS employs the standard diagnostic tests for United States Proof coins of the 1850s when making a Proof vs. a business strike determination on an 1856 Flying Eagle cent:

1. Sharp, squared-off rims and edge.

2. Sharp strike from polished dies, with no signs of die erosion or noticeable die wear.

3. Mirrored surfaces (will vary).

4. Signs of double striking and/or special handling and special manufacture.

The 1856 Flying Eagle cent challenges the above diagnostics by its very nature. The small mintage from several dies with a new design precludes significant die wear. The entire mintage received special handling. The other diagnostics thus demand our attention the most.

We would love to classify all 1856 Flying Eagle cents by die variety, with certain varieties always being business strikes and the others always being Proofs. However, after 16 years of studying them, there does not seem to be hope for this, unless collectors are willing to accept coins as Proofs or business strikes that simply do not give that appearance.

This brings us to market acceptability. All collectors and dealers have basic appearance standards for a wide range of areas. If the majority of numismatists would not accept a given level of quality as "Proof," as a grading service ANACS should not try to impose its own opinion on them. The current consensus for a Proof Flying Eagle cent is one that matches most or all of the previously mentioned diagnostics. To my knowledge, this has not changed in the last decade or two, and it seems unlikely to change significantly in the future.

---

[1] Letter, May 15, 1996.

John Dannreuther (PCGS) commentary:[1]

The issue of Mint State vs. Proof will probably never be resolved, but here is a possible scenario for the striking of the 1856 Flying eagle cents:

Since the act authorizing issuance of the new copper-nickel cents was not passed until February 21, 1857, and not signed into law until May of that year, the "original" 1856 cents struck before that time are technically patterns, and the ones struck later are restrikes.

Q. David Bowers conjectures that the ones struck in 1856 and very early 1857 ("originals") were mainly business strikes struck to show congressmen and others what the new cents would look like. This makes sense. Richard Snow calls most (but not all) originals Mint State coins. Walter Breen states that originals come both Mint State and Proof. Bowers also suggests that they were struck in the Medal Room on Proof or medal presses, rather than high-speed production presses as used in the Coining Room. If the 1856 Flying Eagle cents were in fact struck on Proof or medal presses, maybe they would be best called Proofs, though most of the planchets were obviously not burnished, and the striking technique was not as careful as that used to make other Proofs (such as Proof silver and gold coins of 1856).

Original 1856 Flying Eagle cents are typically satiny to prooflike in their finish and sometimes have "crumbly" and rounded lettering. However, they almost all have square edges and often have wire rims, so they may have been struck with extra care in the same way that Proofs were made. However, original 1856 Flying Eagle cents, no matter how carefully they were made, do not resemble the true Proof Flying Eagle cents of 1857 and 1858.

Another suggestion has been made to call the originals and restrikes "specimens," rather than either Mint State or Proof. The designation of "specimen" is used elsewhere in numismatics—for example among certain special strikings of Canadian coins—to designate coins especially made for collectors, regardless of whether the coins have deep mirror fields. As the typical 1856 Flying Eagle cent neither looks like a frosty business strike Flying Eagle cent of 1857 or 1858 nor like a Proof of those two years, perhaps the "specimen" suggestion has merit.

With specific regard to restrikes, Bowers states that collectors of the second half of the nineteenth century coveted Proofs, just as they do today. Given a choice, most numismatists desired Proof coins and were willing to pay a premium for them.

Snow has concluded that the restrikes are mostly Proofs. Breen suggests that some restrikes are Proofs and others are non-Proofs (*i.e.*, business strikes). The typical restrike 1856 Flying Eagle cent seems to have better lettering (not "crumbly," but not flat either as with most Proof coins) and a surface ranging from satiny to fairly deep prooflike. Does this sound familiar? In reality, there are some originals that look more Proof than some of the restrikes, and there are some restrikes that look more Mint State than some of the originals.

What is the answer? Since the intent of the coiner will never be known, there will be controversy! Let's see: The more things change, the more they are the same. You get the picture—no one knows! One person's satiny or slightly prooflike Mint State coin is another person's carelessly made Proof!

David W. Lange (NGC) commentary:[2]

The Flying Eagle cents dated 1856 have long posed a problem with respect to

[1] Letter, May 16, 1996.
[2] Letter, June 3, 1996.

proper attribution. Just as there is no clear-cut means of distinguishing between original strikes of 1856 and later restrikes, the lines of distinction between Proof and non-Proof strikings are also blurred.

A generation or two ago, Proofs were automatically considered more desirable than non-Proofs, and cataloguers usually gave themselves the benefit of such doubt by listing most specimens as Proofs. In recent years, as the rarity of non-Proofs has become better appreciated, the pendulum may have swung the other way. There is now a desire among many collectors, particularly those collecting Flying Eagle and Indian cents by date, to own a non-Proof in addition to or in place of a Proof.

The job of the graders at NGC is to put these considerations aside and judge each specimen on its own merits. In the absence of indisputable criteria for distinguishing between Proofs and non-Proofs, this requires that they rely on their experience alone. Seeing so many of these coins (and there are quite a few certified) establishes some recurring characteristics which enable them to make an educated determination.

Most of the circulated 1856 Flying Eagle cents appear under the MS (Mint State) heading in the certified population data because there's simply no way to tell the method of manufacture for a coin worn below the Extremely Fine level. Conversely, most of the unworn 1856 Flying Eagle cents are certified as Proofs. This is done with the understanding that Proofs of this issue are usually inferior in overall quality to the much rarer Proof issues of 1857 and 1858. Still, they are recognizable as having been coined with the clear intent of producing Proofs. Such coins have reflective or semi-reflective fields and are usually, though not always, well struck. That they lack the extreme brilliance of conventional Proofs reinforces what has long been suspected: that many if not most of the 1856 Eagle cents were restrikes made in later years to supply the popular demand for this issue. It is also quite possible that the individuals striking them did so clandestinely and were not properly trained in the making of Proofs.

Among the qualities which I demand before labeling a coin as a Proof is the total absence of metal-flow lines. These lines appear only after the dies have produced hundreds of coins since their last polishing. As each die face begins to erode from the movement of planchet metal across its face, these lines or ridges begin to form inside the borders and around the devices, eventually spreading to the entire die face. It is such lines that produce the shimmering effect on non-Proof coins known as mint lustre. As Proofs are produced from polished dies, these lines will not be present, though die-polishing lines may be. These appear on a coin as very fine, raised lines. Unlike flow lines, which typically radiate toward the border from a coin's center and become deeper toward its rim, polishing lines are quite random in direction and of more consistent depth. Early non-Proof strikes made from fresh dies will also have polishing lines in place of flow lines, and these are the coins which create so much work for someone cataloguing coins as either Proofs or non-Proofs. In the case of the 1856 Flying Eagle cents, which were often produced with inadequate die and planchet preparation, there are many coins which fall into this "either/or" category.

Other features which help to distinguish Proofs from non-Proofs are that the former typically have broad, fully formed borders and very flat edges with sharp rims. These qualities, however, are not universal for the 1856 Flying Eagle cents, whether labeled as Proofs or non-Proofs. For that reason, I prefer to fall back onto the criterion described above, in which a Proof must reveal no flow lines.

It's not known whether any of the 1856 Flying Eagle cents were intentionally produced as non-Proofs, though there are clearly some which are so deficient in their Proof qualities that they have been classified under the Mint State heading. As a consequence of their careless preparation, such coins only rarely receive high grades when certified. In fact, very few 1856 Flying Eagle cents have been certified as gems [64 or finer] whether as Proofs or non-Proofs.

It's my belief that there was never any intention of coining the 1856 small cents for circulation and that the many worn examples encountered were placed into circulation years later. This may have been done intentionally, though it is more likely that they were spent by some relative of the original recipient who failed to recognize the date as being worth more than its face value.

Notes

Collecting commentary: Quite possibly the 1856 Flying Eagle cent is the single most famous nineteenth century American coin rarity in a popular and somewhat attainable sense (the storied 1804 dollar is virtually unobtainable, and fewer than a dozen exist outside of museums). Most 1856 business strikes in existence today are in higher circulated grades from VF to AU. Mint State coins typically have dull yellow-brown surfaces. Flashy, lustrous, blazing Mint State gems are virtually unknown.

Coins restruck for collectors were made with prooflike (usually) or Proof surfaces. Whether prooflike pieces should be called Mint State or whether they should be designated Proof is a matter of opinion, as discussed at length above.

Mintage: Mintage of original business strikes estimated at about 1,000 coins struck to inform congressmen, newspaper editors, and others of the design. According to documents in the National Archives viewed by Walter Breen, distribution included the following:[1]

264 pieces or more to congressmen.

200 to Representative S.D. Campbell.

102 to Secretary of the Treasury James Guthrie.

62 to senators.

4 to President Franklin Pierce.

2 to the Mint Cabinet.

In addition to the above 634 coins, additional pieces were given to dignitaries, the Mint staff, interested numismatists, and others. Walter Breen posits that an additional "several hundred were held in stock in the Mint for later distribution to coin collectors, or to trade them for Washington medals for the Mint Cabinet."[2] If one assumes that "several hundred" equates to at least 300, these figures add up to the best part of 1,000 originals, if not even more—a figure more generous than usually given, but probably reasonable. In fact, in view of the quantity of worn specimens in existence today—quite possibly 400 to 800 pieces (including some restrikes that were spent)—a case could be made for the original mintage quantity to have been considerably more than 1,000.

Modern market activity: In 1995 a total of 15 specimens of the 1856 Flying Eagle

[1] Walter Breen, *Encyclopedia of Proof Coins*, p. 245.
[2] QDB note: The Washington Cabinet suggestion is incorrect, as James Ross Snowden did not begin his campaign to add to this display until early 1859. However, the Mint did supply rare coins to collectors at the time, and had been doing so for many years.

cent appeared in leading auction sales. In 1994 the figure was 12, in 1993 it was 19, and in 1992 it was 15. Some of these listings represent repeat offerings of the same specimen.[1]

When you consider that most of the dealer specialists in Flying Eagle and Indian cents do not conduct auctions at all, and that these figures do not represent specimens traded in the off-auction market, it seems evident that an estimate of 30 to 60 1856 Flying Eagle cents bought and sold each year may be reasonable. Here at Bowers and Merena Galleries we handle two or three at private sale for each one we offer at auction.

Harper's Weekly **reviews the 1856 cent:** In its issue of February 7, 1857, the newspaper inserted an illustration of an 1856 Flying Eagle cent and furnished this commentary, in part:

> "You see for yourselves the patriotic design—the wreath entwined with the vine and Indian corn on the one side, and that everlasting American eagle, 'spreading its wings and soaring aloft,' on the other. The bird, by-the-by, has rather an anserine than an aquiline look, and is said to be the same as once was set loose upon golden wings in a previous issue of half eagles, but having been again caged, in consequence of its barn-yard fowl appearance, is now to be turned adrift for a humbler flight...."

The account went on to suggest that the old phrase, "Not worth a red cent," would be of no use now that copper cents were to be replaced, "for the new cent is not red, being of a gray, silvery aspect."

Another contemporary account of the new 1856 cent: *The Buffalo Commercial Advertiser,* January 8, 1857, printed this: "The New Cent: The editor of the Providence, R.I. *Journal* has been permitted to see one of the new cents just struck off at the Mint. He describes it as a little larger than a dime, and nearly twice as thick. On one side is a flying eagle, with the inscription 'United States of America, 1856,' around the circle: On the other is 'One Cent' within a wreath. It is altogether the *handsomest* coin of so low a denomination that we have ever seen."

Market values in 1859: In December 1859, Edward D. Cogan, who called himself the "father of the coin trade in America" and who is generally acknowledged as the first full-time professional numismatist in the United States, offered for sale three varieties of the Proof 1856 Flying Eagle cent:

Copper: $4.

Nickel: $1.

Copper-nickel (the usual issue): $2.

The price of $2 for the standard copper-nickel issue seems to indicate that these were delicacies at the time, and no doubt such a value—equal to more than a day's pay for certain laborers—prompted the Mint to continue making them as a stock item for sale and trade. In fact, as the foregoing were all Proofs and not business strikes, it is likely that they were made after 1856 and already represented restrikes. Among early listings the term "nickel," as opposed to "copper-nickel," was used with abandon and usually simply referred to a regular copper-nickel striking that had a particularly white or pale surface.[2]

Copper-nickel alloy: By July 11, 1856, Mint Director James Ross Snowden had deter-

---

[1] Source: *Auction Prices Realized,* various annual editions, Krause Publications.
[2] Personal observation of pieces in old-time collections, nearly all of which, upon weighing, are found to be about 72 grains and to be the same as ordinary copper-nickel coins.

mined that an alloy of 88 parts copper and 12 parts nickel would "seem to possess all the desirable characteristics for a one-cent piece." As small-diameter 1856 Flying Eagle cent dies apparently had not been made yet, "to prevent expense and delay we have used the half cent dies" (to strike pattern impressions of the new alloy).[1]

On July 18, 1856, James C. Booth of the Mint staff wrote enthusiastically concerning the advantages of the new copper-nickel alloy, noting, in part:[2]

1. It "is made of metals which have as definite a value as the usual articles of commerce, and the supply of which is unlimited. They are copper and nickel." (Strange comment, this, for the then-standard copper "large" cent fit the same definition, except for the nickel content.)

2. "It is sufficiently soft metal to receive a bold impression in coinage." (Almost immediately after copper-nickel was adopted, in 1857, the Mint experienced extreme difficulties with the hardness of the alloy.)

3. "It was [sic] a distinctive color, and cannot be confounded with the metals or alloys used or proposed for coinage."

4. "It will abrade by wear less than copper, gold, or silver, or even than the proposed bronze alloy." (Interesting and little-known reference to bronze alloy being considered at that time; in 1863 when it was re-considered, it was viewed as a *new* idea at the Mint; also see "Rewriting history" comment below in the 1864 bronze Indian cent sub-chapter.)

5. "It will change color, by darkening to a slight extent, but less than the bronzed [sic] cent, and much less than copper. It will alter less than the ordinary silver coin used on the continent of Europe."

6. "It is made up of copper and nickel in such proportions that a cent piece may be made of about 70 grains weight, and yet the seignorage on their manufacture and issue will not be exorbitant, much less, in fact, than the bronze cent proposed. The seignorage will be ample to recall the old Spanish coin from circulation."[3]

7. "The peculiar tone of color will render it difficult of close imitation...." (Booth went on to describe other qualities that would be deterrents to counterfeiting.)

Medal Department proposed: In the 1856 *Mint Report* Director James Ross Snowden, a man with strong numismatic and collecting interests, noted: "The propriety of the organization of a medal office at the Mint is respectfully recommended to your consideration.... The frequent calls upon us to strike medals and to furnish copies of the medals from the dies which are deposited at the Mint, indicate that the establishment of such an office would be of great public benefit."

Actually, facilities of what was later called the Medal Department were in place by March 7, 1855, and by the end of the decade the department furnished special strikings of coins to collectors and others, ostensibly for trade with the Mint Collection (as, indeed, had been done at least since the 1843 exchange of a recently-made 1804 silver dollar with Matthew A. Stickney), but, apparently, also for private profit.

Forgeries: Most forgeries I have seen of the 1856 Flying Eagle cent have been in grades from VF to AU. I urge that while having *any* 1856 Flying Eagle cent authenticated is a good investment, this is essential for coins in the VF to AU range. Sources

[1] Ex. Doc. No. 124, 34th Congress, 1st Session, House of Representatives.
[2] Ex. Doc. No. 128, 34th Congress, 1st Session, House of Representatives.
[3] Another reference to the bronze cent; patterns were struck in various alloys of copper in 1854 and 1855. The reference to Spanish silver coins relates to worn, underweight Spanish coins, then legal tender in the U.S., being exchanged for the new cents; there was enough seignorage or profit in the cent to overcome shortages in silver coin weight.

for authentication include the American Numismatic Association Authentication Bureau (ANAAB) in Colorado Springs, J.P. Martin, manager; and the three leading certification services: ANACS, NGC, and PCGS.

Forgeries are commonly made by either altering the last digit of the date (altering an 1858 cent is usual) to read "1856," or are completely struck from false dies.

Hoards of 1856 Flying Eagle Cents

The following commentary (original text edited and with new text added) concerning three famous hoards of 1856 Flying Eagle cents is primarily by John F. Jones and was published in 1944:[1]

Leeds hoard (cf. John F. Jones, 1944): The first whom we shall mention was R.B. Leeds. He was, at the time of his death, the oldest resident of Atlantic City, N.J. (about 55 miles from Philadelphia). Henry Chapman sold Mr. Leeds' collection on November 27-28, 1906. In the catalogue he stated:

> "For many years he was an ardent collector, turning his attention to accumulating all the examples he could of certain dates, his especial hobby being 1856 Eagle cents of which he had 109 specimens, the greatest collection ever offered of this very rare cent. Mr. Leeds was a firm believer in the rarity and value of this coin, and bought all that he could for many years past. The advance of the past 10 years has proved his judgment to have been correct."

Mr. Chapman, who knew coins and their condition as well as any other expert, listed the Leeds pieces separately as follows:

7 oddities [patterns different from the usual design or in different metals] in Proof, 10 Extremely Fine.

17 Proofs of regular type, 17 Very Fine.

38 [regular type] Uncirculated, 11 Very Good, 9 Good.

The total, 109 pieces, expressed in another way, means only 22% were perfect Proofs, 44% were Uncirculated or Extremely Fine, and 34% had seen service—conclusive evidence that all were not originally issued in *Proof* condition.

In this sale, the Flying Eagle cent without date or legend, in copper, sold at $20; the dated pieces in copper sold from $13.50 to $30 each. The pure nickel piece went for $30. The ordinary [copper-nickel] Proofs sold from $8 to $10.50 each; the Uncirculated, from $6 to $10 each; the Very Fine from $5.50 to $6.50 each; the Good and Very Good, from $4 to $5.50 each; and the whole lot of 109 pieces averaged $7.70 each—certainly a good showing for that sale.

This collection had become a storehouse of rare U.S. coins. Mr. Leeds for years bought every scarce date of U.S. issue that came his way. Among them he had four 1873 gold $3 (only 25 were coined), 12 of the 1815/2 silver half dollars, 12 1852 half dollars, 11 1859 pattern half dollars, and eight 1877 and seven 1878 Proof 20-cent pieces. In large copper cents he had 12 1793s, 12 1804s (among them, one of the finest known), 35 of 1809, 33 of 1811, 60 of 1817 [not a rare date], 70 of 1823, and 130 of the 1857s. He had also 13 1863 pattern two-cents, 11 1854 and 13 1855 pattern cents in different metals, and last but not least, 2,097 half cents dated 1793 to 1857.

[Jones then stated:] Try to equal that today!

Rice hoard (cf. John F. Jones, 1944): George W. Rice, a wealthy building contrac-

---

[1] *The Numismatist,* April 1944. Most of the text is directly from this article, although the present writer has edited it and in some instances expanded the information.

tor of Detroit, Michigan, who began collecting coins in 1864, accumulated the largest hoard of the little 1856 Flying Eagle cents ever gathered together, numbering 756 pieces.

The writer [Jones] spent several days in August 1901 with Mr. Rice at the A.N.A. convention in Buffalo, N.Y., and he then told of his search for that little cent, stating his opinion—from all the information he had acquired—was that only 1,100 pieces were struck of that date, in the regular coinage.

In 1906 Mr. Rice disposed of his main collection of coins (without the 1856 cents) through the St. Louis Stamp & Coin Co. In 1911 he apparently sold this hoard of 756 Eagle cents through Henry Chapman but as yet no catalogue of that sale has been found, although reference to it is made in a Ben Green (of Chicago) sale list after he attended the sale in Philadelphia.

Rice hoard criticized (cf. Commodore W.C. Eaton, 1916): In *The Numismatist,* July 1916, Commodore W.C. Eaton took exception to George W. Rice's hoarding of 1856 Flying Eagle cents, stating that it made the current price of $5 for a specimen "absolutely absurd…for anything under a brilliant Proof," and that such activity was "quite contrary to proper ethics."

Beck hoard (cf. John F. Jones, 1944): Jones' 1944 commentary continues, here expanded and in some parts paraphrased:

John Andrew Beck was born in Chestnut Ridge, Pennsylvania, on January 5, 1859, Beck spent part of his youth with his parents in Texas, but the family was forced to return to the Keystone State because of Indian depredations in the West. In Pennsylvania, Beck's father engaged in drilling for brine (a source of salt) near Pittsburgh. After his father's death, John and his brothers maintained the business. John subsequently acquired 100% interest in the enterprise, and for a number of years traveled around western Pennsylvania selling salt, groceries, and other goods. Later, he went into the oil business and was probably acquainted with numismatist John M. Clapp, who in the late nineteenth and early twentieth centuries was an oil producer in the same state.

At the age of 10 Beck collected his first coins. The passion grew, and as an adult he developed a special interest and hoarding instinct for gold, especially territorial issues, many of which he bought through the Chapman brothers of Philadelphia. At some unrecorded point he became interested in 1856 Flying Eagle cents and decided to hoard them as well.

No doubt Beck bought many of the Leeds and Rice 1856 cents, as we are informed the greater portion of those cents were enclosed in Henry Chapman's envelopes (marked with their cost), proving they came principally from Philadelphia. However, one country coin dealer wrote that "he sold Mr. Beck at least 50 or 60 of his Eagle cents." For years he had a standing offer with all coin dealers of $10 for each 1856 nickel cent obtained, regardless of condition.

Beck, who lived in Pittsburgh, was also an avid collector of American smoking pipes and is said to have had the largest private collection of these in the United States. Indian relics were another focus of interest and upon his death these went to the Carnegie Museum.

John A. Beck passed away on January 27, 1924. His estate was handled by the Pittsburgh National Bank & Trust Company. Beck had been a director of several banks which were merged into this institution.

An inventory of Beck's numismatic estate revealed 531 specimens of the 1856 Flying Eagle cent. The silver composition piece (Lot 2201 in Mickley sale) was believed by John F. Jones to be a part of the Beck holdings, as C.H. Shinkle of Pittsburgh listed such a piece in 1905 in his "U.S. Coin Values and Lists," which was compiled mostly from the Beck Collection, and Jones wrote that "there may be other rarities that have disappeared, also among them."

Jones concluded his 1944 commentary by stating:

> One of the trust companies of Pittsburgh is executor of this estate, and that collection is still intact in their vaults. "Nothing has been sold, and none will be sold," is the reply of the leading official.

> The leading coin dealers of the country have made a well-worn path to that trust company since Mr. Beck's death, without results, but with government, state, and local taxation, and other necessities, there will come a time (if not to the second generation of his family, then perhaps to the third or fourth) when cash they can use will be a prime necessity. When that day comes, there will be plenty of 1856 Flying Eagle cents on the market.

Other Notable Historical Citations (cf. John F. Jones, 1944):

In October 1860 Edward D. Cogan sold four 1856 Flying Eagle cents at auction: two in copper (one was without date or legend on the obverse), one in nickel, and one in copper-nickel.

In October 1867 there was sold in New York City the celebrated collection of Joseph J. Mickley of Philadelphia. Under "pattern pieces" we find five pieces offered," among which was a 1856 half cent—listed under cents. Lot 2201 was interestingly described as follows: "Cent, 1856, struck in a metal resembling silver; fine Proof, extremely rare. This piece must be distinguished from all of the others, for its composition is quite unlike either of them." Lot 2202 was described at "a fine piece of lathe work, executed at the Mint, being the reverse of the nickel cent of 1856, a square piece of brass. Unique."

The Dr. Henry R. Linderman collection sold on February 28, 1888, had two 1856 Flying Eagle cents—one with date and one without date or legend.

The collection of James B. Longacre was sold on January 21, 1870, by M. Thomas & Sons in Philadelphia and had an 1856 copper-nickel half cent and an 1856 cent in copper among other items. [See further description of this sale, 1996 commentary by Thomas K. DeLorey, under the 1870 Indian cent sub-chapter below.]

Dr. R. Coulton Davis of Philadelphia had three specimens of the 1856 Flying Eagle cent.

Lorin G. Parmelee had 10 examples including different varieties.

George D. Woodside, a Philadelphia collector, whose collection was sold on April 23, 1892, had eight different varieties of 1856 Flying Eagle cents in various metals.

Captain Andrew C. Zabriskie, an early president of the American Numismatic Society, New York City, whose collection was sold by Henry Chapman in June 1909, had 14 pieces including varieties.

Judson D. Brenner of Youngstown, Ohio, exhibited 11 different specimens of the 1856 Flying Eagle cent at the American Numismatic Society in 1914.

Burdette G. Johnson of the St. Louis Stamp & Coin Co. wrote us [Jones] regarding the Virgil M. Brand collection of Chicago: "The statement that Mr. Brand [who died in 1926] bought a great many of these Flying Eagle cents is entirely without foundation, as are many other statements about Mr. Brand's collection. I appraised this collection, and in the entire collection there were not over a dozen 1856 Flying Eagle cents of the regular type and possibly ten Flying Eagle patterns."

Col. E.H.R. Green, who nearly cornered the market on the rare postage stamps, had not had his attention properly called to the 1856 Flying Eagle cents, as only about a dozen were included in his immense collection of coins although he had managed to accumulate 12,000 U.S. half dollars in his spare time—all in the finest condition.

QDB note: Jones further noted that the usual copper-nickel variety of the 1856 flying Eagle cent typically appeared at auction over a period of years at the extent of about a dozen to 15 pieces per year—excluding several hoards.

Beck hoard coins offered in 1975: As John F. Jones predicted in 1944, eventually the appeal of the value of the John A. Beck estate coins outweighed any advantage of keeping them in a bank vault. Abner Kreisberg and Jerry Cohen (trading as Quality Sales) offered coins from the Beck Collection for sale on two occasions. The consignor was the Trust Division of the Pittsburgh National Bank. The Quality Sales auction catalogue for January 27-29, 1975, presented 1856 cents with these descriptions:

Lot 781: 1856 An attractively toned Proof specimen. Light golden toning with wire edge visible on both sides. Faint traces of stain or lacquer visible. Few specks. The most sought after date in the small cent series. Ex Henry Chapman, with part of envelope and ticket showing the price Mr. Beck paid: $13.50. [Realized $1,800 at the sale]

Lot 782: 1856 another Brilliant Proof with russet gold toning. The few familiar specks visible under magnification along with very faint handling marks and hairlines. A very appealing coin. [Realized $1,900]

Lot 783: 1856 Choice Uncirculated with some prooflike surfaces. A superbly toned coin with lovely shades of golden brown. Pinpoint planchet flaw between ends of wreath and a pinpoint spot below T in CENT; these two almost invisible except under strong magnification. Supposedly scarcer than the Proof coin. Very valuable. [Realized $2,100]

Lot 784: 1856 Choice About Uncirculated with pale brown toning. Tiny flaw on edge over ICA in AMERICA, which does not detract from the appearance of this valuable coin. [Realized $1,350]

Lot 785: 1856 Sharp Extremely Fine. Very little circulation shows on this specimen. It is seldom that one can find a group of 1856s as nice as these to select from. If you need the date to complete your set of Flying Eagle and Indian Head cents, now is the time to bid and buy. [Realized $1,500]

Lot 786: 1856 Another duplicate, virtually as nice as the preceding lot. Choice Extremely Fine. Sharply struck with full square edge. [Realized $1,400]

Lot 787: 1856 Although all 1856s are considered patterns, they were accepted as regular coinage and circulated freely. This coin will grade Fine to Very Fine with normal wear. Date is recut. Scarce. [Realized $1,000]

Lot 788: 1856 Evenly worn Fine. Very seldom available in lower grades. With an estimated mintage of only 1000 minted, the chances of completing a circulated set becomes difficult. Now you have the opportunity to be one in a thousand! [Realized $1,050]

Lot 789: 1856 This coin has seen much circulation but all important details are clear. If you need a coin in Very Good condition here is your opportunity to place a bid. [Realized $1,025]

Lot 790: 1856 The popular Flying Eagle Cent struck in copper. Judd-181 (AW-205). Plain edge. Beautiful rich brown toning. Uncirculated. Minor dark spot at IC in AMERICA. Almost unnoticeable flaw in edge below date. Rarity 7. [Realized $1,550]

Beck hoard coins offered in 1976: Part II of the John A. Beck Collection was offered by the same cataloguers on February 12-13, 1976. The lot numbers in Part II started with 1, and the 1856 Flying Eagle cents commenced with Lot 734 (the lot numbers were not continuous with the previous sale). Descriptions follow:

Lot 734: 1856 Lightly toned Proof. Pale but attractive shades of reds and purple. Few faded spots in field on obverse, one below tail, another behind wing. Very scarce. [Realized $2,500]

Lot 735: 1856 Choice Uncirculated with a lovely pale purplish red toning. A sharply struck specimen with full square edges of a Proof. Faint spot on wreath at 7 o'clock. Scarce in such an attractive condition. [Realized $1,650]

Lot 736: 1856 Choice Uncirculated with superb toning and equally as attractive surfaces. Full square edge of a Proof striking. Truly scarce in this lovely condition and one of the most appealing from the Beck holding. [Realized $1,850]

Lot 737: 1856 Choice Uncirculated. Lightly toned. Planchet not quite perfect as tiny depression at ST in STATES as struck. Few faint spots on reverse. Partial wire edge. Current trend[1] valuation $2400.00. [Realized $1,700]

Lot 738: 1856 One of the very rarest of the 1856's, STRUCK IN NICKEL. J-183. Rarity 7, with 4 to 12 pieces struck. A trifle weak date as on all specimens struck in nickel. Toned About Uncirculated with very faint signs of handling. Should command a bid in excess of $2,500.00. [Realized $1,350]

Lot 739: 1856 Toned Uncirculated with some prooflike lustre. Tiny hairline behind last S in STATES running vertically through center of eagle. At first glance this coin appears to be a Proof, however, careful examination shows it is definitely Uncirculated. This lovely coin is valued at $2,000.00. [Realized $1,550]

Lot 740: 1856 Choice About Uncirculated with very attractive pale brown toning. Faint flaw on reverse rim at 10 o'clock and tiny edge nick over ME on obverse. Conservatively valued at $1,750.00. [Realized $1,400]

Lot 741: 1856 Sharply struck Extremely Fine. Very pleasingly toned. Planchet flaw at F in OF. Mr. Beck purchased virtually every 1856 offered to him and today you have the opportunity to purchase the "key" coin in the cent series. [Realized $1,375]

Lot 742: 1856 Variety struck in PURE COPPER. Regular die as above. Attractively toned Extremely Fine. Rarity 7. Very scarce, as only 12 were struck. Ex H. Chapman, Jr.[2] [Realized $1,100]

Lot 743: 1856 Very Fine plus. Very well struck with very little wear. Faint handling marks only visible under strong magnification. [Realized $1,400]

Lot 744: 1856 Evenly circulated. Nice Very Fine condition. Pinpoint dig below E in CENT. Should realize $1,250.00. [Realized $1,150]

Lot 745: 1856 Evenly circulated. Fine. Very scarce in lower grades. This is the opportunity you have waited for to complete your circulated set. [Realized $950]

Lot 746: 1856 Very pleasing and strictly graded Very Good. all lettering sharp with just the amount of circulation one would expect of a Very Good specimen. Tiny nick on reverse rim at 6 o'clock. Estimated to realize over $850.00. [Realized $1,200]

---

[1] "Trends" feature of *Coin World.*
[2] Probably purchased by Beck in 1906, when Henry Chapman used the "Jr." designation on his billheads; later this suffix was dropped.

1857 Flying Eagle Cent

Identification:

1857 with obverse letters Style of 1856: Middle serif of E connected to top right serif. Bases of A and M in AMERICA close but not touching. In the O in OF the opening is somewhat "boxy" or "squared" at the corners. Very scarce. Separately described and priced below.

1857 with obverse letters Style of 1857: The "normal" or regular variety as typically seen and offered for sale. Middle serif of E *not* connected to top right serif. Bases of A and M in AMERICA touch. In the O in OF the opening is somewhat rounded at the corners. Common.

1857 with die clashed with Liberty Seated 25¢: Very rare variety. Separately described and priced below.

1857 with die clashed with Liberty Seated 50¢: Rare variety. Separately described and priced below.

1857 with die clashed with Liberty Head $20: Very rare variety. Separately described and priced below.

Business Strikes:

Business strike mintage (all varieties combined): 17,450,000.

Number of business strike obverse dies made (all varieties): 118

Average number of coins struck from typical obverse die: 148,644

Availability in Mint State: Most extant Mint State Flying Eagle cents are of this date. Regular varieties with Style of 1857 letters are relatively easy to find, but high-grade sharply struck gems are elusive. Rare varieties are discussed and priced separately below.

Availability in circulated grades: Readily available in all grades.

Characteristics of striking: Often seen weakly struck, particularly at the eagle's head and tail.

Market Prices

(1857 business strikes, regular dies, obverse letters: Style of 1857):

YEAR	G-4	VG-8	F-12	VF-20	EF-40	AU-50
1938	$0.20	$0.25	$0.40	$0.60	$0.75	$1.00
1944	0.30	0.50	0.75	1.20	1.50	2.00
1965	4.00	7.00	10.00	15.00	25.00	65.00
1996	16.00	21.00	26.00	40.00	110.00	170.00

YEAR	MS-60	MS-63	MS-64	MS-65
1938	$1.50	$1.50	$1.50	$1.75
1944	3.00	3.00	3.00	3.50
1965	90.00	100.00	120.00	135.00
1996	250.00	500.00	900.00	2,200.00

1857 With Style of 1856 Letters

1857 with obverse letters in the Style of 1856. Snow-1 and 2, Fivaz-Stanton 1-001. FND-008 (for obverse with repunched date). Discovered by ANACS; earlier (1921) unknowingly reported by Commodore W.C. Eaton. It is believed that these were made very early in 1857 and were among the first 1857 Flying Eagle cents struck.

Die differences include the following:

Style of 1856 (old style):

Bases of A and M in AMERICA barely touching, base of M aligned slightly high where it meets base of A. Center serif of letter E is solidly connected to upper arm of E. In UNITED the outer edge of the diagonal in N is notched toward the bottom. In the O in OF the opening is somewhat "boxy" or "squared" at the corners (in auction catalogue photographs and other illustrations this feature is often the best for quick identification).

Style of 1857 (new style):

Bases of A and M in AMERICA solidly touching, base of M aligned properly where it meets base of A. Center serif of letter E is not connected to upper arm of E. In UNITED the outer edge of the diagonal in N is perfect. In the O in OF the opening is somewhat rounded on its ends.

Comparisons of certain letters:

Bases of A and M in AMERICA: Style of 1856: Barely touch; bottom of left base of M, if extended, is higher than it should be and touches mid-point of right edge of right base of A. Style of 1857: Touch and are both aligned with each other.

Letter A: Style of 1856: Trapezoid-shaped space in base of A is about twice as wide as it is high. Style of 1857: Space is about 1.5 times as wide, is higher, and overall is larger in area.

Letter E: Style of 1856: Center element of E solidly connects with top arm of E above it and lightly connects to the arm of E below it. Style of 1857: Center element is smaller and barely connects to top arm.

Letter F: Style of 1856: Center element of F connects with top arm of F. Style of 1857: Center element is misshapen and is larger at its top; it does not connect with top arm.

Letter I: Style of 1856: Defective at upper left serif in both appearances in UNITED and AMERICA. Sometimes seen (on 1856 cents) with prominent lump at the upper left of the second I. Style of 1857: Upper left serif is normal.

Letter M: Style of 1856: Bottom of "V" shaped element in center of M is a blob. Style of 1857: Bottom of V is sharply pointed.

Letter O: Style of 1856: "Squarish" center to O. Style of 1857: Center more rounded at top and bottom.

For best identification, both varieties should be examined side by side, although if you simply remember the difference in the O's, you can tell instantly. The early Style of 1856 lettering is much scarcer. A survey of photographs of Mint State 1857 Flying Eagle cent photographs in the Bowers and Merena Galleries archives revealed that only one coin out of every two or three dozen is of the Style of 1856 lettering. In the absence of widespread knowledge concerning these, the chances of finding one at a "regular" price are excellent.

On some (but not all) specimens of the Style of 1856, the right side of each A is thin and irregular (this is a quick test). The right upright of M thin.

There are two obverse die varieties of 1857 style of 1856 cents described in *current* literature, one with a "perfect" date and the other with the date numerals slightly repunched; a third is with the two other published varieties in the Larry R. Steve Collection, and a fourth is rumored.[1] In 1921, it is believed that Commodore W.C. Eaton identified three obverse dies.[2] Possibly, additional dies await numismatic discovery. However, differences among these dies may well be microscopic.

Snow-1 1857 cents with obverse letters in the Style of 1856 occur with fully prooflike surfaces. Richard Snow commented: "These are not Proofs, as sometimes labeled by the grading services."[3] The known Proofs (see Proof section below) of 1857 are with the Style of 1857 letters.

Further, it seems likely that certain letters from the old font(s) were used interchangeably on business strikes with letters from the new or Style of 1857 fonts. I have seen mixed-font specimens with the 1856-style O, but 1857-style A's, in the legend. Whether this represents one or more different hubs or whether it is from the repunching of certain letters to strengthen them has not been determined. Relative to this, Jerry Wysong reported an 1857 cent, Style of 1856 letters, but with the O in OF "oval, not square, and definitely not D-shaped."[4]

Early mintage quantities for 1857 cents: As Flying Eagle cents were first distributed in quantity to the public on May 25, 1857, if the Style of 1856 coins were the

---

[1] Larry R. Steve, letter, April 12, 1996; he had heard of a fourth obverse die in the possession of another numismatist, but had not yet examined it.

[2] However, as Thomas K. DeLorey has pointed out (letter, April 15,1996), Eaton in his various studies of 1857 and 1858 cent varieties did not differentiate between die doubling (important as a variety) and machine doubling (made during the coining process by loose mechanisms; not very important numismatically). Michael Hodder (letter, May 14, 1996) noted that as cataloguer of the Eaton coins when they were sold by Stack's, "I found that Eaton's 'die varieties' were often simply dies with breaks, or coins with incompletely struck devices or letters, and so on; that is why I did not include Eaton numbers in my cataloguing—they were not at all relevant."

[3] Letter, April 10, 1996.

[4] Letter, May 16, 1996; further discussion of his article on lettering, "A Third 1857 F.E. Cent Obverse Die," that appeared in the Summer 1993 issue of *Longacre's Ledger*.

earliest struck, they must have been included among these early deliveries, most probably in the coins on hand as of May 23.[1]

PRODUCTION DATES AND QUANTITIES:

May 23, 1857 (representing the number struck to this date): 2,800,000
May 26, 1857: 350,000
May 27, 1857: 200,000
May 28, 1857: 100,000
May 29, 1857: 150,000
May 30, 1857: 200,000
May total: 3,800,000 Flying Eagle cents

Number of dies used through May: Using the average number of coins struck from typical obverse die in 1857 as 148,644, this means that to the end of May, over 25 obverse dies would have been used to strike 3,800,000 examples of the 1857 cent.

The Paquet punches (1857): Anthony C. Paquet, who later in the same year (on October 20, 1857) was appointed assistant engraver at the Mint (remaining there until 1864, but doing commission work until 1877),[2] cut some new letter punches at the request of Chief Engraver James B. Longacre and shipped them to Director James Ross Snowden on May 27, 1857.[3]

Assuming that Paquet shipped these punches from his shop in New York City, and they arrived at the Mint within a day or two, it probably would not have been until early June that cents could have been struck from dies employing the Paquet letters, if, indeed, they were used on the cent denomination at all.

The possibility has been raised that Flying Eagle cents struck before June 1857 were all of the Style of 1856 letters, and later pieces were from Paquet's font and were of the Style of 1857 letters. However, this most certainly was not the case. As noted, 25 or more different obverse dies must have been used to make 1857 Flying Eagle cents by the end of May 1857. As 118 obverse dies were made for Flying Eagle cents in 1857, this would suggest that if all coins made through May were of the Style of 1856 letters, about one coin in four or five in existence today would be of the Style of 1856 lettering. Thus, in the absence of any such high proportion of Style of 1856 cents known today, it seems that Paquet's letter fonts were used elsewhere, perhaps including for test purposes on other pattern denominations.[4] In summary, the Style of 1857 cents were introduced significantly before Paquet's punches arrived at the Mint.[5]

Market notes: Differences between old-style and new-style alphabets are minor at best, and at present they are not generally known except to Flying Eagle cent specialists, nor do the two major certification services (PCGS and NGC) attribute them. However, they are recognized by ANACS (as are a number of other specialized varieties of this year including clashed dies).

---

[1] From Mint records as located by R.W. Julian, letter, April 11, 1996.
[2] Paquet worked at the Mint as an assistant engraver from 1857 to 1864, but did commission work for the Mint before and after that time.
[3] Letter reproduced in *Flying Eagle and Indian Cent Die Varieties,* Larry R. Steve and Kevin J. Flynn, p. 41; the same reference gives details of the minor differences in the 1856-style and the revised letters. Perhaps the success of his letters was a factor in his later appointment to the Mint staff.
[4] A trial impression illustrating several of these fonts is listed as Pollock-3131.
[5] Thomas K. DeLorey, letter, April 30, 1996, suggested much of this line of reasoning and prompted the author to eliminate Paquet from consideration as the maker of the Style of 1857 letters obverse, at least with regard to the font made by Paquet in May 1857.

The market prices given below are guesses by the author, as no reliable data exist. Larry R. Steve and Kevin J. Flynn suggest that in various grades an 1857 with obverse Style of 1856 and with *repunched date* is worth about 2-1/2 to 3-1/2 times the price of a regular 1857. Larry R. Steve suggests that others should be valued at about 2.0 to 2.6 times the price of a regular 1857 cent.[1]

The "guess prices" below are mine and reflect a modest increment—less than the multiples just mentioned—for the Style of 1856 issue. Actual market prices may vary widely. A point to consider is that even if the Style of 1856 coins are several times rarer than the regular (Style of 1857) letters coins, if there are still hundreds of high-grade coins in numismatic hands, there are more than enough to satisfy *present* demand from specialists. Further, the present mind-set is that most people seeking this variety try to cherrypick one from stocks of "regular" coins.[2]

Whether 1857 Flying Eagle cents with the Style of 1856 letters will catch on with more people than dedicated specialists remains to be seen, but as the differences in the lettering are not very noticeable upon casual glance, I would not bet on it. If NGC and PCGS begin attributing these, and if the variety is listed in the *Guide Book* and other standard price guides, then demand will increase. Absent this, the variety will probably remain a cherrypicking possibility for a long time, but will not merit a strong market premium.

Market Prices

(1857 business strikes, obverse letters: Style of 1856):

YEAR	G-4	VG-8	F-12	VF-20	EF-40	AU-50
1996	$25.00	$35.00	$45.00	$75.00	$200.00	$300.00

YEAR	MS-60	MS-63	MS-64	MS-65		
1996	$350.00	$750.00	$1,300.00	$2,750.00		

1857 Varieties With Clashed Dies

Commentary concerning clashed die varieties: The 1857 clashed die varieties are enthusiastically collected, especially after publicity in the past two decades by Messrs. DeLorey, Fivaz, Flynn, Snow, Steve, and Pilliod.

One variety of 1857 Flying Eagle cent shows on its reverse the outline, in mirror image, of the center of an 1857 quarter dollar reverse die. You can see the eagle's head, neck, and shoulders (top of wings).

Another variety of 1857 Flying Eagle cent shows on its obverse the outline, in mirror image, of the center of an 1857 Liberty Seated half dollar obverse die. You can see parts of Miss Liberty's arm, the liberty cap pole, the drapery of her gown, and other features.

The third variety of 1857 Flying Eagle cent shows on its obverse the outline, in mirror image, of the center of an 1857 $20 Liberty Head gold piece obverse die. You can see nearly all of the left, right, and bottom outlines of Miss Liberty's portrait.

In my opinion these three different varieties are among the most interesting, most

---

[1] Letter, April 17, 1996.
[2] This is the opinion of several contributors to this book including the writer and Thomas K. DeLorey (letter, April 30, 1996).

spectacular in all of the American coinage series. Unlike what I have just said about the 1857 cents with Style of 1856 lettering, I *would* bet on these 1857 clashed die varieties increasing in popularity and, depending upon how many more are discovered, possibly increasing in value as well.

At present, these 1857 clashed die varieties are not recognized by the PCGS and NGC certification services, and the chances are excellent that some undetected examples are in "slabs," with even more to be found in unattributed collections and dealers' stocks. The cherrypicker has a good chance of scoring a home run here! ANACS does attribute clashed die varieties and has helped do much to help recognize these interesting issues.

Price listings are highly subjective for these, especially in higher grades, as very few exist.

Observable realities combined with some opinions and theories concerning these varieties:

1. Matched die sides: The clashes are in all three instances from the same side of the coins. The *obverse* die of a $20 is clashed with an 1857 cent *obverse* die, the *obverse* die of a 50¢ is clashed with an 1857 cent *obverse* die, and the *reverse* die of a 25¢ is clashed with the *reverse* die of an 1857 cent. The clash designs are oriented in the same direction as the cent design; *e.g.,* the Liberty Seated half dollar clash mark on the obverse of an 1857 cent is oriented in an upright position as is the eagle motif on the cent.

2. No bi-denominational coins struck: Because of the foregoing, it seems unlikely that the dies were ever used to strike finished bi-denominational coins in the form of mulings or fancy pieces combining a 25¢, 50¢, or $20 die with an 1857 cent die. Moreover, the dies are of such disparate sizes that no collar could be used to secure the coins during striking in a steam-powered regular production press.

In various instances in Mint history dies of two different denominations have been combined either as standard Mint practice (as in the use of common reverses to strike certain early dimes and $2.50 gold coins) or for pattern purposes (as in the 1853 nickel alloy cent utilizing a $2.50 gold obverse with a pattern cent reverse) or to create oddities for collectors (as in the combination of an 1867 pattern nickel five-cent obverse with an 1866 pattern nickel five-cent obverse; Judd-585, Pollock-646); in such instances the diameters have been more or less the same. However, there seems to have been no intent in 1857 to create, for example, an oddity with the obverse of an 1857 Flying Eagle cent and the reverse consisting of the obverse design of a Liberty Head $20 gold piece.

However, to cover all of the possibilities, I note that Thomas K. DeLorey has commented that if a screw press were used, there would have been no particular need for a collar, and it would have been easier to create oddities from different-sized dies.[1]

3. Special attention required: To create each of these clashed dies required special attention or involved a procedure other than the normal striking of coins.

The same production press used to strike small one-cent pieces was not normally used to strike large-diameter half dollars and $20 gold pieces, but during 1857 when there was a rush to coin millions of new small copper-nickel Flying Eagle cents in a short time, larger presses apparently were used. No doubt, special attention and effort was needed to fit these smaller coins into presses normally used for larger

---

[1] Letter, April 15, 1996.

coins and also—when cent coinage was finished—to reset them for larger denomination coinage.

As obverse is mated to obverse and reverse is mated to reverse in all three instances of the clashed-die 1857 Flying Eagle cents, and the denominations bear no relation to each other, the clash marks did not occur during the regular course of striking coins for circulation. Rather, the marks had to occur before such cent coinage activity.

As each clashed die has the elements of the anomalous denomination punched in lightly and fairly evenly (rather than deeper on one side and lighter on the other), the clashing was probably done when a die of a Flying Eagle cent was in a press at the same time a die for another denomination was there. The two dies, severely mismatched as to their diameters, were each more or less centered. Thus, the clashing was not done on a bench or anvil by hand-impressing an irrelevant die into the die of a Flying Eagle cent; had this been the case, the impressions would vary in their depth, centering, and sharpness in various portions. Rather, the clashing was done when both dies were mounted in a coining press.

4. Not made for numismatists: In 1857 there was absolutely no numismatic interest in coins with clashed dies. If anything, such pieces would have been considered defective and worth *less* than regular issues. Thus it seems unlikely that such pieces were made for numismatic sale or exchange. Moreover, if they had been, they would probably have been made in Proof finish and would have been recorded as having been included in collections in the nineteenth century. As it happened, pieces in existence today are mainly well-worn business strikes and in any event they were not recognized as bi-denominational clashed dies until within the past 20 years.

5. Chris Pilliod's study: In *The Numismatist,* April 1996, Chris Pilliod presented a study, "What Error Coins Can Teach Us About Die Settings." Pilliod, whose credentials in the field of die varieties and attribution are among the finest in numismatics, studied "cud" breaks on various denominations of coins, a "cud" being a blob-like raised section of metal, usually at the rim of a coin, caused when a piece of the die breaks and falls away. As you will see, this has relevance to the 1857 clashed-die cent situation.

If a die in the top or "hammer" position in the press develops a break at the rim, the broken die element will usually fall away, due to gravitational effects. Thus, coins will develop a "cud" (a.k.a. "full cud") along the rim.

If a die in the bottom or "stake" (a.k.a. "anvil") position in the press develops a break at the rim, the broken die element may remain in place, as it is supported from underneath and, further, may be partly restricted by the closed "collar" used to form the outside edge. The collar typically rests against the bottom die. Coins struck from a reverse die with a rim break may still show the broken part of the die in place, and the break will be in the form of a crack, rather than a cud. Chris Pilliod calls these "retained cuds," as the broken die part is retained with the rest of the die.

To summarize the foregoing, if the obverse die of, for example, an *Indian* cent is in the top or hammer die position and the reverse is in the anvil position, if rim breaks develop, these will typically be found on the obverse of an Indian cent and only rarely on the reverse.

In his survey of cuds on *Flying Eagle* cents in numismatic collections, Chris Pilliod found 29 different instances in which full cuds were on the reverse (and no retained cuds) and only one instance with a full cud on the obverse (and five retained cuds). Thus, it can be assumed that for most *Flying Eagle* cents the reverse die was the hammer die and was in the top of the press (for *Indian* cents, the obverse die was the hammer die). The obverse die of the *Flying Eagle* cent was in the anvil position (for the *Indian* cent, the reverse die was in the anvil position).

Here is the significant part:[1]

Chris Pilliod has found that for the denominations clashed with Flying Eagle cent dies, the die positions in the press were as follows:

Liberty Seated quarter dollar of the 1857 era: Obverse in hammer or upper position; reverse in anvil or bottom position.

Liberty Seated half dollar of the 1857 era: Obverse in hammer position; reverse in anvil or bottom position.

Liberty Head $20 gold coin of the 1857 era: Obverse in hammer position; reverse in anvil or bottom position.

6. R.W. Julian's suggestion: Now to the heart of the matter. R.W. Julian has advanced this suggestion:[2]

> It is my guess that these clashed dies had been used as set-up dies for gold and silver coinage. Before a coinage run, dies were adjusted on the press for the best strike and long die life. If too close together, the dies tended to break more quickly, and if too far apart the result was a soft strike.

While I do not necessarily believe that cent dies on their own were used to help set up presses—although, of course, this is a possibility if there were extra cent dies on hand—the preceding does agree with my belief that the clash marks were made during the set-up process.

7. Conclusions: Reiterating the statement made under No. 1 above: The clashes are in all three instances from the same side of the coins. The *obverse* die of a $20 is clashed with an 1857 cent *obverse* die, the *obverse* die of a 50¢ is clashed with an 1857 cent *obverse* die, and the *reverse* die of a 25¢ is clashed with the *reverse* die of an 1857 cent.

Further, when dies are placed into a coining press, the top die is fixed in place, while by means of a chuck or tightening device, the bottom die is adjusted up or down slightly to fit properly with the collar and to optimize striking efficiency. Thus, it seems that these clashed-die pieces were being made when a press was being changed over to accommodate a new denomination of the anvil or *bottom* die.

As presses were being changed from one denomination to another, this also involved fitting new collars on the bottom dies, a further reason for needing adjustments beyond what might have been needed if dies of the same denomination had been replaced.

7a: Scenario No. 1: It is 1857, and a coining press has been used recently to strike $20 gold pieces. A $20 obverse die is in the hammer position and a $20 reverse die is in the anvil position. It is desired to strike Flying Eagle 1¢ pieces using this press, to fill the great demand for this new coin. The public was literally starved for them, and there were shortages for a long time after the first release of the new Flying Eagle cents on May 25, 1857.

The $20 reverse die in the anvil position is removed and replaced with a 1¢ Flying Eagle obverse die. With the newly-fitted 1¢ obverse die in place in the anvil, opposite the $20 obverse still in place in the hammer position, the press is run through a

---

[1] Commentary by QDB using Chris Pilliod's information.
[2] Letter, April 7, 1996.

cycle, and the $20 obverse die in the hammer position strikes the 1¢ obverse die in the anvil position. Clash marks occur on both obverse dies.

The clashed $20 obverse die is removed from the press, put in storage, and a new reverse die for a 1¢ piece is put in the hammer die position. Cents are struck, each of which shows the clash mark of a $20 on its obverse. Whether $20 pieces were ever struck from the now-damaged obverse $20 die is not known; none have been identified thus far by numismatists.

7b: Scenario No. 2: It is 1857, and a coining press has been used recently to strike Liberty Seated 50¢ pieces. A 50¢ obverse die is in the hammer position and a 50¢ reverse die is in the anvil position. It is desired to strike Flying Eagle 1¢ pieces using this press, again to fill the demand for this new denomination.

The 50¢ reverse die in the anvil position is removed and replaced with a 1¢ Flying Eagle obverse die. With the newly-fitted 1¢ obverse die in place in the anvil, opposite the 50¢ obverse still in place in the hammer position, the press is run through a cycle, and the 50¢ obverse die in the hammer position strikes the 1¢ obverse die in the anvil position. Clash marks occur on both obverse dies.

The clashed 50¢ obverse die is removed from the press, put in storage, and a new reverse die for a 1¢ piece is put in the hammer die position. Cents are struck, each of which shows the clash mark of a 50¢ on its obverse. Whether 1857 half dollars were ever struck from the now-damaged obverse 50¢ die is not known; none have been identified thus far by numismatists.

Mint records indicate that half dollars in 1857 were first delivered on June 25, 1857 (50,000 coins) and that deliveries occurred at various times each month through December 29, except for September. Thus, this indicates that the above scenario did not occur before the third week in June, but could have happened any time after then.[1]

7c: Scenario No. 3: It is later in 1857, and a coining press has been used recently to strike 1857 Flying Eagle 1¢ pieces. Now, either the demand for cents has eased, or the demand for 25¢ pieces has taken precedence.

A 1¢ reverse die is in the hammer position and a 1¢ Flying Eagle obverse die is in the anvil position. It is desired to strike Liberty Seated 25¢ pieces using this press.

The 1¢ Flying Eagle obverse die in the anvil position is removed and replaced with a 25¢ reverse die. With the newly-fitted 25¢ reverse die in place in the anvil, opposite the 1¢ reverse still in place in the hammer position, the press is run through a cycle, and the 1¢ reverse die in the hammer position strikes the 25¢ reverse die in the anvil position. Clash marks occur on both reverse dies.

The clashed 1¢ reverse die is removed from the press, put in storage,[2] and a new obverse die for a 25¢ piece is put in the hammer die position. Liberty Seated 25¢ pieces are struck, each of which shows the clash mark of a 1¢ on its reverse. Later, the clashed 1¢ wreath reverse die is combined with a 1¢ Flying Eagle obverse, and Flying Eagle cents are struck showing 25¢ clash marks on the reverse; made in the ordinary manner.

Scenario 7c further suggests that there should be some 1857 Flying Eagle cents with the aforementioned reverse die *before* it received its clash marks, as it was in

---

[1] Delivery dates of 1857 half dollars are detailed in "Philadelphia Coinage Statistics, 1853-1873, Half Dollars," by R.W. Julian, *Numismatic Scrapbook Magazine,* October 1966.

[2] Thus there is the possibility, however remote, that this die could have been used in 1858 in addition to in 1857.

the press prior to the quarters being struck, and must have been used for coinage.[1]

Mint records indicate that quarter dollars in 1857 were first delivered on March 5, 1857 (80,000 coins) and that deliveries occurred at various times each month through December 31.[2] Thus, these figures seem to be of no help in pinpointing a date for the above scenario.

8. Dies used for striking coins: From the foregoing it seems that such clash marks were made in the course of Mint business in the Coining Department. After the die clashes occurred, the Flying Eagle cent dies were routinely used by the Coining Department to turn out a large number of regular business strike cents on a normal production basis. The clashed 25¢ reverse die was later mated with an 1857 25¢ obverse die to create regular Liberty Seated quarters, a specimen of which was identified in 1977.

It could be that the clashed 50¢ obverse die was likewise mated with an 1857 50¢ reverse to make half dollars. Although numismatists have not yet located either an 1857 half dollar or an 1857 $20 with clash marks of a Flying Eagle cent, possibly some of both were produced, although the following should be kept in mind:

Concerning the 1857 $20 with clash marks of the obverse of an 1857 Flying Eagle cent, Larry R. Steve commented:[3] "I question whether any 1857 double eagles were made. Such a clash mark on the $20 would appear as the mirror image of ERICA under Miss Liberty's nose and would be clearly visible—and thus more likely to be removed or reworked before being used for coinage."

Further from Larry R. Steve, this in my opinion being a pivotal argument:

> With the $20 pair of dies presumably in the press at the same time, before the die changeover for the Flying Eagle cent coinage, this would seem to suggest that the production run of $20 pieces had ended—thus freeing up the press—and raises the possibility, in addition to the foregoing comment about die damage, that no further production run of $20 ever took place—hence no clashed $20 pieces were struck. The same argument can be used for the 1857 half dollar coinage from a clashed obverse die. The reverse order of which pair of dies was first in the press, prior to the changeover, for the 25¢ clash, would also explain two things:
>
> 1. Why the clashing shows on the reverse, and
> 2. Why there exist Liberty Seated quarter dollars showing clash marks from the cent.

9. Time of striking: As the clashed die 1857 cents do not have the obverse letters Style of 1856, they were not among the very first 1857 Flying Eagle cents produced in April 1857, but were made after then, with the half dollar being made after the third week of June, for reasons given above. Possibly the 1857 cent with the 25¢ clash marks on the reverse was the last of the three varieties made, also for reasons given above.

10. Summary: The three varieties of clashed-die 1857 Flying Eagle cents were made from dies injured during the die set-up process. The further coinage of cents from the dies was done in the normal course of business, and the resultant pieces were routinely put into circulation.

---

[1] Suggestion of Larry R. Steve, letter, April 16, 1996.
[2] Delivery dates of 1857 quarters are detailed in "Philadelphia Coinage Statistics, 1853-1873, Quarter Dollars," by R.W. Julian, *Numismatic Scrapbook Magazine,* June 1965.
[3] Letter, April 16, 1996, here paraphrased.

The quantities made of each of these is not known today. Inasmuch as 118 business strike obverse dies were made for 1857 cents, the chances of finding one of the cents with the 50¢ or $20 obverse clash mark may be about 1 in 118 in a group of unsorted 1857 Flying Eagle cents.

As there were 129 *reverse* dies made for business strike 1857 cents, the chances of finding a cent with the 25¢ clash mark on the reverse may be 1 in 129, but is probably significantly less as this reverse die seems to have been used to make coins prior to being clashed; thus impressions from the clashed die are only a part of this die's life.

However, if the clash marks were made after the dies had seen some coinage use, many fewer coins may have been produced during what life remained in the dies. In practice, the 1857 with 50¢ clash on the obverse is the most plentiful and by a significant margin, the 1857 with 25¢ clash on the reverse is second most plentiful, and the 1857 with $20 clash on the obverse is the rarest. Thus, the original mintage quantities for each die, after it acquired clash marks, was probably far below average for the 25¢ and $20 clash mark varieties.

For further contemplation: See notes under 1868 (in particular for Chris Pilliod's commentary), 1870, and 1899 for other bi-denominational clashes with Indian cent dies.

Are there any other bi-denominational clash varieties among 1857 cents besides the 25¢, 50¢, and $20 discussed here? Time will tell.

Commentary on 1857 clashed die coins by Thomas K. DeLorey; an alternative theory:[1]

Some notes on the "Midnight Minter":

> After I first identified the 1857 Flying Eagle cent with clash marks on the obverse die from the obverse die for a Liberty Seated half dollar in 1977, I attributed the probable cause of the clash marks to the nocturnal playtime of the Mint's night watchman, Theodore Eckfeldt, who was known to have made and sold several plain-edged 1804 silver dollars c.1858. I suspect that Eckfeldt actually did make our hypothetical cent/quarter, cent/half and cent/double eagle mules in 1857, since several of the dies were later used for normal business strikes, but that the pieces never became known in the hobby as he may not yet have worked up the nerve to attempt to sell them. Theoretically, they could be considered as practice pieces for the Class II 1804 silver dollars, though I doubt if he contemplated that issue in 1857.

> My attribution of these pieces to Eckfeldt is based upon the writings in *The Fantastic 1804 Dollar* by Eric P. Newman and Ken Bressett, and upon those in *The U.S. Mint and Coinage* and *Counterfeit, Mis-struck and Unofficial U.S. Coins* by Don Taxay. I believe that the term "Midnight Minter" was Breen's,[2] and others have applied it to Eckfeldt.

---

[1] Letter, April 16, 1996.

[2] QDB note: The following commentary from Richard Snow (letter, April 10, 1996) explains the origin of the term: "I was the one who coined the term. I told Walter Breen about it at the Seattle ANA convention in 1990. He loved it and asked if he could use it. I said OK. I don't really care about this type of trivia, but I feel the need to set the record straight. While doing research at the National Archives, I found that a Frederick Eckfeldt was a Mint employee during the time in question. He was in the lowest paying position. I felt that Theodore, who was not a Mint employee, but was associated with peddling rarities around Philadelphia, was involved (if in fact there was any 'Midnight Minting' going on). Perhaps one was the outside man and one was the inside man. Perhaps George Eckfeldt was involved too. Pete Smith has furnished me with the Eckfeldt family tree. Since this is all conjecture, I see why you took the approach you did. 'Just the facts, ma'am,' as Sgt. Friday used to say."

1857 CENT WITH 25¢ DIE CLASH ON REVERSE. The head and shoulders of the eagle, incuse and in mirror-image, from the Liberty Seated quarter reverse can be seen above the word ONE. For comparison purposes the reverse of an 1857 quarter dollar is shown as well. (Larry R. Steve Collection)

I have no evidence that Eckfeldt ever actually struck these hypothetical dual-denomination mules in 1857. There are several similar mules in more practical sizes known for the 1866-1870 era, when Eckfeldt still worked at the Mint, and many restrikes are known to have been made, but I cannot say if those were made by Eckfeldt either.

My attribution of these hypothetical 1857 pieces to him is just an intuitive hunch, based upon the accepted knowledge that he crudely produced several 1804 dollars circa 1858 without knowing (or seeming to care) how to apply edge lettering to the pieces. The fact that his father, George Eckfeldt, was the foreman of the Engraving Department in the late 1850s with keys to the die vault may explain how Theodore Eckfeldt obtained access to dies to play with.

All of this is conjecture. However, it is more plausible to me than other conjecture that the dies were damaged in a bizarre die set up procedure involving two mismatched dies not intended to be used together.... There was no reason to test the set up of one die without having the intended opposite die also in the press, as the spacing of the dies would change when the correct opposite die was put in the press.

Descriptions and market commentaries concerning clashed die varieties: 1857 Flying Eagle Cent. Reverse from 25¢ clashed die. Snow-8. Fivaz-Stanton 1¢-005. FND-002.

Average number of coins struck from typical reverse die in 1857: 135,271 (simply a rough guide to the possibility).[1] However, as this reverse die was clashed after it had already been used to strike a number of coins, the number of cents with clash marks made from this die must have been less than the average.

The reverse Flying Eagle cent die with its "agricultural" wreath motif and ONE CENT inscription came into forced contact with the center of a die used to coin the reverse of a Liberty Seated quarter dollar.

The impression from the quarter dollar die is slightly deeper at the top part of the reverse (showing the eagle's head and shoulders) than at the bottom part. All clash marks are within the 1¢ wreath, and none are on the outside. On the left, opposite O in ONE, a clash mark emerges from the wreath, goes through a corn ear leaf, continues upward through tips of wreath elements, passes below the wreath "bud" or tip at top left (called a wheat tip by Breen, but is it the end of an ear of corn?), and enters the bud at top right just below its tip. This represents the shoulder, top of neck, and top of head of the eagle on the reverse of the Liberty Seated 25¢. Another part of the clash mark emerges from wreath on the upper inside right, curves irregularly to the left and downward through the left serif tip of the top right of N, through the upright of the right side of N, curves right to E, continues through E at top area where middle serif of E joins upright of E, extends upward through top arm of E, curves gracefully upward and to the right, then downward to the tip of a corn ear leaf. This represents the bottom of the eagle's head, eagle's neck, and shoulder. These clashes are very distinct. Less distinct are vestiges of shield stripes among the letters C and E and extending to the right of N; also parts of the eagle's lower wing outline and leg below the right of N and extending to the lower left of T.

The clash mark design is oriented in the same direction as the cent reverse design.

Probably somewhere between 15 and 20 are known, but as is the case with oth-

---

[1] Calculated from the figure of 130 reverse dies used in 1857 (see Appendix I) minus one die for Proofs, net 129 reverse dies, divided into the business strike mintage of 17,450.000.

ers in the Snow-7, Snow-8, and Snow-9 trio, I suspect that more await identification. And yet, Thomas K. DeLorey, one of America's best known specialists, has been looking for one since 1977 without success.[1]

Related to the history of this piece is this commentary by Richard Snow:[2] "In 1977 a keen-eyed Jesse Perrotta of New Jersey found an 1857 *quarter* with strange clash marks. He sent the coin to Thomas K. DeLorey, who at the time was editor of "Collectors' Clearinghouse" for *Coin World.* Tom had earlier seen strange clash marks on 1857 coins and had filed the information for future use. The clash marks turned out to match exactly the reverse design of the 1857 Flying Eagle cent!"

In 1991 in his book, *The Comprehensive Encyclopedia of United States Liberty Seated Quarters,* Larry Briggs described the *quarter dollar* (not cent) reverse: "Reverse F. Reverse struck/clashed from reverse of Flying Eagle cent! [Design] seen within shield, also above both wings, and below eagle's left wing!" The same writer called it "one true rarity from this year." By May 1996 Briggs knew of two Mint State and six or seven circulated examples.[3]

In 1986 Bill Fivaz found the related 1857 Flying Eagle cent with quarter-dollar clash marks and described it in *Rare Coin Review* No. 62 (winter 1986). In January 1996, Fivaz, who had earlier purchased the Perrotta quarter and put it into a holder with an MS-64 or finer 1857 Flying Eagle cent with the 25¢ clashed die, sold it, and soon thereafter the set was resold for $7,500.[4]

Market commentary: In 1996 in "How Many Are There, Anyway?" a column in *Longacre's Ledger,* Jerry Wysong recorded the existence of 13 pieces reported to him in the following grades: G-VG 1, Fine 1, VF 3, EF 2, AU 2, MS-60 to 62 1, MS-63 1, and MS-64 1.[5]

As is the case with the other clashed die varieties of this year, market values are highly subjective as there have been relatively few transactions. Listings of these varieties are relatively new on the numismatic scene, many numismatists still do not know about them, and PCGS and NGC (the two leading grading services) do not certify them (but ANACS does). Some particularly dedicated specialists may prefer to wait to cherrypick these varieties from among regular 1857 cents—although, of course, such an opportunity may never occur.

Per contra, probably the publicity given to these varieties in various specialized books including this one will broaden the circle of potential buyers, resulting in a greater demand and, consequently, higher prices in the future.

Market Prices (1857 business strikes, 25¢ clashed die):

YEAR	F-12	VF-20	EF-40	AU-50	
1996	$150.00	$250.00	$450.00	$600.00	

YEAR	MS-60	MS-63	MS-64	MS-65	
1996	$1,200.00	$2,800.00	$4,000.00	$5,250.00	

---

[1] Letter, April 15, 1996;

[2] "The Midnight Minter," *Longacre's Ledger,* January 1991.

[3] Conversation, May 8, 1996, in the author's office.

[4] Letter, April 11, 1996; separately, Richard Snow wrote, April 10, 1996, that he was the seller, and that the cent was valued at $5,000 in the transaction.

[5] Grades were as submitted by his correspondents; these were not graded by the same individual or service.

Another market view: The "Variety Price Guide" feature of *Cherrypickers' News,* May 1996, gave these suggestions for prices: Fine: $75, VF $150, EF $250, AU $400, MS-60 $575, MS-63 $1,250.

1857 Flying Eagle cent. Obverse from 50¢ clashed die. Snow-9. Fivaz-Stanton 1¢-003. FND-003.

Average number of coins struck from typical obverse die in 1857: 148,644 (simply a rough guide to the possibility).

Discovered as a curiosity by Bill Fivaz in 1977 and sent to Thomas K. DeLorey, who attributed the clash mark matrix.[1] Earlier (1921) it was unknowingly reported by Commodore W.C. Eaton.

The obverse Flying Eagle cent die came into forced contact with a die used to coin the obverse of a Liberty Seated half dollar.

This clash is very prominent on the obverse of the Flying Eagle cent. The dies seem to have had absolutely parallel faces when clashing, thus yielding bold impressions. A clash mark extends from the left rim of the cent, upward and diagonally to the right, through the top curved part of the eagle's beak, across the field, to the underside of the wing. A clash mark emerges from the top of the same wing, slightly left of the intersection with the right-side wing, and curves to the left in the direction toward ST, but fades before reaching those letters. The preceding features are part of the leg and far side of Miss Liberty's upraised arm on the 50¢. In the field below TA is a elongated U-shaped clash, combining with another U-shaped clash to its right, the latter extending upward through the second T of STATES and the upper left of the E. This represents part of Miss Liberty's arm, neck, and the liberty cap pole. On the right side of the cent is an especially prominent clash line beginning at the rim above M, continuing downward through the top right of E and progressing deeper into the letters RICA, touching the top tip of the eagle's tail, then turning sharply right for a short distance to exit to the rim, this representing an impression of Miss Liberty's lowered arm. Additional clash marks, lighter in definition, abound in the field above and below the eagle's tail and are Miss Liberty's skirt lines.

The clash mark design is oriented in the same direction as the cent obverse design.

Chris Pilliod commented: "The 1857 Flying Eagle cent clashed with the 50¢ die is found with such regularity in all grades that I am convinced that the clashing occurred prior to any production use. I find this variety to be as common as any other specific 1857 variety I search for, and probably more common."

If the 1857 cent with the 50¢ clash saw an average die use for an 1857 cent, then the production of this issue should have been around 148,644 coins (the mathematical average). By definition, it should be about as available as any other specific variety with average coinage.

Market commentary: Probably about 30 to 60 are known including a few Mint State specimens.[2] This seems to be the most available of the Snow-7, Snow-8, and Snow-9 trio, especially in higher grades.

The market values given below are subjective as there have been very few open market transactions. In 1996 in "How Many Are There, Anyway?" a column in *Longacre's Ledger,* Jerry Wysong recorded the existence of 18 pieces reported to him

---

[1] Bill Fivaz, letter, March 30, 1996; also described in "The Midnight Minter," Richard Snow, *Longacre's Ledger,* January 1991.
[2] Thomas K. DeLorey, letter, April 15, 1996; other reports.

1857 CENT WITH 50¢ DIE CLASH ON OBVERSE. The clash marks between STA and the eagle are incuse mirror-image impressions of Miss Liberty's arm and the liberty cap pole. For comparison purposes the obverse of an 1857 half dollar is shown as well. (Larry R. Steve Collection)

in the following grades: G-VG 4, Fine 2, VF 5, AU 1, MS-60 to 62 1, MS-63 1, MS-64 2, MS-65 1, and MS-66 1. The MS-66 was reported by Richard Snow, was PCGS-certified, and sold by him for $5,750.[1]

Market Prices (1857 business strikes, 50¢ clashed die):

YEAR	F-12	VF-20	EF-40	AU-50		
1996	$120.00	$190.00	$300.00	$400.00		

YEAR	MS-60	MS-63	MS-64	MS-65		
1996	$1,000.00	$1,700.00	$2,500.00	$4,000.00		

Another market view: The "Variety Price Guide" feature of *Cherrypickers' News,* May 1996, gave these suggestions for prices: Fine: $45, VF $100, EF $175, AU $275, MS-60 $450, MS-63 $900, MS-65 $3,500.

1857 Flying Eagle cent. Obverse from $20 clashed die. Snow-7. Fivaz-Stanton 1¢-004. FND-001.

Average number of coins struck from typical obverse die in 1857: 148,644 (but probably fewer than the average were made, as this variety is rarer).

The obverse Flying Eagle cent die came into forced contact with a die used to coin the obverse of a Liberty Head $20 gold piece. This $20 die impressed a positive or coin-like image on the cent die, which created a mirror image (backward) outline on Flying Eagle cents struck from this die.

On the left obverse of the Flying Eagle cent an irregular clash mark begins at the lower left rim and continues upward to the underside of the eagle's head where the lower beak meets the neck feathers; a clash mark exits the top of the beak in front of the nostril and continues through the lower right of U and the upper left of N to the border. This represents the outline of the back of Miss Liberty's hair and hair bun on the $20 die. On the right side of the Flying Eagle cent an irregular clash mark begins at the rim above F and continues irregularly through AME, below RI, grazing the lower part of CA, to the top of the tail. This represents the lower part of the forehead, the nose, the lips, and the chin of Miss Liberty on the $20 die. From the eagle's claw a clash mark curves slightly right and downward to the rim, this representing an outline of Miss Liberty's neck from the $20 die. The facial features of Miss Liberty are dramatic and unequivocal, once you spend a few moments adjusting the alignment of the coin. Parts of the outline of Miss Liberty's neck truncation including a faint J.B.L. (for Longacre's initials) from the $20 die are seen at the bottoms of the 185 numerals of the date.

The clash mark design is oriented in the same direction as the cent obverse design.

This seems to be the rarest issue of the Snow-7, 8, and 9 trio. Most have been found by inspecting "regular" 1857 Flying Eagle cents. This variety is believed to have been discovered circa 1986 by David McCann, who owned a Fine to VF coin.[2] Earlier (1912) unknowingly reported by F.J. Carpenter, although this is not certain (see later commentary). Some have the reverse die rotated slightly to the right of its normal position.[3] Later, the right side of the obverse die breaks away to create a "cud."[4]

---

[1] Letter, April 10, 1996.
[2] Comment by Larry R. Steve in *Longacre's Ledger,* April 1991, p. 8.
[3] *E.g.,* Larry R. Steve Collection specimen.
[4] Specimen owned by Michael C. Ellis.

Market commentary: It is believed that about 15 to 25 specimens are known, with others probably waiting to be identified. This is the most desired of the three clash mark varieties of 1857.

The market values given are highly speculative as there have been very few open market transactions. In 1996 in "How Many Are There, Anyway?" a column in *Longacre's Ledger,* Jerry Wysong recorded the existence of 12 pieces reported to him in the following grades: G-VG 4, Fine 1, VF 5, EF 1, and AU 1. No Mint State coins were noted.

Market Prices (1857 business strikes, $20 clashed die):

YEAR	F-12	VF-20	EF-40	AU-50		
1996	$500.00	$750.00	$1,250.00	$2,500.00		

Another market view: The "Variety Price Guide" feature of *Cherrypickers' News,* May 1996, gave these suggestions for prices: Fine: $375, VF $500, EF $1,000, AU $2,000.

Proof 1857 Cents (regular dies only):

Proof mintage: Mintage: 50 to 100 estimated.

Proof commentary: Most 1857 Flying Eagle cents offered as "Proof" are not. While this is true today (the problem has been diminished sharply by the certification services, however, but these services still have misattributed some prooflike business strikes), it was much more common years ago. Thus, historical prices for 1857-dated Proofs are lower for the 1938, 1944, and 1965 citations below because of business strikes being offered as Proofs. A sharp differential between various levels within the Proof category did not begin in a widespread way until the late 1980s.

True Proofs are very rare, more so than generally realized. Walter Breen, *Encyclopedia of Proof Coins,* p. 104, states most were made in May 1857 from a die with file marks over NI of UNITED, one file mark joining left upright of I to rim. All known 1857 Proofs are of the Style of 1857 lettering. These were probably released to collectors on or after May 25, 1857 (the day that business strikes were first distributed to an eager public).

Reverse with leaf on left at C of CENT high.

It may be the case that fewer than 20 to 30 *true* Proofs are known of this date, and estimates range as low as 10 to 20.

Description of a particular Proof-65 specimen examined by the author:[1] This example exhibits a deep mirror Proof surface on the obverse, with Proof areas within the mouth of the eagle and above the eagle's leg. 1 in date over space between dentils; bottom of 7 over dentil. Reverse is an unquestioned Proof, but from dies not as highly polished as the obverse.

It seems that more information concerning the die characteristics of 1857 Proof Flying Eagle cents is needed. This can only be done by modern examination by specialists of coins that are *definitely* Proof and which are personally examined by *Flying Eagle cent experts* (not by anyone not familiar with technical differences). Old auction catalogue illustrations may include prooflike business strikes. Portions of two famous old-time collections still in private hands as of May 1996 were examined

---

[1] Jay Parrino, owner. Certified as PCGS 2040.65/9777587. Examined May 1, 1996.

1857 CENT WITH $20 DIE CLASH ON OBVERSE. Miss Liberty's neck is seen below the eagle's beak, the front of her face is among the letters of UNITED, the back of her head is seem at AMERICA, and the back of her neck extends from the eagle's talons downward to the border. All features are incuse and in mirror image. For comparison purposes the obverse of an 1857 $20 double eagle is shown as well. (Larry R. Steve Collection)

by the author, and the "Proof" 1857 Flying Eagle cents in each were business strikes that had been carefully polished in the fields by some unscrupulous person decades ago, then retoned. The appearance of each coin was quite deceptive.

In 1857 there was a widespread interest in the new cent, and one would think that numismatists would have desired Proofs, but, apparently, few Proofs were made. Perhaps the popularity of the rare 1856 date eclipsed that of the "ordinary" 1857 and satisfied the need for one coin to illustrate the design. This scenario is all the more likely when it is realized that in early 1857, "rare" cents dated 1856 were still being made.

Market price listings for Proofs are apt to vary dramatically, and quality is also widely variable. In a 1996 issue the *Coin Dealer Newsletter* posted a bid price of $16,500 for a Proof-65 and an ask price of $19,000, and, perhaps a glittering gem would sell in those ranges or even more. However, I doubt if most coins classified as Proof-65 would achieve this mark as most are not of high aesthetic appeal and, as stated, may not be Proofs at all. Further, the true rarity of the 1857 Flying Eagle cent is generally unknown to casual readers of popular texts such as the *Guide Book* and *Coin Dealer Newsletter.*

Market Prices (1857 Proofs)

YEAR	PR-60	PR-63	PR-64	PR-65		
1938	$15.00	$15.00	$15.00	$17.00		
1944	25.00	25.00	25.00	27.00		
1965	1,500.00	1,600.00	1,700.00	1,850.00		
1996	1,250.00	4,000.00	6,500.00	22,000.00		

Notes

Collecting commentary: Cents of the year 1857 offer a rich playground for variety exploration and research, what with the obverse letter styles of 1856 and 1857 and three varieties of clashed dies for starters. What was considered a rather ordinary date years ago has emerged as a focal point of interest for specialists today.

Cent types of 1857: Large copper cents were also struck in this year and are the scarcest date of the decade. The 72-grain copper-nickel Flying Eagle cent was authorized under the Act of February 21, 1857. Distribution began on May 25, but it was a long time until public demand was filled.

Reverse varieties: In his *Complete Encyclopedia* Walter Breen notes that 1857 Flying Eagle cent reverses are of at least two hub types (described in the present text under *1858,* below). These have not been widely studied. If any "Low Leaf" pieces in fact do exist among 1857 cents, they are very rare. All seen by the author (who examined hundreds of photographs in the Bowers and Merena Galleries photo files) have the reverse with the leaf extending up ("High Leaf") to the left of the C in CENT; none was seen with the "Low Leaf." It is significant to mention that Commodore W.C. Eaton (see below) did not find a Low Leaf 1857 cent either. Richard Snow believes this variety to be non-existent.[1]

---

[1] Letter, April 10, 1996.

An early observer of varieties (from *The Numismatist,* February 1912):

Our attention has been drawn by F.J. Carpenter of Mt. Vernon, N.Y. to two varieties of the 1857 [Flying Eagle] cent. Mr. Carpenter writes:

"Will you kindly advise me whether the two 1857 eagle cents, which I enclose, are included in the known varieties of these cents, as I have never seen only the two specimens which I enclose. You will note one has an ear or tongue or tail to the 'U' in the word 'UNITED' [this may have been an early description of what is known today as the obverse clashed with a $20 die, but the description is not complete enough to be sure—QDB], and in the other the 'N' and 'E' of 'ONE' seem to be joined. If these are genuine varieties in your judgment, should they not be added to the list?"

Will not some reader of *The Numismatist,* who has made a special study of the die varieties, kindly reply to Mr. Carpenter. The tongue seems to indicate a break or defect in the die.

The indefatigable Commodore Eaton: Commodore W.C. Eaton of the U.S. Navy took a fancy to minute die varieties of United States cents, and after Lincoln cents were released in 1909 he studied variations of mintmark placement. In 1916, 1920, and 1921 in *The Numismatist* he published a trilogy of articles, "The Eagle Cents of 1858" (see Bibliography and also information under the 1858 listing below). In May 1921 another article appeared under his name, "The Eagle Cents of 1857." To create these studies of 1857 and 1858 cents, Eaton and a collector friend, F.R. Alvord (today best remembered for his fantastic collection of half cents sold at auction by S. Hudson Chapman in June 1924), looked through several thousand Uncirculated cents of these two dates. These were obtained simply enough: by writing to dealers and asking them to forward their stocks. Apparently, Eaton purchased a few pieces considered to be of interest and returned the others after inspecting them. Alvord did most if not all of the research on the 1857 cents, and Eaton compiled the results.

Among 1857 Flying Eagle cents the Eaton-Alvord duo identified 46 distinct die varieties and combinations, the typical issue being identified by one or more characteristics such as a doubling of the date or letters or a die break. Further, 1857 cents were divided into these six groups:

Group 1, coin nos. 1-24: A and M (in AMERICA) joined. Thick high leaf to left of C on reverse. Open 5 in date (ball not touching the part of the numeral above it). Eaton found 24 varieties in this group. Eaton's No. 18 was described as: "Crack on reverse from right bloom to left of wreath; another from small leaf on right through EN and back to wreath above." This may be what we know today as the 1857 cent reverse clashed with a Liberty Seated quarter reverse die.

Group 2, coin nos. 25-35: AM joined; thick high leaf; figure 5 closed. Eaton found 11 in this group. Eaton's No. 30 was described as: "Heavy crack from border over M down through ERICA to tail and then to border; another from middle of wing down through beak to border; suction marks on obverse showing offsets from portions of reverse." This seems to be what we know today as the 1857 cent obverse clashed with a Liberty Seated half dollar reverse die.

Group 3, coin no. 36: Re-engraved date; thick high leaf; AM joined. Eaton found just one.

Group 4, coin nos. 37-43: Thin high leaf; AM joined; open 5. Eaton found seven varieties.

Group 5, coin nos. 44-46: Legend re-engraved as well as date; A and M not joined; AMERICA poorly engraved or punched; A leans too far to the left; wider space between M and E than on previous types; R too high, being above foot of I; I defective at top; open 5; thick high leaf. Eaton found two. One had the "date recut." The other had "date outlined at right; bottoms of letters of UNITED outlined; crack from U through beak to border." Most probably, Eaton's Group 5 coins are what numismatists know today as the 1857 cents with 1856-style obverse letters.

Group 6, coin no. 46: Same as Group 5, but with 5 in date closed. Eaton found just one, it having "crack from U through beak to border." Presumably, this was also an 1857 cent with 1856-style obverse letters.

Denouement to Eaton's research: If the letters on a working die are doubled, this was done when the working die was made from the working hub. At that time the date was not yet in the die. When the date was separately punched later, it probably would not have been doubled. Most likely the coins in Eaton's groups 5 and 6 exhibit what today is called "machine doubling," due to die chatter during the striking process, not due to any characteristics of the dies themselves. Machine doubling probably also accounted for certain other varieties of 1857 and 1858 Flying Eagle cents described by Eaton.

What Commodore Eaton considered separate die varieties of 1857 and also 1858 (which date he studied even more extensively) were in many cases simply artifacts of the coining process, not varieties caused by distinctively different dies.[1]

Eaton Collection sold in 1992-1993: Commodore Eaton's study set of 1857 and 1858 Flying Eagle cent varieties was sold intact to Philadelphia collector Floyd Starr, who was the successful bidder on Lot 547 in Henry Chapman's May 7, 1929 sale, comprising 115 coins. Most of these coins, 114 in all, remained intact and were sold by Stack's in October 1992 and January 1993 as part of the Floyd Starr estate. Most Flying Eagle cent variations proved to be from machine doubling or displayed differences that modern (1990s era) numismatists would not consider to be "die varieties." However, prices were strong, and there were a number of very important pieces sold including these:

1857 Flying Eagle cent graded by Richard Snow as MS-60, was described as "obverse with large cracks from clashed dies," and later identified by Snow as the variety with 50¢ die clash obverse. (Lot 101)

1857 Flying Eagle cents, group of four, one of which was later identified by Richard Snow as being with a 25¢ clashed die reverse and graded by him as AU. (Lot 107).

1858/7 overdate, MS-60. (Lot 13)

1858 Large Letters Proof, regular issue. Proof-63. (Lot 14).[2]

American Life in 1857:

The majority of the following non-numismatic (mostly) news items, quotations, and fillers—including all direct quotes (unless credited otherwise)—are extracted from issues of *Ballou's Pictorial Drawing-Room Companion,* Vol. XII, published in Boston, January 3 to June 20, 1857. Additional information is from *Harper's New Monthly Magazine,* New York City, various 1857 issues, and other diverse historical sources.

---

[1] This note based upon a report of the Eaton coins sold at auction by Stack's in 1992 (as delineated in Rick Snow's Variety Sale No. 1, January 16, 1993) and also a suggestion from Thomas K. DeLorey, April 12, 1996. However, Eaton certainly deserves recognition for his efforts, and no doubt some of his findings inspired or influenced later research.

[2] Sources of information include Stack's two catalogues for these sales; Rick Snow's Variety Sale No. 1, January 16, 1993 (which had a review of the cent part of the sale); Richard Snow, letter, April 10, 1996; and my own conclusions.

This era saw the adoption and first circulation of the Flying Eagle cent.

Economy and business: Pennsylvania was the greatest wheat-producing state with 18,250,000 bushels estimated for 1857, followed by Ohio, New York, Illinois, Wisconsin, and Virginia.

A certain Mr. Gowan deposited documents with the State Department to the effect that "he has discovered a guano [bird excrement, useful for fertilizer] island, called Somuro, containing over 6,000,000 tons, within eight days' sail of New York. The Secretary of State informed him that the government would protect him in his occupation." In an era before chemical fertilizers, the importation of guano was a large business in Eastern ports, and many ships were devoted to the trade.

In the early part of the year the country was riding a wave of speculation in land and in railroad stocks. On August 24, the New York City division of the Ohio Life Insurance & Trust Company failed, followed by its parent company shortly afterward. This triggered a wave of financial crises, banks in some larger cities stopped paying out silver and gold coins, and by year's end several thousand companies were bankrupt. Railroad shares fell precipitously, examples being the January to October fall of Michigan Southern stock from $88 to $15 and Illinois Central from $123 to $79.

On September 12 the sinking in a storm of the steamer *Central America,* enroute to New York City from Panama, resulted in over 400 deaths and the loss of millions of dollars' worth of gold coins and bars, including thousands of freshly-minted 1857-S $20 gold pieces.

Government and politics: On March 4, James Buchanan was inaugurated as the 15th president of the United States, succeeding Franklin Pierce. Before and after the ceremony he was besieged by office-seekers. Washington, D.C., was viewed as an unhealthy place to live, especially during the three warmest months of summer. Lewis Cass, a numismatist and prominent politician, was named as his secretary of state.

It was believed that about 300,000 Indians lived in the United States, mostly in sub-standard condition. In California, many found employment in gold mines and mills.

Slavery was mentioned only occasionally in *Ballou's,* for the newspaper was primarily dedicated to science, literature, travel, and the arts. However, it was noted that in Havana shiploads of slaves were brought over from Africa on American sailing vessels, an activity deplored by the editor.

In other publications such as *Harper's New Monthly Magazine* slavery was a prime new topic. In South Carolina, Governor Adams argued for a large-scale resumption of the slave trade in the United States. The proposed admission of new states into the Union was a balance of pro-slavery and anti-slavery factions, *i.e.,* North vs. South.

This was the year of the Supreme Court's Dred Scott decision which found that the Missouri Compromise was not legal, the government could not prohibit the ownership of slaves, and that a Negro born to parents who were slaves was not a citizen. Black people had virtually no rights in the South. Women of all races were denied the voting privilege except for a few local elections such as for school board candidates in some areas.

The official religion of America seemed to be "high" Christianity, as practiced by established Protestant churches. Catholics were often viewed with disfavor, especially if they were immigrants or poor. Fun was poked at Baptists, especially of the "hard shell" variety. Jews, when mentioned in *Ballou's* or *Harper's,* were in the context of merchants. It must have been difficult for those of non-Christian background to be told incessantly that Christianity, especially Protestantism, was the one and only way to a good life. The top several charities in New York City were bible and missionary societies dedicated to spreading The Word.

Federal income for the year was $75,926,875, while government expenditures added up to $74,064,756, once again yielding a budget surplus. In the same year the Detroit city schools cost $25,354 to operate.

"Arrangements are being made to form a new state out of the northeast corner of Michigan, to be called Superior." This district was a rich source of copper including metal used at the Mint as an alloy for the new copper-nickel cents.

In Utah the Mormons continued to challenge the federal government's authority. Their philosophy was that as Uncle Sam would not let Utah into the Union (mainly because of resentment of the practice of polygamy), the government had no right to conduct courts or any other business in the territory. There were numerous stories of Mormon atrocities to Gentiles (as non-Mormons were called). Meanwhile, there was an anti-Mormon sentiment in many other areas of the United States, as reflected by newspaper articles and clippings.

Crime and law: Crime and the reporting of it became a focal point of interest for the American public. While the great era of sensationalism in the press was still a few decades away, the typical newspaper in 1857—especially if published in New York or another large city—was apt to devote a great deal of space to misdeeds, mysteries, and legal cases. A few samples:

In Irasburg, Vermont, over $1,200 was expended in legal fees concerning a trespass case, the fine for which was $10.

"The *New York Mirror* says that no street in New York is safe after dark, and advises citizens to arm." Garroting (choking) was the most popular way to attack a victim. Proposed solutions included a steel collar with hidden blades or spikes covered with cloth, to cause permanent disfigurement to anyone attempting such an act. Some 4,000 people joined associations to combat the crime and a Committee of Vigilance was proposed, similar to the one recently disbanded in San Francisco.

In Hartford, Connecticut, a clairvoyant, Dr. Reed, helped recover a man's watch and chain—good news so far. However, the police subsequently determined he was the thief who had stolen them.

In Marion County, Ohio, a man rented a house under a year's lease, but left it in a few weeks, believing it harbored ghosts. The landlord took him to court for the rent, but the case was decided in favor of the defendant, who was able to prove that it was indeed haunted.

In Canada a judge ruled that as lottery tickets were illegal there, stealing them could not be a crime.

Typical of a *cause célèbre* of the era, readers of metropolitan newspapers were eager to read day after day the unfolding real-life drama about the curious affair of Dr. Harvey Burdell. A New York bachelor dentist of some substantial financial means, Burdell was found murdered in his home. Soon thereafter, his boarder, Mrs. Emma A. Cunningham, produced a document, signed by clergy and witnessed, attesting that she and the dentist had been married a short time before his demise. Thus, she was entitled to his estate.

The clergyman who had married the couple was called by police to view Burdell's corpse, but could not testify it was the same man he had joined in union with Cunningham, although they were about of the same build. In due course, an 11-day trial established that the foul deed had been committed by Cunningham's lover, John J. Eckel, and that no marriage to Burdell had ever taken place. Cunningham herself was set free.

The matter did not end there. To continue her claim to Burdell's estate, Mrs. Cunningham soon announced she was pregnant by Burdell, even if not married to the decedent, and she displayed ample girth to verify it. Unfortunately for her dreams of riches, the New York district attorney was in constant secret communication with a Dr. Uhl, with whom she had enlisted as her medical adviser.

"She immediately feigned herself in labor pangs [*sic*], and soon a child was produced and identified as hers to bystanders. The police, who had been on the watch, entered at this moment, and arrested her, together with a number of persons whom she had engaged as her assistants.... The infant was taken away and given to its own mother, Mrs. Cunningham persisting in claiming it has her lawful child."[1]

Science and technology: In New York City an exhibition was mounted which showed advances made in electroplating with copper and suggested that an entire wooden ship could be copper-plated. Apropos of the same technique, "A gang of London forgers we see, have been detected in counterfeiting old coins by the electrotype process. Many shrewd antiquaries have been bitten by these impositions."

At the American Institute, New York, a remarkable carpet-sweeping machine was exhibited. It employed a revolving fan that sucked up dust and dirt and carried it into a container partly filled with water. Large particles and fibers were deposited in a separate drawer. The device was said to outlast a thousand brooms.

Night illumination of rooms and public places was mostly by gas fixtures, whale oil lamps, and candles. Electricity was still a novelty, and the first great American oil strike (in Pennsylvania) did not occur until the following year, 1858. The whaling industry flourished out of New England ports.

Maine was a major force in shipbuilding with several large wooden ships recently constructed in excess of 1,000 tons burden each. However, marine insurance companies preferred wooden boats to be slightly smaller, as they seemed to become involved in fewer mishaps. The typical ocean vessel was apt to be all sail (as with clipper ships and most smaller vessels) or a combination of steam with auxiliary sails.

Transportation: There were about 3,000 steamboats in service in America and about 24,000 miles of railroad track. One hazard of steamboats was becoming snagged on underwater stumps and debris on inland waters such as the Mississippi River. In the preceding year, 358 people lost their lives in steamboat accidents, while rail mishaps claimed 195. It took about 40 hours to go from New York City to St. Louis by train. Canals, the great mode of transportation of the 1820s and 1830s, were losing freight business to railroads. In Ohio in 1853, annual revenues for five major canals totaled. $633,203. By 1856 the figure dropped to $427,813.

On the Mississippi River the steamer *Natchez* filled the air with melodies from that new invention, the calliope; the repertoire included *Pop Goes the Weasel, Susannah,* and *Villikens and His Dinah.*

Within cities, omnibus lines were flourishing and consisted of carriages, some-

---

[1] Details were printed in *Harper's,* May 1857, p. 551, and August, p. 547.

times finely appointed, drawn on tracks by horses. Some towns and cities were linked by turnpikes built by stock companies, toll-keepers for which charged a few cents or more for passage.

"The experiment of domesticating camels for the use of the United States Army on the great plains of the Southwest is likely to prove successful. More can be done in the way of transportation, by six camels in five days, than by two six-mule teams in 10 days." (While it might have taken a mathematician to work out such a comparison, in any event the experiment failed, but for many years thereafter there were rumors of wild camels in the desert.)

Balloon ascensions were a popular pastime for the sporting who could afford it. Operators of such devices were called aeronauts.

Communications: An estimated 3,754 newspapers were published in the United States.

The telegraph was the most popular means of rapid communication. The Transatlantic Telegraph Co. stated that $1,750,000 would be required to stretch an underwater cable to London. A section of the proposed cable was on display at the Merchants' Exchange in New York City. It was mused that someday a telegraph cable would link New York and California (which occurred the following decade).

Most people kept in touch with distant friends and relatives by mail. The Post Office was usually quite efficient. Letters were carried by train between many towns and cities, necessitating frequent and sometimes annoying stops for railroad passengers in an era before express (with no intermediate stops) service.

Entertainment: Entertainment consisted of reading, playing cards, dancing, and dining, among other pursuits. Ladies often wore wide crinoline skirts to society functions, prompting some invitations to read "no crinoline," especially if the space were cramped. Such skirts required a wide entrance door, and negotiating flights of stairs was no easy task.

On the stage, Miss Laura Keene was one of the most popular actresses, while Edwin Booth was famed as a tragedian. A few years later in 1865, Miss Keene was before the lights at Ford's Theatre, Washington, in a production of *Our American Cousin,* with President Abraham Lincoln watching from a special box.

In January 1857, the editor of *Harper's* commented: "The lecture season has set in again with the usual severity. There are a few new names, and a very few new subjects.... If people pay two shillings to see white men blackened like Negroes, and singing bad grammar and maudlin sentiment, why should we not hope to see them paying the same sum to hear white men talk sense?"

One of the best-sellers among books was by Dr. Elisha Kent Kane and told of his heroic Arctic adventures. Ironically, Kane died in 1857 in warm Havana and thus did not enjoy the fruits of his literary success. Arctic exploration was all the rage, despite one-way trips by certain explorers (Sir John Franklin being an example) and their crews.

Trips to the cold regions were just a small part of a greater public interest in things exotic. Books about Egypt, wild animals, the mountains of the American West, China, and other places furnished a diversion for many armchair adventurers.

Miss Jane Stuart, daughter of portraitist Gilbert Stuart (designer of the Draped Bust motif for American coinage in 1795), had an art studio in Boston. Fine homes were apt to be decorated by paintings, average homes by lithographs such as those by the recently established partnership of Currier & Ives.

General Tom Thumb, America's most famous midget, was in Europe with impresario P.T. Barnum. Castle Garden in New York City harbor, which had welcomed Jenny Lind a few years earlier in 1850, at the start of her triumphal tour under Barnum, was the main place of disembarkation for immigrants to America.

Games of chance were popular just about everywhere. There were an estimated 2,000 gambling houses and 100 faro banks in New York City.

In an era in which air conditioning was unknown and cities sweltered in the summer, socially prominent easterners were apt to spend their summers at Saratoga Springs (New York), Cape May (New Jersey), or Newport (Rhode Island). Those who could afford it also had their choice of many large hotels in Upstate New York, along the coast of New England, and in the White Mountains region of New Hampshire. Travel was by steamship or rail to a vacation destination, then by livery to the hotel or other establishment.

Chicago, viewed by some easterners as a town full of tree stumps, had its own high society, and in 1857 members of the upper crust were delighted to find that a French count had come to their town to stay. "Many a fair maiden had tried her own Christian name with *Countess* before it, to hear how lovingly it would sound." Hopes were dashed when the Frenchman proved to be an ordinary barber and set up a small shop to pursue his profession.[1]

Health, living, and wellness: Consumption (tuberculosis) was said to be the single leading cause of death and claimed 200,000 annually. Men who worked out-of-doors were said to be more healthy and to live longer than those with sedentary occupations. Whisky and cigars—and in quantity—were necessary accessories for the successful businessman or politicians.

"An excellent institution in New York City, suggested by a similar one in Paris, is the *nursery,* where children can be taken care of while their mothers are sick or at work."

Families were often large, and there was no lack of children. Orphanages were filled to capacity. Adoption was an easy process. In Iowa an orphaned infant was desired by two childless couples, who decided the matter by a card game.

More than just a few American citizens believed that the world would end on June 13 when a great comet was to strike the earth in a fearful cataclysm. The appointed date came and went, and no comet was seen. (Several years earlier a religious sect believed that life on the planet would terminate on May 10, 1854.) "Spirit rapping" a.k.a. "table rapping" was all the rage in America and Europe. Certain spiritually gifted intermediaries would charge clients to sit with them in a room in which a bare table was present. Clients could ask questions of dear departed loved ones and others from the past, and their spirits would communicate by tapping on the table "yes" and "no" answers. These messages from earlier eras had a devastating effect upon some clients, and there were numerous accounts printed during the decade of people committing suicide or being confined to institutions because of the messages they received.

Eating and drinking: Oysters were a favorite delicacy and were served roasted, stewed, boiled, and fried by oyster houses in leading Eastern cities. An estimated 250 vessels engaged in the oyster trade, primarily centered in Baltimore. Put up in tins, Maryland oysters were popular in the California gold fields. In Boston frogs were highly prized in dining rooms and sold for $2.50 per hundred in the market.

---

[1] *Harper's,* July 1857, p. 282.

Coffee was said to constitute one-seventh of the value of all U.S. imports and was estimated at $16,000,000 annually.

Food was often of questionable quality and origin. Milk was often watered. Eggs could be preserved for several weeks or even longer and were regularly shipped to distant places in wooden barrels aboard trains. Ice was in great demand in the summer months, and harvests from New England ponds were shipped from Boston to many distant destinations including San Francisco.

Drugs such as opium were readily available at apothecary shops, but do not seem to have been abused to a great extent. However, in China opium was used by many people, and American and other silver coins received in trade in that country were often shipped to India in exchange for the drug; in India the coins were melted. Alcoholism was rampant just about everywhere in America, and the temperance movement sought to combat it.

Coins and currency: "Darley, the famous artist, has been designing some beautiful figures for some new bills to be issued by the Bunker Hill Bank, Charlestown [in Massachusetts]." There were over 4,000 banks in America, many of which issued their own paper money. Such notes were widely counterfeited, especially those bearing imprints of larger cities. Publications known as bank note detectors or counterfeit detectors were published to aid banks and merchants. Meanwhile, there was no official federal currency in circulation. That would not occur until 1861.

Prof. Benjamin B. Silliman, Jr., a member of the American Association for the Advancement of Science, addressed the problem of photographing bank bills to make counterfeits, and suggested that if a separately printed color such as green (made from the sesqui-oxide of chromium) could be added to notes, a camera would register the green as being black, and accurate copying would not be possible.

"For the first 22 days after beginning to purchase the old Spanish coin, the Philadelphia Mint took in $68,000 worth, chiefly in small sums." (Account dated April 18, 1857, before Spanish coins were exchanged for the new cents; the Mint bought them at a discount in the early months of the year.) Meanwhile, banks were paying 20¢ each for Spanish-American two-bit (25¢) pieces, the same price as at the Mint, and certain merchants allowed 22¢ each for them in payment for merchandise. The exchange rate at the Mint was later raised to 25¢ in swap for new copper-nickel cents.

In Charlotte, North Carolina, and Dahlonega, Georgia, mints turned out a stream of gold coins of the $1, $2.50, and $5 denominations from metal found in those regions. The mints in New Orleans and San Francisco struck silver and gold issues. In California most major gold strikes had already been made, and the era of a fortune-seeker going west was past. Most mining in California was done by corporations, where there were an estimated 63 quartz-stamping gold mills in operation, 30 driven by steam and 33 by water power. In San Francisco, Agostón Haraszthy, former refiner and melter at the Mint, was found guilty of embezzling $151,000 in gold from the institution, a decision that was later reversed.[1]

Short takes: In Springfield, Illinois, the *Register* stated that there were only 12 marriageable ladies in that town, and of that number 11 were engaged; a plea was made for "more female help."

---

[1] QDB note: Haraszthy, who was at one time associated with Wass, Molitor & Co., had a checkered career and was implicated in other misadventures. He had been with the Mint from its inception in 1854, was discharged, and by 1857 had a private assaying business in the same city. After four years of court wrangling, the embezzlement charge was found by a jury to have no merit. More information about Haraszthy appears in the 1982 auction catalogue of the Henry Clifford Collection.

Lawrenceburg, Indiana, was reputed to be a very popular place, for there were no property taxes or other levies. The city government there "had no use for the money."

In London an egg of the extinct great auk sold for £21 at auction.

Further, from *Ballou's:*

"The word *bull,* signifying a ludicrous blunder, became proverbial from the repeated blunders of one Dediah Bull, a London lawyer, in the reign of Henry VII."

"There is a glut of Circassian girls now in the Constantinople market, and the price of handsome ones has come down from $500 to $25."

1858/7 Flying Eagle Cent

OVERDATE: 1858/7 Flying Eagle cent, Snow-1, showing the remains of an early 7 at the upper right of the second 8 in the date.

Business Strikes:

Business strike mintage: Unknown. The typical 1858 die produced on average 106,957 coins. As two obverse dies are known for 1858/7 (Snow-1, the traditional overdate, and another discovered recently), this would give an estimate in the 200,000 to 220,000 range (simply given as a point for discussion).

Number of business strike obverse dies made: At least 2

Average number of coins struck from typical obverse die: 106,957 (average for all 1858 dies, not necessarily for overdate dies)

Availability in Mint State: Very rare. Probably fewer than 15 exist.

Availability in circulated grades: Very rare in comparison to regular 1858 cents. Population probably fewer than 300.

Characteristics of striking for Snow-1: Lightly struck on obverse (actually, the dies were shallowly defined, causing weakness in areas). Tip of wing near border is barely connected, and on late die states it is disconnected, but this is not definitive as other non-overdate cents of this date sometimes occur with broken tip.[1] On the

---

[1] Richard Snow, letter, April 18, 1996.

reverse the two cotton leaves at the upper left are weak on all specimens seen.

The second overdate die was not known when the Snow and Steve-Flynn books were written. Discovered by Mark McWherter, this 1858/7 variety does not have a defective wing tip.[1]

Market Prices (1858/7 business strikes, clear overdate)

YEAR	VG-8	F-12	VF-20	EF-40	AU-50	
1996	$95.00	$180.00	$375.00	$550.00	$1,000.00	

YEAR	MS-60	MS-63	MS-64	MS-65		
1996	$1,750.00	$3,750.00	$7,500.00	$17,500.00		

Notes

Collecting commentary: Large Letters style. Early and late die states, with the early state showing the tip of the under-digit 7 more clearly. On the early die state the right-side tip of the eagle's wing is connected; on later die states the tip appears as a separate "island."

The 1858/7 overdate is not easily distinguished on lower grades, and thus it is not priced in those levels in accordance with its true rarity; demand for overdates without the tip of the 7 visible is low.

There are two obverse dies known. The first has a small triangular (raised) die mark in the field between the date and the eagle's breast; this may have been caused by the inadvertent contact of the upper left corner of the base of the digit 1 in the four-digit date logotype with the working die (a conclusion reached by Chris Pilliod). The second 1858/7 obverse die lacks this triangular mark.

Market prices are highly theoretical for Mint State grades, as very few exist. It could be that a truly superb Mint State coin would bring significantly more than the estimated values given above. The valuation for the MS-65 piece was suggested by Richard Snow; what he would charge *if* he had one at the time (but he didn't have one).[2]

Historical and numismatic notes: Discovered by Walter Breen circa 1957. The variety was slow in being publicized, and when it was, there was little demand for it. Most found by the writer over the years were located as regular (non-overdate) coins, including one in a certified holder in the early 1990s. Made only in business strike form; no Proofs were coined.

Fivaz-Stanton 1¢-006. Listed as No. 3 among the top 20 most popular of all unusual varieties by Larry R. Steve and Kevin J. Flynn in *Flying Eagle and Indian Cent Die Varieties.*

---

[1] Richard Snow, letter, April 18, 1996.
[2] Letter, May 3, 1996.

1858 Flying Eagle Cent

Large Letters

Letter size characteristics:

Large Letters: Bottoms of AM in AMERICA connected. Letters thinner and taller. Eagle's beak with blunt top, thick bottom.

Small Letters: Bottoms of AM do not touch. Letters shorter and thicker; less open in the enclosed spaces. Eagle's beak with sharply pointed tip, thin and pointed bottom. Also, feathers on eagle's neck are more "ruffed" than on the Large Letters variety or on earlier (1856-1857) Flying Eagle cents.[1]

Business strike mintage: 24,600,000 (all 1858 varieties combined).

Business Strikes (1858 Large Letters):

Number of business strike obverse dies made: Part of 230 total made for 1858.

Average number of coins struck from typical obverse die: 106,957

Reverse leaf styles: Business strikes come with both High Leaf and Low Leaf, both are plentiful, but the Low Leaf is slightly the more common of the two. The High Leaf reverse occurs with sub-varieties: E in ONE open (the style usually seen) and E in ONE closed (quite scarce); this information is repeated below as part of a general discussion on reverse styles.

Availability in Mint State (Large Letters): As a date 1858 is much scarcer than 1857, but enough are around that it will not be a stumbling block. The market price is less than might be expected considering it is at least five times harder to find than 1857. In gem grades of MS-64 or finer the 1858 Large Letters is more available than the 1858 Small Letters. Some of the gems may have been those sold as "Proofs" decades ago (see commentary under Proof below).

---

[1] Bill Fivaz, "Definitely a Difference." *Article in Longacre's Ledger,* Summer 1994; follow-up in same publication Fall 1994 suggests that Robert E. Guiles may have been the first to notice this. Also, letter to the author, March 30, 1996.

Among 1858 cents the Large Letters variety is slightly scarcer than the Small Letters.

Availability in circulated grades (Large Letters): Common.

Characteristics of striking (Large letters): Varies.

Market Prices (1858 Large Letters; business strikes)

YEAR	G-4	VG-8	F-12	VF-20	EF-40	AU-50
1938	$0.25	$0.35	$0.50	$0.70	$1.00	$2.00
1944	0.30	0.50	1.00	1.20	1.60	3.00
1965	6.00	8.00	12.00	22.00	35.00	65.00
1996	16.00	21.00	26.00	43.00	112.50	175.00

YEAR	MS-60	MS-63	MS-64	MS-65		
1938	$3.50	$3.50	$3.50	$4.50		
1944	5.00	5.00	5.00	6.00		
1965	140.00	150.00	160.00	175.00		
1996	255.00	525.00	950.00	2,400.00		

Proofs (1858 Large Letters):

Proof distribution (Large Letters): No more than 50 to 100, possibly included as part of the 12-coin copper-nickel pattern sets of the year (and this figure may be overly optimistic), plus extras. Until 1992 PCGS in its *Population Report* listed *all* Proof 1858 cents under the "Large Letters" category, thus distorting their apparent rarity. in actuality, the Large Letters is an extreme rarity in Proof finish.

While Proof 1858 Small Letters cents were included among the restrike sets of 1858-dated patterns made in 1859-1861 (see Appendix II for details), most probably the Proof 1858 Large Letters were only distributed in 1858.

Proof dies: At least two obverse dies were used; one with delicate repunching of letters and with tiny die defects below first 8 and 5 of date; the other with light repunching of the first A in AMERICA.[1] Proofs have the High Leaf style reverse (see commentary on 1858 reverse varieties below).

Proof commentary (Large Letters): Beware prooflike Mint State coins offered as "Proof." In his *Encyclopedia* (1988) Walter Breen stated: "Under 20 Proofs traced." Thus, historical prices for 1858-dated Proofs are lower for the 1938, 1944, and 1965 citations below because of business strikes being offered as Proofs. The *apparent* availability of Proofs is increased by such incidents as this, related by Richard Snow: "There is one die of the 1858 Large Letters which came from 30 or so coins in an Upstate New York hoard. These were sold to [a leading dealer] and marketed as Proofs in the 1940s. They are beautiful prooflike pieces and are the only reason why there is in some listings a higher population of 1858 Large Letter gems as compared to those with Small Letters. These prooflike, but non-Proof coins have a die crack from the eagle's tail down to the rim."[2] No doubt some of these have been certified in

---

[1] Adapted from Richard Snow, *Flying Eagle & Indian Cents,* p. 46.
[2] Letter, April 10, 1996; modified by letter, May 3, 1996.

high Mint State grades since then and may be the source for some of the MS-65 or better Large Letters coins known today.

A sharp differential between various levels within the Proof category did not begin in a widespread way until the late 1980s. (One well-known, now retired, dealer joined the staff of a rare coin company in the 1940s, and as one of his first duties was instructed to sell prooflike Uncirculated Flying Eagle cents as "Proofs" to unknowing buyers.) These may have been from the aforementioned Large Letters die with a tiny crack extending downward to the rim from near the right tip of the eagle's tail.

Further, in past decades the 1858 Large Letters often sold for significantly more money in Proof finish than did specimens of the Small Letters variety. Since about 1960, when collecting coins by basic design types became exceedingly popular, this price difference has narrowed to virtual insignificance. A 1996 issue of the *Coin Dealer Newsletter* had the Proof-65 price of the Large Letters far *below* that of the Small Letters, which seems to be the reverse of the true availability situation (our listings below do *not* reflect this *Coin Dealer Newsletter* opinion). See additional rarity comments under the following 1858 Small Letters sub-chapter.

Stated simply, the 1858 Large Letters Proof cent is a major rarity.

Market Prices (1858 Large Letters, Proofs)

YEAR	PR-60	PR-63	PR-64	PR-65		
1938	$25.00	$25.00	$25.00	$27.50		
1944	35.00	35.00	35.00	40.00		
1965	1,750.00	1,850.00	2,000.00	2,250.00		
1996	1,550.00	4,900.00	7,900.00	18,000.00		

Notes

Collecting commentary: As a date the 1858 cent in higher business strike grades is scarcer than 1857 and usually has less satisfactory lustre, particularly in the fields. However, current market prices do not reflect the higher scarcity of both 1858 issues, nor in general do they reflect the scarcity differences between the two letter sizes of 1858. Thus, the collector of Flying Eagle cents by varieties has a free ride, so to speak, as scarcer issues are available for "type" prices.

Reverse varieties 1856-1858: From 1856 through 1858 there were several different reverse hubs used for certain years, distinguished by several features, including having raised or incuse veins in the cotton leaves (more study of this interesting aspect is needed), having the leaf to the left of the C in CENT high (extending up past the baseline of the C) or low (coming to about the baseline of the C and appearing somewhat small ("High Leaf" and "Low Leaf"), and the tips of the serifs of E in ONE apart ("open") or nearly touching ("closed") on its right side. The Breen, Snow (in particular), and Steve-Flynn books discuss these.

Caveat: If a reverse working hub was punched too lightly into a reverse working die, certain of the lower-relief features would not be sharply impressed into the working die or not impressed at all. Similarly, if a die was relapped or resurfaced after hubbing, certain low-relief features were removed. Such actions were responsible for seeming differences in distance between the serifs on the right side of the E in ONE and the differences in distance between the tips of the "buds" at the top of the wreath; these do not constitute true die *varieties,* but are die *states.*

The High Leaf varieties seem to have been made earlier (and closely follow the style used on the 1854 gold dollar and $3 gold[1] from which this wreath motif was adapted), while in 1858 the Low Leaf varieties seem to have been made for the first time. Presumably, any 1856 cents (such as Snow-4) and, if they exist, 1857 Flying Eagle cents with Low Leaf reverse, are restrikes made 1858 or later. Among the High Leaf varieties there are several sub-varieties.

Synopsis of reverse styles:

High Leaf: Leaf to left of CENT is high and extends above the baseline of the C. One variety has a "thin high leaf" due to either repolishing the die or insufficient depth in punching the working hub into the working die. Leaf below T in CENT higher than on following.

Low Leaf: Leaf to left of CENT is low and small and does not extend above the baseline of the C. Leaf below T is shorter than on the preceding. Several (but not all) Low Leaf varieties seen by the writer have had incised veins in cotton leaves 1 and 2 on each side of the wreath (counting up from the bottom of the wreath). To determine relative rarity of raised vs. incised veins on the Low Leaf reverse an examination of several dozen or more pieces is needed (easy enough to do, but this aspect arose close to press time for this book, and this aspect awaits future research).

Casual observations on "High Leaf" and "Low Leaf" issues 1856-1858:

The following comments are based upon a study of several hundred Flying Eagle cents recorded in the Bowers and Merena photo files:

1856 cents: All originals (Mint State as well as worn pieces) have High Leaf as do nearly all Proofs. Only two coins, both Proofs, were seen with Low Leaf (one of these was observed separately from the aforementioned photo files), these also having the 1856 date on the obverse shallowly punched in the die; presumably, these are clear candidates for having been struck no earlier than 1858; these are unique among 1856 cents in that cotton leaves 1 and 2 on the wreath are incised rather than in relief.

One "High Leaf" variety has the words ONE CENT rotated slightly in a clockwise direction, thus lifting the C in CENT above its normal orientation; in this instance the leaf is long as in the High Leaf style, but it does not extend above the baseline; this is described in Walter Breen's *Encyclopedia of U.S. Proof Coins* (Breen No. 1 from dies 1-A) and in Richard Snow's text (as Snow-1, p. 28).

1857 cents: All with High Leaf.

1858/7 cents: All with High Leaf.

1858 Large Letters cents: Proofs have High Leaf; sometimes the High Leaf is thin or imperfect. Business strikes come with both High Leaf and Low Leaf, both are plentiful, but the Low Leaf is slightly the more common of the two. The High Leaf reverse occurs with sub-varieties: E in ONE open (the style usually seen) and E in ONE closed (quite scarce).

1858 Small Letters cents: Proofs exist of both types, with possibly the Low Leaf

---

[1] The original wax model for the $3 reverse is now owned by Thomas K. DeLorey (letter, April 15, 1996).

the most often seen. Among business strikes, the overwhelming majority are of the Low Leaf variety. The Low Leaf reverse occurs with sub-varieties: E in ONE open (the style usually seen) and E in ONE closed (quite scarce).

Commodore Eaton's studies: Commodore W.C. Eaton, mentioned in the 1856 and 1857 sub-chapters above, had as his first love the 1858 Flying Eagle cents. In three articles in *The Numismatist,* each titled "The Eagle Cents of 1858," published in January 1916, November 1920, and March 1921, he described 76 different die varieties of 1858 Large Letters and Small Letters cents. David U. Proskey and F.R. Alvord assisted Eaton with some discoveries. It fell to Alvord to contact dealers to request to survey their inventories, and in doing so he examined "thousands of Uncirculated 1858s."[1]

Eaton's markers included the High Leaf to the left of the C in CENT, this feature being subdivided into Thin High Leaf (rarer) and Thick High Leaf. The Low Leaf variety extended upward to near the baseline of the C, but not above it.

The 1858 Large Letters business strikes were common with Low Leaf, but fairly scarce if not rare with High Leaf.

The 1858 Small Letters business strike was usually seen with Low Leaf. However, a very few High Leaf pieces were described including one rarity with thin high leaf, with "broken left edge on reverse."

Eaton considered machine-doubled coins (which he described as having repunched letters) and coins with die breaks to constitute separate varieties, which is different from today's view. For further information about Commodore Eaton see 1857 sub-chapter above.

Cent exchanges: As of June 30, 1858, Mint Director James Ross Snowden reported that $16,602 value *by weight* of old large cents had been exchanged for the new Flying Eagle cents in 1857, and that $31,404 value by weight had been exchanged thus far in 1858. Presumably, this equaled about 5 million large cents.[2]

Cent collecting: The following is from *The Bankers' Magazine,* December 1858, and was reprinted from the *Philadelphia Bulletin.* The effect that the new cents had on numismatics is reflected:

> Since the circulation of the new "nickels," coin collectors have been eagerly searching for rare coppers of the old kind, for they will soon be very scarce. We know of one collector who boasts of every copper known to be struck in America, except three or four. Numismatics has become as much as "rage" as opera-going, chess-playing, sailing on the Delaware, rowing on the Schuylkill, exercising in the gymnasium; and the votaries of the fancy pursue it with a zeal and ardor worthy of the immortal old buck.

> One collector was indefatigable enough to pick out from nearly 100,000 coins a cabinet of 400 or 500, which he considered at least worth $500; but just after he had made his selection his premises were broken open, and the rare and precious coins were carried off by some rascally burglar, who valued them at about the price of old copper.

Elsewhere in the hobby: The American Numismatic and Archaeological Society was formed in March of this year, the second coin-collecting group in America, and closely following the establishment of a society in Philadelphia (among whose mem-

---

[1] "The Eagle Cents of 1858," *The Numismatist,* March 1921.
[2] 1858 *Mint Report,* p. 86.

bers was Mint Director James Ross Snowden) on January 1, 1858. Philadelphia, Boston, and New York City were the centers of the rapidly-growing numismatic hobby. Proof coins were openly sold to collectors for the first time, with an estimated 200 to 300 sets of silver Proofs reaching the market.

1858 cent spurs collecting interest: In the course of having several well-known specialists in the field of Flying Eagle and Indian cents review the manuscript, I sent a copy to Sam Lukes, whose reply told how he started in numismatics:[1]

> Like yourself, Dave, I have always enjoyed the Flying Eagle and Indian cent series from way back and can remember finding several pieces looking through rolls here in California back in the early '50s, the oldest being an 1887 which today would probably grade Very Fine.
>
> The first time I ever saw a Flying Eagle cent was in a tiny, upper-story coin shop in Fresno, California, which the dealer had displayed in one of the old Whitman cardboard albums. It was an 1858, probably in Fine or Very Fine grade, and was the Large Letters variety. Who knows if it might have been the rare overdate (1858/7) which Walter Breen had not yet discovered? But I just knew I had to have that coin. The dealer said he would set it aside for me for one week in order to come up with the money which I seem to recall was several dollars, an enormous amount back then for a 12- or 13-year-old!
>
> I begged my dear mother for the funds which I promised I would pay her back with my lawn mowing or shoe shining business, and she finally gave in, warning me not to tell my Dad. I immediately ran back to the coin shop just knowing 'my' coin was already sold. It wasn't, but the dealer was surprised to see me back so soon, and I told him my Mom had loaned me the money. As he handed my very first Flying Eagle, he paused and told me to be sure and 'pay your mother back,' which I later did.

---

[1] Letter, April 8, 1996.

1858 Flying Eagle Cent

Small Letters

Letter size characteristics:

Large Letters: Bottoms of AM in AMERICA connected. Letters thinner and taller. Eagle's beak with blunt top, thick bottom.

Small Letters: Bottoms of AM do not touch. Letters shorter and thicker; less open in the enclosed spaces. Eagle's beak with sharply pointed tip, thin and pointed bottom. Also, feathers on eagle's neck are more "ruffed" than on the Large Letters variety or on earlier (1856-1857) Flying Eagle cents.[1]

The writer has seen no Mint documentation on the 1858 Small Letters cents, a letter style which may have been employed to minimize the metal flow in both directions in the dies, thus permitting the head and tail of the eagle on the obverse to be struck more sharply than on the Large Letters style. I consider it probable that one of Paquet's punch fonts intended for another denomination—possibly the dime—was used to create the 1858 Small Letters cent.[2]

Business strike mintage: 24,600,000 (all 1858 varieties combined).

Business Strikes (1858 Small Letters):

Number of business strike obverse dies made: Part of 230 total made for 1858.

Average number of coins struck from typical obverse die: 106,957.

Reverse leaf styles: Among business strikes, the overwhelming majority of 1858 Small Letters cents are of the Low Leaf variety. The Low Leaf reverse occurs with sub-varieties: E in ONE open (the style usually seen) and E in ONE closed (quite

---

[1] Bill Fivaz, "Definitely a Difference." *Article in Longacre's Ledger,* Summer 1994; follow-up in same publication Fall 1994 suggests that Robert E. Guiles may have been the first to notice this. Also, letter to the author, March 30, 1996.

[2] The inscription UNITED STATES OF AMERICA in three different punch font sizes (apparently intended for the dime, quarter dollar, and half dollar denominations), attributed to Paquet, is seen on Pollock-3131, a one-sided trial striking.

scarce). See commentary under 1858 Large Letters above for 1858 leaf style information. One rare variety of 1858 Small Letters obverse, High Leaves reverse, has the reverse slightly doubled.[1]

Availability in Mint State (Small Letters): Slightly more plentiful than the Large Letters variety in lower Mint state levels, but is rarer MS-64 or finer.

Availability in circulated grades (Small letters): Common.

Characteristics of striking (Small letters): Varies. Some of the Mint State coins have somewhat of a "greasy" appearance on the obverse, instead of deep frosty lustre; often such coins are poorly struck as well.

Market Prices (1858 Small Letters; business strikes)

YEAR	G-4	VG-8	F-12	VF-20	EF-40	AU-50
1938	$0.25	$0.35	$0.50	$0.70	$1.00	$2.00
1944	0.30	0.50	1.00	1.20	1.60	3.00
1965	6.00	7.50	11.00	21.00	34.00	60.00
1996	16.00	21.00	26.00	42.50	110.00	170.00

YEAR	MS-60	MS-63	MS-64	MS-65		
1938	$3.50	$3.50	$3.50	$4.50		
1944	5.00	5.00	5.00	6.00		
1965	135.00	145.00	155.00	170.00		
1996	250.00	550.00	950.00	2,500.00		

Proofs (1858 Small Letters):

Reverse leaf styles: 1858 Small Letters Proof cents exist of both the High Leaf and Low Leaf types, with possibly the Low Leaf the most often seen.

Proof distribution (Small Letters): 100 to 200 for part of the 12-coin copper-nickel pattern sets of the year, some of which were restruck in 1859 and later years. Most Proof 1858 cents seen are of the Small Letters variety.

Proof commentary (Small Letters): Beware of prooflike Mint State coins offered as "Proof." See comment under 1858 Large Letters concerning the historical market price structure.

Moreover, a number of 1858 Small Letters obverse varieties among 1858 pattern cents have distinctly prooflike surfaces—often with myriad parallel die finish lines—and while no doubt were struck as Proofs, are more apt to be called prooflike Mint State by numismatists today. The Eliasberg Collection 1858 Small Letters cent (Lot 609) was described as "MS-65, prooflike," and was from a 12-piece set of (mostly) pattern cents sold in the Richard B. Winsor Collection sale by the Chapman brothers, 1895. Undoubtedly, this was intended as a Proof.

Similarly, Richard Snow commented:[2] "I recently handled a prooflike 1858 Small Letters cent from the same dies as the Proof and pattern pieces. It was not struck

---

[1] Cf. Larry R. Steve, *Coin World,* April 12, 1993, p. 1.
[2] Letter, April 10, 1996.

strongly and thus was not an impaired Proof. I think it was struck for inclusion in one of the pattern sets, but under careless conditions as can be seen on many different varieties of 1858 pattern cents."

Is a coin a Proof because it was struck as one, even though it may appear Mint State; or is it a Proof only if it looks like one? This has been a topic of debate for a long time, as reflected in the earlier discussion in the sub-chapter on 1856 cents.

Description of a particular Proof-65 1858 Small Letters cent examined by the author:[1] This example exhibits a deep mirror Proof surface on the obverse, with Proof areas within the mouth of the eagle but not above the eagle's leg. 1 in date over dentil; second 8 over and slightly to the left of a space between dentils. In U of UNITED left side of upper right serif is missing. Reverse Proof, but not from fully polished die. If the coin is held at a certain angle to the light there are striae diagonally from the upper left to the lower right.

Description of a second Proof obverse by Walter Breen:[2] "Top of U solid, left base of 1 above space. Reverse: Low leaves, open E's, may or may not show minute spine minutely left of tip of upper serif of E in ONE, minute chips at border and rim about 10:30. Beads small, spaced well apart except at top reverse."

The 1996 valuation for Proof-65 was suggested by Brian Wagner, who noted that current population reports suggested fewer Small Letters coins extant Proof-65 than those with Large Letters.[3] However, I counter by saying the jury is out on this one, and I believe that there are more of the Small Letters Proof coins around. In 1977 in his Proof coins *Encyclopedia,* p. 271, Walter Breen estimated possibly 10 to 12 Proofs known of the Large Letters and 15 to 20 known of the Small Letters. The situation will sort itself out as grading services as well as high-level coin buyers become more sophisticated and true populations become better known. In any event, Proofs of this year are extremely rare.

Market Prices (1858 Small Letters, Proofs)

YEAR	PR-60	PR-63	PR-64	PR-65		
1938	$15.00	$1500	$15.00	$17.00		
1944	30.00	30.00	30.00	3500		
1965	1,750.00	1,850.00	2,000.00	2,250.00		
1996	1,200.00	4,000.00	6,500.00	22,000.00		

NOTES

Collecting commentary: See preceding 1858 Large Letters sub-chapter.

[1] Jay Parrino, owner. Certified as PCGS 2043.65/3292074. Examined May 1, 1996.
[2] Walter Breen, Proof coins *Encyclopedia,* 1987 reprint with revisions, p. 330.
[3] Letter, May 3, 1996.

CHAPTER 10
INDIAN CENTS 1859-1909

History and Background

The 1859 Cent Created and Coined

In early 1858 Chief Engraver James B. Longacre and Assistant Engraver Anthony C. Paquet worked to prepare new designs for the obverse of the copper-nickel cent. The Flying Eagle cent, first made in 1856 as a pattern and then in quantity for circulation in 1857 and 1858, was difficult to strike up properly. Often the parts of the eagle nearest the border on the obverse would be lightly defined. One proposed solution to this was a modified small or "skinny" flying eagle cent obverse, the eagle reduced in size and mostly located at the center of the coin. On this coin, the eagle was probably the work of Longacre and the lettering by Paquet.

Several different new reverse designs were made by Anthony C. Paquet and/or James B. Longacre. These consisted of one style with an oak wreath, another with an oak wreath and broad ornamented shield, and a third with an open laurel wreath. The two oak wreath styles each had a few laurel leaves on the bottom of the wreath immediately to the left of the bow.[1] A pencil sketch in the National Portrait Gallery shows a laurel wreath similar to that used on the 1859 cent and is attributed to Longacre; however, as it is not signed, perhaps the attribution is tentative and was assigned to him as chief engraver.[2] Paquet is the other candidate for this reverse motif.

Among 11 pattern designs and die combinations created by Longacre and Paquet in 1858 was one featuring Longacre's fanciful portrait of an

---

[1] These few leaves have been called olive leaves by some, including by 1858 correspondent Howard subsequently quoted, but the berries among the leaves are round, as laurel, not elongated as olive; on the other hand, Heraldic Eagle silver and gold coins of the 1790s and early nineteenth century have an eagle holding an olive branch with incorrectly styled round berries. However, the olive branch held by Miss Liberty on the 1873 trade dollar, designed by William Barber, does appear to have elongated olives, ditto for the olives on the branch on the reverse of the trade dollar. In Appendix II it is noted that on August 20, 1858, in correspondence Longacre called the reverse an "olive wreath," while on November 4, 1858, Director Snowden called it a "plain laurel wreath."

[2] Associative/Decorative Object No. A/D NPG 77.50.24, with modern typed attribution: "Reverse design; wreath of olives, probably for one-cent piece. Maker: James B. Longacre." Copy of image furnished to the author by Thomas K. DeLorey.

Indian on the obverse and Paquet's open laurel wreath on the reverse. The obverse depicted *Miss* Liberty, hardly a Native American, wearing an Indian chief's war bonnet. The facial features bear many similarities to that used on Longacre's 1854 $3 gold coin and to a lesser extent, his 1849 gold $1 and $20—enough to suggest that these were used as sources—but there are differences as well.

Mint Director Snowden described the motif as "an Indian head with a falling crown of feathers."[1]

Quite probably patterns of this format were available by spring 1858, for on April 12 a Mr. Howard wrote to Director Snowden:[2]

> I have learned that a new pattern piece for the cent has been struck off at the Mint, having upon the obverse a head resembling that of the three-dollar piece, and on the reverse a shield at the top of the olive and oak wreath.
>
> I beg leave to inquire of you if you will use your efforts to procure me one specimen only. For which I will give you any price you choose to ask if it is not over five dollars.

Knowledge was certainly widespread by early that summer for R. Coulton Davis (Philadelphia druggist who was an avid collector of pattern coins) wrote to Director Snowden on June 24, 1858, indicating that a Boston newspaper had just carried a favorable story about the proposed new Indian design.[3] On June 26, 1858, Augustus B. Sage, writing on behalf of the newly formed American Numismatic and Archaeological Society, contacted Snowden regarding a specimen of the new Indian Head cent for the Society and another for his own collection.[4]

The Sarah Legend

The *American Journal of Numismatics,* Vol. 41, 1906, pp. 75-76, printed this commentary by J.C.F.:

THE "EMBLEM OF LIBERTY" ON OUR COINS:
In the regulations which determine the devices that may be placed on the coins

---

[1] Snowden, *A Description of Ancient and Modern Coins...*, 1860, p. 120.
[2] Cf. Steve-Flynn, *Flying Eagle and Indian Cent Die Varieties,* p. 213.
[3] Citation from R.W. Julian, letter, April 16, 1996. Additional information from Walter Breen, letter, February 12, 1992. Also, letter from R.W. Julian, March 20, 1992. Robert Coulton Davis was one of the earliest specialists in pattern coins and wrote the first serious study on them, which appeared serially in *The Coin Collector's Journal,* 1885-1887. His collection was catalogued by David U. Proskey and auctioned by the New York Coin & Stamp Co., January 20-24, 1890. Davis had an 1804 silver dollar which the Mint had obligingly certified not only as genuine and original, but actually struck in the year 1804. It was Davis who circa 1858 informed Director Snowden that someone at the Mint was secretly restriking 1804 dollars and peddling them to coin dealers; these were the plain-edge varieties subsequently bought back by the Mint (for details of the plain-edge coins see Newman and Bressett, *The Fantastic 1804 Dollar*). Davis also owned a set of 1866 silver coins without the IN GOD WE TRUST motto, probably struck to his order. Walter Breen stated that druggist Davis secretly supplied laudanum to employees in the Mint Medal Department and in return received many special restrikes and mulings. However, as at the time it was perfectly legal to buy opiates at any drug store, and the supplying of such would not have been a rare favor, it seems unlikely that this would have been a major factor.
[4] Citation provided by R.W. Julian, letter, April 24, 1996.

of the United States, it is provided that they shall bear an "emblem of Liberty." The manner in which this emblem shall be depicted is not prescribed, nor is there any law defining what emblem shall be used. This has been left largely, if not entirely, to the taste of the designers who are charged with preparing the devices to be used in engraving the dies, which, however, must be approved by higher authority before their adoption, and when that approval has been given, the device cannot be changed for a fixed term of years.

As every collector knows, the conventional emblem of Liberty has been, from the earliest days of our coinage, generally confined with the narrow limits of a female head with a fillet or coronet inscribed LIBERTY, or else having the word in the legend above; on some of the silver coins a seated female figure appears, with the national arms beside her, decorated with a ribbon having the same inscription.

The first of the Liberty heads [on 1793 cents], with locks unconfined and floating to the breeze, was no doubt suggested by the famous French device shown on the Libertas Americana medal, and had the liberty cap and staff resting on her shoulder. The staff and cap appear on all the coins which have a seated figure except the trade dollar; and the various modifications of the liberty cap, which began to be used on the first gold coins struck in 1795, and on the silver coinage also early in the last century, had little to commend them. The only exception that seems to have been made to this device was that shown on the small three-cent pieces struck in 1851, which in place of the head bore a star of six points, having the national arms [shield] on its centre, and which required a liberal construction if it was to be regarded as an "emblem of Liberty."

In 1854 the "bonnet," as it was often called—always suggestive of the excesses of the French Revolution, and which had given place to a simple fillet or band in 1838—was abandoned on some of the smaller gold coins [$1 and $3] and an Indian head with a feathered head-dress, sometimes called a panache, was substituted. An Indian head had appeared on the octagonal quarter dollars, struck by private parties in California in 1852,[1] but these pieces were never in general circulation.

The use of the panache in place of the Liberty cap was continued on the gold dollars struck from 1854 to 1889, when the coinage of those pieces was discontinued. It was placed on the three-dollar coins of gold, struck from 1854 to 1889, when they also were discontinued, but was never used on the silver coins. It is, however, familiar to all from its appearance for many years on the cent.

The suggestion of the panache is said to have come from a visit of a delegation of Indians from one of the tribes of the North-west, who came to talk with the "Great Father"[2] in Washington, and while in the East they were taken to see the operations of the Mint. At that time, as the story is told, Miss Sarah Longacre, the daughter of the Mint engraver, was present while the chiefs and their followers were going through the building, and attracted the attention of their leader. In a mood of sportiveness he took his crown of feathers from his head and placed it upon hers. She was a child of five or six years of age, and as she stood for a moment wearing the novel head-dress, someone of the company made a sketch of the little maiden and her feathery cap, and in due time the design was engraved and used upon the coins, dies for which were then in preparation. Such is the story as told by a correspondent of a New York newspaper.

---

[1] QDB note: Any such Indian motif pieces would have been struck at a later time and pre-dated.
[2] QDB note: General name for federal authorities, especially the commissioner of Indian affairs, in charge of relations with Indians (now called Native Americans).

Whether the tale is a true one the writer is unable to say; but certainly the device is far more appropriate to American coins than the conventional cap, which was originally given to the slave who had been freed by his Roman master, the awkward bonnet on our first gold coins, or the equally hideous turbans that so long disfigured the matronly heads on the silver pieces in the later years of the first half of the last century.

The Indian Motif

In a letter dated August 21, 1858, to Mint Director James Ross Snowden, Longacre observed:[1]

I allude more especially to the design on the obverse.... Why should we in seeking a type for the illustration or symbol of a nation that need not hold itself lower than the Roman virtue or the science of Greece, prefer the barbaric period of a remote and distant people, from which to draw an emblem of nationality, to the aboriginal period of our own land?... Why not be American from the spring-head within our own domain?

From the copper shores of Lake Superior to the silver mountains of Potosi, from the Ojibwa to the Araucanian, the feathered tiara is as characteristic of the primitiveness of our hemisphere, as the turban is of the Asiatic. Nor is there any thing in its decorative character, repulsive to the association of Liberty, with the intelligent American.

On November 4, 1858, Mint Director Snowden discussed Longacre's motif in a letter to Secretary of the Treasury Howell Cobb, noting in part:

The obverse...presents an ideal head of America—the drooping plumes of the North American Indian give it the character of North America...and that so far from being modeled on any human features in the Longacre family, or any Indians, these were based squarely on the classical profiles on ancient sculpture.... In any event, the feathered headdress was certainly intended in at least two instances to be that of the Indian, the artists at the Mint evidently not realizing the absurd incongruity of placing this most masculine attribute of the warrior brave on the head of a woman....

Earlier, in 1854, Longacre had used a "feathered tiara" on the new designs for the gold dollar and $3 gold piece. However, it was differently styled than the headdress, typically likened to a war bonnet, used on the 1858 and later Indian cents.

The earlier-quoted legend that Longacre's daughter Sarah posed as the model has long endured, but in actuality the image is probably a composite. Longacre himself stated the facial profile was copied from a statue, *Venus Accroupii* (Venus Crouching), apparently either in a Philadelphia museum or in the Vatican in Italy.[2] The above-quoted letter from

---

[1] Information from Dr. George R. Conger, "The Controversial Feathered Headdress," *Longacre's Ledger*, April 1992; and Joy Goforth, "Who Came First? Goddess, Sarah, or Indian?" *Coin World*, January 4, 1984 (reprinted from Goforth's article in the November 1983 issue of *Mint Press*, there titled "Goddess of Liberty").

[2] Breen, *Encyclopedia*, p. 217, locates the statue "in a Philadelphia museum." Cornelius Vermeule, *Numismatic Art in America*, is the source for the Vatican location. Could there be two versions of the

Snowden to Cobb seemingly addresses the "Sarah question" via the sentence denying the representation of "any human features in the Longacre family."

A photograph of Sarah Longacre (born on February 20, 1828, and thus hardly a little girl when either the 1854 $3 or the 1858 pattern Indian cents were made) taken on her wedding day in 1847 is inconclusive, but shows her face to be an equal or better candidate than the somewhat unlikely profile of the aforementioned Venus (both images are presented in juxtaposition in *Longacre's Ledger*, July 1992, p. 19). The attribution of the portrait will probably never be decided to everyone's satisfaction, especially absent any surviving information from Longacre stating that his daughter Sarah was the model.

With regard to the "absurd incongruity of placing this most masculine attribute of the warrior brave on the head of a woman," history repeated itself in 1907 when Augustus Saint-Gaudens decked Miss Liberty in a feathered headdress on the new $10 gold coin. However, ethnologically correct male Indians in headdresses were used elsewhere in the American monetary system, most notably on the $5 Silver Certificate paper currency in the Series of 1899, Bela Lyon Pratt's designs for the new gold $2.50 and $5 coins of 1908, and James Earle Fraser's Indian-"Buffalo" nickel of 1913.

Director Snowden wrote to Longacre on November 6, 1858, to advise that the Treasury Department had approved the new (Indian) design, the change to take effect on January 1, 1859. Longacre was to prepare the necessary dies. A slight modification was requested in the reverse die.[1]

In due course in 1859 Longacre's Indian Head design became standard on the copper-nickel cent, and 36,400,000 examples were coined for circulation. As it turned out the laurel wreath reverse was only used this year on the cent. It was not forgotten completely, however, and in 1865 it was adapted for use on the new nickel three-cent denomination.

1860: Design Modified

In 1860, for reasons not clear today, the reverse was redesigned to feature a wreath of oak and other leaves with a narrow shield at the top, a motif used in pattern form on certain 1859 cents.

---

statue? Sarah Longacre biographical and portrait information is adapted from "An Argument Favoring Sarah as Longacre's Model," *Longacre's Ledger*, July 1992, which in turn was based upon several cited sources.

[1] Citation per R.W. Julian, letter, April 24, 1996. The slight modification may have referred to the laurel leaves which were increased in number to six per bunch or cluster, from the five used on patterns. This letter does not preclude Longacre's assigning certain work to his assistant, Anthony C. Paquet, as instructions from the Mint director were typically given to the chief engraver, not to assistants.

THE WASHINGTON CABINET: Medal engraved by Anthony C. Paquet to observe the dedication of the Washington Cabinet at the Philadelphia Mint, February 22, 1860. The Washington Cabinet is directly responsible for restrikes being made of many patterns including 1858 cents. These were used in trade to augment the Cabinet, which increased in size from four or five pieces at its inception by James Ross Snowden in early 1859 to 138 pieces by February 1860. (Photograph courtesy of Stack's)

The new oak wreath with narrow shield reverse motif may have been the work of Anthony C. Paquet, alternatively of James B. Longacre, and in any event was adapted from pattern reverses of 1858 (oak wreath with open top and oak wreath with broad ornamented shield at apex). The lettering ONE CENT on the 1860 issues differs from that on the 1859 cent.

The Indian head obverse design and oak wreath and narrow shield reverse remained standard in the series through its end in 1909.

Too Many Cents: an "Evil"

By autumn 1860 there were too many cents in circulation, not only Flying Eagle cents minted for commerce in 1857 and 1858, but also the new Indian Head design first minted in 1859. An article in the *Philadelphia Press,* reprinted in the October 1860 issue of *The Bankers' Magazine and Statistical Register.* advised the following:

> We are requested to state that the Spanish and Mexican fractions of the dollar will not, after today, be received at the Mint at their nominal value, exchanged for the new cents. The main object of the law authorizing these coins to be received at their nominal value of twenty-five, twelve and a half, and six and a quarter cents [Spanish 2-real, 1-real, half real, and medio silver coins], was to retire them from circulation, and thus relieve the community from worn-out and depreciated currency, which materially interfered with our excellent decimal system of coinage.
>
> The object having in a great measure been obtained, and the amount of cents issued being quite large, Mr. Snowden, director of the Mint, recommended that a law should be passed to repeal so much of the former law, on the subject that required these exchanges to be made. This accordingly has been done.
>
> Hereafter the new cents will only be paid out in exchange for gold and silver coins of the United States, and for the copper cent of the former issues. This regulation will undoubtedly be regarded by many of our citizens as a judicious one, inasmuch as the large issue of the new nickel cents has rendered them almost as much of a nuisance as the old Spanish currency. Many persons who have obtained for the latter, at its nominal value, much larger number of the cents than they could legitimately use, have used them to pay bills of one, two or three dollars, and as this custom has been extended, it has caused considerable inconvenience.
>
> The new regulation, by destroying the cause of the over-issue of cents, will no doubt do much to diminish the evil which has resulted from it, and it is hoped that the period is not far distant when the supply of cents will not be graded on the demand for them for use in the small transactions to which silver coins are not adapted....

More About the Flood of Cents

The same issue of *Bankers' Magazine* told more:

> There is much feeling manifested in this city at the persistence of the Philadelphia Mint coinage of cents, the market is so flooded with them. The answer of the Mint is, that there is a constant demand, to meet which they must continue to coin.

This demand comes from those who care nothing for the inconvenience of the community, or who do not experience any of the evils of the great surplus of cents, and are therefore inconsiderate enough to order new pieces from the Mint to meet their payments.

Banks, and a variety of other institutions and establishments which have to provide change, prefer an elegant new cent to a dirty old one, and will order from the Mint a constant supply as fast as their stock is exhausted. Of course, as they are not obliged to receive them back, they care little how many are afloat. Thus the evil goes on increasing every day.

There are 10 million cents at this moment in New York over and above the want of the community, and they serve no purpose except to rob the poor of the daily commission on their hard earnings. There is no way to get rid of them; they are sold every day at a depreciation, and immediately put into circulation to be paid out and sold over again. There is but one way to remedy the evil. Let the secretary of the Treasury order the Mint at once to stop the coinage.

If there is any demand for them, orders can be filled here at this moment, at a discount of one year's interest. Congress should then give the people the privilege of exchanging them at the Mint for silver; this would at once meet the "demand" at the Mint, and the director would take care that there were not too many coined, if the surplus were allowed to go back to its source....

The *Report of the Director of the Mint,* 1860, included this commentary:

The new cents have heretofore been issued in exchange for the fractions of the Spanish and Mexican dollar, and for the old copper cents. As the Spanish and Mexican pieces were received at their nominal value, large amounts of these coins have been brought to the melting-pot, and thus the community has been relieved from an irregular and depreciated currency. But it has required the issue of a large amount of cents, and induced a temporary redundancy of that coin in some of the Eastern cities. They are gradually, however, being distributed to all parts of our country, including a portion of the Southern states, where the copper cent was scarcely known as a circulating medium.

Since the passage of the Act of 25th of June, 1860, the issues have been limited to exchanges for the copper cents, except the supplying of the government offices with the new issue, and distant parts of the country in limited amounts. In order to accelerate the process of relieving the community from the cumbrous and inconvenient copper cents, the Mint now pays the expenses of transportation on them, and will make returns in the new issues. This arrangement will tend to relieve the country from a burdensome currency, without increasing the amount of circulation of that denomination of coins.

The Situation in July 1862

The Bankers' Magazine and Statistical Register, November 1862, reported on events in Philadelphia the preceding July:

The great feature of [July 1862] was the heavy manufacture of cents, of which 3,600,000 were made, of the value of $36,000. There was a great rush to the Mint to procure cents. The *North American* says: "At an early hour in the morning there were not less than 150 boys and men, and 31 young ladies and girls, awaiting a supply of pennies. The boys and men carried shotbags, cigar boxes, baskets, and all sorts of contrivances in which to carry off the much-needed coin. The girls principally carried neat baskets. When the distribution came to be made, the girls were first served, to the intense chagrin of the men, who had been standing on a single foot, alternately, upon the sidewalk for two or three hours. The men and boys were not attended to until the last girl had departed."

Actually, the larger part of the story was left unsaid. The Civil War was raging, and the outcome was uncertain. Some foreign countries (England being the prime example) dallied with the idea of recognizing the Confederate States of America, while others sided with the Union. Meanwhile, as in other times of national emergency, the public tried to squirrel away items of lasting value. In the second week of July, 1862, there was a flurry of hoarding throughout the Eastern and Midwest sections of the United States. By month's end no silver coins were seen in circulation, and copper-nickel cents were "in anxious demand, and we have heard of 2% [premium] in some instances being paid for them."[1] Gold coins had not been seen in general trade since the preceding January.

As a palliative Congress passed the Act of July 17, 1862, stating that ordinary postage stamps could be used as money in paying federal debts up to $5. The intent of this law was subverted soon thereafter, and the Treasury ordered a supply of privately-printed notes popularly referred to as Postage Currency, although there had been no legal provision for them. (Today these are collected as part of the Fractional Currency series.) Postal Currency notes were first distributed to Army paymasters in August 1862 and to the public in September. By early 1863 about $100,000 of these notes reached circulation per day, but the demand remained unsatisfied.[2] Denominations were 5¢, 10¢, 25¢, and 50¢. The first of these notes had perforated edges just like stamps.

Meanwhile, in New York City in mid-July, 1862, there were no silver three-cent pieces, half dimes, or other coins of intrinsic value with which to buy a glass of soda or a mug of beer or a streetcar ride, unless such coins were purchased at a premium from a speculator.

The Treasury Department stopped paying out freshly-minted silver and gold coins and relegated them to bank vaults or sold them at a premium (in terms of paper money) for export. Silver coins did not return to general use until the mid-1870s and were not in generous supply until 1876; gold was back in circulation on a widespread basis by mid-December 1878 (the mandated date was January 1, 1879, but this was anticipated in practice).

For over a decade, beginning in the summer of 1862, substituting in

---

[1] Neil Carothers, *Fractional Money,* p. 187, quoting the July 4, 1862, *Public Ledger.*
[2] Neil Carothers, *Fractional Money,* 177-178.

the place of silver coins were many privately-issued items including tickets and small notes printed in values from 1¢ upward, government postage stamps placed in privately printed envelopes and brass frames (the latter known as encased postage stamps), and a vast flood of small one-cent-size bronze (mostly) and brass tokens.

Indian cents continued to be minted in record numbers in the summer of 1862, and from time to time quantities were released into circulation, as outlined in the newspaper report cited above. The reason why the public clamored for cents in July 1862 is that they were becoming increasingly difficult to find in circulation at the time. Many had been taken off the market, sometimes by being wrapped in paper rolls or packets of 25, 50, or 100 coins, and then stored by those who accepted them in trade. "Bus companies, theatres, and restaurants accepted these rolls everywhere. A retail store in New York received so many that the floor of the room in which they were stored collapsed."[1]

Hoarders had Flying Eagle and Indian cents. The public did not. By July 10, 1862, copper-nickel cents were trading at a 4% premium (in terms of paper money) in New York City, and by July 15 they cost a similar premium in Springfield, Massachusetts.[2] What a change from the glut of 1860!

In his *Fractional Money* study, 1930, p. 187, Neil Carothers commented:

> In a vain effort to satisfy the demand [for copper-nickel Indian cents] the Mint forced itself into a rate of production even higher than that of 1858. By the end of July the weekly issue amounted to 1,200,000 pieces. One-third of this total was reserved for Philadelphia, the remainder going to the other large cities. No applicant anywhere received more than $5 worth.
>
> The coinage jumped from 12,000,000 pieces in the [fiscal] year ending June 30, 1862, to 47,800,000 in the following year. Even this extraordinary value in cents, $478,000, was a small sum which contrasted with the $25,000,000 or more in silver coin that had disappeared. The demand for the cent pieces was never satisfied. The conditions in Philadelphia, which were duplicated in other cities, were described in the *Public Ledger* of July 18th [1862]:
>
> "The difficulty among small shopkeepers, provision dealers in the markets and in the city generally, in making change, has caused an extraordinary demand for cents, and all that can be commanded at the Mint are eagerly bought.... Though many of those who desired cents stood in line for hours, waiting an opportunity to get into the Mint, they had to go home without them, as the supply on hand was exhausted before half the applicants were accommodated."

Carothers went on to note that these cents, called "nickels" or simply "nicks" (in an era before the nickel five-cent piece, introduced in 1866, would assume that name), were in demand because the owner-

---

[1] Carothers, *Fractional Money*, p. 187.
[2] Carothers, *Fractional Money*, p. 187.

ship of a few cents "meant that the owner could ride rather than walk. And, for months after it meant that he could buy a postage stamp without an altercation with the clerk or a cigar without receiving in change a handful of the dealer's own manufactured currency [paper tickets or notes]."

The Scene 1863-1866

By March 1863 the Treasury Department's so-called Postage Currency notes in values of 5¢ to 50¢ had become common in trade and, seemingly, should have alleviated the cent shortage. However, the public still preferred coins, silver and gold remained nowhere to be seen, and attention continued to be focused on the copper-nickel Indian cent. On March 9, 1863, the *Public Ledger* reported that in Philadelphia cents were "so scarce as to command a premium of 20%."[1]

By the end of the Mint's fiscal year on June 30, 1863, copper-nickel cents were sufficiently scarce that Director James Pollock reported that they were "scarcely to be had" in circulation, and stated that he could not guess "as to the amount of cents that will be required to meet the public demand."

Under the provisions of the Act of March 3, 1863, the federal government issued Fractional Currency notes in denominations from 5¢ to 50¢, but this distribution did not begin until October 10 of the same year. At this time the tattered Postage Currency notes began to be gradually retired. In autumn 1864 a new Fractional Currency denomination, the 3¢ note, reached circulation, but never became popular.[2]

Gradually as privately-issued bronze tokens were dumped into circulation by the millions and used for everyday change, Indian cents returned to commercial channels and circulated, but seemingly not in quantity. As late as June 30, 1864, at the end of the Mint's fiscal year, Director Pollock reported, "Large quantities are hoarded, and thus kept from circulation."

Apparently, by autumn 1864 the situation eased somewhat, for little was said later in *Mint Reports* about cent hoarding. By this time the new bronze Indian cent was a reality. In the same year, 1864, the bronze two-cent piece was introduced to help relieve the need for pocket change, and in 1865 the nickel three-cent piece made its debut, followed by the nickel five-cent piece in 1866. Still, silver coins remained in Treasury vaults and did not circulate. However, by 1865-1866 there were enough minor coins in the channels of commerce to satisfy most needs.

---

[1] Carothers, *Fractional Money,* p. 189.

[2] In 1869 another denomination, 15¢, was added to the Fractional Currency lineup, but it, too, was never widely used. Fractional Currency notes of all kinds tended to become tattered and soiled easily and were hard to stack and count. The public called these notes "stamps."

Bronze Cents

Copper-nickel metal was very difficult for the Mint to use. It was extremely hard, did not strike up well, and caused rapid die wear. In 1863 Mint officials noted that the public eagerly used private tokens minted of softer bronze, and pattern Indian cents (Judd-299, Pollock-359) were struck in a related alloy (the Mint alloy was 95% copper and 5% tin and zinc). The new bronze Indian cents, minted under the Act of April 22, 1864, were of lighter weight, thinner, and struck up better than the old-style coins. By the end of May 1864, the copper-nickel cent had been discontinued, and the bronze cent had become standard.

Meanwhile on April 15, 1864, Joseph Wharton, who in 1863 had purchased a nickel mine in Lancaster Gap, Pennsylvania, and who reportedly had $200,000 invested in it, published a pamphlet, "Project for Reorganizing the Small Coinage of the United States of America," which recommended that the use of nickel be *increased,* and denominations of 1¢, 2¢, 3¢, 5¢, and 10¢ be made with an alloy of 25% nickel and 75% copper. Wharton exercised strong influence on certain members of Congress, and at his doorstep can be directly laid the widespread use of nickel in coinage during this era including the new nickel three-cent piece in 1865 and the nickel five-cent piece in 1866 which were made in accordance with his 25% nickel, 75% copper suggestion.[1]

This same Lancaster Gap nickel source, under different ownership, had supplied nickel for copper-nickel cents 1856 onward.[2]

The 1860s and 1870s

After 1865, quantities struck of Indian cents dropped significantly as other minor denominations and Fractional Currency notes took up the slack. From then through 1878 there were only a few years in which the mintage exceeded 10 million: 1868, 1873, 1874, and 1875. For three years—1871, 1872, and 1877—production was less than 5 million annually, with 1877 registering only 852,500 coins.

By 1871 so many cents had accumulated that they had become a nuisance. Congress passed a law allowing them to be redeemed in green-

---

[1] The Wharton School of Business at the University of Pennsylvania is named for him, following his funding in 1881. Wharton (March 3, 1826 - January 11, 1909), well-known in his time for his unflagging efforts to influence legislators, has been largely lionized in print over the years, except in obscure financial and political analyses (Carothers' book being an example). Wharton set up exhibits promoting nickel at international fairs in Vienna in 1873 and Philadelphia in 1876, among other places. He sought to influence various countries—Russia in particular, but his petition was unsuccessful—to substitute nickel alloy for silver in coinage, stating that great profits could be made this way. In an earlier generation—in the mid-1830s—Dr. Lewis Feuchtwanger was a strong advocate of nickel in coinage, and in 1837 he caused many one-cent pieces to be privately made in a silver-appearing alloy containing a significant percentage of nickel.

[2] Carothers, *Fractional Money,* p.197.

Steam-driven coining press used at the Mint in 1885. The pulley at
the left was connected by belting to shafts which in turn were powered by a steam engine at a remote location. (*Visitor's Guide and
History of the United States Mint, Philadelphia, Pa.* A.M. Smith,
1885, P. 20)

backs by the Treasury when presented in amounts of $20 or more. The Act of March 1871 provided for the melting of millions of unwanted two-cent pieces (first coined in 1864) as well as worn copper and bronze cents, with the metal to be used to strike further Indian cents. This piece of legislation resulted in generous mintage figures after 1872.

In 1873 the Treasury's illegal resumption of silver specie payments put silver coins back into commercial channels. By 1876 this severely lessened the demand for minor coins, resulting in lower mintages for the cent, nickel three-cent, and nickel five-cent pieces.[1]

1879-1909

Beginning in 1879, production of Indian cents at the Philadelphia Mint went back over the 10 million mark annually and remained there for the rest of the series through to its end in 1909. The lowest mintage of this interval was 11,765,384 (including 3,790 Proofs) for 1885, and the highest mintage and the only year to cross the 100 million mark was 1907 with a production of 108,138,618 (including 1,475 Proofs). The American economy was in a rapid growth stage during the early twentieth century, coin-operated machines were being made in unprecedented quantities, and Indian cents were needed in record numbers.

Until 1908, production of Indian cents was limited to the Philadelphia Mint. In that year 1,115,000 cents were produced at San Francisco, each coin having a tiny S mintmark below the wreath on the reverse. The first production took place on November 27, 1908.

In 1909 309,000 1909-S Indian cents were made, the lowest business strike production in the Indian series.

Collecting Business Strikes

As a dealer, I have always found it convenient to group Indian cents into several time periods, each of which have their own characteristics. If you are contemplating beginning a set of Indian cents, begin with the less expensive pieces, selecting coins one at a time, and then graduate to the others:

There are no great rarities among copper-nickel Indian cents of the 1859-1864 years. The 1859 is in great demand as it is the only year with the laurel wreath reverse design.

In 1859 an estimated 1,000 or more specimens were made of a transitional pattern (Pollock-272, Judd-228) utilizing the standard 1859 Indian cent obverse in combination with the oak wreath and shield reverse (as

---

[1] The Treasury illegally began silver specie payments, dimes to half dollars, in the spring of 1873; Congress belatedly authorized the action in 1875 (R.W. Julian, letter, April 24, 1996).

regularly adopted in 1860). Unlike most patterns, nearly all strikings were made in business strike format instead of Proof.[1] Over the years some authors and editors have incorporated these into the regular series, most notably in the listing in the 18th (and last) Edition of the *Standard Catalogue of U.S. Coins,* published in 1957. This insertion was at the behest of editor John J. Ford, Jr., successor to Wayte Raymond. The present writer recalls finding several specimens of the Obverse of 1859, Reverse of 1860, transitional cent in dealers' stocks as regular issues. Nearly all specimens are very sharply struck, brilliant, and lustrous. I have never seen a well-worn one, although Walter Breen states (in error in my opinion) that "many survivors are in Fine to EF grades."[2] Richard Snow suggests that many of these pieces may have been stored at the Mint and in the late 1870s distributed to collectors, about the same time that leftover Proof 1862 cents were released.[3]

Among regular-issue Indian cents with the oak wreath and shield reverse motif 1860-1864, the 1861 is the scarcest and usually is seen well struck. The 1864 is not rare, but most are weakly struck. Cherrypicking for quality is advised.

In my opinion, a run of one of each date of copper-nickel Indian cent 1859 to 1864 is beautiful to behold, especially if the coins are in MS-63 or finer preservation.

Bronze Indian cents, first minted for circulation in 1864, must be cherrypicked even more carefully than copper-nickel issues as many are unattractive.

The early range of bronze cents 1864-1878 contains a number of scarce and rare issues, including all dates from 1866 through 1872 plus 1877. The most famous rarities are the 1864 with L on ribbon, 1871, 1872, and especially the 1877.

The later range of cents from 1879 through 1909 is eminently collectible, and just about anyone can afford a complete run of Philadelphia Mint issues in higher grades from EF through, say, MS-64. In my mind, some great buys can be made by cherrypicking such grades as MS-60 through MS-64, as there is often a very wide difference in quality.

The 1908-S and 1909-S are scarce, especially in Mint State. Some specimens of both years, if described as "RB," are apt to have woodgrain toning. Other red and brown coins are somewhat spotty. In the Mint State category you may have to examine several to find just one that you like. This seems to be especially true of 1909-S.

---

[1] Walter Breen, *Encyclopedia,* p. 219, reports just two Proofs known to him; the present writer has also seen just two Proofs (but has owned well over 100 Mint State pieces). Appendix II contains more information on this issue.

[2] *Encyclopedia,* p. 218.

[3] Letter, April 10, 1996.

Counterstamped and Overstruck Coins

Many Indian cents were privately marked with punches and placed into circulation to broadcast a message. Possibly the most curious of these is the variety issued by W. Bell, an Erie, Pennsylvania, dry-goods retailer, who obtained a quantity of 1859 cents, ground off the reverse of each, and counterstamped them with an advertisement for his business.

Dr. G.G. Wilkins of Pittsfield, New Hampshire, stamped many copper-nickel Indian cents and a few early bronze issues with his name. In their time such pieces must have served as advertisement for his dental practice or perhaps for one or another of his activities (operating an eating house, selling patent medicines, etc.). Somewhat rarer are early-date Indian cents stamped OIL OF ICE, apparently a patent medicine, the historical details of which I have never been able to track down. In Blendon, Michigan, in the 1870s, Perry E. Ballou, a phrenologist (a person who examines head bumps and contours and offers conclusions about the personality of the subject), stamped Indian cents and other coins with P.E. BALLOU / PHRENOLOGIST. These pieces are also quite rare, and I have seen only one or two over a long period of years.

Numerous privately-produced Civil War store cards and political tokens of the 1863 era exist overstruck on copper-nickel cents and range in availability from scarce to very rare. Among patriotic-type Civil War tokens, about 65 to 70 different varieties are known.[1] Additional varieties of store cards (advertising tokens) are overstruck and are also scarce to rare.

Parts of the original Indian cent designs and inscriptions are still visible on the store cards if one looks closely, and if you are lucky, the date will be readable as well. The reason for making these is not known, for it seems that little commercial advantage would have been gained by taking current cents at face value, running them through a coining press, and delivering them to a merchant. It can be said that there may have been some advertising advantage, but if so, it would have been easier to have made the same token designs on thin bronze planchets which could have been purchased for less than one cent each. Quite possibly, such overstruck pieces, which exist today to the extent of several hundred or more pieces and usually in Mint State, were made to the order of J.N.T. Levick, Edward Groh (curator of the collection of the American Numismatic and Archaeological Society), and other token aficionados active in the 1860s. It seems likely that these pieces were mainly produced to create token varieties in copper-nickel metal, rather than to specifically make overstrikes, as no special effort seems to have been made to preserve the original Indian cent designs.

---

[1] George and Melvin Fuld, *Patriotic Civil War Tokens,* 4th edition, p. 17.

CIVIL WAR TOKEN OVERSTRIKE: 1863 Civil War token struck over an 1860 copper-nickel Indian cent. The top photographs, enlarged, are oriented to show the Indian cent undertype. Note the "ghost" 1860 date at the lower rim and on the reverse, the shield in ghost form at the horse's tail. Among Civil War tokens this is Fuld catalogue no. F 180-341. Several dozen different varieties of Civil War tokens are known struck over copper-nickel Indian cents. This overstrike is particularly sharp. (Dr. Larkin M. Wilson Collection, Part II, Lot 3519, Bowers and Merena, 1996)

While Indian cents counterstamped with advertisements or overstruck with token dies can have significant numismatic value running in some instances into the hundreds of dollars, much more common are cents that were stamped with stray marks. Such latter pieces bear initials, numbers, or other punches, not attributable as to source today, and are usually considered as damaged coins. For example, a VF-20 grade 1860 Indian cent if counterstamped with OIL OF ICE would be worth over $100—equal to many multiples of the VF-20 price for an unstamped coin—but if marked with a stray punch such as "A" would be considered to be damaged and worth only a dollar or two.

Proof Mintage

Proof 1859 Indian cents, the only year with laurel wreath reverse, have traditionally commanded premium prices over, say, Indian cents of 1860 and 1861 which exist in markedly lower numbers. As the 1859 has been more expensive, more in demand, and more the focus of attention, a proportionately higher percentage of extant pieces have been sent to the certification services.

Government records of the total quantities struck of minor (copper-nickel, bronze, and nickel alloy) Proof coins before 1878 do not exist. Although the *Guide Book* lists estimated mintage figures for Indian cents of the 1859-1877 years, these seem to be based upon the figures for *silver* coins of the same years. While those who bought silver sets usually bought Proof Indian cents as well, many extra Proof cents were sold singly and in groups. In actuality, in my opinion, the mintages of Proof cents as compared to silver coins were often different, sometimes dramatically so. In the sub-chapters for each date I give my opinions of estimated distribution for pre-1878 years. After that time official Mint figures are used.

Among Proof copper-nickel cents of the 1860-1864 years, the scarcest dates are 1860 and 1861, and the most plentiful is 1862. One can suppose that there was a rush for 1862 Proofs because of the circumstances going on in the economy at the time; the earlier quoted rush for Mint State 1862 cents probably created a crossover demand for extra Proofs. Moreover, apparently a group of undistributed Proofs was found at the Mint in the late 1870s and sold to numismatists at that time.[1]

Strangely enough, Uncle Sam would not accept his own "greenback" paper money notes (authorized on February 25, 1862, and first circu-

---

[1] Richard Snow, letter, April 10, 1996; the quantity of 200 Proof cents is suggested. However, R.W. Julian, letter, April 24, 1996, notes "Only a small number of 1862 cents were found in the mid-1870s, not about 200. Also, the large number of Proof cents that piled up [in numismatic hands] were the result of volume buying by dealers, not a Mint action."

lated in April of that year) in payment for Proof coins after mid-1862. To buy them a numismatist had to pay a premium to a bullion dealer or bank for silver or gold coins and send these coins to the Mint! Because of this, it was a nuisance to order Proof coins in 1863 and the next several years, and mintages were reduced accordingly.

In the 1880s the Mint went wild with the striking of Proof cents, and so many unsold pieces piled up that they were wholesaled to Eastern dealers, and supplies remained on the market for generations afterward, at least until the 1950s.

Collecting Proof Indian Cents

Selecting Indian cents for quality is probably even more important for Proofs than for business strikes. While a MS-60 business strike can be very attractive as can a MS-61, in general Proof coins in lower grades such as Proof-60 and Proof-61 tend to be spotted, stained, mottled, or just plain ugly.

Unless you come upon some very special low-grade Proofs, I suggest using Proof-63 as a beginning, at least for the bronze issues. The copper-nickel Proofs 1859-1864 are sometimes decent in grades such as Proof-60 or Proof-61, but bronze Proofs rarely are. In general, Proof copper-nickel Indian cents survived in nicer condition than did Proof bronze cents as bronze is a more chemically active alloy.

Even at the Proof-63 level for bronze cents, and continuing up to whatever higher Proof grades you want to buy, it is essential to cherrypick. While some microscopic "flyspecks" are normal on most Proofs, I would avoid big spots, oxidation and corrosion patches, and other detractions.

There is a strange situation among Proof Indian cents of the bronze series 1864-1909: sometimes a carefully selected brown or red and brown Proof coin can be more attractive than a red one with spots (and a heck of a lot cheaper, too)! I suspect that a very carefully chosen collection of Proof-63 brown and Proof-64 brown Proofs would be a finer assemblage that a quickly purchased run of Proof-65 red coins, especially if the red coins had problems (as they often do).

Among Proof 1864 bronze cents certain Proofs of the usual type without L on ribbon may have been struck on bronzed (dark, as on certain bronzed patterns of this era) planchets and not made with a "red" finish. As is explained in the 1864 bronze cent sub-chapter below, more research needs to be done. However, Proof 1864 cents with L on ribbon were struck with bright or "red" surfaces.

In the 1880s the Mint produced a record number of Proof cents. Many of these were not distributed to the public, but at year's end or early the following year were sold in bulk to dealers. Large numbers, still in thin tissue paper wrappings, remained in hoards through the mid-point of the present century. Today these can often be recognized by having virtually flawless gem surfaces, toned a rich medium brown (from the sulfur in the tissue paper), and with nuances of blue or purple iridescence of incredible beauty. John Dannreuther commented that for Proof cents of 1885 and both types of 1886, purple is the main color for most of the deeply toned coins examined by PCGS.[1]

Writing in the October 1943 issue of *The Numismatist,* Marvin Winsett was enthusiastic about Indian cents. As part of an extended commentary he noted:[2] "Both the Uncirculated and Proof bronze Indian cents are usually toned in a wide variety of color shades. My own 1885 Proof is a brilliant purple color. Perfect brilliant red coins are scarce and usually command a higher price."

The amazing situation today is that such a gem might cost much less on the market than a spotted or defective Proof-65 red coin!

In general, the quality of Proofs made at the Mint declined from the 1880s through the 1890s, and some of the latter decade are very sloppily made.

Michael G. Fahey, senior numismatist at ANACS, commented concerning the fact that relatively few Proofs of the late 1880s have been certified in comparison to their large mintages:[3]

> One possible explanation for such a low percentage is the poor quality of Proof minor coins from this era. There may be hundreds of Proof coins that are trading as business strikes due to their appearance. Also, poorly-made Proofs are typically downgraded, due to their substandard eye appeal.

Choose slowly and carefully. A hurry-up set of miscellaneous quality Proofs could probably be built in a few months, except, perhaps, for the 1864 L rarity. A superb quality set might well take several years to assemble even if your checking account has no limits.

Proofs from about 1902 through 1909, and especially of the year 1903, have the portrait semi-polished rather than frosty. This is normal.

---

[1] Letter, May 16, 1996.
[2] "Collect Indian Head Cents for Pleasure and Profit."
[3] Letter, May 15, 1996.

CHAPTER 11

INDIAN CENTS 1859-1909

•

Date-by-Date Study and Analysis
Arranged in Sub-Chapters

1859 Indian Cent

Laurel Wreath Reverse

Business Strikes:

Business strike mintage: 36,400,000.

Number of business strike obverse dies made: Not known.

Average number of coins struck from typical obverse die: Not known.

Availability in Mint State: Enough were minted that today there is no problem finding one in just about any grade. Brilliant gems are particularly beautiful, even more so if sharply struck.

Availability in circulated grades: Common.

Characteristics of striking: Many are lightly struck.

Market Prices (1859 business strikes)

YEAR	G-4	VG-8	F-12	VF-20	EF-40	AU-50
1938	$0.10	$0.15	$0.25	$0.35	$0.50	$1.00
1944	.25	.40	.50	.80	1.00	2.00
1965	4.00	5.00	9.00	15.00	23.00	40.00
1996	8.00	10,00	12.50	32.50	80.00	150.00

YEAR	MS-60	MS-63	MS-64	MS-65		
1938	$2.00	$2.10	$2.20	$2.25		
1944	3.00	3.25	3.40	3.50		
1965	85.00	87.50	90.00	95.00		
1996	210.00	400.00	950.00	2,750.00		

Proofs:

Proof distribution (estimated): 1,000. Quite a few Proofs were made due to the novelty of the first year of issue.

Proof commentary: When seen, most Proofs are apt to be nice, but there are exceptions. Some prooflike business strikes have been called Proofs, thus diluting the true rarity of the issue. In strong demand for type sets as it is the only year with laurel wreath reverse.

Proofs have laurel leaves in clusters of six; should one be found with leaves in clusters of five it may represent a very early striking or even a pattern.

Note: Proof mintage records do not exist for Indian cents prior to 1878; figures given here are the author's estimate of those actually distributed. There is no way of knowing if larger quantities were made and later melted (such data exist for certain silver coins but few minor issues). However, in 1859 the cost for an individual Proof one-cent piece was face value plus postage; as of 1860 it was twice face value, or 2¢, at the Mint.[1] Prior to 1860 there was no premium attached.

Market Prices (1859 Proofs)

YEAR	PR-60	PR-63	PR-64	PR-65		
1938	$2.50	$2.50	$2.85	$3.25		
1944	7.50	7.90	8.25	9.00		
1965	600.00	635.00	675.00	725.00		
1996	500.00	1,100.00	2,750.00	4,500.00		

Notes

Collecting commentary: A plentiful issue in all business strike grades; rare in Proof. Extremely popular as a one-year type.

Repunched date: One rare variety (Breen-1945, 15-20 estimated to have been identified so far; Snow-1, FND-001) has a dramatically repunched date. Most known specimens are in circulated grades. In March 1995 Sam Lukes "sold the finest known 1859 repunched date (graded ANACS MS-64) for $5,200 to a prominent collector."[2] As of this writing, neither NGC nor PCGS takes note of this variety; thus, there is a great opportunity for the aware specialist to find an example among unattributed coins. The same is true, of course, for most other die varieties in the Indian series.

Only year of type: This date stands alone among regular-issue Indian cents as the only variety with laurel wreath on the reverse.

Numismatic curiosity: The Stuart C. Levine, M.D., Collection (Bowers and Merena, April 1986), Lot 2209, offered an 1859 Indian cent obverse die impression deeply struck on an 1857 silver half dime. The obverse of the half dime was flattened by the cent die. The reverse of the half dime was more or less intact, but wavy; perhaps the half dime had been placed face-up on a piece of leather during the striking process. Described as AU-55, the piece was pedigreed to the George F. Seavey and Lorin G.

---

[1] R.W. Julian, "Notes on U.S. Proof Coinage, Silver and Minor." *Numismatic Scrapbook Magazine,* March 1966; also letter, April 24, 1996.

[2] Sam Lukes, letter, April 8, 1996.

Parmelee collections in the 19th century and to the Charles L. Ruby Collection sale (Superior, 1974).

Cent exchanges: By June 30, 1859, $95,241 value *by weight* of old-style large copper cents had been exchanged at the Mint for new copper-nickel cents.[1]

More on the origin of the design: Chief Engraver Charles E. Barber's commentary on this much-discussed subject: A letter from Barber printed in *The Numismatist*, March 1910, noted that a gentleman still employed at the Mint recalled the time years earlier when James B. Longacre created the Indian Head design and noted that it was not adapted from Longacre's daughter, that Longacre was against using human portraits from life, and that "it is also very clear in his mind that Mr. Longacre's aim was to portray what he considered an ideal head of an Indian female. This he gathered from many conversations upon this subject. This much for the testimony of one who was assistant to Mr. Longacre." Barber further noted that the same face was found on the $3 coin.

The laurel wreath reverse of the 1859 cent is similar to that used on certain 1858 patterns and is believed to have been the work of Anthony C. Paquet.

The curious coins of W. Bell: In 1859 (presumably) a dry goods retailer obtained a supply of new Indian cents, ground off their reverses on a lathe, and stamped on each this inscription: FOR / BARGAINS / IN / DRY GOODS / GO TO / W. BELL'S / 5 EXCHANGE / ERIE PA. Listed by Dr. George Fuld as his catalogue number 360A-1do, the variety is estimated as Rarity-6 (13 to 30 known).

---

[1] 1859 *Mint Report*, p. 5.

1860 Indian Cent

Oak Wreath and Shield Reverse

Business Strikes:

Business strike mintage: 20,566,000.

Number of business strike obverse dies made: Not known.

Average number of coins struck from typical obverse die: Not known.

Availability in Mint State: Fairly scarce at the gem Mint State level.

Two major varieties:

Two main varieties exist for this year:

Narrow Bust: The style of 1859 with Narrow Bust (pointed tip to neck truncation).

Broad Bust: The style of 1860 with rounded neck tip.

The Narrow Bust is considerably the rarer and in grades up through about MS-63 is worth a sharp premium over the rounded neck tip (source: *Coin World* "Trends"; the prices for the Narrow Bust variety given below are from that source). The variety differences are not widely publicized and as of early 1996, neither PCGS nor NGC had taken any notice of them. The 1860 Narrow Bust is thus a prime coin for cherrypicking. Good luck!

Availability in circulated grades: Common.

Characteristics of striking: Most pieces are fairly well struck, but specimens are sometimes seen with pebbly or grainy surfaces due to protracted die use.

Market Prices

(1860 business strikes; Broad Bust with rounded tip to neck;
the usually-seen variety)

YEAR	G-4	VG-8	F-12	VF-20	EF-40	AU-50
1938	$0.10	$0.15	$0.25	$0.35	$0.50	$1.00
1944	.25	.40	.50	.80	1.00	2.00
1965	3.00	4.25	7.50	12.00	18.00	32.50
1996	6.00	7.50	10.00	15.00	45.00	75.00

YEAR	MS-60	MS-63	MS-64	MS-65		
1938	$2.00	$2.10	$2.20	$2.25		
1944	3.00	3.25	3.40	3.50		
1965	60.00	62.00	64.00	67.50		
1996	137.50	205.00	290.00	700.00		

Market Prices

(1860 business strikes; Narrow Bust with pointed tip to neck)

YEAR	G-4	VG-8	F-12	VF-20	EF-40	AU-50
1996	8.50	12.50	17.00	40.00	80.00	140.00

YEAR	MS-60	MS-63	MS-64	MS-65		
1996	225.00	350.00	950.00	3,000.00		

Proofs:

Proof distribution (estimated): 550 (514 with the silver Proof sets, 28 or more individually).[1] However, 1,000 or more Proof cents were coined.

Proof commentary: Beware of prooflike Mint State coins being offered as Proofs. Today Proofs are quite difficult to find. In 1977 in his *Encyclopedia of Proof Coins* Walter Breen stated "only a few dozen can be traced." The same writer went on to say that many published citations of "Proofs" were in fact prooflike business strikes. True Proofs seem to be major rarities and are several orders rarer than are Proof 1859 cents. The reason for this discrepancy is not known.

All Proofs known to specialists today are of the later Broad Bust style.[2] One specimen of the Narrow Bust cent has been certified as a Proof, but "it is blatantly not a Proof."[3]

---

[1] Breen, *Encyclopedia,* p. 220. This assumes that each purchaser of a silver set also acquired a Proof Indian cent; in actuality, this was probably not the case in all instances.
[2] Walter Breen transposed his notes concerning Proof 1860 cents and stated that the narrow-tip variety was the one usually seen; in actuality, none of that style are known in Proof; *all* are of the rounded tip style.
[3] Richard Snow, letter, April 10, 1996.

The first recorded delivery by the coiner of U.S. Proof one-cent places took place on March 8, 1860, when 1,000 or more pieces were included along with 1,000 silver Proof sets.[1] Many of these Proof sets never found buyers. The Mint was optimistic in its production quantities of silver Proof coins (no records exist for copper-nickel cents) in 1859-1861, after which mintages were scaled back to more closely conform with actual sales. It is believed that each silver Proof set sold during the era was accompanied by a copper-nickel cent, and that, in addition, extra Proof cents were minted.

Cost of individual Proof cents at the Mint was 2¢ plus postage.

Market Prices

(1860 Proofs; Broad Bust style with rounded neck tip)

YEAR	PR-60	PR-63	PR-64	PR-65		
1938	$3.00	$3.00	$3.30	$3.75		
1944	7.50	8.00	8.00	8.50		
1965	400.00	450.00	510.00	550.00		
1996	360.00	685.00	1,500.00	3,100.00		

Notes

New type: First year of the oak wreath reverse type, most probably by Anthony C. Paquet, certainly derived from patterns made in 1858. Two main varieties exist for this year: the style of 1859 with Narrow Bust (pointed tip to neck truncation) and the style of 1860 Broad Bust (with rounded tip). See business strike notes above. All Proofs are of the Round Bust variety.

Production notes: [2] After May 1860 so many copper-nickel Flying Eagle and Indian cents were in the channels of commerce that production was lessened, and smaller quantities were made from that time through the following year (1861). Compared to an average cent mintage of about three million per month for the entire year of 1859, the latter part of 1860 saw fewer than 800,000 made in the average month; this was less that 20% of the Mint's capacity to turn out such pieces.

In preparation for making planchet strip, the melter and refiner at the Mint made up ingots.... These were individually tested for conformity to the standard of 88% copper and 12% nickel. In practice, during 1860 and 1861 the nickel content varied from a low of 11.4% to a high of 12.6%. Quoting R.W. Julian, "Each ingot prepared by the melter and refiner produced about 5,500 one-cent pieces. Even for the relatively small coinage of 1860, there were 3,778 copper-nickel ingots prepared." Most copper used in the copper-nickel cents came from melting down old copper "large" cents that had been redeemed. Using these figures, the ingots would have weighed somewhat under 100 pounds each, allowing for certain wastage of planchets and processing.

QDB note: Only about half of the metal in an ingot was finally translated into coin form, due to wastage of the planchet strip remainders, etc.

---

[1] R.W. Julian, "Notes on U.S. Proof Coinage, Silver and Minor." *Numismatic Scrapbook Magazine,* March 1966.
[2] R.W. Julian, "The Cent Becomes Bronze: 1864." *FUN-Topics,* Summer 1987.

Snowden Describes the Minting Process

The following is excerpted from *A Description of Ancient and Modern Coins in the Cabinet Collection at the Mint of the United States,* by Mint Director James Ross Snowden, 1860:

The ingots [of coinage alloy metal] are first brought to a red heat in order to anneal and render them sufficiently ductile to be rolled with facility; they are then passed between hardened steel rollers, driven by a steam engine, which are so arranged that they can be adjusted with the greatest nicety in order to reduce the bar very nearly to the exact thickness required for the coin. In this form they are taken to the *drawing bench,* driven by the same engine, in which the strip is drawn slowly through the *drawing dies,* or plates of the hardest steel accurately adjusted to reduce the strips to their proper thickness. The strip, thus prepared, is next passed through the *cutting press,* also moved by steam, and pieces or *planchets* of the proper size are cut from it. The punch moves with such rapidity that 160 pieces on an average are cut out in one minute. At the completion of this part of the process, which leaves the strip full of holes, it is folded up and returned to the melting pot.

The planchets are now carried to the coining room, where, in order to raise the edge of the planchet to protect the surface of the coin, they are passed through the *milling machine.* The planchets are fed to this machine through an upright tube, and as they descend from the lower aperture, they are caught upon the edge of a revolving wheel and carried about a quarter of a revolution, during which the edge is compressed and forced upon—the space between the wheel and the rim being a little less than the diameter of the planchet. This apparatus moves so nimbly, that 560 half dimes can be milled in a minute; but for large pieces the average is about 120.

The planchets [at least for gold and silver coins] are next to be cleaned, annealed, and whitened....

The planchets are now ready to receive the last impression which is to render them a perfect coin. This most important office is performed by the *coining press,* which we have before mentioned. This machine receives the planchets in a tube from the hand of a workman; as the coin reaches the bottom of the tube it is seized between a pair of fingers and carried forward and deposited within a steel collar between the dies; and while the fingers are expanding and returning for another planchet, the dies close upon the one within the collar, and by a rotary motion are made to impress it silently but powerfully. The fingers, as they again close upon a planchet at the mouth of the tube, also seize the coin, and while conveying a second planchet on to the die, carry the coin off, dropping it into a box provided for the purpose—and this operation is repeated *ad infinitum.* These coining-presses are of various sizes to suit the different denominations of coins. The usual speed of striking is 60 pieces per minute for the half dollar; 75 for the quarter dollar; and 90 for the dime and half dime [and Indian cent].

The coining dies, it will be necessary to state, are prepared by engravers specially maintained at the Mint for the purpose. The process of engraving a die consists of cutting the devices and legends in soft steel, those parts being depressed which on the coin appear in relief. This having been finished and hardened, constitutes an "original die"; which being the result of a tedious and difficult task is deemed too precious to be directly employed in striking coins, but is used for *multiplying dies.* It is first used to impress another piece of soft steel, which then presents the appearance of a coin, and is called a *hub*. This hub being hardened, is used to impress other pieces of steel in like manner, which being exactly like the original die, are hardened and used for striking the coins. A pair of these will, on an average,[1] perform two weeks' work."

Dealer Woodward: William Elliot Woodward, born in Oxford, ME, in 1825 and who moved to Boston in 1848, became a pharmacist by trade, but entered the rare coin business in 1860. He went on to do much research, not only in numismatics but in other disciplines as well, and to publish over 100 coin auction catalogues, the latter beginning inauspiciously with a "poorly catalogued" sale held June 27, 28, 1860. However, he went from that point to turn out some of the most masterful catalogues of his era or any other.[2]

---

[1] Snowden's account was primarily directed toward the coinage of precious metals [as related in extensive parts of his commentary not reprinted here]; certain aspects including die life may have been different for copper-nickel cents.

[2] John W. Adams, *United States Numismatic Literature*, Vol. I, pp. 25 ff.

1861 Indian Cent

Business Strikes:

Business strike mintage: 10,100,000.

Number of business strike obverse dies made: 90

Average number of coins struck from typical obverse die: 112,222

Availability in Mint State: Scarce, but not a rarity. However, sharp, brilliant, frosty pieces are scarce.

John Dannreuther commented:[1] "There was a small hoard of 15 to 30 pieces, I believe, of very choice Mint State coins several years ago. In fact, there was a MS-68 (the only copper-nickel cent ever graded this high by PCGS) and several MS-66 and MS-67 pieces."

Availability in circulated grades: Scarcer than other copper-nickel Indian cents, but in an absolute sense there are many extant.

Characteristics of striking: Usually seen fairly well struck, but there are exceptions.

Market Prices (1861 business strikes)

YEAR	G-4	VG-8	F-12	VF-20	EF-40	AU-50
1938	$0.15	$0.25	$0.35	$0.60	$1.00	$2.00
1944	.60	1.10	2.00	2.75	3.50	4.75
1965	8.00	11.00	17.50	23.00	31.00	55.00
1996	15.00	20.00	25.00	40.00	75.00	160.00

---

[1] Letter, May 13, 1996.

YEAR	MS-60	MS-63	MS-64	MS-65		
1938	$3.50	$4.00	$4.00	$4.25		
1944	7.50	8.50	8.75	9.00		
1965	90.00	92.50	95.00	95.00		
1996	190.00	280.00	330.00	750.00		

Proofs:

Proof distribution (estimated): 400 to 500. Such estimates vary widely, and I have seen numbers as low as 100 and as high as 1,000.

Proof commentary: Date boldly impressed into die. Very scarce today, but not widely recognized as such. In extra demand due to the related low business strike production.

In 1977 in his *Encyclopedia of Proof Coins* Walter Breen stated, "Many marketed as Proofs are in fact early business strikes," and that "possibly only a little over 100" true Proofs survive. The Breen estimates are often on the low quantity side, based upon what he had seen; of course, there were many he had not seen or had reliably reported to him. Still, the Proof 1861 cent seems to be rarer than generally realized, but not as rare as the Proof 1860.

The Proof reverse die was not well made, and coins struck from it lack the deep mirror surface characteristic, for example, of the following year, 1862. Sometimes the rims of Proofs are rounded, rather than sharp or "square."[1]

Market Prices (1861 Proofs)

YEAR	PR-60	PR-63	PR-64	PR-65		
1938	$7.50	$7.85	$8.20	$9.00		
1944	17.50	18.50	19.50	19.50		
1965	500.00	550.00	580.00	650.00		
1996	360.00	725.00	2,000.00	4,500.00		

Notes

Collecting commentary: This date is the lowest mintage copper-nickel Indian cent. The glut of cents that jammed commerce in Eastern cities in 1860 meant that few new coins were needed for business reasons, and the rush by citizens to exchange old copper cents and Spanish-American silver for new small copper-nickel cents was over. However, enough 1861 cents survive today that examples are obtainable in all grades.

Redemption of old coppers: Redeemed half cents and old-style large cents (under the Act of February 21, 1857) provided the sole source for the 88% copper part of the copper-nickel alloy this year.[2] The slowing of such redemptions to a trickle may

---

[1] Richard Snow, letters, April 10 and 18, 1996.
[2] *Annual Report of the Director of the Mint,* 1861.

have been responsible in part for the low mintage figure. Further, all newly-minted cents of this date were paid out in exchange for redeemed coins.

New Mint director: James Ross Snowden left the Mint directorship and was succeeded in May 1861 by James Pollock, who remained in the post until April 1867. He followed James Ross Snowden and preceded William Millward and Henry R. Linderman (see further note under 1866).

Wartime conditions: The Civil War was in progress, but no one knew which side would prevail. The "Trent affair" in which the Union forcibly took two Confederate commissioners from aboard the British ship *Trent* caused a stir. President Abraham Lincoln, desirous of avoiding war with Britain, which had claimed its neutrality had been violated, released the men. General George B. McClellan molded his "Grand Army," but failed to utilize its potential. There was no end in sight to the war. The financial and money markets, often the most sensitive barometer of what is *really* going on, became edgy in December, and in this month hoarding of certain coins began.

W.C. Prime: In his 1861 book, *Coins, Medals, and Seals,* W.C. Prime commented on the untold stories even a recent cent could hold:

> It is a trite, but by no means a worn out idea, that a coin, could it speak, would be able to relate a stranger story than any other article to which imagination might give a voice. Such a thought can never be worn out, for it is inexhaustible in its richness. Human fancy fails utterly to trace the possible advantages of a copper that was coined even last year; and for every month that a coin has been in circulation a lifetime must needs be added to the years that would be required to sum up the incidents in which one can conjecture that coin as an actor."

1862 Indian Cent

Business Strikes:

Business strike mintage: 28,075,000.

Number of business strike obverse dies made: 196

Average number of coins struck from typical obverse die: 143,240

Availability in Mint State: Relatively plentiful.

Availability in circulated grades: Very common.

Characteristics of striking: Among higher grade coins cherrypicking for quality is advised as most are lightly struck, especially in the feather details. Some have grainy or pebbly surfaces from being struck from well-used dies.

Market Prices (1862 business strikes)

YEAR	G-4	VG-8	F-12	VF-20	EF-40	AU-50
1938	$0.05	$0.10	$0.15	$0.15	$0.20	$0.30
1944	.10	.15	.25	.30	.40	0.60
1965	2.00	3.00	5.00	8.00	10.00	17.50
1996	4.00	5.00	7.00	12.00	25.00	50.00

YEAR	MS-60	MS-63	MS-64	MS-65		
1938	$0.50	$0.50	$0.50	$0.55		
1944	1.00	1.00	1.10	1.10		
1965	25.00	26.50	27.50	28.50		
1996	95.00	160.00	280.00	650.00		

Proofs:

Proof distribution (estimated): Estimated number distributed: 2,000 to 2,500.

Proof commentary: Widely available, although most are not choice. Some high-grade pieces have frosty devices and present a cameo-like appearance. In his *Encyclopedia of Proof Coins* Walter Breen tantalizingly mentioned, "a hoard is known," without elucidating; apparently, this referred to a small group, estimated to have been as high as 200 or more, but possibly only a few dozen, that turned up at the Mint in the late 1870s.[1]

Market Prices (1862 Proofs)

YEAR	PR-60	PR-63	PR-64	PR-65		
1938	$2.50	$2.50	$2.75	$3.00		
1944	6.00	7.00	7.20	7.50		
1965	350.00	370.00	410.00	450.00		
1996	345.00	675.00	900.00	1,950.00		

Notes

Collecting commentary: Examples today are readily available in just about any grade.

Hoard of Mint State coins sold in 1918: On January 25 and 26, 1918, Thomas L. Elder conducted an auction featuring the Robert Hewitt and B.C. Bartlett collections. Lot 318 was described: "1862 C. Nickel. Bright. Unc. 125 pcs." This was followed by lots 319 to 323, each described as "Bright Unc." and each containing 100 coins. Then came Lot 324, also of 100 coins, "Unc. red." Apparently, these were toned. Lot 325 featured 50 specimens, "Unc. Bright." To this point 775 pieces of Mint State 1862 cents had been offered. Then followed three lots of 100 coins each, described as containing mixed cents dated from 1857 to 1862, each including "many" 1862 cents, but without the number specified. Accordingly, it is probable that the Elder hoard consisted of about 1,000 specimens of this date.[2]

Historical and numismatic notes: Mintage climbed to 28,075,000 this year due to unprecedented war-driven demand. Hoarding of circulating coinage, which had begun in December 1861, went out of control in the second week of July, 1862, at which time all coins including one-cent pieces disappeared from circulation. The Civil War continued to rage.

The situation at the Mint:[3] The quantity of undistributed Indian cents on hand at the Mint at various times during this era dramatically reflects the scarcity in the summer of 1862:

1861, August 31: 420,505 cents on hand. A comfortable supply.

1861, October 31: 92,290. Supplies were becoming low, and this foretold a larger mintage for 1862.

---

[1] Richard Snow, letter, April 10, 1996 (higher estimate); R.W. Julian, letter, April 24, 1996 (lower estimate).

[2] Catalogue copy furnished by Frank Campbell, American Numismatic Society, New York City.

[3] Adapted from R.W. Julian, "The Cent Becomes Bronze: 1864." *FUN-Topics,* Summer 1987.

1862, January 31: 737,935. A comfortable supply.

1862, April 30: 940,379. A comfortable supply.

1862, August 31: 368.

1862, December 1: 254.

Supplies remained adequate at the Mint through at least July 3, 1862, as evidenced by correspondence from the Mint to a bank, noting that an order for one-cent pieces would be shipped in "a day or two."

In contrast, an order received by the Mint on July 20, 1862, for 5,000 cents was not shipped until September 12! From this time until well into the year 1864, the Mint was not able to ship cents on a timely basis, and delays of up to four months were experienced.

On December 1, 1862, Mint Director James Pollock wrote to Treasury Secretary Salmon P. Chase to inform him that the Mint had the capacity to coin 240,000 or more cents per day, but sometimes only 90,000 were struck, with a good average day's production being about 160,000. Chief among the problems affecting steady coinage was the lack of a reliable supply of nickel, although copper (primarily on hand from melted-down "large" cents) stocks remained adequate. Nickel from the Lancaster Gap mine in Pennsylvania became unavailable (for some unexplained reason) in early autumn 1862, and for several weeks there was no other significant domestic supply. By December 1, the metal was again provided to the Mint. Seeking to diversify the sources, Director Pollock increased the amount of nickel obtained overseas through the agencies of Irving Van Wart & Co., C. Robbins, and Fleitmann[1] & Weirss.

In November 1862 it cost about 48¢ in currency to make 100 copper-nickel cents. Nickel cost about $1.65 to $1.75 per pound when imported from Europe and was not easy to obtain even at that price, as the Civil War in America affected imports and exports. Copper ranged in price from 25¢ to 34¢ per pound and did not pose an acquisition problem. By early 1863, nearly all nickel was being obtained from Europe, although some small quantities may have come from Lancaster County, Pennsylvania.

Dealer Strobridge: In 1862 William Harvey Strobridge entered professional numismatics with a flourish. His initial auction catalogue featured the William Lilliendahl Collection and was laden with rarities. He remained in the trade until a detached retina forced his retirement in 1878.[2]

---

[1] Theodore Fleitmann was at one time a business associate of Joseph Wharton in Camden, N.J.; about 1869 he left Wharton and went on to set up facilities for making nickel and nickel alloy products in the Ruhr section of Germany.

[2] John W. Adams, *United States Numismatic Literature*, Vol. I, pp. 36 ff.

1863 Indian Cent

Business Strikes:

Business strike mintage: 49,840,000.

Number of business strike obverse dies made: Not known.

Average number of coins struck from typical obverse die: Not known.

Availability in Mint State: Relatively common. Mint State coins are often dull or stained and/or are struck from worn dies, giving a "greasy" rather than lustrous aspect, especially in the obverse fields. Cherrypick for quality.

Availability in circulated grades: Very common.

Characteristics of striking: Many are lightly struck, particularly on the feather tips. This and the 1864 copper-nickel are notorious in this regard.

Market Prices (1863 business strikes)

YEAR	G-4	VG-8	F-12	VF-20	EF-40	AU-50
1938	$0.05	$0.10	$0.15	$0.15	$0.20	$0.30
1944	.10	.15	.25	.30	.40	.50
1965	2.00	3.00	4.50	7.00	9.00	14.00
1996	3.25	4.50	6.00	10.00	22.50	40.00

YEAR	MS-60	MS-63	MS-64	MS-65		
1938	$0.50	$0.50	$0.50	$0.55		
1944	.75	.75	.80	.90		
1965	24.00	25.00	26.00	27.500		
1996	80.00	162.50	290.00	700.00		

Proofs:

Proof distribution (estimated): 800 to 1,000. Opinions vary.

Proof commentary: In 1977 in his *Encyclopedia of Proof Coins* Walter Breen considered this to be a bit more plentiful than 1862, but that "many survivors have been cleaned." The present writer considers it to be *much rarer* than 1862 and to be a sleeper, a feeling shared by Richard Snow.[1] Differences of opinion contribute to the fascination of the numismatic hobby. No doubt the widespread availability of the 1863 in *business strike* form has prompted many to consider Proofs common as well.

Market Prices (1863 Proofs)

YEAR	PR-60	PR-63	PR-64	PR-65		
1938	$2.50	$2.50	$2.75	$3.00		
1944	6.50	7.25	7.50	7.50		
1965	325.00	337.50	355.00	400.00		
1996	380.00	750.00	975.00	2,500.00		

Notes

Collecting commentary: With a record mintage of 49,840,000 cents the 1863 is the most plentiful of the copper-nickel issues. Plentiful today in all grades, although coins with needle-sharp detail are scarcer and worth a special premium. Not rare, but many are dull and unattractive. Among Mint State coins a numerical grade may be one thing, but quality may be another thing entirely. I have seen sharp MS-63 coins that have better appearance and aesthetic value than poorly struck MS-65 coins.

Mintage notes: In the year 1863 copper-nickel Indian cents remained scarce despite the widespread availability of other media of exchange including encased postage stamps, privately minted Civil War tokens, and paper Fractional Currency notes.

Years later on June 30, 1925, the Treasury Department stated that a grand total of 200,772,000 copper-nickel cents had been coined in the Flying Eagle and Indian series through 1864, and as of 1925 some 120,043,446 remained outstanding.[2]

In early 1863 nearly all nickel used to make cents was imported from Europe (also see notes under 1862).[3] By March 1863, Mint Director Pollock informed Treasury Secretary Chase that the cost to produce 100 copper-nickel cents was about 60¢ per hundred, not including an estimated 20¢ per hundred for labor. By March 1863, due to uncertainties concerning the outcome of the Civil War, the continued public hoarding of silver coins pushed the price of older silver coins to a 40% premium in terms of federal paper money. In other words, it cost over $140 in federal "greenback" notes to buy $100 face value of silver coins at a bullion exchange or broker.

During the first half of 1863, cent coinage was at a record monthly average pace

---

[1] Letter, April 10, 1996.
[2] 1925 *Mint Report*, p. 10.
[3] Information in this and the following paragraph is adapted from R.W. Julian, "The Cent Becomes Bronze: 1864." *FUN-Topics*, Summer 1987.

of about 4.5 million coins. Despite this, the Mint fell far behind in filling orders. An order for cents received on March 16, 1863, was not filled until mid-September! In late 1863, production of cents slowed somewhat, due to erratic supplies of nickel metal. Meanwhile, privately issued copper and bronze tokens were popular in commerce, thus foretelling the end of the copper-nickel cent.

From the 1863 *Mint Report:*

The coinage and issue of the nickel cent during the year has been very large—almost unprecedented. The demand still continues, and every effort has been made to supply it. This coin has been distributed to every part of the country, and orders for large amounts are daily received. The profits pay all expenses and distribution of the cent.

A great benefit to the country was effected by the Act of 1857, reducing the size of the cent. It is to be regretted that the idea still prevailed that it was necessary to put into the coin, if not an equivalent, at least a large proportion of real value. To this end, and for other reasons, an alloying metal was sought which should command a comparatively high price in the market, without being properly a *precious* metal. Nickel, possessing the requisite value and suitable qualities, was selected. It was then worth about $2 per pound; though it has since been much lower in price....

The change was well intended, but the experience of other countries, and indeed of our own, has taught us that it was an unnecessary liberality; and that all the nickel we have thus used has been so much money wasted. In France, they had formerly a copper *sous,* or five centimes, about the same as our cent in legal value—weighing 154 grains troy; but the five centimes of the present day weighs only half as much. This latter is a mixture called *bronze,* and is composed of 95% copper, the remainder being tin and zinc, which adds nothing to the cost, but gives character and prestige to the coin. The mixture is less oxidizable and more cleanly [sic] than copper."

This account went on to note that even if a cent be made in a new alloy and be intrinsically worth just 1/10 of its face value, it should be made anyway. It would be a cent, by law, to everyone using it. Further:

If any further proof of this fact should be demanded, we have only to refer to our own recent experience when illegal cents [today called Civil War tokens—QDB], or false tokens the size of the legal cent, were made and freely passed—although they contained no nickel, weighed on the average about 51 grains, and worth not more than one-fifth of a cent. Not less than 300 varieties of those false and illegal tokens, or cents, have been made and issued; and until suppressed, were freely used as coin by the public. They were in direct violation of the laws of the United States, and the prosecution of certain parties issuing them have deterred others, and will soon drive them altogether from circulation."

Then followed a plea requesting that nickel should be eliminated from the cent, and, contrary to the paean to nickel coinage given in 1856 (see notes under the 1856 Flying Eagle cent above), now:

"Nickel derives its name from a certain unpleasant allusion, indicating its character, and which, in a metallurgic sense, it honestly deserves. It is very obstinate in the melting pot, requiring the fiercest fire even when in alloy with copper. It commonly makes a hard mixture, destructive to dies, and all the contiguous parts of the coining machinery." Further, nickel found little use in the arts, the director commented.

Thus was laid the foundation for the elimination of nickel in the cent and the implementation of bronze (which would take place the next year, 1864). (For an interesting commentary also see "Rewriting history" in our 1864 bronze cent listing below.)

The same account went on to say that while current copper-nickel (Indian) cents were in strong demand, "they are little used in the Western and Southern states." Of course, the Civil War was going on, and it would have been an unlikely scenario for freshly-minted copper-nickel cents to have been shipped there.

By June 20, 1863, old-style large cents in the value of $287,536.00 had been exchanged for copper-nickel cents. Presumably this value was on a one-to-one exchange; if so, the number of pieces involved was 28,753,600.[1] Copper-nickel cents continued to sell at a premium in terms of paper money and were traded by speculators and brokers. Part of the problem was that federal "greenback" notes were increasingly viewed as being unstable.

This was, perhaps, the most pivotal year of the Civil War.

Bronze patterns: Relative to the problems with copper-nickel, in a letter to Secretary of the Treasury Salmon P. Chase, Mint Director James Pollock said this, December 8, 1863, here lightly edited and quoted in part:

> Bronze, composed of 95% copper, 3% tin, and 2% zinc, makes a beautiful and ductile alloy. This change of material of the cent is not only desirable in itself as an improvement in the quality and appearance of the coin, but becomes an absolute necessity from the advanced, and still advancing, price of nickel...the difficulty of melting, the destruction of dies and machinery, etc., thus increasing the cost of production....
>
> This change in the material of the cent is not only desirable in itself, but has become a necessity from the advance [in the price of] nickel (for a supply of which we are at present entirely dependent upon the foreign market, paying for it in gold or its equivalent), and the great uncertainty of procuring an adequate supply for the future from any source at a price within the legal limit....
>
> It is not proposed to change the size and devices of the cent, only the weight. The weight of the new coin would be 48 grains or 1/10th of an ounce Troy. Enclosed I send you specimens of the bronze cent, which is very superior in every respect to the *slumpy* nickel."

I don't know what *slumpy* means, and a dictionary at hand lists *slummy, slump, slumped,* and *slumping,* but not *slumpy.* However, from its context, we are sure it was intended as a pejorative word. The bronze cents referred to were patterns (today known as Judd-299 and Pollock-359), and Proofs were struck with medal-type alignment with the obverse and reverse dies aligned in the same direction (rather than coin-wise or 180° apart); some non-Proofs—exceedingly rare today—were struck with normal coin-wise alignment.[2] The Proof patterns with medal-type alignment were struck on bronze planchets that were darkened before striking; thus, specimens in cabinets today have a glossy brown surface if they have not been cleaned. Those patterns with coin-wise alignment may have been struck with a brilliant finish.

The new bronze cents weighed 48 grains, a figure devised by Director Pollock as

---

[1] If by weight—which is unlikely due to the logistics and fluctuating values involved—the number was smaller (as the price of copper had risen to the point at which each old cent had more than one cent's worth of the metal).

[2] Richard Snow, letters, April 10 and 18, 1996, after reviewing the present manuscript.

being a convenient measure: 1/10 of a *Troy* ounce, even though the avoirdupois ounce (1/10th of which equals 43.75 grains) was regularly used as the measure for base metals at the Mint. A survey of privately issued copper tokens in circulation revealed that they weighed on average about 51 grains.[1]

Curious 1863 reeded-edge business strike cents: Certain business strike (Mint State surfaces, not Proof) 1863 cents are known with reeded edges and are attributed as Pollock-362 and Judd-300. The Eliasberg Collection specimen sold in May 1996 was described as follows, here excerpted:

Die state and characteristics: Two raised die flaws to the right of and below Miss Liberty's eye. Three raised breaks in hair below Y of LIBERTY. Small breaks are on the obverse rim between 9:00 and 11:00. Quite probably the same die and state could be found among business strike cents. Several other examples—indeed, all other examples—studied in person by Andrew Pollock have had these identical obverse die characteristics. Weight: 70.4 grains.

Notes (forum for discussion): Controversy exists concerning these pieces. Some numismatists believe that the reeded edge feature was applied at the Mint at the time of striking by an edge collar situated in the coining press. Others contend that the edge reeding was privately applied subsequent to issue. Evidence favoring the application of edge reeding by the Mint falls into these historical and technical categories:

Pro:

1) An *Uncirculated* example with edge reeding was offered in a Edward D. Cogan sale of 1865 (as reported by Carl W.A. Carlson). This is significant, as Proof dies, as used on a slow-speed medal press, were usually employed for patterns and collector pieces. The die state of the Cogan coin is not known, and it may have been from different dies than the Eliasberg example.

2) The diameters of all specimens examined are remarkably uniform, between 0.763 and 0.764 inch. This value is substantially higher than that usually seen for regular-issue Indian cent patterns of the period, which typically range from 0.750 to 0.754 inch. The high level of uniformity and the large diameter seem to indicate that the use of a collar having a somewhat larger than usual diameter. If the edges were reeded outside of the mint, the diameter would by definition be no wider than usual and would probably be a bit narrower.

3) Another observation worth mentioning is that the edge is more rounded than usual suggesting, once again, that the collar was ever so slightly too large for the planchet, The reason for the addition of edge reeding in 1863 has not been ascertained. One hypothesis is that the Mint became concerned that plain-edge cents might become subject to fraudulent alteration as a result of increased metal prices during the Civil War.

Puzzlement:

1) The die state with obverse breaks indicates that this variety was probably not among the first few thousand impressions from this obverse die. Thus, to create a reeded edge on this coin its use to strike circulating cents would have had to have been interrupted or terminated.

Needed:

The examination side-by-side of several specimens of this variety and the micro-

---

[1] R.W. Julian, "The Cent Becomes Bronze: 1864." *FUN-Topics,* Summer 1987.

scopic study of minute lines and finish marks in the edge reeding and their topological relationship to letters and devices on the obverse and reverse would probably
settle the question. If all are of the same orientation, virtually certainly they were
made at the Mint. If not, the puzzle continues, especially with regard to the larger
diameter of these pieces. *Longacre's Ledger,* the journal of the Fly-In Club, is encouraged to pursue the matter."

In a later communication, Richard Snow seconded the idea that the reeding was
applied at the Mint and further noted that the dies used were different from those
used to strike Proofs of this year. He noted that he had observed two pieces side by
side, and that the reeding alignment was identical on each.[1]

1863 L cents: Certain pattern 1863 cents in different metals (copper-nickel, aluminum, bronze, and gold[2]) exist with L on the ribbon (cf. Pollock-363 to 367), but I
am not certain these were, in fact, produced prior to 1864; this situation could be
clarified by studying the minute details of the *reverse* die and matching it to the
reverse of one or more regular Proof cents of, possibly, a later year. In any event,
these "1863 L" cents were not generally known to numismatists until years later. The
following communication dated November 8, 1903, was published in *The Numismatist,* December 1903:

> Please find space in December number for a notice of my discovery of the little
> capital 'L' on a nickel cent of 1863. It is usually credited with making its first appear-
> ance on the 1864 bronze cent and is spoken of as 'L on ribbon, etc.'
>
> This little L is extremely small, but is intentionally there to record Longacre's
> artistic design of workmanship. It can be found by using a magnifying glass and
> looking under the middle of the last feather of the helmet and next to the hair. Also
> that a line drawn from "A" in STATES to "C" in AMERICA cuts through this letter 'L.'
> I cannot learn of any other example but this one of mine and it is a Proof. It came
> from our old friend, Wm. P. Brown,[3] among a lot of Proofs.
>
> Very truly yours, Wm. E. Hidden.[4]

Examples of the 1863 L cent I have seen in recent times have the Narrow Bust
style of the 1864 L cents and not the Broad Bust as found on regular 1863 without-L
copper-nickel cents. Thus, the presumption is that 1863 L cents were created *after*
the 1864 L cents and not during the year 1863. However, in my 1959 article, "Transitional Coins of America," I describe a bronze striking of the 1863 L, noting "This coin
has a blunt bust, unlike the 1864 L." Now in the 1990s I do not have my notes for this
1959 article, and all I can state now in 1996 is that in 1959 I was aware of the bust
style differences and, apparently, saw one or more with a blunt (broad) bust. I admit
that this is a bit puzzling to me now, for I would otherwise think that all 1863 L cents
were of the Narrow Bust style.

The 1863 L cents with the Narrow Bust style may have been struck circa 1871
(see note under the 1864 L Proof cent in the sub-chapter for this coin; 1864 L Proof
bronze cents were also restruck circa 1871).

---

[1] Richard Snow, letter, April 10, 1996.

[2] The gold specimen (cf. Michael Hodder, letter, May 14, 1996) most certainly was a delicacy made for
numismatic purposes, not a mint error.

[3] A brief biographical sketch of Brown, a New York City coin dealer for many years, appears in Appendix II of the book, *Louis E. Eliasberg, Sr., King of Coins,* by Q. David Bowers.

[4] Hidden was prominent on the numismatic scene in the early twentieth century, and was once involved in the unfortunate loss of a Templeton Reid $5 gold coin.

1864 Indian Cent

Copper-Nickel

Business Strikes:

Business strike mintage: 13,740,000. However, R.W. Julian has presented evidence that the combined figures for copper-nickel and bronze cents of 1864 are about 1.2 million coins too high.[1]

Number of business strike obverse dies made: Not known.

Average number of coins struck from typical obverse die: Not known.

Availability in Mint State: Relatively easy to find, but well-struck pieces are scarce.

Availability in circulated grades: Scarcer than 1862 and 1863, but still plentiful.

Characteristics of striking: This date is usually seen weakly struck especially at the tips of the Indian's headdress feathers, and cherrypicking is advised. Prices for MS-64 and MS-65 coins given below are for sharply struck pieces; average or weak strikes sell for less.

Market Prices (1864 copper-nickel business strikes)

YEAR	G-4	VG-8	F-12	VF-20	EF-40	AU-50
1938	$0.10	$0.15	$0.25	$0.25	$0.30	$0.30
1944	.50	.40	.75	.80	.90	1.10
1965	5.00	7.00	10.00	15.00	25.00	35.00
1996	13.00	17.50	22.00	27.50	45.00	80.00

[1] R.W. Julian, "The Cent Becomes Bronze: 1864." *FUN-Topics,* Summer 1987. Separately (letter, April 19, 1996), R.W. Julian advised that the total mintage for cents this year was 51,795,000 (from a calendar-year statement located among Mint data in the National Archives) against a *Guide Book* total of 52,973,714. Thus, the business strike figure given in the present text should be adjusted downward by about 2%. Also, R.W. Julian, letter, April 24, 1996.

YEAR	MS-60	MS-63	MS-64	MS-65		
1938	$0.35	$0.40	$0.40	$0.45		
1944	1.50	1.60	1.70	1.70		
1965	60.00	63.00	65.00	67.50		
1996	135.00	195.00	350.00	1,100.00		

Proofs:

Proof distribution (estimated): 800 to 1,000. Estimates of the rarity of this issue vary widely, and some have called it a major rarity. These were struck in the early months of the year and were distributed with Proof sets through at least the end of May 1864 and perhaps later as well (to deplete any inventory).

Proof commentary: Really choice Proofs are scarce. In 1977 in his *Encyclopedia of Proof Coins* Walter Breen stated that possibly 370 or more were struck, but that it is "rarer than mintage figure suggests." The present writer believes this to be the most available wreath-and-shield Proof copper-nickel cent after the 1862. The order of rarity is probably as follows: 1860 (rarest), 1861, 1863, 1864, and 1862 (most available).

The obverse die used to strike these coins was also used to strike bronze Proofs.

Market Prices (1864 copper-nickel Proofs)

YEAR	PR-60	PR-63	PR-64	PR-65		
1938	$3.50	$3.50	$3.75	$4.00		
1944	7.50	8.00	8.50	8.50		
1965	650.00	680.00	740.00	800.00		
1996	380.00	750.00	975.00	2,300.00		

Notes

Collecting commentary: This is the most difficult copper-nickel cent to find with really nice aesthetic appeal. Nowhere else in the copper-nickel Indian cent series is there such a variation in quality among specimens in a given grade (although serious competition for the cellar position is mounted by the 1863).

Time of striking: Copper-nickel cents dated 1864 were struck early in the year with the last coinage occurring in early May.

On March 17, 1864, Mint Director James Pollock sent a copper-nickel cent on a thin planchet, 48 grains, to the Treasury Department as a suggestion that this alloy could be retained for the cent, and bronze could be used for the new two-cent piece.[1]

A British view of our copper-nickel coinage: An interesting commentary was included by John Craig in *The Mint*, 1953, his book about the Royal Mint in London, but which also discusses other countries. Edited excerpt, italics mine:

> The United States of America is generally credited with the first experiment in cupro-nickel coinage. By quaint anticipation [other nickel-content coins were] minted two centuries before Christ in Bactria from a freak ore. The composition adopted by the United States in 1857 was 12 parts of nickel to 88 parts of copper and *the coinage was a failure.* The Swiss mint even before the United States, produced coins of a complicated mixture of copper, zinc, nickel, and a little silver...."

[1] R.W. Julian, letter, April 24, 1996.

1864 Indian Cent

Bronze

Business Strikes:

Business strike mintage: The mintage for 1864-dated bronze cents is given as 39,233,714 in the *Guide Book*. This figure includes an estimated 5,000,000 to 7,500,000 with L on ribbon (see next listing). However as noted under the 1864 copper-nickel cent above, R.W. Julian has presented evidence that the combined figures for copper-nickel and bronze cents of 1864 are about 1.2 million coins too high.[1]

Number of business strike obverse dies made: Not known.

Average number of coins struck from typical obverse die: Not known.

Availability in Mint State: Most plentiful of the early date bronze cents. Mint State coins often show a mixture of orange and brown nicely blended, sometimes with a woodgrain effect. Fully brilliant coins turn up with frequency, more so than any other bronze cents of this era. As with all bronze Indian cents it is important to differentiate between *original* brilliance and *dipped* brilliance.

Availability in circulated grades: Common, but scarcer than the very common issues of the 1879-1909 era.

Characteristics of striking: Most are well struck. However, the 1864 bronze cent marked the introduction of the new reverse hub with the bottom of N in ONE and, to a lesser extent, the tops of EN in CENT shallow in the die; this would continue until a new hub was made in 1870.

---

[1] R.W. Julian, "The Cent Becomes Bronze: 1864." *FUN-Topics,* Summer 1987. Separately (letter, April 19, 1996), R.W. Julian advised that the total mintage for cents this year was 51,795,000 against a *Guide Book* total of 52,973,714. Thus, the business strike figure given in the present text should be adjusted downward by about 2%. This same comment is given under 1864 copper-nickel coins.

Market Prices (1864 bronze business strikes)

YEAR	G-4	VG-8	F-12	VF-20	EF-40	AU-50
1938	$0.10	$0.15	$0.25	$0.30	$0.40	$0.50
1944	.25	.40	0.60	.85	1.25	2.00
1965	2.50	4.75	9.25	13.50	17.00	37.50
1996	6.00	7.50	10.00	22.50	38.00	50.00

YEAR	MS-60BN	MS-60RB	MS-63BN	MS-63RB	MS-63RD	
1938	$0.65	$0.70	$0.70	$0.70	$0.75	
1944	3.00	3.10	3.00	3.20	3.50	
1965	60.00	63.00	60.00	65.00	70.00	
1996	80.00	88.00	82.50	135.00	200.00	

YEAR	MS-64BN	MS-64RB	MS-64RD	MS-65BN	MS-65RB	MS-65RD
1938	$0.70	$0.70	$0.75	$0.70	$0.70	$0.75
1944	3.00	3.50	3.60	3.10	3.50	3.75
1965	63.00	68.00	75.00	65.00	70.00	80.00
1996	100.00	185.00	300.00	195.00	370.00	710.00

Proofs:

Proof distribution (estimated): The *Guide Book* suggests that just 150 Proofs were made, an enticingly low number that is often quoted, but I suspect it may be on the low side. In 1977 in his *Encyclopedia of Proof Coins* Walter Breen stated that 100 or so were struck, also very enticing. My guess: 400 to 500.

Proof commentary: Most extant specimens show brown toning. It has been conjectured that bronzed (with dark brown surface) Proofs may have been issued; certainly this was true of the related bronze Proof patterns dated 1863 (Judd-299, Pollock-359, thin planchet with medal-wise alignment).[1]

Many if not most "red" Proof-63, Proof-64, and Proof-65 coins on the market have been dipped. Richard Snow concurs that Proof 1864 bronze cents were probably issued with bronzed surfaces.[2] Thus, prices given for "red" Proofs below—taken from market listings—should be taken with a large grain of salt; the situation needs more research. It could be that some were issued with brilliant finish and others with bronzed finish.

---

[1] Breen in *Dies & Coinage*, p. 26, described the Boulton & Watt (Birmingham, England) method of bronzing: "[Matthew] Boulton was also responsible for innovations in proofing. Specifically, he began the practice (later carried over to the Philadelphia Mint for medals and some patterns) of striking Proofs on pre-gilded or pre-patinated (bronzed) blanks. Bronzing of copper for this purpose was done by coating the blanks with some copper compound and heating them. A very large number of Soho Mint Proofs are bronzed, as are most of the GOD OUR TRUST patterns of 1861-1863 and some others from the Philadelphia Mint." Of course, this period encompasses the same year (1863) that the above mentioned 1863 pattern bronze Indian cents were struck.

[2] Richard Snow, letter, April 10, 1996.

Proofs are usually of exquisite sharpness of strike.

Proofs were struck from at least three different obverse dies, one of which was used earlier to make copper-nickel Proofs.[1]

Market Prices (1864 bronze Proofs)

YEAR	PR-60BN	PR-60RB	PR-63BN	PR-63RB	PR-63RD	
1938	$4.00	$4.30	$4.20	$4.50	$5.00	
1944	13.00	13.50	13.00	14.00	15.00	
1965	535.00	550.00	540.00	550.00	650.00	
1996	350.00	450.00	640.00	765.00	1,100.00	

YEAR	PR-64BN	PR-64RB	PR-64RD	PR-65BN	PR-65RB	PR-65RD
1938	$4.30	$4.50	$5.25	$4.50	$4.75	$5.50
1944	14.00	14.00	16.00	14.00	14.00	16.00
1965	550.00	590.00	700.00	575.00	625.00	750.00
1996	720.00	2,000.00	4,500.00	1,175.00	3,600.00	13,250.00

Notes

Collecting commentary: Examples are common in all grades up through and including Mint State.

Clashed die two-cent piece: In August 1996 Bill Fivaz reported the discovery of an 1864 bronze two-cent piece bearing the incuse impression of an Indian cent obverse die, adding to the growing list of bi-denominational clashes related to the small cent series. (Illustration courtesy of Bill Fivaz)

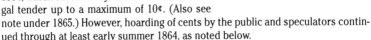

The new cent: The new bronze cent was coined under authority of the Act of April 22, 1864, which set the alloy and made the coins legal tender up to a maximum of 10¢. (Also see note under 1865.) However, hoarding of cents by the public and speculators continued through at least early summer 1864, as noted below.

From the 1864 *Mint Report:* "The substitution of the bronze alloy for the nickel mixture, as authorized by Congress, has been highly successful. The demand for the one- and two-cent pieces has been unprecedented, and every effort has been made to meet it. The demand still continues, although the number issued daily largely exceeds that of any former period. Large quantities are hoarded, and thus kept from circulation. They have also been bought and sold by small brokers at a premium; this has induced individuals to collect them for the purpose of sale, thus producing a scarcity and inconvenience to the public that ought not to exist...."

---

[1] Richard Snow, letter, April 10, 1996.

Following the passage of the aforementioned legislation, coinage of copper-nickel cents continued through early May, to use up supplies of nickel and the alloy on hand.[1] The first bronze ingots for the 48-grain bronze coinage were prepared on May 13, 1864, after which assays were made. The quantity of tin ranged from 3% to 3.2% and zinc about 2.2%, with the balance being copper. On May 20, 1864, a shipment of 50,000 of the new cents went to the Treasury Department in Washington.

In June 1864 a contract was let with Holmes, Booth & Hayden of Waterbury, CT, to supply pre-made bronze planchets for cents and two-cent pieces, these to be used in addition to those made at the Mint. The Connecticut firm supplied its first planchets in July 5 (arrival date at the Mint), and by the end of October over 50 tons of cent and two-cent planchets had been delivered.[2]

Bronze alloy differences: The copper used to coin bronze 1864 (and 1864 with L) cents seems to have been of a special quality, for specimens that are toned brown have an especially rich appearance. Such differences exist elsewhere in the series and are subtle. Doubtless, if extremely refined non-destructive elemental analysis were ever made, the typical bronze cent of 1864, 1907, and 1908-S would all have slightly different metallic compositions.

Wharton busy:[3] Joseph Wharton, owner of America's only significant nickel mine, did not take kindly to the impending adoption of the new bronze format, and in a letter dated February 15, 1864, began a counterattack on the new cent, giving four reasons why the copper-nickel format should be retained:

1. The copper-nickel cent yielded a good coinage profit to the Treasury [but not as great as a bronze cent would yield].

2. He was ready to begin supplying good quantities of nickel to the Mint [but added that he could not completely satisfy the Mint's requirements; meanwhile, foreign supplies were becoming increasingly erratic].

3. The difficulty of coining the hard nickel metal alloy provided a better defense against counterfeiting than would bronze [but in practice, cents never were a popular denomination with counterfeiters; too much trouble for the yield obtained].

4. "Unnecessary changes" in the coinage of a great nation such as the United States should be avoided whenever possible.

A pamphlet dated April 15, 1864, went even further and suggested that as part of a revised coinage system, one-cent pieces should have 25% nickel and 75% copper— or over twice as much nickel as currently in the copper-nickel cent!

Pollock discussed the Wharton letter and other aspects of the Wharton campaign with other Mint officials, and it was agreed that Wharton's political connections to the Treasury Department and to the Mint were so strong, that, indeed, nickel should be continued in cent coinage, but that the copper-nickel cents could be reduced in weight from 72 grains to the same 48 grains that had been proposed for the bronze issue; meanwhile, bronze could be used for a new denomination, the two-cent piece.

Although Treasury Secretary Chase must have been confused by Pollock's turnabout, Chase proposed that the original bill (providing for the new bronze cent) be passed, and it was—as the Act of April 22, 1864. However, while Wharton may have

---

[1] R.W. Julian, "The Cent Becomes Bronze: 1864." *FUN-Topics,* Summer 1987.
[2] Certain additional information is from R.W. Julian, letter, April 24, 1996.
[3] R.W. Julian, "The Cent Becomes Bronze: 1864." *FUN-Topics,* Summer 1987.

lost his anti-bronze-cent campaign, he won the war, and the subsequent advent of the nickel three-cent piece in 1865 and the Shield nickel five-cent piece in 1866 assured that Wharton's coffers would remain overflowing.

Rewriting history: With the advent of the bronze cent the old copper-nickel alloy was a thing of the past. Or, was it? One interesting thing about reading old *Mint Reports* and National Archives data is the finding of numerous inconsistencies, including the re-invention of old ideas and denial of earlier facts. In this vein someone at the Mint, probably not the director (but, who knows?), attempted to rewrite history a few decades later, for the *Annual Report of the Director of the Mint for the Fiscal Year Ending June 30, 1911,* contains this amazing commentary on page 9:

The composition of the [Lincoln] one-cent piece, 95% copper and 5% tin and zinc, is unsatisfactory. The coins soon become dull and dirty in appearance and when exposed to the salt air of the seacoast are rendered unfit for circulation. This is particularly noticeable of coins which lie for a time in slot machines. They are offered for redemption in bad condition and must be remelted. When handled in the Treasury offices and mints an objectionable dust arises from them.

The act adopting the present composition was passed in 1864, prior to which date the one-cent piece was issued under the Act of February 21, 1857, which provided for a composition of 88% copper and 12% nickel. The mint officials have always regarded the change as a backward step, and in the opinion of the bureau the percentage of nickel should have been increased instead of reduced."

This sort of thing makes numismatic research a lot of fun!

1864 L Indian Cent

Bronze; L on Ribbon

Close-up view of the ribbon on the Indian cent showing the addition of a tiny L letter (for engraver Longacre). Bronze cents with L also have a pointed tip to the bust (Narrow Bust), unlike the without-L issues which have a wider tip (Broad Bust).

Business Strikes:

Business strike mintage: Estimated 5,000,000 to 7,500,000. The number of 1864 L cents struck was not separately recorded, but is part of over 39,000,000 bronze cents struck this year. 1864 L cents were made from 18 or more obverse dies.

Number of business strike obverse dies made: Not known.

Average number of coins struck from typical obverse die: Not known.

Availability in Mint State: Fairly scarce. Mint State coins can be very attractive if glossy brown or with a smoothly blended mixture of red and brown, often with a woodgrain effect. Original (undipped, uncleaned) full red specimens are rare.

Availability in circulated grades: Scarce. Very worn 1864 bronze cents with pointed truncation are 1864 L even if the L is worn away, but such coins do not bring any more than a regular bronze coin price.

Characteristics of striking: Usually well struck. Sometimes from clashed dies with traces of the reverse wreath outline visible in the obverse field. The bottom of N in ONE and, to a lesser extent, the tops of EN in CENT are always shallow as on the die; this would continue until a new hub was made in 1870.

Market Prices (1864 L business strikes)

YEAR	G-4	VG-8	F-12	VF-20	EF-40	AU-50
1938	$1.35	$1.75	$2.50	$2.90	$3.25	$4.00
1944	4.50	6.00	7.50	10.00	11.00	14.00
1965	16.00	30.00	60.00	77.50	100.00	150.00
1996	35.00	50.00	80.00	115.00	200.00	230.00

YEAR	MS-60BN	MS-60RB	MS-63BN	MS-63RB	MS-63RD
1938	$8.50	$9.00	$8.50	$9.50	$10.00
1944	18.00	20.00	19.00	20.00	22.00
1965	250.00	260.00	250.00	275.00	300.00
1996	300.00	385.00	320.00	475.00	700.00

YEAR	MS-64BN	MS-64RB	MS-64RD	MS-65BN	MS-65RB	MS-65RD
1938	$8.75	$9.75	$11.00	$9.00	$10.00	$12.00
1944	20.00	20.00	22.00	20.00	22.00	22.00
1965	260.00	285.00	310.00	265.00	290.00	320.00
1996	450.00	700.00	1,500.00	650.00	1,250.00	3,500.00

Proofs:

Proof distribution (estimated): The number of Proofs minted is not known. The *Guide Book* suggests 20 coins, a figure that may be in the ball park as this issue is a prime rarity in Proof format.

Proof commentary: Struck from two different die pairs:[1]

Die Pair 1 (originals): Date farther to the left than on the preceding, with the 1 in date directly below the neck tip. No spine from curl (see Die Pair 2 for comparison). Snow: "The obverse die is polished somewhat unevenly, with more space between the denticles at 3:00 and 9:00 than at 12:00 and 6:00. The reverse die was used earlier to strike some 1864 (without L) bronze Proof cents.[2] This is the original die pair,[3]

---

[1] Die Pair 1 and Die Pair 2 are described by Richard Snow in "The 1864 With L Proof," *Longacre's Ledger,* Summer 1994. Breen's 1977 description in his *Encyclopedia of Proof Coins,* p. 123, is ambiguous and seems to combine features of both dies; apparently, he did not know there were two different: "Date is about centered, peak of 1 nearly even with bust point (unusual), left base of 1 above space between denticles, right base of 4 above center of denticle. *Spine slants down to left, about 1.5mm in length, from curl below ear into neck.* Doubling on much of legend. Reverse: Spine to left from a round leaf tip at very top of right branch. Heavy letters, base of N in ONE not as strong as other serifs, left base stronger than right base (respectively rounded and pointed)."

[2] Richard Snow, letter, April 10, 1996.

[3] Die Pair 1 is equivalent to Die Pair 2 in Richard Snow's *Flying Eagle & Indian Cents* book, 1st edition, 1992; the 2nd edition, when issued, will have the pairings numbered as in the present text. (Cf. Richard Snow, letter, May 3, 1996)

Die Pair 2 (restrikes): Date is significantly to the right of the tip of the neck, with the left side of the 1 in the date being an obvious checkpoint. A tiny spine (about 1.5mm) extends downward to the left from the curl below ear into Miss Liberty's neck. The reverse seems to be from the same die used to strike the 1863 L pattern cents, but in a later state.[1] Richard Snow[2] and I believe these were made for collectors in 1871; *i.e.,* are restrike issues. (Cf. Norweb Collection, Part I, 1987, Lot 156.) John Dannreuther reports that Proof 1864 Small Motto two-cent pieces also exist in restrike form and suggests that they may have been struck around 1871.[3]

Issuing scenario: The scenario for the issuance of Proof 1864 L cents may well have been as follows:

Late in the 1864 year when the new hub with L on ribbon was introduced into the cent series, Proofs produced at that time were made of the new style and routinely sold to collectors who ordered them. Such orders would have straggled in, for traditionally most Proof minor coins in a given year were sold early in the year. *At the time, there was no numismatic interest in or knowledge of the hub change, and no coin collectors noticed that certain late-1864 bronze Proofs had the L on ribbon.* For that reason, the mintage was small and simply limited to those needed to fill orders that came in.

By 1871 collectors were aware of the tiny L on ribbon and sought to buy 1864 Proof bronze cents with this feature, but specimens were few and far between. The solution was a simple one: A new obverse Proof die dated 1864 and with the L on ribbon was created, and additional Proofs were made. The evidence for this is provided by this die sequence in the words of Richard Snow, here lightly paraphrased and expanded:[4]

Among Proof 1864 L Proof cents, the reverse of Die Pair 1 has been matched to the reverse of a regular no-L 1864 Proof bronze cent. Thus, Die Pair 1 can definitely be assigned "original Proof" status. A copper-nickel [pattern; Judd-358, Pollock-429] 1864 L cent I [Richard Snow] have in stock is also a Die Pair 1 coin and was probably struck in 1864.

The aluminum strikings of the 1864 L cent (J-361, P-432) and the 1863 L cents in various metals (J-301, P-363 in bronze; J-302, P-365 in copper-nickel; J-403, P-367 in aluminum) are all paired with the same reverse used to create 1864 L Proof bronze cents from Die Pair 2, but these various patterns are from an earlier die state. This indicates that the 1863 with-L cents were struck before the Die Pair 2 1864 L bronze Proofs.

However—and here is the telling part—this same reverse die can be found on 1869 aluminum strikings (J-671, P-747) and regular-issue Proof 1870 and 1871 bronze cents. The striking order of this reverse die—as observed from coins together at the same time for side-by-side comparison—is as follows:

1863 L in bronze (Narrow Bust) • 1863 L in copper-nickel (Narrow Bust) • 1869 in aluminum • 1870 regular bronze Proof • 1871 regular bronze Proof (variety with 71 apart) • 1864 L regular bronze Proof • 1871 regular bronze Proof (variety with 71 numerals close).

This clearly shows that the Die Pair 2 Proof 1864 L cents were struck no earlier

[1] Richard Snow in "The 1864 With L Proof," *Longacre's Ledger,* Summer 1994.
[2] Richard Snow, letter, April 10, 1996.
[3] Letter, May 13, 1996.
[4] Richard Snow, letter, April 10, 1996; die pairs are per new 1996 designations and are the opposite of Pair 1 and Pair 2 in Snow's 1992 book, as noted.

than 1871 and were made as restrikes for the collector market. It also shows that in 1871 the Mint was making up restrikes for numismatists."

This restriking activity from the 1871 era is not a revelation, as, for example, the so-called Proof restrike 1801, 1802, and 1803 dollars are believed to have been made around this time, and a glance at the Judd or Pollock books will reveal many unusual mulings and off-metal strikes. Of course, restrikes are avidly collected in their own right, and in some instances (such as Proof half cents of the 1830s and 1840s) rare varieties of restrikes sometimes bring higher prices than originals.

Proof notes: One badly stained Mint State coin is in a certified Proof holder and is likely to remain there; beware! Such coins should be repurchased by the grading services as sub-par pieces tend to distort market data when they are offered (opinion here). Some examples of Proof 1864 L cents and other Proof cents after 1864 were called "copper" die trials by Adams and Woodin in their 1913 text. I had occasion to purchase and closely examine many such "copper pattern" pieces from the Woodin estate via Sol Kaplan in the 1950s (see Appendix II). I am skeptical of such "copper" attributions and suspect that elemental analysis will reveal that any such pieces are, in fact, bronze.

Rarity of Proofs: Proof cents of both die pairs seem to be of about the same rarity. A listing of 13 known specimens in Richard Snow's 1994 article reveals that all but two (Marks Collection and Anderson-Dupont Collection specimens) have spots, fingerprints, or other defects.

Over the years I have handled perhaps five or six Proof coins of this issue. Probably fewer than 15 can be traced with certainty, two gems of which are in an Eastern estate not mentioned in previous studies of Indian cents.

Prices of Proofs are highly subjective and should be taken with a grain of salt. Actual prices at auction may vary depending upon the quality of the coin and market conditions at the time.

Unlike the 1864 (without L) bronze Proof cents, most or all of which *may* have been issued with a dark or bronzed surface, the Proof 1864 L cents were definitely issued with a brilliant finish.

Proof prices for 1996 listings are those suggested by Richard Snow.[1]

Market Prices (1864 L Proofs)

YEAR	PR-60BN	PR-60RB	PR-63BN	PR-63RB	PR-63RD	
1938	$40.00	$45.00	$40.00	$50.00	$50.00	
1944	65.00	70.00	70.00	75.00	75.00	
1965	2,100.00	2,150.00	2,250.00	2,400.00	2,750.00	
1996	8,000.00	16,000.00	11,500.00	20,000.00	40,000.00	

YEAR	PR-64BN	PR-64RB	PR-64RD	PR-65BN	PR-65RB	PR-65RD
1938	$40.00	$45.00	$50.00	$40.00	$50.00	$50.00
1944	75.00	75.00	80.00	70.00	75.00	80.00
1965	2,500.00	2,700.00	3,100.00	2,650.00	2,875.00	3,500.00
1996	25,000.00	40,000.00	60,000.00	35,000.00	55,000.000	75,000.00

[1] Richard Snow, letter, April 10, 1996; he noted this: "We sold the Proof-64 RB (PCGS) for $35,000 in 1994 and $40,000 in 1996."

Notes

Collecting commentary: Examples exist in all business strike grades from well worn to Mint State and are not major rarities, although the fame of the variety has given it a special aura and the status of a key issue.

Striking and distribution: Late in 1864 the tiny initial L for the engraver James B. Longacre was added to the ribbon at the bottom of the Indian's headdress.

The tip of the neck truncation is pointed (rather than rounded as on the earlier 1864 bronze cents and copper-nickel cents dating back to 1860); a.k.a. Narrow Bust.

1864 L cents in copper-nickel, points to ponder: A few 1864 cents with L were struck on thick copper-nickel planchets, at least some of them from Die Pair 1 described above under Proofs. Several Proofs are known and at least two Very Fine specimens (the die characteristics for the VF coins have not been studied). This admits of a small possibility that business strike 1864 L cents were struck in the copper-nickel format (listed today as patterns; Judd-358, Pollock-249). If so, this means that the 1864 L hub was in use before the 1864 bronze (without L) circulation coinage. If this was the case, then it would suggest that many 1864 without-L dies had been made early in the year and used for copper-nickel as well as the later bronze coinage, but that one or more 1864 with-L dies were on hand in spring 1864 when copper-nickel coinage was still in progress.

Amateur at the Mint?: Varieties with repunched date numerals are seen with some frequency and may comprise about one-third of known pieces. Several different varieties have the date triple punched. One particularly curious variety (Snow-5, Fivaz-Stanton 1-006.5, FND-005) not only has a triple date, but may be from a working die punched with two working hubs, first with a without-L hub with rounded neck tip and, second, with a with-L hub with pointed neck tip; the jury is still out on this one.

Perhaps a newcomer in the Engraving Department was doing much of the date punching at the Mint, for the repunching has no counterpart in quantity among the earlier copper-nickel Indian cents. Witness as examples the vastly larger mintages of the 1864 copper-nickel and bronze (without L) cents that exist with relatively few repunchings.

It seems likely to the writer that these endemic repunchings on the 1864 L cent can be ascribed to William H. Key, who signed on at the Mint as an assistant engraver in October 1864, which would have been just about right for the 1864 L cent (also see note about Key under the 1877 cent). However, Key was not an amateur, as he had had his own private diecutting business earlier. Thomas K. DeLorey suggests that perhaps an inexperienced person was hired, his ineptness discovered, and Key was hired to *replace* him.[1]

British connection disputed: Walter Breen reports that many 1864 L cents were shipped to England, probably during and after the Civil War, and that thousands were repatriated during the 1950s-1970s era.[2] However, the present writer spent much time in England during the 1960s, bought many American coins, gained an excellent knowledge of which issues were common there and which were not, and is not aware

---

[1] Letter, April 15, 1996.
[2] *Encyclopedia*, p. 220.

of any such preponderance of 1864 L cents, although occasional pieces were seen.[1]

Moreover, to the best of my knowledge, most if not all 1864 L cents were placed into circulation in 1864 in the Union (North) states. There was no particular reason that quantities should have been shipped to England. On the contrary, bronze cents were never international trade coins and, further, as England carried out considerable trade with the Confederacy in the war, due to the cotton from the South needed for British mills, the export of Union-made 1864 L cents seems even more unlikely.

---

[1] Further, R.W. Julian, April 24, 1996, commented that Treasury records do not show bronze coins shipped to England in 1864 or any other year.

1865 Indian Cent

Business Strikes:

Business strike mintage: 35,429,286.

Number of business strike obverse dies made: 107

Average number of coins struck from typical obverse die: 331,115 (a large increase in the average as compared to the figure for the earlier copper-nickel cents of harder alloy)

Plain 5 and Fancy 5 varieties: Date logotypes are of two styles, with "Plain" 5 or "Fancy" 5, discussed in the notes below. Both varieties exist among business strikes. Thus far, the market has paid little attention to these differences.

Availability in Mint State: This and 1864 (without L) are the two most plentiful early bronze cents in Mint State. Fully brilliant or nearly brilliant specimens are especially attractive and are in the distinct minority among Mint State coins. Some have a woodgrain type of toning as also seen on 1864 bronze cents (also see commentary under 1909-S). Original bright red specimens are somewhat on the rare side, but as 1865 is a common date overall (when all grades are considered), bright red coins have never brought high prices.

Availability in circulated grades: Common within the context of its era. As recently as the 1950s, when quantities of unsorted worn Indian cents were common in public hands and were often brought to coin dealers for valuation, it was usual to find 1864 and 1865 bronze cents in multiples.

Characteristics of striking: Usually fairly well struck. The bottom of N in ONE and, to a lesser extent, the tops of EN in CENT are always shallow as on the die; this would continue until a new hub was made in 1870.

Market Prices (1865 business strikes)

YEAR	G-4	VG-8	F-12	VF-20	EF-40	AU-50
1938	$0.05	$0.15	$0.25	$0.30	$0.40	$0.60
1944	.15	.30	.50	.65	.80	1.00
1965	2.25	3.25	5.75	9.00	14.50	20.00
1996	5.00	7.25	10.00	20.00	30.00	42.50

YEAR	MS-60BN	MS-60RB	MS-63BN	MS-63RB	MS-63RD
1938	$0.90	$0.95	$0.90	$0.95	$1.00
1944	1.40	1.50	1.45	1.50	1.65
1965	40.00	42.50	40.00	44.00	47.00
1996	77.50	95.00	82.00	145.00	200.00

YEAR	MS-64BN	MS-64RB	MS-64RD	MS-65BN	MS-65RB	MS-65RD
1938	$0.90	$0.95	$1.00	$0.90	$0.95	$1.00
1944	1.50	1.50	1.65	1.50	1.55	1.70
1965	42.00	45.00	50.00	43.00	46.00	52.50
1996	120.00	175.00	400.00	175.00	330.00	850.00

Doubled Die Reverse: Strongly doubled in sections, quickly identifiable by looking at the left side of the O in ONE and C in CENT. Fivaz-Stanton 1¢-007, rated by them as having high collector appeal and worth a substantial premium. Discovery announced by Marilyn Van Allen in Collectors' Clearinghouse, *Coin World,* July 5, 1989, p. 74. First auction appearance was in the Bowers and Merena sale of the Saccone Collection, November 1989, Lot 2020. By March 1993 19 specimens had been reported to them. As is true of a lot of nineteenth century American die varieties, chances are excellent for finding a specimen among regular business strikes.

Proofs:

Proof distribution (estimated): 750 to 1,000.

Proof commentary: All have Plain 5 in date. Most are toned brown or brown with traces of red. Original bright red unspotted gems are very hard to find.

Market Prices (1865 Proofs)

YEAR	PR-60BN	PR-60RB	PR-63BN	PR-63RB	PR-63RD
1938	$2.80	$2.90	$2.80	$3.00	$3.50
1944	7.00	7.50	7.00	7.50	8.00
1965	290.00	310.00	300.00	325.00	375.00
1996	160.00	175.00	187.50	350.00	375.00

YEAR	PR-64BN	PR-64RB	PR-64RD	PR-65BN	PR-65RB	PR-65RD
1938	$2.90	$3.00	$3.50	$2.90	$3.00	$3.50
1944	7.10	7.50	8.00	7.25	7.50	8.00
1965	320.00	335.00	395.00	340.00	370.00	450.00
1996	260.00	500.00	1,500.00	525.00	1,500.00	5,000.00

Notes

"Plain" and "fancy": Two different date logotype punches were used for 1865 cents, usually called the "Plain 5" and "Fancy 5" varieties.[1]

The Plain 5 issues have the serifs on the base of the 1 shorter, a small projection from the lower right of the upper curve of the 8, a truncated ball at the top of the 6, a somewhat "bent" left side to the upright attached to the top of the 5, and the flag of the 5 with a gently curved top.

Fancy 5 issues have longer serifs at the base of the 1, have no projection on the 8, have a normal knob or ball on the 6, a straight left side to the upright attached to the top of the 5, and the flag of the 5 with the top flat for about 40% of its surface to the left, then dipping in an arc for the remaining 60%.

Richard Snow's book, *Flying Eagle & Indian Cents,* describes these in detail as does *Flying Eagle and Indian Cent Varieties* by Larry R. Steve and Kevin J. Flynn.

The marketplace has taken virtually no notice of these differences, price-wise. Richard Snow reports that the Plain 5 varieties are slightly scarcer than the Fancy 5s.

Inasmuch as Proofs are of the Plain 5 variety and were made beginning earlier in the year, it is assumed that among business strikes the Plain 5 preceded the Fancy 5.

The variety called "1865/4" by Walter Breen[2] and others has been considered by certain authorities to be Plain 5 over Fancy 5, but at present, per Fivaz-Stanton 1¢-007.3, it is simply a repunched Plain 5 date; not an overdate. While, the 1996 edition of the *Guide Book* mentions the 1865/4; it may be on its way to being delisted.

Legal tender: The Act of March 3, 1864, lowered the legal tender of the bronze cent from a maximum of 10¢ per transaction to just 4¢. The intent of the legislation was to prevent large debts from being paid in bulk bronze cents rather than government paper money (such as Fractional Currency notes). At the time silver and gold coins did not circulate except on the West Coast.

Washington portrait cent suggested: In June 1865 the *New York Journal of Commerce* commented:[3]

> But why can we not have the head of Washington on our coinage now? The cent is the coin in most common use, and on that it ought to be placed. We respectfully urge it on the attention of the director of the Mint. Let us have a few patterns with the head of Washington submitted to the Treasury Department, and do a good thing by thus adopting the memory of Washington as a special object of veneration."

Chief Engraver Longacre did not respond with any cent patterns, but this suggestion may have influenced the production in 1865-1866 of several pattern nickel five-cent pieces (in anticipation of the launching of this new denomination in 1866) with the portrait of Washington.

---

[1] Similar "Plain" and "Fancy" 5 varieties exist among 1865 two-cent pieces.
[2] *Encyclopedia*, p. 221.
[3] Quoted by Don Taxay, *U.S. Mint and Coinage*, p. 244.

1866 Indian Cent

Business Strikes:

Business strike mintage: 9,826,500.

Number of business strike obverse dies made: Not known.

Average number of coins struck from typical obverse die: Not known.

Availability in Mint State: Elusive. Most are brown or red and brown. Original (undipped) red specimens are several orders rarer than red and brown pieces. Brian Wagner advises that MS-65 RD gems are especially elusive with a large demand chasing a tiny supply.[1]

Availability in circulated grades: Somewhat scarce.

Characteristics of striking: Often satisfactory, although one rule hardly fits all. The bottom of N in ONE and, to a lesser extent, the tops of EN in CENT are always shallow as on the die; this would continue until a new hub was made in 1870. Three different obverse dies of this year show severe sinking at their centers, causing the obverse of each coin struck from these dies to bulge and to wear rapidly at that point.[2]

Market Prices (1866 business strikes)

YEAR	G-4	VG-8	F-12	VF-20	EF-40	AU-50
1938	$0.20	$0.35	$0.50	$0.65	0.80	$1.25
1944	0.65	1.30	2.00	2.60	3.00	3.85
1965	10.00	15.00	25.00	42.50	55.00	80.00
1996	30.00	34.00	45.00	78.00	137.50	185.00

---

[1] Letter, May 3, 1996.
[2] Thomas K. DeLorey, letter, April 15, 1996.

YEAR	MS-60BN	MS-60RB	MS-63BN	MS-63RB	MS-63RD	
1938	$2.85	$3.00	$2.85	$3.25	$3.50	
1944	5.80	5.90	5.80	6.00	7.00	
1965	134.00	140.00	135.00	142.00	152.50	
1996	235.00	260.00	245.00	335.00	625.00	

YEAR	MS-64BN	MS-64RB	MS-64RD	MS-65BN	MS-65RB	MS-65RD
1938	$3.00	$3.25	$3.50	$3.10	$3.25	$3.50
1944	5.85	6.00	7.00	5.85	6.00	7.00
1965	137.00	145.00	158.00	140.00	150.00	165.00
1996	280.00	540.00	2,000.00	400.00	850.00	6,000.00

Proofs:

Proof distribution (estimated): Estimated number distributed: 850 to 1,100.

Proof commentary: Beginning with this year and continuing through 1872, there was an extra demand for Proofs due to the low mintage of related business strikes.

Proofs have an irregular surface to Miss Liberty's cheek and certain other head and neck features, probably the result of die rust. The obverse die field is more basined than normal. Bright red Proofs are very hard to find. Most "red" Proofs have been dipped (ditto for other red Proofs in the series).

Market Prices (1866 Proofs)

YEAR	PR-60BN	PR-60RB	PR-63BN	PR-63RB	PR-63RD	
1938	$2.90	$3.10	$3.00	$3.30	$3.50	
1944	7.00	7.20	7.00	7.75	8.50	
1965	265.00	285.00	280.00	300.00	350.00	
1996	150.00	170.00	195.00	245.00	320.00	

YEAR	PR-64BN	PR-64RB	PR-64RD	PR-65BN	PR-65RB	PR-65RD
1938	$3.10	$3.30	$3.50	$3.10	$3.30	$3.50
1944	7.00	7.75	8.50	7.00	7.75	8.50
1965	290.00	310.00	360.00	315.00	340.00	425.00
1996	270.00	450.00	1,500.00	480.00	740.00	3,500.00

Notes

Collecting commentary: Fairly scarce as a date, the beginning of the "tough" era of Indian cents that would extend through the early 1870s. In the 1950s when it was not uncommon to find cigar boxes filled with cents, I always picked out the dates from 1866 to 1878 inclusive and set them aside as scarce.

Doubled die: One variety of this year (Snow-1, Fivaz-Stanton 1-007.6, FND-001) has sharp doubling at ERTY in the headband, but is not widely known; actually, the striking is *tripled,* but the tripling can only be seen on well-struck specimens of very early die states.[1] Repunched date varieties also exist of this date and are described by Snow and Steve-Flynn.

Concerning this doubled die variety Sam Lukes commented:[2]

In May of 1993 I cherrypicked this 1866 Snow-1 variety (graded ANACS MS-64 RB), which has since become recognized as the finest known, having a higher percentage of red than a second specimen, also an MS-64 RB, that has less mint color. I was offered $1,500 for mine, which I refused, opting to sell it to a very good client of mine for $850 (I had purchased it for less than $400!). In December 1994 an ANACS MS-62 RB example of the same variety sold for a record $3,150...."

Demand when issued: From the 1866 *Mint Report:* "The demand from the small coin, both bronze [1¢, 2¢] and nickel [3¢, 5¢], was very great during the year, and the coinage was regulated to meet the demand. They were distributed to all parts of the United States, but principally to the Western and Southern states."[3] Part of this was probably due to peace following the Civil War, and the lack of circulating coins in the South (whose merchants and other interests during the Civil War had issued very few private tokens). However, it is doubtful if many were circulated in the *far* West.

New periodical: The *American Journal of Numismatics,* published by the American Numismatic and Archaeological Society, made its debut as the first numismatic periodical in this country and would go on to be published regularly well into the early 20th century.

Millward, forgotten Mint director: 1866, October: William Millward was appointed director of the Mint when the Senate was in recess. The nomination was subsequently sent by President Andrew Johnson to the Senate on January 2, 1867, but was rejected by the Senate on January 26. However, Millward remained in the Mint until Henry Richard Linderman, M.D., was confirmed as director on April 2.[4] Millward's name is omitted from most official accounts of Mint history, possibly because he was never confirmed by the Senate (a procedure which was typically a formality anyway; often Mint directors began serving in the post months before confirmation).

---

[1] Larry R. Steve, letter, April 12, 1996.

[2] Letter, April 8, 1996.

[3] QDB note: This is a departure from the norm; those regions did not usually desire to use minor coins. Could the new demand have been from Northern occupation or Reconstruction? (suggestion of Thomas K. DeLorey, letter, April 15, 1996).

[4] 1971 [*sic*] *Mint Report;* this also appeared in other issues.

1867 Indian Cent

Business Strikes:

Business strike mintage: 9,821,000.

Number of business strike obverse dies made: Not known.

Average number of coins struck from typical obverse die: Not known.

Availability in Mint State: Quite elusive. Most are brown or red and brown. Original bright red specimens were rare years ago and are even more elusive today; most "Brilliant Uncirculated" pieces on the market have been dipped.

Availability in circulated grades: Scarce.

Characteristics of striking: Varies, but usually on the sharp side. The bottom of N in ONE and, to a lesser extent, the tops of EN in CENT are always shallow as on the die; this would continue until a new hub was made in 1870.

Market Prices (1867 business strikes)

YEAR	G-4	VG-8	F-12	VF-20	EF-40	AU-50
1938	$0.20	$0.35	$0.50	$0.65	0.80	$1.25
1944	0.65	1.30	2.00	2.50	2.90	3.70
1965	10.00	15.00	25.00	40.00	55.00	80.00
1996	30.00	34.00	45.00	95.00	135.00	195.00

YEAR	MS-60BN	MS-60RB	MS-63BN	MS-63RB	MS-63RD	
1938	$2.85	$3.00	$2.85	$3.25	$3.50	
1944	4.60	4.75	4.60	5.00	5.30	
1965	125.00	130.00	128.00	132.50	145.00	
1996	250.00	320.00	270.00	360.00	800.00	

YEAR	MS-64BN	MS-64RB	MS-64RD	MS-65BN	MS-65RB	MS-65RD
1938	$3.00	$3.25	$3.50	$3.10	$3.25	$3.50
1944	4.80	5.00	5.50	4.80	5.00	5.50
1965	132.50	136.00	150.00	135.00	140.00	155.00
1996	350.00	550.00	2,000.00	475.00	900.00	7,000.00

1867 REPUNCHED DATE: The 7 digit in particular is dramatically repunched, with the undertype 7 appearing to be smaller and more delicate, perhaps because it was punched only lightly into the die. The "pivot point" for the second and deeper impression of the four-digit 1867 logotype was at the base of the 1; from that point the misalignment becomes greater as the distance increases.

1867 repunched date, a mini-forum: The so-called 1867 over 67, with the last digit being smaller (in my opinion, but I am in the minority, and no consultant to the present book has agreed with me), was first published the February-March 1959 issue of the *Empire Topics* (predecessor of the *Rare Coin Review*). Since then, some have suggested that both 7 digits are the same size, but I am unconvinced this is the case; to my eye, the undertype 7 looks smaller and more delicate. I have an open mind, and very possibly either of the two following views is correct:

Bill Fivaz and J.T. Stanton take the majority view: "We feel it *appears* smaller due to the subsequent logo punch filling in some of the original cavity of the 7 (metal movement to the area of least resistance)."[1] Harry Salyards, M.D., comments that the variation may be due "simply to the depth at which the first punch was hammered into the die, compared to the second punch: analogous to the 1847/7 discussed in *Penny-Wise* #122, July 15, 1989, p. 233."[2]

Larry R. Steve provided his detailed opinion:[3]

The 1867/67 [repunched date] Indian cent specimen I have in my collection is a very early die state which shows a split base of the 1 as well as repunching on the 67. This clearly indicates a four-digit date punch. Also obvious is the fact that it is a pivoted repunching, with the 1 as the pivot point. What is not obvious is that the date punch was tilted when first punched; the punch was 'heeled' on the 1 (*i.e.*, the

---

[1] Bill Fivaz, letter, March 30, 1996.
[2] Letter, April 10, 1995. *Penny-Wise* is the journal of the Early American Coppers club, edited in recent years by Dr. Salyards.
[3] Letter, April 29, 1996.

1 was in contact with the die first with the remaining digits tilted upward away from the die). This is based upon the observation that the first 1 was punched in at nearly the same depth as the second punching of the 1, whereas the depth of the 67 from the first punching is more shallow than the final punching. Now, if a 7 is punched in parallel to the surface of the die it will appear as the same width as the punch itself; if it is punched in at an angle it will appear narrower. This tilting *could* possibly account for the appearance of a smaller 7, but I am not 100% convinced myself. It seems to me to be a more plausible theory than the filling in of the cavity of the first punch; the first punch was more shallow and some distortion of the filling in should have occurred. The possibility of a smaller 7, however, still exists."

Snow-1. Fivaz-Stanton 1¢-008. FND-001. Breen-1974. Market prices are about 50% to 70% higher than regular business strikes (cf. *Coin World* "Trends" by Keith Zaner). Specimens in Mint State occasionally are seen.

Proofs:

Proof distribution (estimated): 850 to 1,100.

Proof commentary: Most are red and brown. Some may have "thin letters" on the obverse (cf. Walter Breen, *Encyclopedia of Proof Coins,* p. 132), but this may be from a lapped or repolished die, certainly it is not a distinct variety.

I reiterate that the certification services routinely call coins "RD" (red) even if they have spots. In all instances, Proof-65 RD coins are scarcer and more desirable if they are spotless.

Market Prices (1867 Proofs)

YEAR	PR-60BN	PR-60RB	PR-63BN	PR-63RB	PR-63RD	
1938	$3.10	$3.20	$3.10	$3.30	$3.50	
1944	7.70	7.80	7.70	8.00	8.50	
1965	225.00	235.00	240.00	250.00	300.00	
1996	152.50	175.00	205.00	230.00	260.00	

YEAR	PR-64BN	PR-64RB	PR-64RD	PR-65BN	PR-65RB	PR-65RD
1938	$3.10	$3.30	$3.50	$3.15	$3.30	$3.50
1944	7.75	8.00	8.50	7.75	8.00	8.50
1965	245.00	265.00	320.00	270.00	300.00	350.00
1996	265.00	390.00	810.00	490.00	900.00	3,500.00

Notes

Collecting commentary: The 1867 is a scarce date in all grades.

Circulation: By 1867, indeed for recent years, minor coins circulated in large numbers and included the Indian cent, two-cent piece, nickel three-cent piece, and the new nickel five cents. Silver coins were absent from the channels of commerce in the Eastern and Midwest United States (but circulated on the West Coast).

Longacre and the coinage of Chile: In 1867 Chief Engraver James B. Longacre, progenitor of the Indian cent motif, and Anthony C. Paquet (by now back in the private sector, but doing contract work for the Mint) redesigned and/or modified certain coins for the government of Chile (none of these motifs bear any resemblance to contemporary American coinage, however). Some Chilean coins dated 1867 and 1868 were sold among other numismatic effects in the sale of the Longacre estate in 1870 (see commentary under 1870).[1]

New Mint director: 1867, April 2: Henry R. Linderman, M.D., began his service as Mint director and would serve until May 1869 and also for a later term, April 1873 to December 1878. Under his administrations many limited-edition patterns and other special pieces were made for private sale by Mint officials to dealers and collectors.

---

[1] Also see commentary on Chilean dies in *World Coin News,* May 31, 1988.

1868 Indian Cent

Business Strikes:

Business strike mintage: 10,266,500.

Number of business strike obverse dies made: Not known.

Average number of coins struck from typical obverse die: Not known.

Availability in Mint State: Rare. Most are fully or at least partly brown. Bright red cents of this date are seen more often than are those of the somewhat comparable (mintage-wise) 1867, but in absolute terms they are extremely rare. As is the case for all "Brilliant Uncirculated" Indian cents, the majority offered as such on the market have been dipped.

Availability in circulated grades: Scarce.

Characteristics of striking: Varies, but often weak or of average sharpness, usually not as sharp as, for example, a typical cent of 1867. The bottom of N in ONE and, to a lesser extent, the tops of EN in CENT are always shallow as on the die; this would continue until a new hub was made in 1870.

Market Prices (1868 business strikes)

YEAR	G-4	VG-8	F-12	VF-20	EF-40	AU-50
1938	$0.20	$0.35	$0.50	$0.65	0.80	$1.25
1944	0.65	1.30	2.00	2.50	2.90	3.70
1965	11.00	16.00	25.00	42.50	57.50	90.00
1996	28.50	32.50	44.00	75.00	122.50	175.00

YEAR	MS-60BN	MS-60RB	MS-63BN	MS-63RB	MS-63RD	
1938	$2.85	$3.00	$2.85	$3.25	$3.50	
1944	4.60	4.75	4.60	5.00	5.30	
1965	160.00	163.00	160.00	165.00	175.00	
1996	225.00	240.00	235.00	265.00	575.00	

YEAR	MS-64BN	MS-64RB	MS-64RD	MS-65BN	MS-65RB	MS-65RD
1938	$3.00	$3.25	$3.50	$3.10	$3.25	$3.50
1944	4.80	5.00	5.50	4.80	5.00	5.50
1965	162.50	167.50	182.00	163.00	170.00	190.00
1996	320.00	495.00	1,000.00	425.00	900.00	3,000.00

Proofs:

Proof distribution (estimated): 750 to 1,000.

Proof commentary: Most are red and brown. Some Proofs—apparently somewhat less than half of the known pieces—have the obverse and reverse dies aligned in the same direction, rather than the usual 180° apart; this has not been widely noticed and bears no significant premium.

On April 27, 1868, 100 Proof Indian cents were delivered along with an equivalent number of silver Proof sets, indicating it was the practice to include these with silver sets at the time. In addition, for 15¢ payable in silver or gold (the government would not accepts its own paper money at par!), a minor Proof set could be purchased, this containing the Indian cent, two-cent piece, nickel three-cent piece, and Shield nickel—total face value 11¢.[1]

Market Prices (1868 Proofs)

YEAR	PR-60BN	PR-60RB	PR-63BN	PR-63RB	PR-63RD	
1938	3.05	$3.20	$3.10	$3.30	$3.50	
1944	7.75	7.85	7.75	8.00	8.40	
1965	265.00	285.00	280.00	300.00	350.00	
1996	155.00	175.00	192.50	240.00	260.00	

YEAR	PR-64BN	PR-64RB	PR-64RD	PR-65BN	PR-65RB	PR-65RD
1938	$3.10	$3.30	$3.50	$3.15	$3.30	$3.50
1944	8.00	8.00	8.50	8.00	8.00	8.50
1965	290.00	310.00	360.00	315.00	340.00	425.00
1996	255.00	380.00	910.00	500.00	900.00	3,500.00

[1] R.W. Julian, "Notes on U.S. Proof Coinage, Silver and Minor." *Numismatic Scrapbook Magazine,* March 1966.

Notes

Collecting commentary: The 1868 along with the 1866, 1869, and 1870 is considered to be semi-scarce in all business strike grades.

1868 NICKEL THREE-CENT PIECE: Obverse with clash marks from the reverse of an Indian cent. Traces of the cent reverse can be seen on Miss Liberty's neck (an oak leaf is prominent) and around UNITED STATES and AMERICA. (Chris Pilliod photograph)

A notable clashed die: An interesting and rare 1868 nickel three-cent piece was discovered by Chris Pilliod and described in *Coin World,* March 4, 1996:[1]

I discovered...in late 1994 at a public auction in Michigan an 1868 copper-nickel three-cent coin with a clover-leaf pattern smack in the middle of Liberty's neck.... The obverse die of this three-cent coin was clashed with the reverse of an Indian Head cent, and what appears as a three-leaf clover is in fact an oak leaf from the wreath of the cent. Several smaller leaves and a portion of the ribbon may be seen in back of Liberty's forehead.

Apparently the clashing also occurred at an oblique angle [rather than during

---

[1] "Collectors' Clearinghouse" column. Article titled "Clashed Dies: Usually Common, There Are Some Bizarre Varieties to Seek."

the die set-up process during which both dies were firmly mounted in the press—QDB]. This piece does not display as much detail of the clashing as the 1870 Shield nickel and as a result cannot command the same of premium.

Additional searching has uncovered several additional examples beyond the discovery piece.... I speculate they occurred when the operator was changing over a minting press from one denomination to a different one. Doubtless the Mint used presses interchangeably for coins of similar diameters. The operator may have inadvertently fired the press before completing the turnover of dies...."

Separately, Chris Pilliod noted that as of early April 1996, he knew of several Extremely Fine specimens and one AU piece. His estimate of scarcity is Rarity-5, or over 30 known.[1]

The Indian cent reverse die was in the anvil or fixed part of the set-up in the coining press, while the obverse for the nickel three-cent piece was in the hammer die position. As Chris Pilliod suggests, this clashing was probably inadvertent and was caused by mismatched dies in the press during the press set-up process (much in the manner that 1857 clashed die Flying Eagle cents were created; see earlier listings).

The question: Is there an 1868 Indian cent showing on its reverse evidence of clash marks from the obverse of a nickel three-cent piece?[2]

Counterpoint: In the May 1996 issue of *2 Times Numismatic Newsletter,* Frank Leone, publisher, discusses this particular 1868 nickel three-cent variety and argues that it has nothing to do with an Indian cent clashed die.

Mint notes: From the 1868 *Mint Report:* "The purchase of the nickel-copper [*sic;* this was common terminology at the Mint at the time; the writer was simply listing the more valuable metal in the alloy first] cents, composed of 88% copper and 12% nickel, still continues, payment being made in the three- and five-cent nickel coins. The amount purchased to the close of the fiscal year [June 30] was $260,482.04. This operation results in a small profit to the United States and serves to reduce the redundancy of cent coins."

Dealer Mason: In 1868 Ebenezer Locke Mason, who had become a rare coin dealer in the late 1850s, published his first auction catalogue for a sale held on October 28-29. By that time *Mason's Coin & Stamp Collector's Journal* was a year old. Mason eventually played the coin circuit and held sales in Boston, New York, and Philadelphia, the leading centers of activity at the time.[3]

1868 large cent: One of the most interesting of all 1868 cents is not an Indian cent at all, but is a latter-day version of the old-style large cent, but minted 11 years after the regular issues ceased to be in February 1857. The 1868 large cent is identical in format to a Braided Hair cent of the 1850s and, presumably, was minted to provide a whimsy for numismatists at the same time a legitimate pattern bronze *three-cent piece* with the same obverse was made. Examples were struck in copper and in nickel alloy. Probably fewer than 20 1868 large cents exist today.

---

[1] Letter, April 12, 1996.
[2] For further information: Chris Pilliod. "What Error Coins Can Teach Us About Die Settings." *The Numismatist,* April 1996.
[3] John W. Adams, *United States Numismatic Literature,* Vol. I, pp. 42 ff.

1869 Indian Cent

Business Strikes:

Business strike mintage: 6,420,000.

Number of business strike obverse dies made: Not known.

Average number of coins struck from typical obverse die: Not known.

Availability in Mint State: Scarce. Usually fully or partly brown. Original red examples are rare.

Availability in circulated grades: Scarce.

Characteristics of striking: Varies, but usually sharp. The bottom of N in ONE and, to a lesser extent, the tops of EN in CENT are always shallow as on the die; this would continue until a new hub was made in 1870.

Market Prices (1869 business strikes)

YEAR	G-4	VG-8	F-12	VF-20	EF-40	AU-50
1938	$0.40	$0.60	$0.75	$1.00	1.25	$2.00
1944	1.00	1.35	2.00	2.25	2.50	2.75
1965	15.00	25.00	50.00	70.00	95.00	160.00
1996	40.00	55.00	160.00	235.00	275.00	360.00

YEAR	MS-60BN	MS-60RB	MS-63BN	MS-63RB	MS-63RD	
1938	$3.20	$3.30	$3.20	$3.30	$3.50	
1944	3.50	3.75	3.50	4.00	4.50	
1965	300.00	310.00	300.00	315.00	330.00	
1996	450.00	490.00	460.00	600.00	900.00	

YEAR	MS-64BN	MS-64RB	MS-64RD	MS-65BN	MS-65RB	MS-65RD
1938	$3.25	$3.30	$3.50	$3.25	$3.30	$3.50
1944	3.80	4.20	4.60	4.00	4.30	4.70
1965	310.00	322.50	340.00	320.00	330.00	355.00
1996	510.00	650.00	2,000.00	625.00	1,250.00	3,500.00

Proofs:

Proof distribution (estimated): 850 to 1,100.

Proof commentary: Most are red and brown. Some were sloppily made. As is true of all Proofs of this era, bright red gems without spots are quite rare.

Struck from at least two different obverse dies, one with very slight repunching of the last date digit. Richard Snow suggests that about one in 20 coins from this latter die are aligned 360°.[1]

Market Prices (1869 Proofs)

YEAR	PR-60BN	PR-60RB	PR-63BN	PR-63RB	PR-63RD	
1938	$3.10	$3.20	$3.10	$3.30	$3.50	
1944	7.70	7.80	7.70	8.00	8.50	
1965	435.00	440.00	445.00	465.00	525.00	
1996	320.00	330.00	340.00	400.00	470.00	

YEAR	PR-64BN	PR-64RB	PR-64RD	PR-65BN	PR-65RB	PR-65RD
1938	$3.10	$3.30	$3.50	$3.15	$3.30	$3.50
1944	7.75	8.00	8.50	7.75	8.00	8.50
1965	460.00	520.00	550.00	475.00	525.00	625.00
1996	490.00	600.00	890.00	600.00	1,000.00	2,300.00

Notes

Collecting commentary: Scarce in all grades. Several varieties of repunched dates exist and in the past have been staunchly defended as overdates; this is especially true of the variety with two "horns" above the final 8 (today classified as Fivaz-Stanton 1¢-008.3, Snow-3, repunched date). The writer suggests that these blunders and also those of 1870 (numerous examples of which are illustrated in the Steve-Flynn book) might be attributed to the inexperience of Charles E. Barber, son of Chief Engraver William Barber, who was hired by the Mint in January 1869 (the same month his father became chief engraver), and who may have been assigned to punching date logotypes into dies for the "least important" of all denominations, the Indian cent (also see note under the 1877 Indian cent). However, as there are a number of repunched dates known for bronze cents before 1869, perhaps William H. Key is

---

[1] "Proof Die Identification for Indian Cents." *Longacre's Ledger,* Fall 1994.

to be thanked (by numismatists today) for these blunders (see note about Key under the 1864 L cent).

Walter Breen in his *Encyclopedia* (p. 222) was aware of repunched dates but specifically noted that in addition there was a true overdate 1869/8.

The 1965 issue of the *Guide Book of United States Coins* gave these values for 1869/8 cents (with the same book's 1869 "regular" cent prices given here in parenthesis: 1869/8 Good $45.00 (regular 1869 $15.50), VG $55.00 ($26.00), F $87.50 ($48.50), VF $125.00 ($70.00), EF $175.00 ($95.00), Uncirculated $450.00 ($300.00). At the time it was generally considered that the "overdate" was about three times rarer than the regular 1869. However, a review of "overdates" offered in the marketplace disclosed that often just about any coin with even the slightest repunching on the 9 digit was sold as an "overdate."

As an artifact of the days when many specimens of the 1869/9 (as they are called today) were called 1869/8 overdates, examples of the 1869/9 have sold for much more than "perfect date" 1869 cents in recent times. However, I predict that as time goes on, the price differential will narrow.

New chief engraver: James B. Longacre, chief engraver since 1844, died on January 1, 1869. William Barber, who had worked as an assistant since 1865, became chief engraver in the same month. Without doubt he punched his share of four-digit date logotypes into Indian cent dies during the 1865-1869 years and possibly later as well. This sketch is from George G. Evans, *Illustrated History of the United States Mint:*

> William Barber, fifth engraver of the Mint, was born in London, May 2, 1807. He learned his profession from his father, John Barber, and was employed on silver-plate work after his emigration to this country [in September 1852]. He resided in Boston 10 years, and was variously employed in his line of work. His skill in this way came to the knowledge of Mr. Longacre, then engraver of the Mint, and he secured his services as an assistant in 1865.
>
> In January, 1869, upon the death of Mr. Longacre, he was appointed as his successor, and continued in that position for the remainder of his life. His death, which resulted from severe chills, brought on by bathing at the seashore, occurred in Philadelphia, August 31, 1879.
>
> Besides much original work on pattern coins, he also produced over 40 medals, public and private. The work on all of them was creditable, but we may specify those of Agassiz, Rittenhouse, and Henry, as very superior specimens of art. Mr. Barber was assisted by Mr. William H. Key, Mr. Charles E. Barber, and Mr. George T. Morgan."

Double weight system: The 1869 *Mint Report* contained an extensive dissertation on the double system of weights employed in the United States. The troy pound is divided into 12 ounces and was used only by the Mint for precious metals, by jewelers, and by apothecaries (druggists). The more popular avoirdupois pound is divided into 16 ounces and was used to measure just about everything else. Further, in the words of Mint Director James Pollock:

> Let me give an idea of how this double system works at the Mint. Gold and silver are weighed by the ounce troy; nickel and copper by the pound avoirdupois. All the weighable accessories and materials, from anthracite coal to acids and chemicals, are measured by the latter. Explanations have to be given, cross calculations made, and mistakes watched against. An ounce troy is 480 grains; the other ounce, 437.5 grains. If we want to bargain for platinum or aluminum, a question arises as to which ounce is to be used. When we sell sweeps [gold and silver dust, chips, and miscella-

neous residue from mint operations], it is by one weight, when we get the returns, it is by another. In short, we are often reminded of the awkward relation of 437.5 to 480, and that a pound avoirdupois is equal to 14.5833 ounces troy...."

Dealer Haseltine: About the year 1869 Captain John W. Haseltine, who had served with distinction in the Civil War, entered the rare coin trade by joining Ebenezer Locke Mason. Soon thereafter he was on his own, and on April 12, 1870, he held his first auction sale, featuring the consignment of his father-in-law William Idler. In the field of small cents Haseltine is perhaps best remembered for bringing the original 1861 Confederate States of America pieces to light in the 1870s by tracking down their maker, Robert Lovett, Jr. Both Haseltine and Idler had close connections with Mint officials and "laundered" many Proofs, patterns, and "special pieces" on their behalf, introducing them to numismatists. (Certain pointed comments about Mint practices in this regard appear in the William Fewsmith Collection sale catalogue by the aforementioned Mason, October 1870) In his time he was nicknamed the "Numismatic Refrigerator," because of all of the delicacies he had in storage. Doubtless, if Haseltine had committed to print all he knew, our information concerning numismatics of the late nineteenth century would be much more accurate. As it developed, it was left to Walter Breen and other researchers to *theorize* what might have happened behind the scenes in the Medal Department, while Haseltine surely *knew*. In the late 1870s in his Philadelphia shop, Haseltine gave employment to the young Chapman brothers, S. Hudson and Henry, thereby launching their remarkable careers.[1]

---

[1] John W. Adams, *United States Numismatic Literature,* Vol. I, pp. 47 ff.

1870 Indian Cent

Business Strikes:

Business strike mintage: 5,275,000.

Number of business strike obverse dies made: Not known.

Average number of coins struck from typical obverse die: Not known.

Availability in Mint State: Most are brown or red and brown. Choice coins are elusive. Original bright red coins are rare and sometimes have a yellowish cast to them, due no doubt to the alloy.

Availability in circulated grades: Quite scarce.

Characteristics of striking: Varies, but can be found well defined. Die characteristics vary. Some have the bottom of N in ONE and, to a lesser extent, the tops of EN in CENT shallow as on the die, from the old hub introduced with the 1864 bronze coinage.

Market Prices (1870 business strikes)

YEAR	G-4	VG-8	F-12	VF-20	EF-40	AU-50
1938	$0.25	$0.40	$0.75	$1.00	$1.50	$2.75
1944	1.50	2.50	3.50	3.80	4.20	4.50
1965	14.00	22.00	37.50	50.00	72.50	110.00
1996	35.00	50.00	140.00	220.00	297.50	350.00

YEAR	MS-60BN	MS-60RB	MS-63BN	MS-63RB	MS-63RD
1938	4.30	4.40	4.50	4.70	$5.00
1944	5.80	5.90	5.80	6.00	7.00
1965	160.00	163.00	160.00	165.00	175.00
1996	400.00	450.00	410.00	545.00	820.00

YEAR	MS-64BN	MS-64RB	MS-64RD	MS-65BN	MS-65RB	MS-65RD
1938	4.50	4.70	$5.50	4.50	4.70	$5.50
1944	5.85	6.00	7.10	5.85	6.10	7.10
1965	162.50	167.50	190.00	165.00	177.50	200.00
1996	500.00	700.00	1,750.00	620.00	1,200.00	4,000.00

Proofs:

Proof distribution (estimated): 850 to 1,100.

Proof commentary: Most are red and brown. Quite a few cleaned specimens are around, seemingly more than for any other date of this immediate era. This date also seems to be susceptible to spotting. Original bright red Proofs are rare.

Proofs exist from the hub with the bottom of the N in ONE and tops of EN in CENT shallowly impressed, and also with a bold N and EN; I have never seen this variety on a want list, and as of this writing there is no price difference between the two. At least two obverse dies were used, one of which shows repunching on the 8 of the date.

Market Prices (1870 Proofs)

YEAR	PR-60BN	PR-60RB	PR-63BN	PR-63RB	PR-63RD	
1938	$3.10	$3.20	$3.10	$3.30	$3.50	
1944	7.70	7.80	7.70	8.10	8.75	
1965	265.00	285.00	280.00	300.00	350.00	
1996	330.00	335.00	330.00	340.00	400.00	

YEAR	PR-64BN	PR-64RB	PR-64RD	PR-65BN	PR-65RB	PR-65RD
1938	$3.10	$3.30	$3.50	$3.15	$3.30	$3.50
1944	7.75	8.10	8.75	7.75	8.10	8.75
1965	290.00	310.00	360.00	315.00	340.00	425.00
1996	370.00	460.00	900.00	525.00	1,100.00	2,300.00

Notes

Collecting commentary: Scarce in all grades, particularly so in Mint State.

Several minor reverse die differences occur and are explained in the introduction to Indian cents and given expanded descriptions below. These variations are not widely collected:

Reverse hub C (introduced in 1864 with the bronze coinage; in use through 1869 and intermittently until 1877): E's with T-shaped serifs at centers. Bottom of N in ONE and tops of EN in CENT in low relief. Style used from 1864 through 1870 and intermittently later (as on 1877 business strikes).

Reverse hub D (introduced in 1870 and used on some cents through 1877 and all after that date): E's with flared or trumpet-shaped serifs at centers. N in ONE in normal relief. Used on most cents through 1909.

Reverse hub D/C: Hub D struck over C, showing doubling, especially at top left of E in CENT. E in ONE has T-shaped serif at center, E in CENT has flared serif. Seen on some 1870 cents.

Misplaced dates: At least two varieties are known which show parts of the date logotype in the denticles below the correct 1870 date, apparently the result of the four-digit punch coming into hard contact with the working die while not being even near the correct position. The most startling in my view is the variety known as FND-001 and Snow-5, which shows the upper part of a 0 protruding from the denticles below the 7 of the date. Less obvious and best seen under strong magnification is FND-004, which shows a garbled mess of digit segments (at least eight according to Larry R. Steve and Kevin J. Flynn) within the denticles.

1870 SHIELD NICKEL: Detail of obverse showing clash marks from the obverse of an Indian cent. Outlines of the headdress feathers can be seen within the vertical shield lines. (Ken Hill photograph supplied by Chris Pilliod)

A notable clashed die: An interesting and rare 1870 Shield nickel five-cent piece was discovered by Ken Hill in 1994. Its obverse shows clash mark impressions of the obverse of an Indian cent. The face and headdress of Miss Liberty appear clearly and in an inverted position in the background areas between the shield stripes on the nickel. The Indian cent obverse die was in the hammer or top movable part of the set-up in the coining press, while the obverse for the Shield nickel was in the anvil or stake position at the bottom. This clashing was probably inadvertent and was caused by mismatched dies in the press during the press set-up process (much in the manner that 1857 clashed die Flying Eagle cents were created; see earlier listings).

The question: Is there an 1870 Indian cent showing on its obverse evidence of clash marks from a Shield nickel? These would probably be in the form of vertical stripes near the head of the Indian.

By April 1996 the variety remained rare, and only one additional specimen has come to light, this in the inventory of Larry Briggs. While the rarity remains to be determined over time as the knowledge of the variety becomes widespread, it is seemingly a candidate for Rarity-7 or Rarity-6 status, but certainly is very scarce.[1]

---

[1] Chris Pilliod. "What Error Coins Can Teach Us About Die Settings." *The Numismatist,* April 1996. Also: Chris Pilliod, letter, April 12, 1996.:

Longacre Sale Contents:

Items from the numismatic estate of Chief Engraver James B. Longacre, who died on January 1, 1869, were auctioned a year later. Thomas K. DeLorey has furnished the following commentary, including the insertion of modern catalogue attributions (Judd numbers):[1]

I happen to own an annotated copy of the catalogue of the James B. Longacre estate sale (M. Thomas & Sons, Philadelphia, January 21, 1870) which included, among others, the following patterns and prices which might be of interest to the reader, especially as it shows how the market for patterns has risen and fallen with collector interests. The multiple coins were all offered as separate lots. The attributions of the patterns are, necessarily, only probable.

1856 half cent struck in nickel, VF, Judd-177. Sold for $4.75.

1856 cent, no date or legend, copper Proof, J-179, $5.00.

1856 nickel [*sic*] cent, Proof, J-180, $1.12. Nine more lots of the same, @ $1.00 each.

1858 nickel cents (2), large eagle, tobacco ["agricultural"] wreath, Proof (apparently the regular issue, called "rare"), $0.65 and $0.62.

1858 nickel cents (2), Large Eagle, oak wreath, Proof, J-192 or 197, $1.62 and $1.12.

1858 nickel cent, Large Eagle, laurel wreath, Proof, J-191 or 196, $0.62.

1858 nickel cents (5), Large Eagle, oak wreath/shield, Proof, J-193 or 198, $0.75 each.

1858 nickel cent, Large Eagle, oak wreath, broad planchet, Proof, very rare (not in Judd, unless a misdescribed J-199), $3.50.

1858 nickel cents (3), Small Eagle, laurel wreath, Proof, J-202, $1.00 each.

1858 nickel cent, Small Eagle, tobacco wreath, Proof, J-206, $0.87.

1858 nickel cents, (2), Small Eagle, oak wreath, Proof, J-203, $1.00 each.

1858 nickel cents, Small Eagle, oak wreath and shield, Proof, J-204, $0.85. Nine more of the same, @ $0.75 each.

1858 [*sic;* catalogued as this date] nickel cent, Indian Head, laurel wreath, broad planchet, without date; Very Fine, very rare, J-214, $8.25.

1858 nickel cents (15), Indian Head, laurel wreath, ordinary planchet, Proof, J-208, $0.55 each.

1858 nickel cents (4), Indian Head, tobacco wreath, ordinary planchet, Proof, J-213, $0.55 each.

1858 nickel cents (2), Indian Head, oak wreath, Proof, J-211, $0.55 each.

1858 nickel cents (12), Indian Head, oak wreath and shield, Proof, J-212, $0.65 each.

Among other items in the sale, an 1836 gold dollar, J-67, brought $6 from Mr. Cogan (nearly certainly dealer Edward D. Cogan); an 1849 half dime, J-112, "undoubtedly a mule, extremely rare," brought $13 from Mr. Thatcher; an 1860 half eagle in copper, J-272, called "remarkably rare," brought $8.50 from Mr. Randall (presumably J. Colvin Randall), while an 1848 $2.50 CAL. described as "Proof" brought $5.50 from Cogan. Pattern half dollars of 1859 in silver, Proof, brought 87¢ to $1 each, while several of the five-cent patterns of 1866 and 1867 brought $7 to $11 each. The highest priced pattern was an 1868 Postage Currency dime in aluminum, J-646, which brought $19. Lot 585 consisted of the obverse and reverse wax models for the $3 gold piece including the wreath later used on the Flying Eagle cent.[2]

---

[1] Letter, April 15, 1996. Conversions were not made to Pollock, Snow, or *Coin World Encyclopedia* (Alexander-DeLorey) numbers as these later references are more detailed as to varieties and attributions would be even more tentative.

[2] In 1996 these models were owned by Thomas K. DeLorey.

1871 Indian Cent

Business Strikes:

Business strike mintage: 3,929,500.

Number of business strike obverse dies made: Not known.

Average number of coins struck from typical obverse die: Not known.

Availability in Mint State: Rare. One of the key issues in the series. Original bright red specimens are exceedingly hard to find, but their market price is dampened by the offering of dipped coins. In general, the 1871 Indian cent can hold its own with the 1872 in any rarity contest, but the latter date is much more publicized.

Availability in circulated grades: Rare in the context of the series. One of the key issues. In fact, in grades from Good through Fine this is believed to be the rarest date in the 1870-1879 span, excluding the 1877.[1] This empirical observation is backed by the relative mintage figures for the decade.

Characteristics of striking: Usually fairly strong.

Date styles: At least two obverse styles for business strikes are known; the style usually seen with 71 noticeably separated (Wide Date) and the other with 71 in date nearly touching (Close Date). These were made from two different four-digit logotype punches; these punches were also used to make working dies for two-cent pieces (see commentary under Proofs below).

All business strike 1871 cents seen in the Bowers and Merena photographic files are of the Wide Date style, although Richard Snow (1992, p. 100) reports that both Wide Date and Close Date examples exist among business strikes. The Close Date pieces must be extremely rare.

---

[1] Jim Reardon, Littleton Coin Co., letter, May 3, 1996. Littleton is probably America's largest-volume seller of circulated Indian cents.

DATE LOGOTYPES on 1871 Indian cents and two-cent pieces exist in two varieties for each denomination, each from the same four-digit logotype punch.

1871 Indian cent, Wide Date (notice separation of digits 7 and 1). This is the style usually seen on cents of this date. This identical four-digit punch was used to create dies for bronze two-cent pieces as well.

1871 Indian cent, Close Date. The 7 and 1 virtually touch. Only a few 1871 cents were made of this style. This identical four-digit punch was used to create dies for bronze two-cent pieces as well.

1871 bronze two-cent piece. Wide Date. From the same date punch used on the cent. Very scarce (just the opposite availability situation from the cent).

1871 bronze two-cent piece. Close Date. The variety usually seen.

Market Prices (1871 business strikes)

YEAR	G-4	VG-8	F-12	VF-20	EF-40	AU-50
1938	$0.50	$0.75	$1.00	$1.60	$1.80	2.75
1944	2.50	3.50	5.00	5.50	5.90	6.50
1965	21.00	30.00	50.00	70.00	90.00	120.00
1996	40.00	70.00	200.00	285.00	312.50	385.00

YEAR	MS-60BN	MS-60RB	MS-63BN	MS-63RB	MS-63RD	
1938	$4.25	4.30	$4.25	$4.50	$5.00	
1944	8.00	8.35	8.00	8.50	9.00	
1965	180.00	183.00	180.00	185.00	200.00	
1996	450.00	500.00	465.00	680.00	1,200.00	

YEAR	MS-64BN	MS-64RB	MS-64RD	MS-65BN	MS-65RB	MS-65RD
1938	$4.25	$4.50	$5.10	$4.25	$4.50	$5.20
1944	8.20	8.65	9.25	8.40	9.00	9.50
1965	182.50	187.50	207.50	185.00	192.50	215.00
1996	565.00	900.00	3,000.00	675.00	2,000.00	8,000.00

Proofs:

Proof distribution (estimated): 850 to 1,100.

Proof commentary: In especially strong demand due to the overall rarity (business strikes plus Proofs) of the date; thus, certification figures are skewed. Choice Proofs are elusive. Many have been cleaned. Many Proofs were carelessly made.

At least two obverse die styles for Proofs were made; one with 71 noticeably separated (Wide Date) and the other with 71 in date nearly touching (Close Date). These were made from two different four-digit logotype punches. These are listed as Snow-1 and Snow-2.

The usually-seen style is the Wide Date; this found on the vast majority of business strikes and most Proofs. Quite rare is the Close Date. A search of the Bowers and Merena photographic files indicates that Close Date Proofs form just a tiny minority, probably less than one in five or 10 Proofs examined. These same two four-digit logotype punches were also used on dies for bronze two-cent pieces; there the rarity is just the opposite: most 1871 two-cent pieces are of the Close Date style.[1]

---

[1] Many dozens of photographs of 1871 nickel three-cent pieces and Shield nickels were examined; all were from different and considerably smaller logotype punches.

Market Prices (1871 Proofs)

YEAR	PR-60BN	PR-60RB	PR-63BN	PR-63RB	PR-63RD
1938	$7.00	$7.10	$7.00	$7.20	$7.50
1944	13.00	13.25	13.00	13.50	14.00
1965	315.00	335.00	325.00	350.00	425.00
1996	325.00	350.00	335.00	350.00	500.00

YEAR	PR-64BN	PR-64RB	PR-64RD	PR-65BN	PR-65RB	PR-65RD
1938	$7.10	$7.30	$7.60	$7.20	$7.40	$7.70
1944	13.30	14.00	15.00	13.50	14.50	16.00
1965	350.00	365.00	412.50	365.00	395.00	500.00
1996	510.00	610.00	1,000.00	610.00	1,100.00	2,200.00

Notes

Collecting commentary: One of the classic scarcities in the series, in a class with the 1872 and slightly scarcer than it. Desired in all grades. Very scarce in Mint State.

Fooling around at the Mint: In this year the Mint restruck specimens of the 1864 with-L Proof bronze cent and certain other delicacies (see notes under 1864 L Proof cent its sub-chapter).

Early study: In *The Numismatist,* April 1910, a study by Charles E. McGirk, M.D., "Varieties of 1871 Indian Cents," was published. The writer reported that in examining 12 cents of this date, "I note that the top of the first 1 in date on two of the specimens is further away from the bust than on the other 10, and that in the two with the 'distant 1' the least measurement from the point of the bust to the margin is 3.5mm...." The article went on to describe a total of three varieties of the 1871 cent.

Numerals: Date numerals widely spaced and in pronounced arc. Last year with date numerals in arc until 1881 (see note).

Metal sources: Up to this year the primary Mint source for copper to refine for coinage into cents was from obsolete copper half cents and large cents redeemed by the Treasury. The copper in 100 lightly worn large cents was sufficient to make over 350 bronze Indian cents.[1]

Copper-nickel cents redeemed: In 1871 copper-nickel Flying Eagle and Indian cents began to be redeemed in very large quantities, although they were only lightly worn in most instances. In this year 8,569,848 were redeemed by the Treasury.

Greenbacks: The Act of March 3, 1871, provided that copper and other token coins (minor coins with no important intrinsic value) could be exchanged for federal greenback notes when presented in quantities of $20 or more. At the time there was a glut of minor coin, and the cent's legal tender limit of 4¢ per transaction (Act of March 3, 1864) made it impossible to use the coins in large transactions.

The redundancy of bronze cents at the time no doubt contributed to the reduced mintage figures for new cents in 1871 and 1872.

---

[1] For a detailed exposition see "President's Report" by Richard Snow, *Longacre's Ledger,* April 1992.

1872 Indian Cent

Business Strikes:

Business strike mintage: 4,042,000.

Number of business strike obverse dies made: Not known.

Average number of coins struck from typical obverse die: Not known.

Availability in Mint State: A key issue. More publicized than the 1871, but ever so slightly less rare. Attractive specimens are hard to find. Some Mint State coins of this era have yellowish orange fields with streaky brown flecks sprinkled over the surfaces, such flecks often being oriented in a particular direction; this is due to imperfectly mixed alloy and distention during the strip-rolling process.

Availability in circulated grades: Rare; a key date. Within the 1870s only the 1877 and 1871 are harder to find.

Characteristics of striking: Most are somewhat indifferently struck; hardly needle-sharp. Specialist Carl Herkowitz observes that about 10 coins out of 35 are notably weak.[1]

Market Prices (1872 business strikes)

YEAR	G-4	VG-8	F-12	VF-20	EF-40	AU-50
1938	$0.70	$0.85	$1.25	$1.75	$2.50	$3.50
1944	2.50	4.00	6.00	7.00	8.00	9.00
1965	24.00	37.50	60.00	85.00	115.00	180.00
1996	57.50	95.00	225.00	275.00	350.00	425.00

---

[1] Letter, February 17, 1996.

YEAR	MS-60BN	MS-60RB	MS-63BN	MS-63RB	MS-63RD	
1938	$5.25	$5.30	$5.25	$5.50	$6.00	
1944	12.10	12.30	12.10	12.50	13.00	
1965	260.00	265.00	260.00	270.00	295.00	
1996	525.00	600.00	550.00	700.00	1,200.00	

YEAR	MS-64BN	MS-64RB	MS-64RD	MS-65BN	MS-65RB	MS-65RD
1938	$5.35	$5.60	$6.10	$5.45	$5.75	$6.25
1944	12.20	12.70	13.25	12.25	12.80	13.50
1965	265.00	305.00	325.00	275.00	320.00	360.00
1996	775.00	1,300.00	3,500.00	1,000.00	3,000.00	11,000.00

Proofs:

Proof distribution (estimated): 850 to 1,100.

Proof commentary: Same market comment as for 1871 Proofs. Beginning with this year, a reverse die with a "blob" or bulge at the top right downward arm of the T in CENT was used to strike Proofs; this die was used for other Proof dates along with other (normal) reverse dies through 1878. This is a die flaw or accident and does not represent an intended change.

On all Proofs seen the date is centered, with the space between the top of the 1 and the neck being about the same as the space between the bottom of the 1 and the denticles.

I believe bright red Proofs are a bit easier to find (but are still rare) for this date than for 1870 or 1871, but opinions differ. Most 1872 Proofs I have seen are a nice blend of red and brown. In anyone's book, a gem Proof of this scarce date is a winner.

Market Prices (1872 Proofs)

YEAR	PR-60BN	PR-60RB	PR-63BN	PR-63RB	PR-63RD	
1938	$7.00	$7.25	$7.00	$7.40	$7.50	
1944	15.50	15.75	15.50	16.00	16.30	
1965	447.50	462.50	455.00	475.00	525.00	
1996	365.00	390.00	385.00	440.00	500.00	

YEAR	PR-64BN	PR-64RB	PR-64RD	PR-65BN	PR-65RB	PR-65RD
1938	$7.35	$7.45	$7.60	7.40	$7.50	$7.80
1944	15.70	15.85	16.50	15.80	16.00	17.00
1965	485.00	550.00	577.50	500.00	565.00	675.00
1996	500.00	625.00	1,250.00	900.00	1,100.00	3,750.00

Notes

Collecting commentary: A highly prized date in all grades. Richard Snow notes that "the scarcity of this date can be additionally attributed to excessive meltage," a situation with which I am not familiar (although the Mint was busy melting quantities of the old *large* cents at the time).

Date numerals: Date numerals are compact and in a straight line; this alignment would continue through and including 1880. The 1872 and 1873 years are in especially small numerals. (The 1872 nickel three-cent piece also has a small, compact date, but it is slightly curved.)

Die varieties: Most business strike 1872 cents have the date positioned very low, with the space between the bottom of the 1 in the date and the denticles being about 1/3 to 1/4th of that from the top of the 1 to the neck. However, a few business strikes have the date slightly higher, but not centered, and a few have the date centered (as on Proofs). The date positions of a Low Date business strike and a Centered Date Proof are dramatically different when the two are compared side by side. A doubled die obverse, discovered by Larry R. Steve, was reported in *Coin World,* April 12, 1993, p. 1.

At the time there were many bronze coins in circulation. Thus, the mintage of new Indian cents dwindled.

Broken-top "D" hub: Certain Indian cents of the 1872-1875 years have the top of the D in UNITED missing. This was caused by a defect in the working hub.[1]

Copper-nickel cents redeemed: In 1872 5,751,073 copper-nickel cents of the 1857-1864 era were redeemed by the Treasury.

Carl Herkowitz and his 1872 cents: In modern times no single collector has been more enamored of the scarce 1872 Indian cent than has Carl Herkowitz. Information concerning his holdings is given below, extracted and edited from the sources noted:

From *Penny Talk,* No. 13:[2] "[We] can now tell you that 'Mr. 1872' is Carl Herkowitz of Detroit, Michigan. His father bought him a nice 1872 Fine while out driving on his linen route one day in 1959. That piece was later stolen from his bedroom drawer along with the rest of his boyhood Lincolns and Indians. Twenty years later Carl began collecting 1872s exclusively without realizing why. The connection was finally made in 1984 while he was writing an article on the 1872 cent for the magazine *The Numismatist,* at which time Carl realized why he had inexplicably selected that date. His father, Fred, had handed him a legacy along with that first 1872, then $16 in Fine, that he brought home from work that day when he was but a kid. Carl has been challenged and occupied with the 'thrill of the hunt' for almost 17 years. His collection of 144 pieces grade from VG-10 to Gem Uncirculated. Half a roll in Mint State, 10 very rare full grade AU, 28 or so Extremely Fine, about 35 Very Fine, 40 coins in Fine, the rest are VG-10 and about Fine."

---

[1] Larry R. Steve. "THE F.IND.ERS REPORT." *Longacre's Ledger,* Winter 1995.

[2] Publication address: Box 443, Scarborough, Maine.

1873 Indian Cent

Closed 3

1873 Closed 3 (left) and Open 3. Note that the Open 3 is slightly more open and the right side of the 3 is slightly thicker. (Photo courtesy of Larry Steve.)

Two date varieties: Indian cents of 1873 were made with Closed 3 in the date (all Proofs plus some business strikes) and Open 3 in the date (no Proofs, some business strikes). At quick glance the 1873 Closed 3 date, made early in the year, resembled "1878," as the knobs on the 3 were close together. The Open 3 was created by filing away most of the bottom knob on the 3 of the date logotype and trimming the knob to a smaller size; dies punched with this modified date logotype are called Open 3.

Business Strikes, Closed 3:

Business strike mintage: 2,000,000 (author's estimate) out of a total of 11,676,500 total cents minted this year.

Number of business strike obverse dies made: 70 of all styles, probably mostly Open 3.

Average number of coins struck from typical obverse die: 166,807

Availability in Mint State: Rare. The elusive nature of Mint State 1873 Closed 3 cents is just beginning to be realized, and this in combination with an increased demand for the variety has pushed prices up sharply in 1995-1996. Original brilliant red specimens are very rare.

Availability in circulated grades: Scarce.

Characteristics of striking: Usually fairly strong.

Market Prices (1873 Closed 3 business strikes)

YEAR	G-4	VG-8	F-12	VF-20	EF-40	AU-50
1938	$0.10	$0.20	$0.35	$0.50	$0.75	$1.25
1944	.25	.60	1.00	1.25	1.60	2.00
1965	5.00	8.00	15.00	22.00	35.00	50.00
1996	14.00	20.00	40.00	62.00	125.00	280.00

YEAR	MS-60BN	MS-60RB	MS-63BN	MS-63RB	MS-63RD
1938	$2.00	$2.00	$2.00	$2.00	$2.00
1944	3.00	3.00	3.00	3.00	3.50
1965	80.00	85.00	85.00	85.00	90.00
1996	390.00	430.00	420.00	510.00	725.00

YEAR	MS-64BN	MS-64RB	MS-64RD	MS-65BN	MS-65RB	MS-65RD
1938	$2.00	$2.00	$2.00	$2.00	$2.00	$2.50
1944	3.00	3.00	3.50	3.00	3.00	3.50
1965	85.00	90.00	90.00	85.00	85.00	90.00
1996	600.00	910.00	2,500.00	800.00	2,500.00	10,000.00

1873 DOUBLED "LIBERTY": 1873 Closed 3, Doubled LIBERTY in headband. Snow-1. The entire word is dramatically doubled, as shown. Discovered in the 1950s, this variety has become one of the most prized issues in the Indian cent series.

Doubled LIBERTY variety: Two varieties:

Type I; Snow-1: This occurs in the sharp "Type I" format with all letters of LIB-ERTY doubled; the most desirable variety. In autumn 1995, Jerry Wysong stated that 102 had been reported to him.[1] This figure included 11 Mint State specimens topped by a single MS-65. No specimen is known with more than 50% original mint red.[2]

Richard Snow calls this "The King of Indian Head Cents." It is listed as No. 1 among the top 20 most popular of all unusual Indian cent varieties, by Larry R. Steve and Kevin J. Flynn in *Flying Eagle and Indian Cent Die Varieties.* Fivaz-Stanton 1¢-009. FND-001. This variety was first published in the October 1958 issue of *Empire Topics* (published by Q. David Bowers and James F. Ruddy trading as Empire Coin Co.) in an article, "Blundered Dies of U.S. and Colonial Coinage," by Walter Breen. At that time just one specimen was known.

In the Market Prices column the 1996 listings for the 1873 Doubled LIBERTY cent represent *Guide Book* and other values. For 1965 the figures are rough estimates as the variety was not well known at the time, few had been discovered, and interest was not high.

Type II; Snow-2: In addition, the so-called "Type II" has the first several letters of LIBERTY slightly doubled; this is scarcer than the preceding but is in lesser demand as the doubling is not as noticeable. Fivaz-Stanton 1¢-009.1, there called "somewhat of a step-sister to Fivaz-Stanton 1¢-009 which exhibits stronger doubling." Jerry Wysong reported the knowledge of 42 pieces in 1995, including 18 Mint State coins, the highest grade of which were two MS-65 coins. Fivaz-Stanton-009.1. FND-002.

As the average number of cents struck from the typical 1873 obverse die was 164,458, this may give a ballpark estimate of the mintage of each of the two Doubled LIBERTY varieties.

Market Prices for Snow-2 are in all instances considerably lower than those given for Snow-1 below.

Market Prices (1873 Closed 3, Doubled LIBERTY, Snow-1)

YEAR	F-12	VF-20	EF-40	AU-50	MS-60BN	MS-63RB
1965	$120.00	$140.00	$225.00	$300.00	$450.00	$650.00
1996	500.00	800.00	2,000	2,950	4,750	12,000.00

1873 S-1 Doubled LIBERTY-iana: Sam Lukes commented as follows:[3]

The late Elliot Goldman[4] owned the 1873 Doubled LIBERTY S-1 which is pictured on the cover of Richard Snow's *Flying Eagle & Indian Head Cents* book. At the time, the coin was housed in a PCGS MS-64 RB holder. Elliot later submitted the coin to NGC, and it was graded MS-65RB, but NGC failed to attribute the variety on the holder, so Elliot sent it back so it would properly be attributed. The coin, unfortunately, never reached NGC as somewhere along the line it ended up being lost or stolen and has not surfaced since.

---

[1] "How Many Are There, Anyway?" Article in *Longacre's Ledger,* Fall 1995.
[2] Richard Snow, letter, April 10, 1996; he further noted that the Mint State coin pictured in color on the cover of his *Flying Eagle & Indian Cents* book belonged to Elliot Goldman, but was later stolen and today is not accounted for.
[3] Letter, April 8, 1996.
[4] Specialist in high quality late nineteenth- and early twentieth-century coins, who passed away unexpectedly in December 1995.

In March of 1995, a client of mine consigned to me another 1873 Doubled LIB-ERTY S-1 which was also graded MS-64RB in a PCGS holder which was superior to Elliot's missing coin. I felt this piece had a great shot at also achieving MS-65RB status, but a dealer friend of mine, David Davidson, informed me that he had a client who was interested in buying the coin, so I sent the coin to him. David eventually sold the coin for a record $19,500, and the new owner promptly submitted the coin to NGC wherein it was upgraded to MS-65RB status.

The coin has since been crossed over to PCGS, retaining the same grade, and is now being offered [on the market] for $50,000. Hence, there are *two* MS-65RB examples of this rarity although one is still missing as mentioned above.

Concerning the history of the lone *NGC* MS-63RB example you have listed of the 1873 Doubled LIBERTY, Dave, keep reading.

I first successfully bid on the coin when it appeared as Lot #1428 in your Ezra Cole Collection auction back in January of 1986. It was described as "MS-60 to MS-63," and I nailed it down for $750, plus the 10% buyer's charge which brought the final figure to $825! I then kept the coin off of the market for several years and then submitted it to NGC where I thought it could grade MS-63RB. Instead, NGC attributed it as MS-62 BN, and although I was disappointed, I tossed it into the vault at the bank, where it reposed until June of 1994 when I sold it to a client of mine for $5,950, assuring him the coin was really a RB and could have graded MS-63.

Nearly a year later, my client phoned to tell me that he had decided to 'crack' the coin out of its NGC holder and submit it to ANACS, which he had already done. Much to his chagrin, ANACS had graded it as an AU-58! I then asked my client (whose original investment had now theoretically dropped from nearly $6,000 to about half that amount) to send his coin back to me so I could send it back to NGC who had graded it originally as MS-62 BN. I submitted the coin right about the same time that David Davidson had set a world record price for his sale, so the "Trends" pricing in *Coin World* leaped to $9,500 for an MS-63RB grade. Much to our delight, my client's coin came back graded exactly what I had submitted it at.... MS-63RB! My client's investment had increased in value nearly 2/3 over what it would have been worth as an AU-58. He immediately sold the coin for $9,500, and it was resold by me to another customer for $10,250!

Richard Snow commented on April 10, 1995: "The single MS-65 specimen is owned by Eagle Eye Rare Coins."

Proofs, Closed 3:

Proof distribution (estimated): 1,500 to 2,000.

Proof commentary: All Proofs minted were of the Closed 3 style. Dies for Proofs were made early in the year when the Closed 3 was the norm; no later dies were produced. Proofs are seen with some frequency today but are still fairly elusive. Bright red gems are especially hard to find.

At least two Proof obverse dies were used, one having the word LIBERTY very faintly doubled—not at all to the degree of the aforementioned 1873 Doubled Die business strikes, but still discernible.[1]

Some Proofs have a high relief "blob" at the right arm of the T in CENT; this die had been in use since 1872 (see note under 1872 Proofs).

---

[1] Larry R. Steve, letter, April 12, 1996.

Market Prices (1873 Closed 3 Proofs)

YEAR	PR-60BN	PR-60RB	PR-63BN	PR-63RB	PR-63RD	
1938	$2.25	$2.35	$2.25	$2.40	$2.50	
1944	4.25	4.40	4.25	4.75	5.00	
1965	225.00	235.00	240.00	250.00	300.00	
1996	120.00	150.00	145.00	230.00	240.00	

YEAR	PR-64BN	PR-64RB	PR-64RD	PR-65BN	PR-65RB	PR-65RD
1938	$2.25	$2.40	$2.50	$2.25	$2.40	$2.50
1944	4.50	4.90	5.20	4.60	5.00	5.50
1965	245.00	265.00	320.00	270.00	300.00	350.00
1996	225.00	380.00	850.00	530.00	650.00	2,800.00

Notes

Collecting commentary: The 1873 Closed 3 cent is much the scarcer of the two date varieties of this year, quite possibly three or four times scarcer than the Open 3 issue. However, many numismatists desire just one specimen of the date and do not collect by varieties; thus, the price differential is not as great as it might otherwise be. Notwithstanding this, the awareness of the Closed and Open 3 varieties in the collecting community has grown by leaps and bounds in recent years, thus widening the price differential. Much of this new demand is due to the dissemination of information in the Snow and Steve-Flynn books plus *Longacre's Ledger*. Years ago, although Harry X Boosel had written extensively about the Closed 3 and Open 3 varieties of this year, the reaction of most collectors was simply an unstifled yawn. Virtually no one had the two date varieties on his or her want list of Indian cents, nor did albums for the series include them. My, how things have changed.

A problem with the date numerals: On January 18, 1873, A. Loudon Snowden, chief coiner at the Philadelphia Mint, wrote to James Pollock, director of the Mint, to state in part:[1]

> I desire in a formal manner to direct your attention to the "figures" used in dating the dies for the present year.

> They are so heavy, and the space between each so very small that upon the smaller gold and silver, and upon the base coins it is almost impossible to distinguish with the naked eye, whether the last figure is an eight or a three....

Snowden recommended that new "sets of figures" be made at an early date. Presumably, there were many dies already on hand with what later became known as the "Closed 3," and these were not destroyed, but were used later in the due course of business, to be replaced at a still later date with the new "Open 3" dies.

On both varieties of the 1873 cent the date numerals are compact and in a straight line; this alignment would continue through and including 1880. The 1872 and 1873 years are in especially small numerals.

---

[1] A copy of this letter is reproduced in *Flying Eagle and Indian Cent Varieties,* by Larry R. Steve and Kevin J. Flynn, pp. 55, 56.

Copper-nickel cents redeemed: In 1873 2,641,157 copper-nickel cents of the 1857-1864 era were redeemed by the Treasury.

Mint titles: Beginning in 1873, the person in charge of the Philadelphia Mint was called the superintendent, and the title of director applied to another person whose office was at the Treasury Department in Washington, D.C., although later directors sometimes spent much time in Philadelphia.

The return of Dr. Linderman: Henry R. Linderman, M.D., who had served as director of the Mint 1867-1869, returned to the post in April 1873 and remained until December 1878. Linderman made or caused to be made many special coins for his private collection and acquired personal ownership of certain Mint dies; certain of these items were later replevined by the government when his numismatic estate was catalogued for auction.

Dealer Proskey: David U. Proskey, born in 1853, entered the rare coin trade in 1873, remaining until 1928.[1] For many years he edited *The Coin Collector's Journal,* which stands today as one of the more readable numismatic publications of the late nineteenth century. In 1888 he joined Harlan P. Smith to form the New York Coin Company, whose brightest day in the sun was undoubtedly the handling at auction of the Lorin G. Parmelee Collection in 1890. Proskey was a person of great numismatic knowledge, but as was later the case with certain other geniuses in the field (Virgil M. Brand and F.C.C. Boyd come to mind), most of what he knew never reached print except in the aforementioned *Journal* and a few auction catalogues. In the 1880s and 1890s he bought many unsold Proof coins including Indian cents from the Mint, and in later years he continued to buy wholesale groups as well. Unfortunately, the specifics of his acquisitions were never recorded.

Richard Snow commented[2] that during the course of an interview with John J. Ford, Jr., successor to many numismatic interests of Wayte Raymond (who was Ford's mentor), Ford related that Raymond stored his stock at his summer home at Montauk, on the ocean at the eastern tip of Long Island. In that moist salt air location many copper coins deteriorated.

---

[1] John W. Adams, *United States Numismatic Literature,* Vol. I, p. 55.
[2] Letter, April 10, 1996.

1873 Indian Cent

Open 3

1873 Closed 3 (left) and Open 3. Note that the Open 3 is slightly more open and the right side of the 3 is slightly thicker. (Photo courtesy of Larry Steve.)

Two date varieties: Indian cents of 1873 were made with Closed 3 in the date (all Proofs plus some business strikes) and Open 3 in the date (no Proofs, some business strikes. At quick glance the 1873 Closed 3 date, made early in the year, resembled "1878," as the knobs on the 3 were close together. The Open 3 was created by filing away most of the bottom knob on the 3 of the date logotype and trimming the knob to a smaller size; dies punched with this modified date logotype are called Open 3.

Business Strikes, Open 3:

Business strike mintage: 9,676,500 (author's estimate[1]) out of a total of 11,676,500 total cents minted this year.

Number of business strike obverse dies made: 70 of all styles, probably mostly Open 3.

Average number of coins struck from typical obverse die: 166,807

---

[1] No precision intended—this figure is the result of deducting an estimated two million pieces (for the Closed 3 variety) from the overall figure to yield an equally imprecise estimate for the Open 3.

Availability in Mint State: Scarce. Bright red specimens are especially so. Brian Wagner commented that in MS-65 RD the 1873 Open 3 is about as rare as the 1867.[1]

Availability in circulated grades: Scarce, but not nearly as scarce as the Closed 3 variety.

Characteristics of striking: Varies; strong pieces can be found.

Market Prices (1873 Open 3 business strikes)

YEAR	G-4	VG-8	F-12	VF-20	EF-40	AU-50
1938	$0.10	$0.20	$0.35	$0.50	$0.75	$1.25
1944	.25	.60	1.00	1.25	1.60	2.00
1965	5.00	8.00	15.00	22.00	35.00	50.00
1996	12.00	16.00	30.00	40.00	97.50	120.00

YEAR	MS-60BN	MS-60RB	MS-63BN	MS-63RB	MS-63RD	
1938	$2.00	$2.00	$2.00	$2.00	$2.00	
1944	3.00	3.00	3.00	3.00	3.50	
1965	80.00	85.00	85.00	85.00	90.00	
1996	190.00	170.00	200.00	245.00	475.00	

YEAR	MS-64BN	MS-64RB	MS-64RD	MS-65BN	MS-65RB	MS-65RD
1938	$2.00	$2.00	$2.00	$2.00	$2.00	$2.50
1944	3.00	3.00	3.50	3.00	3.00	3.50
1965	85.00	90.00	90.00	85.00	85.00	90.00
1996	225.00	380.00	1,400.00	320.00	700.00	7,000.00

Notes

Collecting commentary: This is the usually seen business strike variety. Somewhat scarce in all grades. Beginning with this year, brilliant specimens are seen with more frequency than for any other dates since 1865.

Alignment of date numerals: On both varieties of 1873 cents the date numerals are compact and in a straight line; this alignment would continue through and including 1880.

[1] Letter, May 3, 1996.

1874 Indian Cent

Business Strikes:

Business strike mintage: 14,187,500.

Number of business strike obverse dies made: 66 + 1 Proof die also used to make some business strikes.

Average number of coins struck from typical obverse die: 214,962 (not including business strikes from the aforementioned Proof die).

Availability in Mint State: Fairly scarce. Quite elusive in bright red, especially in comparison to cents of a few years earlier.

Availability in circulated grades: Scarce.

Characteristics of striking: Usually sharp.

Market Prices (1874 business strikes)

YEAR	G-4	VG-8	F-12	VF-20	EF-40	AU-50
1938	$0.10	$0.20	$0.35	$0.50	$0.75	$1.25
1944	.25	.60	1.00	1.25	1.60	2.00
1965	5.00	8.00	15.00	22.00	35.00	50.00
1996	12.00	16.00	30.00	40.00	85.00	120.00

YEAR	MS-60BN	MS-60RB	MS-63BN	MS-63RB	MS-63RD	
1938	$2.00	$2.00	$2.00	$2.00	$2.00	
1944	3.00	3.00	3.00	3.00	3.50	
1965	80.00	85.00	85.00	85.00	90.00	
1996	150.00	170.00	175.00	245.00	350.00	

YEAR	MS-64BN	MS-64RB	MS-64RD	MS-65BN	MS-65RB	MS-65RD
1938	$2.00	$2.00	$2.00	$2.00	$2.00	$2.50
1944	3.00	3.00	3.50	3.00	3.00	3.50
1965	85.00	90.00	90.00	85.00	85.00	90.00
1996	200.00	305.00	900.00	300.00	500.00	2,800.00

Proofs:

Proof distribution (estimated): 1,000 to 1,200.

Proof commentary: Coined from an obverse die having the 4 in the date first punched slightly too low and then corrected. No "perfect date" Proof 1874 has come to light.[1] Bright red gems are quite scarce, in my opinion. I have had very few over the years.

The repunched date Proof 1874 obverse die is also believed to have been used to make some business strikes.[2]

Some Proofs have a high relief "blob" as the right arm of the T in CENT; this die had been in use since 1872 (see note under 1872 Proofs).

Market Prices (1874 Proofs)

YEAR	PR-60BN	PR-60RB	PR-63BN	PR-63RB	PR-63RD	
1938	$2.25	$2.35	$2.25	$2.40	$2.50	
1944	5.20	5.25	5.20	5.35	6.00	
1965	200.00	220.00	215.00	225.00	250.00	
1996	115.00	140.00	135.00	235.00	250.00	

YEAR	PR-64BN	PR-64RB	PR-64RD	PR-65BN	PR-65RB	PR-65RD
1938	$2.25	$2.40	$2.50	$2.25	$2.40	$2.50
1944	5.00	5.50	6.25	5.25	5.75	6.50
1965	230.00	250.00	285.00	240.00	265.00	325.00
1996	210.00	360.00	850.00	425.00	700.00	2,500.00

Notes

Collecting commentary: Somewhat scarce as are other dates in the mid-1870s (1873-1876), but not in the league with the 1871, 1872, or 1877.

Date numeral size: Date numerals larger than in 1872-1873 and in straight line; this alignment would continue through and including 1880.

Copper-nickel cents redeemed: In 1874 3,015,870 copper-nickel cents of the 1857-1864 era were redeemed by the Treasury.

---

[1] Richard Snow, letter, May 3, 1996, noted: "I believe all Proofs have defective dates. I have never seen a perfect date Proof 1874. The 'normal die' listing was an error in my 1992 book."
[2] Larry R. Steve, letter, April 12, 1996. The Proofs are the Snow-1 variety; the business strikes S-2.

1875 Indian Cent

Business Strikes:

Business strike mintage: 13,528,000.

Number of business strike obverse dies made: 65 + 1 Proof die used to make some business strikes.

Average number of coins struck from typical obverse die: 208,123 (does not include the aforementioned Proof die).

Availability in Mint State: Slightly scarcer in all combined Mint State grades than the preceding, but, in my experience, brilliant pieces are slightly easier to find than for the 1874 (opinions differ on this).

Availability in circulated grades: Somewhat scarce.

Characteristics of striking: Usually sharp, but varies.

Market Prices (1875 business strikes)

YEAR	G-4	VG-8	F-12	VF-20	EF-40	AU-50
1938	$0.10	$0.20	$0.35	$0.50	$0.75	$1.25
1944	.25	.60	1.00	1.25	1.60	2.00
1965	5.00	8.00	15.00	22.00	35.00	50.00
1996	12.00	16.00	30.00	40.00	67.00	120.00

YEAR	MS-60BN	MS-60RB	MS-63BN	MS-63RB	MS-63RD
1938	$2.00	$2.00	$2.00	$2.00	$2.00
1944	3.00	3.00	3.00	3.00	3.50
1965	80.00	85.00	85.00	85.00	90.00
1996	200.00	240.00	215.00	275.00	365.00

YEAR	MS-64BN	MS-64RB	MS-64RD	MS-65BN	MS-65RB	MS-65RD
1938	$2.00	$2.00	$2.00	$2.00	$2.00	$2.50
1944	3.00	3.00	3.50	3.00	3.00	3.50
1965	85.00	90.00	90.00	85.00	85.00	90.00
1996	215.00	335.00	960.00	350.00	600.00	2,750.00

Proofs:

Proof distribution (estimated): 1,000 to 1,250.

Proof commentary: Coined from at least three, possibly four, obverse dies, one (Snow-2) having traces of a previous 5 slightly above the 5 in the date, another (Snow-1) with minor evidence of doubling on 1 and 8. In bright red gem preservation this is a very scarce date.

The Proof die for Snow-1, described above, was also used to make some business strikes.[1]

Some Proofs have a high relief "blob" as the right arm of the T in CENT; this die had been in use since 1872 (see note under 1872 Proofs).

Proofs of this year were poorly made; the Mint was derelict in its duties to numismatists. Today, *choice* full-red Proofs are very hard to find.[2]

Market Prices (1875 Proofs)

YEAR	PR-60BN	PR-60RB	PR-63BN	PR-63RB	PR-63RD	
1938	$2.25	$2.35	$2.25	$2.40	$2.50	
1944	5.20	5.25	5.20	5.35	6.00	
1965	200.00	220.00	215.00	225.00	250.00	
1996	120.00	162.50	145.00	295.00	320.00	

YEAR	PR-64BN	PR-64RB	PR-64RD	PR-65BN	PR-65RB	PR-65RD
1938	$2.25	$2.40	$2.50	$2.25	$2.40	$2.50
1944	5.00	5.50	6.25	5.25	5.75	6.50
1965	230.00	250.00	285.00	240.00	265.00	325.00
1996	220.00	450.00	2,100.00	500.00	1,550.00	7,500.00

Notes

Collecting commentary: Popular as a date in the 1870s, but not in the rarity category of 1871, 1872, 1877, or even the 1876.

Date numerals: Date numerals larger than in 1872-1873 and in a straight line; this alignment would continue through and including 1880.

Copper-nickel cents redeemed: In 1875 2,204,701 copper-nickel cents of the 1857-1864 era were redeemed by the Treasury.

---

[1] Larry R. Steve, letter, April 12, 1996.
[2] Richard Snow, letter, April 10, 1996; additional comments May 3, 1996.

Mystery cents of 1875: Where are they?: The following narrative is edited and condensed from "The Case of the Disappearing Cent," in the *Numismatic Scrapbook Magazine,* May 1972, by R.W. Julian:

In the summer of 1875 an aged employee of the Philadelphia Mint was suspected of helping himself to some of the products manufactured there. He confined his activities to that lowly coin, the cent, but the matter was serious and could not be ignored.

His fellow workers informed the foreman of their suspicions and he in turn repeated the information to the coiner. Instead of proceeding further, let us have the coiner tell the story in his own words:

Mint of the United States
Coiner's Department
Philadelphia
August 24, 1875
The Honorable James Pollock, Sup't.
Sir:

Having reported to you my suspicions as to the honesty of X [the name is left out because, as will be seen below, the man was not really a hardened criminal] employed in the coining room of this department and having received from you before your departure into the country authority to suspend him in case my suspicions were confirmed or strengthened, I have the honor to submit the following facts in relation to the further development of the case.

On the morning after our conference I was satisfied from the evidence presented to me that X had taken some of the one cent coins and had them on his person. But being anxious to fix his guilt clearly beyond any cavil or doubt, I instructed him not to use more than one coining press so that X's actions could be the more closely watched and that he should report to me any suspicious actions on X's part. About 11 a.m. Mr. Downing[1] reported that X had been acting in a suspicious manner and that in his judgment he had some of the marked coin on his person. In your absence I sent for Mr. Hickox, acting superintendent, and informed him of all the facts, and requested him to remain with me whilst I sent for and examined Mr. X, which he did.

I sent for X, and after closing the door to prevent our being disturbed I told him that some of the employees suspected him of taking coin out of the coining room. He was little agitated, but laughingly told me that it was a great mistake. I then asked him whether he had any coin on his person and he said he had some, which had been given him by his son. I told him that any coin given him by his son could be designated as the coin of today had been struck upon a marked die.

At this he immediately became very distressed and wanted a private interview. I went with him into the vault connected with my room and he in there confessed that he had recently taken a few cents and begged me to overlook the offense. I told him how much distressed I was to see an old man of his long connection with the Mint detected at such an offense. I sincerely sympathized with his family and himself, but I could not overlook an offense which was known to several of the employees as well as to you, the superintendent.

---

[1] A.W. Downing, foreman of the Coining Room, had been with the Mint since August 1864.

I then took him back to the presence of Mr. Hickox, where he again confessed his fault. I then exhibited to Mr. Hickox two (2) pieces from the marked dies given to me by Mr. Downing and asked X to take out of his pocket the coin he had pilfered. After some trouble he was made to empty his pockets and we found upon him thirty-three (33) cents marked in a similar manner to the ones previously in my possession. These pieces were sealed up in our own presence together with the proper endorsement. Mr. Downing was requested to put up another lot from the same press in an envelope and seal the same which he did. These packages are now in my vault and subject to your examination. I immediately suspended him.

Mr. X tendered his resignation for such action as you may see fit. Mr. X has been connected with this institution almost continuously for over 50 years. He is now a very old man, being upwards of 76 years of age. Of late he has manifested in many ways the weakness of his mind and I think it charitable to say that his grave fault can be attributed to mental decay and weakness more than any other cause.

The feeblemindedness has manifested itself in a marked manner since his recent detection and peculations. At one moment he appears in the very depths of despair and humiliation demeaning himself for the crime. With the very next he speaks of himself as the poor victim of uncharitable people.

I felt it in my duty to present the whole facts for such action as you may deem proper. I will add that from present appearances I do not think X will long survive this terrible blow. His mental suffering I will not attempt to describe. One cannot witness it unmoved.

I am, very respectfully
(signed) A. Loudon Snowden,
Coiner.

The author [R.W. Julian] does not know in what manner the reverse die was marked, but we may assume that it was meant to be reasonably inconspicuous. The most probable action for Downing to have taken was to use a punch and make a tiny hole in the die somewhere around the wreath. If this were done, a small raised dot would appear on the marked cents. It is also perfectly possible that he made some kind of scratch on the die, say between two of the letters in the value. Any numismatist can think of numerous ways that he could have performed this task.

From 1874 through 1876 we find the following numbers of cent dies used at the Mint:

1874: 67 obverse dies (destroyed in January 1875); 93 rev. dies (destroyed in January 1875); 25 rev. dies held over.

1875: 68 obverse dies(destroyed in January 1876); 99 rev. dies (destroyed in January 1876); 9 rev. dies held over.

1876: 39 obverse dies (destroyed in January 1877); 53 rev. dies (destroyed in January 1877); 4 rev. dies held over.

According to this table it would appear that 99 reverse dies of 1875 were destroyed in early 1876. Another nine reverses, still fit for further coinage, were held for 1876.

According to this table and considering the mintage of 13,528,000 business strike cents during the calendar year 1875 and assuming that the 99 reverse dies destroyed represented those used during the year, it would appear that on average approximately 137,000 coins were struck from each die. The uncertainty arises because it is not certain just how much the 25 reverse dies held over from 1874 had already been used, if at all. Nor do we know at present anything about the wear on the nine dies reserved for use in 1876. Further, it could be that some 1876-dated obverses were made, but not used for coinage. Appendix I discusses the matter further.

According to the letter, Downing made a mark on the reverse die to be used on Monday, the 23rd of August. From this we may assume that it was done on Saturday after coining had stopped for the day. Since the die would need to be used for several hours on Monday, it would seem likely that Downing marked a new die. In this way the die would not only last the required number of hours but no suspicion would be aroused by the changing.

Assuming that the cent press began coining at seven o'clock on Monday (it probably began earlier) it would have continued in operation at least four hours before X was apprehended. More than this, it would have continued in operation even while the conference was going on in the coiner's office. From this it is reasonable to say that the marked reverse die was used at least six hours. We are also entitled to think that it was used the rest of the day.

Even if we assume only a six-hour use, there would have been struck in this time over 30,000 cents. If the die was allowed to continue for its full run, then around 137,000 would have been coined altogether. Given the well-known economy of the Mint at all times in its history, it is easy enough to believe that the marked cents were released into circulation in the normal course of Mint business. The Mint was known to have released coins with die breaks, so there would have been little reason to withhold these marked coins. Nor would there have been any reason to remove the distinctive reverse die from service before its useful life ended, for the suspected press operator had already confessed.

Now that collectors are aware of this special 1875 cent, perhaps it can be identified. If so, one can readily envision that a new rarity in the Indian cent series will take its place. It seems that the chances are about 1 in 99 that a given specimen of an 1875 business strike is from the distinctive die. Who will be the lucky finder of the first one? (This concludes R.W. Julian's commentary)

In a column in *CoinWorld* in spring 1996 I synopsized the above and invited readers to examine their 1875 cents for an interesting raised mark on the reverse. This elicited nearly a dozen responses, the most significant of which was from Fred A. Cihon, who submitted a Fine-grade 1875 with an irregular raised prominence in the field to the right of the E in ONE, about two-thirds of the way to the level of the top of the letter; this prominence in the field is about 40% of the distance from the right side of the E to the nearby wreath. If higher grade specimens can be found and examined, perhaps confirmation can be made that this is the long-forgotten "clue."

1876 Indian Cent

Business Strikes:

Business strike mintage: 7,944,000.

Number of business strike obverse dies made: 37

Average number of coins struck from typical obverse die: 214,703

Availability in Mint State: Scarce, especially if fully brilliant and red (original, undipped). In the late 1970s a roll of 50 gem Mint State coins owned by Allen Harriman was dispersed in the market.[1]

Availability in circulated grades: Scarcest date since 1872.

Characteristics of striking: Sometimes lightly struck at the lower part of the portrait.

Market Prices (1876 business strikes)

YEAR	G-4	VG-8	F-12	VF-20	EF-40	AU-50
1938	$0.20	$0.30	$0.50	$0.75	$1.00	$1.50
1944	.50	.80	1.25	1.60	1.85	2.50
1965	7.50	12.00	20.00	30.00	42.50	57.50
1996	20.00	27.50	37.50	55.00	105.00	135.00

YEAR	MS-60BN	MS-60RB	MS-63BN	MS-63RB	MS-63RD
1938	$2.55	$2.65	$2.60	$2.75	$3.00
1944	3.75	3.85	3.75	3.85	4.00
1965	95.00	105.00	100.00	110.00	125.00
1996	210.00	250.00	230.00	325.00	400.00

---

[1] Reported by John Dannreuther, letter, May 16, 1996; a similar roll of 1878 cents was dispersed at the same time.

YEAR	MS-64BN	MS-64RB	MS-64RD	MS-65BN	MS-65RB	MS-65RD
1938	$2.60	$2.75	$3.00	$2.60	$2.75	$3.00
1944	3.85	3.90	4.30	4.00	4.25	4.50
1965	110.00	115.00	135.00	120.00	125.00	142.50
1996	300.00	400.00	1,000.00	400.00	700.00	3,500.00

Proofs:

Proof distribution (estimated): 1,500 to 2,000.

Proof commentary: More Proofs than usual seem to have been minted this year. Perhaps the holding of the Centennial Exhibition in Philadelphia that year increased demand with visitors to the Mint. Bright red Proofs are occasionally seen, much more often than are those of 1874 and 1875.

Walter Breen noted that one variety with a large knob to the top of the 6 in the date had been reported to him; this from a dime date logotype.[1]

Some Proofs have a high relief "blob" as the right arm of the T in CENT; this die had been in use since 1872 (see note under 1872 Proofs).

Market Prices (1876 Proofs)

YEAR	PR-60BN	PR-60RB	PR-63BN	PR-63RB	PR-63RD	
1938	$3.25	$3.30	$3.25	$3.40	$3.50	
1944	5.20	5.25	5.20	5.35	6.00	
1965	150.00	157.50	155.00	160.00	180.00	
1996	127.50	195.00	190.00	240.00	265.00	

YEAR	PR-64BN	PR-64RB	PR-64RD	$3.30	PR-65RB	PR-65RD
1938	$3.30	$3.50	$3.75	$3.30	$3.50	$4.00
1944	5.00	5.50	6.25	5.25	5.75	6.50
1965	165.00	175.00	200.00	170.00	200.00	225.00
1996	290.00	400.00	1,000.00	500.00	625.00	2,750.00

Notes

Collecting commentary: Fairly scarce in all grades.

Silver coin news: Silver coins were plentiful in circulation, the result of the resumption of payments (beginning unofficially in 1873 and sanctioned by Congress in 1875) of long-stored quantities of these coins by the Treasury and the production of new pieces—dimes, quarters, and half dollars—in large quantities. By the end of 1876, this flood of silver lessened the demand for new Indian cents, with an impact on the coinage for the next year, 1877.

---

[1] *Encyclopedia,* p. 223.

Date numerals: Date numerals in a straight line; this alignment would continue through and including 1880. Date usually boldly punched into die.

Copper-nickel cents redeemed: In 1876 3,106,895 copper-nickel cents of the 1857-1864 era were redeemed by the Treasury and melted.[1]

Fractional Currency ceases: 1876, February 23: This day marked the end of the issuance of Fractional Currency paper notes which to this point had been produced to the extent of $368,720,000 face value.

---

[1] *Mint Report;* also *American Journal of Numismatics,* July 1876, p. 12 (latter citation suggested by Michael Hodder, letter, May 14, 1996).

1877 Indian Cent

Business Strikes:

Business strike mintage: 852,500.

Number of business strike obverse dies made: Uncertain, possibly 3.

Average number of coins struck from typical obverse die: 284,167 based upon 3 obverse dies.

Die characteristics: It may be the case that certain 1877 business strikes were made from a die or dies used earlier to make Proofs. At least three obverse varieties of business strikes have been identified, these three having the date somewhat shallowly impressed and the second 7 appearing slightly larger than the first.

Two obverse dies with obvious differences are described below:

1. Dentil below 1 in date, if extended, would reach the lower center-right part of the upright in 1. Space between dentil to left of 1, if extended, would touch tip of left bottom serif of 1. Base of 1 (left and right serifs) much thinner than the following.

2. Dentil below 1 in date, if extended, would reach the center of the upright in 1. Space between dentil to left of 1, if extended, would graze the left of left bottom serif of 1. Base of 1 (left and right serifs) much thicker than the preceding. Date logotype slightly more deeply impressed into the die than on the preceding, thus making the numerals appear to be slightly closer together and accounting for the thickness of the bottom of the 1.

Relevant to the above, Richard Snow has identified two obverse dies and one reverse die used for business strike coinage. "The reverse die clashed early and usually shows a clash mark. This reverse has the shallow bottom to the N in ONE and is the last usage of that hub style."[1]

Larry R. Steve reports the observation of three different business strike obverse dies, "best described as 'thin' (or normal) date, 'medium,' and 'fat'—each with slight differences."[2]

---

[1] Richard Snow, letter, April 10, 1996.
[2] Letter, April 16, 1996.

While it is not my intent to devote the present book to microscopic die differences among business strike issues of various dates, the 1877 is a special situation as no one is sure how many pieces were made or if the *Mint Report* is correct. To the extent that average die use can help resolve the situation, it is useful to know how many obverse dies were employed.

Availability in Mint State: Mint State coins are the rarest of all Indian cent dates. When seen they usually are full or part brown. Original full mint red, uncleaned and undipped coins are great rarities. Certification doesn't help; cherrypicking is a must.

Availability in circulated grades: Rarest of the Philadelphia Mint Indian cents. This is the key to a set of the series.

Cast and struck counterfeits exist as do altered coins; buy only if accompanied by a guarantee.

Characteristics of striking: Most are somewhat lightly struck. Markers for genuine coins:[1] The second 7 in the date is *slightly* larger than the first, this being most noticeable at the bottoms of the 7's. The lower portion of the N in ONE and, to a lesser extent, the tops of EN in CENT on the reverse is weak (shallow). Thomas K. DeLorey advises that these characteristics describe 99% of known business strikes, "but a few business strike coins are known from a non-Proof reverse die with strong central letter details."[2]

In 1996 I saw a high-grade business strike 1877 with OF AMERICA virtually flatly struck, while the other features of the coin were quite sharp. I mention this to remind readers that one price does not fit all coins, and that an impaired piece such as this is worth considerably less than an average or above average strike.

Unexplained rarity: Specimens of the 1877 business strike cent have been especially elusive over the years, possibly even more so than the low mintage would explain, although opinions are mixed. Were some pieces melted and not released? Were Mint figures inaccurate? Did some large group of specimens meet an unknown fate? This is an interesting point to ponder. Or, are 1877 Indian cents rare today simply because relatively few were minted, and they became diluted among vastly larger issues of other dates? Also see Notes below.

Market Prices (1877 business strikes)

YEAR	G-4	VG-8	F-12	VF-20	EF-40	AU-50
1938	$1.00	$1.35	$2.00	$3.00	$4.00	$5.00
1944	5.50	7.50	10.00	12.00	13.50	15.00
1965	100.00	145.00	220.00	350.00	480.00	700.00
1996	370.00	435.00	600.00	750.00	1,250.00	1,750.00

YEAR	MS-60BN	MS-60RB	MS-63BN	MS-63RB	MS-63RD
1938	$7.00	$7.00	$7.00	$7.25	$7.50
1944	19.00	20.00	19.00	20.00	23.00
1965	900.00	925.00	900.00	950.00	1,050.00
1996	2,250.00	2,600.00	2,400.00	2,950.00	4,000.00

[1] Bill Fivaz, letter, March 30, 1996.
[2] Letter, April 15, 1996.

YEAR	MS-64BN	MS-64RB	MS-64RD	MS-65BN	MS-65RB	MS-65RD
1938	$7.00	$7.25	$7.50	$7.00	$7.25	$7.50
1944	22.00	23.00	24.00	22.00	23.00	25.00
1965	925.00	1,000.00	1,150.00	945.00	1,150.00	1,275.00
1996	2,800.00	3,900.00	6,000.00	3,600.00	5,550.00	12,750.00

Proofs:

Proof distribution (estimated): 1,250 to 1,500.

Proof mintage commentary: The mintage of this and other Proofs prior to 1878 is not known, and guesses have been made. The *Guide Book* suggests "900+." I estimate 1,250 to 1,500 pieces. Most probably the 1877 Proof Indian cents, three-cent pieces and Shield nickels were sold in minor sets, and the Proof mintages of all three are the same. However, fewer of the Proof 1877 cents seem to have survived.

Proof die commentary: Struck from at least three different obverse and three different reverse dies, one of which has a blob at the right arm of the T, the die first used in 1872.[1] Unlike the situation with business strikes, the N in ONE and EN in CENT on the reverse are bold on Proofs.[2]

Richard Snow expands on the above:[3] "three obverse, three reverse dies. All are from the bold N reverse die (one is the defective T with blob). One die pair seems to have struck a quantity that are singly struck, exhibiting weak dentils, rounded rims and slight weakness in the headdress. Some of these have made it into circulation and in no way resemble Proofs once they are worn down to EF, although they were intended as such. Counterfeits from transfer dies usually have the bold N reverse (from a later, cheaper date) but using the bold N is not a conclusive way to identify these counterfeits."

Some Proofs (Snow's PR-1) have a high relief "blob" as the right arm of the T in CENT; this die had been in use since 1872 (see note under 1872 Proofs).

Based upon original Mint records in the National Archives, R.W. Julian has concluded that 510 silver Proof sets (which also included minor coins) sold by the Mint in 1877, plus a minimum of 250 minor Proof sets (cent, nickel three-cent piece, and Shield nickel) sold by mail to collectors and dealers, plus an estimated 140 minor Proof sets sold over the counter at the Mint, add up to a minimum approximate figure of 900 coins, which will serve for the nickel three-cent piece and Shield nickel as well.[4]

The 1877 Proof Indian cent is a coin of incredible popularity and demand due to the overall rarity of the date (via related business strikes). Proofs are usually seen toned brown or red and brown, sometimes with a very attractive woodgrain effect.

Beware of the *quality* of certified pieces. For example, I examined a piece certified as "Proof-64 Red" by a leading grading service, but under magnification the entire coin seemed to my eyes to be harshly cleaned, and the obverse had two scratches by the U of UNITED. Of course, there are many nice certified pieces, but it will pay you to inspect them carefully.

---

[1] Richard Snow. "Proof Die Identification for Indian Cents." *Longacre's Ledger,* Fall 1994; updated and revised by a letter, April 10, 1996.

[2] Richard Snow, letter, April 10, 1996.

[3] Richard Snow, letter, April 10, 1996.

[4] R.W. Julian, "The 1877 Indian Head Cent." *Coins Magazine,* October 1992.

Market Prices (1877 Proofs)

YEAR	PR-60BN	PR-60RB	PR-63BN	PR-63RB	PR-63RD
1938	$14.50	$14.75	$14.50	$15.00	$16.00
1944	31.00	31.50	31.00	32.00	35.00
1965	1,425.00	1,475.00	1,450.00	1,500.00	1,650.00
1996	1,600.00	1,800.00	1,875.00	1,925.00	2,220.00

YEAR	PR-64BN	PR-64RB	PR-64RD	PR-65BN	PR-65RB	PR-65RD
1938	$14.50	$15.00	$16.00	$14.50	$15.00	$17.00
1944	31.50	32.00	36.00	31.50	32.50	37.00
1965	1,500.00	1,600.00	1,800.00	1,600.00	1,725.00	2,000.00
1996	2,000.00	2,550.00	3,750.00	2,950.00	3,975.00	7,500.00

Notes

Collecting and historical commentary: From 1873 to 1876 the Treasury's resumption of silver specie payments brought large quantities of coins into the commercial markets and severely lessened the demand for minor coins, resulting in lower mintages for the cent, nickel three-cent, and nickel five-cent pieces.

With a mintage of 852,500 coins the 1877 is the key date among Philadelphia Mint Indian cents. The rarity of the 1877 was recognized by the 1890s, and specimens were sought in circulation, but by that time remarkably few could be found.

It could be that the mintage figure of 852,500 is incorrect, or that some 1877 cents were melted or were shipped to remote areas. Alternatively, the 1877 may be rare simply because only 852,500 were minted.

Breen explains rarity: The low mintage of the 1877 cent was due to a halt in coinage in February of that year in anticipation of Congress' approval of a nickel-content cent (which never materialized).[1] During this era nickel metal faded in and out of numerous Mint and Treasury Department accounts, as Mint officials vacillated on whether nickel was desirable or undesirable for coinage, and nickel-mining interests placed pressure on congressmen.

Julian disputes Breen: Per contra, R.W. Julian in a later study dismissed the nickel-content cent as a "fable" with "no relationship to reality," and went on to note: "The reason for the 1877 cent coinage being very limited was purely economic and had nothing to do with any proposed change in alloy to copper-nickel in place of the bronze (There was such a plan in the early 1880s, but the writer confused the two events)."[2] The real reason was that by 1876 payments of silver coins had been resumed by the Treasury Department (having been suspended from the summer of 1862 until the mid-1870s), and fewer cents were needed to make change. Quantities of Indian cents on hand from previous coinage were ample to meet the needs of commerce. Quantities of nickel three-cent pieces and Shield nickels accumulated in Treasury vaults, leading to the suspension of business strike coinage of these denominations in 1877-1878.

[1] Walter Breen, *The United States Minor Coinage 1793-1916,* p. 14.
[2] R.W. Julian, "The 1877 Indian Head Cent." *Coins Magazine,* October 1992.

An early search for 1877 cents: The following appeared as "He 'Kept Books' on the 1877 Cents," *The Numismatist,* September 1915, p. 319:

A correspondent of the *New York Sun* gives the result of his mathematical computations on the bronze cent of 1877, in a recent issue of that paper, as follows:

Herewith find observations on the humble bronze cent bearing date 1877:

Noticing that this date formed a very small proportion of the dates to be found in a handful of pennies, it occurred to me to start a memorandum record. So in 1881 I began with 1,250 [mixed cents] procured from the bank and found six dated 1877, showing that in the general circulation it then constituted 0.0048% of the output. In 1883, when the number examined had reached 2,950, 11 of that date had appeared, equivalent to 0.0037%. In May 1884, 7,500 had yielded 24, or 0.0032. An intermission then took place, and on February 10, 1896, 10,100 had returned only 24—not one having been found in the additional lot—or 0.0023%. The final entry, November 27, 1897, brought the total to 28,450 with 35 of the 1877, or 0.0012%.

The foregoing shows in a striking manner how the 1877 cent in 16 years had moved toward the vanishing point. What it is today I do not know. I believe, however, that it would take a very long day's work to secure even one out of a batch of 10,000....

QDB comment concerning this search: From the first bronze cent in 1864 through the end of the year 1881 there were about 272,000,000 bronze cents coined. Making the generous assumption that all 1881 cents (mintage: 39.2 million) were in circulation when the search started, this would give a ratio of about one 1877 Indian cent to be found for every 320 bronze cents inspected. It seems that the searcher found about 1 in every 208 cents searched, or *more than expected.* On the other hand, by 1881 many of the earlier-minted bronze cents had disappeared and, without doubt, most of the 1881 cents had not yet been released. The searcher does not indicate whether his 1,250 number included copper-nickel cents (of which slightly over 200 million were made from 1857 through 1864), but if it did, then he found even more 1877 cents, percentage-wise, than mathematically anticipated.

In summation, there seems to be no conclusion to be drawn from the findings of his search. It is interesting to note that by 1897 virtually none were to be found, but by that time additional hundreds of millions of bronze cents had been minted, thus severely diluting the 1877 mintage. Although today it seems that the 1877 Indian cent is even rarer than its low mintage might indicate, in actuality it might be just as rare as it should be.

Rare 1877 cent spent in 1938: In 1938 noted radio personality Harry Einstein, who used the name "Parkyakarkus" on the air, ordered an 1877 Indian cent from a New York City dealer for $20. It arrived at his home in California and was placed on his desk with three or four others. Upon returning to show the prized 1877 to his wife, the entertainer found that the "pennies" had been picked up by the cook and used to pay the milkman.[1]

Date numerals: Date numerals of the 1877 cent are in a straight line; this alignment would continue through and including 1880. The numerals are in shallow relief.

Copper-nickel cents redeemed: In 1877 2,870,433 copper-nickel cents of the 1857-1864 era were redeemed by the Treasury.

Reissuance of earlier bronze cents:[2] A cumbersome system to force the flow of

---

[1] "Record Price For 1877 Cent" *Numismatic Scrapbook Magazine,* October 1938, p. 410. Further, the 1986 Bowers and Merena auction catalogue of the Einstein Collection gives more information about this collector, but not of the missing 1877 cent.

[2] Excerpted from Richard Snow, letters, April 10 and 18, 1996; the words are Richard Snow's.

minor coins had the Mint buying older coins and reissuing them alongside the new coinage. The reason for this reissuance was to move the coinage in quantities greater than the ten-cent legal tender limit back into the commercial channels. The coins flowed into bank and Sub-Treasury vaults and once there, remained on their books as assets. This was clearly an oversight in the legal tender limit provision in the Mint Act of 1857. The special legislation needed came in the form of the Mint Act of March 3, 1871, which required the Mint to buy back the older minor coins in any quantity offered.

At first the coins, which in addition to bronze cents included older copper cents, half cents, copper-nickel cents, bronze two-cent pieces, nickel three cents, and nickel five-cent pieces, were melted and recoined into new coins. As less and less of the pre-1864 coinage was being redeemed it became obvious that the remaining bronze cents and nickel coinage could just be taken in and paid out without going through the recoinage process. The Mint then operated as a clearinghouse for the backlog of minor coins, reissuing them side by side with newly minted coins. Since the coins were already on the books from their original mintage, they were accounted for separately from the mintage of new coinage. A Mint ledger, "Record of Minor Coin Redeemed 1871-83," listed the accounting of this redemption.

1874 14,187,500 minted; 4,051,908 redeemed; 372,500 reissued; total number of bronze cents of various dates paid out this year 14,560,000.

1875 13,528,000 minted; 3,937,872 redeemed; 3,926,000 reissued; total number of bronze cents of various dates paid out this year 17,454,000.

1876 7,944,000 minted; 5,932,723 redeemed; 5,599,500 reissued; total number of bronze cents of various dates paid out this year 13,543,500.

1877 852,500 minted; 9,908,148 redeemed; 9,821,500 reissued; total number of bronze cents of various dates paid out this year 10,674,000.

Linderman book: In this year Henry R. Linderman's book, *Money and Legal Tender,* was published by G.P. Putnam's Sons.

Mint personnel: In 1877 the chief engraver was William Barber, who had served in that position since January 1869, after James B. Longacre's death; his compensation was $3,000 per year. Assistant Engraver William H. Key, a native of Brooklyn, New York, had been at the Mint since October 1864 and was paid $6 per day. Assistant Engraver Charles E. Barber (son of William) had been there since January 1869 and was paid $4 per day. Quite likely, to the last two employees fell the task of punching date logotypes in dies. (Also see note about Key under the 1864 L cent.) George T. Morgan had arrived at the Mint in 1876, having come from England, but as he was hired specifically for artistic reasons, he may be a less likely candidate for such functionary work as stamping date logotypes into working dies for Indian cents, the lowest denomination minor coin.

Dealer Frossard: 1877: Édouard ("Ed") Frossard, born in Switzerland in 1837, came to the United States in 1858 and was a coin collector by 1872. In 1875 and 1876 he edited the early numbers of J.W. Scott's *Coin Collector's Journal,* but hung out his shingle as a professional numismatist in 1877 and began the publication of a journal titled *Numisma.* Although he apparently lived in a glass house from the standpoint of ethics, he was not above throwing stones—and lots of them—at his competitors. Numismatic historians know Frossard as a self-proclaimed numismatic guru and a feisty dealer, but a file of his *Numisma* and numerous auction catalogues yields many items of lasting interest.[1]

[1] John W. Adams, *United States Numismatic Literature,* Vol. I, pp. 68 ff.

1878 Indian Cent

Business Strikes:

Business strike mintage: 5,797,500.

Number of business strike obverse dies made: 30

Average number of coins struck from typical obverse die: 193,250

Availability in Mint State: Many Mint State coins show considerable red. Bright original red pieces are much more available than are those of the late 1860s and early 1870s. In the late 1970s a roll of 50 gem Mint State coins owned by Allen Harriman was dispersed in the market.[1]

Availability in circulated grades: Scarce.

Characteristics of striking: Usually well struck.

Market Prices (1878 business strikes)

YEAR	G-4	VG-8	F-12	VF-20	EF-40	AU-50
1938	$0.20	$0.30	$0.50	$0.75	$0.90	$1.25
1944	.70	1.00	1.50	1.75	2.10	2.80
1965	8.50	13.00	20.00	27.50	37.50	49.00
1996	22.50	30.00	40.00	60.00	100.00	140.00

YEAR	MS-60BN	MS-60RB	MS-63BN	MS-63RB	MS-63RD
1938	$2.10	$2.10	$2.10	$2.25	$2.50
1944	3.75	3.85	3.75	3.85	4.00
1965	82.00	85.00	82.00	87.00	95.00
1996	190.00	210.00	195.00	285.00	525.00

[1] Reported by John Dannreuther, letter, May 16, 1996; a similar roll of 1876 cents was dispersed at the same time.

YEAR	MS-64BN	MS-64RB	MS-64RD	MS-65BN	MS-65RB	MS-65RD
1938	$2.10	$2.25	$2.50	$2.10	$2.25	$2.60
1944	3.85	3.90	4.30	4.00	4.25	4.50
1965	85.00	89.00	102.50	87.00	92.50	110.00
1996	240.00	480.00	900.00	300.00	875.00	2,000.00

Proofs:

Proof mintage: 2,350.

Proof commentary: Not a low-mintage date, but in demand due to the scarcity of related business strikes. Bright red gems are scarce, but are the most available of any Proof Indian cent date up to this point in time.

Proofs were made from at least two obverse dies, one with repunching at base of 1 in date. Some Proofs have "square" or wire rims, while others are rounded, the latter more in the style of a business strike although definitely Proof. Some Proofs have a high relief "blob" as the right arm of the T in CENT; this die had been in use since 1872 (see note under 1872 Proofs).

This is the first year for which precise coinage figures are known for Proof bronze Indian cents. The first Proof mintage figures were a part of the chief coiner's report of January 31, 1878. Earlier mintage figures found in numismatic references (the *Guide Book* is an example) are primarily guesses based upon the number of silver Proofs struck each year, the silver Proof mintages having been recorded from 1859 onward.

Market Prices (1878 Proofs)

YEAR	PR-60BN	PR-60RB	PR-63BN	PR-63RB	PR-63RD	
1938	$3.30	$3.40	$3.30	$3.50	$3.50	
1944	5.20	5.25	5.20	5.35	6.00	
1965	150.00	157.50	152.50	155.00	180.00	
1996	135.00	172.50	165.00	225.00	280.00	

YEAR	PR-64BN	PR-64RB	PR-64RD	PR-65BN	PR-65RB	PR-65RD
1938	$3.30	$3.50	$3.50	$3.30	$3.50	$3.60
1944	5.00	5.50	6.25	5.25	5.75	6.50
1965	165.00	175.00	200.00	165.00	200.00	225.00
1996	300.00	310.00	425.00	360.00	400.00	900.00

Notes

Collecting commentary: Scarce in all grades, the last Philadelphia Mint Indian cent to be in this category, although runners-up include 1885 and 1894. In general, 1878 marks the end of the old order of Indian cents, after which business strike quantities increased dramatically.

Date numerals: Date numerals in a straight line; this alignment would continue through and including 1880.

Copper-nickel cents redeemed: In 1878 1,993,125 copper-nickel cents of the 1857-1864 era were redeemed by the Treasury.

The rise of the Chapmans: The year 1878 saw the inception of the independent business of brothers S. Hudson (born 1857) and Henry (1859) Chapman, who had entered the trade in 1876 in the Philadelphia shop of Capt. John W. Haseltine. From 1878 until well into the twentieth century, the Chapman brothers were front row center in the rare coin business. Under their watch were sold many of the finest collections of the day, with the 1882 catalogue of the Charles I. Bushnell Collection being particularly notable for its innovative writing and for the showmanship with which it was distributed. In 1906 the Chapmans dissolved their partnership and each went his separate way without missing a beat in terms of the collections handled. Henry, who remained in the field long enough to take part in the appraisal of the Virgil Brand estate in the early 1930s, was both a shopkeeper and an auctioneer, and maintained a large retail stock of coins for sale. He was the private sales agent for George T. Morgan in the distribution of certain delicacies from the Philadelphia Mint, among which were limited-production Saint-Gaudens $10 and $20 varieties dated 1907 and mirror Proof Morgan dollars of 1921. S. Hudson Chapman concentrated upon auction sales and coin research, the latter involving some interesting techniques including immersing coins in water in order to reduce glare.

Dealer Steigerwalt: In the same year that the Chapman brothers went into the rare coin business for themselves, in Lancaster, PA, Charles Steigerwalt began in the trade. From that time through the first decade of the twentieth century, he issued fixed price lists and conducted auction sales. Listings of his inventory were his forte, and it is doubtless correct to state that he was one of the leading mail-order rare coin dealers of the 1890s, along with J.W. Scott & Co. and a few others.

1879 Indian Cent

Business Strikes:

Business strike mintage: 16,228,000.

Number of business strike obverse dies made: 76

Average number of coins struck from typical obverse die: 213,526

Availability in Mint State: Readily available, although not as plentiful as some issues of the following decade.

Availability in circulated grades: Common.

Characteristics of striking: Varies. It is difficult in many instances to make a blanket statement about striking quality for issues in which dozens of die pairs were used and for which striking continued over a long period of time during the year.

Market Prices (1879 business strikes)

YEAR	G-4	VG-8	F-12	VF-20	EF-40	AU-50
1938	$0.06	$0.10	$0.20	$0.35	$0.50	$0.75
1944	.30	.50	.75	.80	.90	1.00
1965	2.00	3.50	5.50	8.00	11.00	20.00
1996	4.50	5.00	7.00	14.00	30.00	42.50

YEAR	MS-60BN	MS-60RB	MS-63BN	MS-63RB	MS-63RD	
1938	$0.90	$0.90	$0.90	$0.90	$1.00	
1944	1.30	1.35	1.30	1.40	1.50	
1965	33.00	35.00	33.00	36.00	42.50	
1996	64.00	100.00	66.00	130.00	240.00	

YEAR	MS-64BN	MS-64RB	MS-64RD	MS-65BN	MS-65RB	MS-65RD
1938	$0.90	$0.90	$1.00	$0.90	$0.90	$1.00
1944	1.40	1.40	1.50	1.40	1.40	1.60
1965	34.00	37.00	45.00	35.00	38.50	47.50
1996	80.00	235.00	400.00	100.00	385.00	700.00

Proofs:

Proof mintage: 3,200.

Proof commentary: Coined from at least two obverse dies. One has the date slightly to the left, serif of 1 nearly in line with the bust point. The second has the base of the 1 in date slightly repunched and has traces of slight repunching on the 8 and 9 as well (cf. Breen, *Encyclopedia of Proof Coins*).

High-quality pieces with rich brown-toned surfaces, often with a nuance of iridescent blue (especially when viewed at a certain angle to the light), are from long-term hoards that passed into dealers' hands. Same comment for other issues of 1880s and some of the 1890s, until the Mint began reducing the mintage quantities. Also see commentary under 1883 Proofs.

Market Prices (1879 Proofs)

YEAR	PR-60BN	PR-60RB	PR-63BN	PR-63RB	PR-63RD	
1938	$1.40	$1.40	$1.40	$1.40	$1.50	
1944	2.80	2.85	2.90	2.90	3.10	
1965	75.00	78.00	77.00	80.00	85.00	
1996	110.00	140.00	140.00	150.00	200.00	

YEAR	PR-64BN	PR-64RB	PR-64RD	PR-65BN	PR-65RB	PR-65RD
1938	$1.40	$1.40	$1.50	$1.40	$1.40	$1.50
1944	2.90	2.90	3.10	2.90	2.90	3.15
1965	80.00	83.00	90.00	82.50	85.00	95.00
1996	195.00	210.00	425.00	330.00	400.00	840.00

Notes

Collecting commentary: 1879 inaugurates the long and uninterrupted span extending to the end of the series in 1909 in which Philadelphia Mint Indian cents are all readily collectible, although a few (in particular 1885) are considered slightly scarce.

Numeral alignment: Next to last year with date numerals in a straight line.

Copper-nickel cents redeemed: In 1879 870,342 copper-nickel cents of the 1857-1864 era were redeemed by the Treasury.

New Mint director: 1879, February: Horatio C. Burchard became director of the Mint and would remain in the position until 1885.

New chief engraver: Following the death on August 31, 1879, of Chief Engraver William Barber there was a delay of some months before his son, Charles E. Barber, was named to the post. The younger Barber was not well liked by his superiors, and, apparently, some consideration was given to naming George T. Morgan to the post.[1]

Born in London in 1840, Charles E. Barber came with his family to America in 1852. In 1869 he joined the Mint staff as an assistant engraver, this being the same month that his father, who had been an assistant since 1865, was named chief engraver. Charles E. Barber did not have any important effect upon the Indian cent series as no notable modifications were made during his tenure, except for the routine creation of a new obverse hub in 1886, presumably to replace a worn one in use since 1864. Today, numismatists mainly remember him for his 1883 Liberty Head nickel and the 1892 dime, quarter, and half dollar designs.

For a short time he was assisted by William H. Key and for a very long time by George T. Morgan, who succeeded him as chief engraver decades later in 1917, after Barber's death. Quite possibly Key and Morgan did much of the date logotype punching for Indian cent dies. Barber was primarily occupied with making medals, numerous different designs of which were produced during his tenure.

Demand increases: From the 1879 *Mint Report:* "Owing to the general increased business activity in the country an unusually heavy demand has been created for the minor coins, and the mint at Philadelphia has been called upon to furnish one-cent pieces in excess of its capacity for striking this denomination of coin, and at the same time execute the quota of standard silver dollars [Morgan dollars mandated by the Bland-Allison Act of 1878] required by law."

Further in the same document, Horatio C. Burchard, director of the Mint, recommended that the coinage of nickel three-cent pieces, never a popular denomination, be terminated, and proposed the revival of another denomination: "The amount of one-cent pieces in circulation being already large, and the demand on the mint for a further coinage increasing, the issue of a two-cent piece would probably enable the mint to meet the requirements of the people, and diminish the coinage of one-cent pieces, the demand for which can be more easily relieved if the issue and free delivery of the two-cent piece is authorized." This plaint did not meet a favorable response.

The same report noted that in 1878 there was an estimated $6.50 in coins in circulation per capita. It was also noted that the average immigrant upon coming to America brought about $15 worth of foreign money.

Specie (gold and silver coin) payments, which had been suspended since 1862, were by law to be resumed by the Treasury no later than January 1, 1879, and banks resumed gold payments in exchange for paper in December 1878. Silver specie payments had been resumed unofficially as early as 1873 (and were authorized by Congress in 1875).

---

[1] R.W. Julian, letter, April 24, 1996.

1880 Indian Cent

Business Strikes:

Business strike mintage: 38,961,000.

Number of business strike obverse dies made: 129

Average number of coins struck from typical obverse die: 302,023

Availability in Mint State: Readily available within the context of the 1880s. In general, Mint State cents of the 1880s are often brighter (more brilliant) and less spotted than those of the 1890s, although there are certainly many spotted and stained coins with dates 1880-1889.

Availability in circulated grades: Common.

Characteristics of striking: Varies.

Clashed reverse: One interesting and very rare variety has a prominent arc-like die clash on the reverse extending from the border down past the right side of the shield into E of ONE (Snow-1, FND-001); the obverse of this issue is also slightly doubled. This clash was caused by the obverse die falling out of the top of the coining press and its edge hitting the interior of bottom die at an angle.[1]

Concerning this variety Sam Lukes commented:[2] "In March of 1995 I sold the finest known example of this, PCGS MS-65 RD, for $3,000."

QDB note: In addition, there is an ANACS-graded MS-65 RD in the Larry R. Steve Collection.

Market Prices (1880 business strikes)

YEAR	G-4	VG-8	F-12	VF-20	EF-40	AU-50
1938	$0.05	$0.08	$0.15	$0.20	$0.25	$0.40
1944	.15	.20	.35	.45	.60	.75
1965	1.50	2.50	4.50	6.50	9.00	15.00
1996	2.75	3.50	5.50	7.50	20.00	37.50

---

[1] Thomas K. DeLorey, letter, April 15,1996.

[2] Letter, April 8, 1996.

YEAR	MS-60BN	MS-60RB	MS-63BN	MS-63RB	MS-63RD	
1938	$0.65	$0.65	$0.70	$0.65	$0.75	
1944	1.00	1.00	1.00	1.10	1.25	
1965	27.00	28.00	27.00	30.00	35.00	
1996	62.50	80.00	64.00	110.00	165.00	

YEAR	MS-64BN	MS-64RB	MS-64RD	MS-65BN	MS-65RB	MS-65RD
1938	$0.65	$0.70	$0.75	$0.65	$0.70	$0.75
1944	1.00	1.10	1.25	1.00	1.10	1.25
1965	29.00	32.50	37.50	31.00	35.00	41.00
1996	85.00	165.00	260.00	125.00	350.00	700.00

Proofs:

Proof mintage: 3,955.

Proof commentary: Struck from at least two obverse dies, one with slight traces of repunching at upper part of second 8 in date.

Pieces with rich brown-toned surfaces are from long-term hoards that passed into dealers' hands; see commentary under 1879.

Market Prices (1880 Proofs)

YEAR	PR-60BN	PR-60RB	PR-63BN	PR-63RB	PR-63RD	
1938	$1.00	$1.00	$1.00	$1.00	$1.10	
1944	2.20	2.20	2.20	2.30	2.50	
1965	60.00	61.00	60.00	61.50	62.50	
1996	110.00	142.00	140.00	147.50	200.00	

YEAR	PR-64BN	PR-64RB	PR-64RD	PR-65BN	PR-65RB	PR-65RD
1938	$1.00	$1.00	$1.10	$1.00	$1.10	$1.10
1944	2.20	2.30	2.50	2.20	2.30	2.50
1965	61.00	62.00	63.50	61.00	62.50	65.00
1996	170.00	180.00	300.00	300.00	355.00	820.00

Notes

Collecting commentary: No particular excitement with this or other dates of the era, but collected as part of the later 1879-1909 series.

Date peculiarities: Date logotype on some business strikes and on Proofs is defective and shows some irregularities in the relief of the numerals.

The date 1880 is in a straight line; later years have the date slightly curved to complement the border curve, but in a different arc (1881 is a hybrid; see following).

The large, widely spaced numerals of 1880 are much easier to read than the compact, smaller letters of 1872, the start of the straight-line date sequence.

Copper-nickel cents redeemed: In 1880 577,130 copper-nickel cents of the 1857-1864 era were redeemed by the Treasury.

Many orders: From the 1880 *Mint Report:* "Notwithstanding the large number of cents struck, the demand for this denomination of coin has been so great that the Mint at Philadelphia—the only mint at which minor coins are struck—has been unable to manufacture a sufficient supply to promptly fill the orders received, although the bronze alloy has been purchased in the form of manufactured blanks or planchets ready for striking, and thus greatly lessened the amount of labor required."

1881 Indian Cent

Business Strikes:

Business strike mintage: 39,208,000.

Number of business strike obverse dies made: 95

Average number of coins struck from typical obverse die: 412,716 (the second highest average figure for any date for which Mint figures are available)

Availability in Mint State: Common, although many are spotted; this is especially true of brilliant red specimens.

Availability in circulated grades: Common.

Characteristics of striking: Varies, but sharp examples can be found. On the other hand, some were struck from worn dies and show wavy, granular fields.

Market Prices (1881 business strikes)

YEAR	G-4	VG-8	F-12	VF-20	EF-40	AU-50
1938	$0.05	$0.08	$0.15	$0.20	$0.25	$0.40
1944	.15	.20	.35	.50	.65	.85
1965	1.50	2.50	4.50	6.50	9.00	15.00
1996	2.75	3.75	5.50	7.50	18.00	25.00

YEAR	MS-60BN	MS-60RB	MS-63BN	MS-63RB	MS-63RD	
1938	$0.65	$0.65	$0.70	$0.65	$0.75	
1944	1.30	1.35	1.30	1.40	1.50	
1965	27.00	28.50	27.25	30.00	35.00	
1996	40.00	55.00	42.50	77.50	140.00	

YEAR	MS-64BN	MS-64RB	MS-64RD	MS-65BN	MS-65RB	MS-65RD
1938	$0.65	$0.70	$0.75	$0.65	$0.70	$0.75
1944	1.40	1.40	1.50	1.40	1.40	1.60
1965	29.00	32.50	37.50	31.00	35.00	41.00
1996	75.00	135.00	290.00	115.00	280.00	580.00

Proofs:

Proof mintage: 3,575.

Proof commentary: Pieces with rich brown-toned surfaces are from long-term hoards; see commentary under 1879.

Market Prices (1881 Proofs)

YEAR	PR-60BN	PR-60RB	PR-63BN	PR-63RB	PR-63RD	
1938	$1.00	$1.00	$1.00	$1.00	$1.10	
1944	2.80	2.85	2.90	2.90	3.00	
1965	60.00	61.00	60.00	61.50	62.50	
1996	110.00	140.00	140.00	150.00	205.00	

YEAR	PR-64BN	PR-64RB	PR-64RD	PR-65BN	PR-65RB	PR-65RD
1938	$1.00	$1.00	$1.10	$1.00	$1.00	$1.10
1944	2.90	2.90	3.00	2.90	2.90	3.10
1965	61.00	62.00	63.50	61.00	62.50	65.00
1996	170.00	180.00	300.00	302.50	360.00	825.00

Notes

Collecting commentary: Same remark as preceding.

Date peculiarities: The 1881 date is irregular, with the central 88 dates misaligned, the first 18 digits as if straight, the final 81 as if curved; sort of a hybrid between a straight date (as 1880) and a curved date as used in later years. Curious!

Copper-nickel cents redeemed: In 1881 81,393 copper-nickel cents of the 1857-1864 era were redeemed by the Treasury. By the end of this year the redemption of these old-style cents totaled 31,681,967. Redemption would continue for many decades thereafter, and figures would be listed in the *Annual Mint Report* issues. Quantities diminished sharply over a period of time. By mid-1909 over 80 million had been redeemed, or close to 40% of the total issued. According to Treasury reports, tens of millions of copper-nickel cents are still not redeemed as of the 1990s. Such reports, while interesting, are known to be inaccurate in some areas. For example, during the nineteenth century the Treasury had no record of even a single copper half cent ever being redeemed.

1882 Indian Cent

Business Strikes:

Business strike mintage: 38,578,000.

Number of business strike obverse dies made: 74

Average number of coins struck from typical obverse die: 521,324. Record high figure for the nineteenth-century dates studied; this figure would not be exceeded until 1901.

Availability in Mint State: Common among cents of this era. Gem original red pieces are scarce if unspotted.

Availability in circulated grades: Common.

Characteristics of striking: Varies.

Market Prices (1882 business strikes)

YEAR	G-4	VG-8	F-12	VF-20	EF-40	AU-50
1938	$0.05	$0.08	$0.15	$0.20	$0.25	$0.40
1944	.10	.15	.25	.40	.55	.75
1965	1.50	2.50	4.50	6.50	9.00	15.00
1996	2.75	3.75	5.50	7.50	16.00	25.00

YEAR	MS-60BN	MS-60RB	MS-63BN	MS-63RB	MS-63RD
1938	$0.65	$0.65	$0.70	$0.65	$0.75
1944	1.00	1.00	1.00	1.10	1.25
1965	27.00	28.00	27.00	30.00	35.00
1996	41.00	57.50	43.00	80.00	142.50

YEAR	MS-64BN	MS-64RB	MS-64RD	MS-65BN	MS-65RB	MS-65RD
1938	$0.65	$0.70	$0.75	$0.65	$0.70	$0.75
1944	1.00	1.10	1.25	1.00	1.10	1.25
1965	29.00	32.50	37.50	31.00	35.00	41.00
1996	77.50	140.00	300.00	120.00	285.00	550.00

Proofs:

Proof mintage: 3,100.

Proof commentary: Struck from two or more different obverse dies.

Pieces with rich brown-toned surfaces are from long-term hoards; see commentary under 1879. In this era the Mint made far more Proofs than it could sell during the year. Bright red gems are on the rare side, especially so if without spots.

Market Prices (1882 Proofs)

YEAR	PR-60BN	PR-60RB	PR-63BN	PR-63RB	PR-63RD	
1938	$1.00	$1.00	$1.00	$1.00	$1.10	
1944	1.75	1.80	1.75	1.80	2.00	
1965	60.00	61.00	60.00	61.50	62.50	
1996	105.00	132.50	130.00	140.00	210.00	

YEAR	PR-64BN	PR-64RB	PR-64RD	PR-65BN	PR-65RB	PR-65RD
1938	$1.00	$1.00	$1.10	$1.00	$1.00	$1.10
1944	1.75	1.80	2.00	1.75	1.80	2.10
1965	61.00	62.00	63.50	61.00	62.50	65.00
1996	192.50	177.50	295.00	297.50	350.00	1,000.00

Notes

Collecting commentary: No particular excitement with this or other dates of the era, but collected as part of the later 1879-1909 series.

Misplaced date: One variety shows *two* separate traces of a stray numeral 1 on Miss Liberty's neck at the fourth and fifth beads (counting from the left). An example certified as an MS-65 RB (NGC) regular 1882 cent, was cherrypicked by Vic Bozarth on April 6, 1996, at the Bay State Coin Show, Boston.[1]

Demand: From the 1882 Mint Report: "The demand for small coins, as has been noticed in other countries, increases with business activity, and is a favorable indication of the frequency of actual exchanges and of a prosperous condition of the country."

---

[1] This variety was first discovered by W.O. Walker and first mentioned in the Fall 1996 issue of *Longacre's Ledger*.

Dealer Low: In 1882 Lyman Haines Low issued his first auction catalogue, initiating an activity he would pursue until 1924. Low was a dedicated researcher and is particularly remembered today for his excellent work in the field of Hard Times tokens (issued c. 1832-1844), a monograph concerning which he published in 1899 and portions of which are still widely quoted today. It is indeed unfortunate that Low did not keep a notebook of numismatic events as they happened during his career, for the hobby would have had a rich lode of information as a result.

1883 Indian Cent

Business Strikes:

Business strike mintage: 45,591,500.

Number of business strike obverse dies made: 146

Average number of coins struck from typical obverse die: 312,271

Availability in Mint State: Common. As is true of all dates of this era, bright original red pieces are seen much less frequently than toned examples.

Availability in circulated grades: Common.

Characteristics of striking: Varies.

Market Prices (1883 business strikes)

YEAR	G-4	VG-8	F-12	VF-20	EF-40	AU-50
1938	$0.05	$0.08	$0.15	$0.20	$0.25	$0.40
1944	.10	.15	.25	.40	.55	.75
1965	1.25	2.25	3.50	5.25	9.00	13.00
1996	2.00	3.75	5.50	7.50	16.00	25.00

YEAR	MS-60BN	MS-60RB	MS-63BN	MS-63RB	MS-63RD	
1938	$0.65	$0.65	$0.70	$0.65	$0.75	
1944	1.00	1.00	1.00	1.10	1.25	
1965	24.00	26.00	25.00	27.00	32.50	
1996	41.00	58.00	43.50	81.50	144.00	

YEAR	MS-64BN	MS-64RB	MS-64RD	MS-65BN	MS-65RB	MS-65RD
1938	$0.65	$0.70	$0.75	$0.65	$0.70	$0.75
1944	1.00	1.10	1.25	1.00	1.10	1.25
1965	26.00	28.50	33.50	27.25	29.00	36.00
1996	79.00	132.50	310.00	122.50	295.00	550.00

Proofs:

Proof mintage: 6,609.

Proof commentary: Struck from at least two obverse dies, the scarcer with the 3 repunched.

This is the high water mark for Proof Indian cent mintage. In this year there was a speculative rush at the Mint for Proof nickel five-cent pieces, which were produced in three design types (Shield, Liberty without CENTS, and Liberty with CENTS) to the extent of over 17,000 Proofs(!). Many of these 1883 Proof cents and nickels went to the general public, rather than to numismatists, and today the Proofs are not as common as mintage figures indicate (see study in Appendix IV). It is easy to envision that an excited new collector, eager to get a Proof specimen of the "rare" 1883 Liberty nickel with CENTS, was forced to acquire a "minor Proof set" also containing an Indian cent and a nickel three-cent piece, simply spent the two unwanted denominations.

Many Proofs of this and other high-mintage dates of the era remained unsold and later went in bulk to David U. Proskey and other dealers; old-time dealers Wayte Raymond and William Pukall still had these available in thin paper mint wrappers as late as the 1950s (I recall buying some). Nearly all of these were toned a beautiful medium brown color often with blue iridescent highlights. Also see comment under 1879 Proofs. Bright red Proofs are scarce.

Market Prices (1883 Proofs)

YEAR	PR-60BN	PR-60RB	PR-63BN	PR-63RB	PR-63RD	
1938	$1.00	$1.00	$1.00	$1.00	$1.10	
1944	1.50	1.55	1.50	1.60	1.75	
1965	52.00	53.00	52.00	55.00	57.50	
1996	115.00	142.00	140.00	150.00	210.00	

YEAR	PR-64BN	PR-64RB	PR-64RD	PR-65BN	PR-65RB	PR-65RD
1938	$1.00	$1.00	$1.10	$1.00	$1.00	$1.10
1944	1.60	1.60	1.75	1.60	1.60	1.75
1965	52.00	55.00	58.50	53.00	55.00	60.00
1996	170.00	182.00	305.00	310.00	360.00	1,200.00

Notes

Collecting commentary: The 1883 without-CENTS nickel, mentioned above, was the first coin in American history to excite widespread numismatic and public interest for reasons of anticipated quick profits.[1] Articles in the popular press predicted that the coins would double, triple, or increase even further in value. Vendors of rare coins, mineral specimens, and other collectibles had a field day selling lightly worn specimens of these "rare" nickels for 10¢ to 15¢ each.

Date numerals: Date numerals quite widely spaced; this is also seen on 1883 Shield nickels.

Overdate discredited: In *Walter Breen's Complete Encyclopedia of U.S. and Colonial Coins,* published in 1988, B-2005 is described as "1883, second 8 over 7.... Probably was 1883/79." Today this variety is not considered an overdate by specialists.[2]

---

[1] By contrast, the hoarding of cents in 1862 was due to apprehension as to the financial stability of the nation and the outcome of the Civil War.

[2] W.O. Walker. "A Population Report Rarity Review." *Longacre's Ledger,* Spring 1995.

1884 Indian Cent

Business Strikes:

Business strike mintage: 23,257,800.

Number of business strike obverse dies made: 122

Average number of coins struck from typical obverse die: 190,638

Availability in Mint State: One of the scarcer issues of the 1880s, but there are many in existence. Bright red gems are quite a bit more elusive than generally realized. I have had relatively few over the years.

Availability in circulated grades: Common.

Characteristics of striking: Varies, but usually good.

Market Prices (1884 business strikes)

YEAR	G-4	VG-8	F-12	VF-20	EF-40	AU-50
1938	$0.06	$0.10	$0.20	$0.35	$0.50	$0.75
1944	.15	.25	.40	.55	.70	.95
1965	2.25	3.50	6.00	9.50	13.50	22.00
1996	2.75	4.00	6.00	10.00	20.00	30.00

YEAR	MS-60BN	MS-60RB	MS-63BN	MS-63RB	MS-63RD	
1938	$0.90	$0.90	$0.90	$0.90	$1.00	
1944	1.30	1.35	1.30	1.40	1.50	
1965	36.00	37.50	37.25	38.50	44.00	
1996	53.00	80.00	57.50	120.00	240.00	

YEAR	MS-64BN	MS-64RB	MS-64RD	MS-65BN	MS-65RB	MS-65RD
1938	$0.90	$0.90	$1.00	$0.90	$0.90	$1.00
1944	1.40	1.40	1.50	1.40	1.40	1.60
1965	39.00	41.00	46.00	40.00	43.00	50.00
1996	115.00	235.00	550.00	150.00	335.00	1,750.00

Proofs:

Proof mintage: 3,942.

Proof commentary: Unsold quantities remained at the Mint and were wholesaled. Typically seen with much brown on the surface. See comment under 1879.

Market Prices (1884 Proofs)

YEAR	PR-60BN	PR-60RB	PR-63BN	PR-63RB	PR-63RD	
1938	$1.00	$1.00	$1.00	$1.00	$1.10	
1944	1.75	1.80	1.75	1.90	2.10	
1965	57.00	57.50	57.50	60.00	62.50	
1996	120.00	142.50	140.00	160.00	220.00	

YEAR	PR-64BN	PR-64RB	PR-64RD	PR-65BN	PR-65RB	PR-65RD
1938	$1.00	$1.00	$1.10	$1.00	$1.00	$1.10
1944	1.80	1.85	2.10	1.80	1.90	2.20
1965	57.50	60.00	62.50	57.50	60.00	66.00
1996	200.00	210.00	340.00	285.00	350.00	840.00

Notes

Collecting commentary: The 1884 cent and the 1886 have both been considered as slightly "better" dates in the decade, but not as scarce as the 1885.

1885 Indian Cent

Business Strikes:

Business strike mintage: 11,761,594.

Number of business strike obverse dies made: 44

Average number of coins struck from typical obverse die: 267,309

Availability in Mint State: Scarcest business strike of the 1880s. Usually seen well struck. Gems are elusive, especially if significantly red. In the era when these were made, most collectors bought Proofs and ignored business strikes. By far the majority of Mint State coins are medium brown. The survival of Mint State coins is a matter of chance. Always in strong demand due to its appeal as an elusive date.

Availability in circulated grades: Slightly scarce. Key issue of the 1880s. However, enough exist that finding one will be no problem.

Characteristics of striking: Usually fairly sharp.

Market Prices (1885 business strikes)

YEAR	G-4	VG-8	F-12	VF-20	EF-40	AU-50
1938	$0.15	$0.25	$0.50	$0.60	$0.75	$1.10
1944	.40	.60	1.00	1.35	1.75	2.50
1965	4.25	7.00	12.50	18.00	27.00	37.50
1996	4.00	6.75	10.00	19.00	47.50	65.00

YEAR	MS-60BN	MS-60RB	MS-63BN	MS-63RB	MS-63RD	
1938	$2.00	$2.00	$2.00	$2.00	$2.20	
1944	4.00	4.00	4.00	4.50	5.00	
1965	54.00	55.00	54.00	56.00	58.00	
1996	100.00	135.00	120.00	205.00	370.00	

YEAR	MS-64BN	MS-64RB	MS-64RD	MS-65BN	MS-65RB	MS-65RD
1938	$2.00	$2.00	$2.20	$2.00	$2.00	$2.20
1944	4.00	4.50	5.00	4.00	4.50	5.00
1965	55.00	57.50	62.00	56.00	485.00	65.00
1996	200.00	365.00	600.00	265.00	600.00	1,750.00

Proofs:

Proof mintage: 3,790.

Proof commentary: Struck from at least four different obverse dies, two of which can be readily differentiated by the position of the 1 in the date to the neck tip, one with the 1 directly under the tip and the other positioned farther to the right.[1]

Richard Snow comment: "Many of the Proofs of these high-mintage years were struck only once, leaving rounded rims, weak dentils and weakness on the portrait. Some dies have also been used for regular production after they were retired from Proof production, making attributing some Proofs extremely difficult."[2]

Usually seen with brown surfaces or brown with tinges of red; rarely full red (unless dipped). Pieces with rich brown-toned surfaces are from long-term hoards; see commentary under 1879. Many 1885 and 1886 (both types) Proof cents have rice purple iridescence over brown surfaces.[3] However, 1885 remained in old-time hoards in smaller quantities than some of the others as it was considered to have greater demand (pressure put on Proofs because of the relative scarcity of business strikes), and examples were sold into the market at a more rapid rate.

Market Prices (1885 Proofs)

YEAR	PR-60BN	PR-60RB	PR-63BN	PR-63RB	PR-63RD	
1938	$1.00	$1.00	$1.00	$1.00	$1.10	
1944	5.20	5.25	5.20	5.35	6.00	
1965	77.50	80.00	79.00	82.50	87.50	
1996	130.00	162.50	160.00	170.00	235.00	

YEAR	PR-64BN	PR-64RB	PR-64RD	PR-65BN	PR-65RB	PR-65RD
1938	$1.00	$1.00	$1.10	$1.00	$1.00	$1.10
1944	5.00	5.50	6.25	5.25	5.75	6.50
1965	82.50	85.00	92.50	85.00	87.50	100.00
1996	225.00	235.00	450.00	320.00	355.00	950.00

---

[1] Richard Snow. "Proof Die Identification for Indian Cents." *Longacre's Ledger,* Fall 1994; number of dies modified to four by letter, April 10, 1996.

[2] Letter, April 10, 1996.

[3] Observation of John Dannreuther re: coins submitted to PCGS; letter, May 16, 1996.

Notes

Mint notes: From the 1885 *Mint Report* (covering the fiscal year ended June 30): "40,571,962 cents [were] struck in 1884 at an estimated cost of $20,000, and 17,571,670 struck in 1885 at a cost of some $15,000 (which is about the estimate of the Superintendent of the Mint at Philadelphia) for the reason that the planchets for this coinage are purchased. The cost of coinage therefore is principally the cost of striking."

New Mint director: 1885, December. James P. Kimball became Mint director, a position he kept until 1889.

MILLING MACHINE: By means of this device planchets were squeezed between two surfaces, thus, narrowing their diameter and imparting a raised rim to them, permitting the metal to flow more easily and the strike to be of better sharpness.

1886 Indian Cent

Type I

IDENTIFICATION: On Type I cents (as described here) the last feather of the Indian's headdress points between the I and the C of AMERICA; on Type II it points between the C and the A.

1886 Type I (left) and Type II obverses. Note that on the Type I the last feather of the headdress points between the I and the C, and on the Type II the feather points between the C and the A.

Business Strikes:

Business strike mintage: Estimated 13,000,000. Richard Snow suggests that the business strike mintage of 17,650,000 pieces can be divided into 13,000,000 of the Type I and 4,000,000 or so of the Type II.

Number of business strike obverse dies made: 45 (combined for Type I and Type II).

Average number of coins struck from typical obverse die: 410,465

Availability in Mint State: Scarce, but more often seen than Type II. Bright red gems are rare, especially if problem-free (certification is no help in this regard).

Availability in circulated grades: Slightly scarce within the context of the 1880s decade.

Characteristics of striking: Usually fairly sharp.

Market Prices (1886 Type I business strikes)

YEAR	G-4	VG-8	F-12	VF-20	EF-40	AU-50
1938	$0.07	$0.10	$0.25	$0.40	$0.50	$0.75
1944	.15	.20	.35	.45	.60	.75
1965	2.50	3.75	7.50	12.50	19.00	25.00
1996	3.00	5.00	10.00	27.50	57.50	85.00

YEAR	MS-60BN	MS-60RB	MS-63BN	MS-63RB	MS-63RD	
1938	$0.90	$0.90	$0.90	$0.90	$1.10	
1944	1.00	1.00	1.00	1.10	1.25	
1965	40.00	42.00	40.00	43.00	45.00	
1996	135.00	175.00	160.00	225.00	370.00	

YEAR	MS-64BN	MS-64RB	MS-64RD	MS-65BN	MS-65RB	MS-65RD
1938	$0.90	$0.90	$1.10	$0.90	$0.90	$1.10
1944	1.00	1.10	1.25	1.00	1.10	1.25
1965	41.00	44.50	50.00	42.50	46.00	55.00
1996	225.00	365.00	850.00	385.00	850.00	2,500.00

Proofs:

Proof mintage: Proof mintage reported: 4,290 for Type I and II combined. The Type I pieces are slightly more plentiful in Proof format, based upon a new study by Richard Snow who now estimates a revised Proof mintage of 2,490 for the Type I and 1,800 for Type II.[1]

Proof commentary: Pieces with rich brown-toned surfaces are from long-term hoards; see commentary under 1879. The typical coin has a rich brown surface with some nuances of blue and purple, with the latter color being quite plentiful on Proofs of 1886 (both types) and also 1885.[2] The writer recalls removing quite a few Proofs from this era from their original Mint wrappers, remnants of a hoard bought from an old-time dealer.

While one should *report* market prices, not *predict* them, the figures given below for 1996 Proof values are estimates based upon the *new* information that Type I Proofs are slightly more plentiful than Type II Proofs; as of spring 1996, the Type I Proof, earlier thought to be the rarer of the two, is actually priced a bit higher than the Type II.

[1] Richard Snow, letter, April 10, 1996; this is based upon new studies and is different information from that in his book, *Flying Eagle & Indian Cents* (which suggested a mintage of 1,800 for Type I Proofs and 2,500 for Type II). Snow stated that the Type I Proofs are believed to be slightly more plentiful now. The writer commends Richard Snow on his objectivity and flexibility; all too often, writers take a stand that is later shown to be incorrect, but they stand on false pride and keep defending a position that to others is indefensible.

[2] Observation of John Dannreuther re: coins submitted to PCGS; letter, May 16, 1996.

Market Prices (1886 Type I Proofs)

YEAR	PR-60BN	PR-60RB	PR-63BN	PR-63RB	PR-63RD	
1938	$1.00	$1.00	$1.00	$1.00	$1.10	
1944	1.50	1.55	1.50	1.60	1.75	
1965	60.00	65.00	60.00	72.50	75.00	
1996	125.00	152.50	150.00	160.00	230.00	

YEAR	PR-64BN	PR-64RB	PR-64RD	PR-65BN	PR-65RB	PR-65RD
1938	$1.00	$1.00	$1.10	$1.00	$1.00	$1.10
1944	1.60	1.60	1.75	1.60	1.60	1.75
1965	67.50	74.00	77.50	70.00	75.00	84.00
1996	200.00	210.00	450.00	290.00	400.00	2,000.00

Notes

Collecting commentary: Considered along with 1884 to be a somewhat scarcer date among those of the decade, but, unlike 1885, 1886 when selected from hoards of worn Indian cents years ago did not sell for a premium.

The Type I and Type II varieties of Indian cents were not widely known until the 1950s and not widely collected until recent years when Walter Breen, Richard Snow, the *Guide Book,* and other entities publicized them. The first knowledge of this was attributed to James Reynolds of Flint, Michigan, June 1949, in "Cent Design Changed in 1886," *The Numismatic Scrapbook Magazine.*

The certification merry-go-round: Concerning a particularly nice 1886 Type I business strike cent Sam Lukes commented:[1] "In November of 1991 I purchased an 1886 Type I from Julian Leidman. The coin was NGC MS-64 RB. When I saw the coin, I felt that it had a shot at being graded MS-65 RD, so I sold it 'as is' to a client and coaxed him into breaking it out of the NGC holder and submitting it to PCGS. He did, and it came back as MS-65 RD! I'm sure my client is happy!"

Cent shortage at Macy's: During the 1886 Christmas season at Macy's store in New York City there was a shortage of one-cent pieces. According to an account, Jerome B. Wheeler, a partner in the firm, journeyed to Washington to personally see the secretary of the Treasury and persuade him to secure an order with the director of the Philadelphia Mint for "$10,000 in brand new copper cents."[2]

New Mint director: 1886, May 6: J.P. Kimball, who had served in the post since 1885, was confirmed as Mint director and would remain until 1889.

---

[1] Letter, April 8, 1996.
[2] Edward Hungerford in his book, *The Romance of a Great Store,* as quoted by *The Numismatic Scrapbook Magazine,* April 1944, p. 312. Why a telephone call wasn't placed to Washington or a telegram sent was not explained. However, it makes a good story.

1886 Indian Cent

Type II

IDENTIFICATION: On Type I cents the last feather of the Indian's headdress points between the I and the C of AMERICA; on Type II (as described here) it points between the C and the A.

1886 Type I (left) and Type II obverses. Note that on the Type I the last feather of the headdress points between the I and the C, and on the Type II the feather points between the C and the A.

Business Strikes:

Business strike mintage: Estimated 4,000,000 from a total mintage of the year of 17,650,000.

Number of business strike obverse dies made: 45 (combined for Type I and Type II) + 1 Proof Type II die used to make a few business strikes.

Average number of coins struck from typical obverse die: 410,465 (not including business strikes from the aforementioned Proof die).

Availability in Mint State: Quite scarce, especially in high grades and with good aesthetic characteristics. However, in low Mint State levels and not brilliant, many exist.[1] Worth a strong premium if a gem. Bright red gems are especially elusive. The

---

[1] Richard Snow, Letter, April 10, 1996.

price differential for this vs. Type I is a phenomenon of recent years; earlier, the difference in availability was largely unknown.

Availability in circulated grades: Slightly scarce within the context of the 1880s decade, but common enough in well-worn grades.

Characteristics of striking: Usually sharp.

Market Prices (1886 Type II business strikes)

YEAR	G-4	VG-8	F-12	VF-20	EF-40	AU-50
1938	$0.07	$0.10	$0.25	$0.40	$0.50	$0.75
1944	.15	.20	.35	.45	.60	.75
1965	2.50	3.75	7.50	12.50	19.00	25.00
1996	3.10	6.00	12.50	32.50	70.00	100.00

YEAR	MS-60BN	MS-60RB	MS-63BN	MS-63RB	MS-63RD	
1938	$0.90	$0.90	$0.90	$0.90	$1.10	
1944	1.00	1.00	1.00	1.10	1.25	
1965	40.00	42.00	40.00	43.00	45.00	
1996	210.00	210.00	250.00	455.00	850.00	

YEAR	MS-64BN	MS-64RB	MS-64RD	MS-65BN	MS-65RB	MS-65RD
1938	$0.90	$0.90	$1.10	$0.90	$0.90	$1.10
1944	1.00	1.10	1.25	1.00	1.10	1.25
1965	41.00	44.50	50.00	42.50	46.00	55.00
1996	600.00	1,250.00	2,800.00	800.00	2,800.00	7,500.00

Proofs:

Proof mintage: Proof mintage reported: 4,290 for Type I and II combined. The Type II pieces are somewhat scarcer. The Type I pieces are slightly more plentiful in Proof format, based upon a new study by Richard Snow who now estimates a revised Proof mintage of 2,490 for the Type I and 1,800 for Type II.[1]

One Proof obverse die has a repunched date; this die was also used to make some business strikes.[2]

Proof commentary: Pieces with rich brown-toned surfaces are from long-term hoards; see commentary under 1879 and notes under 1886 Type I Proof. Many 1885 and 1886 (both types) Proof cents have rice purple iridescence over brown surfaces.[3]

---

[1] Richard Snow, letter, April 10, 1996; as stated under notes for Type I Proofs, this is based upon new studies and is different information from that in his book (which suggested a mintage of 1,800 for Type I Proofs and 2,500 for Type II).

[2] Larry R. Steve, letter, April 12, 1996.

[3] Observation of John Dannreuther re: coins submitted to PCGS; letter, May 16, 1996.

Brian Wagner noted:[1] "In seven years of observing certified Indian cents I have *never* seen a red specimen of the 1886 Type II in Proof. I consider this date to be the scarcest of the bronze Indian cents in red Proof except for the 1864 L Proof. This coin is also infrequently encountered in red and brown or even in brown Proof."

The values for high-grade Proofs listed below are thus highly theoretical; actual auction or other transactions may vary widely.

Market Prices (1886 Type II Proofs)

YEAR	PR-60BN	PR-60RB	PR-63BN	PR-63RB	PR-63RD	
1938	$1.00	$1.00	$1.00	$1.00	$1.10	
1944	1.50	1.55	1.50	1.60	1.75	
1965	60.00	65.00	60.00	72.50	75.00	
1996	140.00	170.00	172.50	180.00	1,000.00	

YEAR	PR-64BN	PR-64RB	PR-64RD	PR-65BN	PR-65RB	PR-65RD
1938	$1.00	$1.00	$1.10	$1.00	$1.00	$1.10
1944	1.60	1.60	1.75	1.60	1.60	1.75
1965	67.50	74.00	77.50	70.00	75.00	84.00â
1996	225.00	450.00	2,500.00	460.00	780.00	7,250.00

Notes

Collecting commentary: Although in the 1990s the 1886 Type II is considered to be the rarer of the two types in Mint State, there was no market differential until recent times.

As a date the 1886 has always been considered to be second scarcest of the 1880s (1885 is scarcest).

---

[1] Letter, May 3, 1996.

1887 Indian Cent

Business Strikes:

Business strike mintage: 45,223,523.

Number of business strike obverse dies made: 153

Average number of coins struck from typical obverse die: 295,579

Availability in Mint State: Plentiful for the era. Often with much red, but spotting is a problem (ditto for other dates of this generation).

Availability in circulated grades: Common.

Characteristics of striking: Varies. Sometimes seen softly struck from worn dies, thus giving a granular appearance to the fields, particularly the obverse.

Market Prices (1887 business strikes)

YEAR	G-4	VG-8	F-12	VF-20	EF-40	AU-50
1938	$0.05	$0.08	$0.15	$0.20	$0.25	$0.40
1944	.10	.15	.25	.40	.50	.60
1965	.65	1.25	2.75	4.50	8.00	12.00
1996	1.35	1.75	3.00	5.00	13.00	25.00

YEAR	MS-60BN	MS-60RB	MS-63BN	MS-63RB	MS-63RD
1938	$0.65	$0.65	$0.70	$0.65	$0.75
1944	.85	.85	.85	.90	1.00
1965	21.50	22.50	21.50	23.50	30.00
1996	35.00	50.00	36.00	105.00	130.00

YEAR	MS-64BN	MS-64RB	MS-64RD	MS-65BN	MS-65RB	MS-65RD
1938	$0.65	$0.70	$0.75	$0.65	$0.70	$0.75
1944	.85	.90	1.00	.85	.90	1.00
1965	22.50	25.00	31.50	23.50	26.50	32.50
1996	55.00	125.00	250.00	80.00	325.00	600.00

Proofs:

Proof mintage: 2,960.

Proof commentary: Most Proofs show toning; red Proofs are very rare (see Appendix IV for detailed discussion). Pieces with rich brown-toned surfaces are from long-term hoards; see commentary under 1879. Some Proofs are carelessly made (this cf. Breen, *Encyclopedia of Proof Coins*). Clerks at the Mint were very casual with their handling of Proofs during this era, and quite possibly many coins were fingerprinted or otherwise impaired before leaving the Mint (some readers will remember a related situation occurring at the Royal Canadian Mint in the 1950s, when Canadian cents sold to collectors later developed fingerprints and spots).

Market Prices (1887 Proofs)

YEAR	PR-60BN	PR-60RB	PR-63BN	PR-63RB	PR-63RD	
1938	$1.00	$1.00	$1.00	$1.00	$1.10	
1944	1.75	1.80	1.75	1.80	2.00	
1965	60.00	61.00	60.00	61.50	62.50	
1996	120.00	135.00	135.00	140.00	215.00 .	

YEAR	PR-64BN	PR-64RB	PR-64RD	PR-65BN	PR-65RB	PR-65RD
1938	$1.00	$1.00	$1.10	$1.00	$1.00	$1.10
1944	1.75	1.80	2.00	1.75	1.80	2.10
1965	61.00	62.00	63.50	61.00	62.50	65.00
1996	160.00	180.00	1,250.00	280.00	360.00	4,500.00

Notes

Doubled die: One variety, Snow-1, shows slight doubling at the TY of LIBERTY and at OF AMERICA and is quite rare.

A possibility to look for: In 1887 a number of unused 1886 dies were overdated, including at least three different dies for nickel three-cent pieces (two Proof dies and one business strike) and multiple dies for Morgan dollars. I would not be surprised if an 1887/6 Indian cent turns up someday, but I have never heard even a rumor of one.

Distribution: In 1886-1887 there was a distribution problem with one-cent pieces and other minor coins. They were piling up in Sub-Treasury offices which redeemed them when presented "in sums not less than $20." Meanwhile, remote areas as well as urban centers were suffering from a shortage of the same coins. Adams Express Co. had the contract for shipping minor coins.

The 1887 *Mint Report* noted in part (in "bureaucratese"): "Part of the demand for minor coin, which has arisen to an unprecedented extent during the latter part of the last 12 months [since January 1887], during the first part of which period the coinage of minor coin had not been resumed since February 16, 1885, is at least unreasonable, it having appeared that, in the exercise of a preference for fresh coin, applications to the mint at Philadelphia for large sums of minor coin have been from the very cities where an accumulation was reported in the Sub-Treasuries." (Stated simply, the Mint director felt that it was unreasonable that parties in certain cities should request newly-minted Indian cents and Liberty nickels from the Mint while stocks of these same denominations existed in Treasury facilities in the same cities.)

The account further stated that certain merchants who received large quantities of current coins and turned them into the Sub-Treasuries were the same people who asked for "fresh" coins of the same type from the Mint. Mint Director James P. Kimball suggested, among other ideas, that the Treasury be given the power "to discriminate against unreasonable demands for new coin when current old coin is available."

Cents to the American West: The *American Journal of Numismatics,* July 1887, reported that up to this year, "in San Francisco the smallest coin has been the dime, whilst in St. Louis and New Orleans, nothing circulates less than the 5¢ nickel." It was related that recently merchants had introduced small denominations, "so that large quantities of 5¢ and 1¢ pieces are now forwarded by the Mint to California and Oregon, where they are delivered free of expense, by the government."

1888/7 Indian Cent

(Photo courtesy of Larry Steve)

Business Strikes:

Business strike mintage: Unknown. Probably very small and on the order of just a few thousand pieces.

Number of business strike obverse dies made: At least two (based upon 2 varieties being known today)

Average number of coins struck from typical obverse die: 205,988 (for all 1888 dies; the 1888/7 Variety I may be many fewer, as the die is believed to have failed at a fairly early time).

Availability in Mint State: As of 1996 it is estimated that four Mint State coins exist, one of which was first certified MS-62 RB despite a gash on Miss Liberty's cheek (per correspondence with Sam Lukes reprinted below); now it is graded MS-63 RB (PCGS). Another may grade MS-64 or MS-65. The two discovery coins, each Mint State, have not been certified.

Availability in circulated grades: Very rare. Perhaps only about two dozen worn pieces are known, mostly in lower grades.[1]

Characteristics of striking: Average sharpness.

---

[1] Richard Snow, letter, April 10, 1996; this is based upon new studies and is different information from that in his book, *Flying Eagle & Indian Cents*. Snow stated that the Type I is believed to be slightly more plentiful now; the mintage estimates are by the author (QDB).

Market Prices (1888/7 business strikes)

YEAR	G-4	VG-8	F-12	VF-20	EF-40	AU-50
1996	1,000.00	1,500.00	3,000.00	5,000.00	7,500.00	12,500.00

YEAR	MS-60BN	MS-60RB	MS-63BN	MS-63RB	MS-63RD	
1996	15,000.00	17,500.00	25,000.00	30,000.00	—	

YEAR	MS-64BN	MS-64RB	MS-64RD	MS-65BN	MS-65RB	MS-65RD
1996	—	—	—	—	—	—

Notes

Collecting commentary for 1888/7 Snow-1. Overdate. Two specimens, both Mint State, were discovered by James F. Ruddy in 1970 from a small cache of Indian cents found in the attic of a mansion in Virginia.[1] Both had a distinctive "cud" die break on the left rim at the 9:00 position. One was sold to Robert Marks and the other to Julian Leidman. These remain the finest known and are tentatively represented by the MS-63 RB prices above, although they certainly could grade higher, even *much* higher. I have not seen them in years and do not remember them well enough to equate them to today's numbers.

Since Jim Ruddy's discovery the variety has become widely publicized, but even so, only two more Mint State pieces have come to light plus perhaps up to two dozen worn examples. Snow-1. Fivaz-Stanton 1¢-010. FND-001. The market prices are highly subjective, as specimens are few and far between, especially in higher grades.

Richard Snow commented in April 1996 that "after a diligent search only 13 specimens are known; often called the 'Ruddy Variety.'"[2] The following registry of known specimens was supplied by Snow:

1. MS-65 RD. Sold for a reported $43,000 a few years ago, per Sam Lukes.

2. MS-63 RB (PCGS). Sold by Eagle Eye Rare Coins for $22,000. Until December 1993, this coin was graded 62 RB by ANACS. Presently in the Mick Arconti Collection.

3. Mint State. One of two Ruddy discovery coins; current Mint State numerical designation not known.

4. Mint State. One of two Ruddy discovery coins; current Mint State numerical designation not known.

5. AU-50.

6. EF-40.

7. VF-30.

8. VF corroded.

9. F-15.

10. G-6 (PCGS). Sold by Eagle Eye Rare Coins for $750 in 1992. The plate coin in the Snow book.

11. G-4 (PCGS).

---

[1] Subsequently published in several places including *The Numismatist,* April 1970, p. 531.
[2] Letter, April 10, 1996.

12. G-4.

13. G-4.

Concerning market values for the 1888/7 Snow-1 overdate, these are highly speculative. The figures I give above are mere guesses. See Sam Luke's second commentary below for additional pricing information.

Commentary for second or "Type 2" 1888/7. Snow-2: In addition, a so-called
"Type 2" 1888/7 overdate (also with the added feature of having the first 8 as well as
the second 8 doubled) was discovered by Bill Fivaz and first published in *Longacre's
Ledger,* spring 1991 issue, but is very weakly defined, although high-grade specimens show the overdate unequivocally. Sometimes called the "Fivaz Variety" (as
compared to the "Ruddy Variety" Snow-1).

For some other specimens a measure of faith is needed to make out the overdate,
and on worn examples the overdate features may not be visible at all. This variety
sells for far less due to its lack of overdate sharpness. This variety also has a spur
protruding from the front of Miss Liberty's necklace into the field (an excellent illustration is found in Steve-Flynn, p. 144).[1] Snow-2. Fivaz-Stanton 1¢-010.7. FND-002.

Popularity: The sharper variety (Ruddy Variety, Snow-1) is listed as No. 2 among
the top 20 most popular of all unusual Indian cent varieties, by Larry R. Steve and
Kevin J. Flynn in *Flying Eagle and Indian Cent Die Varieties.*

Commentary by Sam Lukes: The following comment was written in 1993 by small-
cent specialist Sam Lukes, before the great expansion of interest in Indian cents
caused by the Snow and Steve-Flynn books occurred, and reflects the rarity of Mint
State coins as of that time:

> Regarding...the extremely rare Type 1 1888/7 overdate Indian cent... I have
> been tracking this variety ever since Jim Ruddy discovered it in 1970.
>
> None of the original 'discovery' pieces were sold at auction by your firm so far
> as my records ascertain. One was sold to the distinguished Arkansas collector,
> Robert Marks, while the second specimen was acquired by dealer Julian Leidman.

---

[1] Bill Fivaz' discovery specimen was discussed by Walter Breen in *Longacre's Ledger,* April 1991, as part
of a feature by Larry R. Steve in "The F.IND.ERS Report" column, pp. 28-31.

I have before me your Summer 1975 *Rare Coin Review* No. 23, p. 22, where the overdate was offered for $2,995.00. There is an enlarged photo of the last two digits of the date which reveals the underlying 7 as well as a normal-size photograph of the obverse and reverse of the coin. The piece was described as 'Lovely Red and Brown Uncirculated.'

I'm sure you remember the example I sent you for your perusal several years ago which was graded MS-62RB and reposed in an ANACS Cache holder. That coin was sharply struck, was devoid of carbon, and exhibited 85% red on the obverse and at least 90% red on its reverse. What kept it from a higher grade was, unfortunately, a severe gash located directly in the center of Miss Liberty's cheek! The coin was at that time offered to me for $14,000, and later it was reduced in price to $7,500, whereas it immediately was sold.

A fourth specimen (also in Mint State) was offered to me at about that same time from another dealer. The coin, although 'raw,' was fully red and original and graded as MS-65RD by that particular dealer, who was asking $50,000. I declined at that level and was informed within a year that the coin was privately sold for $43,000!

So far as I know, the four coins mentioned are the only Type 1 1888/7 Indian Head cents I am aware of which are in Mint State. I...am unable to turn up any decent looking examples above the grade of Very Good. I remember being offered one that someone had found with a metal detector for $295, but the coin was corroded and quite unattractive—as one might guess.

Second commentary by Sam Lukes:[1]

The 1888/7 Snow-1 which you mention [in your manuscript] is the ANACS MS-62RB which I sent to you for your Research Department years ago. It has since been upgraded to a PCGS MS-63RB (I always felt that *without* the gash on Miss Liberty's cheek, it would have easily graded MS-64RB). It has been offered within the last year for over $40,000 by the owner.

Of course you already know about the two Mint State discovery pieces your former partner James Ruddy found over 25 years ago in a Virginia estate. It would be exciting to know where those two coins are today and what they might grade if submitted to the grading services?...

Further in regard to the pricing structure of the 1888/7 S-1: Several Good examples have traded hands in excess of $1,000-$1,500. In January 1996 I sold the lone PCGS VF-30 example to a client of mine for $7,250, no doubt a record for that grade! I had acquired the coin 'raw' from a customer of mine and informed him that I felt the coin could grade VF, which it did. My selling price was based on several current factors. The first was that another piece had surfaced about that same time and had been submitted to NGC wherein it was encapsulated as AU-50 and was consequently sold immediately (sight-unseen) for a number which approached five figures! The final price for the PCGS VF-30 I sold was insisted upon by my client who owned it.

The VF-30 example was a light to medium tannish-brown with normal circulation wear, no carbon spots, and extremely boldly struck in the area of the overdate, which no doubt was representative of an early die strike.

---

[1] Letter, April 8, 1996.

1888 Indian Cent

Business Strikes:

Business strike mintage: 37,489,832 (includes 1888/7)

Number of business strike obverse dies made: 182 less two for the 1888/7, or net 180 dies.

Average number of coins struck from typical obverse die: 205,988

Availability in Mint State: Available in all Mint State levels, but sharply struck gems are elusive. Bright red gems, if unspotted and never dipped, are in the rarity class. As always, cherrypicking is advised, as coins can be certified as "MS-65 RD" and still have spots. Prices for very high level coins given below are for hand-picked gems; spotty coins, even if graded MS-65 RD, will sell for far less.

Availability in circulated grades: Common.

Characteristics of striking: Varies.

Market Prices (1888 business strikes)

YEAR	G-4	VG-8	F-12	VF-20	EF-40	AU-50
1938	$0.06	$0.10	$0.20	$0.35	$0.50	$0.75
1944	.15	.20	.35	.45	.60	.75
1965	.70	1.50	2.75	4.50	8.00	14.00
1996	1.35	1.80	3.00	5.00	13.25	25.00

YEAR	MS-60BN	MS-60RB	MS-63BN	MS-63RB	MS-63RD	
1938	$0.90	$0.90	$0.90	$0.90	$1.00	
1944	1.00	1.00	1.00	1.10	1.25	
1965	26.00	27.50	26.00	29.00	34.00	
1996	37.00	60.00	40.00	115.00	275.00	

YEAR	MS-64BN	MS-64RB	MS-64RD	MS-65BN	MS-65RB	MS-65RD
1938	$0.90	$0.90	$1.00	$0.90	$0.90	$1.00
1944	1.00	1.10	1.25	1.00	1.10	1.25
1965	27.50	31.00	36.00	29.00	33.00	39.00
1996	100.00	245.00	650.00	130.00	950.00	2,500.00

Proofs:

Proof mintage: 4,582.

Proof commentary: Most Proofs show toning; red Proofs are very rare (see commentary in Appendix IV). Pieces with rich brown-toned surfaces are from long-term hoards; see commentary under 1879. Carelessly made and handled at the Mint.

At least two different obverses were used to coin Proofs this year, one of which displays misplaced digits in the denticles.

Market Prices (1888 Proofs)

YEAR	PR-60BN	PR-60RB	PR-63BN	PR-63RB	PR-63RD	
1938	$1.00	$1.00	$1.00	$1.00	$1.10	
1944	1.50	1.55	1.50	1.60	1.75	
1965	52.00	53.00	52.00	55.00	57.50	
1996	110.00	130.00	130.00	140.00	185.00	

YEAR	PR-64BN	PR-64RB	PR-64RD	PR-65BN	PR-65RB	PR-65RD
1938	$1.00	$1.00	$1.10	$1.00	$1.00	$1.10
1944	1.60	1.60	1.75	1.60	1.60	1.75
1965	52.00	55.00	58.50	53.00	55.00	60.00
1996	165.00	185.00	1,000.00	275.00	425.00	5,000.00

Notes

Collecting commentary: The late Arthur Kelley of St. Louis liked the 1888 date in particular, of all denominations, and bought Proofs whenever he could find them. He was fond of calling these "Oldsmobile coins," for the Oldsmobile automobile was made with an engine called an "88." Kelley handled many rarities in his day and was a very fine person. As he did not conduct auctions, nor was he well known for his writing, he has been largely forgotten by numismatic historians.

Record production: From the 1888 *Mint Report:* "During the fiscal year [ended June 30] the minor coinage was the largest in the history of the Mint at Philadelphia...." It was noted that during the year 275,557.55 pounds of cent planchets had been delivered to the mint, and the cost for these was $74,026.69.

This record production took its toll on accuracy, and a number of dies of this year show repunching or other errors (which, of course, is good news for numismatists).

Where they went: The same report gives an interesting insight into which areas of the country used minor coins. No new Indian cents were sent to Arizona, Idaho, Montana, New Mexico, or Utah. Relatively low amounts were sent to other Western states. The state of West Virginia received more cents than all three West Coast states combined:

Alabama: 120,000 cents distributed.	Mississippi: 4,000.
Arizona: None.	Missouri: 332,000.
Arkansas: 100,000.	Montana: None.
California: 62,000.	Nebraska: 462,000.
Colorado: 87,000.	New Hampshire: 316,000.
Connecticut: 685,000.	New Jersey: 1,183,000.
Dakota: 87,500.	New Mexico: None.
Delaware: 160,000.	New York: 11,016,800.
District of Columbia: 20,000.	North Carolina: 253,000.
Florida: 45,500.	Ohio: 2,747,500.
Georgia: 352,000.	Oregon: 12,000.
Idaho: None.	Pennsylvania: 4,006,500.
Illinois: 4,900,500.	Rhode Island: 515,000.
Indiana: 926,000.	South Carolina: 124,500.
Iowa: 996,000.	Tennessee: 253,000.
Kansas: 441,500.	Texas: 6,000.
Kentucky: 270,000.	Utah: None.
Louisiana: 60,000.	Vermont: 148,000.
Maine: 199,000.	Virginia: 337,500.
Maryland: 987,000.	Washington: 12,000.
Massachusetts: 2,446,000.	West Virginia: 96,000.
Michigan: 1,599,000.	Wisconsin; 852,000.
Minnesota: 790,500.	Wyoming: None.

Statistics such as the above indicate why cents were not struck at Western mints during the 19th century; there was only a trivial demand for them.

Design change proposed: In 1888 Director of the Mint James P. Kimball, who from the expanded size of the *Mint Report* under his tenure was one of the most enthusiastic and conscientious directors, had a bill introduced into Congress to provide for the change of the design of numerous denominations, including the one-cent piece, which he said had not been changed since 1864 [*sic*]. No changes were made. Several years earlier in 1884 the Senate passed a bill which provided in part for the employment, "temporarily, [of] five persons distinguished in departments of art or in knowledge of coinage and medals....who shall investigate and examine the whole subject of our existing system of coinage, with a view to its improvement and greater perfection of execution as to metals, relative value of the minor coins, and also as to devices, legends, and inscriptions...." This bill did not pass the House of Representatives and languished. Also see comment under 1900 listing.

Meanwhile, in Michigan: In Monroe, MI, Dr. Geo. (as he liked to style his first name in print) F. Heath, medical doctor, classical scholar, and coin collector, began publishing *The American Numismatist,* but soon changed it to *The Numismatist* when he learned that another publication had been issued with the "American" name. Later, this became the official publication of the American Numismatic Association (founded in 1891).

1889 Indian Cent

Business Strikes:

Business strike mintage: 48,866,025.

Number of business strike obverse dies made: 223

Average number of coins struck from typical obverse die: 219,130

Availability in Mint State: Available in all Mint State grades; high-grade fully brilliant, undipped, uncleaned coins are scarcer. Bright red, undipped and unspotted gems are particularly elusive.

Availability in circulated grades: Common.

Characteristics of striking: Striking quality varies. Some have pebbly surfaces from worn dies.

Market Prices (1889 business strikes)

YEAR	G-4	VG-8	F-12	VF-20	EF-40	AU-50
1938	$0.05	$0.08	$0.15	$0.20	$0.30	$0.40
1944	.10	.15	.25	.40	.50	.60
1965	.65	1.30	2.40	4.25	6.75	12.00
1996	1.35	1.65	2.75	4.50	12.50	25.00

YEAR	MS-60BN	MS-60RB	MS-63BN	MS-63RB	MS-63RD
1938	$0.70	$0.70	$0.70	$0.70	$0.75
1944	.85	.85	.85	.90	1.00
1965	22.00	23.50	22.00	24.50	26.00
1996	35.00	50.00	37.00	65.00	150.00

YEAR	MS-64BN	MS-64RB	MS-64RD	MS-65BN	MS-65RB	MS-65RD
1938	$0.70	$0.70	$0.80	$0.70	$0.75	$0.80
1944	.85	.90	1.00	.85	.90	1.00
1965	23.00	25.00	27.50	24.00	26.50	30.00
1996	75.00	125.00	475.00	100.00	350.00	2,500.00

Proofs:

Proof mintage: 3,336.

Proof commentary: Often seen spotted. Pieces with rich brown-toned surfaces are from long-term hoards; see commentary under 1879.

Most are from a clashed obverse die with part of the C in CENT visible in front of Miss Liberty. On the reverse in the corresponding area, the outline of Miss Liberty's forehead is seen.

Market Prices (1889 Proofs)

YEAR	PR-60BN	PR-60RB	PR-63BN	PR-63RB	PR-63RD
1938	$1.00	$1.00	$1.00	$1.10	$1.10
1944	1.35	1.40	1.35	1.40	1.50
1965	52.00	53.00	52.00	55.00	57.50
1996	110.00	132.00	130.00	140.00	185.00

YEAR	PR-64BN	PR-64RB	PR-64RD	PR-65BN	PR-65RB	PR-65RD
1938	$1.00	$1.00	$1.10	$1.00	$1.00	$1.10
1944	1.40	1.40	1.50	1.40	1.40	1.50
1965	52.00	55.00	58.50	53.00	55.00	60.00
1996	170.00	175.00	450.00	300.00	325.00	1,100.00

Notes

Collecting commentary: No particular excitement with this or other dates of the era, but collected as part of the later 1879-1909 series.

Requests denied: In order to avoid unnecessary coinage of minor coins, the superintendent of the Philadelphia Mint was instructed to refuse requests from merchants for newly-minted coins if the same people were located in a city with a federal Sub-Treasury that had on hand a supply of older but still current designs.[1]

New Mint director: 1889, December 19: Edward O. Leech was confirmed as Mint director. He had been in the post since October 1889, and he served until 1893.

---

[1] 1889 *Mint Report,* p. 18.

1890 Indian Cent

Business Strikes:

Business strike mintage: 57,180,114.

Number of business strike obverse dies made: 222

Average number of coins struck from typical obverse die: 257,568

Availability in Mint State: Available in all Mint State grades; high-grade fully brilliant, undipped, uncleaned coins are scarcer. *Sharply struck* gems are rare, however, especially if unspotted.

Availability in circulated grades: Common.

Characteristics of striking: Most are indifferently struck.

Market Prices (1890 business strikes)

YEAR	G-4	VG-8	F-12	VF-20	EF-40	AU-50
1938	$0.05	$0.08	$0.15	$0.20	$0.30	$0.40
1944	.10	.15	.25	.40	.50	.60
1965	.65	1.30	2.40	4.25	6.75	12.00
1996	1.35	1.65	2.50	4.50	10.00	22.50

YEAR	MS-60BN	MS-60RB	MS-63BN	MS-63RB	MS-63RD
1938	$0.70	$0.70	$0.70	$0.70	$0.75
1944	.85	.85	.85	.90	1.00
1965	22.00	23.50	22.00	24.50	26.00
1996	35.00	48.00	36.00	65.00	130.00

YEAR	MS-64BN	MS-64RB	MS-64RD	MS-65BN	MS-65RB	MS-65RD
1938	$0.70	$0.70	$0.80	$0.70	$0.75	$0.80
1944	.85	.90	1.00	.85	.90	1.00
1965	23.00	25.00	27.50	24.00	26.50	30.00
1996	67.50	105.00	450.00	85.00	335.00	1,500.00

Proofs:

Proof mintage: 2,740.

Proof commentary: Often seen spotted. Pieces with rich brown-toned surfaces are from long-term hoards; see commentary under 1879.

Market Prices (1890 Proofs)

YEAR	PR-60BN	PR-60RB	PR-63BN	PR-63RB	PR-63RD	
1938	$1.00	$1.00	$1.00	$1.00	$1.10	
1944	1.75	1.80	1.75	1.80	2.00	
1965	52.00	53.00	52.00	55.00	57.50	
1996	85.00	100.00	115.00	140.00	175.00	

YEAR	PR-64BN	PR-64RB	PR-64RD	PR-65BN	PR-65RB	PR-65RD
1938	$1.00	$1.00	$1.10	$1.00	$1.00	$1.10
1944	1.75	1.80	2.00	1.75	1.80	2.10
1965	52.00	55.00	58.50	53.00	55.00	60.00
1996	165.00	195.00	365.00	335.00	410.00	2,000.00

Notes

Collecting commentary: No particular excitement with this or other dates of the era, but collected as part of the later 1879-1909 series.

"Blob" 9: The third digit (9) in the date has the bottom ball touching the top curve of the 9; on worn pieces the connection appears continuous. This blob-type 9 appears on various Indian cents of the 1890s and 1900s until 1909, in which year the 9 was redesigned to an open configuration. The appearance of the 9 on cents from 1890 to 1908 is most blob-like when the date logotype was punched deeply into the working die. On dies with the logotype punched lightly, there is a small separation between the bottom ball and the top curve.

Sources of planchets: In February 1890 the Mint entered into a contract with the Scovill Manufacturing Co., Waterbury, CT, for the supply of 500,000 pounds of one-cent blanks at $0.1994 per pound.[1]

The *American Journal of Numismatics,* April 1890, p. 95, related this:

---

[1] 1890 *Mint Report,* p. 19. Other contracts were let during this era including to Scovill; this citation is representative.

The copper used in the manufacture of pennies is of the very best quality. The metal is shipped in bulk from the mines to the factories of Merchant & Co., in Connecticut. There it is rolled and stamped out in circles of the requisite size. These circles are perfectly plain, with the exception of the raised or milled edge. At this stage the pieces intended for pennies are as bright as gold pieces.... In this condition they are delivered to the Mint.... 100 pennies weigh exactly one pound. When these pieces reach the Mint they are subjected to the finishing process, which consists of stamping them with the denomination, lettering, and characters seen on the coins when they reach the public.... The copper pennies require a pressure of 10 tons avoirdupois....

Design change requested: E.O. Leech, new director of the Mint, continued the request for authorization to change numerous coin designs to more artistic motifs. Once again, nothing came of the move.

1891 Indian Cent

Business Strikes:

Business strike mintage: 47,070,000.

Number of business strike obverse dies made: 172

Average number of coins struck from typical obverse die: 273,663

Availability in Mint State: Available in all Mint State grades; high-grade fully brilliant, undipped, uncleaned coins are scarcer.

Availability in circulated grades: Common.

Characteristics of striking: Varies. In general, cents of the 1890s are not deeply and sharply struck.

Market Prices (1891 business strikes)

YEAR	G-4	VG-8	F-12	VF-20	EF-40	AU-50
1938	$0.05	$0.08	$0.15	$0.20	$0.30	$0.40
1944	.10	.15	.25	.40	.50	.60
1965	.65	1.30	2.40	4.25	6.75	12.00
1996	1.35	1.65	2.50	4.50	10.00	22.50

YEAR	MS-60BN	MS-60RB	MS-63BN	MS-63RB	MS-63RD
1938	$0.70	$0.70	$0.70	$0.70	$0.75
1944	.85	.85	.85	.90	1.00
1965	22.00	23.50	22.00	24.50	26.00
1996	34.00	45.00	34.50	65.00	125.00

YEAR	MS-64BN	MS-64RB	MS-64RD	MS-65BN	MS-65RB	MS-65RD
1938	$0.70	$0.70	$0.80	$0.70	$0.75	$0.80
1944	.85	.90	1.00	.85	.90	1.00
1965	23.00	25.00	27.50	24.00	26.50	30.00
1996	64.00	115.00	350.00	82.50	325.00	1,500.00

Proofs:

Proof mintage: 2,350.

Proof commentary: Fairly scarce at the gem level. Pieces with rich brown-toned surfaces are from long-term hoards; see commentary under 1879. However, 1891 is reduced in mintage quantity from the average of the 1880s, and the downward trend would continue.

Market Prices (1891 Proofs)

YEAR	PR-60BN	PR-60RB	PR-63BN	PR-63RB	PR-63RD	
1938	$1.00	$1.00	$1.00	$1.00	$1.10	
1944	1.75	1.80	1.75	1.80	2.00	
1965	52.00	53.00	52.00	55.00	57.50	
1996	85.00	100.00	115.00	150.00	175.00	

YEAR	PR-64BN	PR-64RB	PR-64RD	PR-65BN	PR-65RB	PR-65RD
1938	$1.00	$1.00	$1.10	$1.00	$1.00	$1.10
1944	1.75	1.80	2.00	1.75	1.80	2.10
1965	52.00	55.00	58.50	53.00	55.00	60.00
1996	165.00	195.00	345.00	325.00	410.00	2,000.00

Notes

"9" punch: The third digit (9) in the date has the bottom ball touching the top curve of the 9; on worn pieces the connection appears continuous. The 1891 is similar to 1890 in this regard. This situation occurs on some later dates as well, especially on business strikes with the date logotype punched deeply into the working die.

Cent not included: On April 4, 1891, the Treasury Department sent a circular letter to artists inviting new designs for silver coins (designs of which had been called "inelegant"), but not mentioning the bronze cent.[1]

---

[1] 1891 *Mint Report*, p. 69.

1892 Indian Cent

Business Strikes:

Business strike mintage: 37,647,087.

Number of business strike obverse dies made: 162

Average number of coins struck from typical obverse die: 232,389

Availability in Mint State: Available in all Mint State grades; high-grade fully brilliant, undipped, uncleaned coins are scarcer.

Availability in circulated grades: Common.

Characteristics of striking: Varies.

Market Prices (1892 business strikes)

YEAR	G-4	VG-8	F-12	VF-20	EF-40	AU-50
1938	$0.05	$0.08	$0.15	$0.20	$0.25	$0.40
1944	.20	.30	.50	.65	.80	.95
1965	0.70	1.45	2.75	5.00	8.50	14.00
1996	1.35	1.65	2.50	4.50	10.00	22.50

YEAR	MS-60BN	MS-60RB	MS-63BN	MS-63RB	MS-63RD	
1938	$0.65	$0.65	$0.70	$0.65	$0.75	
1944	1.30	1.35	1.30	1.40	1.50	
1965	25.00	26.00	25.00	27.00	31.00	
1996	35.00	45.00	36.00	65.00	117.50	

YEAR	MS-64BN	MS-64RB	MS-64RD	MS-65BN	MS-65RB	MS-65RD
1938	$0.65	$0.70	$0.75	$0.65	$0.70	$0.75
1944	1.40	1.40	1.50	1.40	1.40	1.60
1965	26.00	28.00	32.00	28.25	29.00	35.00
1996	62.00	115.00	300.00	77.50	400.00	1,200.00

Proofs:

Proof mintage: 2,745.

Proof commentary: Fairly scarce if gem.

Market Prices (1892 Proofs)

YEAR	PR-60BN	PR-60RB	PR-63BN	PR-63RB	PR-63RD	
1938	$1.00	$1.00	$1.00	$1.00	$1.10	
1944	1.90	2.00	1.90	2.00	2.25	
1965	55.00	55.50	55.00	57.50	60.00	
1996	85.00	100.00	115.00	150.00	175.00	

YEAR	PR-64BN	PR-64RB	PR-64RD	PR-65BN	PR-65RB	PR-65RD
1938	$1.00	$1.00	$1.10	$1.00	$1.10	$1.10
1944	2.00	2.00	2.25	2.00	2.00	2.25
1965	55.00	57.50	61.00	55.00	57.50	62.50
1996	165.00	205.00	290.00	325.00	410.00	800.00

Notes

Possible overdate: Michael Hodder commented:[1] "1892/1. I know it is not accepted, but I was shown one at the 1991 ANA Convention and it looked very convincing to me."

Meltdown: During fiscal year 1892 (ended June 30) Indian cents in the amount of 1,429,087 were made from melted-down uncurrent minor coins, primarily bronze two-cent pieces.[2]

More meltdown:[3] In July 1892 the Mint solicited bids for bronze cent planchets and nickel alloy five-cent from three sources including Benedict & Burnham Manufacturing Co. (of Waterbury, CT, a firm also numismatically remembered for having issued Hard Times tokens circa 1837), Scovill Manufacturing Co. (also of Waterbury and also a former issuer of Hard Times tokens), and Merchant & Co. (of Philadelphia).

When the bids arrived they were found to be "nearly equal" and each a sharp

---

[1] Letter, May 14, 1996.

[2] 1892 *Mint Report*, p. 24.

[3] Information from Henry T. Hettger, "Collusive Bidding on Indian Head Cent Planchets in 1892." *Longacre's Ledger*, October 1991.

advance over the latest contract price, leading Mint Director E.O. Leech, in a letter dated August 25, 1892, to call the bids a "put up job." As a result, Leech ordered the Sub-Treasury in New York City to ship to the Mint $50,000 face value of older bronze cents (five million coins) for melting and recoinage. It seems logical that these cents would have been of earlier dates, perhaps mainly of the 1860s and 1870s, as there would have been no point in returning lightly worn pieces of the 1880s and very early 1890s.

New designs for silver coins: Charles E. Barber's new Liberty Head designs for the dime, quarter, and half dollar made their debut and were struck at the Philadelphia, New Orleans, and San Francisco mints. The public paid little attention to them, however.

At the fair: America was excited about the World's Columbian Exposition, which would throw its gates open to the general public in 1893, a year later than originally planned. In connection with this event, America's first silver commemorative coins were minted: 1892 and 1893 Columbian half dollars. These were sold at the fair for $1 each, but many undistributed pieces were dumped into circulation for face value.

1893 Indian Cent

Business Strikes:

Business strike mintage: 46,640,000.

Number of business strike obverse dies made: 172

Average number of coins struck from typical obverse die: 271,163

Availability in Mint State: Available in all Mint State grades; high-grade fully brilliant, undipped, uncleaned coins are scarcer, although they are more available than are coins from the preceding several years.

Availability in circulated grades: Common.

Characteristics of striking: Varies. Really sharp pieces are in the minority.

Market Prices (1893 business strikes)

YEAR	G-4	VG-8	F-12	VF-20	EF-40	AU-50
1938	$0.05	$0.08	$0.15	$0.20	$0.25	$0.40
1944	.10	.15	.25	.40	.50	.60
1965	.60	1.30	2.40	4.00	6.25	13.00
1996	1.35	1.65	2.50	4.50	10.00	22.50

YEAR	MS-60BN	MS-60RB	MS-63BN	MS-63RB	MS-63RD	
1938	$0.65	$0.65	$0.70	$0.65	$0.75	
1944	.85	.85	.85	.90	1.00	
1965	23.00	25.00	23.00	26.00	30.00	
1996	32.00	43.00	33.00	64.00	115.00	

YEAR	MS-64BN	MS-64RB	MS-64RD	MS-65BN	MS-65RB	MS-65RD
1938	$0.65	$0.70	$0.75	$0.65	$0.70	$0.75
1944	.85	.90	1.00	.85	.90	1.00
1965	24.00	27.00	32.00	25.00	28.00	34.00
1996	60.00	115.00	210.00	72.50	300.00	600.00

Proofs:

Proof mintage: 2,195.

Proof commentary: This was a recession year in the American economy. Presumably, Proof coins were among luxury goods bought in smaller quantities.

Market Prices (1893 Proofs)

YEAR	PR-60BN	PR-60RB	PR-63BN	PR-63RB	PR-63RD	
1938	$1.00	$1.00	$1.00	$1.00	$1.10	
1944	2.20	2.20	2.20	2.30	2.50	
1965	55.00	55.50	55.00	57.50	60.00	
1996	85.00	100.00	115.00	150.00	175.00	

YEAR	PR-64BN	PR-64RB	PR-64RD	PR-65BN	PR-65RB	PR-65RD
1938	$1.00	$1.00	$1.10	$1.00	$1.00	$1.10
1944	2.20	2.30	2.50	2.25	2.35	2.60
1965	55.00	57.50	61.00	55.00	57.50	62.50
1996	165.00	235.00	310.00	325.00	490.00	1,200.00

Notes

At the fair: The World's Columbian Exposition in Chicago inspired the production of America's first commemorative coins, the aforementioned 1892 and 1893 Columbian half dollars and now the 1893 Isabella quarter, priced at $1 retail, the same price as the half dollars. Among souvenirs sold by concessionaires were Indian cents and other coins rolled out (elongated) and impressed with special dies relating to the fair. (Rolled-out "pennies" would be made on hundreds of later occasions as well.)

New Mint director: 1893, November: Robert E. Preston began serving as Mint director, was confirmed by the Senate on January 12, 1894, and remained in the post until February 1898.

1894 Indian Cent

Business Strikes:

Business strike mintage: 16,749,500. Lowest mintage of the decade.

Number of business strike obverse dies made: 55

Average number of coins struck from typical obverse die: 304,536

Availability in Mint State: Readily available, but brings a premium due to its low mintage within the decade. Blazing gems are scarce. Most are orangish in color.

Availability in circulated grades: Common overall, but the least seen of the dates of the 1890s.

Characteristics of striking: Average sharpness.

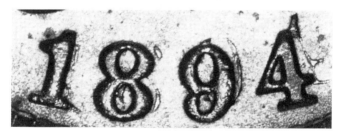

1894 REPUNCHED DATE: Ample traces of an earlier 1894 date can be seen to the right of the final date, oriented slightly higher than the final date figures. This is especially prominent at the 4. Although there are many dozens of repunched date varieties in the Indian cent series, this is considered to be the most dramatic.

Double punched date. This variety is dozens of times scarcer than the regular 1894 cent, but it is not widely known, and demand for it is limited. However, with increased interest in Indian cents in recent years, prices and awareness are both on the ascendancy. The repunching is spectacular, and it certainly is the "king" of repunched dates among Indian cents. Over the years I have located several simply by looking at "regular" 1894 cents. Listed as No. 4 among the top 20 most popular of all unusual Indian cent varieties, by Larry R. Steve and Kevin J. Flynn in *Flying Eagle and Indian Cent Die Varieties.* Snow-1. Fivaz-Stanton 1¢-011. FND-001.

As the average production for an obverse die this year was 304,536 coins, this may give a ballpark guess for the mintage of this variety.

Market Prices (1894 business strikes)

YEAR	G-4	VG-8	F-12	VF-20	EF-40	AU-50
1938	$0.07	$0.08	$0.17	$0.25	$0.30	$0.45
1944	.15	.25	.40	.50	.65	.80
1965	1.75	4.25	7.50	9.50	15.00	23.00
1996	1.75	3.00	7.50	10.00	17.50	32.50

YEAR	MS-60BN	MS-60RB	MS-63BN	MS-63RB	MS-63RD	
1938	$0.70	$0.70	$0.70	$0.75	$0.85	
1944	1.15	1.15	1.15	1.20	1.25	
1965	40.00	42.50	41.00	43.50	47.00	
1996	50.00	65.00	52.00	115.00	170.00	

YEAR	MS-64BN	MS-64RB	MS-64RD	MS-65BN	MS-65RB	MS-65RD
1938	$0.75	$0.80	$0.85	$0.75	$0.80	$0.85
1944	1.15	1.20	1.30	1.15	1.20	1.35
1965	42.50	45.00	50.00	44.00	46.00	54.00
1996	72.00	140.00	300.00	95.00	305.00	630.00

Proofs:

Proof mintage: 2,632.

Proof commentary: Popular due to the low mintage of related business strikes. Bright red gems are especially elusive.

Market Prices (1894 Proofs)

YEAR	PR-60BN	PR-60RB	PR-63BN	PR-63RB	PR-63RD	
1938	$1.00	$1.00	$1.00	$1.00	$1.10	
1944	1.90	2.00	1.90	2.10	2.35	
1965	70.00	73.00	72.50	76.00	80.00	
1996	100.00	130.00	155.00	170.00	195.00	

YEAR	PR-64BN	PR-64RB	PR-64RD	PR-65BN	PR-65RB	PR-65RD
1938	$1.00	$1.00	$1.10	$1.00	$1.00	$1.10
1944	2.00	2.10	2.35	2.00	2.10	2.35
1965	75.00	77.50	85.00	77.50	80.00	90.00
1996	185.00	235.00	310.00	395.00	430.00	1,150.00

Notes

Collecting commentary: Popular as the lowest mintage Indian cent of the 1890s.

Too many: There was a glut of one-cent pieces and nickels, and in April 1894 coinage of these two denominations was suspended. A few months later, cent coinage resumed.[1]

Preston: 1894, January 12: R.E. Preston, who began serving as Mint director in 1893, was confirmed; served until 1898.

---

[1] 1894 *Mint Report,* pp. 11-12.

1895 Indian Cent

Business Strikes:

Business strike mintage: 38,341,474.

Number of business strike obverse dies made: 102

Average number of coins struck from typical obverse die: 375,897

Availability in Mint State: Available in all Mint State grades; high grade fully brilliant, undipped, uncleaned coins are scarcer, but there are enough around that finding one will not be a problem.

Availability in circulated grades: Common.

Characteristics of striking: Usually lightly struck.

Market Prices (1895 business strikes)

YEAR	G-4	VG-8	F-12	VF-20	EF-40	AU-50
1938	$0.05	$0.08	$0.15	$0.20	$0.25	$0.40
1944	.10	.15	.25	.40	.50	.60
1965	.60	1.30	2.50	4.50	7.25	11.00
1996	1.35	1.75	2.50	4.00	10.00	17.50

YEAR	MS-60BN	MS-60RB	MS-63BN	MS-63RB	MS-63RD
1938	$0.65	$0.65	$0.70	$0.65	$0.75
1944	1.00	1.00	1.00	1.10	1.25
1965	18.00	19.00	18.00	20.00	24.00
1996	30.00	40.00	31.00	60.00	110.00

YEAR	MS-64BN	MS-64RB	MS-64RD	MS-65BN	MS-65RB	MS-65RD
1938	$0.65	$0.70	$0.75	$0.65	$0.70	$0.75
1944	1.00	1.10	1.15	1.00	1.10	1.15
1965	18.50	20.50	25.00	19.00	21.00	27.00
1996	55.00	92.50	150.00	65.00	225.00	375.00

Proofs:

Proof mintage: 2,062.

Proof commentary: Fairly scarce. Multiple dies used including one with repunched 9 in date and another with repunched 895. The 1895 Proof set has always been especially popular due to the Barber dime and the rare Morgan silver dollar, these being in demand due to the rarity of business strikes for the dime and the apparent non-existence of business strike dollars.

Market Prices (1895 Proofs)

YEAR	PR-60BN	PR-60RB	PR-63BN	PR-63RB	PR-63RD	
1938	$1.00	$1.00	$1.00	$1.00	$1.10	
1944	1.75	1.80	1.75	1.80	2.00	
1965	52.00	53.00	52.00	55.00	57.50	
1996	85.00	100.00	115.00	150.00	175.00	

YEAR	PR-64BN	PR-64RB	PR-64RD	PR-65BN	PR-65RB	PR-65RD
1938	$1.00	$1.00	$1.10	$1.00	$1.00	$1.10
1944	1.75	1.80	2.00	1.75	1.80	2.10
1965	52.00	55.00	58.50	53.00	55.00	60.00
1996	165.00	190.00	310.00	330.00	430.00	800.00

Notes

Collecting commentary: The 1895 Indian cent blends in with others of its era as having no particularly notable features, although elsewhere in numismatics the silver dollars of this date became scarce to rare.

Strong demand: Herman Kratz, superintendent of the Mint, wrote to R.E. Preston, director, on December 17, 1895:[1]

"The demand for one-cent bronzes is on the increase daily and if it continues at this rate, we will be unable to supply the wants as promptly as should be done from institutions of this character. I have decided if it meets you[r] approval to run the presses until 8 p.m. each day until such time as the orders for one-cent bronzes are filled, to allow each employe[e] who works, over-time at the rate they are paid...."

---

[1] Citation located by Henry T. Hettger; printed in *Longacre's Ledger,* Fall 1993.

1896 Indian Cent

Business Strikes:

Business strike mintage: 39,055,431.

Number of business strike obverse dies made: 130

Average number of coins struck from typical obverse die: 300,426

Availability in Mint State: Available in all Mint State grades; high-grade fully brilliant, undipped, uncleaned coins are scarcer than generally realized. Most are a deep reddish color.

Availability in circulated grades: Common.

Characteristics of striking: Varies; often lightly defined.

Market Prices (1896 business strikes)

YEAR	G-4	VG-8	F-12	VF-20	EF-40	AU-50
1938	$0.05	$0.08	$0.15	$0.20	$0.25	$0.40
1944	.20	.30	.50	.70	.85	1.10
1965	.60	1.30	2.50	4.50	8.00	12.50
1996	1.30	1.75	2.50	4.00	10.00	17.50

YEAR	MS-60BN	MS-60RB	MS-63BN	MS-63RB	MS-63RD	
1938	$0.65	$0.65	$0.70	$0.65	$0.75	
1944	1.85	1.85	1.85	1.90	2.00	
1965	25.00	26.00	25.00	26.50	32.50	
1996	31.00	41.50	31.75	61.00	120.00	

YEAR	MS-64BN	MS-64RB	MS-64RD	MS-65BN	MS-65RB	MS-65RD
1938	$0.65	$0.70	$0.75	$0.65	$0.70	$0.75
1944	1.85	1.90	2.10	1.85	1.90	2.20
1965	26.00	27.50	33.50	27.00	28.50	35.00
1996	67.00	85.00	260.00	100.00	230.00	1,000.00

Proofs:

Proof mintage: 1,862.

Proof commentary: This was the first year since 1877 that the mintage dipped below 2,000 Proofs. All are scarce today, with bright red gems being especially so.

Market Prices (1896 Proofs)

YEAR	PR-60BN	PR-60RB	PR-63BN	PR-63RB	PR-63RD
1938	$1.00	$1.00	$1.00	$1.00	$1.10
1944	2.20	2.20	2.20	2.30	2.50
1965	63.00	67.00	63.00	70.00	72.50
1996	85.00	100.00	115.00	150.00	175.00

YEAR	PR-64BN	PR-64RB	PR-64RD	PR-65BN	PR-65RB	PR-65RD
1938	$1.00	$1.00	$1.10	$1.00	$1.00	$1.10
1944	2.20	2.30	2.50	2.20	2.30	2.50
1965	65.00	71.00	75.00	67.00	72.00	80.00
1996	165.00	190.00	315.00	280.00	400.00	1,200.00

Notes

Dies: In fiscal year 1896 (July 1, 1895, to June 30, 1896) 286 dies for Indian cents were made.[1] It is presumed these were used to strike cents dated 1895 and 1896.

Using some ballpark assumptions (reality probably varied somewhat) this equals 143 pairs of dies. Assuming an average annual coinage during the period of about 39 million cents, and assuming all dies were used, this equates to around 272,000 Indian cents per die pair, a figure that squares nicely with separate figures published by the government. Thus, a particular die variety of the era (*e.g.,* 1894 repunched date) may have been made to the extent of about this many coins.

Bryan in the news: The political election of this year pitted William Jennings Bryan (1860-1925) against William McKinley, and the burning issue of the day was silver. Should the government buy unlimited quantities of it (thus subsidizing Western mines), should a silver dollar be increased in weight so as to contain a full $1 in silver metal, should paper dollars be abolished? These were some of the questions of the moment. McKinley won, but Bryan resurfaced in the 1900 election, again with

[1] 1896 *Mint Report,* p. 203.

the silver question as part of his platform, and, finally, in 1908, this time without silver. Bryan went on to be secretary of state for Woodrow Wilson, resigning in 1915 because of policy differences, became a religious fundamentalist, and later sold his endorsement to various commercial projects and promotions (real estate in Coral Gables, Florida, for example). His last appearance in the public spotlight was as attorney in opposition to Clarence Darrow in the Scopes "Monkey Trial" in Dayton, Tennessee. Bryan died five days after the trial ended.

1897 Indian Cent

Business Strikes:

Business strike mintage: 50,464,392.

Number of business strike obverse dies made: 160

Average number of coins struck from typical obverse die: 315,402

Availability in Mint State: Available in all Mint State grades; high-grade fully brilliant, undipped, uncleaned coins are scarcer. Sharply struck coins are scarcer yet.

Availability in circulated grades: Common.

Characteristics of striking: Usually lightly struck.

Market Prices (1897 business strikes)

YEAR	G-4	VG-8	F-12	VF-20	EF-40	AU-50
1938	$0.05	$0.08	$0.15	$0.20	$0.25	$0.40
1944	.20	.30	.50	.70	.85	1.10
1965	.55	1.20	2.25	4.00	6.25	10.00
1996	1.30	1.75	2.50	4.00	10.00	17.50

YEAR	MS-60BN	MS-60RB	MS-63BN	MS-63RB	MS-63RD
1938	$0.65	$0.65	$0.70	$0.65	$0.75
1944	1.85	1.85	1.85	1.90	2.00
1965	21.00	22.50	21.00	23.00	26.00
1996	30.00	37.50	30.00	50.00	105,00

YEAR	MS-64BN	MS-64RB	MS-64RD	MS-65BN	MS-65RB	MS-65RD
1938	$0.65	$0.70	$0.75	$0.65	$0.70	$0.75
1944	1.85	1.90	2.10	1.85	1.90	2.20
1965	21.50	23.50	27.00	22.00	24.25	29.00
1996	40.00	62.00	85.00	60.00	180.00	500.00

Variety with "spur" from neck: One curious variety (Snow-1, Fivaz-Stanton-011.5, Breen-2030, FND-001) has the left bottom serif of the 1 digit in the date protruding from the neck into the field just above the necklace. A date logotype must have been accidentally tapped against this working die. This error is valued at eight to 10 or more times the price of a regular 1897. Not attributed by PCGS or NGC, thus cherrypicking one for a "regular" price is a possibility!

Proofs:

Proof mintage: 1,938.
Proof commentary: Scarce.

Market Prices (1897 Proofs)

YEAR	PR-60BN	PR-60RB	PR-63BN	PR-63RB	PR-63RD	
1938	$1.00	$1.00	$1.00	$1.00	$1.10	
1944	2.80	2.85	2.90	2.90	3.00	
1965	63.00	66.00	63.00	69.00	72.00	
1996	85.00	100.00	115.00	150.00	175.00	

YEAR	PR-64BN	PR-64RB	PR-64RD	PR-65BN	PR-65RB	PR-65RD
1938	$1.00	$1.00	$1.10	$1.00	$1.00	$1.10
1944	2.90	2.90	3.00	2.90	2.90	3.10
1965	65.00	71.00	75.00	67.00	72.00	80.00
1996	165.00	190.00	315.00	290.00	350.00	1,200.00

Notes

"Blob" 9: On some business strikes the date logotype was impressed too deeply into the working die, and the bottom part of the 9 in the date appears as a blob, with no open area to the right of the ball.

Bank difficulty: On December 23, 1897, the Chestnut Street National Bank in Philadelphia failed, taking with it some $11,465 in draft remittances deposited by the Philadelphia Mint from 97 different banks seeking to purchase minor coins. Eventually, the Mint received 55% of this amount.[1]

---

[1] 1900 *Mint Report,* p. 5

1898 Indian Cent

Business Strikes:

Business strike mintage: 49,821,284.

Number of business strike obverse dies made: 197

Average number of coins struck from typical obverse die: 252,900

Availability in Mint State: Available in all Mint State grades; high-grade fully brilliant, undipped, uncleaned coins are scarcer.

Availability in circulated grades: Common.

Characteristics of striking: Mostly lightly struck.

Market Prices (1898 business strikes)

YEAR	G-4	VG-8	F-12	VF-20	EF-40	AU-50
1938	$0.06	$0.10	$0.20	$0.35	$0.50	$0.75
1944	.20	.30	.50	.65	.80	1.00
1965	.55	1.10	2.15	3.80	6.00	9.50
1996	1.30	1.75	2.50	4.00	10.00	16.50

YEAR	MS-60BN	MS-60RB	MS-63BN	MS-63RB	MS-63RD	
1938	$0.90	$0.90	$0.90	$0.90	$1.00	
1944	1.60	1.60	1.60	1.65	1.75	
1965	18.00	19.00	18.00	19.50	25.00	
1996	30.00	36.00	34.00	47.50	72.50	

YEAR	MS-64BN	MS-64RB	MS-64RD	MS-65BN	MS-65RB	MS-65RD
1938	$0.90	$0.90	$1.00	$0.90	$0.90	$1.00
1944	1.60	1.65	1.75	1.60	1.65	1.75
1965	19.00	21.00	26.00	20.00	22.00	27.50
1996	40.00	85.00	85.00	60.00	180.00	300.00

Proofs:

Proof mintage: 1,795.

Proof commentary: Scarce, as are most of the Proofs of this era.

Market Prices (1898 Proofs)

YEAR	PR-60BN	PR-60RB	PR-63BN	PR-63RB	PR-63RD	
1938	$1.00	$1.00	$1.00	$1.00	$1.10	
1944	2.20	2.30	2.20	2.30	2.50	
1965	60.00	61.00	60.00	61.50	62.50	
1996	85.00	100.00	115.00	150.00	175.00	

YEAR	PR-64BN	PR-64RB	PR-64RD	PR-65BN	PR-65RB	PR-65RD
1938	$1.00	$1.00	$1.10	$1.00	$1.00	$1.10
1944	2.30	2.30	2.50	2.30	2.30	2.50
1965	61.00	62.00	63.50	61.00	62.50	65.00
1996	165.00	190.00	315.00	320.00	350.00	750.00

Notes

New Mint director: 1898, January 26: George E. Roberts confirmed as Mint director, began his duties in February, and served until July 1907 and again 1910-1914.

Across the Atlantic: In England "the outbreak of slot machines was noted as long ago as 1898 as the cause of heavy coinage of pence."[1] Meanwhile, in America a proliferation of coin-in-the-slot devices prompted record coinages of cents and nickels.

San Francisco to Russia: *The Numismatist,* May 1898, printed this item (excerpt):

The little penny is the most agile coin that now bears the face of the Goddess of Liberty. If all the pennies that are now in circulation were piled one upon the other, when the pile was finished it would be 100 times as big as the giant Goddess of Liberty that enlightens a small part of the world in New York harbor. If these same pennies were laid edge to edge they would extend from San Francisco to St. Petersburg. It is also true that the tall pile of them referred to would be 4,000 times the height of the Eiffel Tower, the tallest in the world....[2]

---

[1] John Craig, *The Mint,* 1953, p. 332.

[2] QDB note: Better not look too closely at the above calculations and try to compare the heights of the Statue of Liberty and the Eiffel Tower, the latter apparently being about 1/40th as tall as the New York statue

The government buys the blank coppers on which the design is stamped, from a western firm, each thousand cents costing $1.25. So, 100 cents, with a face value of $1, cost the government less than one-fifth that sum.... A pound of copper, enough to make 108 cents, can be bought for 11¢, so that the counterfeiters can make a good profit if they are skillful enough. So many bad pennies come to the United States Treasury that some of the Secret Service men are at work all the time, looking for the men who make them....

'The hardest-working member of the whole coin family is the penny,' said Supt. Milman of the New York Sub-Treasury the other day as he watched the unloading of an express wagon piled high with canvas bags of the copper coins.... Cents often come to us at the rate of a million a day.... That lot just coming in contains $5,000 worth and represents a day's collection from a single big slot machine company.... Perhaps there are 500,000,000 one-cent pieces here now.... There are kinetoscope views, phonographs, automatic music boxes, candy and chewing gum sellers, weighing machines, lifting machines, and a hundred and one others standing at every hand and coaxing the pennies from their owners' pockets.'...[1]

---

[1] About the cent-grabbing devices: The Kinetoscope (properly capitalized) was an Edison device showing a short "movie" via a film strip. Similarly, the American Mutoscope Company had "movies" via a series of photographic flip cards viewed in rapid succession. While several brands of coin-operated music boxes were in vogue, the market leader was the Regina Music Box Co., of Rahway, New Jersey. Candy and chewing gum vendors were very popular, especially the latter; Zeno was a popular gum brand sold this way. Weighing machines such as the National (a brand which was especially popular in the first decade of the 20th century) were typically made of cast iron and placed on the sidewalk in front of stores, taverns, hotels, railroad stations, and other public places where they could ingest Indian cents 24 hours a day.

1899 Indian Cent

Business Strikes:

Business strike mintage: 53,598,000.

Number of business strike obverse dies made: 116

Average number of coins struck from typical obverse die: 462,052

Availability in Mint State: The most plentiful issue of the 1890s at all Mint State levels including gem bright red.[1]

Availability in circulated grades: Common.

Characteristics of striking: Varies. Mostly lightly struck.

Market Prices (1899 business strikes)

YEAR	G-4	VG-8	F-12	VF-20	EF-40	AU-50
1938	$0.05	$0.08	$0.15	$0.20	$0.25	$0.40
1944	.20	.30	.50	.70	.85	1.10
1965	.50	1.10	2.00	3.50	4.50	12.00
1996	1.30	1.50	2.00	3.50	9.00	16.00

YEAR	MS-60BN	MS-60RB	MS-63BN	MS-63RB	MS-63RD	
1938	$0.65	$0.65	$0.65	$0.65	$0.75	
1944	1.85	1.85	1.85	1.90	2.00	
1965	18.00	18.00	18.00	18.00	20.00	
1996	30.00	37.00	34.00	50.00	73.00	

---

[1] Richard Snow, letter, April 10, 1996.

YEAR	MS-64BN	MS-64RB	MS-64RD	MS-65BN	MS-65RB	MS-65RD
1938	$0.65	$0.65	$0.75	$0.60	$0.65	$0.85
1944	1.85	1.90	2.10	1.85	1.90	2.20
1965	18.00	18.00	21.00	18.00	18.00	22.00
1996	40.00	62.50	85.00	59.00	92.00	275.00

Proofs:

Proof mintage: 2,031.
Proof commentary: Scarce.

Market Prices (1899 Proofs)

YEAR	PR-60BN	PR-60RB	PR-63BN	PR-63RB	PR-63RD	
1938	$1.00	$1.00	$1.00	$1.00	$1.10	
1944	2.80	2.85	2.90	2.90	3.00	
1965	52.00	53.00	52.00	55.00	57.50	
1996	85.00	100.00	115.00	150.00	175.00	

YEAR	PR-64BN	PR-64RB	PR-64RD	PR-65BN	PR-65RB	PR-65RD
1938	$1.00	$1.00	$1.10	$1.00	$1.00	$1.10
1944	2.90	2.90	3.00	2.90	2.90	3.10
1965	52.00	55.00	58.50	53.00	55.00	60.00
1996	165.00	190.00	310.00	240.00	320.00	750.00

Notes

Collecting commentary: Although business strike cents of this era are common, assembling a nicely matched set in Mint State is not as simple a task as it may seem at first, in particular if attention is paid to aesthetic quality.

A possible clashed die: A possible clashed die for the 1899 Indian cent was discovered by Chris Pilliod and described in *Coin World,* March 4, 1996:[1]

It is an 1899 Indian cent reverse that is possibly clashed with [the reverse of] a $2.50 gold quarter eagle. Very little evidence of clashing is evident, and at present it is not confirmed.

Overdate never verified: In *Walter Breen's Complete Encyclopedia of U.S. and Colonials,* published in 1988, B-2033 is described as "1899/7 (?)." Today this variety is not considered an overdate by specialists.[2]

---

[1] Here paraphrased. "Collectors' Clearinghouse" column. Article titled "Clashed Dies: Usually Common, There Are Some Bizarre Varieties to Seek."
[2] W.O. Walker. "A Population Report Rarity Review." *Longacre's Ledger,* Spring 1995.

REVERSE OF 1899 CENT: Detail showing unusual clash marks around and below CE, quote possibly an impression of the reverse of a $2.50 gold piece. (Chris Pilliod photograph)

1900 Indian Cent

Business Strikes:

Business strike mintage: 66,831,502.

Number of business strike obverse dies made: 155

Average number of coins struck from typical obverse die: 431,171

Availability in Mint State: Readily available. A few rolls have come on the market in recent decades. However, bright original red pieces are a bit harder to find than conventional wisdom suggests.[1]

Availability in circulated grades: Common.

Characteristics of striking: Varies.

Market Prices (1900 business strikes)

YEAR	G-4	VG-8	F-12	VF-20	EF-40	AU-50
1938	$0.05	$0.08	$0.15	$0.20	$0.25	$0.40
1944	.10	.15	.25	.40	.50	.75
1965	.50	.80	1.50	2.50	3.50	7.75
1996	1.00	1.20	1.50	2.20	7.00	15.00

YEAR	MS-60BN	MS-60RB	MS-63BN	MS-63RB	MS-63RD
1938	$0.65	$0.65	$0.70	$0.65	$0.75
1944	1.00	1.00	1.00	1.10	1.25
1965	14.00	15.00	14.00	16.00	20.00
1996	22.50	30.00	28.00	40.00	70.00

---

[1] Richard Snow, letter, April 10, 1996.

YEAR	MS-64BN	MS-64RB	MS-64RD	MS-65BN	MS-65RB	MS-65RD
1938	$0.65	$0.70	$0.75	$0.65	$0.70	$0.75
1944	1.15	1.20	1.30	1.15	1.20	1.35
1965	15.00	17.50	22.50	16.00	18.50	24.00
1996	35.00	47.50	80.00	45.00	88.00	275.00

Proofs:

Proof mintage: 2,062 (per Walter Breen, *Encyclopedia of Proof Coins,* who states that the figure of 2,262 published elsewhere is a typographical error).

Proof commentary: Scarce. It is a curious situation that as business strike mintages became larger, Proof mintages trended smaller.

Market Prices (1900 Proofs)

YEAR	PR-60BN	PR-60RB	PR-63BN	PR-63RB	PR-63RD	
1938	$1.00	$1.00	$1.00	$1.00	$1.10	
1944	1.90	2.00	1.90	2.00	2.25	
1965	52.00	53.00	52.00	55.00	57.50	
1996	85.00	100.00	115.00	130.00	165.00	

YEAR	PR-64BN	PR-64RB	PR-64RD	PR-65BN	PR-65RB	PR-65RD
1938	$1.00	$1.00	$1.10	$1.00	$1.00	$1.10
1944	2.00	2.00	2.25	2.00	2.00	2.25
1965	52.00	55.00	58.50	53.00	55.00	60.00
1996	135.00	190.00	310.00	240.00	320.00	750.00

Notes

Oddities: At least three business strike 1900 cents struck on gold quarter eagle planchets exist and were probably made as curiosities (rather than as an unintentional mint errors).[1] Ditto one (verified) or more pieces struck in silver. These are from a slightly rusted reverse die.

One gold striking, 65.8 grains, appeared in the Quality Sales offering of the Beck Collection, January 1975, Lot 609, there pedigreed to the B.G. Johnson and the Col. E.H.R. Green Collection (this must have been an outside consignment to the sale, not from the Beck estate, as Beck died in 1924, at which time Green was just *beginning* his collection; B.G. Johnson assisted with the sale of the Green coins after 1936). This same coin later appeared in Auction '89 (Superior) as Lot 856 then in the 1991 ANA Sale (Bowers and Merena) as Lot 4103, there tentatively given the authorship of George T. Morgan, assistant engraver at the Mint at the time.

---

[1] Michael Hodder, letter, May 14, 1996, reported the knowledge of three pieces, all personally seen, with weights ranging from 65.8 to 67.1 grains.

Branch mints: In 1900 and 1901 George E. Roberts, director of the Mint, recommended that cents and nickels be manufactured at the New Orleans and San Francisco mints, for thus "the demand for the Southwestern and Pacific Coast states and territories could be supplied much more economically than at present."[1] By this time the previously small demand from those sections had increased markedly, but still it was not comparable to demand in the East and Midwest.

Modern mention: Harper Lee's 1960 novel, *To Kill a Mockingbird,* mentions long-hidden 1900- and 1906-dated Indian cents in Chapter 4.[2]

THE MINT COLLECTION: Shown on view at the Philadelphia Mint, Spring Garden Street, 1903. Pattern and regular issue cents were among the displays which included examples of the 1804 dollar, 1849 $20, and other rarities. Years later the exhibit was moved to the "Castle" building at the Smithsonian Institution, Washington, D.C., and still later to its present location in the American History Building. (*The United States Mint at Philadelphia,* James Rankin Young, 1903, p. 80)

---

[1] 1900 *Mint Report,* p. 6; 1901 *Report,* p. 5. Later pleas could be cited as well.
[2] As noted by Thomas K. DeLorey, letter, April 30, 1996.

1901 Indian Cent

Business Strikes:

Business strike mintage: 79,609,158.

Number of business strike obverse dies made: 145

Average number of coins struck from typical obverse die: 549,029. Record high to this point in time (among dates for which information is available). However, it would be surpassed in 1902.

Availability in Mint State: Readily available. A few rolls have come on the market in recent decades.

Availability in circulated grades: Common.

Characteristics of striking: Varies, as might be expected from so many coins struck from so many pairs of dies.

Market Prices (1901 business strikes)

YEAR	G-4	VG-8	F-12	VF-20	EF-40	AU-50
1938	$0.05	$0.08	$0.10	$0.10	$0.15	$0.20
1944	.10	.15	.25	.40	.50	.60
1965	.40	.75	1.15	2.25	3.50	6.00
1996	1.00	1.20	1.50	2.20	7.00	15.00

YEAR	MS-60BN	MS-60RB	MS-63BN	MS-63RB	MS-63RD
1938	$0.40	$0.40	$0.40	$0.40	$0.50
1944	.85	.85	.85	.90	1.00
1965	10.00	11.00	10.00	11.50	15.00
1996	22.50	30.00	28.00	40.00	70.00

YEAR	MS-64BN	MS-64RB	MS-64RD	MS-65BN	MS-65RB	MS-65RD
1938	$0.40	$0.40	$0.50	$0.40	$0.40	$0.50
1944	.85	.90	1.00	.85	.90	1.00
1965	11.00	12.50	17.50	12.00	13.50	20.00
1996	35.00	47.50	80.00	45.00	85.00	275.00

Proofs:

Proof mintage: 1,985.

Proof commentary: One of the lower mintages. As is true of other Proofs of this era, the demand for the 1901 is diminished due to the common nature of related business strikes.

Note about "wipe lines" on Proofs 1901-1907: Richard Snow comment:[1] "Early die state Proofs of this era generally show a crystallized pattern in their fields along with deep mirrors. This is from the die being polished prior to hardening and crystallizing during the hardening process. On cents from 1901 to 1907 (except 1906), there are what I call wipe lines on these early die state coins. When the coin is viewed at one angle, a deep mirror surface is evident. When viewed at another angle there are a profusion of parallel striations which look like hairlines. These are not problems with the coin. These are lines caused by a wiping of the die with a heavy cloth (probably) while the die was soft. The lines then transfer to the coin. After the die has been in use awhile, these lines fade. After the die is repolished they disappear completely." The author (QDB) usually refers to these as "die finish lines." Alternatively to the "wiping" theory, they may have been caused by polishing the die on a buffing wheel.

John Dannreuther noted that similar lines are found on Proof Liberty Head nickels of this decade.[2]

Market Prices (1901 Proofs)

YEAR	PR-60BN	PR-60RB	PR-63BN	PR-63RB	PR-63RD	
1938	$1.00	$1.00	$1.00	$1.00	$1.10	
1944	1.90	2.00	1.90	2.00	2.25	
1965	52.00	53.00	52.00	55.00	57.50	
1996	85.00	100.00	115.00	130.00	165.00	

YEAR	PR-64BN	PR-64RB	PR-64RD	PR-65BN	PR-65RB	PR-65RD
1938	$1.00	$1.00	$1.10	$1.00	$1.00	$1.10
1944	2.00	2.00	2.25	2.00	2.00	2.25
1965	52.00	55.00	58.50	53.00	55.00	60.00
1996	135.00	190.00	310.00	240.00	320.00	750.00

[1] Letter, April 10, 1996.
[2] Letter, May 16, 1996.

Notes

Collecting commentary: No particular excitement with this or other dates of the era, but collected as part of the later 1879-1909 series.

Shuffle off to Buffalo: First year of the 20th century. The Pan-American Exposition was held in Buffalo, NY. Among souvenirs sold were Indian cents in round aluminum "frames" bearing inscriptions relating to the event. Coins later removed from these frames are somewhat "shrunken" in diameter and sometimes also show part of the lettering from the frame impressed on the rim of the cent; the uninitiated sometimes believe these to be "mint errors."

New Mint: The Philadelphia Mint facilities were transferred to a new location, and many devices and procedures were improved and upgraded, permitting increased efficiency of production and record high quantities of coins produced from a given number of dies.

The new Mint occupied a city block bounded by Sixteenth, Seventeenth, Buttonwood, and Spring Garden streets, with the main entrance on Spring Garden Street.

NEW PHILADELPHIA MINT: Occupied in 1901, this building with its main entrance on Spring Garden Street was the third structure to house the facility since the Mint was established in 1792. Indian cents were struck here from 1901 through the end of the series in 1909. The building, constructed by the Charles McCaul Company, remained in use until the late 1960s. (*The United States Mint at Philadelphia,* **James Rankin Young, 1903. Frontispiece**)

1902 Indian Cent

Business Strikes:

Business strike mintage: 87,374,704.

Number of business strike obverse dies made: 148.

Average number of coins struck from typical obverse die: 590,370. Record high figure for the dates for which information is available.

Availability in Mint State: Common. Most are lightly struck (no wonder, considering the record number of coins produced per die). Bright red specimens are scarcer than are those of the preceding several years. Prices for MS-65 RD coins of this era are mostly for "type."

Availability in circulated grades: Common.

Characteristics of striking: Most specimens are lightly struck.

Market Prices (1902 business strikes)

YEAR	G-4	VG-8	F-12	VF-20	EF-40	AU-50
1938	$0.05	$0.08	$0.10	$0.10	$0.15	$0.20
1944	.07	.10	.15	.15	.20	.30
1965	.40	.75	1.15	2.25	3.50	6.00
1996	1.00	1.20	1.50	2.20	7.00	15.00

YEAR	MS-60BN	MS-60RB	MS-63BN	MS-63RB	MS-63RD
1938	$0.40	$0.40	$0.40	$0.40	$0.50
1944	.45	.45	.45	.45	.55
1965	10.00	11.00	10.00	11.50	15.00
1996	22.50	30.00	28.00	40.00	70.00

YEAR	MS-64BN	MS-64RB	MS-64RD	MS-65BN	MS-65RB	MS-65RD
1938	$0.40	$0.40	$0.50	$0.40	$0.40	$0.50
1944	.45	.50	.55	.45	.50	.55
1965	11.00	12.50	17.50	12.00	13.50	20.00
1996	35.00	47.50	80.00	45.00	85.00	275.00

Proofs:

Proof mintage: 2,018.

Proof commentary: Scarce due to the low mintage, but among surviving pieces there are more bright red coins than of other dates of this era.[1]

Some early Proof strikings are seen with "wipe lines," a.k.a. die finish lines (see comment under 1901 Proofs).

Market Prices (1902 Proofs)

YEAR	PR-60BN	PR-60RB	PR-63BN	PR-63RB	PR-63RD	
1938	$1.00	$1.00	$1.00	$1.00	$1.10	
1944	1.90	2.00	1.90	2.00	2.25	
1965	52.00	53.00	52.00	55.00	57.50	
1996	85.00	100.00	115.00	130.00	165.00	

YEAR	PR-64BN	PR-64RB	PR-64RD	PR-65BN	PR-65RB	PR-65RD
1938	$1.00	$1.00	$1.10	$1.00	$1.00	$1.10
1944	2.00	2.00	2.25	2.00	2.00	2.25
1965	52.00	55.00	58.50	53.00	55.00	60.00
1996	135.00	190.00	310.00	240.00	320.00	750.00

Notes

Collecting commentary: Common in all grades, but fully struck pieces with needle-sharp feather detail are scarce.

Fakery: There is said to have been a plague of counterfeit cents during this period, and during fiscal year 1902 some 96,995 pieces were detected by the Treasury Department. Runner-up in "popularity" was the quarter dollar (5,125). Surprisingly, only 11 spurious gold coins were found.[2] Even more surprising is that today in the 1990s, very few collectors are aware of such pieces; certainly the numismatic community would like to know how they differed from authentic pieces.

Coinage press capacities: The *Annual Report of the Director of the Mint,* 1902, told that the amount of pressure required for stamping a silver dollar was 160 tons, while a pressure of 35 tons was needed for a quarter eagle, 155 tons for a double eagle, 98

---

[1] Richard Snow, letter, April 10, 1996.
[2] 1902 *Mint Report,* p. 26.

tons for a half dollar, 35 tons for a dime, and 40 tons for a cent. A large coining press at the Mint was driven by a 7.5-horsepower electric motor running at 950 rpm and could strike 90 coins per minute.

A small coining press—such as one used to strike Indian cents—was run by a 3-hp. motor at 1,050 rpm and could strike 100 pieces per minute. This was equivalent to 6,000 coins per hour, not allowing for down time.

COINING PRESSES IN 1901: Rows of electrically-driven coining presses at the new Philadelphia Mint in 1901. In the foreground are an electric motor and two grinding wheels for instant repairs and adjustments. (*The United States Mint at Philadelphia,* James Rankin Young, 1903, p. 51)

1903 Indian Cent

Business Strikes:

Business strike mintage: 85,092,703.

Number of business strike obverse dies made: 178

Average number of coins struck from typical obverse die: 478,049

Availability in Mint State: Common at all levels.

Availability in circulated grades: Common.

Characteristics of striking: Most are not sharply struck on the feather ends.

Market Prices (1903 business strikes)

YEAR	G-4	VG-8	F-12	VF-20	EF-40	AU-50
1938	$0.05	$0.08	$0.10	$0.10	$0.15	$0.20
1944	.07	.10	.15	.15	.20	.30
1965	.40	.75	1.15	2.25	3.50	6.00
1996	1.00	1.20	1.50	2.20	7.00	15.00

YEAR	MS-60BN	MS-60RB	MS-63BN	MS-63RB	MS-63RD
1938	$0.40	$0.40	$0.40	$0.40	$0.50
1944	.65	.65	.65	.70	.75
1965	10.00	11.00	10.00	11.50	15.00
1996	22.50	30.00	28.00	40.00	70.00

YEAR	MS-64BN	MS-64RB	MS-64RD	MS-65BN	MS-65RB	MS-65RD
1938	$0.40	$0.40	$0.50	$0.40	$0.40	$0.50
1944	.65	.70	.75	.65	.70	.75
1965	11.00	12.50	17.50	12.00	13.50	20.00
1996	35.00	47.50	80.00	45.00	85.00	275.00

Proofs:

Proof mintage: 1,790.

Proof commentary: One of the lower mintages. Portrait lightly polished in the dies, not frosty. Feather tips usually weak.

Some early Proof strikings are seen with "wipe lines," a.k.a. die finish lines (see comment under 1901 Proofs).

Market Prices (1903 Proofs)

YEAR	PR-60BN	PR-60RB	PR-63BN	PR-63RB	PR-63RD	
1938	$1.00	$1.00	$1.00	$1.00	$1.10	
1944	1.50	1.55	1.50	1.60	1.75	
1965	52.00	53.00	52.00	55.00	57.50	
1996	85.00	100.00	115.00	130.00	165.00	

YEAR	PR-64BN	PR-64RB	PR-64RD	PR-65BN	PR-65RB	PR-65RD
1938	$1.00	$1.00	$1.10	$1.00	$1.00	$1.10
1944	1.60	1.60	1.75	1.60	1.60	1.75
1965	52.00	55.00	58.50	53.00	55.00	60.00
1996	135.00	190.00	310.00	240.00	340.00	750.00

Notes

Collecting commentary: No particular excitement with this or other dates of the era, but collected as part of the later 1879-1909 series.

A visit to the Mint: A visitors' guide, *The United States Mint at Philadelphia*, by James Rankin Young, was published in 1903 and contained many views and descriptions of the new (occupied in 1901) Mint facilities. Excerpts relating to one-cent pieces:

> The 25 coining presses now used are supposed to be the best designed machines in the Mint, and represent the gradual development of a press installed in 1874.... Ten new presses were installed when the mint was moved into its new quarters. These presses...were built at the shops of the T.C. Dill Machine Co. in Philadelphia....
>
> The dies are adjusted in the coining press by a skilled operator, the adjustment requiring the services of a man of long experience. The blanks are then fed into a tube at the front of the machine. In doing this the women who feed the machines shake the blanks in the palm of their hands, getting them in a column ready to go

into the tube.... A pair of [mechanical] fingers takes the disc from the bottom of the feed tube and carries it in between the upper and lower die, where it is held in position by a collar.... The stamp then descends. The obverse of the coin is struck on the top of the blank and the reverse on the lower side.... When the pressure is released the lower die forces the coin out of the collar and the fingers force it back into its channel, at the same time carrying a new blank into the collar. Despite the fact that many tons of pressure are put on each coin stamped, this whole operation is done in a moment, and from 80 to 100 coins are thrown into the can at the bottom of the machine every minute....

Since 1899 experiments have been regularly conducted aiming at improvements in the various minting processes. The results of this spirit of enterprise are visible today in every department....

Practically all the nickel comes from the mines at the Gap, in Lancaster County, Pennsylvania, and the copper from the Lake Superior mines. The nickel and copper is received already refined, stamped, and milled [with raised rims], ready to have the design stamped on it by the coining presses, making it coin.... Large box-loads of blanks for pennies are received here daily. The blanks are scooped out and placed in big metal pans [one side of a balance-arm scale], when they are weighed and emptied into trucks [iron-wheeled carts], four or five feet high, in which they are transferred to the coiner. An average of 22 tons of bronze and nickel per month are weighed on these scales....

The five-cent (nickel) and the one-cent (bronze) pieces are all issued from the Philadelphia Mint. The blanks are purchased under contract, and the millions of little pieces sent out yearly are all stamped in the building. The presses are constantly running on these coins, as the demand from the country is a never-ceasing one. The cashier ships daily to banks and business firms throughout the United States thousands upon thousands of the nickel and bronze pieces, the demand being particularly heavy during the weeks preceding the Christmas holidays. For the work thus done the cashier has two office assistants, a shipping clerk, and five to six packers....

Visitors to the Mint invariably find their way to the cashier's office before leaving the building. The visit is not complete unless some newly-minted coins are carried away as 'souvenirs,' the bright cent generally catching the fancy of the stranger....

The actual shipping of coin from the Mint building is done in a room on the north side of the area in the basement. Here the bags of coin are packed into small heavy kegs, about 20 of which constitute a wagon load. From here they are transferred to the various express companies, who are under contract and bond to do all the transportation for the government....

In a single room in the southern end of the second floor of the building is the Medal Room, a department under the coiner though almost an independent mint in itself. All the Proof coins (those given a particularly fine finish) and medals are made in this room.... Against the wall are two electrically driven hydraulic presses, capable respectively of a pressure of 400 and 300 tons to the square inch, and next to them the two hydraulic pumps. Off in an out-of-the-way corner is the old-fashioned hand screw press, with its long arms and heavy weights. The foreman, growing reminiscent, tells how, as a helper, he used to get these arms going round at such a gait that they would move the whole machine.

The Proof sets of coins are made under the government supervision to be preserved for record, or sold to collectors. The face of the dies used in stamping these sets have been given an extra fine finish, and glisten as though they have been nickel-plated. The blanks for coins are annealed and stamped by the hydraulic press....

The "business office" of the Medal Department is in a room on the right side of the corridor as you enter the Cabinet [Mint Collection room]. Proof sets of the half dozen silver and minor coins [Indian cent, Liberty nickel, Barber dime, Barber quarter, Barber half dollar, Morgan dollar] are sold for $2.50, while Proof sets of the four gold coins [$2.50, $5, $10, $20] cost $38.50. Any one of the gold coins can be bought at a premium of 25¢, and a Proof nickel and cent may be had for eight cents, but the Proof sets of silver coins will not be separated....

Coining
Machinery
——AND——
Machine
Tools

T. C. DILL
Machine Co.
INCORPORATED

Somerset and Mascher
Streets : *Philadelphia*

KNUCKLE-ACTION COINING PRESS: 1903 advertisement by T.C. Dill for its coining presses, 10 of which were installed in the new Philadelphia Mint which opened in 1901. This general type of press, with many refinements over the years, had been used since 1836. (*The United States Mint at Philadelphia*, James Rankin Young, 1903)

1904 Indian Cent

Business Strikes:

Business strike mintage: 61,326,198.

Number of business strike obverse dies made: Not known.

Average number of coins struck from typical obverse die: Not known.

Availability in Mint State: Common. A few rolls have come on the market in recent decades. Often Mint State cents of this date are bright orange-red.

Availability in circulated grades: Common.

Characteristics of striking: Varies, but sharp pieces can be found.

Market Prices (1904 business strikes)

YEAR	G-4	VG-8	F-12	VF-20	EF-40	AU-50
1938	$0.05	$0.08	$0.10	$0.10	$0.15	$0.20
1944	.07	.10	.15	.15	.20	.30
1965	.40	.75	1.15	2.25	3.50	6.00
1996	1.00	1.20	1.50	2.20	7.00	15.00

YEAR	MS-60BN	MS-60RB	MS-63BN	MS-63RB	MS-63RD	
1938	$0.40	$0.40	$0.40	$0.40	$0.50	
1944	.45	.45	.45	.45	.55	
1965	10.00	11.00	10.00	11.50	15.00	
1996	22.50	30.00	28.00	40.00	70.00	

YEAR	MS-64BN	MS-64RB	MS-64RD	MS-65BN	MS-65RB	MS-65RD
1938	$0.40	$0.40	$0.50	$0.40	$0.40	$0.50
1944	.45	.50	.55	.45	.50	.55
1965	11.00	12.50	17.50	12.00	13.50	20.00
1996	35.00	47.50	80.00	45.00	85.00	275.00

Proofs:

Proof mintage: 1,817.

Proof commentary: Traces of a misplaced 9 digit in the denticles below the correctly positioned 9.[1]

This date is one of the lower mintages. Especially hard to find in gem red preservation.

Some early Proof strikings are seen with "wipe lines," a.k.a. die finish lines (see comment under 1901 Proofs).

Market Prices (1904 Proofs)

YEAR	PR-60BN	PR-60RB	PR-63BN	PR-63RB	PR-63RD	
1938	$1.00	$1.00	$1.00	$1.00	$1.10	
1944	1.35	1.40	1.35	1.40	1.50	
1965	52.00	53.00	52.00	55.00	57.50	
1996	85.00	100.00	115.00	130.00	165.00	

YEAR	PR-64BN	PR-64RB	PR-64RD	PR-65BN	PR-65RB	PR-65RD
1938	$1.00	$1.00	$1.10	$1.00	$1.00	$1.10
1944	1.40	1.40	1.50	1.40	1.40	1.50
1965	52.00	55.00	58.50	53.00	55.00	60.00
1996	135.00	190.00	310.00	240.00	360.00	850.00

Notes

Date numerals: The 4 in the 1904 date is tilted to the right (business strikes as well as Proofs), so that the base of the 4 is not parallel to the curve of the denticles, but tilts downward to the right (the base of the 4, if extended, would intersect the 0 at its lower right outside curve). By contrast, the base of the 4 in the dates 1864, 1884, 1894 is oriented parallel to the denticles (the 1874 cent has a straight date, and comparisons are not relevant).

Meet me in St. Louis: The Louisiana Purchase Exposition was held in St. Louis this year, and Farran Zerbe had a coin concession there. Among items sold were the first United States commemorative gold dollars, dated 1903, and bearing inscriptions relating to the event.

---

[1] Richard Snow. "Proof Die Identification for Indian Cents." *Longacre's Ledger,* Fall 1994.

1905 Indian Cent

Business Strikes:

Business strike mintage: 80,717,011

Number of business strike obverse dies made: Not known.

Average number of coins struck from typical obverse die: Not known.

Availability in Mint State: Common at all levels.

Availability in circulated grades: Common.

Characteristics of striking: Most are lightly struck on the feather ends.

Market Prices (1905 business strikes)

YEAR	G-4	VG-8	F-12	VF-20	EF-40	AU-50
1938	$0.05	$0.08	$0.10	$0.10	$0.10	$0.15
1944	.07	.10	.15	.15	.20	.30
1965	.40	.75	1.15	2.25	3.50	6.00
1996	1.00	1.20	1.50	2.20	7.00	15.00

YEAR	MS-60BN	MS-60RB	MS-63BN	MS-63RB	MS-63RD	
1938	$0.30	$0.30	$0.30	$0.30	$0.35	
1944	.45	.45	.45	.45	.55	
1965	10.00	11.00	10.00	11.50	15.00	
1996	22.50	30.00	28.00	40.00	70.00	

YEAR	MS-64BN	MS-64RB	MS-64RD	MS-65BN	MS-65RB	MS-65RD
1938	$0.30	$0.30	$0.35	$0.30	$0.30	$0.35
1944	.45	.50	.55	.45	.50	.55
1965	11.00	12.50	17.50	12.00	13.50	20.00
1996	35.00	47.50	80.00	45.00	85.00	275.00

Proofs:

Proof mintage: 2,152.

Proof commentary: Scarce. Some early Proof strikings are seen with "wipe lines," a.k.a. die finish lines (see comment under 1901 Proofs).

Market Prices (1905 Proofs)

YEAR	PR-60BN	PR-60RB	PR-63BN	PR-63RB	PR-63RD	
1938	$1.00	$1.00	$1.00	$1.00	$1.10	
1944	1.50	1.55	1.50	1.60	1.75	
1965	52.00	53.00	52.00	55.00	57.50	
1996	85.00	100.00	115.00	130.00	165.00	

YEAR	PR-64BN	PR-64RB	PR-64RD	PR-65BN	PR-65RB	PR-65RD
1938	$1.00	$1.00	$1.10	$1.00	$1.00	$1.10
1944	1.60	1.60	1.75	1.60	1.60	1.75
1965	52.00	55.00	58.50	53.00	55.00	60.00
1996	135.00	190.00	310.00	240.00	360.00	750.00

Notes

Collecting commentary: No particular excitement with this or other dates of the era, but collected as part of the later 1879-1909 series.

John Dannreuther reported that a large group of "Uncirculated" 1905 cents came on the market, but that these were circulated pieces that had been treated, possibly with cyanide or another etching agent, and then given a brilliant color; the color will wipe off the coins![1] Such coins would have little value to the serious numismatist.

At the Mint: In fiscal year 1905 the Treasury's supply of silver bullion for coinage into dollars was exhausted, and no dollars were made after (calendar year) 1904, thus freeing certain mint facilities. The 1905 *Mint Report* commented:

> We took advantage of this state of things to experiment on the manufacturing of blanks for minor coins. These experiments were so satisfactory that the resumption of manufacturing these blanks was entered upon. The work was done in the Mint years ago, although with somewhat unsatisfactory results.... New and improved machinery has been installed [and we believe] we can manufacture the minor coin blanks at less cost to the government than the price heretofore paid to private manufacturers." (During fiscal year 1905 the Mint purchased 360,000 pounds avoirdupois of bronze cent blanks from an outside supplier for $86,400.)

---

[1] Letter, May 16, 1996.

1906 Indian Cent

Business Strikes:

Business strike mintage: 96,020,530.

Number of business strike obverse dies made: Not known.

Average number of coins struck from typical obverse die: Not known.

Availability in Mint State: Common at all levels. Philadelphia Mint coins of this decade are usually priced as "types" rather than by dates. Although some are scarcer than others, there are still enough around to fill the demand.

Availability in circulated grades: Common.

Characteristics of striking: Varies.

Market Prices (1906 business strikes)

YEAR	G-4	VG-8	F-12	VF-20	EF-40	AU-50
1938	$0.05	$0.08	$0.10	$0.10	$0.10	$0.15
1944	.07	.10	.15	.15	.20	.25
1965	.40	.75	1.15	2.25	3.50	6.00
1996	1.00	1.20	1.50	2.20	7.00	15.00

YEAR	MS-60BN	MS-60RB	MS-63BN	MS-63RB	MS-63RD
1938	$0.30	$0.30	$0.30	$0.30	$0.35
1944	0.35	0.35	0.35	0.35	0.40
1965	10.00	11.00	10.00	11.50	15.00
1996	22.50	30.00	28.00	40.00	70.00

YEAR	MS-64BN	MS-64RB	MS-64RD	MS-65BN	MS-65RB	MS-65RD
1938	$0.30	$0.30	$0.35	$0.30	$0.30	$0.35
1944	0.35	0.35	0.40	0.35	0.35	0.40
1965	11.00	12.50	17.50	12.00	13.50	20.00
1996	35.00	47.50	80.00	45.00	85.00	275.00

Proofs:

Proof mintage: 1,725.

Proof commentary: One of the lower mintages. Dies typically fully mirrored; no "wipe lines" seen on early states of these Proofs.[1]

Market Prices (1906 Proofs)

YEAR	PR-60BN	PR-60RB	PR-63BN	PR-63RB	PR-63RD	
1938	$1.00	$1.00	$1.00	$1.00	$1.10	
1944	1.75	1.80	1.75	1.80	2.00	
1965	52.00	53.00	52.00	55.00	57.50	
1996	85.00	100.00	115.00	130.00	165.00	

YEAR	PR-64BN	PR-64RB	PR-64RD	PR-65BN	PR-65RB	PR-65RD
1938	$1.00	$1.00	$1.10	$1.00	$1.00	$1.10
1944	1.75	1.80	2.00	1.75	1.80	2.10
1965	52.00	55.00	58.50	53.00	55.00	60.00
1996	135.00	195.00	310.00	240.00	360.00	750.00

Notes

Collecting commentary: Again we have the situation—prevalent for the 1890s and 1900s—that an issue is plentiful in business strike form but truly scarce in Proof.

Oddity: One specimen is known struck in gold, undoubtedly a delicacy made for numismatic sale (see related entry under 1900 sub-chapter), not as a mint error.[2]

Planchets: In 1906, for the first time in many years, planchets for one-cent pieces were made within the Philadelphia Mint. However, 216,000 pounds avoirdupois of ready-made planchets were purchased from the outside for $59,540.[3]

Branch mints: The Act of April 24, 1906, provided that minor coins including cents could be struck at the branch mints (San Francisco, Denver, and New Orleans). However, such coinage did not materialize until San Francisco struck cents in 1908, and Denver produced them in 1911. New Orleans never produced minor coins.

---

[1] Richard Snow, letter, April 10, 1996.
[2] Michael Hodder, letter, May 14, 1996, who reported he had personally inspected the coin.
[3] 1906 *Mint Report*, p. 36.

New cent design in the offing?: *The Numismatist,* May 1906, carried an article, "New Design for Copper Cent," which contained some information and mis-information. Excerpts:

> A change in the design of the small bronze cent, which has made its appearance each year since its adoption, in 1864, is being considered by a Congressional committee, and experiments are also underway looking to the use of a new metal, either pure nickel or aluminum, to take the place of that now used, which is 95% copper and 5% zinc.

> The contemplated change is the outcome of the agitation in favor of new designs for United States coins of all denominations, not a single one of the present series seeming to meet with general favor. Expert numismatists go so far as to say that never in the history of this country has it been represented by a less artistic set of coins....

> In 1808 the old style of Liberty Head, with flowing hair and face to the right, was superseded by a new and handsome head, with hair bound, facing to the left.... There was not a really handsome head borne by any cent issued after 1809 [*sic;* actually, the design of 1808, called the Classic Head today, was continued through 1814], each succeeding year the design apparently becoming more indifferent than its predecessor, while in 1839 there appeared varieties now known to collectors by the titles of 'Booby Head' and 'Silly Head' cents....

> Though no cents were issued in the year 1815, still a pattern cent was made at the Mint. This showed a coronet head surrounded by very small stars, but none was issued.... [QDB note: All of the information about the 1815 pattern is false.]

> Of recent years very few pattern cent dies have been made, though quite a number of cents have been struck at the Mint from the regular dies in various metals other than those ordinarily used. It would thus appear that the designers are now content with the present style of cent, but many of those interested in coins are not so well pleased, and will gladly welcome a change.

As it turned out, a number of shield-design cents were made in 1896. While some were sold to collectors, many dozens were retained at the Mint and exchanged with William H. Woodin circa 1910. Years later in the early 1950s, these turned up in or near Woodin's home in Berwick, Pennsylvania, and were acquired by Robert K. Botsford, of Nescopeck, Pennsylvania, and sold to the present writer.

1907 Indian Cent

Business Strikes:

Business strike mintage: 108,137,143. Record high mintage for any United States coin issue from 1793 up to this date.

Number of business strike obverse dies made: Not known.

Average number of coins struck from typical obverse die: Not known.

Availability in Mint State: Common at all levels. A few rolls have come on the market in recent decades.

Availability in circulated grades: Common.

Characteristics of striking: Varies.

Market Prices (1907 business strikes)

YEAR	G-4	VG-8	F-12	VF-20	EF-40	AU-50
1938	$0.05	$0.08	$0.10	$0.10	$0.15	$0.20
1944	.07	.10	.15	.15	.20	.30
1965	.40	.75	1.15	2.25	3.50	6.00
1996	1.00	1.20	1.50	2.20	7.00	15.00

YEAR	MS-60BN	MS-60RB	MS-63BN	MS-63RB	MS-63RD
1938	$0.40	$0.40	$0.40	$0.40	$0.50
1944	.65	.65	.65	.70	.75
1965	10.00	11.00	10.00	11.50	15.00
1996	22.50	30.00	28.00	40.00	70.00

YEAR	MS-64BN	MS-64RB	MS-64RD	MS-65BN	MS-65RB	MS-65RD
1938	$0.40	$0.40	$0.50	$0.40	$0.40	$0.50
1944	.65	.70	.75	.65	.70	.75
1965	11.00	12.50	17.50	12.00	13.50	20.00
1996	35.00	47.50	80.00	45.00	85.00	275.00

Proofs:

Proof mintage: 1,475.

Proof commentary: Paradoxically, while 1907 has the highest mintage of any business strike Indian cent, it has the lowest Proof mintage of its era. There was a financial panic that year, and many buyers of Proof coins sat on the sidelines. Several years ago a client, John Jay Pittman, spent several years trying to find a nice Proof of this date. Bright red Proofs are especially elusive.

Many Proof strikings are seen with "wipe lines," a.k.a. die finish lines. The 1907 is particularly well known in this regard. (See comment under 1901 Proofs.)

Market Prices (1907 Proofs)

YEAR	PR-60BN	PR-60RB	PR-63BN	PR-63RB	PR-63RD	
1938	$1.00	$1.00	$1.00	$1.00	$1.10	
1944	2.20	2.20	2.20	2.30	2.50	
1965	52.00	53.00	52.00	55.00	57.50	
1996	85.00	100.00	115.00	130.00	165.00	

YEAR	PR-64BN	PR-64RB	PR-64RD	PR-65BN	PR-65RB	PR-65RD
1938	$1.00	$1.00	$1.10	$1.00	$1.00	$1.10
1944	2.20	2.30	2.50	2.20	2.30	2.60
1965	52.00	55.00	59.00	54.00	56.50	61.00
1996	135.00	210.00	400.00	270.00	395.00	1,250.00

Notes

Collecting commentary: The most common Indian cent in terms of business strikes. Available in all grades.

Proofs are quite scarce as, indeed, are most Proof issues of the 1890s and 1900s. However, the price structure is such that more plentiful Proofs of the 1880s often sell for higher prices.

Gold striking: At the 1952 convention of the American Numismatic Association, California dealer Abe Kosoff sold Eastern dealer Bill Mertes a 1907 Indian cent struck in gold. The price was $40, which was about 15 times the amount a bronze Proof of the same date might have sold for at the time. The *New York Times* carried a story in its August 19th edition stating that "a 1907 Indian cent" had sold for $40, neglecting to mention it was in gold. Other newspapers picked up the news. For the next several days coin dealers were deluged with telephone calls and visits from members of the public who had ordinary bronze 1907 cents—the commonest date of the series, a coin worth about five cents if well worn—hoping to get $40 for it.

The *Numismatic Scrapbook Magazine,* September 1952, told of the incident and went on to give a theory concerning the origin of the gold issue:

"There are several Indian cents of various dates known that are struck in gold. During the time that the Indian head type was being struck the Mint was also coining gold coins. The gold cents happened the same way that a nickel on a cent blank turns up occasionally today; a stray blank planchet in the wrong press." (Also see commentary under the 1900 cent listing above.)

Planchets: Manufacture of bronze cent planchets continued within the Mint, but in fiscal year 1907 190,000 pounds avoirdupois of finished blanks were purchased on contract for $65,550.[1]

New Mint director: 1907, September. Frank A. Leach became director of the Mint (was confirmed by the Senate later, on February 12, 1908) and was on hand when the famous MCMVII Saint-Gaudens $20 pieces were first made and when the 1908 Pratt $2.50 and $5 coins made their first appearance. In early 1909 he facilitated the introduction of the Lincoln cent. He left the post in November 1909 and was succeeded in the same month by A. Piatt Andrew, who served less than a year.

What might have been: Working in his studio in Cornish, New Hampshire, America's best known living sculptor, Augustus Saint-Gaudens, was busy redesigning the nation's coinage. By the time of his death in the summer of 1907 he had completed most work for his Indian $10 gold and "Victory" $20 gold designs and had sketched new motifs for a one-cent piece. While the $10 and $20 pieces were made in coinage form by the end of the year, his designs for the new cent were not developed sufficiently to be utilized.

---

[1] 1907 *Mint Report*, p. 35.

1908 Indian Cent

Business Strikes:

Business strike mintage: 32,326,317.

Number of business strike obverse dies made: Not known.

Average number of coins struck from typical obverse die: Not known.

Availability in Mint State: Generally considered to be a slightly scarcer date, but this is not borne out in population checks. Readily available in Mint State, although I do not recall ever having had a full Mint State original roll.

Availability in circulated grades: Common.

Characteristics of striking: Varies, mostly average, neither sharp nor weak.

Market Prices (1908 business strikes)

YEAR	G-4	VG-8	F-12	VF-20	EF-40	AU-50
1938	$0.05	$0.08	$0.10	$0.10	$0.10	$0.15
1944	.07	.10	.15	.15	.20	.30
1965	.50	.90	1.30	2.40	3.75	7.50
1996	1.00	1.20	1.50	2.20	7.00	15.00

YEAR	MS-60BN	MS-60RB	MS-63BN	MS-63RB	MS-63RD	
1938	$0.30	$0.30	$0.30	$0.30	$0.35	
1944	.45	.45	.45	.45	.55	
1965	13.50	14.00	13.50	15.00	20.00	
1996	23.50	32.00	29.00	42.00	75.00	

YEAR	MS-64BN	MS-64RB	MS-64RD	MS-65BN	MS-65RB	MS-65RD
1938	$0.30	$0.30	$0.35	$0.30	$0.30	$0.35
1944	.45	.50	.55	.45	.50	.55
1965	14.50	16.00	22.50	15.50	17.00	25.00
1996	36.50	48.50	82.00	47.00	86.00	280.00

Proofs:

Proof mintage: 1,620.

Proof commentary: Very low mintage for the era. Sometimes seen red with brown blotches. Assembling a beautiful set of Proof Indian cents dated in the 1900s is far more difficult than putting one together from the 1880s.

Market Prices (1908 Proofs)

YEAR	PR-60BN	PR-60RB	PR-63BN	PR-63RB	PR-63RD	
1938	$1.00	$1.00	$1.00	$1.00	$1.10	
1944	1.75	1.80	1.75	1.80	2.00	
1965	52.00	53.00	52.00	55.00	57.50	
1996	85.00	100.00	115.00	130.00	165.00	

YEAR	PR-64BN	PR-64RB	PR-64RD	PR-65BN	PR-65RB	PR-65RD
1938	$1.00	$1.00	$1.10	$1.00	$1.00	$1.10
1944	1.75	1.80	2.00	1.75	1.80	2.10
1965	52.00	55.00	58.50	54.00	56.00	61.00
1996	135.00	190.00	300.00	240.00	320.00	750.00

Notes

Collecting commentary: Readily available, but always considered to be a slightly better date in Mint State.

No longer exclusive: First year of non-exclusivity of cent striking by just one mint. The San Francisco Mint produced cents for the first time (1908-S).

1908-S Indian Cent

Close-up view of the tiny S mintmark on the reverse of the 1908-S Indian cent, the first branch mint coin of this denomination.

Business Strikes:

Business strike mintage: 1,115,000.

Number of business strike obverse dies made: Not known.

Average number of coins struck from typical obverse die: Not known.

Availability in Mint State: In Mint State 1908-S Indian cents are fairly scarce, but are more available than the low mintage implies, as collectors saved them. In over 40 years of being a rare coin dealer I have seen only one original bank-wrapped roll of 50 pieces, and this was a roll owned by James F. Ruddy in the mid-1950s. However, I have always thought that the 1908-S is harder to find than the 1909-S Indian, and in terms of rarity in Mint State it far eclipses the celebrated 1909-S V.D.B. Lincoln cent.

These and 1909-S Indian cents (and also 1909-S V.D.B. Lincoln cents) were struck on bronze planchets of a somewhat more yellowish-appearing straw-colored alloy, different to the experienced eye from the deeper red used for Philadelphia Mint cents (this difference can only be seen on cents that have not been cleaned, dipped, or retoned). Sometimes these have a woodgrain type of toning, but not as prominent as on later 1909-S Indian cents.

Availability in circulated grades: Rare in the context of the Indian series. A key issue. Circulated specimens are most often seen in grades from Fine to VF or EF. Well worn (Abt. Good and Good) pieces are rarer but not more desirable.

Characteristics of striking: Average. The reverse is usually sharper than the obverse. The feather tips are nearly always weak, but there are scattered exceptions. Richard Snow reports seeing an original roll of 50 Mint State coins with all pieces having the final A in AMERICA very weak.[1]

Market Prices (1908-S business strikes)

YEAR	G-4	VG-8	F-12	VF-20	EF-40	AU-50
1938	$0.50	$0.65	$0.75	$1.00	$1.25	$2.00
1944	.70	.90	1.25	1.50	1.75	2.25
1965	22.00	30.00	37.50	50.00	62.50	90.00
1996	35.00	40.00	46.00	50.00	82.00	125.00

YEAR	MS-60BN	MS-60RB	MS-63BN	MS-63RB	MS-63RD
1938	$2.25	$2.25	$2.25	$2.25	$2.50
1944	3.50	3.50	3.50	3.70	4.00
1965	120.00	125.00	120.00	127.50	135.00
1996	190.00	225.00	280.00	300.00	400.00

YEAR	MS-64BN	MS-64RB	MS-64RD	MS-65BN	MS-65RB	MS-65RD
1938	$2.25	$2.25	$2.50	$2.25	$2.25	$2.50
1944	3.50	3.70	4.00	3.50	3.70	4.00
1965	125.00	130.00	137.50	127.50	132.50	150.00
1996	295.00	395.00	650.00	365.00	600.00	1,125.00

Notes

Collecting commentary: The first branch mint coin of this denomination. Always in demand. This issue is scarcer in Mint State than generally believed, due no doubt to most pieces being put into circulation before widespread public interest arose in "rare" cents, the latter occasioned by the release of the new Lincoln cents on August 2, 1909. The 1909-S V.D.B. Lincoln cent was soon recognized as a rarity, but by that time anyone wanting to find Mint State 1908-S Indian cents probably could not do so, at least not very easily.

No minor coins at other mints: In the American West most transactions were in silver and gold coins, and on the West Coast one-cent pieces were rarely seen, nor was there a call for them. Because of this, no minor coins were struck at western mints until the 1908-S cent.

David Sundman proposes that streetcar fares and sales taxes were catalysts to the coining of Indian cents for the first time in San Francisco.[2] In *The Story of the Bank of California,* by Neill C. Wilson, it states:

---

[1] Richard Snow, letter, April 10, 1996.
[2] David Sundman letter and book excerpt, September 1996.

Among the changes wrought by the Depression upon the Pacific Coast was the disappearance of gold money, and its replacement by paper currency. When the government called in all gold and locked it into vaults at Fort Knox, the eight-decade rule of King Gold and Queen Silver on the Coast came to an end. Another western custom also had been disappearing—the aversion to pennies. Once all settlements even at the banks, had been made to the nearest nickel. The rise of street car fares from five cents to six had made copper pennies essential. Sales tax also rushed the trend along. The great Mint at Fifth and Mission streets in San Francisco, which had coined over $103 million in gold in one year before the Fire, and never a copper penny until 1908, at last turned energetically to the task of making one-cent pieces.

From the 1909 (*sic*) *Mint Report:* "The manufacture of United States minor coin was instituted at this mint during the year [1908], and on November 27, 1908, the first one-cent pieces ever made at the San Francisco Mint were delivered by the coiner to the superintendent. The one-cent bronze pieces struck during the [1909 fiscal year extending from July 1, 1908 to June 30, 1909] amounted to $14,240.... The bronze coins manufactured at this mint during the year were made on the silver presses. Two new presses for bronze coining are now being installed to handle this class of work."

A specimen of the 1908-S cent was subsequently added to the Mint Collection in Philadelphia. This cabinet did not normally include branch mint coins (of earlier issues in the silver and gold series), nor did the 1908-S inclusion signal a major policy change. It developed that by 1914 no 1909-S Indian cent had been added.[1]

Die varieties: The May 1912 issue of *The Numismatist* contained this comment from Commodore W.C. Eaton, who earlier had published several commentaries on varieties of *Lincoln* cents:

I find that in my various listings of the sub-varieties of the San Francisco cents I have missed one. Mr. Henry Mitchell of Philadelphia has kindly written me concerning his discovery that there are two varieties in the position of the mint mark in the S.F. Indian Head of 1908. In one the 'S' is midway between the ribbon end on the left and the stem on the right; in the other the 'S' is nearer the ribbon end. I do not know how I overlooked this variety as I find I have both, my duplicates all being of the latter type.

If all collectors were as obliging as Mr. Mitchell in reporting their discoveries we would be pretty certain to make this list complete.[2]

---

[1] *Catalogue of Coins, Tokens and Medals...*[in the Mint Collection], 1914, p. 82.
[2] More information about Commodore Eaton will be found earlier under the sub-chapter on 1857 Flying Eagle cents.

1909 Indian Cent

Business Strikes:

Business strike mintage: 14,368,470.

Number of business strike obverse dies made: Not known.

Average number of coins struck from typical obverse die: Not known.

Availability in Mint State: One of the most plentiful of all Indian cents despite its somewhat low mintage. Undipped, uncleaned brilliant Mint State coins are reddish orange and are colored different from the 1909-S. Bright red specimens are among the most common issues, although this date has sometimes been called "scarce" in this regard, no doubt by cataloguers who look at the mintage figure and consider little else.

Availability in circulated grades: Slightly scarcer date in worn grades due to its lower mintage.

Characteristics of striking: Varies, but usually better than average.

Market Prices (1909 business strikes)

YEAR	G-4	VG-8	F-12	VF-20	EF-40	AU-50
1938	$0.05	$0.08	$0.10	$0.10	$0.10	$0.15
1944	.07	.10	.15	.15	.20	.30
1965	.85	1.25	2.00	3.00	5.00	8.75
1996	1.55	2.00	3.10	3.75	8.75	17.00

YEAR	MS-60BN	MS-60RB	MS-63BN	MS-63RB	MS-63RD	
1938	$0.30	$0.30	$0.30	$0.30	$0.35	
1944	0.35	0.35	0.35	0.35	0.40	
1965	14.00	15.00	14.50	15.50	22.00	
1996	31.00	44.00	35.50	45.00	80.00	

YEAR	MS-64BN	MS-64RB	MS-64RD	MS-65BN	MS-65RB	MS-65RD
1938	$0.30	$0.30	$0.35	$0.30	$0.30	$0.35
1944	0.35	0.35	0.40	0.35	0.35	0.40
1965	15.50	17.50	24.00	17.00	19.00	27.00
1996	52.00	65.00	85.00	50.00	90.00	285.00

Proofs:

Proof mintage: 2,175.

Proof commentary: Fairly scarce. Usually a rich red-orange color if brilliant. This date has often sold for a premium, due not so much to its scarcity as to its position as the last year in the series.

Market Prices (1909 Proofs)

YEAR	PR-60BN	PR-60RB	PR-63BN	PR-63RB	PR-63RD	
1938	$2.50	$2.50	$2.50	$2.50	$2.50	
1944	3.20	3.30	3.20	3.30	3.50	
1965	63.00	67.00	63.00	70.00	72.50	
1996	85.00	100.00	115.00	160.00	195.00	

YEAR	PR-64BN	PR-64RB	PR-64RD	PR-65BN	PR-65RB	PR-65RD
1938	$2.50	$2.50	$2.50	$2.50	$2.50	$2.50
1944	3.30	3.30	3.50	3.30	3.30	3.50
1965	65.00	71.00	75.00	67.00	72.00	80.00
1996	185.00	210.00	300.00	320.00	365.00	750.00

Notes

Collecting commentary: The 1909 is the last of the Indian cents and is in slightly greater demand as such. However, the issue is not particularly scarce in higher grades.

Master die: Beginning this year the date was included in the master die and impressed at the same time as the other design features into the working die. Thus, from 1909 onward—including in the Lincoln series—there are no more repunched date numerals (later doubled die obverses are from the entire die being double punched, not just the date).

In 1909 the initial L (for Longacre) on the headdress ribbon was enlarged slightly.

The 9 in the date, which often displayed blob-like characteristics on coins dated from 1890 through 1908, was reconfigured to a more open appearance, with greater separation between the bottom ball and the top curve. See expanded commentary under the 1890 sub-chapter.

Planchets: For the first time in many years *all* planchets were made within Mint facilities.[1]

---

[1] 1909 *Mint Report*, p. 43.

1909-S Indian Cent

Business Strikes:

Business strike mintage: 309,000.

Number of business strike obverse dies made: Not known.

Average number of coins struck from typical obverse die: Not known.

Availability in Mint State: Fairly scarce, although more available by far than Mint State coins of higher mintages such as 1866-1872 and 1877. This is because there was an awareness of numismatics and low mintages in 1909 that was not present earlier.

Planchets usually have light straw-colored or yellow streaks, sometimes subtle, sometimes giving a woodgrain toning effect similar to that seen on bronze cents of the mid-1860s (although the cents of the 1860s are reddish, not yellowish, in cast). This characteristic is probably true of all undipped original 1909-S Indian coins (the same planchet characteristics are seen on the later 1909-S V.D.B. Lincoln cents).

Availability in circulated grades: Rare. Usually seen Fine or better. Struck and cast counterfeits exist as do pieces with phony mintmarks added later; buy with a written guarantee, without exception.

Characteristics of striking: Usually lightly defined and always lacking feather tip details, not due to striking, but to lack of definition in the working die. On the reverse the shield is usually well struck, however.[1]

Market Prices (1909-S business strikes)

YEAR	G-4	VG-8	F-12	VF-20	EF-40	AU-50
1938	$0.75	$0.90	$1.20	$1.50	$2.00	$3.00
1944	2.50	4.00	5.00	6.00	7.00	8.00
1965	77.50	95.00	130.00	165.00	200.00	290.00
1996	225.00	265.00	300.00	325.00	360.00	410.00

[1] Richard Snow, letter, April 10, 1996. He further commented: "The only one I have ever seen with full feather tips was certified as MS-65 RD, but I informed [a leading certification service] that the S was added later." The service bought the coin from him.

YEAR	MS-60BN	MS-60RB	MS-63BN	MS-63RB	MS-63RD	
1938	$4.25	$4.25	$4.25	$4.50	$5.00	
1944	11.00	11.00	11.00	11.50	12.50	
1965	325.00	350.00	335.00	360.00	380.00	
1996	470.00	520.00	510.00	610.00	750.00	

YEAR	MS-64BN	MS-64RB	MS-64RD	MS-65BN	MS-65RB	MS-65RD
1938	$4.25	$4.50	$5.00	$4.25	$4.50	$5.00
1944	11.00	11.50	12.50	11.00	11.50	12.50
1965	340.00	365.00	385.00	350.00	375.00	410.00
1996	600.00	850.00	1,100.00	700.00	1,100.00	2,200.00

Notes

Collecting commentary: Lowest mintage of any regular issue in the series; just 309,000. Numismatists were aware of the desirability of the variety, and quite a few coins were saved (in contrast, business strike 1877 cents were ignored in the year of their issue and became very rare). However, the old-style 1909-S Indian cents were vastly eclipsed by the new Lincoln cents released on August 2, 1909, and they soon were forgotten by all but a few.

Second time: The 1909-S Indian cent represents the second year of cent production at the San Francisco Mint.

Reminiscence: In the early 1950s I received a price list from B. Max Mehl, the famous Fort Worth, Texas dealer (1884-1957) who was then in the twilight years of his illustrious career. Offered for sale was an Uncirculated 1909-S cent for $10. Mehl at that time issued such lists only occasionally and did not necessarily keep up with the rapidly advancing rare coin market. Recognizing the 1909-S as a bargain I telephoned him in Fort Worth to order one. He responded with a cheery commentary that went something like this:

> I know the 1909-S Indians are worth a lot more than ten dollars now, but I have had these for a long time. I like to read your ads in the *Numismatic Scrapbook,* and I wish you luck in your career. How many 1909-S cents do you want?

Additional Comments and Summary

Indian cents minted from 1859 to 1909 became quite popular beginning in the early 1990s. This activity came after about 20 years of lassitude. Still, even today there are some Indian cents that are priced no higher than they were back in the 1970s!

As has been the case with collecting Flying Eagle cents, the publication of Richard Snow's book, *Flying Eagle & Indian Cents,* in 1992 and the debut of Larry R. Steve and Kevin's book, *Comprehensive Guide to Selected Rare Flying Eagle and Indian Cent Varieties,* in 1995 no doubt have spurred a lot of interest in Indian cents, as has the Fly-In Club and its information-filled journal, *Longacre's Ledger.*

On August 2, 1909, the new Lincoln cent made its debut, and the long-lived Indian cent design became part of history.

APPENDIX I
DIE QUANTITIES FOR EACH YEAR

Commentary and Analysis

R.W. Julian's Research

Introduction

The following information concerning dies is adapted from data gathered by R.W. Julian in the National Archives and furnished to the author. (Following the Julian data and commentary are other figures taken from a different source, the A.W. Downing notebook.)

Figures are given each year for the number of obverse and reverse dies destroyed for each year. As obverse dies were dated, they were destroyed early in January of each year following. On the other hand, reverse dies could be held over for further use. For example, early in 1863, dies used in 1862 were destroyed, amounting to 197 obverses and 296 reverses. Thus, these constitute the 1892 figures.

It seems likely that the Mint made dies as they were needed, rather than in large groups on speculation that they might be used. Thus, obverse dies for lower mint-age dates such as 1877 and 1894 were made in smaller quantities. It was probably the case that, despite this practice, not all dies were used.

The average business strike production from obverse dies for a given year can be determined by dividing the mintage total by the number of dated obverse dies made. In most if not all instances, this number is probably slightly higher than the actual average, for some of the dies may not have been used and others may have been Proof dies not used for circulating coinage. Moreover, it was Mint practice to prepare some dies in December for the following year's coinage; for example, it seems likely that in late December 1885 certain 1886-dated obverse cent dies were made (see explanation under A.W. Downing notebook, 1886 die listing, below; this study follows the R.W. Julian data).

Records are available for certain years 1856 through 1898 inclusive.

Business Strike and Proof Dies

The Mint records show these die figures for each year. For a few years Proof dies are listed separately, but these do not necessarily represent all of the Proof dies used that year. For years in which Proof dies are not given separately, figures include a few Proof dies. Author's commentaries are in parentheses:

1856: Flying Eagle: "4 experimental dies for small cents" (Comment: Apparently equivalent to two pairs; this would mean that other dies for 1856 Flying Eagle cents were made later, possibly included under figures for other later dates.)

1857: 119 obverse dies, 130 reverse dies. (Comment: From this point until the late 1870s it appears that obverse dies were replaced less often than reverse dies.)

1858: 232 obverse, 266 reverse.

1859-1860: not available.

1861: 92 obverse, 85 reverse.

1862: 197 obverse, 296 reverse.

1863-1864: not available.

1865: 109 obverse, 144 reverse.

1866-1872: not available.

1873: 72 obverse, 87 reverse; 16 reverse dies were held over for the next year. (In addition to these "holdover" figures, certain other reverse dies were held over from time to time, as reflected by the evidence on coins studied by specialists; in other words, these Mint figures are not complete.)

1874: 67 obverse, 93 reverse; 25 reverse dies were held over.

1875: 68 obverse, 99 reverse; 9 reverse dies were held over.

1876: 39 obverse, 54 reverse; 4 reverse dies were held over.

1877: 3 obverse, 6 reverse; 4 reverse dies were held over [apparently, this did not include Proof dies].

1878: 32 obverse, 45 reverse; 2 reverse dies were held over.

1879: 77 obverse, 64 reverse; 5 reverse dies were held over. (From this year onward the trend was for reverse dies to outlast obverse dies.)

1880: 130 obverse, 115 reverse; plus 1 obverse Proof die and 1 reverse Proof die listed separately.

1881: 97 obverse, 97 reverse; 1 reverse die was held over.

1882: 75 obverse, 63 reverse.

1883: 149 obverse, 137 reverse.

1884: 124 obverse, 130 reverse.

1885: 47 obverse, 47 reverse; plus 1 obverse Proof die and 1 reverse Proof die listed separately.

1886: 48 obverse, 48 reverse.

1887: 154 obverse, 161 reverse.

1888: 185 obverse, 123 reverse.

1889: 224 obverse, 183 reverse.

1890: 224 obverse, 166 reverse.

1891: 175 obverse, 127 reverse.

1892: 165 obverse, 133 reverse.

1893: 173 obverse, 137 reverse.

1894: 57 obverse, 51 reverse.

1895: 105 obverse, 101 reverse; plus 1 obverse Proof die and 1 reverse Proof die listed separately.

1896: 133 obverse, 133 reverse; plus 1 obverse Proof die and 1 reverse Proof die listed separately.

1897: 160 obverse, 140 reverse; plus 1 obverse Proof die and 1 reverse Proof die listed separately.

1898: 197 obverse, 152 reverse; plus 1 obverse Proof die and 1 reverse Proof die listed separately.

1899: 117 obverse, 98 reverse; plus 1 obverse Proof die and 1 reverse Proof die listed separately.

1900: 157 obverse, 135 reverse.

1901: 149 obverse, 140 reverse.

1902: 150 obverse, 125 reverse.

1903: 179 obverse, 147 reverse.

From this time *combined* obverse and reverse die production was given by the Mint for *fiscal* years (July 1 through June 30). Thus these numbers cannot be precisely matched with calendar year mintage figures:

1903-1904 (fiscal year): 264 cent dies.

1904-1905 (fiscal year): 404 cent dies.

1905-1906 (fiscal year): 626 cent dies.

1906-1907 (fiscal year): 557 cent dies.

As the number of obverse dies in a given year rarely equates to the number of reverse dies and in most years is not even close, the policy at the Mint must have been to replace dies when they broke or showed too much wear, at which time dies were replaced not in pairs but one die at a time.

Proof Obverse Dies

Not recorded in Mint archives are Proof dies for all other dates, nor are the figures complete for the dates that are recorded. However, we know that in every instance at least one Proof obverse die was made each year, and in some instances there were several. For example, in his 1994 study Richard Snow found two or more obverse die varieties for certain dates in the Indian cent series (Flying Eagle cents were not studied). The Downing die notebook (cited separately below) does not list Proof dies for certain Indian cent dates; the figures were mixed with business strike dies.

Further, some Proof dies were also used to coin business strikes. At the very least the data are "fuzzy," but they are all we have to work with. In time, numismatic study will probably supersede the Mint figures.

Obverse die counts based upon observation of specimens in numismatic hands include the following:[1]

1859: 2 obverse dies

1860: 2

1861: 2

1862: 1

1863: 1[2]

1864: 5 = 3 without L and 2 with L

1865: 2, both Plain 5

1866: 1

1867: 1

1868: 1

1869: 2

1870: 2

1871: 3

1872: 1

1873: 2; Closed 3 style[3]

---

[1] "Proof Die Identification for Indian Cents." *Longacre's Ledger,* Fall 1994. Cited here are Richard Snow's numbers for the years ending with 1903.

[2] Pattern 1863 bronze cents are from a different die.

[3] Larry R. Steve, letter, April 12, 1996, mentioned a second obverse die, not cited by Richard Snow, which is *very slightly* doubled in the word LIBERTY (but is not a Proof version of the famous Doubled Die of this year).

1874: 1[1]
1875: 3[2]
1876: 2
1877: 3[3]
1878: 2
1879: 1
1880: 2
1881: 2
1882: 1
1883: 3
1884: 2 (one pair, probably dated 1884, delivered on December 19).[4]
1885: 4[5] (one pair delivered on January 5).[6]
1886: 5 = 2 of Type I and 3 of Type II
1887: 1
1888: 3 (one pair delivered on January 11).[7]
1889: 1
1890: 2
1891: 3
1892: 3
1893: 1
1894: 2
1895: 4
1896: 4
1897: 1
1898: 1
1899: 2
1900: 2
1901: 4
1902: 2
1903: 1

Number of Business Strike Obverses Each Year

To approximate the net number of obverse business strike dies for each year I take the total number of obverse dies and deduct from these figures the number of different obverse dies known to have been used on Proof coins (per Richard Snow's previously cited figures and other sources). The number of Proof obverse dies is probably slightly larger than given here, as certain Proof dies have not been numismatically identified and published. Moreover, in some instances Proof dies were also used to make business strikes.[8] Further, as explained in the introductory

---

[1] Richard Snow, letter, May 3, 1995; earlier the same writer had thought there were two obverse dies, one without recutting.
[2] QDB note: Possibly four obverse dies are known. Richard Snow cites three different.
[3] Richard Snow, letter, April 10, 1996.
[4] Per A.W. Downing die notebook.
[5] Richard Snow, letter, April 10, 1996.
[6] Per A.W. Downing die notebook.
[7] Per A.W. Downing die notebook.
[8] Larry R. Steve, letter, April 12, 1996.

remarks to Appendix I, it is possible that certain figures may include dated dies made in advance for the next year. However, these numbers are no doubt useful in a general sense, even though absolute dating precision cannot be applied to them.

This procedure yields the following:

1856: 2 obverse dies made during this calendar year.

1857: 118 dies (119 per Mint figures, minus 1 die known on Proofs)

1858: 230 dies (220 less 2 known on Proofs).

1859-1860: information not available.

1861: 90 (92 less 2)

1862: 196 (197 less 1)

1863-1864: information not available.

1865: 107 (109 less 2)

1866-1872: information not available.

1873: 70 (72 less 2)

1874: 66 (67 less 1)

1875: 65 (68 less 3)

1876: 37 (39 less 2)

1877: 3 (estimated; the Mint figures on obverse dies cannot be correct this year for more business strike and Proof die varieties are known than the combined total of 3 in Mint records)

1878: 30 (32 less 2)

1879: 76 (77 less 1)

1880: 129 (131 less 2)

1881: 95 (97 less 2).

1882: 74 (74 less 1)

1883: 146 (149 less 3)

1884: 122 (124 less 2)

1885: 44 (48 less 4)

1886: 43 (48 less 5)

1887: 153 (154 less 1)

1888: 182 (185 less 3)

1889: 223 (224 less 1)

1890: 222 (224 less 2)

1891: 172 (175 less 3)

1892: 162 (165 less 3)

1893: 172 (173 less 1)

1894: 55 (57 less 2)

1895: 102 (106 less 4)

1896: 130 (134 less 4)

1897: 160 (161 less 1)

1898: 197 (198 less 1)

1899: 116 (118 less 2)

1900: 155 (157 less 2)

1901: 145 (149 less 4)

1902: 148 (150 less 2)

1903: 178 (179 less 1)

Number of Business Strikes Per Die Each Year

From the preceding it is possible to obtain the average number of business strikes made from each obverse die each year by dividing the number of dies into the business strike mintage.

The numismatic importance of these figures is mainly to estimate the average mintage of a given die variety. For example, of a given specific die variety of 1858— such as the 1858/7 overdate with the die chip above the date—the estimated mintage is 106,957. Of course, the die could have broken after a few hundred coins were struck, or it could have been kept in use for a longer than average time and, say, 150,000 could have been made. However, it seems reasonable that a rounded-off average mintage of 100,000 to 110,000 pieces is reasonable.

In the same vein, there is one known 1894 obverse die with a sharply double-punched date. On the average, as there were 55 obverse dies used that year, it seems that the chances of finding one of the double-punched date variety among a group of unsorted 1894 cents would be about 1 in 55. And, it seems that a mintage of, say, 300,000 to 310,000 for this variety might be a reasonable estimate.

On the other hand, if a die variety is general and was used on many different dies—such as 1858 Flying Eagle cents with Large Letters and Small Letters or 1886 Indian cents of the Type I and II formats—then these figures are not useful. For example, probably 100 or more 1858 obverse dies were of the Large Letters type. However, as within the 1858 Large Letters cents there are two *specific dies* for the 1858/7 overdate known, it is reasonable to estimate a coinage of about 100,000 to 110,000 from each of these dies, or a total overdate mintage of 200,00 to 220,000. Of course, if a third 1858/7 overdate die were to be identified by numismatists, then the estimate would increase.

Further, as noted in the introduction to Appendix I, some dies may have been made up in advance, thus distorting the figures slightly.

1856: 2 dies / 900 estimated business strikes = 450 coins per die (average). Commentary: Pattern, not a regular issue. These dies were probably used in later years to make restrikes.

1857: 118 / 17,450,000 business strikes = **148,644 coins per die.** Commentary: Copper-nickel.

1858: 230 / 24,600,000 = **106,957 coins per die.** Commentary: Copper-nickel.

1861: 90 / 10,100,000 = **112,222 coins per die.** Commentary: Copper-nickel.

1862: 196 / 28,075,000 = **143,240 coins per die.** Commentary: Copper-nickel.

1865: 107 / 35,429,286 = **331,115 coins per die.** Commentary: This is the first bronze Indian cent for which figures are known. The softness of the new bronze alloy apparently accounted for a greater number of coins struck per die. From this point onward, the averages are higher than for the 1857-1862 copper-nickel issues.

1873: 70 / 11,676,500 = **166,807 coins per die.**

1874: 66 / 14,187,500 = **214,962 coins per die.**

1875: 65 / 13,528,000 = **208,123 coins per die.**

1876: 37 / 7,944,000 = **214,703 coins per die.**

1877: 3 / 852,500 = **284,167 coins per die.** Commentary: This figure is highly theoretical, as 1877 cents seem to be much rarer than an original business strike mintage of 852,000 would indicate. See discussion under sub-chapter for 1877 cents.

1878: 30 / 5,797,500 = **193,250 coins per die.**

1879: 76 / 16,228,000 = **213,526 coins per die.**

1880: 129 / 38,961,000 = **302,023 coins per die.**

1881: 95 / 39,208,000 = **412,716 coins per die.** Commentary: Highest figure to this point in time for the dates studied.

1882: 74 / 38,578,000 = **521,324 coins per die.** Commentary: Record high figure for the nineteenth century dates studied; this figure would not be exceeded until 1901.

1883: 146 / 45,591,500 = **312,271 coins per die.**

1884: 122 / 23,257,800 = **190,638 coins per die.**

1885: 44 / 11,761,594 = **267,309 coins per die.**

1886: 43 / 17,650,000 = **410,465 coins per die.**

1887: 153 / 45,223,523 = **295,579 coins per die.**

1888: 182 / 37,489,832 = **205,988 coins per die.**

1889: 223 / 48,866,025 = **219,130 coins per die.**

1890: 222 / 57,180,114 = **257,568 coins per die.**

1891: 172 / 47,070,000 = **273,663 coins per die.**

1892: 162 / 37,647,087 = **232,389 coins per die.**

1893: 172 / 46,640,000 = **271,163 coins per die.**

1894: 55 / 16,749,500 = **304,536 coins per die.**

1895: 102 / 38,341,474 = **375,897 coins per die.**

1896: 130 / 39,055,431 = **300,426 coins per die.**

1897: 160 / 50,464,392 = **315,402 coins per die.**

1898: 197 / 49,821,284 = **252,900 coins per die.**

1899: 116 / 53,598,000 = **462,052 coins per die.**

1900: 155 / 66,831,502 = **431,171 coins per die.**

1901: 145 / 79,609,158 = **549,029 coins per die.** First year of operation at the new Philadelphia Mint building and facilities.

1902: 148 / 87,374,704 = **590,370 coins per die.** Record high figure for the dates studied.

1903: 178 / 85,092,703 = **478,049 coins per die.**

Discussion of Die Combinations

Within a given year it is apparent that the obverse and reverse dies in a coining press were replaced as needed and at different times from each other.

Indian cents are not normally collected by minute differences (such as die polish lines) on their reverses, but are collected primarily by obverse varieties due to the individual characteristics of the date locations. However, as the dies were not re-placed by pairs at the same time, the rarity of a given obverse and reverse die combination can be much greater than the averages indicate.

Take for example the Indian cent of 1892. According to R.W. Julian's figures, modified to deduct Proof dies, there were 162 obverse dies used in 1892, and each struck an average of 232,389 coins. In practice, some dies struck more and some struck less, but this was the average.

In the same year, 1892, there were 133 reverse dies used—per the records of dies destroyed in January of the following year—but this might not include Proof dies, which might have been held over. If one estimates that two Proof dies were expended, this would leave a net of 131 business strike dies used. If so, then considering the business strike mintage for 1892 (37,647,087) and dividing by 131, the average number of coins struck per reverse die was 287,392.

As Larry R. Steve has pointed out,[1] the identification of every obverse die would be an arduous task, and for reverse dies it would be next to impossible unless high-grade specimens were available of each, as die markers would be very subtle and could not be seen on worn coins.

Among half cents, large cents, Connecticut copper coins, and numerous other early American series it is customary to assign specific obverse dies with numbers and reverse dies with letters. Thus the designation 1-A would represent Obverse Die 1 in combination with Reverse Die A.

Now, to a hypothetical scenario involving cents of 1892. It is early in the year, and Indian cents are to be struck for the first time. Over the next month or so, many coins are struck. The coiner keeps a record of the number of pieces struck from each obverse and reverse die and notes the following:

Obverse die No. 1: 210,008 (or a bit less than the average of 232,389 coins per obverse die).

Obverse die No. 2: 294,631 (more than average)

Obverse die No. 3: 14,032 (far fewer than average; the die broke unexpectedly after brief use)

Obverse die No. 4: 297,775 (more than average)

Obverse die No. 5: 345,499 (many more than average)

Concerning the reverse dies, production quantities are as follows:

Reverse A: 374,332 (more than the average of 287,392 per reverse die).

Reverse B: 74,537 (far fewer than average; the die broke).

Reverse C: 376,974 (more than average)

Reverse D: 334,032 (more than average)

Reverse E: 364,025 (more than average)

To continue the illustration, if the dies were used with each other in the above sequence, being replaced as they wore out or broke, coinage figures from each *die pair* would be as follows:

1-A: 210,008 (after which Obverse 1 was replaced by Obverse 2; however, Reverse A still a useful life of 164,324 impressions remaining)

2-A: 164,325 (at which time Reverse A broke and was replaced by Reverse B; Obverse 2 still had a useful life of 130,306 impressions remaining)

2-B: 74,537 (after which Reverse B broke and was replaced by Reverse C; however, Obverse 2 still had a useful life of 55,769 impressions remaining)

2-C: 55,769 (after which Obverse 2 broke and was replaced by Obverse 3; however, Reverse C still had a useful life of 321,205 impressions remaining).

3-C: 14,032 (after which Obverse 3 broke unexpectedly and was replaced by Obverse 4; however, Reverse C still had a useful life of 307,173 impressions remaining)

4-C: 297,775 (after which Obverse 4 broke and was replaced by Obverse 5; Reverse C still had a useful life of 9,398 impressions remaining)

5-C: 9,398 (after which Reverse C broke and was replaced by Reverse D; Obverse 5 still had a useful life of 336,101 impressions remaining)

It is seen from the above that combinations 3-C and 5-C are very rare and, in fact,

---

[1] Letter, April 16, 1996.

are over 30 times rarer than combination 4-C. However, taken on their own, Obverse 5 and Reverse C are both common.

It can be further seen that if the above were Indian cents, Obverse 2 would be mated with three partners, Reverses A, B, and C, and combinations of these would be of greatly differing rarity.

A.W. Downing's Die Records
1880-1886

The following information concerning cent dies is extracted from a notebook of dies kept at the Philadelphia Mint 1880-1886 by A.W. Downing, foreman of the Coining Department, verified by A.W. Straub, foreman of the "Die Makers' Room."[1]

Detailed extracts are given from the records for 1880 and 1886. In addition, summaries are given for other years 1881-1885. The figures differ in some instances from those located in the Archives by R.W. Julian, but this is not necessarily unusual, as the Downing notebook is not complete. All such material contributes something to our knowledge, but cannot be considered definitive.

1880-1886 Proof dies:

For Proof dies these numbers are given for the years in question:

1880: No Proof cent dies specifically recorded in the Downing-Straub figures.

1881: No Proof cent dies recorded.

1882: No Proof cent dies recorded.

1883: No Proof cent dies recorded.

1884: One pair of Proof dies delivered on December 19 (the obverse may have been dated 1885, as by this time many Proof cents dated 1884 had already been made).

1885: One pair of Proof dies delivered on January 5.

1886: One pair of Proof dies delivered on January 11 (presumably of the Type I style); no other Proof dies are recorded for the year.

1880-1886 business strike dies:

For unspecified dies—mostly business strikes, but probably including a few Proofs—these numbers are given for the years in question:

1880: 132 obverse, 108 reverse dies (compare to R.W. Julian: 130 and 115).

1881: 97 obverse, 97 reverse dies (same as R.W. Julian's figures).

1882: 75 obverse, 63 reverse dies (same as Julian's figures).

1883: 149 obverse, 137 reverse dies (same as Julian's figures).

1884: 123 obverse, 129 reverse dies (Julian: 124, 130); the Proof die pair delivered on December 19 was not recorded in this part of the ledger.

1885: 47 obverse, 47 reverse dies (same as Julian's figures); the Proof die pair delivered on January 5 was not recorded in this part of the ledger.

1886: 47 obverse, 47 reverse dies (Julian: 48, 48); the 47 figures probably include a pair of Proof dies delivered on January 11.

---

[1] As Straub identified himself at the end of the die records for the year *1884.*

1880 business strike dies (details):

1880, January 2: 3 reverse dies returned as unused to the Engraving Department.

1880, January 2: 5 obverse dies and 5 reverse dies received from the Engraving Department.

1880, January 6: 2 obverse, 2 reverse dies received.

1880, January 13: 3 obverse, 3 reverse dies received.

1880, January 16: 1 obverse, 1 reverse die received.

1880, January 21: 5 obverse, 4 reverse dies received.

1880, January 27: 1 obverse, 1 reverse die received.

1880, February 3: 5 obverse, 5 reverse dies received.

1880, February 24: 1 obverse, 1 reverse die received.

1880, March 16: 6 obverse, 6 reverse dies received.

1880, March 22: 2 obverse dies received.

1880, April 13: 4 obverse, 4 reverse dies received.

1880, April 27: 6 obverse, 6 reverse dies received.

1880, May 11: 5 obverse, 5 reverse dies received.

1880, May 25: 6 obverse, 6 reverse dies received.

1880, July 13: 6 obverse, 6 reverse dies received.

1880, July 31: 5 obverse, 5 reverse dies received.

1880, August 13: 4 obverse, 4 reverse dies received.

1880, August 20: 6 obverse, 6 reverse dies received.

1880, September 3: 4 obverse, 4 reverse dies received

1880, September 10: 6 obverse dies received.

1880, October 6: 8 obverse dies received.

1880, November 4: 6 obverse, 6 reverse dies received.

1880, November 11: 6 obverse, 6 reverse dies received.

1880, November 20: 6 obverse, 6 reverse dies received.

1880, December 3: 6 obverse, 6 reverse dies received.

1880, December 9: 3 obverse, 3 reverse dies received.

1880, December 9 (2nd receipt of the day): 3 obverse dies received.

1880, December 17: 3 obverse, 3 reverse dies received.

1880, December 21: 4 obverse, 4 reverse dies received. Could some of these (and also the following delivery) have been dated 1881?

1880, December 22: 2 obverse dies received.

1880, December 23: 2 reverse dies received.

Total obverse dies: 132 received.

Total reverse dies: 108 received.

1886 Business strike dies (details):

Delivery of cent dies in the year 1886 is particularly interesting as the records seem to indicate that most or even all coinage must have taken place later in the year in autumn or early winter. This ostensibly means that the Type I business strikes were also made at that time.

However, records for *1885* show that there was intense delivery of cent obverse (but not reverse) dies in the waning days of that year; namely, four obverses on December 22, 1885, followed by four more on December 23. Could it be that most if not all of these were dated 1886? At the time it was often the practice to make up dies in November and December for use in the following year. For example, on November 11, 1873, six pairs of trade dollar dies were shipped to San Francisco for 1874 coinage, followed on November 14 by six pairs of dies shipped to Carson City for 1874 trade dollar coinage.[1]

If this is the case, then coinage of 1886 Type I cents could have taken place early in 1886 from dies prepared in late December 1885.

1886, January 11: 1 obverse, 1 reverse die received. These were probably Proof dies of the Type I style.

1886, September 18: 2 obverse dies, 2 reverse dies received.

1886, September 20: 2 obverse dies, 2 reverse dies received.

1886, September 29: 2 obverse dies, 2 reverse dies received.

1886, October 11: 2 obverse dies, 2 reverse dies received.

1886, October 21: 3 obverse dies, 3 reverse dies received.

1886, October 26: 2 obverse dies, 2 reverse dies received.

1886, November 1: 4 obverse dies, 4 reverse dies received.

1886, November 8: 3 obverse dies, 3 reverse dies received.

1886, November 12: 1 obverse die, 1 reverse die received.

1886, November 15: 3 obverse dies, 3 reverse dies received.

1886, November 20: 3 obverse dies, 3 reverse dies received.

1886, November 27: 4 obverse dies, 4 reverse dies received.

1886, December 1: 4 obverse dies, 4 reverse dies received.

1886, December 6: 3 obverse dies, 3 reverse dies received.

1886, December 13: 4 obverse dies, 4 reverse dies received.

1886, December 27: 4 obverse dies, 4 reverse dies received.

Total obverse dies: 47 received.

Total reverse dies: 47 received.

---

[1] Source: R.W. Julian; these and other trade dollar die figures are quoted in my book, *Silver Dollars and Trade Dollars of the United States: A Complete Encyclopedia.*

Prelude to the Flying Eagle Cent

◀ 1837 Feuchtwanger's Composition one-cent piece privately issued by Dr. Lewis Feuchtwanger, proponent of his variety of "German silver." This was the first of several nineteenth-century proposals for a small diameter cent to replace the "large" copper cent. He petitioned Congress to adopt his alloy, but nothing came of it.

1850 annular or "ring" pattern cent, ▶ perforated at the center in the style of Chinese coins.

◀ 1853 pattern cent, small diameter, utilizing an obverse die for a regular issue gold $2.50 piece in combination with a new pattern reverse cent.

1854 pattern cent with the Liberty ▶ Seated motif on the obverse. The obverse die was made by mechanically reducing the image of an 1854 silver dollar. In the process much design detail was lost, and the 1854 date appears as "1851." The reverse is of a pattern style created for the occasion.

◀ 1854 pattern Flying Eagle cent utilizing the eagle created by Christian Gobrecht and first used on pattern half dollars dated 1838. The eagle has slightly different features from that used on Gobrecht's 1836 silver dollar and on the 1856 Flying Eagle copper-nickel cent. The reverse is somewhat similar to that used on the contemporary copper "large' cent, but smaller and differently proportioned. Struck in copper and bronze.

1855 pattern Flying Eagle cent similar ▶ to the 1854 and also using Gobrecht's 1838 eagle. The reverse is somewhat similar to the 1854 pattern, but has a more luxuriant wreath. Struck in copper and bronze.

APPENDIX II
PATTERN SMALL CENTS

Introduction

Pattern "Birch," silver-center, and other cents were struck at the Philadelphia Mint in 1792 before federal coinage began. These led to the circulating coinage of copper "large" cents which commenced in February 1793 (with the first delivery taking place in March), but not using any of the pattern motifs. From that time forward, copper cents were struck for circulation through the year 1857.[1]

Beginning in 1850, patterns were produced in an effort to reduce the cent size and weight and to test certain designs. Such pieces were made in many different styles and formats through 1859 and later and today are interesting to study and collect.

Sources for detailed information are several and include *United States Pattern, Trial, and Experimental Pieces,* Edgar H. Adams and William H. Woodin, 1913; *U.S. Mint and Coinage,* Don Taxay, 1966; *United States Pattern, Experimental and Trial Pieces,* Dr. J. Hewitt Judd and A. Kosoff, 7th edition, 1982; *Flying Eagle & Indian Cents,* Richard Snow, 1992; *United States Patterns and Related Issues,* Andrew W. Pollock III, 1994; and *Coin World Comprehensive Catalog & Encyclopedia of U.S. Coins,* 1995.[2] Rather than reiterate the detailed die descriptions found in the preceding, I simply refer you to them for further study and appreciation.

My own interest in pattern cents dates from about 1954, when I found it very curious that while an 1856 pattern Flying Eagle cent was worth about $300 on the market, an 1858 pattern Indian cent—even rarer and to my eyes just as interesting— could be bought for $50 to $100, or even less (I once bought one for $5 from dealer Cathy Bullowa). From this point I sought every scrap of information I could find on patterns, which in the mid-1950s mainly consisted of the 1913 Adams-Woodin book (available in a reprint edition from Dayton, Ohio dealer James Kelly) and articles in the *American Journal of Numismatics, The Numismatist,* and a few other places. The most enlightened numismatic publisher of the time was Lee F. Hewitt, and his *Numismatic Scrapbook Magazine* contained much particularly useful information. Hewitt had a missionary zeal for the hobby and devoted much time and space to promoting numismatics, including arcane specialties such as patterns, tokens, and minute die varieties of American coinage.

Dealers in patterns were few and far between, and only the firms that handled major collections were apt to even have a copy of the Adams-Woodin book. There

---

[1] Although some cents were coined in 1815, they were dated earlier; no cents dated 1815 were made. Otherwise the production of cent dates was continuous from 1793 to 1857.

[2] Although the *Coin World Encyclopedia* covers the entire U.S. series, its section on patterns, primarily the work of Thomas K. DeLorey and consultant David A. Novoselsky, is quite extensive and contains much useful information. Coins are given "E" number designations.

were three dealers who had significant stocks of them: Sol Kaplan in Cincinnati, who had by far the most; A. Kosoff in California, who was a partner in Kaplan's pattern stock, but who also had his own supply in California; and James Randall, a Chicago dealer who later moved to Florida and whose supply, I believe, mainly came from the King Farouk auction held in Cairo in 1954. The Farouk collection was an array of dissimilar things if there ever was one; there were world-class gems and rarities, and there were also lots of dregs.

The pattern stock of Sol Kaplan was immense. Basically, it consisted of undistributed pieces obtained by the late William H. Woodin from the Philadelphia Mint through the offices of John W. Haseltine and Stephen K. Nagy in 1910, augmented by purchases by Kosoff from F.C.C. Boyd in the 1940s and by Kaplan and Kosoff at the 1954 Farouk sale in Cairo.

In the mid-1950s, certain patterns such as the 1856 Flying Eagle cent, 1859 and 1860 transitional half dimes, 1836-1839 Gobrecht silver dollars, and 1879-1880 stellas were in great demand, mainly because they were listed among regular issues in the *Guide Book,* the familiar red-covered volume which at the time was the one-book "library" of most collectors, even those who were advanced and spent a lot of money on coins.

Because of this ready market, such coins struck in their intended metals (Gobrecht dollars in silver, $4 stellas in gold, etc.) were mostly gone from Kaplan's stock by the time I delved into it. However, other issues abounded and were often represented in depth. While I do not recall the exact numbers now, I know that Kaplan had from a few to a dozen or two of most of the commoner Indian cent and Flying Eagle cent pattern varieties of 1858.

Abe Kosoff liked to "talk patterns" and often featured them in his sales. His client Dr. J. Hewitt Judd, of Omaha, was persuaded by Abe to update the quite obsolete Adams-Woodin book, but progress was slow. Dr. Judd, a very cordial fellow, was not a technical student or researcher in the sense that Walter Breen or R.W. Julian were and that Don Taxay and others would become. Rather, Dr. Judd wrote letters to various collectors of patterns and kept a file of notes, later corresponding with many specialists including Breen and me about die varieties.

Although it seems strange to recount this now in the 1990s, back in 1954-1955 very few people cared about patterns, and no one at all was interested in minute die differences. I noticed that the 1858 pattern Indian cent with laurel wreath reverse, which over a period of time I had hoarded to the extent of dozens of pieces, occurred in several different variations. In the late 1950s I communicated some of this information to Dr. Judd, who mentioned this in a footnote.

In the February-March 1959 issue of *Empire Topics* my article, "Transitional Coins of America," was the first effort in print to discuss in detail various die varieties of the 1858 pattern cent and related issues.

I came to love patterns. Cents were my favorites among these, more by necessity as these were the least expensive in an era in which my budget as a beginning coin dealer could not afford the luxury of owning, for example, a gold 1880 $4 Coiled Hair stella.

A few years later, when my business was better known and I was recognized as a pattern specialist, my business partner at the time, Jim Ruddy, and I bought from Abner Kreisberg the Major Lenox R. Lohr collection of patterns, the largest ever formed. It contained nearly one of everything. Well, not quite, but there were over 1,400 *different* varieties within all denominations! I found it amusing that a certain pattern nickel five-cent piece called "unique"—just one in existence—by Adams and Woodin was represented by *four* specimens in the Lohr Collection! There were seven different patterns of the rare 1792 year.

Since those numismatic days of long ago much has happened in the field of patterns. A new generation of highly competent researchers arose, new methods of analysis were developed, prices rose dramatically, and other developments occurred. Today, patterns, while not in the forefront of numismatics, are at least widely collected, and it is very enjoyable for me to read what modern scholars such as Andy Pollock and Richard Snow have found out about the little copper-nickel pattern cents of 1858.

We all build upon foundations laid by others, and doubtless a future generation of numismatists will know more than we do now. Meanwhile, pattern cents—especially of the 1858 year—remain a particularly fascinating area of interest to me.

Ring Patterns of 1850-1851

In the late 1840s the combination of rising copper prices plus increased costs of production resulted in copper half cents and cents becoming increasingly expensive to produce. On January 9, 1849, Chairman Samuel F. Vinton of the Ways and Means Committee in Congress sent this proposed wording for a bill to Robert Maskell Patterson, director of the Mint:

> Resolved, that the Committee of Ways and Means take into consideration the propriety of reporting a bill for reducing the size of the one-cent piece, & to authorize the coining of a three-cent piece—both to be composed of copper and some other precious metal.

In 1850 the Mint struck patterns in a ring-shaped ("annular" was the Mint's term) format, perforated at the center, and of smaller diameter than the current copper "large" cent. The alloy used was billon, a mixture of 90% copper and 10% silver (which is just the reverse of the standard silver alloy of the time for half dimes to dollars, which consisted of 90% silver and 10% copper).

The obverse design was simple and bore the inscription CENT above the central hole and the date 1850 below the hole. A rosette was at either side of the coin. The reverse had U.S.A. above the hole and in small letters, ONE TENTH SILVER below the hole. The intention was not to create a finished design for circulation, but to illustrate what a small cent format would look like. In the pattern form here described the coin weighed 25 grains (compared to 168 grains of copper for the regular "large" cent of the time) and was the same diameter as a dime. The hole in the center was intended to permit quick identification of the coin. The *Philadelphia North American and United States Gazette,* May 14, 1850, remarked on the utility of such pieces:

> [The new cent] is as small as could be desired for such a coin; it affords a distinctive mark by which the piece may be recognized and safely paid out even by touch; it affords a facility to retailers to put the pieces up in parcels, say of a hundred or thousand, by stringing them, or putting them on an upright stake or file....

While the Mint struck such patterns in the aforementioned billon alloy and also a few in copper (some of the latter being silver-plated at the Mint), most known today are restrikes probably made in 1859 or later. Some restrikes are unperforated. Such pieces were made in a variety of metals.

In 1851 additional ring-format cent patterns were made and, again, these were restruck in several metals after early 1859.

Patterns of 1853

From 1853 through 1855 pattern cents were made in several different unrelated styles. Most numerous today are the Liberty Head and Flying Eagle copper cents of 1854-1855.

The series commences with an interesting and somewhat rare small-diameter issue of 1853, this being made by utilizing a $2.50 Liberty Head gold coin die in combination with a seemingly hastily contrived reverse, the latter consisting of a wreath enclosing ONE CENT (Judd-149, Pollock-178, and related pieces). The inscription UNITED STATES OF AMERICA is not to be seen. These were struck in a nickel-alloy of some sort, resembling so-called German silver, and reminiscent of the "Feuchtwanger's Composition" small-diameter cents issued by Dr. Lewis Feuchtwanger in 1837.

Inasmuch as this cent is not of the ring style and is of small diameter, it has some credentials as the first normal-format "small cent" in federal coinage, although it is upstaged by Feuchtwanger's private 1837 coins, as noted.

This ONE CENT reverse was resurrected in 1857 and combined with a pattern obverse die for a $2.50 gold coin, to create an 1857 pattern "cent," but this was probably not really a pattern, but was most probably a curiosity made for numismatic purposes (Judd-186, Pollock-222, etc.). This variety, as interesting as it may be today, apparently did not capture the fancy of collectors during the restriking period (beginning circa 1859) and was not made in quantity for that market. Specimens are exceedingly rare today.

1854 Liberty Seated Cent

By any account one of the most curious productions of the Philadelphia Mint in the decade of the 1850s is the 1854 Liberty Seated cent pattern.

To create this piece, the Engraving Department at the Mint took an already struck 1854 Liberty Seated silver dollar (not a model, not a hub, but an actual coin, and not of the cent denomination) and used a reducing lathe to transfer its design to a cent die slightly less than the diameter of a quarter dollar.

The transfer was made in extreme haste, with the result that the tracing point on the dollar and the rapidly rotating cutting head on the other end, recorded just the basic details of the dollar obverse. The stars appear as stretched-out blobs, and in the date the 4 is indistinct, causing it to read as "1851."[1] Under low magnification the spiral path of the cutting head is seen on the obverse of the finished pattern coins.

The reverse consists simply of a wreath enclosing 1 CENT, again without any mention of the United States of America. Most were struck in a bright white nickel-content alloy in the German silver style.

As if this were not enough to say about this strange dollar-cent pattern, it is further curious to note that at the Mint a number of additional pieces are said to have been made in copper by the electrotyping process, rather than striking from dies!

1854-1855 Patterns

In 1854 and 1855 many copper alloy patterns were made in two basic styles:

The obverse of the first employed the portrait of Miss Liberty as seen on the contemporary "large" copper cent.

---

[1] Opinion is divided as to what date of silver dollar was used, and some believe it to have been an 1851 (cf. Andrew W. Pollock III, note, April 17, 1996).

The second was a re-use of Christian Gobrecht's flying eagle design superficially similar to that used on the 1836 Gobrecht silver dollar, but styled more closely to Gobrecht's eagle on pattern half dollars dated 1838 and 1839 (the neck is differently contoured and has ruffed feathers, the feet are in a slightly different position, etc.). Both obverses were mated with reverse dies similar in general design to the standard cent of the period, but of reduced diameter and with the wreath more delicately cut.

Patterns of both these years were made in fairly large numbers, probably by the hundreds for the more plentiful varieties. Some were restruck, but apparently not in quantity.

1856 Flying Eagle Cents

The 1856 pattern Flying Eagle cent in copper-nickel is, of course, the subject of its own sub-chapter earlier in the book. These were made in several combinations of obverse and reverse dies. The basic design is as follows:

Obverse with eagle flying left, copied from the reverse of the 1836 Gobrecht silver dollar. UNITED STATES OF AMERICA is in an arc around the border, date 1856 below.

Reverse with "agricultural" wreath of corn (most prominent), wheat, cotton, and tobacco—called a "cereal" wreath by Mint Director Snowden.

Struck in alloy of 88 parts copper and 12 parts nickel, called copper-nickel. Small diameter (0.75 inch), plain edge. 72 grains.

These were produced in original and restrike form to the extent of an estimated several thousand pieces, from obverse dies believed to have been made in 1856 or very early 1857, and from various reverse dies of the 1856-1858 period.

In addition several other varieties of 1856-attributed patterns are listed in the Adams-Woodin, Judd, Pollock, and *Coin World Encyclopedia* pattern references. Some are off-metal (different alloys) strikings of the preceding dies. Others represent different combinations.

One particularly well-known style depicts on the obverse the same flying eagle, but with no description or date. This is combined with the agricultural wreath reverse (Judd-178, Pollock-206, etc.)

Another variety combines the preceding inscriptionless obverse with another obverse, apparently made in 1858, with an eagle and UNITED STATES OF AMERICA, but also lacking a date. This could have served no pattern purpose and was made as a numismatic curiosity (Judd-219, Pollock-209; possibly unique).

Another variety, most certainly struck no earlier than 1858, combines a dated 1856 Flying Eagle cent obverse with a pattern reverse illustrating an oak wreath with ornamented shield, this being a popular die widely used for 1858-dated patterns (*e.g.,* Judd-184, Pollock-220).

1858 Pattern Cent Sets

In 1858 and continuing for several years thereafter, a popular "commodity" coming out of the Mint and into the hands of collectors and dealers was the 12-coin set consisting of 11 1858-dated pattern copper-nickel cents and a Proof of the regular 1858 Flying Eagle design (and usually of the Small Letters style). The number of these sets minted is not known and has been variously estimated as from 60 to 200.

In addition, certain patterns were struck individually in larger numbers; this is particularly true of the 1858 Indian cent, exact obverse and reverse designs of 1859. The following pattern and regular dies were used to make the sets as well as pieces that may have been sold separately, but are of the same basic designs as those in the sets. The pieces listed are all on regular-size copper-nickel planchets (off-metal strikes and other curiosities are not listed):

Obverse 1a: Flying Eagle cent die ("Large Flying Eagle" as used on regular coinage), Large Letters, regular die. At least two obverse dies were used; one with delicate repunching of letters and with tiny die defects below first 8 and 5 of date; the other with light repunching of the first A in AMERICA. By James B. Longacre.

Obverse 1b: Flying Eagle cent die, Small Letters, regular die. Richard Snow further divides the Small Letters obverse into those with incomplete serif to U in UNITED (left side of serif on right upright of U; this is the style usually seen; this was in the working hub and was used to make multiple dies) and those with complete serifs. The specimens I have seen from the latter "perfect U" die are from incompletely polished Proof dies with many raised die lines visible under magnification. By James B. Longacre.

Obverse 2: Small or "skinny" pattern Flying Eagle, more formally called "Small Flying Eagle." Central eagle probably by Longacre (the formation of the eye details and certain other features are essentially the same as on the regular Flying Eagle cent, although the configuration of the bird is different), lettering attributed to Anthony C. Paquet. The vertical elements in the obverse letters are thicker than normal and are exaggerated vertically; for example, the interior of the letter 0 is a thin, narrow, straight-sided rectangle and the A is very tall; this feature is traditionally ascribed to Paquet as, for example, on the lettering on the reverse of the 1857 pattern quarter dollar J-188, P-255. This lettering font appears to be from the same hand that created the font for the 1858 Small Letters obverse (although the letters in each font are different; there are certain similarities, however, including the shape and irregularity of the top serifs in the letter T).

Obverse 3a: Indian Head design dated 1858, of the type later adopted on 1859 cents, Narrow Bust (per current terminology) or neck point as also used in 1859, date low and close to dentils; original Indian design. Lower right serif tip of final A in AMERICA is enlarged or blob-like at its tip, unlike the other A letters in the legend (in contrast, Obverse 3b has normal serif tip to final A). By James B. Longacre. This die was ready and apparently pieces had been struck by March 1858.[1]

Obverse 3b: Indian Head with Broad Bust as introduced in early 1860. Date centered between bust and dentils; this type of die, although dated 1858, was most likely not made before early 1860, hence *any cents from this die were probably made in 1860 or later.* Studying these in the 1950s, the author identified five die varieties of this style, but did not keep a list of them. In 1996, an inspection of the several patterns in the Eliasberg Collection yielded three different dies for Obverse 3b.[2] An

---

[1] Steve-Flynn, *Flying Eagle and Indian Cent Die Varieties,* p. 213, quoting a Mr. Howard who sought to purchase a specimen.

[2] Identification of the Eliasberg Collection coins: Sub-variety 1: 1 in date: If division between two denticles is extended, it will intersect the center of the 1; First 8: If division between two denticles is extended, it will intersect slightly to the right of the center bottom of the digit; 5 is over denticle; Second 8 is over denticle. Digit 1 more or less centered and about the same distance from denticles as from portrait. High wire rim on part of reverse. • Sub-variety 2: 1 in date over denticle; First 8: if division between two denticles is extended, it will intersect slightly to the left of the center bottom of the digit; 5: If division between two denticles is extended, it will intersect slightly to the right of the center of the bottom of the digit; Second 8 is over denticle). Digit 1 slightly below center and slightly

additional variety was found by the writer when examining a group of 20 coins held by dealer Julian Leidman in April 1996. I suspect that careful inspection of a wider field of examples would yield additional varieties. By James B. Longacre.

Reverse Aa: "Agricultural" wreath as used on 1858 cents; regular die, High Leaf at C (style of 1856, but also used in 1858). By James B. Longacre.

Reverse Ab: "Agricultural" wreath as used on 1858 cents; regular die, Low Leaf at C (style introduced in 1858). By James B. Longacre.

Reverse Ba: Laurel wreath; laurel leaves arranged in clusters of five leaves each, style used only on patterns. Possibly by Anthony C. Paquet, although a sketch of a similar wreath in the National Portrait Gallery bears a modern attribution to Longacre.

Reverse Bb: Laurel wreath as later adopted on 1859 cents; laurel leaves arranged in clusters of six leaves each, style used on patterns as well as on regular-issue 1859 Indian cents. Possibly by Anthony C. Paquet; if not, then by James B. Longacre. *Most if not all pattern 1858-dated cents with this reverse were probably mostly made c. 1859 or later.*

Reverse C: Oak wreath pattern; primarily oak leaves, but with a few leaves of another species (laurel?) at the lower left. Possibly by Anthony C. Paquet, whose wreaths were especially luxuriant (cf. the 1859 pattern $20, J-257, P-305).

Reverse D: Oak wreath pattern with broad ornamented (also called ornamental, wide, and ornate) shield. The shield style was rejected for regular coinage use as Director Snowden felt that it too closely resembled a harp.[1] The wreath part of the reverse is essentially the same as the wreath on Reverse C up to about opposite the word CENT, after which there are differences; the wreath on Reverse D is smaller in order to make room at the top for the shield. Possibly by Anthony C. Paquet; in any event, by the same engraver as Reverse C. This die was ready by March 1858 and, apparently, pieces had been struck.[2]

1858 Patterns: Basic Types

Utilizing the preceding, these *basic* 12 combinations would have been possible and, indeed, constituted a set of 12 1858 Proof cents (one regular issue and 11 patterns) as sold and traded by the Mint. It could have been in some instances that sets of 11 pieces, excluding the authorized design (1-A in the listing below), were made up, as Snowden referred to 11 combinations when discussing these.[3]

BASIC SET OF 12 1858 PATTERN CENTS:

1-A: Flying Eagle / Agricultural wreath.

1-B: Flying Eagle / Laurel wreath.

---

closer to denticles than to portrait. Raised die scribe line at inner border of denticles under 185 and extending to the left. High wire rim on part of reverse. • Sub-variety 3: 1 in date: If division between two denticles is extended, it will intersect the center of the 1; First 8: If division between two denticles is extended, it will intersect slightly to the right of the center bottom of the digit; 5 over denticle; Second 8 is over denticle. Digit 1 more or less centered and about the same distance from denticles as from portrait. No die scribe line. High wire rims at left obverse and corresponding part of the reverse.

[1] Snowden, *A Description of Ancient and Modern Coins...*, 1860, pp. 120-121. The various dies are illustrated on his Plate XV. The 1858 regular issue obverse on the plate is of the Small Letters style and the 1858 Indian obverse has the Low Date position, undoubtedly significant.

[2] Steve-Flynn, *Flying Eagle and Indian Cent Die Varieties*, p. 213, quoting a Mr. Howard who sought to purchase a specimen.

[3] Snowden, *A Description of Ancient and Modern Coins...*, 1860, p. 120, specifically called this a "cereal" wreath.

1-C: Flying Eagle / Oak wreath.

1-D: Flying Eagle / Oak wreath with ornamented shield.

2-A: "Skinny" or Small Flying Eagle / Agricultural wreath.

2-B: "Skinny" or Small Flying Eagle / Laurel wreath.

2-C: "Skinny" or Small Flying Eagle / Oak wreath.

2-D: "Skinny" or Small Flying Eagle / Oak wreath with ornamented shield.

3-A: Indian Head / Agricultural wreath.

3-B: Indian Head / Laurel wreath.

3-C: Indian Head / Oak wreath.

3-D: Indian Head / Oak wreath with ornamented shield.

1858 Patterns: Die Variety Differences

However, within any given set of 12 1858 Proof pattern cents there were and are minute differences in die varieties. The *possibilities* for die combinations of the various obverse and reverse combinations are listed below, although quite possibly some were never struck.

Rarity ratings on the Sheldon Scale are from Andrew W. Pollock III's *United States Patterns and Related Issues* and other sources. Those listed as Rarity-5 (31 to 75 known) are the varieties mostly likely encountered in a typical 12-piece set. Listings of the usually seen die varieties are prefaced with a dot: •.

The designation "ambiguous" after a Judd, Snow, or Pollock number indicates that these authors did not divide a particular variety into the technical variety now described and that their numbers referred to more than one possibility.

The notation "EXISTENCE NOT VERIFIED" means that as of press time, no specimen of this particular technical variety has come to light (accounting in some instances why a given variety is not listed in the Snow or Pollock guides); perhaps these varieties were never struck. Further, the die combinations for unknown pieces and possible non-existent varieties are listed in parentheses.

1858 Large Flying Eagle Obverse, Large Letters, Combinations:

1a-Aa: Flying Eagle, Large Letters / Agricultural wreath, High Leaf at C. *Same as the regular-issue Proof cent of this year.* Judd (not listed as it is of the regular issue type). Snow I-1a (obverse with die defect below first 8 and 5) and Snow 1-1b (repunched left foot of first A in AMERICA), Pollock (not listed as it is of the regular issue type). Rarity-6.

(1a-Ab): Flying Eagle, Large Letters / Agricultural wreath, Low Leaf at C. *Same as the regular-issue Proof cent of this year.* Judd (not listed as it is of the regular issue type). Snow (not listed), Pollock (not listed as it is of the regular issue type). EXISTENCE NOT VERIFIED.

1a-Ba: Flying Eagle, Large Letters / Laurel wreath with 5-leaf clusters. Judd (ambiguous, type of J-196), Snow IV-1a, Pollock-227. Rarity-8.

(1a-Bb): Flying Eagle, Large Letters / Laurel wreath with 6-leaf clusters. Judd (ambiguous, type of J-196), Snow (not listed), Pollock (not listed). EXISTENCE NOT VERIFIED.

1a-C: Flying Eagle, Large Letters / Oak wreath. Judd-197, Snow III-1, Pollock-228. Rarity-8.

1a-D: Flying Eagle, Large Letters / Oak wreath with ornamented shield. Judd-198, Snow II-1a, Pollock-229. Rarity-6 to 7.

1858 Indian Cent Obverses and Reverses

1858 Indian cent obverse by James B. Longacre. Earliest version with 1858 date close to border and distant frombust.

1858 Indian cent obverse. Later version (used on restrikes) with 1858 date centered between border and bust. Several minute die varieties exist of the centered date issue.

1858 reverse, the "agricultural wreath" as used on regular issues as well as patterns. Style with Low Leaves below CENT.

1858 reverse, oak wreath and ornamental shield (a.k.a. "Harp Shield") used only on patterns.

1858 reverse, laurel wreath as also used on the 1859 regular issue. Two styles of leaves were used on 1858 cents, with five-leaf clusters and with six-leaf clusters.

1858 reverse, oak wreath used only on patterns.

1858 Large Flying Eagle Obverse, Small Letters, Combinations:

•1b-Aa: Flying Eagle, Small Letters / Agricultural wreath, High Leaf at C. *Same as the regular-issue Proof cent of this year.* Judd (not listed as it is of the regular issue type). Snow VI-1a, Pollock (not listed as it is of the regular issue type). Snow estimates this as Rarity-6.

1b-Ab: Flying Eagle, Small Letters / Agricultural wreath, Low Leaf at C. *Same as the regular-issue Proof cent of this year.* Judd (not listed as it is of the regular issue type). Snow V-1, Pollock (not listed as it is of the regular issue type). Snow estimates this as Rarity-7. Eliasberg:609 had many parallel die finish lines on the reverse.

•1b-Ba: Flying Eagle, Small Letters / Laurel wreath with 5-leaf clusters. Judd (ambiguous, type of J-191), Snow IX-1a and IX-2, Pollock-233. Rarity-5. *All were probably made after 1858.*

1b-Bb: Flying Eagle, Small Letters / Laurel wreath with 6-leaf clusters. Judd (ambiguous, type of J-191), Snow X-1a, Pollock-234. Rarity-7.

•1b-C: Flying Eagle, Small Letters / Oak wreath. Judd-192, Snow VIII-1, Pollock-235. Rarity-5.

•1b-D: Flying Eagle, Small Letters / Oak wreath with ornamented shield. Judd-193, Snow VII-1a, Pollock-236. Rarity-5. Eliasberg:123 was described: "Magnification reveals some Mint-caused die lines on both surfaces."

1858 "Skinny" or Small Flying Eagle Obverse Combinations:

(2-Aa): "Skinny" or Small Flying Eagle / Agricultural wreath, High Leaf at C. Judd (ambiguous; type of J-206), Snow (not listed), Pollock (ambiguous; type of P-242). EXISTENCE NOT VERIFIED.

•2-Ab: "Skinny" or Small Flying Eagle / Agricultural wreath, Low Leaf at C. Judd (ambiguous; type of J-206), Snow XI-1a, Pollock (ambiguous; type of P-242). Rarity-5.

•2-Ba: "Skinny" or Small Flying Eagle / Laurel wreath with 5-leaf clusters. Judd (ambiguous, part of J-202), Snow XIV-1a, Pollock-245. Rarity-5. *All were probably made after 1858.*

2-Bb: "Skinny" or Small Flying Eagle / Laurel wreath with 6-leaf clusters. Judd (ambiguous, part of J-202), Snow (unlisted), Pollock-246. Rarity-6 or 7. Apparently, only a few were made, possibly after 1858.

•2-C: "Skinny" or Small Flying Eagle / Oak wreath. Judd-203, Snow XIII-1, Pollock-247. Rarity-5.

•2-D: "Skinny" or Small Flying Eagle / Oak wreath with ornamented shield. Judd-204, Snow XII-1a, Pollock-248. Rarity-5.

1858 Indian, Narrow Bust, Low Date, Obverse Combinations:

3a-Aa: Indian Head, Narrow Bust, low date / Agricultural wreath, High Leaf at C. Judd (ambiguous, type of J-213), Snow XXIV, Pollock-251. Rarity-7.

3a-Ab: Indian Head, Narrow Bust, low date / Agricultural wreath, Low Leaf at C. Judd (ambiguous, type of J-213), Snow XXIII-1, Pollock-252. Rarity-6 to 7.

3a-Ba: Indian Head, Narrow Bust, low date / Laurel wreath with 5-leaf clusters. Judd (ambiguous, type of J-208), Snow XXVII-1, Pollock-253. Rarity-7.

3a-Bb: Indian Head, Narrow Bust, low date / Laurel wreath with 6-leaf clusters. Judd (ambiguous, type of J-208), Snow XXVIII-1, Pollock-254. Rarity-7.

3a-C: Indian Head, Narrow Bust, low date / Oak wreath. Judd (ambiguous, type of J-211), Snow XXVI-1, Pollock-255. Rarity-7.

3a-D: Indian Head, Narrow Bust, low date / Oak wreath with ornamented shield. Judd (ambiguous, type of J-212), Snow XXV-1, Pollock-256. Rarity-7. Apparently, coins from this die combination had been struck by March 1858.[1]

1858 Indian, Broad Bust, Centered Date, Obverse Combinations:

3b-Aa: Indian Head, Broad Bust, centered date / Agricultural wreath, High Leaf at C. Judd (ambiguous, type of J-213), Snow (not listed), Pollock-257. Rarity-7.

•3b-Ab: Indian Head, Broad Bust, centered date / Agricultural wreath, Low Leaf at C. Judd (ambiguous, type of J-213), Snow XVIII-1 and XVIII-2 (with date farther to the right), Pollock-258. Rarity-5 in my opinion (Pollock: Rarity-6).

•3b-Ba: Indian Head, Broad Bust, centered date / Laurel wreath with 5-leaf clusters. Judd (ambiguous, type of J-208), Snow XXI-1 and XXI-2 (date farther to the right; this being slightly more easily found), Pollock-259. This is the most plentiful variety among 1858 pattern cents and was probably restruck for a longer time as a stock in trade item at the Mint. Richard Snow suggests that unsold supplies of these may have been released into circulation under the directorship of James Pollock, who succeeded Director Snowden in 1861.[2] Rarity-3.

3b-Bb: Indian Head, Broad Bust, centered date / Laurel wreath with 6-leaf clusters. Judd (ambiguous, type of J-208), Snow XXII-1 and XXII-2 (date farther right), Pollock-261. The Snow reference gives no rarity rating but notes that "many are worn" of XXII-1; Pollock calls it Rarity-7.

•3b-C: Indian Head, Broad Bust, centered date / Oak wreath. Judd (ambiguous, type of J-211), Snow XX-1 (date to right), Pollock-262. Rarity-5 (Pollock: Rarity-5 to 6).

•3b-D: Indian Head, Broad Bust, centered date / Oak wreath with ornamented shield. Judd (ambiguous, type of J-212), Snow XIX-1a and XIX-1b (date farther right), Pollock-263. Rarity-5.

1858 Pattern Cent Mintages

At the outset, apparently just 20 coins were made of each basic pattern type, the prelude to a much more extensive coinage before year's end. On August 20, 1858, James B. Longacre notified Mint Director James Ross Snowden that 20 each had been made of the following issues. The numbering sequence is Longacre's; comments in brackets are by the author:[3]

No. 1. Emblematic head of America [Indian head]. Oak wreath with shield.

No. 2. Emblematic head of America. Oak wreath without shield.

No. 3. Emblematic head of America. Olive wreath. [This is what numismatists call a laurel wreath today; it seems that Longacre may have considered it to have been a different species; in any event, it may have been the work of Paquet.]

No. 4. Emblematic head of America. Corn/cotton [the cotton leaves resemble maple leaves][4] wreath [a.k.a. agricultural wreath; Director Snowden called it a cereal wreath, others called it a tobacco wreath].

---

[1] Steve-Flynn, *Flying Eagle and Indian Cent Die Varieties,* p. 213, quoting a Mr. Howard who sought to purchase a specimen.

[2] Letter, April 10,1996.

[3] Information from R.W. Julian, letter, April 24, 1996. Mintage quantities of pattern coins were not listed in annual *Mint Reports,* but were sometimes mentioned in departmental correspondence and records. Similar information is found in "The Adoption of the Indian Head Cent," Walter Thompson, *Numismatic Scrapbook Magazine,* July 1961.

[4] What with olive-laurel and cotton-maple differences in nomenclature past and present, perhaps numismatics needs a botanist to assign specific terms!

No. 5. Flying Eagle — new pattern [Small Eagle, a.k.a. "skinny" eagle]. Oak wreath with shield.

No. 6. Flying Eagle — new pattern. Oak wreath without shield.

No. 7. Flying Eagle — new pattern. Olive wreath.

No. 8. Flying Eagle — new pattern. Corn/cotton wreath.

No. 9. Old Flying Eagle in use [regular die]. Oak wreath with shield.

No. 10. Old Flying Eagle in use. Oak wreath without shield.

No. 11. Old Flying Eagle in use. Olive wreath.

No. 12. Old Flying Eagle in use. Corn/cotton wreath. [This is the regular issue Flying Eagle design of the year, probably with Large Letters obverse.]

On November 4, 1858, Mint Director James Ross Snowden wrote to the Treasury Department to seek approval of the "ideal head of America" obverse in combination with a "plain laurel wreath" reverse,[1] indicating that at least Snowden considered the reverse to be laurel.

The Eliasberg 1858 Pattern Set

The Louis E. Eliasberg, Sr. Collection, sold at auction in May 1996, included a 12-piece set of 1858 pattern cents which traced its pedigree to the Richard B. Winsor Sale, Lot 1121, sold by the Chapman brothers in December 1895. While there is no way of knowing whether this was an intact original set as purchased from the Mint or whether it was assembled at a later date piece by piece, an inventory of it includes the following (those with the • being Rarity-5 and other plentiful issues):

1b-Ab, •1b-Ba, •1b-C, •1b-D, •2-Ab, •2-Ba, •2-C, •2-D, 3a-Ab, 3a-D, 3b-Ba, and •3b-C.

It is seen that the collection is somewhat of a mixture. All four of the Flying Eagle cents are of the Small Letters obverse style. Among the Indian cents two are of the earlier Narrow Bust style and two are of the later Broad Bust format.

Commentary: 1858 Pattern Sets

If present-day availability is a guide, most sets (or at least most coins sold in one way or another) seem to have had 1858 Flying Eagle cents with the 1b (Small Letters) rather than the 1a (Large Letters) obverse; each set probably had one or the other, but not both.

It seems likely that pattern Indian cents actually struck in 1858 had the Narrow Bust (a.k.a. pointed-neck, pointed bust) and low date. Only one obverse die has been identified of this style. Pattern Indian cents restruck 1859 and later from new dies probably had the Round Bust format and centered date. At least four or five different obverse dies of this style are known, and more possibly remain to be discovered.

Laurel wreath reverse pattern cents actually made in 1858 probably had 5-leaf clusters—as this was the earlier style, while those made after 1858 probably had 6-leaf clusters—this was the style used on regular-issue 1859 cents. However, both could have been used at the same time.

In all instances, an earlier die (such as the Indian obverse with Narrow Bust and 5-leaf cluster laurel wreath reverse) *could have been made* after 1858 from dies on hand, but later dies (such as round-bust Indian cents and 6-leaf cluster laurel wreath

---

[1] Citation provided by R.W. Julian, letter, April 24, 1996.

cents) *were most probably made* no earlier than 1859. Today, the latter are much more plentiful, suggesting they may have constituted the larger part of Snowden's restrikes.

Among the various coins associated with the pattern sets of 1858 it is seen that combinations 1a-Aa, 1a-Ab, 1b-Aa, and 1b-Ab are regular issue 1858 Large Letters and Small Letters Proof Flying Eagle cents.

As 1858-dated pattern sets as well as extra individual coins were made over a period of time, there are variations. The 1a-A and 1b-A issues employ regular Proof Flying Eagle dies, but not always fully polished. Strikings of 3-B, the exact type of the 1859 Indian Head cent but dated 1858, were especially popular, were produced in extra quantities, and multiple obverse and reverse dies were made. As many of these show wear today, it is likely that additional quantities were made to distribute to Congressmen and others in order to acquaint them with the forthcoming Indian Head motif; the same rationale as for the distribution of 1856 Flying Eagle cents. Despite a few suggestions to the contrary appearing in numismatic literature, I do not believe any 1858 transitional cents were ever deliberately made for circulation.

In addition, some rare varieties of 1858 cent patterns were made—including dateless issues and pieces in alloys other than copper-nickel—but were not a part of the aforementioned sets, nor were they sold widely.

Most dies for the foregoing pieces did not receive deep, brilliant polish. As a result, the majority of coins in existence today show mint lustre, parallel die striations, and frosty patches. This is normal and is the way the coins were produced, giving rise to the theory that some may have been intended as business strikes— which I consider to be highly unlikely.

Some 1858 pattern cents have high wire rims (a.k.a. "knife rims" or "fins") which give them a thick appearance when viewed edge-on. As a general rule, the regular-issue Flying Eagle obverse dies are more prooflike than the Small Eagle (a.k.a. "skinny eagle") obverse and Indian cent obverse dies.

Traditionally, all 1858 copper-nickel patterns, if not worn or damaged, have been catalogued as "Proof." The extensive discussions as to what constitutes a "Proof" 1856 Flying Eagle cent and what defines "Mint State" (see earlier sub-chapter on 1856 cents) has not extended to the 1858 pattern copper-nickel cents, but if it does the same problems will arise. I venture to say that no sets of 1858 patterns were ever issued with deep mirror Proof surfaces of the quality found on contemporary gold or silver Proofs, and that nearly all "Proofs" have die finish lines, frosty patches, incomplete areas, or some other "Mint State" characteristics.

Over the years a few sets of 12 cents (11 patterns and one regular issue) of this year have come on the market. The aforementioned Eliasberg Collection set came from the December 1895 sale of the Richard B. Winsor Collection and was sold to Pennsylvania oil magnate John M. Clapp (and in 1906 passed to his son, John H. Clapp, and in 1942 to Louis E. Eliasberg, Sr.). Ben Green's auction of December 10, 1905, saw another set of 1858 pattern cents fetch $30.

Although as a dealer I believe I have handled as many patterns—if not more— than just about anyone living today, I have only ever had two 12-coin sets of 1858 cents. The first was early in my numismatic career, and I have often regretted that I did not make notes concerning the minute die characteristics of the pieces (but this was in the mid-1950s and before the reawakening of interest in patterns, and few people cared about die varieties). The second is the Winsor-Clapp-Eliasberg set.

The Brenner Collection described below also had one of these 1858 sets. Again, in the absence of documentation there is no way of knowing if such a set was as issued or was acquired piece by piece on the market.

The Brenner Pattern Collection

The Numismatist, issue of September 1912, described the collection of patterns owned and displayed by Judson Brenner of DeKalb, Illinois. In view of the various issues discussed in the present Appendix II, the Brenner Collection coins provide an interesting glimpse of a group which would be difficult if not impossible to duplicate today. As it was described in 1912:

> This represents the largest collection of minor patterns in existence....
>
> Of 1850 he showed no less than 12 different varieties of the pattern cent of that year, both perforated and unperforated, in silver, copper, copper-nickel and pure nickel. Some of the designs show only one side. Of the cents of 1851 showing the obverse of the quarter-dollar [actually a reduction from a Liberty Seated silver dollar and today in the 1990s attributed to 1854] with the reverse of one cent, he had two specimens, one in copper and the other in nickel.
>
> He showed two varieties of the 1853 nickel cent on thin and thick planchets.
>
> Of 1856 he showed a cent without date, flying eagle, reverse tobacco wreath, in copper. Of the same year, with the flying eagle and dated, with the reverse of oak wreath and broad shield, he showed one in copper and one in copper-nickel; with the dated, tobacco wreath, he showed specimens in copper, copper-nickel, and pure nickel.
>
> Of 1857 there was a cent with the quarter eagle obverse and a reverse same as that on the cent of 1853. These pieces are in copper-nickel.
>
> A full series of the cents of 1858 were shown, with one having a broad planchet. An excessively rare cent of this year was that with the small flying eagle, tobacco wreath reverse, in pure nickel. A rarity of 1859 showed no date, but was struck from the regular dies on a broad planchet, in copper. Of 1860 he showed one cent from the regular dies, in pure nickel....
>
> Of 1863 from the regular dies he showed specimens in bronze, copper, copper-nickel, and aluminum.... Of 1864, from the regular dies, he showed specimens in aluminum, brass, bronze, copper and copper-nickel, one on a thick planchet, the other on an ordinary planchet. Of 1864 he showed one of the rarest and most desirable of the cent pieces, which bears the regular Indian obverse design of the year and the reverse design of the large flying eagle of 1858. This was in copper-nickel....

Comments on Artistry

Certain similarities between motifs used on pattern and regular cents of the 1856-1858 years, elements of which were designed by James B. Longacre and Anthony C. Paquet, and other patterns and medals have been noticed.

While engravers at the Mint often copied each other's work, used plasters or brass castings from "stock," and kept motifs and punches on hand for long periods of time, and while there are only so many ways that an engraver can cut an oak leaf or other motif, the following observations may offer a path for further research. Similarities are not necessarily conclusive, as is evident, for example, by studying elsewhere the many portraits of George Washington used on coins, tokens, and medals of the 1860s and 1870s for which the products of many different engravers look often look remarkably alike.[1]

1855 Longacre medal: In 1855 Longacre created the reverse die for the Commander Duncan Ingraham medal (Julian NA-26), which on the reverse had a wreath composed of laurel (on the left) and oak (right) leaves, the leaves in each instance being differently configured than on the cents of 1858. Longacre medal designs are few and far between. This description is inserted to indicate that the cent leaves were not copied from Longacre, at least not from any medals seen by the writer.

1859 medalets by Paquet: Certain medalets of the era including the 1859 Commencement of Washington Cabinet (Julian MT-22) are ascribed to Paquet and have an *olive* wreath on the reverse, this bearing no resemblance to the *laurel* wreath. The reverse inscription reads: A MEMORIAL OF THE WASHINGTON CABINET MAY 1859.

1859 pattern $20 by Paquet: Anthony C. Paquet's pattern $20 of 1859 affords the opportunity to examine that artist's techniques. The feathers of the eagle on the obverse are quite detailed, but in a manner entirely unlike found on either the 1856 Flying Eagle cent or the 1858 "skinny" or Small Eagle pattern. The neck feathers, rather than being separate elements as on Longacre's aforementioned cent eagles, are in fur-like strands. The depiction of Miss Liberty is hardly elegant in the sense that Longacre's and William Barber's patterns of the ensuing two decades were. On the reverse of the 1859 pattern $20 the luxuriant wreath is composed of oak leaves (with raised veins) and laurel leaves (also with raised veins), by no means a close copy of the oak wreath used on 1858 cent patterns, but similar in some regards and different in others. This pattern $20 and other coinage die efforts may have prompted Don Taxay to note this in *U.S. Mint and Coinage,* p. 215: "Paquet possessed a very modest talent, and his dies, with one brief exception (the 1861 $20 reverse), were never adopted on the coinage. A peculiar ugliness in portraiture, stiffness in anatomy, and tall, thin lettering distinguish the work of this artist. Paquet designed a pattern double eagle in 1859, and the following year *Longacre* contributed a beautiful pattern half eagle showing Liberty with a starry cap. It is unfortunate that the latter was never adopted."[2] Taxay was a consistent admirer of Longacre's engraving talent. Another Taxay citation comments on the current gold coins of the late 1850s: "Gobrecht's [Liberty Head] designs still remained on the $2.50, $5, and $10 pieces, and seem vastly inferior to Longacre's work."[3]

1860 Assay Commission medal by Paquet, Julian AC-1: The obverse is Longacre's Liberty Head as used on 1859 pattern half dollars. The reverse is a laurel wreath which "appears to have been reduced from an original [brass casting] for a pattern cent (Judd-208) of 1858" (Julian). This die is similar to the *6-leaf* cluster type of 1859 reverse. The same reverse design was used on the 1861 Assay Commission medal, AC-2., and 1867, AC-3.

1860 Japanese Embassy medal by Paquet: In 1860 Paquet produced the Japa-

---

[1] R.W. Julian's masterwork, *Medals of the United States Mint: The First Century 1792-1892,* has been a valuable aid to this study as has been Andrew W. Pollock III's *United States Patterns and Related Issues.*
[2] Italics added. From *U.S. Mint and Coinage* it is not clear if Taxay was aware of Paquet's extensive repertoire of Mint medals, many of these quite artistic and none with the clumsiness of Miss Liberty as on the 1859 pattern $20.
[3] Taxay, p. 215. Probably, Taxay is in the minority among modern commentators in suggesting that Longacre's Liberty Head (for example on the $20) was by implication vastly superior to Gobrecht's Liberty Head motif. There is no accounting for numismatic tastes, and what one person condemns, another likes—which is as it should be in a land of free expression.

nese Embassy medal (Julian CM-22, 76mm) which featured on the reverse an oak wreath with certain stylistic similarities (leaf and acorn details) to that on the 1858 pattern cent and 1859 pattern $20 reverses.

1860 Washington Cabinet medal by Paquet: Related to the 1859 Washington Cabinet medalet is the large size (59mm) Washington Cabinet medal by Paquet (Julian MT-23) observing the dedication of the Cabinet on February 22, 1860 (Washington's birthday). Another large-size (79mm) medal by Paquet is dated 1859 (Julian MT-3) and depicts Mint Director Snowden on the obverse and an angular view of the Mint building on the reverse. This medal was done as a tribute to the director at the behest of other officers of the Mint, who selected Paquet for the work.[1] This chronology of the two medals relating to the Washington Cabinet, June 1859 to February 22, 1860, might well represent one of the most intense periods of restriking to gain items in trade for the Mint display.

1861 Washington medalet by Paquet: On a small medal of George Washington (Julian PR-27) a *5-leaf* cluster-style laurel wreath encircles the inscription TIME IN-CREASES HIS FAME, and is signed AP (for Paquet) on the obverse. Apparently, these were first struck in autumn 1861. The Washington obverse was muled with a reverse die of Andrew Jackson (signed P for Paquet) and struck on October 23, 1861, "solely to create additional varieties of Washingtoniana." These medals were an instant success. Large numbers were sold immediately. As this was well into the directorship of James Pollock, it illustrates that Snowden's successor in office was not above making "fancy pieces" strictly for numismatic sales. This reinforces the belief that restriking of 1858-dated pattern cents and other delicacies continued under Pollock's tenure.[2]

1865-1871 Indian Peace medals by Paquet: Paquet remained at the Mint through part of 1864, then left, but continued his work as an outside supplier on a fee basis. He designed two Indian Peace medals, including the Andrew Johnson medal (Julian IP-40) for which he went to Washington in September 1865 and sketched President Johnson from life.[3] The second medal, portraying Ulysses S. Grant, was dated 1871, and was completed in August of that year. None of the Indian Peace medals bear motifs similar to those found on cents.

The assigning to Assistant Engraver Anthony C. Paquet the work for the foregoing medals, among others, illustrates that he was held in high esteem by Director Snowden. Further, only a small number of the many Paquet medals are described here. During the time Paquet was employed at the Mint and also as an outside contractor, his output of medals far exceeded that of Chief Engraver Longacre. One might conclude that Paquet saved Longacre a lot of work, that Longacre was not primarily interested in coinage designs of the era anyway (as evidenced by his copying his and others' earlier motifs), and that as the cent was the most "lowly" of all denominations it was never a showcase for the chief engraver's prowess. Longacre's name is associated with some higher-denomination patterns, particularly of the 1860s, none of which has drawn collectors' acclaim in the manner that certain Gobrecht, William Barber, and George T. Morgan patterns have.[4] Thus, quite possibly Longacre

[1] Julian, p. 180.
[2] Julian, p. 100.
[3] Julian, p. 60.
[4] Longacre's most numerous patterns are found in the rather repetitious Standard Silver series of the end of the decade, most produced after his January 1, 1869 death. Acclaimed patterns by other engravers include Gobrecht's Liberty Seated and flying eagle issues of 1836-1839, William Barber's 1872 "Amazonian" and 1879 "Washlady" series, and Morgan's illustrious 1879 "Schoolgirl" dollar, 1882 "Shield Earring" silver patterns, and various pattern half dollars of 1879.

was content to let Paquet do a lot of the design work for one-cent patterns in addition to making multiple letter and numeral fonts. However, in the absence of specific documentation the precise authorship of certain cent dies may never be known.

Cents Made to Order in 1859-1861

It is my opinion that restriking of 1856 and 1858 pattern cents began in earnest in 1859. By that time the market price of the 1856 Flying Eagle had risen to $1 to $2, and the Mint had run short of extra pieces. In addition, the recently coined 1858 patterns were in short supply. Most probably, such pieces continued to be made in quantity through 1860, perhaps to the end of the Snowden directorship in spring 1861, with selected pieces produced in smaller numbers after that time, almost certainly through the early 1870s and perhaps even later.

On January 22, 1859, Mint Director James Ross Snowden wrote the following telling letter to Howell Cobb, secretary of the Treasury:[1]

> Sir, we are daily pressed upon, by collectors of coins from all parts of the country either by letter or in person, for specimens of pattern pieces of coin, and rare types. A few of these have been in every case issued—some of them got into the hands of dealers and are sold at excessive prices. I propose with your approbation, to check this traffic, and at the same time gratify a taste which has lately increased in this country, and seems to be increasing every day, namely by striking some of each kind and affixing a price to them, so that the profits may inure to the benefit of the Mint Cabinet of coins and ores which is the property of the United States; an exact amount of which will be kept and rendered to the Department.'

Snowden was a numismatist possessing good general knowledge of the subject. His specialty was tokens and medals relating to George Washington, and to this end he set about with fervor building a display of these within the Mint Cabinet (being the official collection begun at the Mint in June 1838 and continued since that time). Snowden sponsored, lent his name to the title page, and partially wrote two excellent books, each elegantly illustrated, *Description of Ancient and Modern Coins in the Cabinet Collection of the Mint of the United States,* published in 1860, and, in 1861, *A Description of the Medals of Washington: The Medallic Memorials of Washington in the Mint of the United States.* In an era in which there was very little literature on United States coins and related pieces, these two works were well received. Even today both books can be reviewed for the excellent information they contain.

In his letter of January 22, 1859, Snowden reveals that when collectors have requested that specimens of "patterns" and "rare types" have been in "every case issued" when requested by collectors. At the time the Mint had an abundant supply of back-dated dies on hand, and when a die could not be found, a new one was often made. Snowden, apparently without thought of personal gain, suggested that such coins should be restruck on a more formal basis, assigned prices, and the profits should go to augment the Mint Cabinet.

In January 1859, coin dealer John K. Curtis asked Snowden if the Mint could supply a specimen of the very rare 1851 Liberty Seated dollar, and the director replied that "one could be struck from the dies of that year." Today we know that two new obverse dies for the 1851 dollar were made up, each differing in minute details from the original 1851 die, which, apparently, had either been lost or rendered unserviceable.

---

[1] This and other quotations under this heading are from the National Archives, edited from the copies reprinted by Eric P. Newman and Kenneth E. Bressett, *The Fantastic 1804 Dollar,* 1962; by Don Taxay, *Counterfeit, Mis-Struck and Unofficial U.S. Coins,* 1963; and by Taxay, *U.S. Mint and Coinage,* 1966.

In the same vein is Director Snowden's response to a letter from a P. Clayton, who made this request:

> Dear Sir,
> If you have specimens in copper of the new $20, also model half & quarter dollars & specimen cents struck last year before settling on the new device now used—& can spare them without detriment to the public interest, I would like to have them. My object is to give them to a friend who seems to have a passion for specimens of coins.

Snowden's reply, dated January 24, 1859, bore the notation "Unofficial" and commented:

> Dear Sir,
> I have rec'd your note of the 22nd inst. and learn from it that you are acquiring a personal knowledge of the "passion for specimens of coins" which possesses so many people in our country. On Saturday I had nine applications of a similar character—today (now 12 o'clock) I have had three. It was in view of this increasing, as well as troublesome, taste that I made the request mentioned in my official letter of last Saturday (22nd inst.) which I hope will deserve the sanction of the department.
> In reference to the specimens you ask for I have to state that the trial piece in copper of the double eagle of 1859 which I left at the Department is the only one I had: I have a few of the specimen cents but not all the varieties. I could send you two or three of these, but perhaps it will be best to defer sending them until the new arrangement is made, when your friend, and all other collectors of coins, AND THEIR NAME IS LEGION, can be supplied to their heart's content.

This letter specifically states that Snowden's stock of "specimen cents" made the preceding year, 1858, was diminished to the point of having only "a few" coins, possibly only two or three different, but that a "new arrangement" was in the offing under which "collectors of coins...can be supplied to their heart's content."

It would seem that no further proof is required to demonstrate that the Mint in 1859 intended to restrike 1858-dated cents and other rarities.

While today in the 1990s, it might be viewed that such practice was a "naughty" one, at the time the Mint had a long history of accommodating the wishes of collectors. However, before long the situation would go "underground," and various employees of the Mint would make coins for their private profit, not for the enrichment of the Mint Cabinet. Along the way, the Mint would issue many phony denials, misleading statements, false authentications, and other inexcusable statements, soon earning the enmity of much of the collecting community—especially those who did not have privileged connections to Mint insiders. However, in January 1859 Snowden's motives seemed to have been selfless.

It has been suggested by Don Taxay, Walter Breen, and others that Snowden was engaged in some illegal activity, particularly in view of coinage laws dated 1792 and 1837 which stated that "all coins bear the year of their issue." However, in practice the Mint violated these laws countless times. In fact, even in our own era in the late twentieth century the Mint continues to do this, as in the restriking of denominations from Lincoln cents to Kennedy half dollars in the mid-1960s from earlier-dated dies, the *pre*-striking of 1976 Bicentennial coins beginning in 1974, etc., etc. The list is a long one.

Notwithstanding the seeming openness of Snowden's January 1859 communications, before long there were abuses and, apparently, restrikes in various series were being sold—at least by second-hand parties—without disclosing that they were of recent manufacture. On June 14, 1859, dealer Edward D. Cogan wrote to Director Snowden:

> I have been applied to by a great many collectors of American coins wishing to be informed whether the report now current—that there are many of the pattern cents being restruck at the Mint for the purpose of exchanging them for Washington pieces is true.
>
> The only answer I can give is that the many pieces shown me lately would tend to confirm the report. A rumor of this kind uncontradicted will tend to depreciate the value of every fine piece in whatever collection it may be found and I should be glad if you would give it the most unqualified denial.

Snowden continued his posture of free dissemination of information by replying:

> It is quite true that I have caused a number of pattern or specimen cents to be struck for the purpose of exchanging them for Washington pieces whenever opportunities to do so occur.
>
> If you possess any Washington pieces I would be much obliged if you will send me a list of them, and if there are any among them which I desire for the Cabinet I would be pleased to procure them by giving you in exchange other interesting medals or coins.

Other Restrikes at the Mint

Meanwhile at the Mint, and apparently without the knowledge of Director Snowden, certain profit-minded individuals were using old dies to make their own restrikes. In its May 1868 issue (which was 10 years after the alleged incident) the *American Journal of Numismatics* commented:

> It is perhaps not generally known that in 1858 certain dollars of 1804, re-struck from the original dies, without collars, and therefore having plain edges, found their way out of the Mint. Major Nichols, of Springfield, had one of these at the cost of $75 and Mr. Cogan had one, but both were on solicitation returned to their source.

Similarly, in June 1882, Ebenezer Locke Mason, in his *Coin Collector's Magazine,* recalled that he "was offered by young Eckfeldt three genuine U.S. 1804 dollars at $70 each, and nearly all the rare 1/2 cents in dozens of duplicates were purchased."

The identity of "young Eckfeldt" is not known with certainty, but it may have been a son of Mint employee George Eckfeldt. Newly restruck 1804 silver dollars were offered to the dealer community, but without knowledge of Snowden. The unfavorable reaction to this caused Snowden to demand an accounting of old dies at the Mint and to put them under seal. However, certain old dies could still be maintained "in use," but the director was to be furnished descriptions of these "cabinet coins," the quantities struck, and the recipients of them.

Years later, Henry R. Linderman, M.D., then director of the Mint, found two sealed boxes of dies, but not an inventory of their contents. Linderman commented:

> On the 8th of July 1859 several experimental dies were boxed, sealed, and placed in the vault in the cabinet by the then director of the Mint and a list thereof was filed in the Director's Office. Another sealed box of experimental dies was placed in said vault July 30, 1860, and a list filed in the same office. Neither of these papers can now

be found, and the director deems it proper to have the boxes opened and again sealed up. It is ordered that the boxes referred to shall be opened this day in the presence of the director, chief coiner & engraver. A list of the dies shall then be made, immediately after which the dies shall be replaced in the boxes and sealed up under the official seals of the director and engraver.

Linderman, of whom more will be said in subsequent paragraphs, was a numismatist, and no doubt it was with a measure of thinly disguised glee that he found these dies, representing possibilities for his own profit.

In the meantime, after James Ross Snowden left his Mint office in early 1861, he continued his numismatic activities in the private sector. Snowden had been a member *ex officio* of the Numismatic and Antiquarian Society of Philadelphia when he was Mint director. After spring 1861 he became a dues-paying participant. In 1864 his 72-page monograph, *The Coin of the Bible and Its Money Terms* was published.

Director Pollock

When Abraham Lincoln entered the White House in 1861 he selected as the new director of the Mint James Pollock, a former governor of Pennsylvania.

Apparently, the good feeling that collectors must have felt in January 1859 when former director Snowden openly expressed willingness to supply "specimen coins" had deteriorated sharply by November 12, 1861, when the new director, Pollock, was sent this letter signed by members of a collectors' group:

> The undersigned, a committee of the Boston Numismatic Society, were instructed to call your attention to the abuses which have of late years been practiced at the Mint of the United States whereby a number of pattern pieces and coins from dies of former years have been freely struck and disposed of by employees of the Mint to dealers who have in turn disposed of them at great prices.
>
> Two years since members of this Society were offered specimens of the dollar of 1804 of which, previously, only three or four examples were known; on applying to the director of the Mint, he peremptorily replied that none had been struck; further investigation resulted in the fact being proven that three specimens had been struck, two of which had been sold for $75.00 each; various pattern pieces, in large numbers, have also been issued without the sanction of the proper officers. Under these circumstances, we respectfully urge the expediency of destroying the dies of the current coin, and also of pattern pieces at the close of each year.

To this Pollock sent this reply on November 21, 1861:

> Gentlemen,
>
> Yours of the 12 inst. has been rec'd. The abuses to which you refer, if they have ever had an existence, can no longer be practiced in this Institution. The practice of striking pattern pieces and coins from dies of former years cannot be too strongly condemned, and great care is now taken to prevent the recurrence of any such abuse.
>
> All the dies of former years are secured in such a manner that it is impossible for any one to obtain possession of them without the knowledge of the Director. The dies of the current coins and of pattern pieces will be destroyed at the close of the year. The dies of the past few years have also been destroyed.

Notwithstanding this declaration of restriking innocence and the passing suggestion that restrikes were never made to begin with, "fancy pieces" continued to be produced. If Pollock was not directly involved, certainly others under his supervision were. Under his watch quite a few off-metal strikes, unusual mulings, and other pieces were made, among which were the various GOD OUR TRUST and IN GOD WE TRUST serial issues of 1861-1865 which were unofficially, but not very secretly, peddled to dealers and collectors.

In Massachusetts, dealer W. Elliot Woodward, far from Philadelphia and not an insider to Mint favors, penned this commentary in his October 1880 catalogue of the Ferguson Haines Collection relative to 1861-dated GOD OUR TRUST patterns (made under Pollock's directorship) and other issues:

> Judging from my own experience, I believe that the purchaser of an 1804 dollar, or any one of many of the rarest American coins, has no guarantee that the son of some future director or chief coiner of the Mint will not, at an unexpected moment, place a quantity on the market. "What man has done man may do"; and the ways of the Mint are past finding out, though transactions, such as restriking 1804 dollars, 1827 quarter dollars, and rare half cents, and speculations in rare experimental coins designed, engraved, and struck at the expense of the government, have become too frequent not to be well understood. What the lords of the Treasury will do next is "what no feller can find out." We will wait and see.
>
> In these days of investigation, an inquiry into past conduct of some of its officials, would, if properly conducted, be fruitful in results; and if properly reported, would furnish what Horace Greeley used to call "mighty interesting reading."
>
> As the government is fond of illustrating its reports, as a frontispiece is suggested a view of a son of a late official of the Mint, as he appeared at the store of the writer, when, on a peddling expedition from Philadelphia to Boston, he drew from his pocket rolls of (1861) "God Our Trust" patterns, and urged their purchase at wholesale, after sundry sets had been disposed of at $100 each to collectors of rare coins, with the assurance that only a very few had been struck, and that the dies were destroyed....

Dr. Linderman as Director

Henry Richard Linderman, M.D., assumed the Mint directorship in April 1867 and served until 1878 (except for about four years). Under his administration the production of special coins assumed major proportions. Linderman was a numismatist and was very aware of the profits to be made.

Linderman outdid every previous Mint director in this department, and unlike Snowden and Pollock, made many pieces for his own personal enrichment. In June 1878 a congressional subcommittee made charges of misconduct against him, which he denied. Linderman died on January 27, 1879, at the age of 53. The charges were never resolved.

In addition to Linderman, various others at the Mint produced special pieces on occasion over a period of many years. The 1885 Indian cent in aluminum, struck from regular Proof dies, is a tail-end example of a long list of shenanigans. Historical details of such productions are extremely fascinating, but are beyond the scope of the present book.

Restriking Summary

In the early 1990s Walter Breen suggested that 1804 dollars and other delicacies were made without the knowledge of Director James Ross Snowden by parties Breen (following a suggestion by Richard Snow) called the "Midnight Minters" (George and Theodore Eckfeldt[1]), from 1858 to the summer of 1860, and again April 1867-April 1869, during the first Mint directorship of Dr. Richard Henry Linderman. Breen further noted:[2]

> George Eckfeldt was the foreman in the coining room, and would have had access to dies for Snowden's projects. What Snowden objected to—and why he confiscated the pattern dies in August 1859 and the others July 30, 1860—was George Eckfeldt's unauthorized use of the dies for private profit. The example of Franklin Peale, fired for similar activity with medal dies, was probably still fresh in Snowden's mind.[3]

Walter Breen made these additional comments concerning the Eckfeldts:[4]

> Few people at the Mint would have had ready access to blank planchets as it was Mint practice to treat second process (upset rims) planchets of *silver or gold* as money. As this did not apply to base metals, clearly the "Midnight Minters" [Theodore and George Eckfeldt] could have easily made copper coins and "trial pieces."

> I therefore postulate that the "Midnight Minters" had to obtain silver or gold planchets from outside the Mint, and that this fact (for fact it certainly is; witness the 1804 silver dollar overstruck on an 1857 Bern shooting taler, an extant 1838 Gobrecht dollar on an 1859 dollar, one specimen of an 1851 restrike dollar on an 1855 dollar and another on an unspecified New Orleans Mint dollar,[5] 1827 restrike quarters on 1806 and other Draped Bust quarters, etc.) accounts not merely for these overstrikes but for the variable weights of other silver restrikes. That the restrike half cents vary so greatly in weight indicates that the "Midnight Minters" most likely cut blanks from strip of atypical thickness; probably few normal 84-grain blanks were left over from 1857....

> I have long since stopped taking as fact anything that either James Ross Snowden, Archibald Loudon Snowden, or Henry R. Linderman ever said about how many pieces were made, or when, or about die destruction.

It is not clear whether Mint Director James Ross Snowden or the "Midnight Minters"—or both—made the 1856 Flying Eagle cent restrikes. Most of the emphasis in the preceding Breen commentary relates to higher denomination silver and gold issues. The multiplicity of specimens of the 1856 Flying Eagle cent, all on *normal* planchets, does suggest that Snowden was in charge of these. Significantly, no 1856 Flying Eagle cent dies were among those seized in 1859 or 1860.[6] Further, Snowden

---

[1] In *The Fantastic 1804 Dollar: 25th Anniversary Follow-Up,* Eric P. Newman and Kenneth E. Bressett, 1987, the suggestion was made that George Eckfeldt's son was named Cater; whether Cater was a nickname for Theodore, or whether he was a different person, is not known.

[2] Letter from Walter Breen to the author, April 21, 1992. Certain of this information is from Bowers, *Silver Dollars and Trade Dollars of the United States: A Complete Encyclopedia.*

[3] QDB note: Franklin Peale, a gifted technician and artist, brought many innovations to the Mint, but at the same time he used Mint facilities to run his private business of making and striking medals. Don Taxay in *U.S. Mint and Coinage* gives details.

[4] Specific contribution by Breen to the two-volume study, *Silver Dollars and Trade Dollars of the United States: A Complete Encyclopedia,* Bowers, 1992.

[5] QDB note: This 1851 restrike is reported to have been certified as an "1851-O" dollar by a grading service.

[6] As stated, George Eckfeldt was the foreman of dies in the coining room. His son Theodore is said to have been the Mint's night watchman. The third conspirator (who accompanied Theodore on ped-

was open about the restriking of 1858 cents. A more likely scenario for the production of certain limited-edition pieces is that while Snowden was openly producing pieces for exchange or sale to enhance the Mint Cabinet, others at the Mint, without his knowledge, were far more deeply engaged in restriking activities of items other than pattern cents.

After Snowden left the Mint in early 1861, his successors or people working at the Mint under them continued to make restrikes and fancy pieces for collectors, through at least the year 1885, but in smaller quantities and not openly.

1859 Pattern Cent a Regular Issue?

One of the most interesting patterns (putatively) of this era is the transitional copper-nickel Indian cent, regular planchet alloy and thickness. The obverse depicts Longacre's Indian motif, UNITED STATES OF AMERICA surrounding, and the date 1859 below. The date logotype is curved to follow the bottom border, a contrast to the straight alignment of 1858 patterns. The reverse, instead of being the laurel wreath as used on circulating business strike Indian cents of 1859, depicts an oak wreath with narrow shield—the style regularly adopted in 1860. This variety is known as Judd-228 and Pollock-272.

The origin of this coin is related by a letter from Director Snowden to the Treasury Department, December 13, 1859, stating that a modification of the reverse design would be desirable, and enclosing specimens to illustrate the new concept. On December 14, 1859, Secretary of the Treasury Howell Cobb approved the new design. As no further action was necessary (no act of Congress, for example), the design was official as of that point.

Quite probably, 1,000 or more of these were struck in December 1859 from at least two different obverse and two different reverse dies. A few were struck as samples to send to the Treasury as per the December 13 letter cited above, but the purpose for a larger quantity is not known. I have seen no indication that members of Congress, newspaper editors, and others of influence needed to be educated or informed about the new motif, which to the casual observer was just a minor design change. Nor have I come across any accounts of these being a focal point of numismatic interest in 1859 (the limelight at the time seems to have been focused upon 1856 Flying Eagle cents and 1858-dated patterns of various combinations). Nor do I have any indication that these 1859 pieces were ever restruck.

In my 1959 study, "Transitional Coins of America," I noted this:

> As to rarity there is a story told to us by a former Illinois dealer concerning the existence of 12 rolls of Uncirculated specimens—a hoard which was broken up in the late 1930s. We would estimate from this, as well as from the number we have seen, a population of from 700 to 800 pieces. A Boston collector presently owns 51 of these.... There are two minor reverse variations...only of interest to the specialist."

Over a period of years in the 1950s and early 1960s, when I spent quite a bit of time buying, selling, and studying pattern small cents of the 1850s, I learned that almost without exception 1859 cents with reverse of 1860 available in the market were brilliant Uncirculated business strikes. I probably handled about 100 to 200

---

dling trips to coin dealers as far away as Woodward's in Roxbury, Massachusetts) has not been identified. Theodore Eckfeldt sold half cent restrikes through Ebenezer Locke Mason, Jr.'s coin shop, in a building owned by Montroville Wilson Dickeson, M.D. (author of *The American Numismatical Manual*, 1859), near the corner of North 2nd and Buttonwood streets, Philadelphia. Also, letter from Walter Breen to the author, February 12, 1992.

pieces, with not a worn piece or Proof among them.[1] The 51 pieces mentioned above in my 1959 article were mostly sold by me to Dr. R., a Boston research physician who took a fancy to this issue. For all I know, he probably bought others after the above article was printed.

Around the same time there were scattered groups of these in dealers' hands including 17 pieces which I tried to buy from John J. Ford, Jr., but he had taken a liking to these and, in fact, caused them to be listed among business strikes in the 1957 (and final) edition of the *Standard Catalogue of United States Coins.* John felt that these transitional pieces indeed had special status and may have been intended as circulation strikes, but were struck in small numbers and never passed out.

During the preparation of this book, Richard Snow suggested that a group of such Mint State coins remained undistributed at the Mint, along with a cache of 1862 Proof regular-issue cents, and came on the market through dealers in the late 1860s or early 1870s. I don't recall having heard or read about this before.[2] I do not know if this Mint hoard is related to the 12 rolls (600 coins) alluded to earlier.

As these 1859 transitional pattern cents were and are found in business strike rather than Proof format, they were occasionally incorporated into old-time collections to fill the 1859 regular-issue space in a "National" (Wayte Raymond) or other brand of album. In the 1950s, when few dealers knew about or cared about patterns, I found a few of these patterns among regular 1859 cents in dealers' stocks.

If Mint documentation or other evidence is ever found that this 1859 transitional cent is in fact a regular business strike issue, it will probably become one of the most highly prized of all American small cents.[3] It is at least twice as rare as the 1856 Flying Eagle cent, but unlike the latter it is usually found in lustrous gem Mint State grades.

Transitional Patterns

Before moving on past 1859 I share a few comments about what I consider to be "special" Flying Eagle and Indian cent patterns, struck on regular copper-nickel planchets and dated 1856-1859. From the time in 1953 when I first "discovered" the Adams and Woodin book on pattern coins, I found it quite unusual that the 1856 transitional pattern Flying Eagle cent was famous, expensive ($200 to $300 for a nice one), and in demand, but few people even knew about the other transitional issues of the era. A few years later I wrote an article, "Transitional Coins of America," for *Empire Topics* magazine, the issue of February-March 1959.

A quick definition of a transitional pattern cent is as follows:

1. The obverse of the coin bears the identical motif and letter arrangement of an adopted issue, but the date may be earlier than the year the motif was first used for circulation. If the obverse is of the currently circulating type, then the reverse was first used on regular issues at a later date.

2. The format—planchet alloy, thickness, weight—is the same as the standard 72-grain, copper-nickel (88% copper, 12% nickel) cent of the era. The edge is plain.

EXCLUDED from the above are strikes in various other alloys (such as bronze),

---

[1] In general, "Proofs" I have seen offered for sale have been business strikes that have been automatically listed as Proofs because they are patterns.

[2] Richard Snow, letter, April 10, 1996.

[3] However, R.W. Julian, letter, April 29, 1996, expressed the opinion that weekly or other frequent mintage/delivery records for late 1859 no longer exist. Thus, further facts may never be learned.

pieces with reeded edges, coins with one side not conforming to a motif ever used for circulation (such as the oak wreath without shield style).

A quick overview and reiteration of the transitional patterns follows:[1]

1856 Flying Eagle cent, design of 1857. Large flying eagle motif obverse combined with agricultural wreath reverse identical to the 1857 design, but dated a year earlier. This, of course, is the famous 1856 Flying Eagle cent, the glory of which has been derived from long-term listings among regular issues in reference books on U.S. coins (to find out about the *other* transitional pattern cents, a technical reference on patterns had to be consulted by interested numismatists). The 1856 Flying Eagle has had time on its side and was recognized as an object of numismatic desire from the very time of its issue. Today this is far and away the most plentiful of the transitional issues, ditto for being the most expensive and most publicized. Specimens were restruck at later times using original obverse dies. Most struck in 1856 or very early 1857 had a business strike or "Mint State" finish; examples struck later are all believed to have been made with Proof finish, but typically from incompletely polished dies.

1858 Flying Eagle cent with laurel wreath reverse. This is the standard 1858 obverse, Large Letters (rarer) or Small Letters style, combined with the laurel wreath reverse as first regularly used on circulating cents in 1859. Specimens were restruck at later times. These were made with Proof finish, usually from incompletely polished dies showing many parallel striations. In 1959 in my article, "Transitional Coins of America," I estimated that 80 were known of this general style, with "the Large Letters obverse rarer by a considerable margin"; of course, this is now "ancient" history in the field of pattern research; no differentiation was made at the time concerning leaf positions on the reverse.

1858 Indian cent with agricultural wreath reverse. This combines Longacre's new pattern Indian cent obverse with the standard agricultural wreath reverse being used on Flying Eagle cents of the era. Of the transitional patterns listed here, this is among the scarcest. Specimens were restruck at later times. Struck with Proof finish, usually from incompletely polished dies. In my 1959 article I estimated that 80 were known of this general style.

1858 Indian cent with laurel wreath reverse. This combines Longacre's new pattern Indian cent obverse with the laurel wreath reverse as first regularly used on circulating coins in 1859. Of the transitional patterns listed here, this is the third most plentiful (after the 1856 Flying Eagle cent and the 1859 transitional cent). Specimens were restruck at later times. Struck with Proof finish, usually from incompletely polished dies. In my 1959 article I estimated that 200 were known of this general style, about 50 or 60 of them being Proofs. Since that time I have seen more and believe that the population is somewhat larger than this. Also, probably all were struck as Proofs, but most do not have full Proof surfaces; the same is true of the other Proof pattern cents of this year.

1859 Indian cent with oak wreath and shield reverse. This combines the regular-issue Indian cent obverse of 1859 with the oak wreath and narrow shield reverse as first regularly used on circulating coinage in 1860. Nearly always seen in lustrous Mint State preservation. The second most available transitional pattern (after the 1856 Flying Eagle). I doubt if any were restruck. Of the several 1858 and 1859 transi-

---

[1] For detailed die descriptions and attribution numbers for 1856-1858 patterns see 1856 sub-chapter for 1856 cents and earlier paragraphs in the present Appendix II for 1858 issues; also Judd, Snow, and Pollock texts.

tional issues listed here, this is the only one that has a claim to being a circulation strike rather than a pattern. The final chapter on the status of this coin has yet to be written.

Later Pattern Indian Cents

Pattern cents related to the Indian series and dated after 1859 include these important (in my opinion) pieces made to test proposals, alloys, formats, or other aspects related to the business strike production of one-cent pieces:[1]

The 1863 thin-planchet bronze Indian cent, a transitional issue and precursor to the regular 1864 48-grain bronze cent. These seem to have been struck on bronzed (darkened by a special process prior to striking) planchets, with obverse and reverse dies aligned in the same direction. These pieces are discussed earlier in the present work. Most (but not all) of these seem to be originals dating from 1863. Judd-299, Pollock-359.

The 1863 copper-nickel Indian cent with reeded edge, a mysterious piece discussed earlier under the 1863 sub-chapter. My own feeling is that this variety was made up for some experiment or other purpose the details of which are not known today, and that this is not a special coin made for numismatic sales. Judd-300 (ambiguous; description also covers other possibilities), Pollock-362.

1864 thin-planchet copper-nickel cent: On March 17, 1864, Mint Director James Pollock sent a copper-nickel cent on a thin planchet, 48 grains, to the Treasury Department as a suggestion that this alloy could be retained for the cent, and bronze could be used for the new two-cent piece.[2]

1863-1864 oroide and other metallic experiment cents. Prior to adopting the bronze alloy, the Mint struck Indian cents in several experimental metals. Best known is one called oroide, a popular golden-hued ("oro" is the Spanish word for gold) alloy of copper with a generous measure of tin, used to make cheap watch cases, jewelry, and other mass-market consumer goods.[3] These oroide alloy coins seem to have been made in small numbers, with business strike (not Proof) finish, and were not restruck for collectors. Varieties are dated 1863 and 1864. In the latter year the Mint created patterns in several experimental alloys including 95% copper and 5% aluminum, 92.9% copper and 7.1% aluminum, and 90% copper and 10% aluminum, some of which at the time of striking resembled bright yellow gold. On June 8, 1864, the assayer's office at the Mint reported that aluminum-bronze alloy was unsuitable for coinage, primarily because it was difficult to roll into strips to make planchets.[4]

Many of these patterns may have later toned to resemble Mint State regular issue bronze cents, and quite probably there are some acquired as such in collections today. Elemental testing is required to differentiate various experimental alloys, and few numismatists have the facilities or inclination to do this.[5]

---

[1] Certain *basic* patterns listed here are given Judd and Pollock numbers; those same texts can be consulted for many if not most of the other patterns mentioned. The Snow text delineates many related specifically to the Indian series.

[2] R.W. Julian, letter, April 24, 1996; this is also cited earlier in the present text under the 1864 copper-nickel cent sub-chapter.

[3] Products fabricated in oroide were extensively advertised during this era, watch cases in *Harper's Weekly* being an example.

[4] R.W. Julian, letter, April 24, 1996.

[5] Pollock, *United States Patterns and Related Issues,* pp. 123-124, gives much additional information concerning the aluminum-content pieces.

Patterns Made for Collectors

Patterns in the above-titled category are not really patterns inasmuch as they were not made to test proposals, new alloys, or any other such traditional purpose. Rather, they were delicacies created especially for sale or trade to dealers and collectors. None of these were made in especially large quantities, and all seem to have been distributed in a *sub rosa* manner; *clandestine* is the word Walter Breen preferred.

Just as a king or queen or even a head figure of a religion can come from less than ideal parental circumstances, many highly desired coins in various areas of the market were created under less than historically ideal circumstances. Or, if examined closely, their date of birth is different from the date on the coin. While I am not an apologist for the actions of the Mint in the nineteenth century or any later era, I am a realist, and I believe that a coin can be highly desirable, no matter what its circumstances of birth. For example, all but a few 1879-dated $4 gold stellas were struck in 1880 or later, but just about anyone would be happy to own one.[1]

Anachronistic copper-nickel cents: By the end of May 1864 the copper-nickel cent was history. The Mint switched over to the new thin bronze format for regular coinages as well as for Proof strikes sold openly to collectors, singly or as part of sets. However, as the years passed it apparently required no great measure of marketing acumen to determine that dates after 1864, if struck in the old copper-nickel format, would be readily salable to collectors. Accordingly, such Indian cents as 1865, 1866, 1867, 1868 and 1869 were made on copper-nickel (sometimes called "nickel") planchets as were some other dates, some specimens of which are of questionable authenticity.[2] Not content with making them look like regular copper-nickel cents, those who were fooling around at the Mint also made examples with reeded edges and on light weight copper-nickel planchets with the latter being the main style from about 1866 onward (by which time regulation 72-grain copper-nickel planchets were no longer readily available). The listing of some of these in various Scott *Standard Catalogue* issues created a demand for them (see Appendix III).

1863 L cents: The 1863 cents with L on ribbon were probably made years after the 1863 year, although the 1863 L situation is not completely clear to me (see discussion under the notes for the 1863 cent sub-chapter).

Other fancy pieces and off-metal strikes: A list of fancy pieces related to the Indian-motif cents includes these delicacies, any one of which would draw enthusiastic bidding at an auction and each of which is a rarity:

The previously mentioned 1863 cents with L on ribbon, struck in various metals other than bronze, are a very exciting and numismatically desirable patterns, but were virtually certainly struck significantly later than 1863, quite probably in 1871, the latter year being an active time for restriking various issues including Proof coins of the preceding decade.[3]

Various Indian cents struck in aluminum from regular Proof dies are likewise fancy

---

[1] See comment about $4 gold stellas under the 1856 Flying Eagle sub-chapter.

[2] In my opinion the vast majority of *non-Proof* "nickel" and "copper-nickel" cents dated after 1866 and of weights within a grain or two of 48 grains (the bronze standard) are in fact discolored regular bronze strikings. Over the years I have encountered many of these, including some that were in the King Farouk Collection. Any such offerings should be authenticated by an expert in *pattern* coins.

[3] Restrikes include 1864 Large Motto two-cent pieces struck from new dies employing the new obverse hub introduced in 1871 (see Breen, *Encyclopedia,* 1988, pp. 238, 240), and possibly the 1867 With Rays Proof Shield nickel (conversation with John Dannreuther, May 1996).

pieces. In my opinion, all of these were struck as special pieces for collectors, nearly all in very limited numbers.

Various mulings and illogical pieces have their place as well and, perhaps, are epitomized by a coin having on one side the obverse die of an 1858 Flying Eagle cent and on the other the obverse die of an 1864 cent (Judd-362, Pollock-428).

Other Cent Pattern Designs

A perusal of the Judd and Pollock books on pattern coins and the *Coin World Encyclopedia* will reveal a rich selection of pattern cents not related to the Indian motif. These include late nineteenth-century coins made up to test new designs, metals, formats, etc.

A partial list includes 1869 nickel-alloy cents of small diameter and with a Liberty Head design to match the current nickel three-cent piece (a matching pattern was also made for the nickel five-cent piece, the thought being that the 1¢, 3¢, and 5¢ coins would all match in the same way that Liberty Seated silver coins were related to each other); 1884 and 1885 pattern cents with a hole at the center (this experimental format was also tried for nickel five-cent pieces); and the extensive shield-motif cent patterns dated 1896.

In addition to such pieces made for pattern purposes, some of these dies were muled or made in other metals for sale to collectors.

Among other fancy pieces made for collectors one of my favorites is the 1868 copper large cent, a coin virtually identical in appearance to an 1843-1857 era Braided Hair large cent in every respect except the date. Obviously, the Mint was not contemplating the reissue of the large cent design in 1868, thus this was made as a post-dated rarity, sort of like having a 1920 Indian cent or a 1945 Buffalo nickel, if such existed![1]

---

[1] Although to be objective I mention that new styles of the one-cent piece were being considered in 1868 and that a pattern 10¢ piece using the same cent-style obverse was made. For expanded information see Don Taxay, *U.S. Mint and Coinage,* p. 247, as well as the Judd and Pollock pattern references. I have always liked the 1868 large cent and over the years have owned several specimens.

APPENDIX III
SCOTT CATALOGUE LISTINGS

The Rise and Fall of Scott Catalogues

I draw upon various *Standard Catalogues* issued in the late nineteenth and early twentieth centuries by J.W. Scott & Co. and the Scott Stamp & Coin Co., Ltd., for the following commentaries. When the first list cited, 1878, was published, the Indian cent series still had more than three decades to go.

The Scott catalogues were prepared very erratically, as the following listings demonstrate. Such data have very little research value today, except to show what type of information a beginning collector was apt to encounter in popular catalogues. At one time Scott had it all, as there were no other regularly issued price guides in existence. However, poor numismatic content and editorial arrangement cost Scott dearly, and most collectors and dealers found the price guides to be inaccurate, irrelevant, or both.

Titles varied and are given as they appeared on the catalogue covers.

1878 Scott Listings

The Standard Coin Catalogue (Copper). 1878. Indian cents were listed in three grade categories: Fine, Uncirculated, and Proof. In 1878 there were no universally accepted published grading guidelines of any kind for such coins, nor would there be throughout the life of the Scott guides. Note that the 1864 L cent is not listed, although this variety was known to numismatists as early as 1871. Prices listed in 1878 were as follows:

1859: Fine $0.05; Uncirculated $0.10; Proof $0.25.

1860: Fine $0.05; Unc. $0.10; Proof $0.25.

1861: Fine $0.05; Unc. $0.10; Proof $0.25.

1862: Fine $0.05; Unc. $0.10; Proof $0.25.

1863: Fine $0.05; Unc. $0.10; Proof $0.25.

1864 Copper-nickel: Fine $0.05; Unc. $0.10; Proof $0.25.

1864 Bronze: Fine $0.05; Unc. $0.10; Proof $0.25.

1865: Fine $0.05; Unc. $0.10; Proof $0.25.

1866: Fine $0.05; Unc. $0.10; Proof $0.25.

1867: Fine $0.05; Unc. $0.10; Proof $0.25.

1868: Fine $0.05; Unc. $0.10; Proof $0.25.

1869: Fine $0.05; Unc. $0.10; Proof $0.25.

1870: Unc. $0.05; Proof $0.25.

1871: Unc. $0.05; Proof $0.25.

1872: Unc. $0.05; Proof $0.25.

1873: Unc. $0.05; Proof $0.25.

1874: Unc. $0.05; Proof $0.25.

1875: Unc. $0.05; Proof $0.25.

1876: Unc. $0.05; Proof $0.25.

1877: Unc. $0.05; Proof $0.25.

1878: Unc. $0.05; Proof $0.25.

1879: Unc. $0.05; Proof $0.25.

Commentary: The preceding listing is hardly informative, but is simply a listing of dates 1859-1869 with the same prices for each, with a price break in 1870 followed by more similar prices through 1879.

Such listings were of little use to collectors, and dealers likewise ignored them. (I condense certain consecutive repetitive listings in the following citations to save space, now that the 1878 demonstrates the original appearance of such duplicated numbers.)

1880 Scott Listings

The Standard Coin Catalogue (Copper). 1880. These listings are vastly different from those of 1878 inasmuch as certain dates—1877 being an example—are now recognized as scarce issues.

For some unexplained reason, the "Fine" grade category of the 1878 edition is now replaced with "V. Good" (Very Good) and "Good," with even this being backward, as the later years—the ones less likely to be encountered well worn—are listed in the lower "Good" classification.

1859: V. Good $0.05; Uncirculated $0.25; Proof $0.50.

1860: V. Good $0.05; Unc. $0.20; Proof $0.35.

1861: V. Good $0.05; Unc. $0.25; Proof $0.50.

1862: V. Good $0.05; Unc. $0.20; Proof $0.30.

1863: V. Good $0.05; Unc. $0.15; Proof $0.25.

1864 Copper-nickel: V. Good $0.05; Unc. $0.15; Proof $0.25.

1864 Bronze: V. Good $0.05; Unc. $0.15; Proof $0.25.

1865: V. Good $0.05; Unc. $0.15; Proof $0.25.

1866: V. Good $0.05; Unc. $0.25; Proof $0.50.

1867: Good $0.05; Unc. $0.25; Proof $0.40.

1868: Good $0.05; Unc. $0.20; Proof $0.35.

1869: Good $0.05; Unc. $0.20; Proof $0.35.

1870: Unc. $0.20; Proof $0.40.

1871: Unc. $0.20; Proof $0.40.

1872: Unc. $0.25; Proof $0.50.

1873: Unc. $0.20; Proof $0.35.

1874: Unc. $0.15; Proof $0.35.

1875: Unc. $0.15; Proof $0.35.

1876: Unc. $0.15; Proof $0.35.

1877: Unc. $0.35; Proof $0.75.

1878: Unc. $0.05; Proof $0.25.

1879: Unc. $0.05; Proof $0.25.

Commentary: The preceding shows some market knowledge. Note that 1872 is valued more highly than 1871, but in a later edition (see following) the opposite would be true. Arguably, this is the best of the early Scott catalogues from a numismatic arrangement viewpoint except for the illogical substitution of "V. Good" and "Good" for the earlier "Fine" category. From this point, editions became increasingly erratic in their listings and price structures.

During the nineteenth century most Scott catalogues bore on the cover a notation which read as follows:

> This catalogue gives the market value of every American copper coin...in various degrees of preservation, with prices at which they can be purchased of the publishers.

In practice, Scott's inventory was stored in paper envelopes in which various dates of Indian cents were casually placed, Proofs mingling with Uncirculated pieces and these coming into contact with worn coins. Scott, whose main business was stamps, sought to supply Indian cents by dates rather than by degrees of grade. The Scott firm's coin stock was incomplete, and any orders for rarities were simply returned with a statement that these pieces were not available. Scott issued stamp catalogues on the same premise: list everything and price it for sale, whether or not it is *really* in stock for sale.

1887 Scott Listings

Scott's Standard Catalogues. Copper Coins. 1887 Edition. Indian cents were listed in three grade categories: Good, Bright (presumably meaning Uncirculated, but with Scott, who knows?), and Proof. Prices were as follows:

1859: Good $0.05; Bright $0.10; Proof $0.20.

1860: Good $0.05; Bright $0.10; Proof $0.20.

1861: Good $0.05; Bright $0.10; Proof $0.25.

1862: Good $0.05; Bright $0.10; Proof $0.30.

1863: Good $0.05; Bright $0.10; Proof $0.20.

1864 Copper-nickel: Good $0.05; Bright $0.10; Proof $0.20.

1864 Bronze: Good $0.05; Bright $0.10; Proof $0.20.

1865: Good $0.05; Bright $0.10; Proof $0.20.

1866: Good $0.05; Bright $0.15; Proof $0.30.

1867: Good $0.05; Bright $0.10; Proof $0.20.

1868-1871, each: Good $0.05; Bright $0.15; Proof $0.30.

1872: Good $0.05; Bright $0.10; Proof $0.25.

1873: Good $0.05; Bright $0.10; Proof $0.20.

1874-1876, each: Good $0.05; Bright $0.10; Proof $0.15.

1877: Good $0.10; Bright $0.20; Proof $0.40.

1878-1885, each: Good $0.05; Bright $0.10; Proof $0.15.

1886: Good $0.05; Bright $0.08; Proof $0.10.

Commentary: It is seen that among coins in circulation (Good grade) there are just two dates with a significant premium value, the 1871 and 1877, both listed at 10¢. The others listed at 5¢ were not worth that, but simply were valued as such to reflect a dealer's handling costs.

Among "Bright" coins several are valued at 15¢ each, with most at 10¢ each. The 1872 has retrogressed from its listing in the 1878 edition and now appears as a common date. The 1877 at 20¢ leads the pack as the most valuable "Bright" date, but the observer of today in the 1990s has no hint as to the reason for its fall in price from the 1878 edition.

Among Proofs, the 1877 is the leader at 40¢, and the 1862 (today in the 1990s considered to be the most plentiful of its era) is the most costly of the copper-nickel issues.

1893 Scott Listings

Scott's Standard Catalogues. No. 5. Copper and Nickel Coins. 17. 1893. Indian cents were listed in three grade categories: Fine, Uncirculated, and Proof. The "Good" grade had disappeared without explanation, and "Fine" was back again. "Bright" was nowhere to be seen, but "Uncirculated" seems to have taken its place. Note that the 1864 with L on ribbon is now listed.

Certain pattern coins were mixed among the regular issues in this edition, but the author of the Scott listings did not identified them as patterns. Doubtless, this influenced many collectors of the era to seek such patterns and explains, at least in part, why many auction offerings of Indian cents in the 1890s included such non-regular issues. However, it also confused other collectors, as such patterns were extremely rare, not seen in circulation, and not properly a part of a regular set.

1859 Copper-nickel [regular issue]: Fine $0.05; Uncirculated $0.25; Proof $0.50.

1859 Copper [laurel wreath reverse; pattern]: Unc. $2.50; Proof $4.00.

1859 Copper-nickel [oak wreath and shield reverse; pattern]: Unc. $1.50; Proof $2.00.

1860: Fine $0.05; Unc. $0.25; Proof $0.50.

1861: Fine $0.05; Unc. $0.30; Proof $0.65.

1862: Fine $0.05; Unc. $0.15; Proof $0.30.

1863 Copper-nickel [regular issue]: Fine $0.05; Unc. $0.15; Proof $0.40.

1863 Bronze [pattern]: Unc. $1.00; Proof $1.50

1864 Copper-nickel: Fine $0.05; Unc. $0.10; Proof $1.00.

1864 Bronze [without L]: Unc. $0.10; Proof $1.25.

1864 Bronze. L on ribbon: Fine $0.05; Unc. $0.15; Proof $0.85.

1865 Copper-nickel [pattern]: Fine $2.50; Unc. $3.50; Proof $4.00.

1865: Fine $0.05; Unc. $0.15; Proof $0.40.

1866: Fine $0.05; Unc. $0.15; Proof $0.40.

1867: Fine $0.05; Unc. $0.15; Proof $0.40

1868: Fine $0.05; Unc. $0.15; Proof $0.40

1869: Fine $0.05; Unc. $0.15; Proof $0.35.

1870: Fine $0.05; Unc. $0.15; Proof $0.35.

1871: Fine $0.05; Unc. $0.20; Proof $0.35.

1872: Fine $0.05; Unc. $0.25; Proof $0.35.

1873: Fine $0.05; Unc. $0.15; Proof $0.30.

1874: Fine $0.05; Unc. $0.10; Proof $0.30.

1875: Fine $0.05; Unc. $0.10; Proof $0.25.

1876: Fine $0.05; Unc. $0.10; Proof $0.25.

1877: Fine $0.10; Unc. $0.75; Proof $0.75.

1878: Fine $0.05; Unc. $0.10; Proof $0.20.

1879: Fine $0.05; Unc. $0.10; Proof $0.20.

1880: Unc. $0.10; Proof $0.25.

1881: Unc. $0.10; Proof $0.30.

1882-1891, each: Unc. $0.10; Proof $0.15.

1892: Unc. $0.05; Proof $0.10.

Commentary: The recently-listed 1864 L cent had established no market stature at this point, and, in fact, a Proof striking was said by Scott to be worth $0.85, or substantially less (relatively speaking) than the $1.25 at which a regular bronze Proof of the same year was valued. Two issues crossed the $1 mark for the first time: the 1864 regular issue copper-nickel Proof at $1 and the aforementioned regular issue bronze in the same category.

Among coins in circulation the only one of significant premium was the 1877 at $0.10. The 1871, valued in the 1887 catalogue at the same price as the 1877, fell from grace and was relegated to the status of a common date. However, in Uncirculated grade the price rose, and this date was one of the more valuable issues.

1907 Scott Listings

J.W. Scott's Standard Coin Catalogue No. 2. Copper Coins of the World. 1907. Indian cents were listed in three grade categories: Proof, Uncirculated, and Good. The "Fine" grade had disappeared once again, and the "Good" grade, in use in the 1887 catalogue, bounced back. Quite probably, either "Good" or "Fine" simply meant "an average coin taken from circulation," but once again the Scott catalogue offered no clues to its readers.

An exception was 1859 which was priced in Uncirculated, Fine, and Good grades, with Proof omitted. Certain pattern coins continued to be mixed among the regular issues.

1858 Copper-nickel [pattern; listed, but unpriced in any grade]

1858 Copper [pattern; listed, but unpriced in any grade]

1859 Copper-nickel [regular issue]: Good $0.05; Fine $0.25; Unc. $0.50 [Proof category not listed; Proofs commenced with 1860]

1859 Copper [laurel wreath reverse; pattern; listed, but unpriced in any grade]

1859 Copper-nickel [oak wreath and shield reverse; pattern]: Unc. $1.50; Proof $2.00.

1860: Good $0.05; Unc. $0.25; Proof $0.50.

1861: Good $0.05; Unc. $0.30; Proof $0.65.

1862: Good $0.05; Unc. $0.15; Proof $0.30.

1863 Copper-nickel [regular issue]: Good $0.05; Unc. $0.15; Proof $0.40.

1863 Bronze [pattern]: Unc. $1.00; Proof $1.50

1864 Copper-nickel: Good $0.05; Unc. $0.10; Proof $1.00.

1864 Bronze [without L]: Unc. $0.10; Proof $1.25.

1864 Bronze. L on ribbon: Good $0.05; Unc. $0.15; Proof $0.85.

1865 Copper-nickel [pattern]: Good $2.50; Unc. $3.50; Proof $4.00.

1865: Good $0.05; Unc. $0.15; Proof $0.40.

1866: Good $0.10; Unc. $0.15; Proof $0.40.

1867: Good $0.10; Unc. $0.15; Proof $0.40

1868: Good $0.05; Unc. $0.15; Proof $0.40

1869-1872, each: Good $0.05; Unc. $0.15; Proof $0.35.

1873: Good $0.05; Unc. $0.15; Proof $0.30.

1874: Good $0.05; Unc. $0.10; Proof $0.30.

1875: Good $0.05; Unc. $0.10; Proof $0.25.

1876: Good $0.10; Unc. $0.10; Proof $0.25 [same value given for Good and Unc.!]

1877: Good $0.20; Unc. $0.75 [Proof listed, but not priced]

1878-1889, each: Good $0.05; Unc. $0.10; Proof $0.20.

1890: Unc. $0.05; Proof $0.15.

1891-1907, each: Unc. $0.05; Proof $0.10.

Commentary: Although there are a few changes here and there among 1907 prices versus those of 1893, most remained the same, and it seems that the contributor to this section of Scott's reference was lazy, and little effort was made to reflect true values. Because of this, most active buyers used dealers' price lists and auction sale realizations for guides.

1913 Scott Listings

J. W. Scott's Standard Coin Catalogue No. 2. Copper Coins of the World. 1913. Indian cents were listed in three grade categories: Proof, Uncirculated, and Fine, the last grade having taken the place of "Good" found in the 1907 version. Consistency was not a precept at Scott's editorial office.

Exceptions were 1858 and 1859 which were priced in Uncirculated, Fine, and Good grades, with Proof omitted. As before, certain pattern coins were mixed among the regular issues.

1858 Copper-nickel [pattern with Indian obverse, laurel wreath reverse]. Fine $3.00; Unc. $4.00.

1858 Copper [pattern as preceding; listed, but unpriced in any grade]

1858 Copper-nickel [pattern with Indian obverse, regular cereal wreath reverse of the year]. Unc. $5.00.

1859 Copper-nickel [regular issue]: Good $0.05; Fine $0.15; Unc. $0.35 [Proof category not listed; Proofs commenced with 1860]

1859 Copper [laurel wreath reverse; pattern; listed, but unpriced in any grade]

1859 Copper-nickel [oak wreath and shield reverse; pattern]: Unc. $3.50; Proof $5.00.

1860: Fine $0.05; Unc. $0.15; Proof $0.20.

1861: Fine $0.10; Unc. $0.30; Proof $0.75.

1862: Fine $0.05; Unc. $0.15; Proof $0.25.

1863 Copper-nickel [regular issue]: Fine $0.05; Unc. $0.10; Proof $0.20.

1863 Bronze [pattern]: Unc. $3.00; Proof $4.00

1864 Copper-nickel: Fine $0.05; Unc. $0.10; Proof $0.20.

1864 Copper-nickel, thin planchet [pattern]: Unc. $3.00; Proof $4.00.

1864 Copper-nickel, oroide [pattern]: Proof $10.00.

1864 Bronze [without L]: Fine $0.05; Unc. $0.10; Proof $0.20.

1863 Bronze. L on ribbon [pattern]: [listed but not priced].

1864 Bronze. L on ribbon: Fine $0.15; Unc. $0.25; Proof $0.35.

1865 Copper-nickel, thick planchet [pattern]: [listed but not priced]

1865 Copper-nickel, thin planchet [pattern]: Unc. $4.00; Proof $6.00.

1865: Fine $0.05; Unc. $0.10; Proof $0.25.

1866 Copper-nickel [pattern]: [listed but not priced]

1866: Fine $0.15; Unc. $0.30; Proof $0.40.

1867 Copper-nickel [pattern]: [listed but not priced]

1867: Fine $0.10; Unc. $0.15; Proof $0.40

1868: Fine $0.10; Unc. $0.20; Proof $0.35.

1869: Fine $0.10; Unc. $0.20; Proof $0.35.

1869 Aluminum [pattern]. [listed but not priced]

1870: Fine $0.15; Unc. $0.25; Proof $0.30.

1871: Fine $0.40; Unc. $0.75; Proof $1.00.

1872: Fine $0.15; Unc. $0.30; Proof $0.50.

1873: Fine $0.05; Unc. $0.15; Proof $0.20.

1874: Fine $0.05; Unc. $0.15; Proof $0.25.

1875: Fine $0.10; Unc. $0.15; Proof $0.25.

1876: Fine $0.10; Unc. $0.20; Proof $0.30.

1877: Fair $0.20; Fine. $0.75 [not priced in higher grades]

1878: Fine $0.05; Unc. $0.10; Proof $0.50.

1879: Fine $0.05; Unc. $0.10; Proof $0.50.

1880: Fine $0.05; Unc. $0.10; Proof $0.25.

1881-1907: Fine $0.10; Unc. $0.15; Proof $0.35.

1908: Unc. $0.05; Proof $0.35.

1908-S: Unc. $0.75.

1909: Unc. $0.15; Proof $0.75.

1909-S: Unc. $0.40.

Commentary: The 1913 prices must have confused just about everyone. Proof 1864 copper-nickel and bronze cents were posted at $0.20 each, a small fraction of the $1.00 and $1.25 values of 1907. The exceedingly rare 1864 L Proof, formerly at $0.85, is now at $0.35. Rare patterns that few people had ever seen and few wanted to add to their date sets confused the listings even more.

For good measure, the 1877 Indian cent was priced in just Fair and Fine grades with Uncirculated and Proof ignored.

In the early 1930s Wayte Raymond, associated with Scott & Co., issued a new series of *Standard Catalogues.* However, these later books, issued in 19 editions through the year 1957, were well researched and bore no resemblance to the early Scott catalogues quoted above.

APPENDIX IV
THIRD-PARTY GRADING

Third-Party Grading

Since the founding of the Professional Coin Grading Service (PCGS) by David Hall in 1986, the Numismatic Guaranty Corporation of America (NGC) by John Albanese in 1987, and several others since then, the encapsulation of coins in plastic "slabs" has become an important part of the marketplace.

These services for a fee (typically ranging from about $10 to $25) will render an opinion as to the numerical grade of a Flying Eagle cent, Indian cent, or other coin. Although in Mint State and Proof ranges, the designations BN (brown), RB (red and brown), and RD (red) are given in addition to the number, no information is transmitted as to the aesthetic desirability of a coin, its striking, or overall numismatic quality. In other words, a designation such as "MS-64 RB" yields very little useful information as to the aesthetic desirability or the market value of a given coin.

Basically, if you are a serious numismatist—as I hope you already are, or will be after reading this book—you have no advance indication as to whether a given coin slabbed "MS-64 RB" will be spotted, or have a gently blended reddish-brown surface, or will have a patch of corrosion.

These third-party grading services have especially good value for the *beginner* in *certain series* in which there are not large differences in quality. For example, among Morgan silver dollars dated 1881-S (San Francisco Mint), virtually all are brilliant and are sharply struck. Thus, an 1881-S Morgan dollar certified, as MS-63 typically yields a brilliant, well-struck coin of pleasing appearance. A MS-64 is better, and a MS-65 is better yet.

However, the specialist in Indian cents will find that the foregoing is not true for that series, and even with accompanying "BN," "RB," and "RD" designations, it is difficult to determine or even guess whether a given coin will be worth adding to your collection.

As mentioned earlier in this book, *connoisseurship* is the key and will bring you home safely. Not to worry if you take the time to study the series and buy carefully. In fact, you can turn this uncertainty to your economic advantage by cherrypicking for quality. As stated in Chapter 5, use certified coins as a beginning, and from that point study each coin carefully to determine its aesthetic qualities or lack thereof.

An Interview

In 1995 the *Rosen Numismatic Advisory*—a monthly periodical oriented toward investors rather than to numismatic specialists—carried interviews by Maurice Rosen with Richard Snow and David Davidson.[1] Both respondents have been active in the Indian cent series.

Maurice Rosen summarized:

> What comes out of these two interviews are three messages:
>
> 1. Collectors demand rules.
> 2. True red gem Mint State and Proof pieces are much rarer than even the population reports indicate.
> 3. Less than 50% of slabbed red gem Mint State and Proof [MS-65 RD and Proof-65 RD] pieces are correctly graded. As intimately familiar with slab grading as I am, I must admit I was a bit surprised by these findings. They tell me that while a strong case can be made that properly graded coins are rarer than many believe, they also vividly alert us to the necessity of becoming a knowledgeable consumer because of the many questionably-graded pieces that reside in certified holders.
>
> Dave and Rick echo here the feedback they get from their collector customers who are, after all, the end users of all slabbed coins, the ultimate buyers of the coins we investors hold. It's prudent for us to heed their messages.

Maurice Rosen then asked, "What makes Flying Eagle and Indian cents so popular, though they be small, copper coins?"—an interesting question as it seems to infer that there is something "wrong" with small copper coins (a popular notion among investors, but certainly not among collectors).

The answer by Richard Snow:

> They're popular because, but for the early ones, they are copper, widely available in low grades allowing many collectors to get involved. For those who can afford the high grades, the beauty of the coins is a powerful attraction. I realize many investors avoid copper coins, but by doing so they lose sight of one thing: who's going to buy their coins when they want to sell? That could be another investor or a collector. Frankly, I'd rather have a coin that later on will be sought by a collector because he's always involved in coins, not so for investors who can be very fickle.

The Rosen question, "How has slabbing changed the climate for their trading and collecting?" brought these responses:

> Richard Snow: It has created a two-tier market: one, a strong market for correctly-graded coins that trade quickly at what seem to be very high levels; two, substandard coins which in collectors' eyes don't make the grade, and which are tougher to sell, thus are priced much cheaper. There might be a real nice MS-65 RD of a certain date priced at $1,000, and another offered at $600. Due to the superior attributes of the $1,000 coin it will sell a lot faster than will the $600 one.
>
> David Davidson: It has produced mixed results. You rarely hear of counterfeits in slabs. Then there's color; it means everything with Mint State and Proof Indians. Often there's a huge price difference between the colors Brown, Red Brown, and Red. You want a Red coin to stay Red in its holder. PCGS backs its Red grade; if it turns to RB in their holder, which it's not supposed to do, they arrange a settlement for you. I've done it many times, and find it a positive thing about slabbing.

The question from Maurice Rosen, "What percentage of slabbed and Mint State and Proof Indians are clearly overgraded?" drew a reply from David Davidson noting

---

[1] *Rosen Numismatic Advisory,* Box 38, Plainview, NY 11803. Used with permission.

in part that neither of the two leading certification services "grade by strict collector standards, just as they don't use *Early American Cents* [1949 book by William H. Sheldon] standards when they grade large cents."

Maurice Rosen: "Let's refine that to only Mint State and Proof-65 Red or better grades. What percentage now?"

David Davidson: Probably only about 40%, that's for grade and color. I think the services sometimes get overly enthusiastic, see a coin with 90% or so full Red and call it full Red, though it should be graded Red/Brown. So, if a certain date shows a combined population of, say, 50 Full Red 65 or better pieces, only about 20 would make the grade again if resubmitted....

Maurice Rosen asked, "What are your recommendations for Proof Indian Cents?"

Richard Snow: One of the reasons that the Proofs are so difficult is that buyers must sift through many uglies to find a nice coin. The key word here is *nice*. There are plenty of spotted and ugly coins lurking in dealers' cases, slabbed or raw. They sell them only to other dealers because no collectors want them. The only reason to buy a Proof Indian with a big black spot is because it's cheap. But you can't impress anyone with a discounted price.

What's in the market? About half of the slabbed Proof-65 RDs are unacceptable. They have carbon spots, some are overgraded, and some are really Red Brown, but graded as full Red.

Maurice Rosen: Rick, give me an example of just how relatively scarce nice Proofs are:

Richard Snow: Take the 1889, a typical Proof Indian cent date. The PCGS and NGC population reports show that 269 were graded from an original mintage of 3,336. Of those 269, 92 are Proof-65 or better, any color. And of those 92 Proof-65s, only 17 are Red (none higher). Of these 17 1889 Proofs, there are probably two or three with ugly spots. Of what's left, maybe four or five are just plain overgraded: 64s in 65 holders. Then you have two or three with less than full Red; they are really Red Brown. What are you left with? Maybe only seven or eight correctly-graded, true Proof-65 Red pieces of the 17 listed. And this is an average date!

By the way, don't think that you'll be able to buy a solid full Red Proof-65 common date for anywhere near the Bluesheet's [*Certified Coin Dealer Newsletter's*] $500 bid. Such beauties go for about $600-$800; solid Proof-66 Reds go for about $850-$1,000.

Apropos of the foregoing Rosen interview, Bill Fivaz, well-known researcher and variety specialist, commented: "One of the statements I always use in our grading seminars is: 'There are quality differences in every grade.'"[1] This applies to all series of older coins in all metals and in all grades.

Certification "Populations"

Among recent reference books published on different American coin series, the inclusion of data from the *PCGS Population Report* (issued by the Professional Coin Grading Service) and the *Numismatic Guaranty Corporation of America Census Report* has been a popular practice. The *Population Report* issued by ANACS has been less

---

[1] Letter, March 29, 1996.

widely quoted, but is very valuable for its listings of certain die varieties not delineated by the larger PCGS and NGC services. For reasons of broadening the appeal of the present book and also extending some caveats and explanations and enlightening present readers, I include *selected* PCGS, NGC, and ANACS population data in Appendix IV (from early 1996 reports; here used by permission). The ANACS information is discussed separately, following the PCGS and NGC analysis.

I say "selected," as such data if not explained can be very misleading. Let me give some examples from the March 1996 *PCGS Population Report:*

PCGS Population Data for the 1877 Cent

1877 Indian cent (rare date) and the number certified in each grade:

Business Strikes:

Poor to Good: 98 certified.	MS-62 BN: 8
VG: 41	MS-62 RB: 12
Fine: 31	MS-62 RD: 0
VF: 72	MS-63 BN: 16
EF-40: 49	MS-63 RB: 55
EF-45: 36	MS-63 RD: 1
AU-50: 38	MS-64 BN: 6
AU-53: 6	MS-64 RB: 50
AU-55: 16	MS-64 RD: 13
AU-58: 19	MS-65 BN: 0
MS-60 BN: 1	MS-65 RB: 16
MS-60 RB: 2	MS-65 RD: 13
MS-60 RD: 0	MS-66 BN: 0
MS-61 BN: 1	MS-66 RB: 1
MS-61 RB: 1	MS-66 RD: 2 (highest graded)
MS-61 RD: 0	

Reviewing the preceding population numbers, Harry Salyards, editor of *Penny-Wise* and a long-time observer of early copper large cents (1793-1857) and other areas of numismatics, commented in part:[1]

From AU-55 through MS-62 RD there are 60 pieces; from MS-60 BN through MS-62 RD there are only 25 pieces; and in the combined categories of MS-61 and MS-62 there are only five pieces. However, in higher grades of MS-63 through MS-65 there are 170 pieces. I find it statistically unbelievable that among an unhoarded, randomly-distributed late nineteenth century business strike date, nearly *three-quarters* of the coins with realistic claims to Mint State should fall into the magic MS-63, MS-64, and MS-65 categories!

Lengthy experience with earlier U.S. series would suggest that, if there really were a couple of dozen MS-65s, there should be *hundreds* of MS-60s, not just three.

An explanation was provided by John Dannreuther of PCGS:[2]

---

[1] Letter, April 10, 1996, here paraphrased.
[2] Letter, May 16, 1996, here paraphrased.

As the 1877 Indian cent was recognized as a rare issue in the nineteenth century, more were saved in higher grades. Mint State coins would have been especially coveted and cared for. In addition, most people tend to send in their higher quality coins to PCGS, hoping for such grades as MS-64 and MS-65.

Further, among Mint State coins, all small-denomination series show fewer bagmarks than large denomination ones, and thus Mint State coins tend to be in higher average grades. However, higher denomination coins such as half dollars, silver dollars, gold $20, etc., are heavier and more susceptible to damage and are skewed the other way, with most Mint State coins in the lower ranges due to bagmarking and contact marks.

Proofs:

Proof-60 BN: 0
Proof-60 RB: 0
Proof-60 RD: 0
Proof-61 BN: 0
Proof-61 RB: 1
Proof-61 RD: 1
Proof-62 BN: 9
Proof-62 RB: 1
Proof-62 RD: 1
Proof-63 BN: 9
Proof-63 RB: 42
Proof-63 RD: 5

Proof-64 BN: 5
Proof-64 RB: 72
Proof-64 RD: 15
Proof-65 BN: 2
Proof-65 RB: 23
Proof-65 RD: 12
Proof-66 BN: 0
Proof-66 RB: 2
Proof-66 RD: 4
Proof-67 BN: 0
Proof-67 RB: 0
Proof-67 RD: 1 (highest graded)

PCGS Population Data for 1907 Cent

1907 Indian cent (common date) and the number certified in each grade:

Business Strikes:

Poor to Good: 0 certified
VG: 0
Fine: 0
VF: 0
EF-40: 1
EF-45: 1
AU-50: 1
AU-53: 0
AU-55: 0
AU-58: 1
MS-60 BN: 0
MS-60 RB: 0
MS-60 RD: 0
MS-61 BN: 0
MS-61 RB: 2
MS-61 RD: 0
MS-62 BN: 2

MS-62 RB: 3
MS-62 RD: 1
MS-63 BN: 8
MS-63 RB: 87
MS-63 RD: 35
MS-64 BN: 6
MS-64 RB: 201
MS-64 RD: 235
MS-65 BN: 1
MS-65 RB: 52
MS-65 RD: 134
MS-66 BN: 0
MS-66 RB: 1
MS-66 RD: 18
MS-67 BN: 0
MS-67 RB: 0
MS-67 RD: 3 (highest graded)

Proofs:

Proof-60 BN: 0

Proof-60 RB: 0

Proof-60 RD: 0

Proof-61 BN: 0

Proof-61 RB: 0

Proof-61 RD:

Proof-62 BN: 1

Proof-62 RB: 1

Proof-62 RD: 0

Proof-63 BN: 5

Proof-63 RB: 34

Proof-63 RD: 1

Proof-64 BN: 2

Proof-64 RB: 42

Proof-64 RD: 6

Proof-65 BN: 0

Proof-65 RB: 18

Proof-65 RD: 9

Proof-66 BN: 0

Proof-66 RB: 2

Proof-66 RD: 6

Proof-67 BN: 0

Proof-67 RB: 1 (highest graded)

If you are a mathematician-numismatist and love numbers, and do not know anything other than what you read in population reports and investment advisory sheets, you may conclude the following:

1. In worn grades such as Good, VG, and Fine, the 1877 cent is readily available, but the 1907 is non-existent or, at the very least, is a formidable rarity.

2. At the various AU levels only two specimens of the 1907 cent have been certified, indicating great rarity, but 41 specimens of the "common" 1877 have been certified.

3. Among MS-65 red cents, there have been 13 1877 Indian cents certified, but 134 examples of 1907 have been certified in the same grade. Obviously, 1877 is scarcer in MS-65 red than is the 1907.

4. However, as 72 cents dated 1877 have been certified in Proof-64 brown grade, this date is much more plentiful at this level than the 1907, of which only 42 have been certified.

5. Further, per Dr. Salyards' comment above (under the 1877 business strike listing), you might believe that low-level MS-61 and MS-62 1877 Indian cents are far rarer than gems at the MS-65 level.

However, in actuality the truth is as follows concerning the above five conclusions:

1. False. Well-worn 1907 Indian cents are worth $1 to $5 or so each, or less, and for this reason it would be foolish to pay $10 to $25 to have one certified. Thus, worn 1907 cents appear to be "rare" in the population report, but in fact they are extremely common. On the other hand, a well-worn 1877 cent can be worth several hundred dollars, and it is more reasonable to pay $10 to $25 to have one certified.

2. False. Even in AU grade it may cost more to certify a 1907 cent than the coin is worth. On the other hand, an AU 1877 can be worth close to $2,000 or even more.

3. True. However, the fact that the 1877 is worth several thousands of dollars in MS-65 red grade (if aesthetically desirable) and the 1907 just slightly over $100 is not reflected by the data.

4. False. Proof-64 brown cents of 1907 are worth just a tiny fraction of the value of Proof-64 brown 1877 cents, so fewer have been certified.

5. False. There are many more low-level Mint State coins in existence than there are gems.

An Invitation to Analysis

Introduction

Through the courtesy of PCGS and NGC selected additional data from 1996 population and census reports are given below. Using these figures you can formulate your own ideas of rarity. However, as the preceding "conclusions" demonstrated, numbers alone have relatively little meaning. Notwithstanding this, there is some useful information to be gleaned from *certain* elements of the data. Here are some of my ideas, an invitation for you to do your own analysis:

Certification Cost

PCGS and NGC charge various prices for their services, with prices in the $15 to $25 range being typical; higher for fast turnaround, photographs (such as NGC Photo Proof and PCGS Coin Profile), or extra services. Thus, currently it would be a waste of time to send a coin with a market value of, say, under $50 or $75 to be certified. Because of this, common Indian cents in low grades appear to be "rare" in the population charts.

Market Timing

Around 1989-1990, common Indian cents in high grade levels sold for very expensive prices compared to market levels of 1996. Thus, an Indian cent of 1907 (the highest mintage date) was valued at $750 or more in MS-65 RD grade, or about triple the price of 1996. Accordingly, in 1990 there was more economic incentive to certify certain common dates than there is now. On the other hand, some of the better dates and varieties in choice grades sell for more now (to specialists representing the new wave of buyers, as opposed to investors of the 1990 era), and more of these are now being certified.

Like vs. Like

When comparing the rarity of a given coin with another, compare two coins of similar qualities—such as similar market values and similar grades. Like vs. like. Comparing two coins of significantly different market values or rarity is meaningless.

Examples of like vs. like include these three studies:

Study 1

1857 and 1858 Flying Eagle cents in MS-63, MS-64, and MS-65 grades sell for about the same price. Thus, data can be compared. The PCGS data show that the 1857 is more plentiful in MS-63 and MS-64, but the 1858 is slightly scarcer in MS-65. Not stated is the fact that the 1858 cents are collected by two varieties—Large Letters and Small Letters—not attributed by PCGS. Thus, the 1858 population figures have to be divided. The conclusion is therefore that either an 1858 Large Letters or 1858 Small Letters cent in MS-63 to MS-65 grade is rarer than a comparable 1857.

The NGC data are divided into 1857 cents, 1858 unclassified cents,[1] 1858 Large

---

[1] In the early days of its existence NGC classified all 1858 cents under just one category (*e.g.*, August 1, 1990, *Census Report*).

Letters cents, and 1858 Small Letters cents. The figures cumulatively are similar to PCGS findings in that Mint State coins of each date are about the same degree of availability. However, within the 1858 Large Letter and Small Letter categories, the Large Letters is the more plentiful of the two—just slightly in the MS-63 and MS-64 ranges, but more than half again as more plentiful in the MS-65 range. Conclusion: In MS-65 grade the 1858 Small Letters cent is somewhat of a sleeper.

Study 2

1877 Indian cents are highly valued in Mint State, and thus in all recent markets many of them have been certified. Among coins in MS-65 grade, how available are brilliant (MS-65 RD) coins in comparison to ones toned brown (MS-65 BN) or red and brown (MS-65 RB)?

PCGS data tell us that MS-65 BN coins are rare (none certified), red and brown coins have been certified to the extent of 16 coins, and brilliant ones, 13 coins.

NGC data tell us that MS-65 BN coins are rare (1 certified), red and brown coins have been certified to the extent of 18 coins, and brilliant ones, three coins.

A glance at other Mint State ranges shows that "brown" coins are scarce elsewhere, too. It can be concluded that of the MS-65 coins in numismatic hands, most show enough mint red to be called RB or RD. Ones called RB are more plentiful than those called RD, especially among PCGS coins.

As MS-65 BN coins, despite their rarity, are not worth as much as those with red and brown or with full red surfaces, where to go from here?

Study 3

In the market until recent times (when buyers have become more sophisticated) most Proof Indian cents dated from 1878 to 1909 were priced as "types" rather than by dates, with 1878 being an exception. We begin with 1878 as this is the first year for which Proof cent mintages are known.

Are there any Indian cents in this range that seem to be particularly rare in Proof-RD preservation? Bear in mind that PCGS has certified more coins than has NGC, thus PCGS figures can only be compared with other PCGS figures and NGC figures with other NGC figures.

Let's take a look:

PCGS data for Proof-65 RD coins 1878-1909 show these dates to be the 10 most plentiful:

43 coins certified: 1880 The most common date.

39: 1881 Second most common date.

34: 1902

34: 1892

33: 1884

32: 1878

30: 1899

28: 1879

25: 1895

25: 1903

The PCGS data also show these to be the 10 lowest populations in Proof-65 RD PCGS coins, in order from the rarest upward toward the most plentiful:

2 coins certified: 1888 Rarest date.

4: 1887 Second rarest.

6: 1882

7: 1886

7: 1891

8: 1897

8: 1890

9: 1907 Although this has the lowest mintage, it is not the rarest.

10: 1896

11: 1883

11: 1885

Conclusions for Study No. 3: The 1888 (2 certified) and 1887 (4 certified) Proof-65 RD cents are clearly winners in the sweepstakes and are much harder to find than are, for example, 1880 (43 certified) or 1881 (39 certified) cents of the same preservation.

Curiously, the Proof mintages are as follows:

1887: 2,960 Proofs struck.

1888: 4,582.

1880: 3,955.

1881: 3,575.

At the very least, the reader might say, "Hey, there's more to the situation than mintage figures. What happened?"

However, a glance at the 1887 and 1888 PCGS figures for Proof BN and Proof RB in Proof-63, Proof-64, and Proof-65 grades shows these to be very common! Thus, Proofs of this date are rare only if they have red (RD) surfaces. Obviously, something must have happened to tone the surfaces. That "something" was probably the storage of the pieces in thin tissue paper which toned the coins (see commentary under the 1879 Indian cent listing in the main text).

Other factors which could have influenced the toning of the pieces include the source of the planchet stock. If an examination of records in the National Archives were to show an unusual source for metal for planchets for these two years, such planchets may have been more chemically active than, say, those of 1880 or 1881 (variable copper sources affect the surface coloration of early U.S. large cents and have been discussed in detail in that series).

For purposes of your own study, PCGS and NGC data are presented on the following pages at the conclusion of which will be found a combined summary of certain grades.[1]

---

[1] Grades given here range from 60 to 66; a few stray coins have been graded higher and are not cited.

PCGS Data

Mint State Coins (March 1996, PCGS)
1856-1858 FLYING EAGLE CENTS

PCGS	1856	1857	1858/7	1858
MS-60	6	33	1	17
MS-61	8	43	0	29
MS-62	30	220	5	138
MS-63	38	402	9	310
MS-64	26	361	12	305
MS-65	8	84	0	95
MS-66	2	6	0	15

Mint State Coins (March 1996, PCGS)
1859-1864 COPPER-NICKEL INDIAN CENTS

PCGS	1859	1860	1861	1862	1863	1864
MS-60	13	8	6	11	22	17
MS-61	14	4	8	11	26	12
MS-62	90	56	45	120	210	72
MS-63	246	169	115	243	372	226
MS-64	183	198	132	284	285	158
MS-65	46	81	70	91	60	25
MS-66	6	15	13	21	5	3

Mint State Coins (March 1996, PCGS)
1864-1873 BRONZE INDIAN CENTS

PCGS	1864 Br.	1864L	1865	1866	1867	1868	1869	1870	1871	1872	1873Op 3	1873Cl 3
MS-60 BN	1	3	6	0	0	2	2	1	0	0	0	1
MS-60 RB	0	1	2	0	0	1	0	0	2	0	0	0
MS-60 RD	0	0	0	0	0	0	0	0	0	0	0	0
MS-61 BN	0	2	2	1	0	1	3	1	1	2	3	0
MS-61 RB	0	2	0	0	0	1	0	2	0	0	1	1
MS-61 RD	0	0	0	0	0	0	0	0	0	0	0	0
MS-62 BN	8	7	9	2	6	7	6	2	3	6	3	1
MS-62 RB	6	14	12	7	13	8	8	4	13	9	7	3
MS-62 RD	1	0	0	0	0	0	0	0	0	0	0	0
MS-63 BN	22	24	10	8	15	5	17	3	11	7	13	0
MS-63 RB	54	80	88	42	51	57	44	51	36	44	49	11

PCGS	1864 Br.	1864L	1865	1866	1867	1868	1869	1870	1871	1872	1873Op 3	1873Cl 3
MS-63 RD	6	4	7	2	6	3	5	4	1	0	5	0
MS-64 BN	20	11	6	8	3	6	8	3	3	5	2	2
MS-64 RB	162	94	139	82	91	67	100	70	50	45	84	11
MS-64 RD	42	15	65	6	24	22	17	29	11	11	17	3
MS-65 BN	13	2	5	2	1	2	2	0	0	0	1	0
MS-65 RB	108	26	30	21	14	29	32	25	9	17	19	4
MS-65 RD	49	13	31	7	5	12	11	11	6	4	5	4
MS-66 BN	0	0	0	1	0	0	0	0	0	0	0	0
MS-66 RB	7	0	1	0	1	0	0	2	1	0	0	0
MS-66 RD	18	2	7	1	1	0	2	2	0	1	2	2

Mint State Coins (March 1996, PCGS)
1873 Dbl. Die—1884 BRONZE INDIAN CENTS

PCGS	1873 Dbl.	1874	1875	1876	1877	1878	1879	1880	1881	1882	1883 N	1884
MS-60 BN	1	0	1	1	1	2	1	1	2	0	0	0
MS-60 RB	0	0	2	1	2	0	1	0	0	0	0	0
MS-60 RD	0	0	0	0	0	0	0	0	0	0	0	0
MS-61 BN	0	1	0	1	1	0	0	0	0	0	0	1
MS-61 RB	0	0	0	1	1	4	0	1	0	1	1	0
MS-61 RD	0	0	0	0	0	0	0	0	0	0	0	0
MS-62 BN	1	3	2	4	8	3	4	1	1	0	1	0
MS-62 RB	1	9	4	8	12	5	5	3	4	7	5	5
MS-62 RD	0	0	0	0	0	0	0	0	0	0	0	0
MS-63 BN	2	9	6	6	16	9	15	7	5	5	5	7
MS-63 RB	2	53	60	46	55	54	85	44	45	34	39	44
MS-63 RD	0	4	5	5	1	0	7	6	5	8	16	5
MS-64 BN	0	8	3	3	6	1	10	7	7	7	9	7
MS-64 RB	3	101	89	76	50	77	89	97	88	85	84	91
MS-64 RD	0	15	24	16	13	20	32	32	48	44	64	19
MS-65 BN	0	0	2	1	0	0	0	0	2	4	2	5
MS-65 RB	1	34	20	22	16	24	38	20	19	31	21	21
MS-65 RD	0	15	16	8	13	20	27	33	32	41	35	14
MS-66 BN	0	0	0	0	0	0	0	0	0	2	0	0
MS-66 RB	0	1	0	0	1	0	1	0	1	0	1	0
MS-66 RD	0	2	4	6	2	5	9	6	8	8	16	5

Mint State Coins (March 1996, PCGS)
1885-1895 BRONZE INDIAN CENTS

PCGS	1885	1886	1887	1888/7	1888	1889	1890	1891	1882	1893	1894	1895
MS-60 BN	1	0	0	0	1	0	0	1	0	0	0	0
MS-60 RB	0	0	0	0	1	0	1	0	0	0	0	0
MS-60 RD	0	0	0	0	0	0	0	0	0	0	0	0
MS-61 BN	0	0	0	0	0	0	0	0	0	0	0	0
MS-61 RB	0	0	0	0	0	0	0	0	1	0	2	0
MS-61 RD	0	0	0	0	0	0	0	0	0	0	0	0
MS-62 BN	3	1	0	0	1	0	2	0	1	1	1	1
MS-62 RB	2	8	4	0	2	3	4	7	2	3	6	5
MS-62 RD	0	0	1	0	0	0	1	0	0	0	0	0
MS-63 BN	5	8	3	0	6	1	4	5	2	8	3	5
MS-63 RB	32	37	27	1	34	36	45	47	38	46	59	41
MS-63 RD	0	3	10	0	1	6	9	5	6	6	9	11
MS-64 BN	13	6	2	0	3	5	4	2	1	5	6	5
MS-64 RB	51	47	57	0	40	53	49	55	43	60	46	60
MS-64 RD	24	22	53	0	21	40	32	50	47	54	57	72
MS-65 BN	1	0	0	0	0	2	0	0	0	0	1	3
MS-65 RB	24	13	4	0	3	7	9	8	4	6	6	6
MS-65 RD	15	12	32	0	11	12	21	20	23	37	31	65
MS-66 BN	0	0	0	0	0	0	0	0	0	0	0	0
MS-66 RB	1	0	0	0	0	0	0	0	0	2	0	0
MS-66 RD	6	5	11	0	5	2	2	3	3	11	13	10

Mint State Coins (March 1996, PCGS)
1896-1906 BRONZE INDIAN CENTS

PCGS	1896	1897	1898	1899	1900	1901	1902	1903	1904	1905	1906
MS-60 BN	0	0	0	1	0	0	0	0	1	0	0
MS-60 RB	0	0	0	0	0	0	1	0	1	0	0
MS-60 RD	0	1	0	0	0	0	0	0	0	0	0
MS-61 BN	0	0	1	0	0	0	0	0	0	0	0
MS-61 RB	0	0	0	2	0	0	0	0	2	1	0
MS-61 RD	0	0	0	0	0	0	0	0	0	0	0
MS-62 BN	2	0	0	0	0	1	0	0	0	1	1
MS-62 RB	1	3	4	4	5	8	4	5	2	8	4
MS-62 RD	0	1	0	0	0	0	0	2	1	1	0
MS-63 BN	3	2	6	7	2	7	2	5	0	1	4
MS-63 RB	43	30	42	95	26	68	65	64	54	68	64
MS-63 RD	8	11	9	20	7	25	23	17	13	31	12

PCGS	1896	1897	1898	1899	1900	1901	1902	1903	1904	1905	1906
MS-64 BN	1	2	3	0	4	6	7	9	5	7	14
MS-64 RB	45	58	99	263	92	159	154	171	158	173	180
MS-64 RD	59	59	70	122	82	190	144	136	150	184	157
MS-65 BN	1	0	2	1	1	4	2	0	1	0	0
MS-65 RB	7	14	13	51	32	43	38	31	38	23	54
MS-65 RD	19	35	51	86	59	89	74	89	131	99	88
MS-66 BN	0	0	0	0	0	0	0	0	0	0	0
MS-66 RB	0	0	0	2	1	2	1	1	0	0	0
MS-66 RD	5	7	25	31	27	25	21	31	20	11	8

Mint State Coins (March 1996, PCGS)
1907-1909-S BRONZE INDIAN CENTS

PCGS	1907	1908	1908-S	1909	1909-S
MS-60 BN	0	1	7	1	4
MS-60 RB	0	0	1	1	1
MS-60 RD	0	0	0	0	0
MS-61 BN	0	0	2	1	0
MS-61 RB	2	0	5	0	0
MS-61 RD	0	0	0	7	0
MS-62 BN	2	0	7	2	5
MS-62 RB	3	6	14	8	19
MS-62 RD	1	1	0	42	0
MS-63 BN	8	4	19	6	25
MS-63 RB	87	75	111	113	103
MS-63 RD	35	43	7	78	15
MS-64 BN	6	6	6	5	11
MS-64 RB	201	205	140	237	172
MS-64 RD	235	251	95	455	97
MS-65 BN	1	1	0	2	1
MS-65 RB	52	52	46	73	47
MS-65 RD	134	126	96	333	71
MS-66 BN	0	0	0	0	0
MS-66 RB	1	0	0	2	0
MS-66 RD	18	20	10	65	6

Proof Coins (March 1996, PCGS)
1856-1858 FLYING EAGLE CENTS

PCGS	1856	1857	1858 LL	1858 SL
Pr-60	8	1	1	0
Pr-61	13	0	0	1
Pr-62	36	1	1	5
Pr-63	50	8	2	4
Pr-64	54	11	7	12
Pr-65	14	5	6	4
Pr-66	0	0	0	0

Note: These data are virtually meaningless, for until 1992 PCGS grouped ALL Proof 1858 Flying Eagle cents under the Large Letters heading. In actuality, 1858 Large Letters Proofs are several times rarer than Small Letters Proofs.

Proof Coins (March 1996, PCGS)
1859-1864 COPPER-NICKEL INDIAN CENTS

PCGS	1859	1860	1861	1862	1863	1864
Pr-60	0	0	1	1	0	0
Pr-61	1	1	1	2	0	0
Pr-62	5	3	3	6	4	9
Pr-63	19	11	24	24	21	33
Pr-64	70	18	14	86	46	44
Pr-65	25	16	6	61	18	23
Pr-66	6	0	0	14	3	8

Proof Coins (March 1996)
1864-1874 BRONZE INDIAN CENTS

PCGS	1864 Br.	1864L	1865	1866	1867	1868	1869	1870	1871	1872	1873Cl 3	1874
Pr-60 BN	0	0	0	0	1	0	0	0	0	0	0	0
Pr-60 RB	0	0	0	0	0	0	0	0	0	0	0	0
Pr-60 RD	0	0	0	0	0	0	0	0	0	0	0	0
Pr-61 BN	0	0	0	0	0	0	0	0	0	0	0	0
Pr-61 RB	0	0	0	1	0	0	1	1	0	2	1	0
Pr-61 RD	0	0	0	0	0	0	0	0	0	0	0	0
Pr-62 BN	0	0	0	0	1	1	1	0	0	2	0	0
Pr-62 RB	0	0	3	1	1	1	2	1	5	3	2	1
Pr-62 RD	0	0	0	0	0	0	0	0	0	0	0	0
Pr-63 BN	4	0	2	3	3	2	6	4	3	2	1	5
Pr-63 RB	5	2	13	12	14	11	16	18	18	20	17	16

PCGS	1864 Br.	1864L	1865	1866	1867	1868	1869	1870	1871	1872	1873Cl 3	1874
Pr-63 RD	0	0	2	7	1	1	0	0	3	5	5	3
Pr-64 BN	2	0	3	3	4	4	5	2	2	6	5	1
Pr-64 RB	18	1	35	38	37	37	40	42	57	63	67	45
Pr-64 RD	4	0	6	6	13	12	12	14	14	10	24	12
Pr-65 BN	1	0	0	2	2	2	0	0	2	2	2	1
Pr-65 RB	21	2	6	30	18	16	21	14	22	36	25	15
Pr-65 RD	4	0	8	8	8	7	14	16	17	5	11	8
Pr-66 BN	2	0	0	0	0	0	0	0	0	2	0	0
Pr-66 RB	4	0	0	1	1	2	0	2	1	36	0	1
Pr-66 RD	1	0	0	0	1	1	1	1	0	5	1	7

Proof Coins (March 1996, PCGS)
1875-1886 BRONZE INDIAN CENTS

PCGS	1875	1876	1877	1878	1879	1880	1881	1882	1883	1884	1885	1886
Pr-60 BN	0	0	0	0	0	0	0	0	0	0	0	0
Pr-60 RB	0	0	0	0	1	0	0	0	0	0	0	0
Pr-60 RD	0	0	0	0	0	0	0	0	0	0	0	0
Pr-61 BN	1	0	0	0	0	0	1	0	1	0	1	0
Pr-61 RB	0	0	1	0	0	1	1	0	1	0	0	0
Pr-61 RD	0	0	1	0	0	0	0	0	0	0	0	0
Pr-62 BN	1	1	1	5	1	0	0	3	1	2	0	1
Pr-62 RB	4	4	9	4	5	5	5	3	6	5	1	4
Pr-62 RD	3	0	1	0	0	0	0	0	1	0	0	0
Pr-63 BN	0	4	9	4	1	5	7	9	14	8	12	9
Pr-63 RB	23	25	42	39	32	42	40	25	55	24	24	25
Pr-63 RD	3	3	5	5	4	7	4	3	2	4	0	1
Pr-64 BN	3	1	5	4	13	6	9	21	38	11	22	42
Pr-64 RB	45	57	72	78	94	110	102	60	121	90	76	71
Pr-64 RD	5	16	15	39	20	24	31	14	20	32	8	17
Pr-65 BN	0	0	2	0	2	2	2	22	28	12	29	17
Pr-65 RB	6	23	23	27	47	31	43	46	61	73	65	49
Pr-65 RD	3	11	12	32	28	43	39	6	11	33	11	7
Pr-66 BN	0	0	0	0	1	0	1	6	5	3	11	1
Pr-66 RB	1	3	2	1	10	4	4	12	17	24	17	1
Pr-66 RD	1	3	4	8	15	12	14	8	2	16	6	0

Proof Coins (March 1996, PCGS)
1887-1898 BRONZE INDIAN CENTS

PCGS	1887	1888	1889	1890	1891	1892	1893	1894	1885	1896	1897	1898
Pr-60 BN	0	1	0	0	0	0	0	0	0	0	0	0
Pr-60 RB	0	0	3	0	1	0	1	0	0	0	0	1
Pr-60 RD	0	0	0	0	0	0	0	0	0	0	0	0
Pr-61 BN	0	0	0	0	0	0	0	0	1	0	0	0
Pr-61 RB	0	0	0	1	0	1	0	0	0	0	1	0
Pr-61 RD	0	0	0	0	1	0	0	0	0	0	0	0
Pr-62 BN	2	1	0	2	0	0	1	0	1	0	0	1
Pr-62 RB	0	4	2	8	4	4	6	0	2	2	1	4
Pr-62 RD	0	0	0	1	1	0	0	0	0	0	0	0
Pr-63 BN	16	14	11	2	5	4	6	7	8	6	5	5
Pr-63 RB	33	28	29	43	32	33	43	31	25	17	22	18
Pr-63 RD	2	3	1	2	3	7	4	6	2	2	3	2
Pr-64 BN	31	36	22	7	11	3	5	10	8	19	12	7
Pr-64 RB	56	52	52	66	66	84	56	68	63	46	61	50
Pr-64 RD	6	11	12	25	35	31	27	19	21	17	14	26
Pr-65 BN	19	15	15	2	2	1	0	1	3	3	9	1
Pr-65 RB	32	19	29	13	20	18	11	13	16	19	28	33
Pr-65 RD	4	2	13	8	7	34	17	14	25	10	8	23
Pr-66 BN	3	1	0	0	0	0	0	0	0	1	2	0
Pr-66 RB	4	2	4	1	0	5	0	0	4	5	8	6
Pr-66 RD	1	1	0	1	3	8	3	7	10	3	8	9

Proof Coins (March 1996, PCGS)
1899-1909 BRONZE INDIAN CENTS

PCGS	1899	1900	1901	1902	1903	1904	1905	1906	1907	1908	1909
Pr-60 BN	0	0	0	0	0	0	0	0	0	0	0
Pr-60 RB	0	0	0	0	1	0	0	0	0	0	0
Pr-60 RD	0	0	0	0	0	0	0	0	0	0	0
Pr-61 BN	0	0	0	0	0	0	0	0	0	2	0
Pr-61 RB	0	1	0	0	0	1	0	0	0	1	0
Pr-61 RD	0	0	0	0	0	1	0	0	0	0	0
Pr-62 BN	0	2	0	0	1	2	2	0	1	0	0
Pr-62 RB	1	4	1	2	4	4	4	4	1	4	2
Pr-62 RD	1	0	0	0	0	2	0	1	0	0	1
Pr-63 BN	3	1	3	1	3	3	4	6	5	2	5
Pr-63 RB	15	20	23	15	27	28	27	24	34	28	34
Pr-63 RD	6	2	3	4	3	3	2	2	1	2	4

PCGS	1899	1900	1901	1902	1903	1904	1905	1906	1907	1908	1909
Pr-64 BN	6	7	6	5	4	3	9	3	2	10	8
Pr-64 RB	56	69	52	66	57	39	53	77	42	66	68
Pr-64 RD	28	22	19	29	33	36	15	14	6	25	23
Pr-65 BN	3	3	2	3	0	0	1	3	0	0	4
Pr-65 RB	32	24	45	29	15	17	19	14	18	28	23
Pr-65 RD	30	22	16	34	25	12	13	16	9	17	19
Pr-66 BN	2	0	0	0	0	0	0	0	0	0	1
Pr-66 RB	11	5	11	8	3	0	2	2	2	2	5
Pr-66 RD	16	8	10	15	16	3	7	6	6	5	8

NGC Data

Mint State Coins (January 1996, NGC)
1856-1858 FLYING EAGLE CENTS

NGC	1856	1857	1858/7	1858 Misc	1858 LL	1858 SL
MS-60	0	4	1	0	0	0
MS-61	3	11	0	1	4	4
MS-62	1	39	2	14	12	12
MS-63	7	145	8	48	31	28
MS-64	23	334	16	82	79	74
MS-65	0	101	1	23	45	27
MS-66	0	5	0	4	6	5

Mint State Coins (January 1996, NGC)
1859-1864 COPPER-NICKEL INDIAN CENTS

NGC	1859	1860	1861	1862	1863	1864
MS-60	2	0	0	0	0	1
MS-61	5	5	2	8	16	11
MS-62	22	18	14	41	52	41
MS-63	76	53	33	75	123	88
MS-64	160	101	85	190	194	105
MS-65	48	65	57	67	73	36
MS-66	3	12	15	14	3	5

Mint State Coins (January 1996, NGC)
1864-1873 BRONZE INDIAN CENTS

NGC	1864 Br.	1864L	1865	1866	1867	1868	1869	1870	1871	1872	1873 Cl 3	1873 Op 3
MS-60 BN	0	0	0	0	0	0	0	0	0	0	0	1
MS-60 RB	0	1	0	0	1	0	0	0	0	0	0	0
MS-60 RD	0	0	0	0	0	0	0	0	0	0	0	0
MS-61 BN	0	2	1	3	2	2	2	0	0	0	0	2
MS-61 RB	1	1	0	0	0	0	0	0	1	2	0	2
MS-61 RD	0	0	0	0	0	0	0	0	0	0	0	0
MS-62 BN	10	15	8	4	6	4	4	3	2	4	1	6
MS-62 RB	2	2	1	0	1	1	3	4	4	6	1	1
MS-62 RD	0	0	0	0	0	0	0	0	0	0	0	0
MS-63 BN	12	16	12	14	2	5	7	4	3	10	3	10
MS-63 RB	20	17	17	21	15	10	12	13	10	8	3	9
MS-63 RD	2	2	2	1	3	1	1	1	1	4	0	1
MS-64 BN	23	10	12	13	13	12	14	6	14	8	1	7
MS-64 RB	59	64	57	35	39	51	38	33	32	23	9	36
MS-64 RD	14	12	24	7	7	6	6	8	3	7	0	10
MS-65 BN	22	6	7	10	4	4	7	1	3	5	1	4
MS-65 RB	98	38	60	35	41	39	45	28	26	20	8	33
MS-65 RD	26	8	16	3	4	12	10	6	3	2	1	5
MS-66 BN	5	2	1	0	1	0	0	0	0	2	0	0
MS-66 RB	26	6	3	6	3	4	4	0	1	1	0	1
MS-66 RD	6	2	2	0	0	1	0	0	0	0	0	1

Note: 1873 Open 3 numbers include coins specifically attributed as Open 3 in the NGC report plus coins simply listed as 1873. Thus, these numbers may include a few of the rarer 1873 Closed 3 coins.

Mint State Coins (January 1996, NGC)
1873 Dbl. Die—1884 BRONZE INDIAN CENTS

NGC	1873 Dbl.	1874	1875	1876	1877	1878	1879	1880	1881	1882	1883	1884
MS-60 BN	1	0	0	1	0	0	0	0	0	0	0	0
MS-60 RB	0	0	0	0	0	0	1	0	0	0	0	0
MS-60 RD	0	0	0	0	0	0	0	0	0	0	0	0
MS-61 BN	0	0	0	0	1	0	1	0	0	0	0	1
MS-61 RB	0	0	0	0	0	0	1	0	0	0	0	0
MS-61 RD	0	0	0	0	0	0	0	0	0	0	0	0
MS-62 BN	0	2	2	7	2	4	1	2	1	0	1	5
MS-62 RB	0	1	2	0	1	0	4	2	3	2	1	0
MS-62 RD	0	0	0	0	0	0	0	0	0	0	0	0
MS-63 BN	0	7	7	5	9	6	11	6	3	10	5	4

NGC	1873 Dbl.	1874	1875	1876	1877	1878	1879	1880	1881	1882	1883	1884
MS-63 RB	1	13	15	12	7	10	15	16	13	5	8	10
MS-63 RD	0	1	2	0	1	0	1	0	2	1	1	2
MS-64 BN	2	10	5	7	8	7	11	15	7	20	14	15
MS-64 RB	0	45	65	33	26	36	58	56	60	54	37	35
MS-64 RD	0	8	14	5	1	9	6	6	20	16	18	6
MS-65 BN	0	6	3	1	1	3	12	8	9	14	6	14
MS-65 RB	0	30	47	30	18	28	33	29	55	46	32	41
MS-65 RD	0	10	6	7	3	4	14	7	17	15	26	14
MS-66 BN	0	0	0	1	0	0	0	1	0	3	1	3
MS-66 RB	0	6	2	6	1	5	13	7	7	8	8	12
MS-66 RD	0	1	2	1	1	2	1	5	2	5	15	5

Mint State Coins (January 1996, NGC)
1885-1895 BRONZE INDIAN CENTS

NGC	1885	1886 Misc	1886 Ty II	1887	1888	1889	1890	1891	1882	1893	1894	1895
MS-60 BN	0	1	0	0	0	0	0	0	0	0	0	0
MS-60 RB	0	0	0	0	0	0	0	0	0	0	0	0
MS-60 RD	0	0	0	0	0	0	0	0	0	0	0	0
MS-61 BN	0	0	0	1	0	1	0	0	0	0	1	1
MS-61 RB	0	0	0	0	0	0	0	0	0	0	0	0
MS-61 RD	0	0	0	0	0	0	0	0	0	0	0	0
MS-62 BN	4	5	0	0	4	3	1	1	0	0	5	1
MS-62 RB	0	3	0	2	2	0	2	1	4	0	0	0
MS-62 RD	1	0	0	0	0	0	0	1	1	0	0	1
MS-63 BN	3	10	1	5	6	9	4	4	3	2	6	2
MS-63 RB	4	6	3	11	9	15	11	14	11	8	8	7
MS-63 RD	1	1	0	1	1	2	2	5	3	1	1	1
MS-64 BN	7	10	0	13	10	11	13	12	6	6	10	10
MS-64 RB	24	23	7	26	34	35	51	30	27	37	37	29
MS-64 RD	6	7	0	16	10	33	14	20	19	19	17	27
MS-65 BN	9	3	0	2	1	11	3	3	1	8	5	7
MS-65 RB	26	20	7	14	17	21	26	20	17	17	18	20
MS-65 RD	7	11	1	13	8	13	8	16	6	11	15	20
MS-66 BN	0	1	0	0	0	0	1	0	0	1	0	0
MS-66 RB	5	0	0	0	1	0	1	1	3	0	1	2
MS-66 RD	1	1	0	3	1	1	0	0	1	2	3	3

Mint State Coins (January 1996, NGC)
1896-1906 BRONZE INDIAN CENTS

NGC	1896	1897	1898	1899	1900	1901	1902	1903	1904	1905	1906
MS-60 BN	0	0	0	0	0	0	0	0	0	0	0
MS-60 RB	0	0	0	0	0	0	0	0	0	0	0
MS-60 RD	0	0	0	0	0	0	0	0	0	0	0
MS-61 BN	0	0	0	1	0	0	0	1	1	0	1
MS-61 RB	0	0	0	0	0	0	2	0	0	0	0
MS-61 RD	0	0	0	0	0	0	0	0	0	0	0
MS-62 BN	1	2	0	1	1	1	2	1	1	1	2
MS-62 RB	0	2	2	2	2	2	2	1	1	2	3
MS-62 RD	0	0	0	0	0	2	2	2	0	2	0
MS-63 BN	1	3	3	7	2	5	5	4	4	9	6
MS-63 RB	11	19	14	11	13	18	24	16	8	26	16
MS-63 RD	0	3	1	2	1	14	16	2	4	6	8
MS-64 BN	7	7	5	20	8	10	18	13	11	12	19
MS-64 RB	37	41	47	80	46	99	86	67	65	64	64
MS-64 RD	16	20	18	36	39	50	56	38	49	88	72
MS-65 BN	3	5	3	7	7	15	9	7	5	3	9
MS-65 RB	21	31	31	78	33	58	44	53	27	42	53
MS-65 RD	17	13	21	43	46	46	77	44	42	149	55
MS-66 BN	0	0	2	1	0	2	2	0	0	0	0
MS-66 RB	0	5	3	10	2	10	8	3	4	2	4
MS-66 RD	2	7	13	17	13	14	79	16	7	51	6

Mint State Coins (January 1996, NGC)
1907-1909-S BRONZE INDIAN CENTS

NGC	1907	1908	1908-S	1909	1909-S
MS-60 BN	0	0	0	0	0
MS-60 RB	0	0	0	0	0
MS-60 RD	0	0	0	0	0
MS-61 BN	0	2	1	1	4
MS-61 RB	0	0	1	0	0
MS-61 RD	0	0	0	0	0
MS-62 BN	0	0	9	1	2
MS-62 RB	4	0	6	0	4
MS-62 RD	0	0	0	2	1
MS-63 BN	5	0	12	5	9
MS-63 RB	26	22	16	29	26
MS-63 RD	7	7	1	15	7

NGC	1907	1908	1908-S	1909	1909-S
MS-64 BN	14	6	13	16	6
MS-64 RB	91	82	58	106	64
MS-64 RD	63	104	31	148	28
MS-65 BN	5	5	2	12	3
MS-65 RB	58	55	39	60	47
MS-65 RD	51	82	48	115	21
MS-66 BN	0	1	0	0	0
MS-66 RB	0	5	2	7	2
MS-66 RD	7	12	12	11	1

Proof Coins (January 1996, NGC)
1856-1858 FLYING EAGLE CENTS

NGC	1856	1857	1858 Misc	1858 LL	1858 SL
Pr-60	3	0	0	0	0
Pr-61	1	0	0	0	1
Pr-62	6	2	1	0	1
Pr-63	21	1	1	0	0
Pr-64	33	8	3	7	1
Pr-65	3	1	0	1	3
Pr-66	0	0	0	1	0

Proof Coins (January 1996, NGC)
1859-1864 COPPER-NICKEL INDIAN CENTS

NGC	1859	1860	1861	1862	1863	1864
Pr-60	0	0	0	0	0	0
Pr-61	0	0	0	0	0	0
Pr-62	0	1	4	2	0	3
Pr-63	17	1	7	11	14	13
Pr-64	49	8	14	54	27	31
Pr-65	13	7	9	51	19	20
Pr-66	8	3	0	11	5	2

Proof Coins (January 1996, NGC)
1864-1874 BRONZE INDIAN CENTS

NGC	1864 Br.	1864L	1865	1866	1867	1868	1869	1870	1871	1872	1873Cl 3	1874
Pr-60 BN	0	0	0	0	0	0	0	0	0	0	0	0
Pr-60 RB	0	0	0	0	0	0	0	0	0	0	0	0
Pr-60 RD	0	0	0	0	0	0	0	0	0	0	0	0
Pr-61 BN	0	0	0	0	0	0	0	0	0	0	0	0
Pr-61 RB	0	0	0	0	0	0	0	0	0	0	0	0
Pr-61 RD	0	0	0	0	0	0	0	0	0	0	0	0
Pr-62 BN	0	0	0	0	0	1	0	0	1	1	1	0
Pr-62 RB	0	0	2	1	0	0	0	1	1	1	1	2
Pr-62 RD	0	0	0	0	0	0	0	0	0	0	0	0
Pr-63 BN	1	0	0	1	2	1	0	1	0	4	1	1
Pr-63 RB	1	0	5	3	6	5	4	4	8	9	9	1
Pr-63 RD	0	0	1	2	0	0	1	1	0	1	2	3
Pr-64 BN	1	1	6	3	3	4	4	1	1	4	6	2
Pr-64 RB	18	2	11	12	16	14	14	18	17	20	27	22
Pr-64 RD	4	0	5	2	9	3	5	14	6	9	4	6
Pr-65 BN	2	0	2	1	5	1	4	3	2	6	1	3
Pr-65 RB	5	0	13	17	12	16	12	15	12	10	17	13
Pr-65 RD	0	0	4	6	6	2	7	5	12	7	2	8
Pr-66 BN	2	0	1	0	1	0	0	0	0	2	0	0
Pr-66 RB	4	0	5	2	5	3	1	1	2	2	3	8
Pr-66 RD	1	0	0	2	2	2	1	1	0	1	2	2

Proof Coins (January 1996, NGC)
1875-1886 BRONZE INDIAN CENTS

NGC	1875	1876	1877	1878	1879	1880	1881	1882	1883	1884	1885	1886
Pr-60 BN	0	0	0	0	0	0	0	0	0	0	0	0
Pr-60 RB	0	0	0	0	0	0	0	0	0	0	0	0
Pr-60 RD	0	0	0	0	0	0	0	0	0	0	0	0
Pr-61 BN	0	0	0	0	0	0	0	0	1	0	0	0
Pr-61 RB	0	0	0	0	0	0	1	0	0	0	0	0
Pr-61 RD	0	0	0	0	0	0	0	0	0	0	0	0
Pr-62 BN	1	0	0	0	2	0	2	2	3	2	1	0
Pr-62 RB	0	0	0	2	2	3	2	0	3	3	1	2
Pr-62 RD	0	0	0	0	0	0	0	0	0	0	0	0
Pr-63 BN	2	2	1	4	5	6	4	3	11	2	3	5
Pr-63 RB	7	9	11	7	8	14	7	2	10	10	3	7
Pr-63 RD	4	0	0	0	1	0	0	0	0	0	0	0

NGC	1875	1876	1877	1878	1879	1880	1881	1882	1883	1884	1885	1886
Pr-64 BN	2	3	4	4	9	6	8	11	32	4	15	19
Pr-64 RB	25	21	26	34	28	39	33	32	31	35	23	21
Pr-64 RD	6	8	6	13	2	9	4	4	6	5	2	2
Pr-65 BN	1	3	8	4	4	6	7	13	24	13	29	28
Pr-65 RB	6	20	17	28	36	34	36	33	57	45	31	28
Pr-65 RD	3	7	7	16	10	16	19	4	4	12	2	3
Pr-66 BN	0	0	0	0	1	2	2	11	11	8	16	4
Pr-66 RB	0	5	3	0	13	12	13	6	16	19	15	11
Pr-66 RD	0	2	1	2	5	4	5	1	1	8	1	2

Proof Coins (January 1996, NGC)
1887-1898 BRONZE INDIAN CENTS

NGC	1887	1888	1889	1890	1891	1892	1893	1894	1885	1896	1897	1898
Pr-60 BN	0	0	2	0	0	0	0	0	0	0	0	0
Pr-60 RB	1	0	0	0	0	1	0	0	0	0	0	0
Pr-60 RD	0	0	0	0	0	0	0	0	0	0	0	0
Pr-61 BN	0	0	1	1	0	0	0	1	0	0	0	0
Pr-61 RB	0	0	0	0	0	1	1	0	0	0	0	1
Pr-61 RD	0	0	0	0	0	0	0	0	0	0	0	0
Pr-62 BN	0	1	2	0	0	2	2	1	3	0	2	0
Pr-62 RB	0	3	0	2	2	1	1	1	1	4	2	0
Pr-62 RD	0	0	0	0	0	0	0	0	1	0	1	1
Pr-63 BN	5	7	8	2	1	2	4	0	3	3	7	1
Pr-63 RB	8	9	6	12	6	7	13	4	6	5	7	4
Pr-63 RD	0	0	2	1	3	3	4	3	0	0	0	0
Pr-64 BN	16	11	16	4	7	5	6	5	7	4	4	5
Pr-64 RB	15	15	16	34	34	35	25	26	18	22	18	21
Pr-64 RD	4	1	5	9	10	9	12	16	3	7	4	8
Pr-65 BN	21	9	10	1	2	1	2	2	4	4	4	3
Pr-65 RB	22	16	9	19	27	23	12	10	20	17	23	31
Pr-65 RD	1	2	2	2	6	5	7	8	10	4	5	6
Pr-66 BN	5	2	5	0	0	0	5	2	1	1	3	0
Pr-66 RB	4	3	5	1	1	4	2	4	4	2	5	8
Pr-66 RD	1	0	0	0	2	3	7	1	3	1	2	3

Proof Coins (January 1996, NGC)
1899-1909 BRONZE INDIAN CENTS

NGC	1899	1900	1901	1902	1903	1904	1905	1906	1907	1908	1909
Pr-60 BN	0	0	0	0	0	0	0	0	0	0	0
Pr-60 RB	0	0	0	0	0	0	0	1	0	0	0
Pr-60 RD	0	0	0	0	0	0	0	0	0	0	0
Pr-61 BN	0	0	0	0	0	0	0	0	0	0	0
Pr-61 RB	0	0	0	0	0	0	0	0	1	0	0
Pr-61 RD	0	0	0	0	0	0	0	0	0	0	0
Pr-62 BN	0	0	1	0	0	0	1	1	0	1	1
Pr-62 RB	0	1	0	1	0	0	0	0	1	0	3
Pr-62 RD	0	0	0	0	0	0	0	1	0	0	0
Pr-63 BN	2	0	2	1	1	2	4	1	1	0	3
Pr-63 RB	5	5	8	5	8	5	3	6	5	4	6
Pr-63 RD	1	1	2	1	0	3	7	0	1	0	0
Pr-64 BN	4	4	5	1	7	2	2	1	4	2	5
Pr-64 RB	18	21	24	24	25	9	18	23	23	13	17
Pr-64 RD	9	6	4	15	10	12	7	3	3	5	12
Pr-65 BN	5	2	5	0	2	0	2	3	2	5	3
Pr-65 RB	22	14	33	21	11	13	18	14	11	21	23
Pr-65 RD	13	10	9	10	11	7	10	10	4	12	9
Pr-66 BN	2	1	4	1	0	0	0	0	1	0	1
Pr-66 RB	4	8	9	9	4	0	5	1	4	7	6
Pr-66 RD	10	3	1	10	6	3	6	3	6	5	5

SUMMARY of certain PCGS + NGC Data

Combined listings for Proof 1878 to 1909 cents

YEAR	1878	1879	1880	1881	1882	1883	1884	1885	1886	1887	1888	1889
Total Proof Mintage	2,350	3,200	3,955	3,575	3,100	6,609	3,942	3,790	4,290	2,960	4,582	3,336
Total PCGS + NGC Proofs certified	360	460	443	446	360	594	503	425	377	312	268	282
Certified total as % of Proof mintage	15%	14%	11%	12%	12%	9%	13%	11%	9%	10%	6%	8%
# of Proof-64 & 65 RD certified by PCGS + NGC	100	60	92	93	28	41	82	23	29	15	16	32
# of Proof-64 & 65RD as % of Proof mintage	4.3%	1.9%	2.6%	2.6%	0.9%	0.6%	2.0%	0.6%	0.7%	0.5%	0.3%	1.0%

YEAR	1890	1891	1892	1893	1894	1895	1896	1897	1898	1899	1900	1901
Total Proof Mintage	2,740	2,350	2,745	2,195	2,632	2,062	1,862	1,938	1,795	2,031	2,262	1,985
Total PCGS + NGC Proofs certified	270	292	335	283	260	273	224	269	278	305	266	298
Certified total as % of Proof mintage	10%	12%	12%	13%	10%	13%	12%	14%	15%	15%	12%	15%
# of Proof-64 & 65 RD certified by PCGS + NGC	44	58	79	63	57	59	38	31	63	80	60	48
# of Proof-64 & 65RD as % of Proof mintage	1.6%	2.5%	2.9%	2.9%	2.2%	2.9%	2.0%	1.6%	3.5%	3.9%	2.7%	2.4%

YEAR	1902	1903	1904	1905	1906	1907	1908	1909
Total Proof Mintage	2,018	1,790	1,817	2,152	1,725	1,475	1,620	2,175
Total PCGS + NGC Proofs certified	310	291	209	242	240	194	267	299
Certified total as % of Proof mintage	15%	16%	11%	11%	14%	13%	16%	14%
# of Proof-64 & 65 RD certified by PCGS + NGC	88	79	67	45	43	22	59	63
# of Proof-64 & 65RD as % of Proof mintage	4.4%	4.4%	3.7%	2.1%	2.5%	1.5%	3.6%	2.9%

Commentary concerning combined Proof data:
All Proof grade levels Proof-60 to Proof-66:

1. For Proofs from 1878 to 1909, for most dates the percentage certified *at all grade levels* Proof-60 to Proof-66 combined is about 10% to 15% of the number minted. However, as coins are often resubmitted as well as crossed over from one service to another, in all instances the number certified is not less than the numbers shown and is probably more.

2. The scarcest Proofs in terms of the percentage certified at all grade levels are these with percentages below 10%: 1883 9%, 1886 9%, 1888 6% (lowest of all percentages, and 1889 8%. All of these have fairly large Proof mintages, but only a small percentage have survived today in Proof-64 and 65 RD. This is probably due to several factors including these:

a. They are 20 to 30 years older than certain dates later in the series and thus have been subjected to atmospheric influences longer. Thus, more have become damaged or lost and are less likely to be certified.

b. They were wrapped in sulfur-content paper when issued by the Mint and thus tended to tone brown. Thus, they appear to have lower value today and are less likely to be sent in to be certified.

c. Large numbers were sold to the general public (1883 in particular) and once the novelty of coin collecting passed, were not carefully preserved and thus are less likely to be certified.

d. In summation, many Proofs have disappeared or have become damaged or deeply toned and for these reasons have not been available for certification or have not been deemed valuable enough to merit certification.

3. The most plentiful dates in terms of numbers certified are these with 15% or more: 1878 15%, 1898 15%, 1899 15%, 1901 15%, 1902 15%, 1903 16% (tied for highest), and 1908 16% (tied for most common). This is probably due to several factors including these:

a. The 1878 is a more valuable date due to the related low business strike mintage, and is thus more apt to be certified.

b. The other dates are later in the series and are either of low Proof mintage or survive in finer grades, thus making them more valuable and more likely candidates to be certified.

Commentary concerning combined Proof data:
Higher Proof grade levels Proof-64 and 65 RD:

1. For Proofs from 1878 to 1909, for most dates the percentage certified *at Proof-64 and 65 RD levels* is very small, typically less than 4%. Those with certification levels below 1% are these: 1882 0.9%, 1883 0.6%, 1885 0.6%, 1886 0.7%, 1887 0.5%, and 1888 0.3% (lowest of all percentages). This is probably due to several factors including these:

a. Some issues were poorly struck and poorly handled at the Mint (1887 and 1888 are in this category), thus fewer survived in high levels.

b. Proofs were issued wrapped in sulfur-content tissue paper which toned the coins.

c. Many were sold to the general public (this is especially true of 1883) and were not carefully handled.

1. For Proofs from 1878 to 1909, the most plentiful (proportional to mintage) dates certified *at Proof-64 and 65 RD levels* are these with 4% or more of the original Proof mintage: 1878 4.3%, 1902 4.4%, and 1903 4.4%. This is probably due to several factors including these:

     a. 1878 is a valuable date and was apt to be more carefully preserved by numismatists than the commoner dates of the 1880s and 1890s.

     b. 1902 and 1903 cents are later in the series and have not been subjected to toning influences as long as older issues have.

Final remarks concerning PCGS and NGC data:

The preceding numbers can be analyzed all sorts of ways and are interesting to contemplate in this regard. While such numbers may not be a guide to the availability of *quality* coins, as even high-grade pieces in some instances are spotted, they are certainly a guide to the *relative availability* of various issues at various grade levels.

ANACS Data

General comments

Among high-grade Flying Eagle and Indian cents, ANACS has certified far fewer than have PCGS and NGC. However, unlike the last two services, ANACS has certified many specialized die varieties. Thus, a collector seeking certification for the clashed die varieties of 1857 cents would likely submit coins to ANACS, which will specifically identify them as such on the holders. ANACS has carved a market niche for itself in the identification of varieties attributed to Breen and Snow numbers and also the identification of mint errors.

The following commentaries by the present author pertain to selected excerpts from Mint State and Proof Flying Eagle and Indian cents described in the ANACS *Population Report* dated February 1996. In addition, data are given for several varieties in worn grades as specifically cited.

1856 Flying Eagle cent: 12 certified in Mint State (two of which are specifically designated as Snow-3); 10 in Proof finish. Highest grades: MS-64 (1 coin), Proof-64 (1 coin).

1857 Flying Eagle cent with rim clip: 1 certified as MS-61, an instance of someone submitting a Mint error and requesting certification.

1857 Flying Eagle cent with Style of 1856 letters (Snow-2): 1 certified, an MS-64.

1857 Flying Eagle cent with unspecified style letters (presumably, Style of 1857): 146 in Mint State, the highest being 10 specimens clustered at the MS-64 category.

1857 Clashed die with 25¢ (Snow-8): EF-40 2, EF-45 2, AU-55 2, MS-62 1.

1857 Clashed die with 50¢ (Snow-9): Good 1, VG 2, F-12 1, F-15 1, VF-20 4, VF-30 1, VF-35 3, EF-45 3, MS-64 1, plus 3 certified as genuine only (surfaces impaired, so no numerical grade given).

1857 Clashed die with $20 (Snow-7): VG 1, F-12 2, VF-35 2, AU-58 1.

1858/7 overdate (Snow-1): MS-61 1, MS-62 2, MS-63 1.

1858 Flying Eagle cents: In Mint State, 20 of the Large Letters and 31 of the Small Letters coins have been certified. Among Proofs, 1 has been certified without any designation as to letter size, and 4 Small Letters coins have been certified.

Indian cents in Mint State: In all numerical grade levels combined, 1,346 have been certified with Brown surfaces, 4,721 with Red and Brown, and 869 with Red. (These data are not particularly meaningful with ANACS or any other grading service, as many Brown coins of lower values, and of very common dates, have not been submitted due to the cost of certification vs. the coins' market value.)

Indian cents MS-65: 68 Brown, 422 Red and Brown, 135 Red. (Same comment as preceding.)

Indian cent varieties: Many are listed by Snow and Breen numbers, among which are numerous repunched dates, clashed dies, etc. Among 1865 cents the Plain 5 and Fancy 5 varieties are differentiated. One Fancy 5 coin, MS-64, has been certified as an 1865/4 overdate. Among various types of mint errors certified for various years are clipped, broadstruck, off-center, and rotated die varieties.

Proof Indian cents: Total coins certified include 251 Brown, 940 Red and Brown, and 126 Red. (Doubtless, many Brown coins were never submitted due to low market values; thus these figures have little research value; ditto for similar figures of other grading services.) Among 1868 Proof cents, 13 have been certified with (presumably) regular die orientation, while 3 are specified as having rotated dies. Among certified 1886 Proofs, 10 are specified as Type I and 6 as Type II.

BIBLIOGRAPHY

Abbott, Waldo. "Making Money: The Mint at Philadelphia." *Harper's New Monthly Magazine,* March 1861:

Adams, Edgar H. Untitled commentary about pattern cents in *The Numismatist,* July 1912, pp. 246-247. Basic descriptions of 34 different patterns. Terminology included "tobacco wreath" for what is called "agricultural wreath" in the present text.

Adams, Edgar H. and William H. Woodin. *United States Pattern, Trial, and Experimental Pieces.* New York: American Numismatic Society, 1913.

Adams, John Weston. *United States Numismatic Literature.* Vol. I. Mission Viejo, CA: George Frederick Kolbe Publications, 1982. A masterwork on the subject of early coin dealers and their publications, particularly their auction catalogues.

Alexander, David T., Thomas K. DeLorey, and Brad Reed. *Coin World Comprehensive Catalog & Encyclopedia of United States Coins.* Sidney, OH: Coin World, 1995.

American Journal of Numismatics. New York, NY: American Numismatic Society. Various nineteenth century issues as cited.

Annual Report, Director of the Mint. Washington, DC: Government Printing Office. 1836 to 1910; titles and printers vary (*e.g.,* the 1859 report was published by B.F. Mifflin, Philadelphia); later issues by the G.P.O. Contains much information, but primarily on coinages in precious metals (silver and gold); relatively little on cents. Cited as "Mint Report."

Ballou's Pictorial Drawing-Room Companion, Vol. XII. Boston: 1857. Reflections upon the American scene in the year that the Flying Eagle cent first reached circulation.

Barber, Charles E. "Manufacture of Dies." *Twenty-Fourth Annual Report of the Director of the Mint to the Secretary of the Treasury. For the Fiscal Year Ended June 30, 1896.* Washington: Government Printing Office, 1897.

————— Letter about the origins of Longacre's Indian motif as used on the 1859 cent. *The Numismatist,* March 1910, p. 75.

Barrett, Don C. *The Greenbacks and Resumption of Specie Payments, 1862-1879.* Cambridge, MA: Harvard University Press, 1931. Study of the monetary situation of the era, but with an imperfect understanding of coinage (*e.g.,* p. 77 states erroneously that bronze cents were introduced in 1864 because "the bullion value of the nickel cent was worth more than its mint value").

Becker, Thomas W. *The Coin Makers.* Garden City, NY: Doubleday & Company, 1969. Overview of die making and coinage processes.

Bowers, Q. David. Various as cited.

Boyd, F.C.C. "Engravers of the U.S. Mint In Philadelphia." *The Numismatist,* July 1940.

Breen, Walter H. "More About Longacre's Indian Cent Model." *Numismatic Scrapbook Magazine,* April 1951. [Breen signed his name as Walter H. Breen in certain early works, the H being for Henry; later, he dropped the H.]

—— *Proof Coins Struck by the United States Mint 1817-1921.* New York: Wayte Raymond, Inc., 1953.

——*The United States Minor Coinage 1793-1916.* New York: Wayte Raymond, Inc., 1954.

—— *The Secret History of the Gobrecht Coinages 1836-1840.* New York: Wayte Raymond, Inc., 1954.

—— "Blundered Dies of U.S. and Colonial Coins." *Empire Topics,* October 1958. First publication of the 1873 Doubled LIBERTY cent.

—— *Dies & Coinage.* New York City: QWERTYUIOPress [one of Robert Bashlow's various ventures], 1962.

——*Complete Encyclopedia of U.S. and Colonial Proof Coins.* Albertson, NY: F.C.I. Press, 1977; reprint and update by Bowers and Merena Galleries, Wolfeboro, NH, 1989. "Encyclopedia of Proof Coins" citations.

——*Walter Breen's Complete Encyclopedia of United States and Colonial Coins.* New York: Doubleday & Co., 1988. A superb guide to varieties, history, and rarity. "Breen" numbers. "Encyclopedia" citations.

Bressett, Kenneth E. (editor). *A Guide Book of United States Coins.* Racine, WI: Various modern editions. The standard introductory guide to American coinage, a best seller for decades.

Bressett, Kenneth E. and A. Kosoff; introduction by Q. David Bowers. *The Official American Numismatic Association Grading Standards for United States Coins.* 4th edition. Colorado Springs, CO: American Numismatic Association, 1991.

Briggs, Larry. *The Comprehensive Encyclopedia of United States Liberty Seated Quarters.* Lima, OH: Larry Briggs Rare Coins, 1991. Discusses the reverse of the 1857 quarter dollar showing clash marks from an 1857 Flying Eagle cent.

Brown, Martin R., and John W. Dunn. *A Guide to the Grading of United States Coins.* Oklahoma City, OK: Published by the authors, 1963.

Carothers, Neil. *Fractional Money.* New York, NY: John Wiley & Sons, Inc., 1930. Essential text about nineteenth-century monetary conditions in America.

Cherrypickers' News. Published by J.T. Stanton, Savannah, GA. The May 1996 issue was consulted for several items including suggested values for 1857 clashed die Flying Eagle cents.

Coffin, Joseph. "Christian Gobrecht." *The Numismatic Scrapbook Magazine,* November 1944. Biographical notes.

Cogan, Edward D.. "Concerning the Coin Trade In America." *American Journal of Numismatics,* Vol. 1, No. 11, 1867. Reminiscences of the writer's early days as a coin dealer and mention of the 1856 Flying Eagle cent.

Coin & Paper Money Calendar. Iola, WI: Krause Publications, 1995 (1996 cover date). Contains many historical U.S. coinage dates.

Coin Dealer Newsletter. Torrance, CA (currently; other locations earlier): 1963 to date.

Coin World Almanac. Sidney, OH: Coin World, 1976 and later editions.

Coin World. Sidney, OH: Amos Press. Various issues. Various issues. Also, "Trends" column by Keith Zaner, various issues.

Coinage Laws of the United States 1792-1894, The. Committee on Finance of the U.S. Senate, Washington, D.C., 1894. Reprint, 1990, with new foreword by David L. Ganz. Bowers and Merena Galleries, Inc.

COINage. Ventura, CA: Miller Publications. Various issues.

Coins magazine. Iola, WI: Krause Publications. Various issues.

Comparette, T.L. *Catalogue of Coins, Tokens and Medals in the Numismatic Collection of the Mint of the United States at Philadelphia, Pa.* Washington, D.C.: Government Printing Office, 1914.

Conger, George R. "The Controversial Feathered Headdress," *Longacre's Ledger,* April 1992.

———— "An Argument Favoring Sarah as Longacre's Model." *Longacre's Ledger,* July 1992.

Cooper, Denis R. *The Art and Craft of Coinmaking, A History of Minting Technology.* London: Spink & Son, 1988.

Craig, John. *The Mint: A History of the London Mint from A.D. 287 to 1948.* Cambridge, England: The University Press, 1953. Describes minting processes.

Davis, Robert Coulton. "Pattern and Experimental Issues of the United States Mint." *The Coin Collector's Journal,* series beginning in July 1885; issue of September 1885 includes information on cent patterns of the 1850s.

DeLorey, Thomas K. "Was Mischief Afoot in 1857 Die Clashes?" "Collectors' Clearinghouse," *Coin World,* July 1, 1977.

———— "Longacre, Unsung Engraver of the U.S. Mint." *Longacre's Ledger,* January 1992. Illustrates models used for the Indian obverse and the "agricultural" wreath reverse, discusses engraving techniques, and gives much other valuable information. Reprinted from *The Numismatist,* October 1985.

Downing, A.W. Notebook of dies at the Philadelphia Mint each year 1880-1886. Downing was general foreman of the Coining Department and kept the notebook; certain pages were countersigned at the bottom by A.W. Straub, a machinist in the Engraving Department (who by 1884 identified himself as foreman of the Die Makers' Room). Copy furnished by Dr. Richard Doty, Smithsonian Institution.

Eaton, W.C. "The Eagle Cents of 1858." *The Numismatist,* January 1916.

———— "The Eagle Cents of 1858." *The Numismatist,* November 1920 (update of 1916 article).

———— "The Eagle Cents of 1858." *The Numismatist,* March 1921 (further update of 1916 article).

———— "The Eagle Cents of 1857." *The Numismatist,* May 1921. Most research for this article was done by F.R. Alvord.

Eckfeldt, Jacob R., and William E. DuBois. *A Manual of Gold and Silver Coins of All Nations, Struck Within the Past Century.* Philadelphia, PA: Assay Office of the Mint, 1842.

Errorscope. Journal of the Combined Organizations of Numismatic Error Collectors of America (CONECA).

Evans, George G. *Illustrated History of the United States Mint.* Philadelphia, George G. Evans, 1885 (and other editions).

Fivaz, Bill. "Never In My Wildest Dreams." *Rare Coin Review* No. 62. Description of the discovery of the 1857 Flying Eagle cent with clash marks from a Liberty Seated quarter dollar.

——— "Definitely a Difference!" *Longacre's Ledger,* Summer 1994. Description of the differences in the neck feathers on the letter size varieties of the 1858 Flying Eagle cent.

Fivaz, Bill, and J.T. Stanton. *The Cherrypickers' Guide to Rare Die Varieties.* 3rd edition. Wolfeboro, NH: Bowers and Merena Galleries, 1994. "FS" and "Fivaz-Stanton" citations. A treasure trove of information, complete with prices, rarity ratings, and enlarged illustrations, of many die varieties, each selected for its significance.

Flynn, Kevin. "Two Obverse Types Used on 1858 Flying Eagle Cents." *Numismatic News,* April 2, 1996.

Fuld, George and Melvin. *U.S. Civil War Store Cards.* Token and Medal Society, 1972.

——— *Patriotic Civil War Tokens.* 4th edition. Token and Medal Society, 1982,

Gengerke, Martin. *American Numismatic Auctions.* Three volumes. New York: Various dates 1980s onward.

Gerhardt, Paul W. "Proof Cents and Nickels, 1878-1916." *Numismatic Scrapbook Magazine,* February 1946. Mintage figures obtained from the superintendent of the Mint. (Related information appeared under the title of "Mint Record of Early U.S. Proof Coinage" in the same publication, September 1948.)

Goforth, Joy. "Goddess of Liberty." *Mint Press,* November 1983; reprinted as "Who Came First? Goddess, Sarah, or Indian?" *Coin World,* January 4, 1984. Discussion of the Indian headdress motif on the cent including citations from Mint correspondence.

Harper's New Monthly Magazine. New York: Harper & Brothers, various issues circa 1856-1862.

Harper's Weekly. New York: Harper & Brothers, various issues circa 1857-1887..

Hauptman, Wesley. "The Flying Eagle Cent of 1856." *The Numismatist.* September 1938. (This article had many inaccuracies and was superseded by John F. Jones' article of April 1944.)

Hettger, Henry T. "Collusive Bidding on Indian Head Cent Planchets in 1892." *Longacre's Ledger,* October 1991.

Hewitt, Lee F. (unsigned). "Cent Design Changed in 1886." *Numismatic Scrapbook Magazine,* June 1949.

——— "Feuchtwanger Bid on Making 3-Cent Nickel Blanks." *Numismatic Scrapbook Magazine,* February 1963.

Howard-White, F.B. *Nickel: An Historical Review,* Princeton, NY, D. Van Nostrand Company, Inc., 1963.

Indian Central. Various issues 1995 and 1996. Seahurst, WA: Eagle Eye Rare Coins, Inc.

Jones, John F. "The 1856 Flying Eagle Cent." *The Numismatist.* April 1944.

Judd, J. Hewitt. *United States Pattern, Experimental and Trial Pieces.* 7th edition. Racine, WI: Western Publishing Co., 1982.

Julian, R.W. "Philadelphia Coinage Statistics, 1853-1873, The Quarter Dollar." *Numismatic Scrapbook Magazine,* June 1965.

——— "Notes on U.S. Proof Coinage: Silver and Minor." *Numismatic Scrapbook Magazine,* March 1966.

——— "Philadelphia Coinage Statistics, 1853-1873, The Half Dollar." *Numismatic Scrapbook Magazine,* October 1966.

—— "The Case of the Disappearing Cent." *Numismatic Scrapbook Magazine,* May 1972.

—— *Medals of the United States Mint: The First Century 1792-1892.* El Cajon, CA: Token and Medal Society, Inc., 1977.

—— "The Flying Eagle Cent." *COINage,* October 1987.

—— "The Indian Head Cent." *COINage,* May 1988.

—— "The Cent Becomes Bronze: 1864." *FUN-Topics,* Summer 1987.

—— "The 1877 Indian Head Cent." *Coins Magazine,* October 1992.

Kreisberg, Abner, and Jerry Cohen. John A. Beck Collection auction sale catalogues, 1975 and 1976. Offerings of 1856 Flying Eagle cents.

Linderman, Henry R. *Money and Legal Tender.* New York: G.P. Putnam's Sons, 1877.

Longacre's Ledger. Journal of the Fly-In Club. Contains much information on die varieties, rarity ratings, etc.

McGirk, Charles E., M.D. "Varieties of 1871 Indian Cents." *The Numismatist,* April 1910.

Newman, Eric P., and Kenneth E. Bressett. *The Fantastic 1804 Dollar.* Racine, WI: Whitman Publishing Co., 1962.

—— *The Fantastic 1804 Dollar: 25th Anniversary Follow-Up.* Coinage of the Americas Conference at the American Numismatic Society, New York, 1987.

Numismatic Guaranty Corporation of America Census Report. Various issues. Parsippany, NJ: Numismatic Guaranty Corporation of America.

Numismatic News. Iola, WI: Krause Publications. Various issues. Also, "Coin Market" column various issues (these by Bob Wilhite).

Numismatic Scrapbook Magazine. Chicago, IL, and Sidney, OH: 1935-1976.

Numismatist, The. Current address: Colorado Springs, CO; other addresses earlier. Various issues 1888 to date.

Penny Talk. Newsletter. Scarborough, Maine.

Pilliod, Chris. "What Error Coins Can Teach Us About Die Settings." *The Numismatist,* April 1996. Description of the 1870 Shield nickel with Indian cent clash marks; also a valuable discussion of die positions in coining presses. This was an exceedingly important article which influenced the thinking of the writer of the present book (QDB) on the mystery of the 1857 clashed-die cents.

PCGS Population Report, various issues. Newport Beach, CA: Professional Coin Grading Service.

Pollock, Andrew W. III. *United States Patterns and Related Issues.* Wolfeboro, NH: Bowers and Merena Galleries, 1994.

Population Report. Columbus, OH: ANACS. February 1996 issue.

Rare Coin Review. Wolfeboro, NH: Bowers and Merena Galleries, Inc. Various issues.

Rare Coins of the United States. New York: Guttag Brothers, 1924. Listing of the Guttag firm's buying prices for Uncirculated coins including small cents.

Raymond, Wayte. *Standard Catalogue of United States Coins and Paper Money* (titles vary). Scott Stamp & Coin Co. (and others): New York, 1934 to 1957 editions. In particular the 1935, 1938 and 1944 editions were studied for prices and a page was reproduced from the 1941 edition.

Rosen, Maurice. *Rosen Numismatic Advisory.* October-November 1995 issue re: Indian cents.

Ruddy, James F. *Photograde.* 19th edition. Racine, WI: Western Publishing Co., 1990.

Schilke, Oscar G., and Raphael E. Solomon. *America's Foreign Coins: An Illustrated Standard Catalogue with Valuations of Foreign Coins With Legal Tender Status in the United States 1793-1857.* New York, NY: Coin and Currency Institute, Inc., 1964.

Schultz, William J. "The Flying Eagle Cent of 1856; The Origin of the Copper-Nickel Half Cent." *The Numismatist,* October 1938. Reprints Mint correspondence on these subjects.

Scott Stamp & Coin Co., Ltd., also Scott & Co. and J.W. Scott Co., Ltd. *Standard Catalogue* (various titles). 1878-1913. Selected editions as quoted in Appendix III.

Sellers, George Escol. *Early Engineering Reminiscences (1815-40) of George Escol Sellers.* Eugene S. Ferguson, editor. Washington, DC: Smithsonian Institution, 1965. Sellers' reminiscences of Mint events were memorialized decades after they occurred and must be taken with a grain of salt when studied today; however, they are very interesting and informative.

Sheldon, William H. *Early American Cents.* New York: Harper, 1949. Describes Sheldon's market formula including rarity scale and numerical grading. Updated by *Penny Whimsy,* 1958.

Sholley, Craig B. "Inexperience, Not Die Steel, Caused Problems at Early US Mint." Manuscript furnished by the author; published in *Penny-Wise.*

Sinnock, John R. "Making Dies At the Philadelphia Mint." *The Numismatist,* October 1941.

Smith, A.M. *Coin Collectors' of the United States, Illustrated Guide.* Philadelphia, January 1886. Contains grading scale.

Snow, Richard. "The Midnight Minter." *Longacre's Ledger,* January 1991.

—— "High Leaves, Low Leaves." *Longacre's Ledger,* April 1991.

—— *Flying Eagle & Indian Cents.* Tucson, AZ: Eagle Eye Press, 1992. Photographs by Chris Pilliod. Uses "S" numbers. This master work defined and accelerated interest in minute die varieties as well as early small cents in general. Much numismatic and historical information is given as well. An essential work for the dedicated specialist.

—— Rick Snow's Variety Sale No. 1. Tucson, AZ: January 16, 1993. Contains report of the Floyd Starr group of Flying Eagle cents.

—— *"Proof Die Identification for Indian Cents."* Longacre's Ledger, Fall 1994. The author uses the position of the edge of the left bottom serif of the 1 in date in relation to the dentils as a guide to descriptions.

Snow, Richard, and Brian Wagner. "Pricing Proof-65RD Small Cents (1856-1909). *Longacre's Ledger,* Fall 1993.

Snowden, James Ross. *A Description of Ancient and Modern Coins in the Cabinet of the Mint of the United States.* Philadelphia, PA: J.B. Lippincott, 1860. Mostly researched and written by George Bull (then curator of the Mint Cabinet) and William Ewing DuBois.

—— *A Description of the Medals of Washington.* Philadelphia, PA: J.B. Lippincott, 1861.

Stack's. Floyd T. Starr Collection. Sale catalogues, October 1992 and November 1993. Contained coins earlier from the Commodore W.C. Eaton set of Flying Eagle cents.

Steinberger, Otto C. *Indian Cent Date Varieties. Numismatic Scrapbook Magazine.* Serial feature commencing with the December 1961 issue, later reprinted as a monograph.. Emphasizes various date placements within certain years, such being identified by the position of the 1 with relation to the neck truncation point, etc.

Steve, Larry R. "THE F.IND.ERS REPORT." *Longacre's Ledger,* various issues. Reports and updates concerning new discoveries and significant varieties.

Steve, Larry R., and Kevin J. Flynn. *A Comprehensive Guide to Selected Rare Flying Eagle and Indian Cent Varieties.* Jarrettsville, MD: Nuvista Press, 1995. Excellent historical background, illustrations and detailed descriptions of selected die varieties, price guide to the varieties. Uses "FND" numbers, some of which are cited in the present text. An essential work for the dedicated specialist.

Straub, A.W. See Downing, A.W.

Taxay, Don. *Counterfeit, Mis-Struck and Unofficial U.S. Coins,* New York City, ARCO Publishing Company, Inc., 1963

——— *U.S. Mint and Coinage.* New York: Arco Publishing, 1966. Definitive book on the inside workings of the Mint.

Thompson, Walter. "The Copper Nickel Cent." *Numismatic Scrapbook Magazine,* September 1960.

——— "The Adoption of [the] Indian Cent." *Numismatic Scrapbook Magazine,* July 1961.

2 Times Numismatic Newsletter. May 1996. Published by Frank Leone, College Point, NY. Contains discussion of the so-called "clashed die" 1868 nickel three-cent piece in which the writer believes it is not clashed with an Indian cent die.

United States Treasury Register, Containing a List of Persons Employed in the Treasury Department. Washington: Government Printing Office, 1877.

Vermeule, Cornelius. *Numismatic Art in America.* Cambridge, MA: Belknap Press of Harvard University Press, 1971. Detailed artistic and technical discussion of the iconography of the Flying Eagle and Indian cents.

Wade, Mr. Senate report, May 23, 1856, examining the petition of Franklin Peale (who had been fired in 1854) for compensation said to be due him for a vast number of improvements made at the Mint.

Wagner, Brian, and Richard Snow. "Pricing MS-65 RED Bronze Indian Cents." *Longacre's Ledger,* Winter 1993.

Wexler, John A. *The Encyclopedia of Doubled Dies.* Fort Worth, TX: Robert C. Wilharm, News Printing Co., 1981.

Wharton, Joseph. "Project for Reorganizing the Small Coinage of the United States of America," April 15, 1864. (Copy not seen, just references to it.)

——— *Memorandum Concerning Small Money and Nickel Alloy Coinage, with Illustrations and Descriptions of Existing Alloy Coins.* Camden, NJ: American Nickel Works, 1877. (Copy not seen, just references to it.)

White, W.O. "A Population Report Rarity Review." *Longacre's Ledger,* Spring 1995.

Wysong, Jerry. "A Third 1857 F.E. Cent Obverse Die." Article in *Longacre's Ledger,* Summer 1993.

——— "How Many Are There, Anyway?" Article in *Longacre's Ledger,* Winter 1996. Reported numbers of certain die varieties.

Yeoman, Richard (editor). *A Guide Book of United States Coins.* Racine, WI: Various editions beginning with 1946 (1947 cover date). The 1965 edition in particular was used in the present work. Kenneth E. Bressett has been editor in recent years and is current editor.

Young, James Rankin. *The United States Mint at Philadelphia.* Philadelphia, PA: Capt. A.J. Andrews [sales agent; publisher not given], 1903.